D0165889

TOURISM AND ENTREPRENEURSHIP

International Perspectives

ADVANCES IN TOURISM RESEARCH

Series Editor: **Professor Stephen J. Page**

University of Stirling, UK

s.j.page@stir.ac.uk

Advances in Tourism Research series publishes monographs and edited volumes that comprise state-of-the-art research findings, written and edited by leading researchers working in the wider field of tourism studies. The series has been designed to provide a cutting edge focus for researchers interested in tourism, particularly the management issues now facing decision-makers, policy analysts and the public sector. The audience is much wider than just academics and each book seeks to make a significant contribution to the literature in the field of study by not only reviewing the state of knowledge relating to each topic but also questioning some of the prevailing assumptions and research paradigms which currently exist in tourism research. The series also aims to provide a platform for further studies in each area by highlighting key research agendas which will stimulate further debate and interest in the expanding area of tourism research. The series is always willing to consider new ideas for innovative and scholarly books, inquiries should be made directly to the Series Editor.

Previously published titles in this series include:

International Perspectives of Festivals and Events
ALI-KNIGHT

Tomorrow's Tourist: Scenarios & Trends
YEOMAN

Asian Tourism: Growth and Change
COCHRANE

Developments in Tourism Research
AIREY

New Frontiers in Marine Tourism
GARROD

Battlefield Tourism
RYAN

Travel Medicine: Tales Behind the Science
WILDER-SMITH

The Critical Turn in Tourism Studies
ATELJEVIC

Tourism and Politics
BURNS

Tourism in the New Europe
THOMAS

Hospitality: A Social Lens
LASHLEY

Micro-Clusters and Networks
MICHAEL

Related Elsevier Journals — sample copies available on request

Annals of Tourism Research
International Journal of Hospitality Management
Tourism Management
World Development

TOURISM AND ENTREPRENEURSHIP

International Perspectives

EDITED BY

JOVO ATELJEVIC and STEPHEN J. PAGE

Amsterdam • Boston • Heidelberg • London • New York • Oxford
Paris • San Diego • San Francisco • Singapore • Sydney • Tokyo
Butterworth-Heinemann is an imprint of Elsevier

ELSEVIER

Butterworth-Heinemann is an imprint of Elsevier
Linacre House, Jordan Hill, Oxford OX2 8DP, UK
30 Corporate Drive, Suite 400, Burlington, MA 01803, USA

British Library Cataloguing in Publication Data
A catalogue record for this book is available from the British Library

Library of Congress Cataloging-in-Publication Data
A catalog record for this book is available from the Library of Congress

ISBN: 978-0-7506-8635-8

For information on all Butterworth-Heinemann publications visit
our web site at www.elsevierdirect.com

Transferred to Digital Printing 2009

Working together to grow
libraries in developing countries

www.elsevier.com | www.bookaid.org | www.sabre.org

ELSEVIER   BOOK AID International   Sabre Foundation

Contents

Part Three   Tourism Entrepreneurship Mediating the Global–Local Divide

Part Four **Sectoral Strategies and Policy Issues for Tourism Entrepreneurship**

List of Figures

List of Tables

List of Contributors

Alastair Durie, Department of History, University of Stirling and formerly Senior Lecturer in History, University of Glasgow (mail contact is Stephen Page)

Andreas Walmsley is Senior Lecturer in Business Management, York St John University, York, UK. A.Walmsley@yorksj.ac.uk

Anne-Mette Hjalager is a Senior Researcher Advance/1, Science Park Gustav Wiedsvej Aarhus C. Denmark. hjalager@advance1.dk

Arvid Flagestad, Norwegian School of Management, Oslo, Norway. Arvid.flagestad @bi.no

C. Michael Hall is Professor at the Department of Management, College of Business & Economics, University of Canterbury, Christchurch, New Zealand and Docent, Department of Geography, University of Oulu, Oulu, Finland. michael.hall@ canterbury.ac.nz

David Gallagher is an Independent Consultant for Business/Regional Development, based in Sarjevo, BiH. davidg@developmentaction.com

Dimitrios Buhalis is Professor of Tourism, International Centre for Tourism & Hospitality Research, Bournemouth University, UK. dbuhalis@bournemouth.ac.uk

Douglas Pearce is Professor of Tourism Management, Victoria Management School, Victoria University of Wellington, New Zealand. douglas.pearce@vuw.ac.nz.

Edward H. Huijbens is Director of Icelandic Tourism Research Centre – Borgum v/ Nordurslod, Akureyri, Iceland. edward@unak.is

Elizabeth Chell is Professor of Entrepreneurship & Entrepreneurial Behaviour, Small Business Research Centre, Kingston University London, Kingston Hill, Kingston upon Thames, KT2 7LB, UK. e.chell@kingston.ac.uk

Hilary C. Murphy is Professor of Information Technology & E-marketing Ecole hôtelière de Lausanne Le Chalet-à-Goblet, Lausanne, Switzerland. Hilary. MURPHY@ehl.ch

Ian Fillis is a Senior Lecturer in Marketing, Management School, University of Stirling, UK. i.r.fillis@stir.ac.uk

Irena Ateljevic is Associate Professor in Socio-Spatial Analysis, Wageningen University, the Netherland, Irena.Ateljevic@wur.nl

Jovo Ateljevic is Lecturer of Entrepreneurship, Stirling Management School, University of Stirling, UK. Jovo.ateljevic@stir.ac.uk

Julie Franchetti is Tourism Innovation Manager, Scottish Enterprise, Glasgow, UK. Julie. Franchetti@scotent.co.uk

Lan Li is Associate Professor of Hospitality Administration, School of Family, Consumer and Nutrition Sciences, Northern Illinois University, DeKalb, USA. lanli@niu. edu

Linda Peeters, the Socio-Spatial Analysis Group at Wageningen University, the Netherlands. linda.peeters@wur.nl

Marko Koščak (PhD) is an independent consultant and advisor for Rural Development in Slovenia. Currently he is Project Manager of the Dolenjska and Bela krajina Heritage Trails Partnership in SE, Slovenia. marko.koscak@siol.net

Patricia N. Joubert (Dr) University of Swaziland Faculty of Commerce

Peter Björk is Professor at the Swedish School of Economics and Business Administration, Vasa, Finland. peter.bjork@hanken.fi

Peter Rosa is the George David Chair of Entrepreneurship and Family Business, and Head of the Entrepreneurship and Innovation Group at the Edinburgh University Business School, Edinburgh, UK. Peter.Rosa@ed.ac.uk

Rhodri Thomas is ITT Chair of Tourism and Events Policy, UK Centre for Events Management, Leeds Metropolitan University, UK. r.thomas@leedsmet.ac.uk

Sara Nordin, European Tourism Research Institute Östersund, Sweden. sara.nordin@ etour.se

Stephen Doorne is a Director of Wrighton Doorne Limited consultancy and Associate Professor at the University of the South Pacific, Fiji. wrighton_doorne@yahoo. co.nz

Stephen J. Page, Scottish Enterprise Professor of Tourism Management, Stirling Management School, University of Stirling, UK. s.j.page@stir.ac.uk

Thomas Forbes is a Senior Lecturer of Management and Public Policy, Department of Management, Stirling Management School, University of Stirling, UK. t.m.forbes@stir.ac.uk

Tony O'Rourke is Director of the Finance & Investment Seminar Programme, University of Stirling, UK. a.r.orourke@stir.ac.uk

Acknowledgements

The editors would like to thank: the London Transport Museum, for permission to reproduce the image from the 1915 poster; Totally Wellington, for permission to use the map of the Central Stage Macro Tourism Region, New Zealand; and the United Nations, for permission to use the map of Bosnia and Herzegovina (Drina Valley Tourism Region).

Chapter 1

Introduction

Jovo Ateljevic and Stephen Page

Background

Tourism development provides an avenue for overall economic development and a boost for local entrepreneurship. As a result, the encouragement of entrepreneurship and sustainable tourism development has emerged as core areas for policy support and donor-assisted funding across both developed and the developing world. The academic contribution to identifying and understanding a range of issues critical to tourism entrepreneurship and tourism development has remained a largely neglected area for research. To date the links between tourism and entrepreneurship, with a few exceptions, remain divergent themes that are not addressed in any way which draws upon the inherent synergies between the two areas.

The result is that the two themes of tourism and entrepreneurship have progressed on different paths and rarely has any major crossover occurred in each of their literatures to cross-fertilize the development of the subject areas. Yet in almost every country across the world, the critical linkages between tourism and entrepreneurship remain key policy objectives to grow the indigenous capability of the tourism sector to create new business development. In many settings, policies exist to seek to grow tourism SMEs and micro-businesses through encouraging local entrepreneurship, but there have been few critical studies which draw upon the experiences in this area in both a historical and contemporary context. Where literature reviews exist in both tourism and entrepreneurship as disparate subjects, they are not integrated to derive wider understandings of these two integral areas that are critical to growing future tourism businesses.

Tourism and entrepreneurship courses have increased in number over the past few decades and have become more integrated into the mainstream university curriculum. Increasing numbers of students are studying tourism and entrepreneurship courses at undergraduate and postgraduate levels, and there has also been an increase in Ph.D. research in this area. The two areas of study strongly complement each other; tourism programmes are increasingly introducing entrepreneurship courses, and entrepreneurial studies treat tourism as a distinctive context. Tourism as both economic and social phenomenon spans different industries, economic sectors and social domains; therefore an interdisciplinary approach is critical to understanding tourism and entrepreneurship, not least because of the interconnections between the two areas.

One of the aims of this book is to reach not only scholars but all those concerned with tourism development, including practitioners and policy-makers at international, national and regional levels who are increasingly looking to the scholarly community for assistance. There is, of course, a plethora of scholarly monographs, textbooks and edited volumes written either by academics or policy-makers on both subjects. Some of these titles give students, researchers and practitioners a reasonable introduction into the subject of entrepreneurship in the tourism and associated fields but serious scholars, students and practitioners would require additional and wider sources of material to gain a complete understanding of the phenomenon and specific topics complemented by current business case studies. In order to accommodate changes taking place in the business environment, mainly driven by globalization and the ICT revolution, the business/entrepreneurship paradigm has been significantly changed. Moreover, almost none of the exiting contributions have an integrative approach to tourism development. This book represents an initial response to these calls by providing a synthesis of an interdisciplinary literature on tourism development and entrepreneurship in a format that students, researchers and other users can access and use easily.

The book provides a fresh and innovative approach to tourism and entrepreneurship, reflecting on the most recent trends in tourism development. The central theme of our book is the role of entrepreneurship in the context of regional/local tourism development. The book engages with the top scholars in the tourism and entrepreneurship area to give the text a high degree of credibility among potential adopters of the book. Contemporary themes of major significance highlighted include the importance of individual and collective entrepreneurship in both private and public sectors. These are put into a broad context of economic, social and cultural environments as well as tourism development models from across the world. One of the distinctive features of this book is the inclusion of institutional entrepreneurship (the concept derived from institutional and organizational theories), which explains how institutional entrepreneurs use resources/assets exchanges and mobilization of allies to further their goal. These and other aspects associated with tourism development and entrepreneurship are dealt with in the relevant chapters.

The central aims of the book are achieved by following these objectives:

- to explain the impact of tourism entrepreneurship on places and overall regional/ destination development;
- to examine the role of the public sector in facilitating the need for sustainable tourism development (institutional and public sector entrepreneurship);
- to examine the effects and implications of funding schemes and support programmes beyond the immediate interest in the success or failure of the firm, and with particular attention to the facilitation of entrepreneurship;
- to explore specific issues, from the perspective of the owner/manager/entrepreneur, as the starting point of analysis;
- to seek to contextualize developments within the context of tourism against both their structural backdrop and against the dynamics of sustainable tourism development in other economic and cultural environments; and lastly
- to assist practitioners and policy-makers through up-to-date case studies of best practice tourism development across the world.

Structure of this Book

At a general level the themes that hold this book together are related to a broader context of tourism development and entrepreneurship articulated through the following concepts and issues: tourism, innovation and entrepreneurship; the role and nature of individual and collective entrepreneurship in different contexts (e.g. business, institution, organization); the role of tourism in responding to development opportunities created by global forces; and finally, issues associated with tourism strategies and policies. In order to simplify the complexity of the themes presented in the individual chapters, the book is divided into four parts that essentially reflect the most relevant areas of tourism entrepreneurship today. These are:

- Part One – Understanding the conceptual basis of tourism entrepreneurship;
- Part Two – Creative use of entrepreneurship and processes of social innovation;
- Part Three – Tourism entrepreneurship mediating the global–local divide; and
- Part Four – Sectoral strategies and policy issues of tourism entrepreneurship.

All chapters are structured so as to provide a solid and essential theoretical understanding of the related concepts. The link between theory and practice is one of the main features of all the chapters, which is achieved through a blend of contrasting geographical contexts from different spatial scales (local, regional, national and international). Diversity of cases provides the reader with an opportunity to compare cases from different perspectives and see how the process of tourism development/entrepreneurship is shaped by a multiplicity of factors in specific geographical settings.

Part One – Understanding the Conceptual Basis of Tourism Entrepreneurship

Chapter 2 provides a general understanding of three important areas of tourism entrepreneurship including: tourism-related concepts (e.g. tourism industry, tourism product, and tourism forms); tourism development and growth since the end of the Second World War; and existing research in the field of tourism entrepreneurship.

Chapter 3 unravels the complexity of issues related to the entrepreneur and the entrepreneurial process. The chapter covers early research on entrepreneurs and their characteristics, and enhances our understanding of the key theoretical models of entrepreneurial behaviour, the nature of the process that drives entrepreneurship, and some of the most important policy measures that could be put in place in order to increase the 'stock' of entrepreneurs.

Part Two – Creative Use of Entrepreneurship and Processes of Social Innovation

From a number of different disciplines, Chapter 4 effectively communicates issues associated with innovation and entrepreneurship where tourism is clearly treated as a distinctive context linked to the social, cultural, economic, institutional and regulatory environment. The central theme of the chapter is the power structures and relations in the process of tourism development and innovation, articulated though a number of examples related to tourism and tourism product development across the Nordic countries.

Chapter 5 contributes to our understanding of women entrepreneurship in tourism, both conceptually and empirically. In connecting women entrepreneurship in tourism and the empowerment of women, this chapter aims to approach the issue of women's empowerment in a positive way instead of the usual 'a priori victimizing' approach. The authors have also made an attempt to unravel the real meaning behind the terminology of community development, social change, and preservation of cultural and natural heritage.

Chapter 6 gives the reader a unique opportunity to understand the way the public sector shapes and creates an environment conducive to tourism innovation. This chapter introduces the importance of knowledge management in the tourism context through individual cases from Scandinavia and Scotland.

Chapter 7 outlines the concept of institutional entrepreneurship, an emerging field that is highly relevant to the tourism context. The chapter provides an analysis of two examples of institutional entrepreneurship from which readers can compare and relate to the broader issues of entrepreneurship. It also provides a link between entrepreneurship and institutional entrepreneurship, and the implications of these activities for the broader field of tourism.

Part Three – Tourism Entrepreneurship Mediating the Global–Local Divide

Chapter 8 gives a critical account of the cultural and economic importance of the craft industry, and highlights links between the craft sector and tourism. The chapter explains how the craft sector provides a source of creativity and innovation in relation to the process of entrepreneurship by using examples of typical craft firms from the Celtic cultural context.

Chapter 9 is about tourism entrepreneurship and regional development. The chapter, based an empirical research conducted in a region in New Zealand, identified the key factors that steer the process of tourism development. In order to better understand such a complex process the bottom-up theory provides the conceptual base.

Chapter 10 identifies and discusses entrepreneurial opportunities of the African sub-Saharan wildlife. A number of important issues are addressed and explained including the dual role of tourism resources in terms of the protection and commercialization of the wildlife, as well as the main obstacles that prevent local communities benefiting more from wildlife resources. By understanding the nature of the impact of the media industry on the African wildlife, and the role of international organizations and institutions in protecting the resources, this chapter illuminates the way tourism entrepreneurship mediates the global–local separate.

Chapter 11 explains and dismisses some of the main misconceptions related to an alternative form of tourism development in a context where tourism is regarded as one of the main sources of income and vehicles for local devilment. By using a Fiji island as an example, this chapter critically assesses the process of tourism entrepreneurship with all the key issues and implications. It provides an understanding of the cultural detachment between local consumers and local producers. Both the theoretical and practical lessons from Indigenous Entrepreneurship on Vatulele Island, Fiji, might be applicable in other similar contexts worldwide.

Chapter 12 provides a novel approach to explaining regional tourism development and institutional/social entrepreneurship, in the specific political and historical context of the Balkans, where various internal and external political influences and personal interests inevitably burden the process of regional development. In this chapter an international NGO is presented as a leading force in enhancing entrepreneurship through social capacity building (SCB) with the ultimate objective of helping local communities to convert their economic and social weaknesses into strengths.

Part Four – Sectoral Strategies and Policy Issues of Tourism Entrepreneurship

Chapter 13 provides a comprehensive coverage of the public policy context of tourism and its innovative development. The chapter systematically explains the complexity of the tourism policy system, and how tourism entrepreneurs and firms are embedded within institutional structures in which the activities of government and the state are dominant.

Chapter 14 explores methods by which sustainable rural development takes an integrated approach in terms of how start-up, implementation and development is supported by and benefits from the notion of a core of multiple stakeholders. Primarily this relates to a model, based on international precedents, which was developed in Slovenia – a country that joined the European Union in 2004.

Chapter 15 explains the context of Information Communication Technologies (ICTs) within the tourism entrepreneurship, focusing on small-to-medium-sized tourism enterprises SMTEs, which play an important role in the process of tourism innovation. The chapter explores the strategic strengths and weaknesses of SMTEs related to the ICT applications, as well as the diffusion of innovations and the different stages of ICT engagement in the tourism sector at whole.

Chapter 16 is concerned with issues connected to the delivery of financing structures which match the demands and requirements of tourism entrepreneurs. More specifically, this chapter tends to focus on the micro- and small-scale tourism sector whilst at the same time providing examples from similar issues facing tourism SMEs in a selection of European transition economies.

Chapter 17 assesses the complexity and importance of the tourism distribution value chain. It identifies the most recent theoretical contribution and empirical research on tourism distribution systems as well as assessing the impact of technological change (the Internet and associated technologies) on tourism distribution. Innovation in New Zealand tourism through improved distribution channels is the empirical context of the chapter.

Chapter 18 addresses and explores the gap in knowledge, related to the tourism graduate career decision-making, by investigating the entrepreneurial intentions of tourism students who had undertaken a year's work placement in tourism SMEs. Although the discussion takes place largely within a British context, the insights offered into entrepreneurial intentions are likely to be of wider relevance. The discussion is based on the theoretical context of the Shapero's Model of the Entrepreneurial Event and Ajzen's Theory of Planned Behaviour.

By using specific sources of historical data, such as newspapers, Chapter19 explains the role of crisis in the business environment, and demonstrates how one large entrepreneurial and international company, Thomas Cook & Sons Ltd, responded to a major crisis. The chapter also identifies the challenges posed by operating in a wartime setting where travel is not able to operate in a free market setting and government intervention is a dominant feature in order to meet national wartime efficiency objectives.

Part 1

Understanding the Conceptual Basis of Tourism Entrepreneurship

Chapter 2

Tourism Entrepreneurship – Concepts and Issues

Jovo Ateljevic and Lan Li

Learning Outcomes

After reading this chapter, you should be able to:

- Gain a general understanding of tourism as a distinctive social and economic phenomenon;

- Understand the key tourism concepts such as tourism as a social phenomenon, tourism as an industry or collections of industries, tourism product, tourism forms, tourism development and planning, and tourism entrepreneurship;

- Expand the theoretical understanding of different phases of tourism development and growth since the end of the Second World War; and

- Understand the characteristics of entrepreneurship research in the field of tourism and identify entrepreneurship research progress and potential for tourism scholars.

Introduction

This chapter, after reflection upon the structure of the book and the underling issues, provides the necessary understanding of concepts that are used throughout the book. Certainly, most of the concepts related to tourism development and entrepreneurship are not new; however this is a new approach to explain an increasingly complex relationship, and the process of tourism development and innovation.

Tourism is a broad and confusing concept and means different things to different people. An inconsistency also exists amongst scholars who tackle tourism from a range of disciplinary perspectives. The complex nature of tourism and its interdisciplinary nature are the key reasons for the lack of an adequate theoretical foundation for understanding tourism as a distinctive social and economic phenomenon. From the perspective of entrepreneurship, tourism provides a specific context that is perceived to be different from other industrial sectors in terms of identification of entrepreneurial opportunities and the process of their conversion into a consumable tourism product. In this process there is more often a multiplicity of stakeholders with individual motivation for a coordinated approach to develop a vital component of the economy through a strategy that is focused on economic yield while considering environmental, social and cultural values.

Even though tourism seems to be a rewarding sector for investors and entrepreneurs the concept of tourism entrepreneurship has not been adequately understood. The limited literature in the area of the tourism entrepreneurship suggests there is little entrepreneurial behaviour in the sector. The reality, however, proves the opposite. The hospitality and tourism industry has been a fertile field for entrepreneurial business. Thomas Cook's tour packages, Ray Kroc's McDonald's, Walt Disney's theme parks, J.W. Marriott's and Conrad Hilton's hotels are just a few classic entrepreneurial brands in the world of hospitality and travel enterprises. Driven by an inner need to succeed and to make a difference in some way, these truly successful entrepreneurs focused on their opportunities and pursued them with great dedication and courage in the face of opposition and setbacks. All of these entrepreneurial leaders have engraved their names and businesses in the history of the hospitality and travel industry.

We are also witnessing new approaches by both the private and public sectors in the creation of innovative businesses as well as tourism development models worldwide. These novelties may not, however, be always visible or measurable by strict business criteria. The tourism product is often intangible and secondary to main commercial tourism activities; and it is therefore difficult to prove its market value. The ever-increasing scale of tourism, one of the fastest growing sectors of the global economy, is not only driven by human needs and a desire for travel but also by business opportunities to respond to increasingly complex human needs and curiosities (Lee and Crompton, 1992). These opportunities are realized through the commercialization of nature, culture, traditions, history, religions as well as other commercial activities and human achievements. In order to examine the level of entrepreneurship and the factors that underpin such behaviour in the tourism sector, it is necessary to understand the industry structure that is more complex, as opposed to other industrial sectors and, to a greater degree, integrated into a wider social and economic context.

The main objective of this chapter is to reflect upon the distinctiveness of the tourism sector with the ultimate aim of contributing to the better understanding of tourism entrepreneurship. The chapter will start with an explanation of tourism concepts, followed by a discussion of tourism products, tourism development and planning, and, finally, entrepreneurship.

Tourism: Concepts, Forms and Significance

Although tourism is a field of study in its own right, the context has frequently been used across disciplines that try to explain this social and global phenomenon from different perspectives, linked to its expansion and complexity (see Page and Connell, 2006). Indeed, tourist movement and activity that sustains it have experienced steady growth in the preceding 50 years, underpinned by a number of interrelated factors including technological advancement (e.g. transportation, digital technologies) and various forms of global exchange accelerated by the world trade liberalization. For example, tourism as a form of international trade has significantly benefited the establishment of the WTO (World Trade Organization), which places particular emphasis on the liberalization of international trade in services (Cornelissen, 2005). In such a liberalized business environment, the mobility of financial and other forms of capital have contributed to the growth of travel, creating opportunities for an increasing number of small-to-medium-sized tourism businesses.

At the same time, as Cornelissen (2005) explains, capital coagulation through intra/trans-sectoral merges has also increased, providing greater opportunities for large multinationals. These organizations, individually or through strategic alliances within and outside the tourism sector facilitated by ICT (information and communication technology), are able to shape both tourism demand (e.g. cheap travel packages) and supply (i.e. investment taking advantage of weak local economies, subcontracting and outsourcing).

Generally speaking, tourism is a social phenomenon associated with human travel for different pursuits including business, leisure, pleasure, religion, education, security and politics. This definition only provides part of the explanation as tourists or travellers enter a range of activities before, during and after the travel experience, in return creating an increasing number of interconnected activities in economical, social, political, policy and educational forms. As a consequence of the complexity of tourist motivation, there is a number of tourism forms defined according to the purpose of travel or other common features related to both the supply and demand sides. Any such definition is essentially incomplete yet pragmatic; it reveals little of many forms that tourism can take. The most common forms of tourism are now discussed.

Nature-based Tourism

This form of tourism is often considered a segment of rural tourism and referred to as nature-based tourism, ecotourism or sometimes recreation-based tourism. Nature-based tourism attracts people interested in visiting natural areas for a variety of reasons. Nature-related and rural tourism cover a broad range of activities including hiking, backpacking, bird watching, camping, kayaking, fishing, hunting, nature photography, scuba diving, and visiting parks, farms and orchards. Such types of tourism are inadequately developed in many countries despite very favourable natural resources. This is due to the lack of adequate facilities, infrastructure and creativity of local people.

The concept of ecotourism was initially used to describe nature-based *travel* to undisturbed areas with an emphasis on education. The model of ecotourism has, however, been broadened and has taken a scientific turn in its approach to planning, management and development of sustainable tourism activities. It is an approach that creates a range of quality tourism products that are environmentally and ecologically sustainable, economically viable, and socially acceptable.

Mountain and Winter (or Ski) Tourism

Mountain and winter (or ski) tourism are relatively recent phenomena, particularly ski tourism which began to be more organized in the 1930s with the invention of cable cars for the vertical transportation of skiers in the Swiss, Austrian and French Alps. In fact, the development of the cable car system has, over time, influenced the development of other forms of mountain tourism such as hiking, mountain biking and other outdoor pursuits. This type of mountain tourism is highly spatially diffused; it does not have the same concentration of visitors' flow effects nor the economic impact that the ski resorts have in winter. It also requires much more innovation and skills by those involved in its development.

Competition for mountain tourism is increasingly strong around the globe. Recent evidence suggests that 10% of towns and tourist centres attempt to develop this form of tourism. Only in the European Alps are there more than 50 medium-to-large-sized tourist centres. Marketing campaigns (International Institute for Tourism, 2005) for this form of tourism include a range of points to attract visitors which includes: the diversity and high quantity of resources; mountains; history; climate; lifestyle; hospitality; peacefulness; authenticity; and art, crafts and culture.

Adventure and Youth Tourism

The context of these forms of tourism, particularly adventure tourism, are very much associated with the above mentioned forms of tourism, as most of the adventure activities are nature-based. However, adventure and youth tourism are more management and marketing constructs, with the aim of creating business opportunities with the improvement of existing products. Although wildlife and nature play important roles, adventure travel is not synonymous with ecotourism as the factors of risk and challenge are typically involved. Adventure tourism is not a monoculture because the players are involved in many different kinds of soft and hard adventure activities (from trekking, canoeing, whitewater rafting to parachuting, bungee jumping and flying fighter jets). As with entrepreneurs, the demographics of adventure travellers are rather broad. Personality, as well as ideology and political beliefs, is an important characteristic of both, as they are influenced by politics and similar risks. This form of tourism has created an increasing number of small and mid-sized companies.

The 'youth traveller' is defined as a young person, aged 30 or under, who is travelling outside the family structure but not for business, and not primarily to visit friends or relatives, and whose travel includes at least one overnight stay. Youth travellers are normally free and independent travellers (FIT) embarking individually or in groups for different purposes, including education and personal development. This is the most dynamic market in terms of growth interests and spatial movements (e.g. over 200,000 youths from New Zealand travel overseas every year). Youth travellers tend to stay longer on a single trip (sometimes for a year or more, frequently changing places), stay in budget accommodation establishments (hostels, backpackers), and experiment with different experiences including adventure activities and attending special events.

Spa and Wellness Tourism

Although once considered a luxury, spas have recently become a more accessible means of achieving physical, mental and spiritual restoration. Sports, fitness exercises, hot natural mineral waters, massage, alternative therapies, saunas, and a range of other services and facilities are all designed to help the human body recover from a busy lifestyle. This is often complemented with a healthy and balanced diet. Many people no longer see the spa as a luxury, but as a prerequisite to staying healthy and looking good. In many countries spas have been transformed and developed alongside the increase in fitness and leisure centres and the growing trend for more luxurious facilities.

The spa market has shown strong growth in the last decade, attracting a wide range of markets such as teenage females, young professionals and other business people. Evidence suggests that in the last couple of years, spas saw an influx of teenage girls seeking beauty treatments and the thrill of a luxurious spa experience. Business opportunities are being increasingly realized; the number of spa locations doubles in number every four years and the number of locations has increased by an average of 20% annually over the last eight years.

Urban, City and Cultural Tourism

The World Tourism Organization predicts that international tourist arrivals are expected to reach 1.6 billion by the year 2020. The forecast is based on a modest growth rate of between 4.3% and 6.7%, which is less than the current growth rate. It is also predicted that most of this increase will have to be absorbed by cities which don't include domestic tourism movements.

Indeed, one of the most important trends in world tourism over the past decade has been the rise in short-break trips, mainly to easily accessible cities. This has been reflected in the reduction of the average length of tourist trips to most destinations worldwide. Various interlinked factors have contributed to such traveller behaviour. These include changes in lifestyle, irregular working patterns, job insecurity and lack of time on the one hand, and consumer interest in heritage and urban development and travellers' search for things to do and spending opportunities, on the other. Consequently, people tend to choose destinations that can be reached easily and quickly. This trend in the tourist movement has benefited short-haul, accessible destinations and has contributed to the growth of short-break, city or urban tourism. Policy-makers seeing tourism as an avenue for overall economic development have also increasingly promoted a growing trend in urban areas.

Transport access is a crucial infrastructure component for a successful tourism industry. The impact of low-cost airlines, like Ryanair and easyJet from Europe, has had a major influence on the increasing popularity and accessibility of cities. Tourists visit cities and urban localities for different purposes, often combining two or more in a single visit. Culture, history, education, business and visit in transit are the most common motivators for city visitors. Research shows that about 20% of city tourists in Europe rate culture as their prime motivator; however, far more city visitors are actually involved in cultural activities while on a city trip. Nevertheless, shopping, consumption of food and beverages, and entertainment are the fundamental desires of typical tourists visiting cities.

Business tourism is an important and distinctive market segment providing disproportionate benefits to a country's urban centres. High spending levels by conference delegates, for example, result in a disproportionate contribution to local income and employment, and have the effect of boosting tourism spending during off-season periods.

The quality of tourism in cities significantly contributes to the sustainable development of urban as well as regional areas by creating diverse tourism products and services.

The development of city tourism largely depends on the local authorities and their entrepreneurial ability to respond to new tourism trends.

Religious or Pilgrimage Tourism

This is one of the oldest forms of tourism, which is still growing strong. Religious tourism forms an integral part of the tourist industry. This form of tourism generates more than US $18 billion for the US tourism industry (Larkin, 2008). Other evidence suggests that religious tourism remains a focal point of tourism (Hitrec, 2006).

Religious tourism is associated with spirituality offering to believers a facility to exercise their worshipping. Both religion (e.g. Hinduism, Islam, Judaism, Christianity, Buddhism) and spirituality (e.g. the spiritual philosophies of East Asia) are among the most common motivations for travel. Many tourism destinations have developed largely as a result of their connections to sacred people, places and events. Sociologies, on the other hand, view religious tourism as an opportunity for some people to access sacred art and unique architecture.

Both the demand and supply side have contributed to a growing popularity of religious and pilgrimage tourism. While travellers have been seeking more authentic experiences, such as spiritual and cultural traditions, there has been an emergence of more diverse tourist products. This is due to national tourism organizations and individual region and tourism-related businesses that seek to extend the traditional tourist season. An increasing number of travel agents offer religious tourism and pilgrimage tours where people seek more unusual holidays or more diversification within a single trip.

Maritime Tourism

The most ubiquitous form of tourism is associated with sea, sand and sun. It can be defined as 'maritime tourism'. This form of tourism is a very significant economic and social force in Mediterranean countries. Factors contributing to the expansion of maritime tourism include the existence of a sunny climate and sandy beaches, close proximity to the growing markets of Western Europe, relative low prices in some destinations and the development of low-cost package holidays. Despite the shifting tourist demand from the so-called 'old-passive' to the 'new-active' and diverse, seaside tourism is still increasing and representing more than one-third of the total tourist demand in Europe (IPK International, 2005).

An increasing number of low-fare airlines, in alliance with accommodation and land transport companies, have additionally contributed to a steady growth of this type of tourism. Decreasing airfare costs in general has contributed to the growing competition amongst coastal tourist destinations. Emerging new destinations in southeast Europe (e.g. Romania, Bulgaria), Asia (e.g. Vietnam, Laos) and the Caribbean (e.g. Cuba) offer more choices for European's summer holidaymakers (the worlds' largest tourist market). Such trends have begun to force traditional destinations in the Mediterranean region to reinvent their conventional 'sea, sand and sun' product by introducing value-for-money strategies such as better customer service and better quality food. Relaxation and 'doing nothing' (attributes associated with the traditional summer holiday) are the main motivators for the majority of seaside holidaymakers, therefore higher quality accommodation, food, and entertainment are the key competitive advantages for coastal destinations.

The forms of tourism discussed above provide only part of the full picture of tourism movements, as the human desire and motivation for travel is much broader and complex. Understanding human behaviour is the key requirement for tourism industry suppliers to fulfil travellers' complex needs and wants. These complex desires then need to be skilfully translated into a range of individual tourism products.

The Tourism Product: What Makes It Specific?

The concept of the tourism product, despite its importance, is the least understood area of all tourism-related topics. Mainstream tourism literature is more focused on destination as an amalgamation of individual tourism products and services, while the individual tourism experience has been somewhat neglected (Komppula, 2001).

The tourism industry, which encompasses a number of individual sectors, includes a range of fulfilments from a single fulfilment or tourist need (e.g. meal, bed, transportation) to fulfilment of a traveller's entire holiday needs (e.g. packaged holiday). The 'package' is perceived by the tourist as an experience, available at a price, and has been defined as the so-called 'components model' of a destination consisting of five components: destination attractions, destination facilities, accessibility, images and price. As such, the tourist product is divided in two levels: a) the total level referring to the total tourists experience (from the time one leaves home to the time one returns), and b) the specific level referring to a discrete product offered by a single business (Komppula, 2001).

There are a number of additional features that make the tourism product unique: most tourism products or services are often intangible and inhomogeneous, they can not be standardized as many factors may shape the tourist experience, and it is, for example, unlikely that any product can ever be perceived equally by all customers. Most tourism-related products or services involve only the actions on behalf of the customer and have little tangible substance. Tangible products can be related to either a single tourist activity or need, such as horse riding, accommodation, and transportation, or the combination of a number of activities and needs.

As opposed to other industries where products have a more clearly defined utility or used value (and this can be seen or felt before the act of consumption), in tourism, the product utility is more often based on the tourists' perception and curiosity. Understanding human curiosity is, in fact, an essential precondition to understanding tourism entrepreneurship as manipulation of human curiosity for commercial purposes is at the very heart of the entrepreneurial ability. In the context of tourism, human curiosity is well depicted in the following quote:

> The miraculous power that will drive man to the far reaches of the universe isn't anything tangible...the power that will get men there comes from within. It is called curiosity. We travel on an endless road, motivated by the excitement we experience with each new discovery...
>
> (Ward, 2007, p. 1)

Many examples prove that human curiosity is indeed the core pillar of many tourism products and services. A tourism product can be almost anything that provokes human curiosity and as long as that 'anything' is named, described, priced and offered.

By taking advantage of human nature, tourism destinations and individual businesses try hard to commercialize history, traditions, nature, cuisines, religions and the community spirit in order to create tourism products. To create a successful tourism business model or destination, a number of distinctive activities and innovative approaches must be undertaken, and often through a collective action by both private and public sectors. Sweden's Icehotel in Lapland is a good example that demonstrates how entrepreneurs, through a private–public partnership, have exploited human curiosity; the product is closely associated with snow and ice. The hotel has also triggered a number of additional innovative tourism products including the Ice Church and Ice Theatre.

There has been relatively little contribution by tourism literature to the area of product development in assisting existing and new tourism businesses to create their competitive position in the volatile tourism market. The research on product development in tourism is dominated by research on destination development, representing planning approach in most cases. The existing research does not offer any explanation on how the new innovations are developed into product concepts in individual tourism companies. Innovative tourism business models are, as Hjalager et al. (2008, p. 11) believe, those where 'innovation can hardly be seen as the targeted action of an individual tourism organization'; such a limited view does not therefore provide a full picture of innovative activity in the industry. Tourism development, tourism product development and other related themes are comprehensively discussed in many chapters of this book.

Tourism: An Industry, Economic Contributors, Process of Development

Tourism, as an industry, gained international recognition in the 1960s due to, primarily, its economic and political significance. However, as the industry encompasses a range of tourism services it inevitably questions the concept of tourism as a single industry. Some scholars argue that 'global tourism production involves an overlay of different types of industries and economic activities' (Cornelissen, 2005, p. 80). Tourism industry, as a generic term, has never been based on any serious theoretical interpretations but mainly 'relied on simplistic propositions' (Leiper, 2008, p. 239). Leiper seriously challenges the validity of 'the tourism industry' as a singular concept arguing that 'it is an overly simplistic, mistaken and misleading idea, which should be replaced, in generic contexts, by the plural term, 'tourism industries' (2008, p. 237). Moreover, the International Standard Industrial Classification (ISIC) framework also regards tourism as tourism-related activities (ISIC, 1990).

The 'tourism industry' as a singular concept fails a number of theoretical tests including: the test of evidence, the test of internal consistency, the test of consistency with other well-tested theories and the check on the problem (to what extent the theory can solve the problem) (Champion, 2005). It fails the test of evidence due to empirical research showing that many businesses supplying goods and services directly to tourists have no industrial relationship to tourism (Firth, 2002). The tourism industry does not have an internal consistency as its consumers cannot be clearly defined. Other theories suggest that the tourism industry is a pluralistic concept as it lacks consistency regarding substitutes, cooperation and strategic management, applied to identify industries. From the perspective of the demand-side, the tourism industry includes an increasing number of suppliers which are not necessarily related to tourism, implying that many suppliers have only a revenue-collecting role and not an industry one (Leiper, 2008). Likewise, Tremblay (1998) argues that tourism is an increasingly dynamic and fragmented system of production consisting of a number of diverse firms that serve a wide range of customers, not only tourists.

The singular concept ('the industry') has both pragmatic and political justification as it 'simplifies dialogue between governments, public sector bureaucrats, industrial interests, and lobbyists representing industrial interests in dealing with governments and public servants' (Leiper, 2008, p. 239). Public justification campaigns are backed up with statistical claims to show that the industry is large and valuable with potential for growth, and therefore requires government assistance. However, this very pragmatism and simplification is the main cause of confusion in terms of measuring tourism impacts, as well as defining the level of tourism entrepreneurship.

Although the concept of 'the tourism industry' has been widely adopted by scholars and practitioners, some countries use it loosely. For example, Australia does not recognize tourism as an individual industry and has no definition for 'tourism' as such, but instead an incorporation of diverse industries or sectors that directly or indirectly cater to the tourist needs. In this country there are five direct commercial sectors under the umbrella of the tourism industry: accommodation, transport carriers, attractions, tour operators and wholesalers, promotions and distributions, and retail services. Such structure is sometimes arbitrary as some activities (e.g. various forms of arts and museums) from other industries could easily fall into a section under the tourism sector, thus further complicating the notion of the tourism product (March, 2003).

Economic Significance: The Problem of Measurement

More than anything else, tourism is an important economic activity. As a result of domestic and international travel, the scale of its economic benefit is enormous. Many economies around the globe almost entirely rely on the tourism sector. However, due to the secondary effects or multipliers created by tourism, the economic impact is often difficult to measure (see Archer, 1982). The concept of tourism's multipliers, developed by Archer (1977), explains how tourism, as a result of its diverse production structure, has the ability to generate revenue in multiple ways: money spent by tourists stimulates spending by residents, businesses and government in the locality which in return generates the flow (Cornelissen, 2005).

As a result of the problem associated with its economic evaluation, tourism in many countries suffers from a lack of political and popular support because its true economic significance has often been underestimated. It has hitherto been approached mainly as a consumer activity, hence the focus of analyses on the traveller, trip characteristics and other demand-side aspects.

While other industries, such as agriculture or manufacturing, are classified in accordance with goods and services they produce, tourism is defined by the characteristics of the customer demanding tourism products. As such an economic benefit created by tourism requires alternative measurement systems. Tourism Satellite Account (TSA)[1] has been introduced to measure the economic contribution of tourism to the gross domestic product (GDP) and to provide analysis of the national tourism industry. Now there is increasing awareness of tourism's role as a productive activity and its potential in generating employment, government income and other benefits whether directly or through induced effects in the economy.

The real economic benefit is greater in larger specialized tourist economies because of their ability to support linked specialist services and manufacturing (Shaw and Williams, 1998). Forms and scales of tourism activities are important parts of the equation; smaller locally owned tourism firms are less likely to create profit leakages as multinational tourism organizations do.

To ensure that tourism benefit is maximized and balanced with broader economic, social and environmental objectives, its development requires a holistic strategic approach by both private and public sectors at all spatial levels. Less entrepreneurial tourist destinations, e.g. certain countries, regions and places, face challenges of how to fully exploit their tourism potential and opportunities. Many fail to create suitable tourism products; instead they put more emphasis on marketing activities, thus leaving out possibilities for unwanted types and scales of tourism development. The following section focuses on tourism development and its evolution since the emergence of mass tourism after the Second World War.

Tourism Development: From Boosterism to Sustainability – From Entrepreneurship to Entrepreneurism

Since the emergence of mass tourism in the late 1950s and early 1960s, tourism development has gone through a number of distinctive phases: from simplistic planning (to yield economic benefit), the saturation stage in the late 1980s (tourism implications impacts assessments) and the current phase of sustainable tourism development characterized by an increasing number of innovative models and approaches. Tourism

---

1. Input–output tables which give a detailed picture of the economy broken down by industry, product, primary input and final demand category, provide the starting point for deriving final accounts. The following main variables are used. *Direct Tourism Demand* is equivalent to tourism expenditure, excluding VAT. *Indirect Tourism Demand* is the value of intermediate inputs used in the production of goods and services sold to tourists. *Tourism Product Ratio* represents the proportion of the supply of a product purchased by tourists. TSA is also a powerful database that makes it possible to quantify tourism's economic impacts. This function entails the constant collaboration of National Tourism Administrations with other government ministries and bodies (such as central banks, national statistical offices, Ministries of Finance, and migration authorities). http://stats.oecd.org/glossary/index.htm

development is not an isolated socio-economic process but an integral part of a broader cultural, political, socio-economic structural transformation. In the past five decades a number of theories highlight strong links between tourism and development that are connected by different types of factors and common activities in the area of consumption, production and institutional infrastructure.

Against this backdrop four distinctive phases of tourism development are identified:

* Boosterism;
* Expansion of mass tourism;
* Tourism as resource user; and
* Alternative approaches to tourism development.

Phase One: Boosterism

The early approach to tourism development was characterized by the emergence of mass tourism – package tours based on products mainly associated with summer holidays and sea resorts. This form of tourism, in theory, is labelled as boosterism (Hasse, 2001), with an emphasis on the economic benefit without questioning possible negative impacts. This was a reactive approach to tourism development with the ultimate objective of accommodating the growing demand, particularly from Western European countries. Tourism planning and development was mainly initiated and executed at top government levels without involvement of the local community in the decision-making process (Hall et al., 1997).

This period of tourism development coincides with the modernization theory, or discourse of Enlightenment, in the late 1940s and early 1950s, reflecting the period of fundamental political and economic changes in Western Europe. The term 'modern' denotes the model of social progress (Gardner and Lewis, 1996). As such the modernization theory ignores contextual differences related to, for example, local cultures and traditions, which in fact were regarded as obstacles to progress and development.

Phase Two: Expansion of Mass Tourism

Tourism in the 1960s and 1970s was consumed on a mass scale created by fast social and economic changes (Ionides and Debbage, 1997). Advanced technology, transport in particular, for the most part facilitated the replication of mass tourism on a global scale (Pearce, 1987). As such tourism displayed almost all the characteristics of the manufacturing sector; that is to say it was standardized and rigidly packaged (Poon, 1993). Being recognized as an agent for economic growth, tourism development gained political significance, making tourism one of the top priorities for politicians and policy-makers (Williams and Shaw, 1991). The emphasis from planning that prevailed during Phase One was shifted on to the area of marketing and market diversification.

This phase of development is associated with the dependency theory based on Marxist and neo-Marxist critical views of capitalism (Schuurman, 1996). The paradigm has major implications in tourism devolvement addressing the problems of core-periphery relations, highlighting the issues of the negative impacts on natural resources in local communities, and criticizing the aggressive approach of multinationals which, by pursuing unsustainable development, take advantage of natural resources and economically depressed localities (Britton, 1991). Despite a variety of theories that had proposed models to solve the growing problems, these academic efforts did not make much impact in practice (Gardner and Lewis, 1996).

Phase Three: Tourism as Resource User

Full-scale mass tourism was reached by the mid-1970s. Tourism overdevelopment and evidence of its negative impacts, on the natural environment in particular, became increasingly visible. This created space for scholars to assume that tourism is a resource user and its development should be defined in environmental terms. Studies addressing environmental, social and other impacts made by uncontrolled tourism activities started to proliferate. Planning for tourism replaced the term 'tourism planning' as the purely economic approach to tourism development became superseded (Pearce, 1996).

Shifts in tourism development in the post-Ford era were a direct consequence of the macroeconomic crises and declining rates of corporate profit in the manufacturing sector during the 1970s. In fact, tourism has benefited directly from the new economic order that emerged in the post-industrial society, in which tourist activity has become a privileged production space turning into one of the most sophisticated occupations and business opportunities of high value-added service industries (Montanari and Williams, 1995). On the other hand, global transition has been instrumental for travel, tourism and leisure activities where tailor-made tourism products and services can be offered to a growing number of sophisticated and experienced travellers (Morgan and Pritchard, 2000).

During this period scholarly debates began about the failure of 30 years of conventional, technocratic, top-down development programmes in many countries (Hasse, 2001). At the end of the 1980s, the neo-liberal development doctrine of structural economic adjustment came into being. This was followed by government restructuring giving more autonomy to local authorities obligated to serve the best interests of the local economy (Hirst, 1997). The deregulation of the welfare state and the 'mean–lean' policy by many developed and developing countries pushed an increasing number of individuals to pursue entrepreneurial opportunities in the steady growth of the tourism industry (Ateljevic, 2002). In fact, both private and public sectors saw entrepreneurship and innovation as a way forward.

Having emerged as autonomous entities with inadequate funding and revenue sources, local governments have become more proactive in collaboration with the private sector in their respective areas. Public–Private Partnership (PPP) grew rapidly during the macroeconomic dislocation of the late 1970s and throughout the 1980s and 1990s has become particularly strong in the tourism sector.

Phase Four: Alternative Approaches to Tourism Development

This phase is characterized by sustainable tourism development,[2] giving more power to the community in the process of development. Many scholars also discuss alternative forms of tourism development that are in line with the principles of sustainability. The concept of alternative tourism refers to nature-based, ecological, environmentally friendly, green, cultural and indigenous tourism (Mowforth and Munt, 1998). One of the key principles of the alternative form of tourist development is participation by various stakeholders in the decision-making process.

Alternative forms of tourism development have also been influenced by the tourism demand and emergence of so-called 'new' travellers (Poon, 1993) seeking more alternatives. Such changing traveller behaviour (e.g. manifestation in lifestyle expression, individualism and self-enhancement) is a direct consequence of an invisible social process shaped by various forces. 'New' more knowledgeable travellers look for different destinations and new forms of experience translated into the desire for adventure and authenticity. In the context of this shift, and the corresponding demand for differentiated, 'tailor-made' tourism products, opportunities have been created worldwide for a wider array of specialized smaller-scale tourism firms.

The shift moved from a professional paradigm focusing on things such as physical infrastructure and industrial work in the 1950s and 1960s, towards the new paradigm from the early 1990s onwards focusing on people – reversing the direction of tourism development from top-down to bottom-up – making the process of the development more diverse, complex and dynamic (Chambers, 1997). The contemporary development theory, often labelled as post-modernism[3] or post-development, was an inevitable shift from the neo-liberal paradigm in which the role of the state has changed; 'it is not all powerful in progress only from a plurality of sources of power into dialogue and the state is not wealthy in itself therefore should promote shared wealth' (Curtis, 1997). The changing state involvement in economic (tourism) development has meant greater mobility and more opportunities for different actors including international non-governmental organizations (NGOs) trying to fill in the gaps those governments either will not, or cannot.

Nevertheless, government involvement in tourism planning and development remains vital. In order to take advantage of the intensification of international and domestic tourist movements, national governments have introduced innovative policies and major institutional changes. Old inefficient and bureaucratic institutions and organizations have been replaced by more dynamic, entrepreneurial and market-oriented ones capable of recognizing new travel trends and responding to the fast-changing business environment. Governments may take actions that are expressed through specific tourism policies that are implemented by various government agencies at national, regional and local levels.

---

2. The World Tourism Organization defines sustainable tourism as 'tourism which leads to management of all resources in such a way that economic, social and aesthetic needs can be filled while maintaining cultural integrity, essential ecological processes, biological diversity and life support systems.'
3. The post-modernist approach is associated with diversity and cultural relativity, complex diversity of the real world of development, social construction of reality and other aspects related to human nature and its behaviour.

Pearce (2001) implies that there are frequently no clear-cut responsibilities and well-developed policies for tourism planning and development. The institutional environment has been further enhanced by various forms of partnership with the private sector. The emergence of new markets as well as tourist destinations has brought new types of development opportunities as well as challenges for individual businesses and places; therefore a collective action by various stakeholders in destinations has become increasingly important. This gives rise to opportunities for entrepreneurship in tourism.

Tourism and Entrepreneurship

Entrepreneurship: A General Overview

Entrepreneurship research is a relatively young field. Some scholars argue that it is in its adolescence (Low and MacMillan, 1988), others that it is still emerging (Busenitz et al., 2003). Supporting these positions are arguments suggesting that entrepreneurship is a field: (1) in which the search for a distinct theory of entrepreneurship continues; (2) that is characterized by low paradigmatic development (Ireland et al., 2005). Scholars have also frequently evaluated its progress and status as an independent field of study (Davidsson, 2003; Sarasvathy, 2004; Smith et al., 1989).

The notion of entrepreneurship is often associated with new and innovative economic activity, and innovation per se is very broad, encompassing a number of entrepreneurial principles: innovation materializes in new products, new services, new processes, new raw materials, new organizational forms and new markets (Schumpeter, 1934). Entrepreneurship has been studied for more than a century and across a number of disciplines. Such a multidisciplinary character has most likely contributed to a lack of consensus in defining and conceptualizing entrepreneurship. Due to its complexity, the concept of entrepreneurship is almost impossible to accommodate in one single definition.

One of the problems in defining entrepreneurship is related to the fact that it involves the nexus of two phenomena: the presence of lucrative opportunities and the presence of enterprising individuals (Venkataraman, 1997; Shane and Venkataraman, 2000). By defining the field in terms of the individual alone, entrepreneurship researchers have generated incomplete definitions that do not withstand the scrutiny of other scholars (Gartner, 1988). The definition of an entrepreneur as a person who establishes a new organization is an example of this problem. Because this definition does not include consideration of the variation in the quality of opportunities that different people identify, it leads researchers to neglect opportunities. Consequently, empirical support (or lack of support) for attributes that differentiate entrepreneurs from other members of society is often questionable because these attributes co-found the influence of opportunities and individuals. In contrast to previous research, Venkataraman (1997) defines the field of entrepreneurship as the scholarly examination of how, by whom, and with what effects opportunities to create future goods and services are discovered, evaluated, and exploited.

As entrepreneurship is a direct consequence of human behaviour that is underpinned by a range of attributes (Kirby, 2003), this further complicates the possibility of providing a more consistent and lasting definition. Given the dual character of entrepreneurship, economic and human engagement, three classes of theoretical perspectives have been identified. The first perspective refers to the economic school and theorists on the role of the entrepreneur in economic development. Second, the socio-behavioural theorists are concerned with the personal characteristics and traits and the social environment. The greatest contributor in the study of entrepreneurship is Max Weber, who argues that charisma and leadership are the key characteristics as the charismatic leader is not constrained by tradition or law and he or she is able to establish customs and roles in order to bring about changes. The third theoretical context is associated with the physiological perspective that is concerned with entrepreneurial personality; behavioural characteristics advocate that entrepreneurs are risk-takers and have a high need for achievement, control and autonomy.

The behavioural approach, based on activities and behaviours of entrepreneurs, appears to be the most popular amongst scholars (Gartner, 1990) who have identified a wide range of business behaviours that might be associated with entrepreneurship and entrepreneurial activities such as, for example, new venture creation, innovation, business ownership, business growth, and managing a larger business. In the early stage of its development the entrepreneurship field was viewed as a new venture creation (Schumpeter, 1934; McClelland, 1961; Vesper, 1980; Gartner, 1985). The position of this view has become weaker as business growth and innovation, the two essential components of entrepreneurship, vary significantly from venture to venture. Different activities may vary in degree of entrepreneurship depending upon underlying requirements or characteristics, such as opportunity perceptions (Kirzner, 1973, 1979), creativity (Torrance and Horng, 1980), innovation (Schumpeter, 1934), risk-taking (Knight, 1921; Begley, 1995; Stewart and Roth, 2001), locus of control (Perry et al., 1986), need for achievement (McClelland, 1961) and need for autonomy.

Motivation is an important factor to look at but it can delude us from the core principles associated with entrepreneurship. Motivation cannot easily change personality, which is the key driver within the entrepreneurial context; therefore it is not a good starting point in explaining entrepreneurial behaviour. However, the two are not mutually exclusive. Why some individuals are more entrepreneurial than others is a difficult question to answer. Many scholars suggest that personality is an important factor (see Chapter 4).

Entrepreneurship is often mixed up with the small business, although the two are not synonymous (Stewart and Roth, 2001). A new venture, which usually starts small, is more visible and measurable, therefore those launching and owning a new business are more likely to claim an entrepreneurial attribute. Indeed, in many new firms a limited degree of innovation might take place but not necessarily at the formation stage. The tourism context is not an exception. Although they have been greatly lauded in the context of regional development, sustainable development and economic diversification, only a small percentage of STFs (Small Tourism Firms) are truly entrepreneurial.

It is also inappropriate to link entrepreneurial to managerial capacity and vice versa. Schumpeter's principles remind us that entrepreneurship is associated with something innovative and original that could be the business idea and the business model. Entrepreneurship that is associated with innovation is highly complex and it is difficult to define. However, many scholars agree that innovation is related to the introduction and application of new ideas and practice within a role, group or organization (King, 1992).

Institutional and Collective Entrepreneurship

Studies of entrepreneurship tend to be preoccupied with the individual and the purely economic aspects of starting a new enterprise and subsequent business development (Spear, 2000, p. 1). In the context of tourism development, entrepreneurship is more complex and includes many interlinked forms of innovation undertaken by different actors – individual or collective. Successful tourism development in a locality is underpinned by common goals (which are mainly to make a destination appealing and to attract visitors), therefore involving an increasing number of stakeholders working in different forms of partnership. The collective entrepreneurship in tourism is not a new practice but one that, in the last decade or so, has been intensified due to strong competition between destinations, changing market trends and, above all, to shrinking direct government financial support that has forced the key stakeholders to be more entrepreneurial.

Spear (2000) defines collective entrepreneurship as: 'pluralistic entrepreneurship underpinned by common goals but not necessarily driven by the collective motivation'. From the position of human nature, everyone involved in tourism or other local development has his or her own personal motivation and interests. Collective entrepreneurship is largely associated with institutional entrepreneurship, deriving from the organization theory, and provides a suitable theoretical frame to explain the collective approach to economic (tourism) development.

Institutional[4] entrepreneurship represents the activities of different actors or organizations, from both private and public sectors, who have an interest in particular institutional arrangements and who leverage resources to create new institutions or transform existing ones (DiMaggio, 1988; Fligstein, 1997). Those entrepreneurs who in the end create new enterprises also put pressure on traditional institutions to change, thus creating more opportunities and a more hospitable environment for new and entrepreneurial firms. Those labelled as institutional entrepreneurs are characterized by charisma, leadership and vision, in addition to other attributes linked to the commercial or business context. To translate this into the context of tourism development, these individuals can be, for example, the manager of RTO, local authority representatives, the leader of a religion, etc. – all institutions that are linked directly or indirectly to tourism (see Chapter 9).

Entrepreneurship Research in Tourism: How Far Has it Gone?

The study of entrepreneurship within the field of tourism has begun to gather some momentum in recent years. Student texts such as those produced by Thomas (1998) and Morrison et al. (1999) have aided the growth of courses on entrepreneurship and small business management within hospitality and tourism degree programmes. The status of entrepreneurship scholarship has not been evaluated systematically, which prompts us to ask the questions: How much entrepreneurship research has been published? What are

---

4. Institutions are sets of common habits, routines, established practices, rules, or laws that regulate the relations and interactions between individuals, groups and organization. They are the rules of the game. Examples are patent laws and norms influencing the relations between universities and firms (Edquist, 2001, p. 5).

some of the characteristics of entrepreneurship research? What is the research progress and potential for scholars?

To explore these issues, we analysed entrepreneurship research published in major hospitality and tourism management journals from 1986 to 2006. We were fundamentally interested in the status of entrepreneurship scholarship in terms of volume of publications, research methods, and research focal areas, which may indicate importance, sophistication, and expectation.

Several studies in the management discipline have referenced and discussed entrepreneurship in terms of its development. Harrison and Leitch (1996) found that entrepreneurship research published in management journals from 1987 to 1993 represented a very small percentage of all published entrepreneurship research. Aldrich and Baker (1997) compared management and entrepreneurship research published from 1990 to 1995 and concluded that progress toward coherence in paradigm development in entrepreneurship research has been limited. No powerful unifying paradigm exists, nor are there multiple coherent points of view. Entrepreneurship studies tend to be less sophisticated in sampling methods; hypothesis development, statistical analysis, and dynamic longitudinal analysis then are organizational studies in the more established disciplines (Aldrich and Baker, 1997).

Several scholars have discussed the legitimacy issue of entrepreneurship research, referring to the extent to which research in entrepreneurship advances useful knowledge (Busenitz et al., 2003). Harrison and Leitch (1996) indicated that entrepreneurship research had to create a distinct position in the context of existing structures to achieve academic legitimacy. Entrepreneurship becomes a more distinct field of research when new theory is articulated, which is then recognized by scholars in other fields of research (Busenitz et al., 2003). Distinctiveness is better established when questions, concepts, and relationships are identified that are different from those proposed by scholars in other disciplines and are unanswerable by them using their research lenses. Such theoretical contributions serve to identify and bracket new concepts and relationships.

To better understand the progress and potential of entrepreneurship research in the hospitality and tourism context, this section intends to review the visibility of entrepreneurship research in major hospitality and tourism research journals. The study proceeds as follows. First, we will evaluate how many entrepreneurship articles have been published in the past. Second, we will examine the sophistication of research methods, including data collection and analytical tools, in the entrepreneurship publications. Finally, we will evaluate the core subject matter published to reveal the focal areas of entrepreneurship research in major hospitality and tourism management journals.

For the purpose of this volume we identified and analysed a set of entrepreneurship articles published in the hospitality and tourism management journals. Using four major databases – Hospitality and Tourism Index, Sage Journals Online, ScienceDirect, and Emerald Insight – articles were searched according to three criteria:

1. Publication in one of seven refereed academic journals in the field of hospitality and tourism management: *Cornell Hotel and Restaurant Administration Quarterly (CHRAQ), International Journal of Hospitality Management (IJHM), Journal of Hospitality and Tourism Research (JHTR), International Journal of Contemporary*

Hospitality Management (IJCHM), Annals of Tourism Research (ATR), Tourism Management (TM). The seven journals were selected because of the top rating of the perceived research quality by over 500 tourism and hospitality experts reported in the study of McKercher et al. (2006);

2. Use of one or more keywords related to entrepreneurship in the article or abstract, i.e. entrepreneur (founder, entrepreneurial individual), small business (emerging business), family business, new venture (emerging venture); corporate entrepreneurship (intra-preneurship). Two major reviews of entrepreneurship research by Ireland et al. (2005) and Brusenitz et al. (2003) used the same keywords and terms;

3. Publications over the past 21 years (between 1986 and 2006) to identify the research trends.

Articles were then categorized as either empirical or theoretical. 'Empirical studies were classified as those that included some kind of data or data analysis in the study. These included both statistical and qualitative analyses' (Chandler and Lyon, 2001). Literature reviews, untested theoretical models, and proposed mathematical models were defined as theoretical studies (Chandler and Lyon, 2001). All editor notes, book reviews, review articles on the entrepreneurship domain, and replies to published articles were omitted from this survey so the data would contain only articles and research notes that were non-invited and were peer reviewed.

Numbers of Articles Published

Ninety-seven articles met the selection criteria. Of the total 4917 articles published in the seven hospitality and tourism journals during the time frame of this study, 97 addressed entrepreneurship (about 2%). Going by each journal, for all years included in the study, the numbers varied from a low of six articles in *Journal of Hospitality and Tourism Research* (*JHTR*) to a high of 28 articles in *Tourism Management* (*TM*). *TM* also had the highest percentage of entrepreneurship articles for the 21-year period, at 2.82% of all published articles, closely followed by the *International Journal of Hospitality Management* (*IJHM*) at 2.80% of all published articles. *Cornell Hotel and Restaurant Administration Quarterly* (*CHRAQ*) had the lowest percentage (1.33%) of articles dedicated to entrepreneurship research.

Types of Research Undertaken

'Evidence of a growing body of entrepreneurship articles could lend support to the view that entrepreneurship is emerging as an important research domain. Active scholarship in theory development followed by empirical testing could signal the maturity of the entrepreneurship research' (Busenitz et al., 2003, p. 291). Of 97 entrepreneurship articles published over the past 21 years, 72 articles are empirical research (74%), while 25 are theoretical articles (26%). A regression analysis was conducted to statistically investigate the trends of the number and type of entrepreneurship articles over the years. Controlling for the total number of articles published, the results do not indicate a significant increase in the number of theoretical entrepreneurship articles published in major hospitality and tourism journals over time, nor a significant positive trend in the number of empirical entrepreneurship articles published over time. Overall, the findings reveal that entrepreneurship research has not been aggressively pursued in the field of hospitality and tourism management.

Research Methods and Analytical Procedures Used. To examine the sophistication of the research method in entrepreneurship study, data collection and analytical procedures of 72 empirical studies were analysed. Over 50% of empirical studies used surveys for data collection and made it the most popular choice among researchers. Interview was the second most popular data collection method (26%). About 17% used secondary sources, which included newspapers, archival company financial records, industry records, and government records. Field observation was the least used method of data collection among scholars (4%).

The use of descriptive statistics accounted for about 33% of the studies. In about 29% of the articles, researchers used qualitative methods, such as case study, focus group, and content analysis of documents. Multiple Regressions (12.5%) was the third most popular analytical tool of the entrepreneurship research, followed by ANOVA (8%) and factor analysis testing (8%). However, the use of more sophisticated analytical tools such as structural equations modelling was very limited with only one article in 2006.

Focal Areas

Another window into understanding the development of entrepreneurship is to evaluate the core subject matter published in entrepreneurship research among the major hospitality and tourism management journals. While searching for a number of keywords, or terms, we found out that the 97 articles fit predominantly into seven categories.[5] For example, 'corporate entrepreneurship' and 'intrapreneurship' were combined to form the corporate entrepreneurship category. Some studies, of course, deal with more than one single topic. In these instances, the author placed the article into the category representing the study's primary focus. For example, Jogaratnam's research (2002) studied entrepreneurial behaviour among a sample of small restaurant businesses. As the entrepreneurial behaviour was the major theme of the research, the paper was categorized as 'entrepreneurial behaviour' not 'small business'.

Eighteen articles focused on entrepreneurial behaviour or activities, and six articles focused on entrepreneurship education and training. 'Corporate entrepreneurship' has the least coverage in the seven leading journals. Overall, the data reports a range of research areas in entrepreneurship, but a majority of the publications concentrate on two areas: small business and entrepreneurial behaviour (activity), which make up about 63% of total research in the field.

---

5. The seven categories are: 'small business', 'entrepreneurial behaviour and activities','individual or entrepreneur', 'entrepreneur education and training', 'family business', 'new venture', and 'corporate entrepreneur'.

Research Directions

Given the traditional importance of small business and entrepreneurial spirit in the hospitality and travel industry, it was expected that there would be an upward trend in the number of entrepreneurship articles appearing in the major hospitality and tourism journals. However, the findings of our study did not support this assumption. Findings revealed that the percentage of entrepreneurship-related articles appeared less than anticipated, only 2% of the total 4917 published articles. The amount of entrepreneurship research in the leading hospitality and tourism management journals has not increased over the past 21 years, even though *Tourism Management*, *International Journal of Hospitality Management*, and *International Journal of Contemporary Hospitality Management* have published more entrepreneurship research than other journals.

Among 97 entrepreneurship publications in hospitality and tourism journals, 74% are empirical research, while theoretical work remains at a consistently low level (26%). This finding is consistent with trends in the field of generic entrepreneurship research. Koppl (2007) stated that, 'Entrepreneurship research today is rich in fact but poor in theory'. Entrepreneurship scholars have produced many important empirical results. No broad theoretical framework has yet emerged. Koppl (2007) concludes that there are many empirical works in entrepreneurial studies but no unifying theory. This claim should not be taken to imply that all those empirical works are, somehow, theory free. They often have quite strong theoretical grounding, but there is little or no theoretical consistency from one scholar to the next nor one study to the next (Koppl, 2007).

The root cause of this unproductive form of theoretical diversity is the 'struggle' between disciplinary research and a separate domain of entrepreneurship research. On one hand entrepreneurship research is pursued within established disciplines like economics, psychology, sociology and management, but there are few contingencies of interest to entrepreneurship scholars that are not contained in existing disciplines (Landstrom, 2005). As a consequence, entrepreneurship scholars from different disciplines use existing theories of their disciplines to test explanatory value in the entrepreneurial context (Landstrom, 2005). However, there is no guarantee that this research approach will focus on the most central questions of entrepreneurship. On the other hand, entrepreneurship is regarded as a complex phenomenon. Existing theories may not always be optional for addressing these characteristics, which indicates a need to post new questions and build concepts and models to explain the phenomenon (Landstrom, 2005). Future researchers of entrepreneurship need to learn more theories from different disciplines, combine disciplinary knowledge, and form research collaboration.

Of course, methodological issues are as important as theory development. This study also presents a systematic analysis of methodological issues in the body of hospitality entrepreneurship literature. Findings reveal that the use of surveys is the most popular choice for data collection among hospitality entrepreneurship researchers, which mirrors the generic entrepreneurship literature reviewed by Ireland et al. (2005) and Davidsson (2004). Ireland et al. (2005) conclude, 'Convenience, cost and incomplete secondary data sources are among factors that may contribute to the frequent use of surveys among scholars across research areas' (pp. 560). In addition, the findings indicate that general descriptive statistics is the dominant analytical approach of entrepreneurship research in the leading hospitality and tourism journals.

Although descriptive statistics can be accurate and systematic, the research cannot reveal casual connection between variables, and the results are rarely of great interest in their own right. On the other hand, the findings also show that the use of regressions has been on the rise in recent years (2005 and 2006) and is an appropriate tool for examining entrepreneurship-related research questions (Ireland et al., 2005). Future research should use more sophisticated analytical tools (for instance, use of structural equations modelling).

The popular use of qualitative methods in hospitality research is consistent with the findings of generic entrepreneurship literature. Ireland et al. (2005) found that the use of qualitative methods was increasing among entrepreneurship researchers. Qualitative methods are often used inductively – for exploration, theory building, and description. With their emphasis on understanding complex, interrelated, and/or changing phenomena, qualitative methods might be particularly relevant to the challenges of conducting entrepreneurship research. Future scholars might combine qualitative methods with quantitative ones that will provide particularly rich and robust inquiries in entrepreneurship research.

And last, but certainly not least, the study reveals the main focal areas of the entrepreneurship articles published in the hospitality and tourism journals. Some of the areas gained much research attention; other areas might have potential for future research opportunities. Among them, 'small business' has been the preponderant focal area in hospitality entrepreneurship research. The researchers' interest concentrated on issues such as the importance of small firms in job creation and regional economic impact. Wanhill (2000) provided empirical findings of small tourism enterprises in job creation. Sharma (2006), Sharpley (2002), Dahles and Bras (1999) investigated the contribution of small business in regional development. In addition, government support for small firms has been an important aspect of policy in many countries. Wanhill (2000) examined the effectiveness of government support for small and medium tourism enterprises. Future research calls for more studies on improvements in the ways in which incentive policy for small businesses can be carried out.

Another aspect of small business research is the relationship between the size and survival of firms, and constraints on firm growth. Researchers empirically identified the potential role of capital and financial constraints on firm growth. Roberts (1987) reported that 90% of UK tourism and leisure companies were too small to be quoted on the UK stock exchange – poor finance represents important constraints on growth. Özer (1996) investigated the financial sources of 101 small hotels and found that personal funds were the main source of initial investment, while retained earnings were the most important finances in the ongoing operation.

These findings are consistent with the credit constraint theory developed by Evans and Jovanovic (1989) in generic entrepreneurship research. According to the theory of credit constraint, banks lend in proportion to a firm's assets rather than on the basis of its expected cash-flow profits. Since collateral tends to fall with business size, a given loan demand is less likely to be supplied to a smaller business. Such constraints cause entrepreneurs to invest a larger proportion of their assets in the business and to reinvest earnings back into the business. However, undercapitalization might reduce profit, and it is expected that small firms will be more likely to fail as a result of credit constraints.

Alongside this theme, studies examined how failure evolved among the small firms. Wilke (1996) conducted a longitudinal analysis of restaurant failure. Cullen and Dick (1989) reported that in the restaurant sector, nearly half of all new restaurants failed in the first year of operation and 85% closed within five years. Generic research on entrepreneurship (Cressy, 2006) showed that the

> first two and half years of a firm's life were the most risky, but that if entrepreneurs survived this initial 'valley of death,' their long run chances of failure were rather low. Factors influencing the position of this have now begun to emerge, but a fascinating finding is that initial size matters only in the short run; in the long run other factors take over and the failure curves of big and small entrants converge on low asymptotic rates. (p. 189)

Future research might elaborate these findings on the datasets of hospitality firms to refine the underlying theory.

These findings show that scholars appear to be increasingly interested in studying questions regarding entrepreneurial behaviour and activities. The research of entrepreneurial behaviour is to identify what entrepreneurs do and what entrepreneurs are like. Entrepreneurial behaviour describes a universal aspect of human action related to an individual's ability to perceive opportunities for potential changes (Minniti, 2007). Through a series of qualitative case studies of destinations' development, Bussell and Faulkner (2004, 1999) examined how entrepreneurs in small businesses spot opportunities during times of chaos. Keith and Malcolm (1997) explored aspects of the entrepreneurs' motivation and its effect on the decision to exploit entrepreneurial opportunities in small hotels. Another group of scholars examined the influence of entrepreneurship behaviour on hospitality organizations. For instance, Jogaratnam et al. (1999) conducted an empirical analysis of top management's entrepreneurial behaviour and firms' performance in independent restaurants. Williams and Tse (1995) investigated the relationship between entrepreneurial behaviour and strategy in small hospitality organizations.

All the above studies still limited their samples to small and individual businesses. However, while hospitality firms grow larger, they tend to develop bureaucratic and control system impediments to innovation. How can large firms still keep their entrepreneurial spirits and simulate and foster innovation? Corporate entrepreneurship deserves the attention of hospitality researchers. Currently, 'corporate entrepreneurship' had the least coverage in the seven leading hospitality and tourism management journals. There are numerous future research opportunities on this topic. For instance, under what conditions might organizational structure, culture, and leadership be conducive to corporate entrepreneurship? How can large hospitality corporations encourage employees' participation in entrepreneurial process? How can employees' entrepreneurial behaviour be supported by reward systems and the management process? Future research might collect data from large hospitality firms, and findings will have practical application for hospitality corporations that are attempting to become more entrepreneurial.

Another area that has been under-researched in the hospitality industry is 'family business'. The research on family business overlaps in many ways with that pertaining to small business, but there are a number of key differentiating components. Intergenerational ownership transference accounts for about 20% of the family business literature (Getz and Carlsen, 2000). The interactions between family dynamics and business operation, such as gender roles (Lynch, 1998), dealing with family issues (Getz and Carlsen, 2000), and paternalistic management, are important topics unique to family business research. In addition, from family business, the roles of female entrepreneurs and ethnical minority entrepreneurs have appeared as research areas in generic entrepreneurship research. However, the knowledge of the nature and extent of entrepreneurial activity among different minority groups is very limited in the hospitality sector. For example, what are particular issues minority groups face when deciding to start a business? Future research might study them from different perspectives, such as culture, personal characteristics, motivation and organizational behaviour.

Today, women and ethnical minority entrepreneurs are recognized as driving forces in the hospitality industry, whether measured by the number of businesses owned, the revenues generated, or the number of people employed. Research about them is needed to inform both academics and practitioners about their approaches to research and education. Worldwide policy-makers are also increasingly interested in learning more about how to encourage and promote women's and ethnic minorities' entrepreneurship as a means of advancing wealth creation, innovation, and general economic development. The demand for the knowledge is readily acknowledged, but the pace of the research still needs to be advanced.

Overall, the findings of this study suggest that entrepreneurship research remains understudied in the field of hospitality and tourism management. Scholars of the hospitality and tourism field need research collaboration with scholars in different disciplines to map a course of study and to develop theoretical frameworks specific to the entrepreneurship domain. When a solid theoretical base is established, empirical studies will test and validate the theories in the hospitality and tourism discipline. The good news from the findings is that there are abundant opportunities for scholars in the hospitality and tourism field to explore the field of entrepreneurship as a viable research paradigm.

Questions for Discussion

1. Why is tourism a unique context to study?
2. What are the key reasons and motivations for travel?
3. What are the main features of the tourism product and how is it different from products and services from other industries?
4. Can the tourism sector be classified as a single industry?
5. Which area(s) of tourism entrepreneurship research is mostly neglected?
6. What are the possible future research topics in tourism entrepreneurship?

References

Hjalager, A.M., Huijbens, E.H., Björk, P., Nordin, S., Flagestad, A., and Knutsson, O. (2008). Innovation Systems in Nordic tourism. *NORDEN, Nordic Inovation Centre*, Oslo, Norway.

Komppula, R. (2001). New-product development in tourism companies – case studies on nature-based activity operators. Paper presented at *The 10th Nordic Tourism Research Symposium,* October 18–20, Vasa, Finland.

Shane, S. and Venkataraman, S. (2000). The promise of entrepreneurship as a Field of research. *Academy of Management Review,* 25 (I), 217–226.

Smith, K.G., Gannon, M.J., and Sapienza, H.J. (1989). Selecting methodologies for entrepreneurial research: tradeoffs and guidelines, *Entrepreneurship: Theory & Practice,* 14 (1), 39–49.

Venkataraman, S. (1997). The distinctive domain of entrepreneurship research: An editor's perspective. In J. Katz and R. Brockhaus (Eds.), *Advances in entrepreneurship, firm emergence and growth*, vol. 3, pp. 119–138. Greenwich, CT: JAI Press.

Chapter 3

Introduction and Overview to the Entrepreneur and Entrepreneurial Process

Elizabeth Chell

Learning Outcomes

After reading this chapter, you should be able to:

- Identify and understand an early research on entrepreneurs and their characteristics;
- Understand the key theoretical models of entrepreneurial behaviour;
- Understand the nature of the process that drives entrepreneurship; and
- Identify and explain some of the most important policy measures that could be put in place in order to increase the 'stock' of entrepreneurs.

Introduction

Current economic policy underscores the importance of innovation and entrepreneurship for the development of new industry, the replacement of the old and for improved prosperity for all. Developing economies with attractive natural assets – beautiful landscapes, pristine territory, wildlife, and warmth that draws interest from people located in colder climes – have an interest in developing entrepreneurship, in particular in the hotel, leisure and tourist industry. But can the supply of entrepreneurs be identified to meet demand? Underpinning any governmental policy are assumptions that should be based on research and understanding of key elements of entrepreneurship theory and process. Much governmental policy has been based on 'rate' research, that is the rates at which new businesses are created, sustained, grow or fail. 'Trait' research was much criticized in the 1980s; however, many of the original criticisms have been overcome and there is a growing interest in psychological aspects of entrepreneurship (Baum et al., 2007; Chell, 2008).

There is, however, one 'old chestnut' that should be considered as an assumption that, if true, would affect the supply of, and consequently policy toward, entrepreneurs. If 'entrepreneurs are born' with the appropriate attributes then the pool of entrepreneurs would be limited and could not be changed by economic policy; all that could be done would be to provide incentives to enable potential entrepreneurs to make their appearance in the market place rather than (as may be the case for some) rest in a chosen career and, arguably, initially at least, more comfortable employment conditions. Certainly some governments have attempted to flush out entrepreneurs in this way. On the other hand, if it is assumed that 'entrepreneurs are made' then it might be argued that the pool of potential entrepreneurs is unlimited and that 'anyone can become an entrepreneur' (Hashemi and Hashemi, 2002).

Whilst one may not subscribe to the latter sentiment (that anyone could become an entrepreneur), research should demonstrate the conditions that are supportive of entrepreneurship and enable people to develop appropriate skills, behaviours and attitudes. Clearly, governments may instigate various measures to promote increased or enhanced entrepreneurship in practice. If one assumes that entrepreneurs are born then probably governments are limited to fiscal measures: tax breaks and incentives to encourage entrepreneurship. However, if one assumes entrepreneurs are made, then there are a lot more measures that could be put in place; these include, importantly, education and training at all levels – to adopt the vernacular – 'from cradle to grave'.

So what have we learnt about the entrepreneur and the entrepreneurial process that will help policy-makers, practitioners and students of entrepreneurship integrate theory and practice for the benefit of economic development and the increased prosperity of their citizens? Early research, which focused almost exclusively on the identification of single traits or a profile of traits that purportedly characterized an entrepreneur, has fared less well than research that recognized the importance of economic and environmental pressures, which such individuals would be operating within.[1] But there is a resurgence of interest in the psychological aspects of entrepreneurship. However, arguably, the power of the psychological approach to entrepreneurship is enhanced by the integration of economic and sociological perspectives that increase the understanding of the context and its psychological component (Rauch and Frese, 2007). Further, knowledge of industry, markets and the economic (competitive) situation are all salient aspects of the context, especially salient in relation to understanding entrepreneurial decision-making and attitude toward, and management of, risk (Shane, 2003).

In this chapter, I shall outline psychological models of entrepreneurial behaviour that focus on both person and situation, discuss research that has been carried out to further our understanding of particular approaches and emergent issues that are pertinent to entrepreneurship. Next, I will consider alternatives to the traditional conceptualization of traits and couch the outcome of this discussion in a model of the process of entrepreneurship. This will enable me to highlight the socio-psychological aspects of the individual–opportunity exchange process – in particular the behaviour and person characteristics, such as skills and

---

1. The very detailed work of McClelland (1961), which focused on the achievement, motivation and calculated risk-taking of entrepreneurs, recognized the socio-economic context of the entrepreneur. From a psychodynamic perspective, Kets de Vries (1977) identified the familiar and situational pressures that he argued shaped the psychological character of the entrepreneur. In contrast, the work of Brockhaus (1980) and Hornaday and Aboud (1971) typified the 1970s and early 1980s period in which they sought to identify essential traits of entrepreneurs.

abilities, and the type of decision taken. I then consider some criticisms of the approach that may produce profiles of entrepreneurs as 'larger than life' figures. Finally, I seek to address the question of whether entrepreneurship is culture bound or whether there are some aspects that might be considered universal, regardless of culture.

The Psychology of the Entrepreneur

The models of the psychology of entrepreneurship have been influenced by work originated by Lewin (1951), who took into consideration the field forces that he argued influence an individual's behaviour. The models may be differentiated as follows: $B f P$; $B f S$; and $B f P, S$ ($P \times S$), where B = behaviour, P = personality traits, S = environment/situation, and $f =$ function (Chell, 1985). Translating such models as a basis for entrepreneurship research, we have:

(i) expressed entrepreneurial behaviour as a function of the inherent personality traits of the individual psyche;
(ii) expressed entrepreneurial behaviour as a consequence of environmental and situational forces surrounding the individual;
(iii) expressed entrepreneurial behaviour as a consequence of personality traits, situational factors *and* the interaction between personality traits and the situation.

Model (i) B f P

Expressed entrepreneurial behaviour, such as the pursuit of opportunities to introduce a new product into the market place (and thereby create wealth), would be assumed to be a consequence of the personality trait or traits of the individual, for instance, his or her need for achievement (NAch), locus of control (LOC), risk propensity, need for autonomy and/or self-efficacy (Stewart et al., 1998).[2] Such an individual is assumed to be born to be an entrepreneur. There are a number of criticisms of such research (apart from the underlying assumption) concerning the sampling, the measures used, and the research design, including sampling on the criterion variable (e.g. Chell, 1991; Johnson, 2001; Thornton, 1999; Wortman, 1989). Clearly, it is crucial to design the research correctly to avoid such criticisms.

Hansemark (2003), for instance, carried out a 'before-and-after study' on a sample of trainees before any had founded a business, and measured both NAch and LOC before the training and after an 11-year period. She found no evidence to support the claim that need for achievement has predictive ability in respect of starting one's own business, but did find evidence to support LOC, but for male subjects only. The mixed evidence and often equivocal results of research that has assumed this model have led many psychological researchers to build more sophisticated models that take into account environmental factors as described below in model (iii).

---

2. It is beyond the scope of this chapter to review all the research on this, the traditional trait approach. The instances given are indicative only.

Model (ii) B f S

The notion that expressed behaviour is a function solely of environmental or situational factors received scant support from psychologists (Bowers, 1973). Initially the model was supported by Mischel (1968), but he soon developed a more thoughtful model that took account of both psychological aspects of situations and the psychology of the individual. The entrepreneur's situation may be said to vary dependent on the economic theory that the research assumes.

For example, Schumpeter (1934) describes a very dynamic environment that creates shocks within the system. Within this context an innovative entrepreneur may create new business opportunities in which the old industry is destroyed, the conditions for the innovative entrepreneur are highly competitive and uncertain, and it is the ability to produce a radical innovation that enables the entrepreneur to secure both a competitive advantage of the innovation and that of time, before others can adapt and possibly catch up. Yet, despite this focus on the economies of the situation, Schumpeter also believed that the personality of the entrepreneur was important – along the lines of the 'Great Man Theory of Leadership' (Baum et al., 2007, p. 8).

Schumpeter was not the only economist to assume the importance of environmental or situational characteristics. Kirzner (1973) has emphasized 'alertness to opportunities', whereby an individual perceives a situation that constitutes an opportunity to create wealth and should be alert if he or she is to recognize the opportunity. However, Kirzner did not conceive 'alertness' as a personality characteristic.

Networking research, arguably, loses sight of the entrepreneur, placing emphasis on the structure of economic situations. This work was initially influenced by sociological studies, in particular the work of Granovetter (1973), who discussed the importance of 'weak ties' in facilitating the introduction of new knowledge and opportunities for entrepreneurial/economic development. This has been developed by, for example, Burt (1992) in his work on 'structural holes'. Arguably, where this work has influenced entrepreneurship, the skills associated with networking behaviour have been emphasized (Birley, 1985; Chell and Baines, 2000; Johannisson, 1987).

In addition, social psychologists have emphasized the relationship between the entrepreneur and their personal network, which require skills associated with information gathering, opportunity spotting, the management of social influence processes and impression management (Chell, 1985). Littunen (2000) suggests also the importance of studying how informal networks influence personality, whereas Delmar and Davidsson (2000) test a model of the impact of social and human capital on venture discovery and exploitation and subsequent success. Thus, the idea that networking behaviour of entrepreneurs is solely a situational phenomenon has already been questioned.

From a psychological perspective, however, there tends to be an absence of definition and distinction between 'environment' and 'situation', and in particular the psychological aspects of engagement by the entrepreneur with either. To discuss 'environmental shocks', as indeed does Casson (1995), there is a need to move away from the merely mechanical interaction – whereby the individual is apparently buffeted by such 'shocks' and responds in a predictable way, just as a billiard ball responds when struck in a certain way by the action of the cue – to considering the cognitive thoughts processes and affective responses that may be apparent as a consequence of the circumstance in which the entrepreneur finds him- or herself embroiled. The recognition of such psychological processes has suggested the greater importance of interactionism and by and large has knocked situationism 'on the head' as far as psychology is concerned. There are, however, always exceptions and social constructionists, such as Rom Harré (Harré, 1979; Harré and Gillett, 1994), would fall into this category.[3]

Evolutionary theory, whilst not specifically psychological, but sociological, in origins, also tends to focus on the environment, the strategy of the enterprise, and the factors that cause it to operate in certain ways. Here the level and unit of analysis is the organization and not the individual entrepreneur. Evolutionary theory lacks predictive capability and, one assumes, is intended as an explanatory framework for explaining survival, growth or demise of an organization. The dynamic force that brings about change in the organization's fortunes is the strategy adopted, which is attributed anonymously to the organization (or firm) rather than to the entrepreneur, the team or head. Hence, evolutionists focus on populations of firms rather than on personal characteristics of the individuals that make the decisions.

Model (iii) B f P, S (P × S)

This model emphasizes the importance of personality, situation and their interaction. Clearly this is a more complicated model than either of the above. Statistically, measures would seek to analyse the varying importance of these three variables, whereas psychologists would tend to argue for the importance of the interaction (Argyle, 1976; Pervin, 1990). This model resulted from a strong critique of trait theory in the 1960s and 1970s by Mischel (1968), which countered the assumption generally made at the time that a single trait would predict a single behaviour. The upshot, as summarized by Epstein and O'Brien (1985, pp. 515–7), was that of the importance of aggregating items (i.e. observations of behaviour) over different situations and occasions in order to measure traits that are broad and stable (Chell, 1985).

Traits measured in this way allow for the prediction of broad dispositions, but they do not enable the prediction of a single behavioural act. When the interaction of personality and situational variables is taken into account the result is higher predictive power of traits (Endler and Magnusson, 1976; Magnusson, 1981). It is also possible within this model to consider the effects of strong situations (e.g. a storm where people tend to run for cover) or strong personality (e.g. where an extrovert may dominate discussion in a group). Entrepreneurs experience both strong situations (e.g. economic downturns) – and arguably are strong personalities (e.g. doggedly determined to make a success of their business) – and

---

3. Social constructionists generally do not subscribe to the notion of an essential, inner personality. For example, Hampson (1988) suggested that personality ascription resides in the relationships between people. Harré & Gillett (1994) likewise consider personality to be an outcome of discourse and that it is likely to be unique to the individual in the situation. This contrasts with trait psychology that assumes a dispositional tendency that is measurable and typifies the individual's response to situations.

the interaction effects of both personality and situation (e.g. where they show tenacity and resilience in the face of economic difficulties).

Furthermore, Rauch and Frese (2000) argue that it is important to distinguish between broad (distal) and specific (proximal) traits. As such, proximal traits are likely to be more powerful predictors of behaviour. This is highly pertinent to entrepreneurship research: headway has been made in establishing an agreed five broad traits that form the basis of personality (Costa and McCrae, 1988); however, such traits indirectly affect business outcomes through their influence on more specific (entrepreneurial) traits.

Mischel and Shoda (1998) have gone further by linking personality constructs to personality dynamics. Their approach separates the cognitive and affective elements of personality and shows the individual 'behavioural signatures' that arise through charac-teristic modes of interaction between the person and situation (discussed further in Chell, 2008). Moreover, interactionism suggests a linear model of personality–situation variables and outcomes: in other words a deterministic model. Rauch and Frese (2007, p. 43) suggest that being too ambitious, too risk-oriented, or too self-efficacious, for example, may not yield successful performance outcomes. Thus, it is important to consider and research these possibilities. Entrepreneurs are invariably judged by their performance – a lack of success often throwing doubt over whether the individual is truly entrepreneurial – hence rigorous measures are needed to analyse such cases (Chell, 2008).

A fundamental problem that pertained in research examining the entrepreneurial personality was not only small sample sizes and lack of rigor of the measures, but that the statistical power was extremely low. Several studies have now been undertaken using meta-analysis, which show that by taking several studies together the results are clearer and significantly higher. Johnson (1990) reviewed 23 studies of the achievement motive and entrepreneurship, and found an entrepreneurial inclination in 20 of those studies. This led him to conclude that there is a relationship between nAch and entrepreneurial activity. Furthermore, he argues for the development of rigorous, theory-driven multidimensional research models that include 'consideration of individual behaviour along with firm-level outcome measures with explicit attention given to contextual or environmental variables (Johnson, 1990, p. 50). However, Johnson's review was a 'narrative review' whereas that of Collins et al. (2004) is a meta-analysis that enabled them to show the magnitude of the relationship between nAch and entrepreneurial activity.

Rauch and Frese (2007), in a model of entrepreneurial characteristics and success, identify five classic, specific entrepreneurial traits that are evident through the entre-preneur's action strategies that are goal-oriented and affected by environmental variables. Their results indicate that:

- The need for achievement is positively correlated with business success;
- There is a curvilinear relationship between risk-taking and entrepreneurial behaviour in which moderators are likely to affect business outcomes (specifically success);
- The effects of risk-taking propensity are small, but nonetheless positive and significant;
- Innovation is directly related to business creation and positively correlated with success;
- The need for autonomy is positively correlated with success, but autonomy may have a negative impact on business growth, although there is a lack of empirical evidence to examine this relationship;

- A small positive correlation was found between internal LOC and success, however other factors may moderate this relationship; and lastly
- There is a very high correlation between self-efficacy and success ($r = .419$).

These authors conclude that there is sufficient evidence from meta-analyses of need for achievement, risk propensity, innovativeness and internal locus of control to support the view that there is a need to include measures of such personality variables in models that examine factors in business success.

However, perhaps one should sound a note of caution; there are a number of issues that previous reviews of entrepreneurial personality research have highlighted and which the use of meta-analyses does not exactly dispel. First, a closer examination of the above noted results suggests that only in the case of need for achievement, innovativeness and self-efficacy are the correlations sufficient to warrant Rauch and Frese's conclusion. Second, there are issues of validity of the measures; risk-taking propensity is a case in point. A risk-taker is someone 'who in the context of a business venture, pursues a business idea when the probability of succeeding is low' (Chell et al., 1991, p. 42).

However, how do people think of risk when faced with a situation characterized by uncertainty of outcomes? Of course, there are the 'risk averse' who, when faced with such a situation, decide that they do not wish to pursue it. The person with a high-risk propensity, however, is presumed to secure entrepreneurial outcomes (successfully securing their objective) and hence a high correlation would be the resultant datum. This analysis takes no account of situational or contextual variables. A novice entrepreneur may be prepared to go all out to secure their goal because the potential gains far outweigh any losses (in other words they have little to lose). However, a more experienced entrepreneur with an extant business would most certainly have something to lose if their 'gamble' didn't pay off.

Researchers sampling different types of business owner and ignoring descriptive data, such as how long they have been in business, have compromised the conceptual basis of risk-taking and its measurement. Clearly, entrepreneurs, business owners and, indeed, business managers take risks and some may have a risk-taking propensity; however, more carefully compiled data-sets are required before conclusions can be drawn about the relationship between risk-taking as a personality variable and outcomes such as business founding or business performance.[4]

Further, the concept of 'innovativeness' as a personality variable is not yet established. The theoretical basis of this construct would appear to be based on Schumpeter's approach, which includes the introduction of new products, services, new processes, opening new markets, and new technologies with a view to achieving a competitive edge on rival firms. One aspect of innovation is creativity, which occurs in relation to a context and a specific goal (Amabile, 1990, 1998). Contextual factors such as size of extant

---

4. Saravathy et al. (1998) provided more detailed discussion of the perception of risk by entrepreneurs and bankers. They see the issue of perception and the cognitive construction of risk as more important than the issue of whether entrepreneurs are risk averse or have a higher than average risk propensity. The construction of the 'problem' and how it is framed in relation to the incumbent's *personal values* is deemed critical to its resolution and the management of perceived risks.

business are fundamental if the innovative entrepreneur is to have a direct impact on business performance. Furthermore, Schumpeter assumed radical innovation and that the entrepreneur was both innovator and decision maker, i.e. that they were responsible for the success or otherwise of the firm.

However, the majority of innovations are not radical, but are incremental and may be developed by employees within the business. Thus, much of the research on innovation has been at the firm level of analysis, not the individual. Clearly, there is a case for research designs that measure individual creativity and innovativeness of nascent[5] entrepreneurs, and for assessing performance over a period of five years or even longer. It would be essential, however, to include measures of pertinent contextual variables in order to assess the potency of the personality dimension.

Although Rauch and Frese (2007, p. 52) report 'small, positive, and significant differences between owners' and non-owners' internal LOC', using meta-analysis on 20 studies, there have been problems reported of the measure of LOC (e.g. Furnham), the use of different scales (Furnham, 1986; Levenson, 1973; Rotter, 1966) and research using a before and after design that showed significant results only for male subjects (Hansemark, 2003).

Hence, there is a problem with the quality of some previous research studies that meta-analysis would only serve to obscure. Undoubtedly, Rauch and Frese (2007) are right to suggest that it is likely that some personality variables do have direct effects on business founding and performance in small entrepreneurial starts and, I would add, nascent entrepreneurially-led business propositions. However, to strengthen such research, the design should use and develop measures of proximal personality variables that are assumed to have a direct impact on the entrepreneurial process and outcomes. Further, the entrepreneurial process needs to be better understood and researchers should focus on different aspects of it, as different personality factors are likely to be influential at these different stages. This would follow the general tenet of interactionism and ensure that greater care is taken in understanding and measuring situational variables.

The model of personality should be broadened to take into account a wider range of personality attributes, such as attitudes (Robinson et al., 1991), skills (Baum and Locke, 2004), cognitive factors (Baron, 1998, 2004) and affect (Chell, 2008; Goss, 2005; Mischel and Shoda, 1998). The outcomes of the process – business founding or business performance (not simply success) – should be considered in the research design in order to develop a fine-grained analysis of the impact of specific, proximal measures of personality on each of these outcomes. There continues to be a need to develop the theoretical underpinnings of the measures in relation to a depth of understanding of the entrepreneurial process (Chell, 2008). Environmental and situational variables may include strategies, tasks and goals and, where they do, the level of analysis is crucial. In summary, Rauch and Frese (2007) have made a case for more research that examines the impact of personality on entrepreneurial process and outcomes but, by their own admission, a great deal more work is required before we can be confident of the results.

---

5. 'Nascent' entrepreneurs are those individuals who have expressed explicitly an intention to engage in entrepreneurship and have taken some steps to further their intention (see Aldrich, 1999).

The Conceptualization of Traits

The above discussion has focused on research that assumes a relatively conventional understanding of the trait as a behavioural disposition to behave in ways consistent with the construct. This leaves some flexibility as to how an individual might behave given a particular circumstance and shows that behaviour may be adaptable, within the limits of the narrowly, or broadly, defined construct. Hence, behaviour is influenced by the situation. Too few studies have attempted to measure the interaction between person and situation. This represents a gap in knowledge which, if addressed, would improve the predictive capability of the measure. Entrepreneurship researchers, in particular, strongly believe in the influence of environmental circumstances and the personal situation of the entrepreneur (Krueger and Carsrud, 1993).

Research has also questioned the narrow definition of personality based on trait terms alone. A more holistic view of personality suggests that it comprises cognitive and affective elements that interact dynamically to produce behavioural expression that are unique to an individual (Mischel and Shoda, 1998). The earlier work of Mischel (1973, 1981) suggested a reconceptualization of personality constructs to include: personal constructs, competencies, expectancies, values and self-regulatory strategies and plans. This meant he viewed people as having a developing set of: constructs or ways of viewing the world; abilities and skills; learned expectations of other people's behaviour and their own in particular situations; a set of preferences, showing their likes and dislikes; and goals of what they may wish to achieve in life. People thus learned through their inter-action with others in situations. Moreover, the emotional element acts as the driver in the dynamics of personality expression, as people modify their behaviour according to circumstance. Few people would look overjoyed at a funeral and are more likely to express sadness; this applies to the more extrovert individuals too – a good example of situation dominating personality expression. Likewise an entrepreneur whose business has won an important order is more likely to be happy and energized than one who has just lost a major customer (Chell, 1985).

In this analysis trait terms are a convenient way of encapsulating dispositions to behave in particular ways and whose basis is in language. As such people use adjectives to describe behaviour; from such an adjectival set of terms psychologists have attempted to more rigorously define traits for research and also consultancy purposes (Hampson, 1988; Allport and Odbert, 1936). Research on the impact of the entrepreneur on the entrepreneurial process has to some degree moved away from an exclusive focus on traits to one that focuses on the cognitive and affective elements (Baum and Locke, 2004; Locke and Baum, 2007). In the next section I shall describe these elements and develop our understanding of the psychology of the process.

The Entrepreneurial Process

The basic model of the entrepreneurial process that includes personality factors is shown in Figure 3.1. Current research suggests that personality should be conceived in terms of cognitive factors (Mitchell et al., 2002) that may be construed as thoughtful, skilled engagement with the process of opportunity recognition, development and formation within a specifiable entrepreneurial environmental context, and, moreover, such engagement also comprises an affective set of behaviours that help direct and energize the entrepreneur (Chell, 2008).

This model assumes person–situation interaction and is developed from a social psychological perspective. The person is conceived in terms of 'cognitive' factors described as:

- *Knowledge* including experience and beliefs;
- *Skills* that are acquired through training and education and are relevant to the entrepreneurial process;
- *Abilities* that the entrepreneur has, such as musical or creative ability, that may be drawn upon to facilitate innovation and opportunity development in a known field;
- *Constructs*, specifically the label set that enables the individual to describe their world, their situation and the objects and people around them and, at a higher level, form schema for understanding and describing complex phenomena, events and circumstances; and
- *Plans* that include strategies and tactics devised by the incumbent to enable them to negotiate their world.

The person's make-up also includes *affect*, i.e. the *emotions* and feelings that accompany all behaviour, whether these are suppressed, repressed or expressed; *emotions* help *drive* behaviour along a desired pathway to enable the person to secure their goals; *emotions* and *drive* are accompanied by *attitudes* based on beliefs and values, showing the interconnectedness of cognitive and affective behaviour; and finally, affect also comprises *values*, which are often deeply held and express the individual's estimation of an object's or a person's worth to them. All behavioural expression has thus a dynamic basis to it (Mischel and Shoda, 2005).

People interact with the social-task environment, within a larger environmental context. Such engagement is revealed through their dispositions to behave in particular ways as expressed through their behavioural signature. Other persons viewing such behaviour would tend to label it using trait-like terms; these would comprise both descriptive adjectives and adverbs, indicating how the behaviour was enacted. It is possible, through reflection, for the individual and the observer to evaluate what behaviours are effective in specifiable situations. The incumbent of an entrepreneurial role, for example, is judged often on their effectiveness, though often only once the outcomes of that behaviour are known – in other words these are post hoc judgements. Entrepreneurial behaviour is intentional and goal-directed (Bird, 1988; Krueger and Carsrud, 1993); entrepreneurs operate with implicit strategies and intuitive feelings about what opportunities and plans to pursue (Allinson et al., 2000; Alvarez and Busenitz, 2001; Gaglio and Katz, 2001). Entrepreneurial outcomes should be distinguished, as the business founding/creation process suggests different attitudes, skills and behaviours that would achieve different business performances such as growth, success or indeed, failure.

In general, Figure 3.1 depicts what I believe to be the overall process of entrepreneurship at the level of the individual. However, to understand in greater detail how

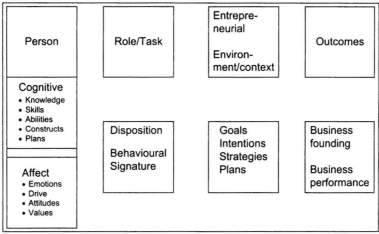

Source: Chell, 2008.

Figure 3.1: The basic model of the entrepreneurial process that includes personality factors.

entrepreneurs identify and develop opportunities, a more fine-grained analysis is required on that aspect of individual–situation interaction.

The Individual–Opportunity Interchange

The notion of opportunity recognition has been extensively researched (Gaglio and Katz, 2001; Gaglio, 2004). Shane (2003) maintains that opportunities exist within the market place and industry to be discovered by alert entrepreneurs. Furthermore, his thesis suggests that entrepreneurs with prior knowledge of an industry, market and technologies will be better placed to spot opportunities (Shane, 2000). Thus, Shane emphasizes the importance of industry context, where industry includes all aspects that potentially affect the development of opportunities for new products, services and processes. In this he appears to follow Kirzner (1973), whose thesis focuses upon the individual who is alert to opportunities. For example, he suggests one difference between the latter's position and that of Schumpeter is that Schumpeter's entrepreneur appears to be 'willing to make decisions on very little evidence' (Shane, 2003, p. 21).

However, he then surprises by suggesting that Schumpeterian innovation would most likely occur in large organizations, because it depends on both the creation of new information and recognition (ibid, p. 22). His term for this process is the 'individual–opportunity nexus'. However, it is suggested that 'entrepreneurs play a more prominent role in markets that are not already occupied by large firms' (Park, 2005, p. 741). Certainly it would appear important to consider the role of the nascent entrepreneur in the process of opportunity identification and exploitation (Arenius and Minniti, 2005).

The individual–opportunity interchange describes a process in which innovation (that is the creation of something new or novel) occurs (Chell, 2008). An innovation may refer to something that is new to the individual and the market for which it is intended. However, innovations are not restricted to products or services. The process may be captured in stages (Ardichvili et al., 2003; Haugh, 2007), for example ideation, opportunity recognition, opportunity formation and opportunity exploitation, resulting in various outcomes (Chell, 2008). There are both cognitive and affective aspects to each stage of this process, pertaining to the successful entrepreneur or innovator which comprise:

1. *Ideation* draws on the insight and private thought processes of the individual, as he or she mulls over the idea and makes an intuitive, subjective judgement to pursue the thought further; these thoughts are energized by positive feelings towards the subjective vision or idea.
2. *Recognition* takes that insight further, by considering the social-economic and contextual aspects of the opportunity; intuitively the individual believes that the idea is an opportunity and in his or her subjective judgement should be pursued further; such thoughts are underpinned by an empathetic understanding of people and the market place to be served.
3. *Formation* is governed by more explicit thought processes and behaviours, as the individual considers what they should do to develop the opportunity. This may include consulting others, garnering initial resources and possibly identifying a partner or team to support opportunity development; affect is social and interpersonal, comprising positive persuasive attitudes and the constructive evaluation of the opportunity;
4. *Exploitation* draws further on a mix of explicit and implicit knowledge that shapes further the subjective decision to continue the development of the opportunity. At both the formation and exploitation stages, the entrepreneur should be sensitive to the feelings and evaluations of others, but is likely to be governed by feelings of conviction (the intuitive belief that the opportunity is a real one). This is a delicate stage of the process where fine and accurate judgement is needed, and where over confidence may result in lack of success or even failure (Baron, 2004).

This process will vary in time and space; temporally opportunities can be exploited in months in certain industries (ICT, media, andt) or years (pharmaceuticals, aerospace). Spatially, the entrepreneur draws upon their personal network, which should include remote ties (Granovetter, 1973; Birley, 1986). The entrepreneurial opportunity should also be embedded in the location, to further its successful exploitation and development (Jack and Anderson, 2002).

What might be the characteristics of the entrepreneur in the successful process labelled the individual–opportunity interchange? Criticisms abound of extensive lists of such entrepreneurial characteristics – a chief complaint being that they fuel the idea of the entrepreneur as 'hero' (Ogbor, 2000), a 'larger than life figure' or 'Great Man', as Schumpeter would have it. However, there is a tradition of practical entrepreneurship, which seeks to understand characteristics that enable *successful* entrepreneurial performance (Timmons et al., 1985; McClelland, 1987). This seeks to identify the skills, motivation and abilities of successful entrepreneurs, as well as traits that might be considered to be more enduring (Baum and Locke, 2004).

In my model, the process of individual–opportunity interchange shows the socio-structuring (situation/context) of behaviour, the characteristics of the entrepreneur that facilitate leverage of opportunities from the perceived context or situation, and the nature of the decisions made over time (Chell, 2008, Chapter 9). Table 3.1 presents a simplified version of the entrepreneur–opportunity interchange characteristics based on Chell (2008).

The Impact of Culture and the Socio-economy

The socio-economic environment provides a structure that shapes socio-economic situations perceived by the alert entrepreneur (Sarason et al., 2006). The socio-economy is also shaped by culture, for example: locally (Jack and Anderson, 2002); at industry level (Shane, 1993); at corporate level (Thiessen, 1997); at country/national level (Mueller and Thomas, 2000; Mitchell et al., 2002) and globally (Lee and Peterson, 2000). To what extent might culture

Table 3.1: The characteristics of a successful entrepreneur and the socio-economic structure in different phases of the individual–opportunity interchange process.

Stage	Socio-structural behaviour	Entrepreneurial characteristics	Decision type
1. Ideation	Socio-economic situation; market situation	Insight, imagination creativity, energy	Intuitive
2. Opportunity recognition	Opportunity identification; empathetic understanding; preliminary envisaging	Social/ market awareness; positive feelings; drive	Intuitive, implicit
3. Opportunity formation	Synthesis of information; evaluation; engagement in the socio-economy	Networking, counter-factual thinking; positive commitment and application	Implicit and explicit
4. Opportunity exploitation	Garnering of capitals and support; human resource; Financial and coping strategies deployed	Resourcefulness; resilience, conviction; discernment; risk management	All types

Source: Based on Chell (2008, Table 9.1).

affect the behavioural expression of entrepreneurs? Do entrepreneurs from different cultures behave and think differently? Whilst these are huge questions and beyond the scope of this chapter to answer fully, they are worth posing; and thus, in the remains of this section, we will consider disentangling some of the threads of the argument.

The environment or socio-economy in which entrepreneurs operate structures their behaviour, providing a context for engagement, a set of opportunities and also constraints; according to Giddens, the individual's behaviour both structures and is structured by the environment that is constituted in the social sphere by institutions (Giddens, 1984). From a social psychological perspective this has been termed 'organismic interactionism', where the meaning and interpretation of a situation is the salient element in person–situation interaction. The socio-economic environment may be considered to operate at three distinct levels – micro, meso and macro – and it is with the micro-level that we are principally concerned; however, the three levels are sources of influence at both vertical (between strata) and horizontal levels (across strata between structure and agency) (Chell, 2008). Engagement, as noted above, is at the four distinct stages of ideation, opportunity recognition, formation and exploitation. Hence, the question is: are there distinctive entrepreneurial behaviours that may be associated with this process regardless of culture? Turning this question on its head: does culture matter?

Culture has been variously defined as ways of being and ways of doing, based on deeply held values and beliefs that shape the approach to addressing societal problems and issues. Arguably, entrepreneurship is a culturally-based phenomenon embedded in capitalism, which provides a structure for engagement. Within this system there are choices to be made, ways of garnering resources, engaging with a wider personal network, and developing a product or service with a competitive edge on rivals. At the local level, entrepreneurs, if they are to be successful, should adapt their behaviours to suit local conditions (Jack and Anderson, 2002). Thus, empathetic understanding, sensitivity and social skills are critical (Chell, 2008). A particularly apposite paper considers two dimensions of national culture – individualism and collectivism – and their relationship with two entrepreneurial functions, complex behaviours termed 'variety generation and resource leverage' (Thiessen, 1997). When 'unpacked' these complex functions draw on creativity and initiative (at the level of the individual) and the leveraging of resources through greater efficiency, networking and flexible responsiveness (at firm level).

Since the seminal work of McClelland (1961), the argument is that individualism is aligned with independent and autonomous individuals, who seek to achieve in an environment that is uncertain, and that these behaviours are fundamental to entrepreneurship. But, work on national cultures (Hofstede, 1980) has shown that countries may be classified as either individualistic or collectivist in orientation. Thiessen argues that these two categories of culture should be considered as independent variables (not two ends of a continuum) and as such collectivist countries may also engage in entrepreneurial activities (ibid, p. 372). The prediction would be, for example, that entrepreneurs in individualist countries would engage in business creation and innovation, whereas within collectivist countries, innovation would occur through corporate venturing.

Lee and Peterson (2000) suggest that culture may be supportive (or not) of entrepreneurial orientation (EO) at individual and firm levels. Following Lumpkin and Dess (1996) they argue that EO comprises:

- *Autonomy* – independent spirit and freedom to create ventures;
- *Innovativeness* – the creative process in which ideas and novel solutions to problems are supported;
- *Risk-taking*, where individuals are willing to assume risks in the face of uncertainty;
- *Proactiveness* – the ability to take initiative through the pursuit of opportunities; and
- *Competitive aggression* – where entrepreneurs are highly achievement-oriented and competitive.

Social, political, economic and legal factors frame society's institutions, which, in any particular country, may support or hinder entrepreneurship. Developed economies, transition economies and emerging economies are showing increasing signs of support for entrepreneurial behaviours (Lee and Peterson, 2000). Thus, cultures are not immutable; they change and may be seen to embrace entrepreneurship.

Mueller and Thomas (2000) also address the issue of entrepreneurial personality – in particular internal locus of control (ILOC) and innovativeness in relation to culture. They argue that there should be a psychological predisposition to engage in the opportunity-recognition process that suggests a need to feel in control. Further, they cite evidence in support of the view that innovativeness is a characteristic of successful entrepreneurs. The underlying mechanism, they suggest, is that culture influences the development of cognitive schema, i.e. values and beliefs, that shape specific behavioural patterns – a process supported by Hofstede (1980) and Mitchell et al. (2000). As cultural values vary, it would not be surprising that, in general, some cultures would be more closely aligned with entrepreneurship. However, cultures are not completely uniform; indeed an intriguing study by McGrath and McMillan (1992) showed that a sample of 700 entrepreneurs drawn from nine countries, characterized as Anglo (individualistic), Chinese (Confucian) and Nordic (socialist), shared beliefs and values *in common* that were very different from those of others in their society. This, they argued, suggested a set of functional and dysfunctional behaviours that might be said to characterize entrepreneurs *across cultures* (McGrath and McMillian, 1992, pp. 426–7).

Mueller and Thomas' (2000) conclusions were slightly at variance with these studies. Testing their hypotheses on student samples from 25 universities in 15 countries, they found that ILOC was significantly more prevalent in individualistic cultures; Entrepreneurial Orientation (a combination of ILOC and innovativeness) was more likely in cultures characterized by low 'uncertainty avoidance'[6]; and individualism was greatest in cultures that were low on UA and highly individualistic. The prevalence of innovativeness was *not* found to be associated with *any* particular culture.

There are a number of observations that may be made in respect of these findings. First, a separate measure of the extent to which the culture (e.g. at governmental levels) was supportive of entrepreneurship would be helpful, as their measure EO was intended to be a proxy for entrepreneurial supportiveness. Second, as ILOC has a chequered

---

6. *Uncertainty avoidance* is indicative of a culture where members of the population feel threatened by unknown and uncertain situations. A low score on this would indicate that members felt less threatened by uncertainty.

history as a measure of entrepreneurial behaviour, ESE (entrepreneurial self-efficacy) might be a better measure. Third, these so-called 'traits' are in fact learned behaviours and they are not necessarily immutable, thus training programmes can help support and develop their appropriate entrepreneurial attitudes, skills and behaviours. The study is of course limited to the extent that it used a student sample, where one might argue there is inherent latent potential or at best some signs of nascent entrepreneurship. However, comparative cross-cultural research studies such as these do yield some interesting, indeed valuable, insights.

Summary and Conclusions

Countries around the world are turning to entrepreneurship as a means by which they can develop and enhance economic growth. In this chapter, I have argued that it is crucial to get the assumptions underpinning policies right if such an end is to be achieved. Furthermore, I have highlighted important developments in the psychology of entrepreneurship and systematically considered research associated with three distinct models. The traditional trait model is thinly supported in entrepreneurship research; there has been much equivocal evidence and mixed results. The situation model tends not to operate at the level of the individual; rather research that has successfully identified behavioural factors influencing the process of entrepreneurship has tended to focus on the firm, for example networking theory and evolutionary theory. These approaches omit the individual and yet it is people who make decisions and take actions with respect to entrepreneurship. Model three, which I have labelled interactionist, has been much more successful. This model emphasizes the importance of 'person', 'situation' and the interaction between person and situation influences on behaviour. This basic model is developed to deal with the complexities of the entrepreneurial process.

Rauch and Frese (2007) argue for a more conventional approach in which proximal traits affect entrepreneurial behaviours. A slightly different approach that is supported by the fundamental psychological research of Mischel (1973), Chell (1985) and Mischel and Shoda, 1995) reconceptualizes the nature of 'person' into cognitive and affective elements. This approach is consistent with current entrepreneurship research that, in particular, has focused on the cognitive aspects of entrepreneurial behaviour (e.g. Mitchell et al., 2002). Affect also addresses the motivational aspects of entrepreneurial behaviour, where drive and commitment are key behaviours (Locke and Baum, 2007). However, for those that prefer conventional trait measures of 'person', further work is needed to develop valid, proximal measures of what are thought to be key traits – risk propensity being a case in point.

There may also be a case for careful deconstruction of composite measures of constructs such as 'innovativeness'; perhaps it may be more effective to measure distinct elements, such as 'creativity', 'proactivity' and 'intention'. There is also a tendency to persist with the 'big three' (need for achievement, ILOC and risk propensity) despite the mixed evidence. This should prompt more careful conceptualization of the process and behaviours associated with entrepreneurship at the early stages (and throughout the process) of opportunity development, and a consideration of (a) whether extant measures do validly measure attributes at all or any of these stages; (b) whether new measures should be devised; and (c) whether sampling is appropriate to the particular objectives and design of the research.

Within entrepreneurship, there is a particular process that I have labelled the individual-opportunity-interchange. This separates out the initial ideation from opportunity recognition, formation and exploitation and considers the mix of knowledge, skills and abilities of the entrepreneur as he or she engages in this process (Chell, 2008). Moreover, the psychology of this process is directed through meaningful engagement with perceived situations, yielding decision outcomes made in a variety of ways – intuitively, implicitly and explicitly, where others are also involved.

But does such a process apply to entrepreneurs across cultures? This is an enormous question which cannot be answered definitively in this chapter. However, research has begun to ask whether and to what extent culture affects behavioural expression. Implicitly, entrepreneurship is itself a culturally developed phenomenon bound up with capitalism; thus, the more countries engage in free market economics, the more one would expect to see the development of entrepreneurship and the rise of entrepreneurs in those economies. Evidence from transitional and emerging economies suggests that this is indeed what is happening (Lee and Peterson, 2000).

But culture is complex and operates at many levels within society. At the micro-level the question is whether individuals have the freedom to engage in entrepreneurial activities and whether the state supports such activity and provides incentives to encourage the individual–opportunity interchange. More work is needed in transitional and emerging economies to test the model of the individual–opportunity interchange and the socio-psychological and economic processes that underpin it. In adopting cross-cultural and cross-national research designs, it will be possible to begin to map out the behavioural profile of successful entrepreneurs and develop appropriate training programmes, supported by research that recognizes the cognitive and affective nature of the process that drives entrepreneurship, in order to increase the supply of entrepreneurs.

Questions for Discussion

1. What are the main contributions by social psychologists to the study of entrepreneurship?
2. Is the entrepreneur made or born? Provide arguments for and against.
3. Is entrepreneurship a culturally-based phenomenon?
4. What are the key lessons that we have learnt from the chapter about the entrepreneur and the entrepreneurial process that will help policy-makers, practitioners and students of entrepreneurship integrate theory and practice for the benefit of economic development and growth?

References

Aldrich, H.E. (1999). *Organizations Evolving*. London: Sage.

Allport, G.W. and Odbert, H.S. (1936). 'Trait names: a psycho-lexical study', *Psychological Monographs*, 47, whole no 211.

Argyle, M. and Little, B. (1972). 'Do personality traits apply to social behaviour?' *Journal for the Theory of Social Behaviour*, 2 (1), 1–35.

Baron, R.A. (1998). 'Cognitive mechanisms in entrepreneurship: why and when entrepreneurs think differently than other people'. *Journal of Business Venturing*, 13(4), 275–94

Baum, J.R., Frese, M., and Baron, R. (2007). *The Psychology of Entrepreneurs*. Mahwah, NJ and London: Lawrence Erlbaum Associates.

Burt, R.S. (1992). The social structure of competition, In *Networks and Organisations: Structure, Form, and Action*, (N. Nohria and R. G. Eccles, eds), Cambridge, MA: Harvard University Press, pp 57–91.

Costa, P.T. and McCrae R.R. (1988). From catalog to classification: Murray-s needs and five factor model. *Journal of Personality and Social Psychology*, 55, 258–265.

Costa P.T. Jr. and McCrae, R.R. (1992). Four ways five factors are basic, *Personality and Individual Differences*, 135, 653–665.

Delmar, F. and Davidsson, P. (2000). Where do they come from? Prevalence and characteristics of nascent entrepreneurs. *Entrepreneurship & Regional Development*, 12(1), 1–23.

Epstein, S. and O'Brien, E.J. (1985). The person-situation debate in historical and current perspective, *Psychological Bulletin*, 98, 513–537.

Gaglio, C.M. (2004). 'The Role of Mental Simulations and Counterfactual Thinking in the Opportunity Identification Process', *Entrepreneurship Theory & Practice*, 28(6), 533–552.

Hornaday, J.A., and Aboud, J. (1971). 'Characteristics of successful entrepreneurs', *Personnel Psychology*, 24, 141–153.

Jack, S.L. and Anderson, A.R. (2002). The effects of embeddedness on the entrepreneurial process, *Journal of Business Venturing*, 17, 467–487.

Johannisson, B. (1987). Anarchists and organizers: entrepreneurs in a network perspective, *International Studies of management & Organisation*, 17, 49–63.

Johnson, B.R. (1990). 'Towards a multidimensional model of entrepreneurship: the case of achievement motivation and the entrepreneur.' *Entrepreneurship Theory & Practice*, 14(1), 39–54

Kets de Vries, M.F.R. (1977). 'The entrepreneurial personality: a person at the crossroads', *Journal of Management Studies*, 14(1), 34–57.

Levenson, H. (1973). 'Multidimensional locus of control in psychiatric patients', *Journal of Consulting and Clinical Psychology*, 41(3), 397–404.

Lewin, K. (1951). In *Field theory in social science: selected theoretical papers*, (D. Cartwright, ed), New York: Harper Row.

Littunen, H. (2000). Entrepreneurship and the characteristics of the entrepreneurial personality, *International Journal of Entrepreneurial Behaviour and Research*, 6, 295–306.

Locke, E.E. and Baum, J.R. (2007). Entrepreneurial Motivation, In *The Psychology of Entrepreneurship*, (J.R. Baum, M. Frese, R.A. Baron, eds), Mahwah, N.J.: Lawrence Erlbaum Associates, chapter 5, pp. 93–112.

McClelland, D.C. (1987). 'Characteristics of successful entrepreneurs', *Journal of Creative Behavior*, 21(3), 219–233.

Minniti, M., Bygrave, W.D. and Autio, E. (2005). *Global Entrepreneurship Monitor*, Babson College, Babson Park, MA and London Business School, London, UK.

Mischel, W. (1973) 'Toward a cognitive social learning reconceptualisation of personality', *Psychological Review*, 80(4), 252–283.

Mischel, W. and Shoda, Y. (1998). 'Reconciling processing dynamics and personality dispositions', *Annual Review of Psychology*, 49, 229–258.

Saravathy, D.K., Simon, H.A. and Lave, L. (1998). 'Perceiving and managing business risks: differences between entrepreneurs and bankers'. *Journal of Economic Behavior & Organization*, 33(2), 207–225.

Stewart, W.H., Watson, W.E., Carland, J.C., Carland, J.W. (1998). 'A proclivity for entrepreneurship: A comparison of entrepreneurs, small business owners, and corporate managers.' *Journal of Business Venturing*, 14(2), 189–214.

Thornton, P. (1999). The sociology of entrepreneurship, *Annual Review of Sociology*, 25, 19–46.

Timmons, J.A., Smollen, L.E. and Dingee, A.L.M. (1985). *New Venture Creation*, 2nd ed. Homewood, III, Irwin.

Wortman, M. S. (1986). 'A unified framework, research typologies, and research prospectuses for the interface between entrepreneurship and small business', *The Art and Science of Entrepreneurship*, Cambridge, Mass.: Ballinger, 273–331.

Part 2

Creative Use of Entrepreneurship and Processes of Social Innovation

Chapter 4

Sustaining Creative Entrepreneurship: The Role of Innovation Systems

Edward H. Huijbens, Anne-Mette Hjalager, Peter Björk, Sara Nordin and Arvid Flagestad

Learning Outcomes

After reading this chapter, you should be able to:

- Understand broad meanings and the importance of innovation and entrepreneurship;
- Recognize and explain social, cultural, economic, institutional and regulatory contexts of different industries' innovation systems;
- Gain a conceptual understanding of innovation systems in tourism;
- Understand the most recent trends in tourism entrepreneurship and innovation;
- Understand the power structures and relations in the process of tourism development and innovation; and
- Identify the key features of Nordic tourism and the innovative models adopted to boost its development and growth.

Introduction

Innovation in tourism takes place continuously. New services and products emerge, and there is substantial creativity in the private sector as well as in public segments of the industry. However, innovation can hardly be seen as the targeted action of an individual economic entity or organization, or a single entrepreneur; such a limited view does not provide a full and precise picture of innovative activity in the tourism industry, or any other industry for that matter. In many senses innovation in tourism, as elsewhere, is collaborative action, where suppliers, employees, consumers and various less formal players take part.

   This chapter builds upon a joint cross-Nordic research project on innovation systems in tourism. The assumption was that in well-established welfare economies collaborative and interactive processes would be especially pronounced, thus lending themselves to theories of innovation systems. The purpose was to investigate cases, and to reassess the innovation systems literature and theories in a tourism context based on the empirical findings (for a more detailed account see Hjalager et al., 2008).

The collaborative and interactive processes documented in the above-mentioned study make prominent the role of individual entrepreneurs and entrepreneurship. As Drucker (2006), in his classical book *Innovation and entrepreneurship* makes clear, innovation is inextricably linked with entrepreneurship. Entrepreneurship remains a central issue in writings about innovation systems. In a tourism context, the composite product and the sequential purchase and consumption process enhance the notion of entrepreneurship, as gaps in the value chain are constantly created, filled, reopened and remodelled. In contemporary industries, innovation takes place in social, cultural, economic, institutional and regulatory environments, i.e. innovation systems. The process of harvesting ideas and transforming them into commercial successes and sustainable businesses relies on the existence of transcending organizational, cultural and social structures, a capacity manifest in entrepreneurial activities.

The first section of this chapter will present and discuss the theoretical framework of innovation systems in a tourism context. The second section will draw on examples from rich case studies in all the Nordic countries. The cases analysed are:

- The Beitostølen ski resort, Norway;
- The Opplev Oppdal Company, Norway;
- The Icehotel corporation, Sweden;
- The Mountain Destination of Åre, Sweden;
- The Siida Nature Initiative, Finland;
- Santa Claus Village, Finland;
- The Roskilde Festival, Denmark;
- The Seatrout Funen, Denmark;
- Whale Watching in NE Iceland;
- White Water Rafting in NW Iceland.

Section I: The Architecture of Innovation Systems

The theoretical genealogy of innovation systems can be traced to Joseph Schumpeter (1934) who in his book *Theory of Economic Development* describes how innovation must be seen as a process of development. His understanding was that the driving force of the economy was the continual rearrangement of its constituent parts for more profit. Later Schumpeter (1942, p. 83) goes further and explains that obsolescence and innovation are *the main* driving forces of the economy. At the same time he reduces his emphasis on individual actors, but places more on the understanding of innovation as part of development and therefore not always something radical or unforeseeable. He explains this with reference to his observation that imitators are more likely to succeed than those leading change. Those that follow are namely able to polish and fine-tune the innovation and are thus better equipped to introduce it to the market. Fagerberg (2005, p. 13) builds on this understanding and says:

Imitators are much more likely to succeed in their aims if they improve on the original innovation, i.e. become innovators themselves. This is more natural, because one (important) innovation tends to facilitate (induce) other innovation in the same or related fields. In this way innovation diffusion becomes a creative process in which one important innovation sets the stage for a whole series of subsequent innovation.

Innovation is thus, in nature, a development process, activating a number of processes and individuals through a kind of chain reaction. It is disseminated amongst individuals who take up new practices or adjust them to a new innovation. In other words, innovation is social, described by Trott (1998, p. 11) as:

"Not a single action but a total process of interrelated sub-processes. It is not just the conception of a new idea, nor the *invention* of a new device, nor the development of a new market. The process is all these things acting in an integrated fashion."

The notion of innovation systems was introduced by Lundvall (1992) and Nelson (1993), and it has been refined and developed in various academic and political contexts over the years, for example by national authorities and international actors such as the EU and OECD (Moulaert and Sekia, 2003; OECD 2005). Here only selected key theoretical sources are scrutinized to a limited extent, as the literature on innovation systems is quite vast. We especially draw on Edquist (2001, p. 14), who defines an innovation system as 'all important economic, social, political, organizational, and other factors that influence the development, diffusion, and use of innovation.' Accordingly, Edquist's broad definition focuses on the determinants of innovation, and not on the specific outcomes in terms of, for example, new products. His focus is upon the specifications of different functions within a system's framework. Later Edquist (2005) identifies 10 of these determinants:

- Research and development;
- Competence building;
- Formation of new product markets;
- Articulation of user needs;
- Creation and change of organizations;
- Networking around knowledge;
- Creating and changing institutions;
- Incubating activities;
- Financial resources;
- Consultancy services.

A list like this can never be complete and already authors have pointed out glaring omissions from Edquist's original (Nooteboom, 2000). Nonetheless this approach is of particular value in policy related studies, as researchers will have to address these determinants and make sense of what they are and how they function. In terms of the research presented here, research and development plays a major role in tourism, in the same way as in numerous other service industries (Malerba, 2004).

The function of the above outlined determinants forms the basis of Lundvall's (2005a, 2005b) critique on Edquist. Lundvall argues for the value of case specificity and empirical data, and explains his approach and thus what underpins the functions of each determinant in his opinion:

> I would see learning through research and learning through human and organisational interaction as the central activities at the core of the innovation system. *Important for how these* activities take place and with what outcomes are organisational forms, institutional framework and the production structure. *The processes and the organisational form* will reflect the wider setting in terms of the national welfare regime and the markets for labour and finance. *Outcomes of the system* may be innovation and competence building and in the last instance economic growth and development. (p. 40, authors' emphasis)

While Edquist focuses on determinants, Lundvall complementarily points out the importance of the embeddedness and the 'structuration' of innovative practices. Drawing on Freeman (1987, 1995) and Lundvall (1992, 2005a), Flagestad et al. (2005, p. 24) define the basic innovation system that:

> ...consists of actors and relations between those actors which through collective processes create the innovation performance within the system. Innovations normally emerge through incremental and cumulative processes but may appear as radical and unexpected events.

This quotation serves as our preliminary understanding of an innovation system, drawing on Lundvall's practice-based and grounded theory approach, but with an eye on the determinants as set forth by Edquist to lay out a 'system' that nonetheless is amorphous and hard to explain in a systematic fashion.

National, Regional, Sectoral and Technological Innovation Systems

In order to apply the notion of innovation system to the tourism cases studied, some practical guidelines needed to be drawn. Any system must have some kinds of outer boundaries – otherwise it is hardly a system (Henten et al., 2006). On the most general level, four categories of boundaries have been outlined and may guide any empirical inquiry. The four categories of boundaries are: national, regional, sectoral, and technological settings, all of which have their specific conceptual backgrounds that will be addressed in the following section.

The first seminal writings about innovation systems revolved around *national* innovation systems (Lundvall, 1992; Nelson, 1993). 'A national innovation system can be perceived as a historically grown subsystem of the national economy...' (Balzat and Hanusch, 2004, p. 197). According to the literature, the nation state – with its numerous institutional set-ups, complexity of traditions and tacit cultural arrangements – is influencing the innovation patterns substantially for better or worse. For example the banking systems, patent laws, labour market regulations and educational resources are normally national in their nature. This intriguing complexity of institutional arrangements at the national level is of great importance to commercial innovation activity. None of the tourism innovation systems identified in this study are national in this sense, and none of the five Nordic countries possesses an overarching national innovation system that embraces the tourism sector in a distinctive way.

The investigation of national innovation systems has, in the literature, led to closer inquiries into the occurrence and nature of *regional* innovation systems (Cooke et al., 1997). The questions are similar, but with a smaller geography in mind. References are often made to early studies of 'industrial districts' and 'industrial clusters' (Camagni and Capello, 1999; Feldman and Florida, 1994; Porter, 1990) – all characterized by dynamic economic development, sometimes in contrast to national trends. The notion is that a rapid reorientation and response to external changes could hardly take place with such efficiency without the spatial proximity of many actors and institutions at the regional level (Braczyk et al., 1998). The milieus with many loosely coupled links and alliances were found to be particularly appropriate to promote innovative activity.

Recently, an attempt has been made to deal with tourism destinations as regional innovation systems, albeit with several reservations (Flagestad et al., 2005; Nordin, 2003; Sundbo and Gallouj, 2000). For example ownership structures in tourism destinations are often dispersed, leading to a lack of regional connectivity and commitment from the actors (Hjalager, 2000).

Innovation system studies have generally struggled with the fact that geographical boundaries are highly permeable for economic activity. Dynamic national or regional environments are not cut off from the forces of globalization. Johnson and Lundvall (2000) argue that sustainable national and regional innovation systems are those able to enhance institutional learning and build social capital on a continual base in spite of – or even as a positive consequence of – global orientations. Being able to integrate global knowledge and networks into local innovative processes is of crucial importance, and the existence of an absorptive capacity and learning atmosphere is therefore needed in a contemporary innovation system (Asheim and Isaksen, 2002). The globalization of the economy is a continual challenge for the concept of the spatially oriented regional innovation systems.

Drawing on Amin's (2002) spatial ontology for a globalized world, it is emphasized that the nation, and region for that matter, are constituted through a topology of overlapping near and far connections and relations that are 'produced through practices and relations of different spatial stretch and duration' (p. 389). Thus a nation and region together constitute a form of 'place making, through the myriad network practices and memorializations that mark the sites we choose to call places' (Amin, 2002, p. 392; see also Amin, 2004, p. 40). The geographical units we make in our minds are 'places [that] are also the moments through which the global is constituted, invented, coordinated, produced' (Massey, 2004, p.11).

Because any geographical demarcation is so highly malleable and uncertain, the scope of research has recently been broadened to investigations of 'sectoral' innovation systems (Malerba, 2004). Sectoral innovation systems are based on the idea that different industries and sectors operate under different knowledge, regulatory and technology regimes, and that they are characterized by particular 'combinations of opportunity', through mobilizing their specific constellation of regimes. The driving forces may be highly integrated into national or even regional dynamics but may also transcend spatial boundaries. Geels (2004) emphasizes the institutionalization as a determining factor, particularly in sectoral innovation systems, and the linkages with users and regulators are considered crucial for dynamics and continuity, particularly if technologies are crucial ingredients. The conceptualizations of sectoral innovation systems may seem to be more relevant for tourism, and research may well be drawn and widened from this perspective.

When looking at the technological innovation systems, the definition focuses on (a group of) generic technologies with general application to many industries. Carlsson et al. (2002) mention that a technological innovation system leads to the creation of other types of collaborative communities and stronger buyer–seller relations; they mention microwave technology as a good example of a rapidly developing technological system that has affected many industrial sectors. When studying technological innovation systems there is a focus on the building of absorptive capacity and capacity to apply technologies in creative ways, rather than on the development of the basic technologies. In tourism, technological innovation is an emerging field, notably in terms of infrastructural developments and IT.

All four categories of innovation systems represent valuable contributions to understanding the facilitators of innovation. They are not mutually exclusive (Oinas and Malecki, 2002), although the delineation of the systems varies; how these apply to tourism will be demonstrated later on in this chapter.

Components in Innovation Systems

So far in this chapter the concern has been with what an innovation system is, and the problems of delimiting the systems *vis-à-vis* its environment or wider setting. It is, however, also vital to examine a number of definitions of what constitutes the innovation system and its actors. Generally, the whole notion of innovation systems is based on the statement that single entrepreneurs seldom innovate in isolation; they are all part of networks as stated above. Whilst innovation signals discontinuity and a break from what is established, a system represents a stable structure – something fixed (Lundvall, 2005).

Innovation systems usually have an evolutionary history where future development depends on historical trajectories, as innovation is normally a cumulative and path-dependent process (Morgan, 2004). The implication is that it is difficult, if not impossible, to create an innovation system by means of political will and intention. Innovation systems emerge as a function of innovative practices; the notion of system is thus heuristic and offers 'a broad and flexible framework for organizing and interpreting case studies and comparative analysis' (Lundvall, 2005, p. 20). When analysing innovation systems, the task is to assess which components are present and mobilized, and thus track the route actors navigate whilst innovating.

It is generally recognized that innovation systems, no matter whether they are national, regional, sectoral or technological, are *heterogeneous*, and that the variation of actors in itself is one of the driving forces. Edquist (2001, p. 5) distinguishes between 'organizational' and 'institutional' components:

> Organisations are formal structures with a purpose. They are players or actors. Some important organisations in innovation systems are the business companies, universities, venture capital organisations, public innovation policy agencies, NGO's, and many others.

Institutions are sets of common habits, routines, established practices, rules, or laws that regulate the relations and interactions between individuals, groups and organisation. They are the rules of the game. Examples are patent laws and norms influencing the relations between universities and firms.

Often in the literature, networks between actors are suggested as main components of innovation systems. Edquist's approach includes networks in his theory, through different notions of collaboration. 'Organizations' include explicit collaborations. In tourism this may be single enterprises in the sector, e.g. accommodation, catering or attractions. But without doubt these need to establish collaborative linkages with, for example, retailing, the public sector, construction and the educational sector. 'Institutions' contain networks that are more like 'citizenships' of a community. In tourism, important issues such as established norms for the use of natural resources, and mechanisms of resource exchange with the voluntary sector, could be mentioned here but will be visited in the case study analysis.

Usually, the private sector business enterprises are regarded as having major importance in the performance of innovation, while the other organizational actors to a greater extent are considered facilitators. However, as mentioned by Johnson and Lundvall (2000), 'commoditization' of previously tacit knowledge, for example originating in the public sector, is gradually taking place and gaining importance. The roles of many organizations are blurring and changing, and it is not so clear who are innovators and who are facilitators. This commoditization process might be beneficial to the systems in the first place. Potentially, though, it might eventually undermine the cohesion of the system, but it is surely one component.

Relations in Innovation Systems.   The components are important units of analyses and so are the relations between the components. Relations in an innovation system may be of a 'market' or a 'non-market' kind.

Market relations can be manifold. The literature on business networks mentions, for example, sales and purchases of components and services, investments, franchising and licensing agreements and joint ventures (Håkansson, 1986). There are, of course, differences in the duration and commitment of the relations. The innovation system literature often emphasizes that market relations are of a particular, permanent nature in the successful innovation systems, and that especially well-grown and trust-based supplier–customer relations can be springboards for innovation. Accordingly, involved and reflective customers, who are also close in terms of space or culture, may facilitate innovation processes. In addition, it is often emphasized in research on innovation systems that informal relations are particularly dense and frequent in those systems that function well (Schienstock and Hämäläinen, 2001). These interactions, through formal market and trade relations, and the social capital that they represent, serve as important channels for knowledge diffusion.

These market relations are typically relations between individual organizations. However, we also need to take into consideration the surrounding institutions – the cultural glue (Markusen, 1999). Edquist (2001, p. 6) describes the relations between organization and institutions in this way:

> Organisations are strongly influenced and shaped by institutions; organi-
> sations can be said to be 'embedded' in an institutional environment or set
> of rules, which include the legal system, norms, standards, etc. But insti-
> tutions are also embedded in organisations. Examples are firm-specific
> practices with regard to book keeping or concerning the relations between
> managers and employees; a lot of institutions develop inside firms. Hence,
> there is a complicated two-way relationship of mutual embeddedness
> between institutions and organisations, and this relationship influences
> innovation processes and thereby also both the performance and change of
> systems of innovation.

Not only is there a complex two-way relationship between institutions and organizations through embeddedness, but there also exist mutually supporting relations between different institutions, e.g. labour regulations and educational policies. Alternatively, 'rules of the game' could be contradictive, conflicting and counterproductive, supposedly compromising the innovation system's efficiency.

The way in which organizations and institutions are mutually embedded does indeed function to qualify the extent and nature of innovative practices. That leads to speculations about the 'function' of relations, beyond the above-mentioned distinction between market and non-market relations. In a conceptual way, the fundamental functions of creating and maintaining relations between components in an innovation system could be as follows, drawing on Edquist (2001):

- To create new knowledge or new ideas;
- To enhance the search and diffusion of knowledge and ideas;
- To create human capital;
- To supply resources, such as capital, competencies, raw materials, etc.;
- To test and implement new products or services;
- To ensure synergy with other economic activities;
- To control competition;
- To facilitate the formation of markets;
- To create new organizations;
- To create and legitimize new institutions;
- To legitimize and promote the system vis-à-vis the environment;
- To wipe out obsolete organizations and institutions.

Paraphrasing, Johnson (2001) supplies the following functions:

- To stimulate/create markets;
- To reduce social uncertainty;
- To counteract resistance to change;
- To guide the direction of the search for markets, resources, information, etc.

The relative importance of these functions is not easy to determine, and they are of course not uniform across innovation systems. However, in tourism it is fair to point out that high volatility may jeopardize the maintenance of relations and level down positive impacts. The innovation systems are, though, structures that to some extent compensate for many closures/start-ups in the tourism sector.

Innovation Systems and their Complexity

Many analyses stress the complexity of innovation systems and their dynamic nature (Archibugi et al., 1999; Edquist et al., 2001; Fisher and Frölich, 2001). It is not easy to provide a concise picture of the evolution of an innovation system; many factors impact it, requiring the system to have certain abilities as listed below:

- The ability of the innovation system to adjust continually and to grasp the opportunities that present themselves from the environment;
- The ability to ensure cross-fertilization and enhance the speed of innovation processes within the system;
- The ability to transform in qualitative ways – modernizing and increasing the sophistication of the relations and the outcomes such as products and knowledge systems;
- The ability of the innovation system to transform itself radically in response to major external challenges, such as new technologies or nature catastrophes;
- The ability of the innovation system to add on and enlarge itself into the surrounding environment, and to increase its capabilities, complexities and importance.

It is not unlikely that dynamic innovation systems will, over time, merge with or get absorbed by other innovation systems. For example, some sectoral systems of innovation seem to become more and more globalized as a result of the activities of multinational corporations, and regional innovation systems may be affected by the redefinition of local areas into cross-border functional regions.

Section II: Innovation Systems in Tourism

Basically, tourism is a specific, and to some extent a well-defined, economic sector and, accordingly, it would be logical to explain 'sectoral innovation systems' specific to tourism, without downplaying the relevance of national or regional innovation systems. In his outline of sectoral systems of innovation Malerba (2004) observes that private business enterprises in a related product group are the main drivers of the innovation processes. The continual tendency to renew products and services and to create market positions leads to interactions in the sectoral system, which is dominated by commercial players. Uniform economic mechanisms promote an entrepreneurial spirit in institutions and organizations in the vicinity (functionally or geographically), according to Malerba. The innovation literature is not explicit on the topic of local innovation systems and certainly non-existent in the context of a place or tourist destination (Flagestad et al., 2005). However, Flagestad et al. (2005,

p. 256) suggest 'that a tourist destination with its boundaries of place should qualify as a category of local innovation system'.

Tourism innovation systems can be found in a Nordic context (Sundbo and Gallouj, 2000; Hjalager, 2006), and it is possible to witness dense relationships that are platforms for radical new products and services in the sector, as will be shown in greater detail in the following discussions. However, we assume that the commercial segments of the tourism system play a somewhat less pronounced role than in other innovation systems. In tourism a variety of voluntary and public organizations are catalysts for development as tourism activity is usually embedded in wide ranging societal institutions. Under these circumstances private tourism enterprises may primarily play a role in the follow-up phase, when first concepts are established and launched, and when a demand starts to manifest itself.

Through focusing on topics outlined in Table 4.1 below, an analysis of all 10 Nordic cases was done in order to relate tourism more effectively as a sectoral innovation system to the literature presented above. The table is largely inspired by Edquist's (2001) outline of fundamental functions creating and maintaining relations in innovation systems, detailed above, and the dynamics impacting innovation systems.

In Table 4.1, structures in terms of organizations and institutions, entrepreneurs and relations underpin driving forces of innovation, resulting in various outcomes as documented in detail by Hjalager et al. (2008). In this chapter the intention is to focus solely on dimensions related to entrepreneurship.

Some Basic Common Features of Innovation Systems

A major finding among the tourism innovation systems case studies in the Nordic countries is that they have been in operation for a considerable length of time. All share the trait that they have been able to ensure a continuous launching of new products and services, a variety of spin-off opportunities for new entrepreneurs, and development opportunities for other actors over time.

Additionally, innovation systems share the following common characteristics:

- *A multitude of actors.* There are strong entrepreneurial forces in all innovation systems, but the outcomes are generally not the sole achievements of persons operating on their own.
- *A diversity and density of relations.* The projects draw on many types of personal backgrounds, knowledge and connections. Actors efficiently bridge cultural, social and institutional gaps. The actors feel a belonging to the geographical area, and this increases the density of long-term and trusted relations.
- *Mobilizing role of key actors.* A key role is played by visionary entrepreneurs who have been able to facilitate the growth and stabilization of the projects as parts of an innovation system, drawing on a host of resources. These visionary actors also emerge as the powerful focal points for the systems, which can also be a weakness.
- *Open resource access.* The enterprises enjoy an open and inviting atmosphere, and a willingness to share resources and knowledge. A tacit 'linux' philosophy is embedded in many of the innovation systems.

Table 4.1: The general framework for analysis of the cases.

Structures, entrepreneurs and relations	Driving forces for innovation	The outcomes
Nature of relations – strong, weak, formal or informal	External pressures for changes in the innovation system	Products and services for the tourists
Mobilizing role of entrepreneurs – how are new relations created	Second comers, entrepreneurial opportunities	Educational spin-offs
Diversity of relations	Profit motives	New managerial methods and competencies
Power of relations	Altruistic-ego	Networks with players; new ways of mobilizing
History of relations	Public sector role	Reversed innovation – innovation in the hinterland – beneficial for the population
	Professional/scientific development that goes hand in hand with the innovation system	Reversed business spin-offs
	Family ties	
	Trust	Tourism secondary innovation
	Tourism policies	
	Policies in other fields	
	Role of customer	
	Societal ethos and altruism	
	Synergetic driving forces	
	Balance in the institutions; volatility and stability	

- *Second comers to innovation being promoted.* A common theme in the systems is that the companies involved often reap the benefit from innovation tried and tested by a pioneer who failed.
- *Keen competition.* Competition occurs for resources and customers among the actors. But at the same time the actors cooperate on various issues in the spirit of collaboration: a type of *co-opetition* (a combination and balance between competition and cooperation) (Nalebuff and Brandenburger, 1997) is implicit in them.
- *Public sector role.* In all cases the public sector has a decisive role, be it in a hampering or facilitating manner. In the same way all specific tourism policy is conspicuous by its absence, whereas policies in other fields come to the fore in the tourist enterprises.
- *An increasing global outreach.* The numerous players involved increasingly invite knowledge, capital and ideas into the system as well as linking up to larger communities for marketing and resource purposes.
- *An increasing cross-sectoral outreach.* The spin-offs from the innovative activities of the actors involved increasingly affect other sectors, for example science, business, education, leisure, charity, health and environmental policy, and these affect them in turn.

Under the surface of these commonalities there are different emphases. Generally, in order to remain successful the enterprises studied have had to be faithful to their origins, but open to acceptance of corrective and supplementary driving forces from other fields. In the following section a closer analysis with further examples will illustrate the role of entrepreneurs and their relations, and how entrepreneurial spirit and vision is a key driving force in innovation systems.

Entrepreneurs and Their Relations

In tourism innovation systems, relations are not necessarily advanced in terms of knowledge and power, but are nonetheless crucial for the existence of continuous dynamics and development of the system.

The following significant relation types were documented in the Nordic cases.

Family Ties and Clan Structures.   The Icelandic cases serve as examples of two very close-knit extended family networks. The nature of these close-knit family ties influences the operational mode of the innovation system developing around these companies. Everybody seems to be involved in nearly all work tasks, and there is high transparency in almost all operations amongst members of the clan. Strictly speaking there is a kind of oligopoly, where flow of information from each of the two family-based companies is somewhat restricted, while internal flows are allowed at a higher pace.

Corporate Ties.   Over the years – with an emphasis on the last 10 years – the organizational and ownership structure at Beitostølen ski resort has grown from fragmented ownership to a more consolidated one consisting of one major owner of commercial operations and one other major real estate developer. An almost similar centralization has taken place in Åre. This transition can be described as emergence from (a fragmented) 'community model' of a tourism destination to an almost consolidated ownership 'corporate model'. Åre is, a public–private sector network, led by private actors but with strong support from the public sector.

Publicly Dominated Cooperative Networks. In the Seatrout Funen, the Siida and the Santa Claus village cases, public actors had, and still have, a very dominant initiating and coordinating role. They took the initiative to get involved, and they invited others. The Santa Claus village was distinctly and decisively institutionalized by public actors. The environmental ingredient in the Seatrout Funen case has a strong public involvement, and a continuous mediating of resources and access to the national resources. In these cases private initiatives are enthusiastically welcomed, but public sector actors serve as 'gatekeepers'.

Leisure and Voluntary Organizational Ties. The Roskilde Festival is deeply embedded in the local area's sports, cultural and other voluntary organizations and associations. Members of these groups contribute ideas and practical work and, indirectly, they enjoy the fruits of the surplus from the festival. The network is dense, but fluctuates around a stable core of charismatic leaders. Also in the Siida case, there is a strong involvement of associations, particularly those with a Sami background. Here the innovation systems efficiently link the public and the voluntary sectors together.

We also observe that both formal and informal relationships are found in all the cases without exception, and that these types of relationships complement each other. Business relationships are usually formalized to a degree where public actors or voluntary organizations operate. Trust and personal ties lessen the need for costly contracts and legal arrangement (Boschma, 2005). In this respect tourism innovation systems have features that are identical to many other industrial cluster and innovation systems.

Mobilizing New Relations and Resources. Over time, the innovation systems in this study have developed and grown in size and complexity. New resources have been utilized, and new relations have been forged. There are several ways to mobilize resources, but mainly this will follow from the nature of existing relations and structures. In some situations, local relations have to be supplemented with relations from outside to provoke and ensure dynamism. These shifts in scale and scope are of particular interest in the understanding of innovation systems.

Flexible Opportunity Creators. The Roskilde Festival and the Santa Claus village occupy a particularly open and inviting attitude towards new resources. Every year, for example, the festival makes space and creates opportunities for cultural entrepreneurs and others who want to test business and cultural concepts at the festival. There is a fruitful dialogue, which is usually helpful for the festival as well as the entrepreneurs. Some of the new elements turn out to be successful, others not. New resources at the Santa Claus village contribute to the diversification of the place and are consistent with the line of operation and the image.

Symbiotic Resource Mobilization.   The Icelandic whale watching operation, the Seatrout Funen, and the Siida are all innovation systems that not only enhance the tourism product, but become involved in a symbiotic relationship (i.e. one help in balance) with society. In the Seatrout Funen case, resource constellation includes a range of environmental organizations. In many respects the environmental resource systems are more resource affluent than the tourism system, and their proximity indirectly helps the tourism system. In the Siida case, the Finnish forestry authorities represent a similar power of resources, and the symbiosis is fruitful for the modest tourism activities. In the case of whale watching, whaling is a permanent issue, recently with a higher political and media profile. The tourism entrepreneurs can, by capitalizing on this feature, access resources not otherwise available to such small operators.

Strategic Business Expansion.   In the Icehotel, Beitostølen and Opplev Oppdal, where the corporate element is significant, the resource acquisition takes place on a larger financial and labour market. Yet the Icehotel has been able to sustain its smallness in some respect, having kept some of the advantages of a small firm where more or less everyone is involved and knows one another. The Åre ski destination is presently in a development phase where private and public resources are being consolidated within a Vision 2011 strategy for the future, now replaced by a new vision for 2020. Thus, the area is attempting to utilize its existing resources more economically and sustainably, and in the process gaining access to more economic resources and a better symbiosis of private and public powers.

External Resources Mobilization.   There are several examples that the innovation systems, at some stage in their development, need 'new blood' (Hjalager, 2007). The whale watching destination got a new vision about the opportunities by inviting an international tour specialist. Likewise, the Roskilde Festival, in smooth operation in the 1990s, adopted the cluster concept introduced by the Ministry of Trade and Industry. Other innovation systems also had their 'moments of truth', where lock-ins and tunnel vision features were challenged.

From this analysis it becomes clear that mobilizing strategies differ in the innovation systems. The 'playful' innovation systems with an extensive degree of voluntary work and effort allow very experimental procedures, as new innovation systems also do. The more 'oligopolic' and more commercial innovation systems draw to a greater extent on the standard resource acquisition methods.

Diversity of Relations and Structures.   A diversity of relations was a criterion for the selection of the cases in this study. However, a closer analysis demonstrates that the management of this diversity is not uniform.

Formalization.   Some of the innovation systems analysed have found it necessary to formalize groups and committees that overarch and are in a position to handle great diversity efficiently. The Santa Claus Village joint committee has quite firm control over the main relations, particularly between the regulating authorities and other external factors on the one hand and local actors on the other.

Informal Charismatic Leadership. The rafting and the whale watching enterprises suggest that in small innovation systems, the existence of a charismatic and visionary leader is crucial for building bridges across various borders and to undertake coordination. The personality of the informal leader is crucial. It is necessary for him or her to be inclusive and open-minded towards different cultures, such as those seen in Siida where the Sami visions of cultural heritage have to coexist with elements of preservation and an environmental agenda. In Beitostølen a visionary and highly esteemed entrepreneur has for several decades been able to make the best of diverse relations. A major expression of success in this respect is the fact that he has been able to build bridges between the health care sector and tourism. Charismatic and visionary leadership has, moreover, played a central role at the Icehotel where the managing director is credited greatly for its success and development, as is the case for whale watching in Iceland.

Overlapping Membership. The Roskilde case is an example of a fluid organization and the management of diversity. There are many organizations, committees and boards in the town that manage tourism activities, the festival business, and numerous voluntary organizations, and many local actors are active in several boards and groups across the private, public and semi-public sphere. The diversity is, in other words, integrated in a complex and dynamic organizational picture. The Roskilde case is also characterized by continual reorganization. If a committee or a board has done its work, or if it has become obsolete, it is dissolved without pity. Thus the diversity is allowed to flourish in continuously new forums supplied with fresh energy and knowledge.

The innovation examples, mentioned above, are not mutually exclusive, so whilst overlapping memberships might be a characteristic of one innovation system, this feature could be explained by the presence of informal charismatic leaders.

Power Structures in the Relations. In the tourism innovation systems, we expected to find low power distances and ease of communication across all thinkable boundaries. However, there are nevertheless power displays taking place in the innovation systems. Power cannot be ignored as a part of a successful development process, as it guides and controls relations (Fuchs and Shapiro, 2005).

Power of Persistence. The entrepreneurs and initiating actors in the innovation systems tend to possess, what is called first mover advantage (i.e. those businesses first into the sector and first to innovate). For example the whale watching operation is still the key provider, and newcomers have difficulty in keeping up and gaining the same external and internal reputation. In the Seatrout Funen case, the county council is a principal participant, investing its capacities in waterway resources and funds for restoration without which the innovation system could hardly persist. The county council exercised its muscle in order to overcome conflicts involving various categories of anglers and between tourism operators and local landowners.

Power of Knowledge.   Knowledge is a legitimate base for influencing relations in an innovation system. In all the tourism innovation systems the official knowledge actors – the universities – are latecomers in forging relationships with other players. In Roskilde and the Santa Claus Village, for example, the educational sector is moving in slowly. In Beitostølen, however, medical knowledge became an early stage factor for the development of the place, but also because the medical experts go skiing as a main leisure activity. Thus, Beitostølen represents a very prominent example of knowledge transfer across scientific borders.

In some case studies we identify examples of knowledge conflicts. Much knowledge is embedded in legal procedures and public planning. The Icehotel and the whale watching operations have had their controversies. They found the knowledge possessed and empowered by the authorities to be outdated and obsolete.

Power of Values.   The Roskilde festival evolved out of a hippie culture and leftist, even anarchistic, 1970s movements where any aggressive power was not accepted. Basically, the egalitarian norms adopted in the festival organization, and beyond it, are much in debt to the original ideas. There is an open distribution of information, and a very inviting style of management. A consensus-seeking attitude is dominant, and there is a (sometimes tacit) reference to the general values in the area. Values can also act as a compass for the development of the innovation systems. The values of the Sami culture in the Siida case are also an example.

The Power of Capital.   The innovation systems have clear economic objectives and, in all of them, any altruism and mutual responsibility are paired with the need and will to create a financial success for the benefits of the owners and/or the local population. In the skiing destinations and Santa Claus Village, commercial objectives are most prevalent and the investor power dominates in the development of relations. Skistar, a major international ski resort operator, is deeply involved in Åre, for example, and the public authorities sometimes find it easier to establish relations with this dominant player rather than smaller actors. The Icehotel building alliances with the Swedish Absolut Vodka is another example of a strategic alliance that is rather the result of the earning potential and marketing benefits than the need to create local or regional partnerships.

An Entrepreneurial Spirit as a Driving Force

As argued in the introduction, the driving forces are in many ways the element that maintains the momentum of relations that constitute the innovation system. The emphasis is on the creation, expansion, maintenance and – in some cases – rejuvenation of the innovation systems. As often pointed out in the cluster and innovation system literature, a basic entrepreneurial spirit is a major driving force (Maskell and Malmberg, 1999). For entrepreneurs it is important to see things grow and develop, and they are keen to launch new projects and activities when old ones are put out of operation. In spite of this common intention, the entrepreneurial spirit does not uniformly apply to all cases.

Single Entrepreneurship. The Icehotel, Opplev Oppdal, Beitostølen, whale watching and white water rafting are all stories about a *single* entrepreneur with impressive energy and clear vision. Characteristic of these entrepreneurs is their ability to tap alternative sources to develop their resource base and turn the disadvantages of a remote area into an attraction. Through a societal vision and general altruism, these entrepreneurs are drawing others – employees, family, locals and business partners – into the system, which gradually results in its expansion in scale and scope. They are not lone riders, but inspirational first movers in teams of actors.

Social Entrepreneurship. Other cases suggest a wider model for entrepreneurship – a more *collective* and *cooperative* entrepreneurial spirit. It is interesting to see that the descendants of the hippie culture in connection with the Roskilde Festival are also able to foster a genuine project drive fully comparable to the more commercially based entities. The Roskilde projects often have a wider objective and are more inclusive in their organizational forms than in the cases where single entrepreneurs are the main driving forces.

Public Entrepreneurship. The 'public sector' is usually not considered an entrepreneurial force. However, this assumption cannot be confirmed by the case studies. The Seatrout Funen innovation system is a creation of the minds of very entrepreneurial civil servants, and the Siida project would hardly have been such an innovative concept without the continual project development of the heritage custodians. Also, in the case of Santa Claus, the public authorities were first movers, driven by a need for regional development in the area.

Corporate Entrepreneurship. The 'corporations' operating as key components in some of the cases analysed have traditional development departments and innovation service centres central to their operations. These use classic business methods of innovating such as corporate sponsored study tours, customer feedback analysis teams, think tanks and other systematic creative processes.

Entrepreneurial spirit – the second tier. Innovation systems are dynamic. Initial entrepreneurs may lose energy and direction, and others then have to take over ideas and resources, or come in and gear up the process. There are several examples of changes of momentum in the 10 case studies.

Filling Gaps in the Value Chain. A tourism product is composed of a number of elements, not necessarily delivered by one enterprise alone. In the Nordic peripheries gaps in the product value chain are most often in terms of accessibility. Transportation to the Santa Claus Village and the development of the transportation system in and around Rovaniemi and Kittilä are good examples of this. Santa Claus as a global phenomenon attracts people from all over the world. Rovaniemi airport has been rebuilt to match the heavy traffic during November, December and January. In terms of the Icehotel, Kiruna airport is of key importance in bringing in customers. Making a destination available and attractive is thus often a matter of simple infrastructural amendments.

Shifting the Commercial Momentum.   The Åre Ski resort is the main example of a shift of momentum by Skistar, a major player in the ski resort business. In Åre, with the introduction of this large player, the focus and driving forces of relations were shifted into higher gear in terms of professionalism and commercialization.

Shifting the Scope.   Until 2001 the Roskilde Festival was repeated annually almost in the same format, although it grew massively in scale and reputation. Creation of the state-supported growth environment 'Musicon Valley' in 2001 led to denser and wider ranging organizational structures with the aim of nurturing business spin-offs more consistently. The educational and research sectors became more closely engaged and initiatives were launched for a series of training opportunities that address the needs of the experience economy. The scope developed from festival to community development.

The Icehotel is planning to move into 'Space tourism' as a new, but not unjustified, development. Their location near the Esrange, the launching site of the Swedish Space Corporation, and the involvement of local as well as global players in the aviation business, is of key importance for such a step. Saab is also a new collaborative partner where some drivers of Saab cars are invited to the Icehotel to test the cars on ice. This is, however, part of a greater experience at Icehotel.

Opening the Media Umbrella.   One of the innovation systems which has invited new actors of particular relevance for the tourism sector is the media. The Siida example shows how small-scale tourism, small ethnic groups and the media can work in collaborations for the wider public good. The peak season at the Santa Claus Village is about six weeks in November, December and January. One hundred and eighty thousand visitors representing 185 nationalities is the result of a well-planned media strategy. Integrated marketing communication is practised and the website of Santa Village does today include online video and streamed materials produced by Santatelevision.com. Roskilde Festival always receives considerable media attention, and the festival attempts to make the best of it. The festival and the area are moving into a new era of media collaboration, relying on more direct communication with visitors online.

In another vein, the media can also be seen as a resource when it comes to marketing through their coverage of related matters. Beitostølen has, as well as actors competing fiercely to attract the organizers of the World Cup, activities like cross-country skiing and the biathlon. More than 20 TV channels in Europe are represented at Beitostølen during these events.

Summary and Conclusion

Emerging clearly throughout the chapter is how entrepreneurs, through mobilizing relations and the system dynamics of their 'destination-based innovation systems', shape and remodel the supply of products and services. The spirit and vision of single entrepreneurs is a pertinent driving force, but being thoroughly embedded in organizations and institutions, as explained through Edquist above, these never act alone. Organizations and institutions, as the two key components of innovation systems, along with commercialization, are set within a certain national and regional framework.

Through mobilizing in different ways families, corporate actors, public sector actors and institutions along with NGOs and various voluntary bodies, the entrepreneurs effectively maintain the innovation system in their particular aims. These aims and visions are often driven by a wholly different idea than the one manifest in the products or services supplied, but these ideas nonetheless drive the mobilization of relations. The specific mobilizing practices documented above revolve around how the entrepreneurs operate in smaller-scale, less formal settings, flexibly adapting to external stimuli or drawing upon a collaborative relationship with a range of other actors. In a denser setting, where relations are more commercialized, the development of business relations becomes prominent and external resources are mobilized in a more strategic manner. With the difference documented between 'denser' or more commercial relations and those that are more informal, the power of relations starts to emerge.

One of the key conclusions to emerge though is the role of the entrepreneur in filling gaps in the value chain. Due to the cross-sectoral nature of the tourist industry, an entrepreneur has considerably wider scope to draw resources from, but at the same time complements the value chain of their own service and product supply. The organizations and institutions of innovations systems, tied on their national, regional and/or sectoral saddle, are cross-mobilized by entrepreneurs in a tourism destination/attraction setting. The notion of entrepreneurship is thus enhanced through tourism and further studies following this vein might be of benefit to other cross-sectoral studies of entrepreneurial activities.

Questions for Discussion

1. What theory or theories provide best explanation of innovation systems?
2. Why does tourism provide a unique context for innovations and entrepreneurship?
3. What are the main characteristics of the Nordic tourism sector?
4. Identify and explain the actors' relationships between different groups in tourism development in Nordic countries.
5. Explain how and why public actors have a dominant role in the tourism development in the Nordic area.

References

Drucker, P. (2006). *Innovation and entrepreneurship*, 2nd edn. New York: Harper Collins.

Etzkowitz, H., and Leydesdorff, L. (2000). 'The Dynamics of Innovation: from National Systems and 'Mode2' to Triple Helix of University-Industry-Government Relations', *Research Policy*, 29, 109–123.

Flagestad, A., Hope, C.A., Svensson, B., and Nordin, S. (2005). 'The Tourist Destination; a Local Innovation System? The Creation of a Model', In *Innovation in Tourism – Creating Customer Value*, (P. Keller and T. Bieger, eds), Brainerd: AIEST.

Freeman, C. (1987). *Technology Policy and Economic Performance*. London: Pinter.

Freeman, C. (1995). 'The National Innovation Systems in Historical Perspective', *Cambridge Journal of Economics*, 19, 5–24.

Johnson, A. (2001). 'Functions in Innovation Systems Approaches', DRUID paper. www.druid.dk

Lundvall, B-Å. (2005). 'National Innovation Systems – Analytical Concept and Development Tool', Paper Presented at the DRUID Conference in Copenhagen.

Lundvall, B-Å. (2007a). 'National Innovation Systems – Analytical Concept and Development Tool', *Industry and Innovation*, 14(1), 95–119.

Lundvall, B-Å. (2007b). 'Innovation Systems: Theory and Policy', In *Companion to Neo-Schumpeterian Economics*, (H. Hanusch, ed), Cheltenham: Edward Elgar.

OECD (1999). *Boosting Innovation. The Cluster Approach*. Paris: OECD.

OECD (2005). *Innovation Policy and Performance. A Cross-Country Comparison*. Paris: OECD.

Chapter 5

Women Empowerment Entrepreneurship Nexus in Tourism: Processes of Social Innovation

Linda W.J. Peeters and Irena Ateljevic

Learning Outcomes

After reading this chapter, you should be able to:

- Understand the concept of women entrepreneurship and its relation to the broader issues of social innovation and community development;

- Perceive women empowerment in a positive way as opposed to the usual 'a priori victimizing' approach;

- Identify hidden entrepreneurship behind the terminology of community development, social change and preservation of cultural and natural heritage;

- Explain the link between women entrepreneurship and tourism;

- Understand how entrepreneurship empowers women.

Introduction

The objectives of this chapter are threefold with the first two contributing to the entrepreneurship field of study and the third to the gender field of study. The first objective is to contribute to the under-researched area and lack of coherent understanding of women entrepreneurship in tourism both conceptually and empirically. Secondly, through this first objective, our understanding of entrepreneurship will be expanded to the area of (women) empowerment which leads to community development, social innovation and change. Women empowerment has become even more important nowadays as it has gained political importance since being acknowledged by UNWTO. In connecting women entrepreneurship in tourism and women empowerment, this chapter approaches the issue of women empowerment in a positive way instead of the usual 'a priori victimizing' approach. A lot of literature on empowerment discusses empowerment from the a priori idea that someone is a victim, a marginalized, poor person not having choices. However, by looking at empowerment and human possibilities positively, and connecting them to entrepreneurship, the chapter shows there is a lot of 'hidden' social entrepreneurship behind community development, social change and preservation of cultural and natural heritage.

The consequence of connecting women entrepreneurship in tourism and women empowerment is the expansion of our understanding of entrepreneurship as a business in the traditional sense to the notion of social innovation and change. In other words, our definition of 'being entrepreneurial' expands to the civil society organizations (NGOs), which often very innovatively create economic and social opportunities at the individual and community level.

Finally, this chapter contributes to gender studies in tourism by paying attention to women leadership, entrepreneurship and creativity as opposed to the dominant tendency in literature to describe constraints, inhibiting factors and marginalization, from the female point of view, in the areas of women as hosts and employees, women as travellers, and tourist images (Kinnaird and Hall, 1994).

In the light of those arguments the chapter will begin with an overview of the current state of affairs on (women) entrepreneurship (in tourism) to be followed by the main debates in the area of community development and women empowerment in tourism. Currently, literature on community development and women empowerment in tourism is divorced from the entrepreneurship literature. Many development examples in community development and empowerment are not seen as entrepreneurship and because of that are overlooked by entrepreneurship research, which focuses on profit-making enterprises. This theoretical conceptual discussion will then be supported by a range of selective case studies from around the world that will illustrate the central argument of this conceptual chapter, which is to expand the definition of tourism entrepreneurship into the area of social innovation and change.

Mapping the Literature

This literature review will cover four big areas, namely: (tourism) entrepreneurship, women entrepreneurship, women entrepreneurship in tourism, and community development and women empowerment in tourism.

(Tourism) Entrepreneurship

As discussed by Ateljevic and Li in Chapter 2 of this book, entrepreneurship research in general is a relatively young field studied within a variety of disciplines. Because of this multidisciplinary nature of entrepreneurship research there has been no agreement so far on the conceptualization or definition of entrepreneurship. Chapter 2 also asserts that the possibility of providing a more lasting and consistent definition of entrepreneurship is further complicated by the notion that human behaviour that is supported by a range of attributes directly influences entrepreneurship. Nevertheless, Chapter 2 was able to identify three areas of theoretical perspectives:

1. The first theoretical perspective refers to the economic school and theorists on the role of the entrepreneur in the economic development;

2. The second theoretical perspective refers to the socio-behavioural theorists that are concerned with the personal characteristics/traits and the social environment;
3. The third theoretical context is associated with the psychological perspective that is concerned with entrepreneurial personality and his or her behavioural characteristics, advocating that entrepreneurs are risk-takers and have a high need for achievement, control and autonomy.

According to Gartner (1990), the second theoretical perspective has received most attention from scholars. Spear (2000, p. 1) argues that 'studies of entrepreneurship tend to be preoccupied with the individual, and the purely economic aspects of starting a new enterprise and subsequent business development'.

Next, Chapter 2 narrows its discussion by continuing with the issue of entrepreneurship research in tourism, arguing that 'in the context of tourism development, entrepreneurship is more complex and includes many interlinked forms of innovation undertaken by different actors – individually or collectively'.

Terms used to describe how successful tourism development in a locality is based on common goals (and therefore includes a growing number of stakeholders working in different forms of partnership) include 'collective entrepreneurship', 'pluralistic entrepreneurship' and 'institutional entrepreneurship'. As the status of entrepreneurship research has not been studied systematically, Ateljevic and Li conducted a study to evaluate tourism entrepreneurship scholarship in the period 1986–2006 by identifying and analysing a set of entrepreneurship articles published in seven refereed academic journals in the field of hospitality and tourism management in this period. The main findings were categorized according to the number of articles published, the types of research, the research method and analytical procedures, and the focal areas of study; these are discussed in Chapter 2. Among the research areas that gained much attention, 'small business' has been the dominant area in hospitality entrepreneurship research. Within this area researchers have concentrated on topics such as the importance of small businesses in regional economic impact and job creation. Venkataraman (1997) raised an important point arguing that small business is often mixed up with entrepreneurship, but that the two, however, are not synonymous.

Women Entrepreneurship

In order to complete the literature review concerning the specific issues discussed in this chapter, a literature review has been carried out concerning women entrepreneurship research in general, which will first be presented shortly, followed by a more specific literature review on women entrepreneurship in tourism, which will be discussed in more detail. When we look at the women entrepreneurship literature in general we see it covers a whole wide range of areas. Several main observations can be made.

A huge area of research within the literature on women entrepreneurship concerns the barriers and constraints women face in the process of becoming, and being, entrepreneurs (Roomi and Parrot, 2008; Brindley, 2005; Moore and Buttner, 1997; Blanchard et al., 2008; Becker-Blease and Sohl, 2007; Botha et al., 2006; Heidrick and Johnson, 2002;

Bates, 2002; Winn, 2005; Della-Giusta and Phillips, 2006). Women do not only face barriers and constraints in the process of becoming entrepreneurs; barriers and constraints women face as employees also push them towards becoming an entrepreneur, highlighting the positive aspects and opportunities of being a female entrepreneur (Heilman and Chen, 2003; Moore and Buttner, 1997; Mattis, 2004). Often studies on barriers, constraints and opportunities link their discussion to the second big area of research: the differences between female and male entrepreneurs (Becker-Blease and Sohl, 2007; Carter and Bennett, 2006).

Thus, another big area of research is the focus on the differences between female and male entrepreneurs with regard to several aspects, such as access to capital, personal characteristics and motivations (Watson and Robinson, 2003; Buttner and Rosen, 1988; Watson and Newby, 2005; DeMartino and Barbato, 2003; Runyan et al., 2006; Fuller-Love et al., 2006; Walker and Webster, 2007; Catley and Hamilton, 1998), which can be linked to the three theoretical perspectives within the general entrepreneurship literature. What is of specific interest here, with regard to the topic of this chapter, is the difference in motivations and characteristics between female and male entrepreneurs.

As explained in the literature review on general entrepreneurship, there is no agreement on the definition and conceptualization of entrepreneurship, but nevertheless 'studies of entrepreneurship tend to be preoccupied with the individual, and the purely economic aspects of starting a new enterprise and subsequent business development' (Spear, 2000, p. 1). This can be linked to the difference in motivations and characteristics between male entrepreneurs and female entrepreneurs, as male entrepreneurs are mainly motivated by economic orientations and female entrepreneurs mainly by social orientations (McClelland et al., 2005). McGehee et al. (2007) give an example of this, stating that in the case of an alternative agriculture enterprise men are focused on income-generating motivations and women on cost-reducing motivations.

All these comments point to a tendency to put male notions about what constitutes entrepreneurship to the forefront, while 'neglecting' or 'seeing as different from the norm' the female notions about what constitutes entrepreneurship (see, for example, Buttner and Rosen [1988] whose study results confirmed their hypothesis that characteristics attributed to successful entrepreneurs were more commonly ascribed to men than to women). Bruni et al. (2004, p. 256) wrote an interesting article in this regard arguing that:

> Social studies of women entrepreneurs tend to reproduce an androcentric entrepreneur mentality that makes hegemonic masculinity invisible. They portray women's organizations as 'the other', and sustain social expectations of their difference, thereby implicitly reproducing male experience as a preferred normative value.

Research about characteristics and motivations of female entrepreneurs has also been carried out without comparing these to the male entrepreneur's characteristics and motivations, in combination with the issues on constraints, barriers and opportunities (Lerner et al., 1997; Still and Walker, 2006; Gray and Finly-Hervey, 2005). One particular issue that can be observed within this literature is the way that these female entrepreneurs handle their work–life balance and renegotiate gender roles (Walker et al., 2008). In some studies female entrepreneurs across and within countries or regions have been compared (McClelland et al., 2005; Lituchy and Reavley, 2004; Hisrich and Öztürk, 1999). The GEM (Global Entrepreneurship Monitor) (Allen et al., 2008, p. 8), for example, 'labels those individuals who start a business to exploit a perceived business opportunity as opportunity entrepreneurs, and those who are, by contrast, pushed to start a business because all other options for work are either absent or unsatisfactory as necessity entrepreneurs' and also applies this labelling to female entrepreneurs.

Das (1999) classifies women entrepreneurs not in two but into three different categories: 'chance', 'forced' and 'created or pulled' entrepreneurs and Anna et al. (1999) investigate the differences between women business owners in traditional and non-traditional industries.

Following the pattern observed in the general entrepreneurship literature, small business has also been a dominant area within the literature on women entrepreneurship (see for example Fielden and Davidson, 2005).

Several reports and publications on certain projects are available on the internet, published by certain organizations such as the GEM and the ILO (International Labour Organization). The GEM, for example, is a not-for-profit academic research consortium which aims at producing high quality international research data on entrepreneurial activities and making these data available to as many people as possible. One of their reports concerns the Global Entrepreneurship Monitor study on women's entrepreneurship (Allen et al., 2008, p. 4) which focuses on measuring differences in the level of entrepreneurial activity among countries, uncovering factors leading to entrepreneurial behaviour, and suggesting policies that may enhance national levels of entrepreneurial activity.

The ILO has published several documents concerning their WEDGE project (2008), which is part of the ILO's SEED programme. According to the ILO, the WEDGE approach is based on:

- Developing a knowledge base on women entrepreneurs;
- Promoting representation, advocacy and voice;
- Developing innovative support services for women entrepreneurs;
- Strategic alliances;
- Gender mainstreaming.

The development of entrepreneurship among women with disabilities is one of the more specific concerns of the ILO, as well as the position of women entrepreneurs in certain developing regions and countries.

Beside these reports and articles, a whole range of books has been published, each of which covers most of the issues concerning women entrepreneurship discussed here and shows how extensive attention has been paid to women entrepreneurship in general (Butler, 2003; Brush et al., 2006; Smith-Hunter, 2006; Wells, 1998; Kyro et al., 2008; Fielden and Davidson, 2005; Allen and Truman, 1993; Coughlin and Thomas, 2002; Ericksen et al., 1999; Heffernan, 2008; Smith, 2005; Radovic Markovic, 2008; Hughes, 2005).

Women Entrepreneurship in Tourism

Although the literature on women entrepreneurship in general is extensive, in Chapter 1 Ateljevic and Page point out that the role of female entrepreneurs is rather neglected in tourism entrepreneurship research. Indeed, when searching more specifically for literature on women entrepreneurship in tourism, it soon becomes obvious that surprisingly little has been done in this specific area. For this reason it is rather difficult to observe the emergence of specific key issues or areas in the literature on women entrepreneurship in tourism, one of the main reasons being that when the topic is discussed at all, it rarely is the focus of the study concerned.

Many studies, for example, discuss the extent and nature of women's employment in the tourism industry and employment opportunities for women in this sector (Samir El-Sharif Ibrahim et al., 2007; Iverson and Sparrowe, 1999; Doherty and Manfredi, 2001; Kempadoo, 2001; Roehl and Swerdlow, 2001; Ng and Pine, 2003; Gibson, 2001), with entrepreneurial activities sometimes mentioned as one of these opportunities (Elmas, 2007; Gentry, 2007; Apostolopoulos and Sönmez, 2001; Cohen, 2001; Hall, 2001; Walker et al., 2001). However, most of these discussions do not expand on this opportunity and quickly turn to focus on the sexualized labour division in the tourism industry, in which women mostly hold low-paying, low-skilled positions.

Thus, the positions that women hold as employees in the tourism sector has been the focus of discussion in the tourism employment literature, pointing out that these female employees tend to be concentrated in positions that are an extension of their traditional domestic roles (Apostolopoulos and Sönmez, 2001; Timothy, 2001; Elmas, 2007; Hall, 2001; Walker et al., 2001). Gentry (2007) addresses this issue by discussing the employment experiences of Belizean women in alternative, mass and non-tourism businesses in order to find out if the alternative sector addresses the criticism which is attributed to employment in mass tourism. Although it is not the focus of her article, Gentry discusses the opportunities and advantages for women of owning their own business as part of the general discussion on employment benefits and disadvantages.

When looking at the few studies that focus more or less specifically on women entrepreneurship in tourism, it is interesting to notice that most of these studies concern positions of women entrepreneurs in the tourism sector that could also be regarded as an extension of traditional domestic roles. The host family sector or the commercial home enterprise is an example of this. Several scholars (Lynch, 1998; Harris et al., 2007; Long and Wall, 1995; Li, 2003) have investigated this accommodation sector in which they studied women playing an important role, as the work is carried out within their own home environment mirroring their traditional domestic roles. Lynch (1998), for example, reports on the motivations of hosts providing an accommodation service from their own home, using the literature on female entrepreneurship as a conceptual lens. Long and Wall (1995) discuss the improved mobility and status of women who run home-stays in Bali; Li (2003) examines how women in a village in China (re)negotiate their identity in the face of tourism development, being actively engaged in tourism business through inviting tourists to their Dai-styles bamboo houses and selling crafts at home; and Harris et al. (2007)

report on the personal experiences of commercial home hosts in New Zealand with a focus on issues of work–life balance and *copreneurship* (couples [with a marital or pseudo-marital link] who share ownership of, commitment to, and responsibility for, a venture).

Within the literature on women entrepreneurs in tourism, another example of women extending their traditional domestic roles is the relatively large representation of studies which focus on agritourism entrepreneurship (Bouquet, 1982; Garcia-Ramon et al., 1995; Brega, 1998; Jennings and Stehlik, 1999; Overbeek, 2003; McGehee et al., 2007). Garcia-Ramon et al. (1995) discuss the changing position of women in the novel economic activity of farm tourism (accommodation) in Spain and their role within the economic production of the family unit. They point out women's opportunities to interact with the outside world by commodifying their domestic work to provide services for tourists, while at the same time preserving their landscape. Bouquet (1982, p. 227) also points to this mirroring of the domestic role in agrotourism, elaborating on the transformation of women's roles from mainly working within agriculture to mainly working within the domestic domain:

> Women's contemporary domestic labour on the farm is of two sorts: on behalf of the family (reproductive labour) and for tourists (productive labour) accommodated within the house.

Overbeek (2003) analyses and explores the consequences of the process of economic individualization for women who are married to the owner of a business or who own a business in tourism or agriculture. The purpose of McGehee et al.'s (2007) study is to investigate the possibly gendered nature of motivations for agri-tourism entrepreneurship among Virginia farm families, testing the alternative agriculture paradigm developed by Chiappe and Flora (1998) as a potential theoretical framework.

Although not specifically focused on female entrepreneurs, literature on family business, which often also includes the host family sector and the agritourism sector, is very much related to female entrepreneurs. Getz et al. (2004) edited an important book within this area titled *The Family Business in Tourism and Hospitality*. Besides discussing issues such as the scope and significance of family business, the link between entrepreneurship and family business, motivations and goals, gender challenges and issues in balancing family and business through the life cycle, they also discuss the different forms of family businesses such as farm-based family business, family-owned and -operated small hotels, family-owned nature-based resorts, family-owned and -operated tour companies, and family-owned tourist attractions and wineries. Langreiter's (2004) paper deals with the employees and families working in family-run hotels and catering industries focusing especially on the 'proprietresses', and Tucker (2007, p. 88) refers to the opportunities for women entrepreneurs in family-run businesses arguing:

> Small and microenterprises, and especially family run businesses, have been found in many settings to be relatively beneficial to women because of the opportunities they offer for women to earn extra income and improve their status both within and outside of the household.

A second issue mentioned in the literature (Mills, 2004; Bras and Dahles, 1998; Wilkinson and Pratiwi, 1995; Tucker, 2007) is the importance of the informal sector providing opportunities for women, both employees and entrepreneurs. Bras and Dahles (1998), for example, have studied the impact of tourism and tourism policy, with its changing government regulations and measures, on the employment opportunities of women entrepreneurs in the informal sector in Sanur, Bali. Tucker (2007) discusses the case of a woman in Turkey who runs an informal *pansiyon* (Turkish term for tourist accommodation establishment with fewer than 10 rooms) business and a report by the United Nations (1999) presents cases of entrepreneurial activities of which some started off as an informal sector initiative and then became a registered business involving more people.

Finally, an interesting work worth mentioning here is the bibliography *Women – The Invisible Pioneers in Recreation and Leisure Research* (Markham, 1997). This bibliography is the result of a discussion within the academic world on the state of research and writing about 'Women – the Invisible Pioneers in Recreation and Leisure'. However, Markham points out that it was felt that 'an edited book might not be appropriate until more knowledge existed in our literature'. A workshop held at the International Congress on Women and Leisure at the University of Georgia further prompted the need to establish an understanding of the state of knowledge of these pioneers. Thus, the purpose of Markham's bibliography is to focus on women pioneers in leisure services. As an example, Markham refers to an email conversation she had with Elery Hamilton-Smith who argued that 'women were of immense importance in tourism because of their role as guest house proprietors and hoteliers'. According to his research:

> While the histories of tourist resorts often describe the role that men played in shaping the industry, the accommodation directories for the areas all name women as the proprietors of the guest houses and hotels.

Community Development and Women Empowerment in Tourism

The last area that will be covered in this literature review is community development and women empowerment in tourism. This big area of literature can be divided into two sub-areas, namely tourism community development and tourism women empowerment. Literature on community development is very huge and broad, but also very general and often very dispersed. The word 'community' alone, for example, can be defined in several ways looking at geographical, religious, cultural, ethnical or other common interest relationships (León, 2006). How the term should be defined has been an important point of discussion during the years (Richards and Hall, 2000). Joppe (1996, p. 475) argues

> ...for the most part, 'community' is self-defining in that it is based on a sense of shared purpose and common goals. It may be geographical in nature or a community of interest, built on heritage and cultural values shared among community members.

The concept of development has also been a point of discussion in the literature as it is not easy to grasp and understand (Lackey, 1990). Nevertheless, there has been an increasing stream of literature on community development in tourism in recent years as a consequence of the recognition that the development of tourism can be influenced by communities (Richards and Hall, 2000). Richards and Hall refer to Murphy's (1985) classic review of community tourism (which shaped the basis for many subsequent studies), who stressed it was necessary for each community to connect tourism development to local needs. As a result of this basic argument, subsequent studies of community-based tourism have gradually expanded the notion of community-based tourism to incorporate a wide range of issues, such as local participation and democracy and ecological aspects. Thus, as Richards and Hall (2000, p. 5) point out,

> Although the concept of community has shifted in meaning and application in the tourism field over the years, the recent rediscovery of the 'local' and the growing importance of identity have placed 'community' at the fore-front of discussions about tourism development.

In these discussions on tourism community development four key areas can be discerned (León, 2006; Richards and Hall, 2000; Murphy, 1985; Beeton, 2006):

1. *Community participation.* Important points of discussion within this main area in the literature are the definition of community participation, the level of community participation in tourism development initiatives and how it has been and should be implemented. The level of applying a bottom-up approach, which is seen as a characteristic of the participatory development approach, or a top-down approach within development processes has been discussed and criticized heavily. Pretty (Pretty and Hine, 1999), for example, has identified six types or levels of participation and Tosun (2000; 2001) identified four important constraints or limits in fully achieving community participation, which he followed by developing the framework 'Stages in the emergence of participatory tourism approach in the developing world' in a later work (2005). Mitchell and Reid (2001) developed the 'Integration tourism framework' in order to investigate how public participation and related external and internal factors possibly influence or determine planning processes for a certain tourism project.
2. *Sustainability.* Richards and Hall (2000, p. 5) argued that 'The local community has become for many the appropriate context level for the development of sustainable tourism'. Community participation is often linked to the concept of sustainability, as this generally is seen as a prerequisite for tourism to develop in a sustainable way. Mowforth and Munt's (2003) criteria for sustainability in tourism, for example, include the criterion 'local participatory'. Community empowerment is an important concept within this sustainability and participation debate. However, often it is not questioned what or who exactly is being empowered within the community (Scheyvens, 2000).
3. *Economic/regional development.* The first and second areas within the literature on tourism community development ('community participation' and 'sustainability') are

linked to the third area ('Economic/regional development') as several scholars have criticized the so-called sustainability level of tourism community development, especially with regard to the community participation issue, as 'tourism continues to be driven by levels of government rather than community interests' (Joppe, 1996, p. 475). Governments, especially in developing countries, have seen the economic potential of tourism as a way to create jobs, reduce debts and encourage economic and regional development, pushed and inspired by international organizations such as the United Nations and the World Bank. The many reports and papers published by these kinds of organizations on this issue are an indication of this.

4. *Cultural heritage.* Striving for economic/regional development through tourism community development by governments implies the notion of the community as a commodity (Joppe, 1996). It is the community that is the tourist attraction and it is the community that needs to be sold to tourists. Thus the issue of cultural heritage plays an important role in literature on tourism community development. How cultural heritage in a community can be and is being commoditized to meet the need of the tourists (Joppe, 1996) is discussed as well as how this can be a way to preserve the community's cultural heritage on the one hand, but can also alter a community's cultural heritage as a result of the interaction with tourists on the other hand. Notions such as staged authenticity or communicative staging are also part of these discussions (Chhabra et al., 2003; Williams, 2004; MacCannell and Lippard, 1999; Mowforth and Munt, 2003).

However, in spite of this extensive research on tourism community development, gender is rarely a part of the discussion within these areas. In addition, also other power structures at play are being ignored (Joppe, 1996, p. 478):

> the research undertaken on community tourism development has all but ignored the broader political dimension of tourism development, the power structure in decision making, the implications of excluding certain interest groups from decision making processes, and why non-decisions occur.

In order to understand gender in tourism issues three central aspects need to be taken into account, Kinnaird and Hall (1994 in Myers and Hannam, 2007, p. 176) argue:

> First, tourism processes are constructed from gendered societies ordered by gender relations. Second, gender relations over time inform and are informed by interconnected economic, political, social, cultural and environmental dimensions of all societies engaged in tourism development. Third, power, control, and equality issues are articulated through race, gender, class and gender relations in tourism practices.

This brings this literature review to the second sub-area within women empowerment in tourism community development: tourism women empowerment. Literature on women empowerment is usually part of gender studies and is often not linked to the tourism community development literature, although there have been some attempts to link these gender issues and women empowerment to tourism community development in particular

(Momsen, 2004) and community development in general, such as the book *Myth of Community: Gender Issues in Participatory Development* (Guijt and Shah, 1998). Scheyvens (1999) has provided a framework presenting the different forms of empowerment in order to determine the impacts of ecotourism initiatives on local communities, which does not include an explicit discussion on gender issues:

1. Economic empowerment;
2. Psychological empowerment;
3. Social empowerment;
4. Political empowerment.

However, in one of her later works (Scheyvens, 2000) she reconsiders these four forms of empowerment including gender issues. A lot of literature on empowerment discusses empowerment from the a priori idea that someone is a victim, a marginalized, poor person not having choices. When looking at the literature covering tourism women empowerment, three key areas of research can be observed (Kinnaird and Hall, 1994; Timothy, 2001; Pritchard et al., 2007; León, 2006; Berger, 2005; Gibson, 2001):

1. *Gendered employment/hosts (women as employees/hosts)*. Women entrepreneurship in tourism can be seen as part of this area of research and has already been discussed earlier in this chapter, where it was argued that the literature on tourism women employment has mainly been concerned with the positions that women take as employees in the tourism sector, 'ignoring' the positions that women (can) take as employers or entrepreneurs. Hosts as prostitutes are an important issue within this part of the literature on gendered hosts. Furthermore, literature on gendered hosts discusses how hosts 'construct and reconstruct their sense of meaning of gender throughout their involvement in the tourism development' (León, 2006), possibly interfering with the traditional social practices, societal values and cultural norms.
2. *Gendered travellers (women as travellers both in business and leisure)*. According to Timothy (2001) and Gibson (2001) there is less written about women as consumers of tourism compared to women as producers of tourism. The few accounts on women as travellers deal with issues such as the difference in needs, preferences and experiences between male and female travellers, the difference in male and female roles as tourists, the relevance of social class, societal and cultural environments, lifestyle characteristics, family life-cycle stage and safety, and the constraints and opportunities women from developing countries face in their travel opportunities.
3. *Tourism as gendered construction*. Many scholars have investigated the way in which certain destinations and people are marketed and promoted using gendered stereotypes: 'gendered and sexualized representations in tourism marketing are one way the tourism industry uses gendered and often racial and ethnic forms to construct images of a destination or vacation package' (Gibson, 2001, p. 36). Northern destinations, for example, are being presented in a masculine way, while many islands are being presented in a feminine way (Berger, 2005).

The Nexus?

Currently, literature on community development and women empowerment in tourism is divorced from the entrepreneurship literature. Many development examples in community development and empowerment are not seen as entrepreneurship, and because of that are overlooked by entrepreneurship research, which focuses on profit-making enterprises. However, there have been a few exceptions in the literature which more or less present a similar kind of argument as presented in this chapter, using for example the notion of social entrepreneurship (Oppedisano, 2004; Lee-Gosselin and Grisé, 1990). However, these are not focused on tourism entrepreneurship.

It needs to be stressed that this chapter does not want to ignore structural inequalities and injustices. However, by looking at empowerment and human possibilities positively and connecting it to entrepreneurship, this chapter shows there is a lot of hidden entrepreneurship behind the terminology of community development, social change and preservation of cultural and natural heritage. Thus the following part of this chapter will discuss some positive case studies in the area of women empowerment through entrepreneurship in tourism with the main objective of expanding our notion of entrepreneurship into the area of social innovation and change.

Method

In order to write this chapter, the method of desk research was employed, as it principally is a conceptual chapter. This chapter is a combination of a conceptual literature review accompanied by a selection of 'successful' case studies from Asia and Africa which illustrate the way the notion of entrepreneurship can be expanded into the area of social innovation and change. With regard to the 'successful' case studies, this chapter needs to acknowledge the work of the Academic Cluster Project of Wageningen University completed in June 2008. The main objective of this research was the collection of successful stories of women's empowerment through tourism around the world (Africa, Asia, Eastern Europe, Middle East and Latin America) in order to show the connection between tourism and the socio-economic development of women. As there are different types of empowerment, this research emphasized the importance of extra disciplinary knowledge. In carrying out the research the following three steps were followed:

1. Browsing through major search engines on the World Wide Web by typing in the four main keywords 'women', 'empowerment', 'tourism' and the name of a certain country or region. This did not produce the desired results.
2. Identifying international and local NGOs which are either related to tourism or are involved in women's empowerment projects, using a website listing non-governmental organizations all over the world.
3. Writing emails to selected NGOs requiring further information.

After all the cases were collected, they were grouped into similar type of projects per region followed by a document analysis using both qualitative and quantitative approaches accompanied by a macro-regional analysis for each region. In the final part an overall world-view was provided comparing cases, processes and regions in order to discover the overall regional performance and the key to success in women empowerment projects. Because the objective of this chapter is to extend our understanding of entrepreneurship to the area of social innovation and civil society, the focus has been primarily on NGOs.

Case Studies

This part of the chapter provides three case studies from Africa showing women who 'have been entrepreneurial in their social commitment' (Oppedisano, 2004, p. 174) and illustrates how the notion of entrepreneurship can be expanded to the area of social innovation and change. Each case study will provide information on the geographical location, the NGO involved and a short entrepreneurial analysis of the activities carried out.

Case Study One

Location: Kenya, East Africa
Organization: A local tourism organization called Ol Lentille offering four holiday houses, a restaurant, pool, library and a lot of activities. They are working together with four local women's groups as one.

Entrepreneurial Analysis.   These four local women's groups build and host a craft *manyatta* (village) for guests. The women are being trained, employed and financially supported in all kinds of issues, varying from book keeping, managing and developing new projects, community health work in community medical programmes, setting up an egg project and developing microbusinesses. In this way these women are socially and economically innovative, bringing together resources for the good of the community. The women of these local women's groups have to utilize entrepreneurial skills to create organizations for social good, as they are themselves responsible for the construction, organization, farming and marketing. Furthermore they are thinking about employing a trained Masai woman from outside to help them manage their projects and develop new projects, which means that if they proceed with this initiative, they will become not only self-employed, but an employer as well.

Case Study Two

Where: Uganda, East Africa
Organization: The main organization is Community Based Tourism Initiative (COBATI), a local NGO that has managed to establish partnerships with international and other local NGOs, government, private sector, development agencies, communities and individuals. COBATI is a local tourism NGO that is empowering local communities and individuals to engage in community tourism as an alternative for income generation. COBATI's mission is to enhance the capacity of local people living in areas endowed with natural and cultural resources, but disadvantaged by poverty, to improve their livelihoods through community tourism in the framework of small-scale enterprises.

Entrepreneurial Analysis.   COBATI can be regarded as a truly entrepreneurial organization and the founder of COBATI, Maria, as a true entrepreneur. Maria has created a niche as a capacity developer for communities to come up with innovative ideas that generate income through tourism and that help them to use their endowments that were otherwise idle. This inspiring woman is producing economic as well as social innovation, utilizing entrepreneurial skills to create organizations for social good, through which resources are brought together and distributed equally between tourism operators and host communities to ensure improved livelihoods, social security and an enriched tourism product in Uganda. Entrepreneurial aspects can be recognized in the process through which this is achieved, starting with education and training given to the local people to acquire the necessary tourism entrepreneurial skills, followed by guiding the local people in establishing the hospitality enterprises, and finally by linking the local people's enterprises to mainstream tourism (the market).

Case Study Three

Where: Uganda, East Africa
Organization: A local non-governmental organization called Uganda Community Tourism Association (UCOTA) which was established in July 1998. To date UCOTA has grown into 50 member-groups countrywide, representing about 1200 individuals of whom 63% are women and 37% men. They empower local communities in sustainable development through the provision of accommodation, guiding services, cultural performances and handcraft enterprises.

Entrepreneurial Analysis.   The groups, which for the bigger part consist of women, operate small enterprises ranging from accommodation, guiding services and restaurants to craft shops and music, dance and drama performances. So, one could more or less say that UCOTA is the parent company with the small enterprises being the subsidiaries. This means that entrepreneurial skills are being employed to guide this organization and its subsidiaries, producing economic as well as social innovation since the income is reinvested back into the communities and most UCOTA groups also fund a community project. UCOTA achieves this economic and social entrepreneurial innovation through five core (entrepreneurial) activities: capacity building, marketing, advocacy, networking and conservation.

Conclusion

This chapter has highlighted the under-researched area of women entrepreneurship and the lack of coherent understanding of it in tourism both conceptually and empirically. It has also highlighted the dominant tendency in the literature to describe constraints, inhibiting factors and marginalization, from the female point of view, in the areas of women as hosts and employees, women as travellers, and tourist images. By paying attention to women's leadership, entrepreneurship and creativity, this chapter has contributed to this under-researched area of women entrepreneurship, as well as to gender studies, by approaching the topic in a positive manner.

Through connecting women entrepreneurship in tourism and women empowerment, our understanding of entrepreneurship as business in a traditional 'masculine' sense has been expanded to the notion of social innovation and change, the third objective of this chapter, as feminine ideas about what constitutes entrepreneurship are being incorporated. In other words, our definition of 'being entrepreneurial' has expanded to the civil society organizations (NGOs) which often very innovatively create economic and social opportunities at the individual and community level. This definition of 'being entrepreneurial' is very much related to the notion of lifestyle entrepreneurship, in which 'non-economic motives have been recognized as significant stimuli for tourism entrepreneurship and growth of the small-business sector' (Ateljevic and Doorne, 2000).

The focus on NGOs in this chapter challenges the capitalistic view of businesses as the major units of entrepreneurship. Civil society creations of NGOs actually illustrate a form of self-employment and more ethical careers, which contribute to the well-being and the future sustainability of humanity. Furthermore, entrepreneurship is also perceived to go beyond the triple bottom line of profit-making and possibly the future of work aspirations. Therefore this chapter wishes to encourage innovative research in the area of (women) tourism entrepreneurship.

Questions for Discussion

1. What are the main forms of empowerment that determine the impacts of ecotourism initiatives on local communities, and how are these related to the context of gender?
2. Why does tourism provide an interesting context to study women entrepreneurship and their empowerment?
3. What are the comment issues/themes that link the three case studies in terms of entrepreneurship and social innovation?

References

Bruni, A., Gherardi, S., and Poggio, B. (2004). Entrepreneurial-mentality, gender and the study of women entrepreneurs, *Journal of Organizational Change Management*, 17(3), 256–268.

Carter, S. and Bennett, D. (2006). Gender and entrepreneurship. In: Carter, S., Jones-Evans, D. (Eds.), *Enterprise and Small Business Principles, Practice and Policy*. FT Prentice Hall, England New York, pp. 176–191.

Coughlin, J.H. and Thomas, A.R. (2002). *The Rise of Women Entrepreneurs: People, Processes, and Global Trends*. Quorum Books, Westport, Connecticut, London.

MacCannell, D. and Lippard, L.R. (1999). *The Tourist: A New Theory of the Leisure Class. Berkeley and Los Angeles*. University of California Press, California.

Myers, L. and Hannam, K. (2007). Women as backpacker tourists: a feminist analysis of destination choice and social identity. In: Hannam, K., Ateljevic, I. (Eds.), *Backpacker Tourism: Concepts and Profiles*. Channel View Publications, Clevedon, UK, pp. 174–187.

Runyan, R.C., Huddleston, P., and Swinney, J. (2006). Entrepreneurial orientation and social capital as small firm strategies: A study of gender differences from a resource-based view, *Entrepreneurship Mgt*, 2, 455–477.

Chapter 6

Entrepreneurs, Institutions and Institutional Entrepreneurship: New Light through Old Windows?

Thomas Forbes

Learning Outcomes

After reading this chapter, you should be able to:

- Understand the concept of institutional entrepreneurship and relate to the broader issues of entrepreneurship;

- Grasp the process of institutionalization and identify the causal mechanisms that lead to its stability/instability;

- Understand how institutional entrepreneurship brings about change in concrete institutions, for example global climate change policy; and

- Explain the relevance of institutional entrepreneurship in the context of tourism.

Introduction

This chapter outlines the concept of institutional entrepreneurship and will relate the concept of the institutional entrepreneur to the wider entrepreneurship literature. The chapter is organized as follows. Section One examines entrepreneurship at a general level and some of the key attributes that are associated with this activity. Section Two then provides a discussion of the theory behind the nature of 'institutions' and institutional processes from which the concept of institutional entrepreneurship has emerged. Section Three consists of two case studies analysing institutional entrepreneurship from both an individual and collective perspective. Finally, Section Four will provide a link between entrepreneurship and institutional entrepreneurship and examine the implications of these activities for the broader field of tourism entrepreneurship.

Section I: Entrepreneurship

Entrepreneurship has emerged in the last 35 years as a relatively new and exciting area for academic study. It is often associated with a number of diverse activities ranging from new business development, including small businesses and family run businesses, to the setting up of what are perceived as successful organizations such as Virgin or Amstrad. Timmons (1994) argues that entrepreneurship is concerned with the creation and building of something of value out of nothing, while for Morrison (2006) entrepreneurship is the process of creating or identifying opportunities and pursuing them. Entrepreneurship as an activity is also somewhat vague with no objective definition that can clearly identify who are entrepreneurs and what they actually do (Bridge et al., 2003). This may also explain why some areas of entrepreneurial activity are more successful than others.

The classic view of entrepreneurs sees them as individuals who set up new firms or companies as a result of identifying opportunities to exploit in particular markets, often in the presence of adversity. An opportunity is therefore seen as a prerequisite for the entrepreneur but is in itself not sufficient for entrepreneurial activity. The entrepreneur must be able to exploit the opportunity. This begs the questions why, when and how some people are able to exploit opportunities and other not. It also suggests the opportunities are out there 'waiting to be found' when in fact what is required from the entrepreneur is the nuances associated with an understanding of the environment and the interpretation and/or perception of opportunities. Nuances not all aspiring entrepreneurs possess (Ardichvili et al., 2003). This has been linked to the nature of the opportunity and to the characteristics of individual entrepreneurs (Venkataramen, 1997).

Entrepreneurial opportunities vary in a number of ways and are also related to the value of the opportunity. Given the current concerns over the costs of oil, for example, a device that saves fuel by up to 25% in a car will have a higher perceived value than a similar device that improves the safety of elderly people living on their own. This exploitation of the opportunity also requires that the entrepreneur considers that the value of his or her profit will more than compensate for the time and effort that went into the endeavour. The risk aversion of the entrepreneur is a final factor in relation to entrepreneurial activity, with several studies indicating that individual differences in attitudes to risk are key influencing factors in the decision to exploit entrepreneurial opportunities (Khilstrom and Laffont, 1979).

Entrepreneurship is also associated with the idea of innovation (Schumpeter, 1934) with economic growth based on the introduction of new technologies effectively making obsolete existing technology through a 'gale' of creative destruction. This creative destruction leads to the opportunities which are then exploited by entrepreneurs who are alert enough to take advantage of them. This innovation can be in areas such as developing new services, improving the quality of products and focusing on niche market opportunities to develop business (Baumol, 1993).

Casson (1982) argues that there can be high and low forms of entrepreneurship with high entrepreneurship consisting of substantial innovation and low entrepreneurship being nothing more than creating a new business which may or may not be innovative. All of this implies change or deviation from existing ways of working, some of which will not be readily accepted by incumbent businesses or markets. To be successful in this environment, entrepreneurs have to get their ideas accepted as the norm and as such a 'legitimate' area of activity amongst a wide range of social groups (Aldrich and Fiol, 1994).

Having indicated that the entrepreneurship literature tends to imply an individual pursuit, often in terms of 'heroic' efforts against adversity, there are also examples of 'collective entrepreneurship; in areas such as cooperatives (Young, 1987), entrepreneurship in a number of alternative contexts including social entrepreneurship (Badelt, 1997) and public sector entrepreneurship (Casson, 1995). Here the goals of entrepreneurship differ, with the term itself perhaps being too limiting as it focuses on economic activity at the expense of other forms of entrepreneurship that also leads to change.

In social entrepreneurship, for example, individuals are challenging traditional forms of business activity and replacing it with an alternative 'social' purpose rather than one for financial gain. Likewise the public sector entrepreneur contributes to social welfare, which then confers status on the entrepreneur and attracts a particular type of person to the activity. Entrepreneurship in this context involves actors who attempt to transform existing institutional activities or who shape emerging institutions leading to change. This is no mean feat given the complexities involved in changing individual behaviours or organizational activities. These actors can be viewed as institutional entrepreneurs 'who have an interest in particular institutional arrangements and who leverage resources to create new institutions or to transform existing ones' (Maguire et al., 2004, p. 657). Institutional entrepreneurship has thus emerged as an area of study developed from institutional theory and seeks to explain how change can occur in organizations. As such we now turn our attention to institutional theory before returning to institutional entrepreneurship in more detail.

Section II: Institutions

Institutions consist of organizations, individuals and groups suspended in a *web* consisting of shared values, norms and taken for granted assumptions. This web provides the blue print for organizing by specifying which particular activities, behaviours and social arrangements actors and their organizations can engage with (DiMaggio and Powell, 1983). Deviating from the given arrangements can often incur sanctions or be costly (Jepperson, 1991). Institutions are also socially constructed and are maintained through a process of negotiation which constrains the options or possibilities for action encouraging certain types of behaviour and discouraging others (Meyer and Rowan, 1977; Scott et al., 2000; Greenwood et al., 2002).

Under a variety of conditions institutionalized practices and behaviours can be highly susceptible to challenge, rejection or replacement, which can lead to the adoption of new practices and behaviours – what Oliver has termed 'deinstitutionalization' (Oliver, 1992). Organizations as a result exist in an environment which often exerts pressure on them, constrains their behaviour, confers legitimacy and offers support for maintaining the status quo (Scott, 1995). Scott develops this theme further by developing the notion of 'institutional pillars'. There are three institutional pillars: *regulatory*, which conveys legitimacy and applies sanctions or coercion to behave in a certain manner; *normative*, which defines acceptable behaviour and provides the morals and ethics of the business; and *cognitive*, which acts as a 'road map' for organizations to interpret and act in their environment.

The Role of Interest and Agency

Institutional theory attempts to identify the causal mechanisms that lead to organizational stability or change on the basis of a preconscious understanding that organizational 'actors' share independent interests. It provides explanations of phenomena that do not reflect the behaviour of rational actors driven by clearly perceived interests. We prefer certainty and predictability in life. However, institutional processes emerge, reproduce and decline on the basis of interest and group behaviour. This suggests that organizational structure and behaviour are independent of self-interest.

Institutionalization is a product of the political efforts of actors to accomplish their own ends, and the form a resulting institution develops is dependent on the relative power of the actors who support, oppose or attempt to influence it. The success of an institutional process creates new sets of legitimated actors who in pursuing distinct interests deinstitutionalize aspects of institutional forms to which they owe their autonomy and legitimacy. This also creates a paradox in relation to how institutionalization is often considered. As an 'outcome' it places structures and practices beyond the reach of interest and politics. On the other hand, as a 'process' institutionalization is seen as political and represents the relative power of organized interests. Creating new institutions, as entrepreneurs often do, is expensive and requires high levels of both interest and resources.

Organizational Fields

In attempting to change behaviours and activities we must also consider the environments that organizations, individuals and indeed entrepreneurs inhabit. This can be termed an 'organizational field'. DiMaggio and Powell (1983) describe fields as being composed of institutions and networks of organizations that taken together constitute a recognizable area of life. A field is a community of actors and organizations who relate to each other through a common system of meanings, understandings and organizing principles which can be referred to as an institutional logic (Friedland and Alford, 1991; Scott, 1994; Lawrence and Philips, 2004; Reay and Hinings, 2005). Fields emerge through patterns of social action that produce, reproduce, and transform the institutions and networks within it, what Barley and Tolbert term 'structuration' (Barley and Tolbert, 1997) – effectively an 'ordering' of social relationships.

Fields consist of dominant and dominated actors and institutions which 'attempt to usurp, exclude, and establish monopoly over the mechanisms of the field's reproduction and the type of power effective in it' (Bourdieu and Wacquant, 1992, p. 106). It is at the level of an organizational field where consideration can be given to the contextual pressures that maintain stability as well as the dynamics that can lead to change (Greenwood and Hinings, 1996). The force of habit, history and tradition can therefore cause institutional practices and behaviours to acquire an almost rule-like status that can render them highly resistant to change (Berger and Luckman, 1967; Zucker, 1977; Hinings and Greenwood, 1988).

Institutional Entrepreneurship

Institutional theory is often criticized for inadequately providing an explanation of how change occurs within organizational fields, how new institutions form and how organizational innovation and diffusion occur (DiMaggio and Powell, 1991). The concept of institutional entrepreneurship has emerged to help address these issues (Maguire et al.,

2004). Institutional entrepreneurship represents the activities of actors or organizations who have an interest in establishing institutional arrangements and who leverage resources to create new or transform existing institutions (DiMaggio, 1988; Fligstein, 1997; Rao et al., 2000). Institutional entrepreneurs create a whole new system of meaning that ties the functioning of disparate sets of institutions together (DiMaggio, 1988) and seek to define, legitimize, combat, or co-opt rivals to succeed in their change projects (Scott, 1995). Assuming the role of change agents, institutional entrepreneurs energize efforts toward collective action and devise strategies for establishing stable sequences of interaction with actors and their organizations to establish new practices institutions (Aldrich and Fiol, 1994).

Acts of institutional entrepreneurship effectively attempt to deinstitutionalize existing beliefs, norms and values embedded within organizations and replace them with new practices and behaviours based upon an alternative view of the world. Institutional entrepreneurs therefore lead efforts to identify political opportunities, frame issues and problems, and mobilize constituencies creating an environment conducive for change (Rao et al., 2000). This is also reflected in the mainstream entrepreneurship literature where opportunities are identified to exploit new products and develop new markets by creative entrepreneurs. Fligstein (1997) argues that the creation of institutions is a messy, manipulative, instrumental, conscious and devious battle often fought in political and cognitive realms requiring astute political skill.

Attempts to bring about change in either an institution or institutional field thus require an ability to study the interactions between the microactions of actors and emerging macroinstitutional structures (Fligstein, 1997). The concept of institutional entrepreneurship as such focuses attention on the struggles that take place within institutions and the manner in which actors attempt to influence their institutional contexts (DiMaggio, 1991; Fligstein, 1997; Beckert, 1999). The critical relationships are between interests, agency and institutions (DiMaggio, 1988). Institutional change is therefore political in nature and involves processes reflective of the power and interests of organized actors and their institutions, who they have the ability to mobilize competing institutional logics and resources to frame and serve their interests (Seo and Creed, 2002).

Institutional Entrepreneurship in Mature and Emerging Fields. The key variable that links institutional theory and institutional entrepreneurship is the organizational field. Fligstein has argued that the successful use of particular skills and strategies by institutional entrepreneurs 'depends very much on whether or not an organizational field is forming, stable or in crisis' (Fligstein, 1997, p. 398). Mature fields represent relatively well-structured configurations of actors involved in a common enterprise among which there are identifiable patterns of interaction demonstrating domination, subordination, conflict, and cooperation (DiMaggio and Powell, 1983). Emerging fields, on the other hand, are forming and lack such an established order. This then may establish a degree of uncertainty in the existing institutional order that can provide scope for institutional entrepreneurs to be opportunistic (DiMaggio, 1988; Fligstein, 1997).

With fields that are in crisis, actors may attempt to use existing templates of understanding to legitimate current practices and behaviours maintaining the status quo

(Fligstein, 1997). Such a situation could occur as a result of social, economic or political pressure which threatens or challenges established institutionalized practices or behaviours. In a crisis, circumstances may alter and individuals or groups can challenge the status quo, leading to the opportunity to bring about institutional change (Rao et al., 2000).

We have seen that institutional entrepreneurship is an important area of study because it can help understand how fields get constructed, how new institutions arise and how existing institutions are transformed – activities that are also associated with more traditional forms of entrepreneurship. Sections two and three will provide examples of how institutional entrepreneurship has been enacted at two levels: individual and collective. We will then discuss how combining the entrepreneurship and institutional literature may provide scholars with the opportunity to ask questions about how and why new practices occur, how they develop over time and how they become established.

Section III: Case Studies

Case Study One: The European Union's Single Market Programme

This case study example by Fligstein (2001) illustrates how a crisis provided the opportunity for the European Union (EU) Commission to act as an institutional entrepreneurship to develop the European Single Market Programme (SMP). The emergence of a crisis is often the trigger or 'shock' that can lead to the building of new institutions. The term 'crisis' in this context implies that the rules governing how individuals or groups interact with each other over time fail to bring the same benefits from the existing 'system'. Often the building of new institutions is very much dependent on previous experience or arrangements, what is known as path dependency. For new institutions to develop, change has to occur in the 'institutional logic' of organizational actors and groups.

During a crisis a new institutional logic can emerge which then guides behaviour and activities in a reordering or rethinking of a given situation. Institutional entrepreneurs take advantage of such crises to produce new interests based on their interpretation of an event or events, and try to convince others that their interpretation is correct and in everyone's interests, using skills to form new supporting coalitions. The key role for the institutional entrepreneur is to form a new cultural frame within a given field and have it accepted as a legitimate course of action. This case study tracks the development of such a new cultural frame in creating a new order of shared understandings, rules and relationships that formed the SMP. Fligstein weaves his story around three related areas: how the EU produces agreements; the particular crisis engulfing the EU at the time; and what possibilities this crisis generated for new institution creation.

The EU Context.   The EU consists of a number of political arenas where each member state, the EU Commission and other interest groups meet. The EU Commission is central to the process of framing new EU legislation and brokering agreements between various national interests to form new institutional projects. The Commission itself is not a united body but consists of 20 members and 23 Director Generals, with each Director General responsible for a specific area. The production of new legislation is heavily dependent on the President of the Commission, the EU member states and other organizations who straddle the member states. This forms a series of very complex relationships, all of which have to respond and agree to new EU Directives.

Ultimately the success of this process is dependent on the EU Commission bringing (often disparate) groups together through building consensus that leads to the acceptance of new Directives. New Directives often develop from grievances from member states or from business, which are taken up by the member states who then lobby the Commission. The end stage would be that the Commission might then consider developing a new Directive. Significant negotiation is thus required to get agreement. Once agreement is reached then specific projects can be taken forward to get the attention of the Commission President and then on to the heads of the member states where further negotiations occur: often EU member states may seek to control any process leading to change. It was becoming clear at the end of 1983 that EU member states were unable to reach an agreement that would lead to the creation of a Single Market.

The EU under Crisis.   In the case of the EU 'field' in the early 1980s there was not one but in fact a number of crises. A slowdown in the economies of many EU member states had left many with sluggish growth and trading conditions. As a result the economic policies of many EU member states were struggling to provide enough stimulation to grow their economies. The sheer size of the EU should have provided significant potential for collective action. However EU member states were beginning to question the role of the EU in finding a solution to the downturn in the economy, which led to disagreement in ways to tackle the problem.

Two major projects at the time were being considered: institutional reform and monetary union. The main problem for the Commission that stymied increased cooperation was the normative pillar (Scott, 1995) of unanimous voting over matters by the EU Council. Any potential changes in legislation could be effectively blocked by a number of member states. Secondly, monetary union was planned as an attempt to link member state currencies to try to stabilize exchange rates between member states. These two projects ran into problems over individual sovereignty of member states who saw such moves as attacks on their ability to control their own political destiny – a cognitive pillar (Scott, 1995). As a result neither project had backing from the leaders of the member states.

In effect a political crisis had emerged with no member state being able to agree initiatives and, in some instances, with factions within member states deliberately blocking initiatives. The EU institutional field maintained existing arrangements and allowed member state actors to veto decisions. The SMP therefore began life as a potential institutional project which was then pushed as a mechanism to launch cooperation by member states. The catalyst to the SMP was a ruling by the European Court of Justice in 1979 that prohibited the banning of the sale of products or services between EU member states even if there were differences in technical and quality standards and such products or services whether or not they were safely produced or delivered. This introduced a new regulatory institutional pillar which attempted to change behaviour and legitimize free trade.

The key actor at the beginning of the evolution of the SMP was Karl Narjes, an EU Director. Narjes began with a limited proposal to consolidate the internal market by removing customs and transit formalities within the EU. This Directive originated with the idea that a single market would essentially be a market without borders. This concept was rapidly expanded to include 30 Directives after presentation to the European Parliament, thus bringing other actors on board to support the proposal. The EU Parliament approved the project viewing it as an excellent vehicle for obtaining more cooperation between member states. These Directives were passed from the Commission to the Council in December 1982. Narjes was attempting to deinstitutionalize existing patterns of behaviour and activities by *framing* the SMP as a means of improving cooperation and kick-starting the economies of the member states.

Narjes attempted to build a broader political coalition around the concept of the single market. The issues taken up in the Directive were relatively similar: establishing a European-wide passport which would allow free movement; equalizing value-added taxes across states thus removing tax as a source of competitive advantage; and proposals to simplify border formalities. The Commission argued that removing these *rules* would add up to 7% to European GDP. To improve EU competition with other parts of the world, it was argued that opening markets would lead to improved competition, the efficient allocation of resources and economic growth. The planned extension of the Single Market immediately met with French opposition who argued that the Single Market would benefit both EU and non-EU producers who sought to maintain the existing institutional arrangements.

An EU meeting in Copenhagen during 1982 ended with agreement to push the Single Market initiative forward, but there was still continued opposition from the French, which led to further delays. However, The EU Parliament continued to support the SMP as did the business community. The Permanent Conference of Chambers of Commerce and Industry of the EU – who represented the large European businesses – argued for the extension of the Single Market. At a summit in June 1983, the issue was again discussed at some length and progress made on a number of the Directives. However, by mid-1984, only 15 of the 30 proposals had been passed by the Council. Narjes again made an appeal to the Council that the SMP would have positive economic effects and be resource neutral without any regulatory costs on the member states.

The Single Market was a key institutional project which over time gathered momentum across many organized groups. It now had the support of the Parliament and, significantly, more and more European business groups. Although the Single Market idea had originated within the Commission, it now had developed into a key mechanism that many important groups saw as having the potential to kick-start the revival of the EU and member state economies. The Directive successfully linked several issues together and, significantly, did not create an expensive new regulatory apparatus. The support of various transnational business groups through a snowballing process also pulled key groups together. Business interests were well represented in the SMP and member states were under increasing pressure to accept it as a workable solution. The Single Market was a new institutional logic that both brought together disparate groups under a common goal, yet provided these groups with different things.

When Delors took office as the President of the EU in 1985, the completion of the Single Market was now the highest priority of the Commission. The Union of Industries of the European Community Council of Presidents (UNICE), which had representatives from the largest firms in Europe, formally endorsed the Single Market Programme. The Single Market idea was originally developed and pushed by Narjes acting as an institutional entrepreneur in bringing groups with disparate interests together, which was subsequently continued by Delors. Narjes let the idea evolve, thus allowing time for a political coalition to develop based on powerful business groups and others in the EU who wanted to see more European cooperation.

Lord Cockfield subsequently took over from Narjes. Both Cockfield and Delors now had the opportunity to change the shape of the EU. The impass over institutional reform and monetary union had left the EU struggling for legitimacy. The Single Market Programme contained three main ideas that tried to overcome these problems: the construction of a programme that carefully avoided trying to open markets where strong opposition existed; the passage of legislation that did not create any new regulatory apparatus; and the use of 'mutual recognition' as a mechanism to negotiate Directives. All three ideas attempted to create new institutional processes that would allow change.

Cockfield recognized that setting up the SMP would require getting round the expected political opposition. Opposition to any of the Directives was now viewed as opposition to the whole project. This had the positive effect of making it difficult for member states to block any single Directive as they could be seen as compromising the SMP, a change in EU member state normative and cognitive pillars. Delors had also managed to address the issue of institutional reform to the SMP by changing the voting rules from unanimous to majority voting for all Directives, effectively deinstitutionalizing the existing institutional processes. At a summit in 1985, the issue was again considered. After many machinations, the negotiations resulted in the Single European Act at the end of 1985. This was followed by a revision of the treaty that established the EU, which subsequently changed the voting procedures in the EU Council from unanimous to a qualified majority for issues concerned with the Single Market. This had the effect of changing the EU institutional field.

Between 1980 and 1988, the SMP had changed the attitudes of member states over cooperation in European matters. Member states agreed to change the voting rules and in the Treaty on European Union they agreed to extend those changes to most issues and to form a monetary union. These changes were only made possible because the entire framework in which discussions were occurring had been transformed by the idea of the SMP. Member states thus went from viewing EU cooperation in a negative sense to seeing it as a requirement for economic growth. This was achieved through Narjes, Cockfield and Delors acting as institutional entrepreneurs in shaping the future direction of the EU by bringing about institutional change.

Case Study Two: Collective Institutional Entrepreneurship – Global Climate Policy

The Emergence of Global Climate Policy.   Global climate change policy is a contemporary topic with which to examine institutional entrepreneurship. Many studies of institutional entrepreneurship tend to focus on individual acts of institutional entrepreneurship. However, in this example Wijen and Ansari (2007) demonstrate how institutional entrepreneurship can also occur at a collective level, and develop a conceptual framework to analyse this process.

Climate change has gathered momentum in the last 25 years as scientists have increasingly warned that the Earths' temperature has been slowly rising. The main cause of climate change has been identified as resulting from the combustion of fossil fuels such as coal and oil which release greenhouse gases including carbon dioxide. The removal of large swaths of forest in other parts of the world, which normally act as a *sink* to absorb these gases, has led to a progressive warming of the Earth, with the gases, having nowhere to go, warming up the atmosphere; hence the term 'greenhouse' effect.

One result of this 'heating' of the Earth's atmosphere has been changes to the world's climate with droughts, floods, the melting of polar icecaps and associated human and natural wildlife catastrophies. The institutional field of climate change is complex. Much recent effort has focused on discouraging use of fossil fuels in both the developed West and developing East including India and China. However, there are many people with vested interests who have been keen to see the status quo remain and who wish to see their economies and living standards grow. Many of these countries rely heavily on fossil fuels both as suppliers and consumers, and reducing their production and consumption patterns has proved to be extremely difficult. This is sometimes called a coercive action dilemma because there is the requirement for major change in both the production and consumption of fossil fuels.

Global Climate Change Institututionalized.   The first attempt to harness support in developing a climate change policy began in 1988 with the setting up of the Inter-governmental Panel on Climate Change (IPCC). This panel began to collect and use scientific evidence that climate change was indeed occurring – prior to this the evidence was fragmented with no clear message making a convincing argument. At the 1992 Rio Earth Summit 188 countries accepted a United Nations Framework Convention on Climate Change which set the scene for all subsequent policy developments on climate change and created a major institutional field.

This Convention attempted to stabilize the production of greenhouse gases by establishing responsibilities for the production of gases, with developing nations taking the lead role. A number of subgroups were set up through the Convention, including a Conference of Parties, or COP, to oversea progress on an annual basis and to monitor the plans of each country that signed the Convention in terms of how they were meeting agreements in the production of gases, with institutional pressure to maintain the status quo. There has always been disagreement on the exact cause and levels of production of the gases. However, it was an IPCC report in 1995 that clearly identified a direct human link with the production of the gases and subsequent changes in the earth's climate. A COP meeting in Kyoto in 1997 led to the development of the now famous Kyoto Protocol.

The Kyoto Protocol for the first time attempted to put a cap or ceiling on worldwide emissions of gases and at an individual country level each country committed itself to specific targets that they should meet over a period of time. No such targets were set for developing countries. The Kyoto Protocol should be seen not as a prescribed set of policies but rather as a set of flexible implementation mechanisms. This included emission trading and the joint resourcing of methods to reduce the production of gases in both developed and developing countries.

A further innovation of the Kyoto Protocol is that it allowed for the overproduction of gases in one year to be compensated for in subsequent years and for the *banking* of unused gas emissions for the future. Non-compliance can lead to a 30% reduction surcharge in these figures, but the Kyoto Protocol has no direct means to ensure compliance in the figures. This was to have a detrimental effect on these targets ever being met. The USA, which represented a third of all industrialized countries, rejected the Kyoto Protocol in 2001 and, to ensure that at least 55% of all countries and 55% of all industrialized countries came on board, Russia would have to comply. 156 countries eventually accepted the broad blueprint of the Kyoto Protocol. Countries which did not comply included the USA, China, India, Australia and South Korea; instead they signed a 'complementary agreement' with each other to pursue changes to the world's climate via economic means and using 'clean' technology. In effect this was an alternative to the Kyoto Protocol and attempt by incumbent actors to maintain the integrity of the existing institutional logic.

Section IV: Bringing in the Collective in Institutional Entrepreneurship

We now expand Wijen and Ansari's framework to demonstrate how collective institutional entrepreneurship brought about change in the institutional field of global climate change policy. Their framework consists of six drivers, all of which are internal to any given situation or organization, and seeks to explain how a number of often disparate and competing groups can overcome their differences – the collective action dilemma – to promote collaboration. The drivers in themselves are not mutually exclusive but when combined bring about change. The drivers are:

- *Manipulating power configurations* – Power differences between actors in a field can prevent the formation of collaborative relationships. If such power differences can be moulded to reduce the diversity of opinion this can then lead to collaboration and change.
- *Creating common ground* – This involves effectively developing tactics to bridge any divide that presents itself between actors to allow the development of alliances between groups. Tactics include 'framing' which attempts to identify common ground around the topic; 'agenda setting' which gives every group an interest in the issue; developing task-orientated goals; and establishing 'cognitive legitimacy' for specific issues which ensures groups become familiar with issues and accept them as important.
- *Mobilizing band wagons* – A snowballing of participants behind a cause or issue, which develops a collective desire for action through a general diffusion of ideas.
- *Devising appropriate incentive structures* – Ensuring that the costs of acting alone far outweigh the benefits of collaboration. This includes economic benefits and costs associated with non-compliance.
- *Applying ethical guidelines* – Behaviour is shaped by social norms. Actors respond not because of normative conformity but out of the 'right thing to do'. Collective institutional entrepreneurship thus motivates actors by appealing to the *right thing to do* in terms of equity, fairness and altruism.
- *Using implementation mechanisms* – Particularly in relation to ensuring joint agreements are carried out. This can involve the sharing of information, providing technical assistance, funding projects and managerial advice.

Manipulating power configurations. Approximately 200 countries became involved in the moves to establish a global climate policy. Attempting to get agreement from such a large number would be a challenge. This was not helped by the fact that many of these countries had major domestic issues to contend with indicating that the climate change institutional field was externally influenced by other fields. OPEC countries were sympathetic to measures that would not affect their economic interests, while EU countries lined up alongside developing countries in arguing that the big contributors to gas emissions needed to be closely regulated. Eventually three major coalitions formed: the EU countries, the G77 countries, and a group consisting of the USA, Norway, Japan, Australia, New Zealand, Canada and Switzerland. The fact that negotiations were now able to be made with three large groups, rather than 200 individual countries with diverse interests, made talks significantly easier. This in turn led to consensus with power distributed amongst the three groups.

Creating common ground. Given the diversity of interests represented, it can sometimes prove difficult to focus on a number of key issues. Use was made of the increasing scientific evidence to *frame* the issues deinstitutionalizing the existing logic by claiming that damage was being done to the Earth's atmosphere by gas emissions and that work had now to be done to prevent further damage. The use of scientific evidence reduced the politicking between countries who could no longer deny that the damage was man-made.

Each of the three main groups representing the 200 countries had different viewpoints on how to tackle gas emissions. Over time diverse views were reduced to three through negotiation through which it was hoped that the big prize, the development of binding targets for reducing gas emissions for industrialized countries, would be reached. Here the key social skills of the institutional entrepreneur were employed.

Dutch officials (Holland Chaired the EU in 1997) engaged in intensive negotiations with EU countries to iron out any differences. NGOs and academia lobbied hard through the media to keep the main issue on the news agenda, which was successful in influencing negotiations. Different actors created a common ground by their persistence in ensuring climate change had a voice. Key politicians like Tony Blair of the UK kept climate change on the agenda when he chaired the influential G8 Group. Dutch Environment Minister Pronk ensured that climate change was always discussed at later COP meetings and the Chair of the Kyoto Conference, Estrada-Oyuela, ensured only convergent talks had voice, which led to common agreement in developing the protocol.

Mobilizing band wagons. Although there was often disagreement, leading to a number of deadlocks in the negotiations with even the threat of complete withdrawal by some countries, with the ever-increasing media coverage and peer pressure, consensus eventually emerged with no country wishing to be seen as dragging their feet in a key world problem in the glare of a world media circus. A bandwagon thus developed allowing several diverse views on climate change to merge in a common cause.

Devising appropriate incentive structures. Negotiators at Kyoto used a number of incentives to ensure compliance with the Kyoto Protocol. A number of binding targets were introduced for the industrialized countries of the world which carried a 30% emission surcharge if not met. There was criticism from the developing countries that industrialized countries could circumvent their *home* targets by complying abroad and buying off their commitments. However, this was resolved by the industrialized countries funding technology to be used by the developing countries to reduce gas emissions. A major coup was obtaining ratification from Russia, a key producer of greenhouse gases, who eventually agreed to the Kyoto Protocol after the EU indicated it would support Russia's desire to become a member of the World Trade Organization. A key political role for the institutional entrepreneur is the ability to use political influence to reach change and this is a good example of the process.

Applying ethical guidelines.   A key issue was the establishment of 'fair shares' in relation to gas emissions and most countries were happy with the final number worked out on their behalf. However, the main ethical factor was based on the now scientific basis for ensuring future generations would be protected from climate change, with most countries having a joint interest. This led to a moral acceptance in complying with the Kyoto Protocol and making sure gas emission targets were met.

Using implementation mechanisms.   The Kyoto Protocol introduced three important monitoring processes to ensure compliance. These were emission trading, technology transfers and the joint implementation of emission reduction in developing countries. This led to the Kyoto Protocol having a much greater impact than previous treaties. Additionally, funds and know-how were made available to developing countries to allow them to fully participate in this agenda.

We have seen that Wijen and Ansari (2007), through use of their six point framework, have demonstrated how collective institutional entrepreneurship can create agency in the face of fragmented and hostile groups – and move from collective inaction to collective action. This was achieved by engaging different groups of divergent stakeholders at different points in time using a combination of approaches rather than simply applying a limited number from a change management 'tool kit' to a chosen smaller target group. This included appealing to like-minded groups, building consensus through coalitions of interests and using incentives and inducements to ensure compliance and building capacity to monitor and implement change.

Discussion and Conclusion

This chapter has examined the emerging concept of institutional entrepreneurship and some of the key concepts associated with this relatively new area of organizational research. In Chapter 2, Ateljevic and Li argued that most studies of entrepreneurship focus on the behaviour of individual entrepreneurs in developing new business growth by exploiting opportunities in products, markets or services. This chapter suggests that while this might be the case in certain circumstances, entrepreneurs may well work better and achieve more by working with individuals and groups which can then carry their change projects with them. This by its nature ensures that entrepreneurship is also a political process and fits with the concept of institutional entrepreneurship.

Tourism is an area ideally suited to this approach. Tourism tends to be a pluralistic and fragile activity – outbreaks of civil or international conflict, disease or acts of terrorism can devastate communities engaged within the tourism industry. As a result successful tourism entrepreneurship is heavily dependent on a number of groups working together to make destinations attractive for this type of economic activity. With the increased economic power of tourists and ease of transportation, there has been fierce competition from many destinations for patronage. There is therefore the need for increasing numbers of stake-holders to work together to ensure that the destination 'experience' is worthwhile for tourists who will then return and indeed spread the word about the experience.

The chapter also introduced concepts associated with institutional theory to allow us to flesh out the theory behind institutional entrepreneurship in more detail and locate it within tourism entrepreneurship. This included a discussion of the nature of institutions, institutional fields and the idea of an institutional logic. The work of the institutional entrepreneur has an important role to play here in ensuring all stakeholders do indeed share common goals and work together in partnership to achieve these goals. Institutional entrepreneurs successfully work on mobilizing 'social movements' in ensuring that this occurs and are politically astute in bringing what can often be diverse groups together to deliver on this agenda. Acting as individuals or collectively we have seen how this can be achieved by the use of persuasion and appropriate incentives to ensure compliance.

The tourism 'institutional field' is not insular but subject to external pressure and influence, which we also saw with our case studies, and which will inform the institutional logic for change to make improvements in delivering tourism. Often this is likely to be constructed from existing relationships and processes which will need to be 'framed' in such a way to gather support. Stakeholder interests have to converge if this is to be successful and stakeholder management – as seen with the European SMP and global climate change policy – is an important task for the institutional entrepreneur to facilitate.

The chapter also raises important questions about the nature of entrepreneurship itself. It is not simply the acts of individuals creating or exploiting opportunities for economic growth. While economic growth is important, the means by which entrepreneurs achieve this is also worthy of investigation. They may act alone and be viewed as 'heroic' but there is also the need to convince others of the potential of their labours and of the benefits of new products or services. This is particularly important in mature fields where incumbent groups have well-established institutional logics and frames which guide behaviour and relationships and who may prefer stability to change. Mature fields are also more difficult to break down due to the existence of powerful incumbants.

Influencing skills are important as is the need for astute political awareness with the ability to recognize when the institutional field is ready for change – in crisis – or indeed if attempts are made to deinstitutionalize exisiting organizational arrangements. Fields in a crisis on the other hand provide opportunities for change as the status quo, or existing modus operandus, is perhaps not delivering the way it should and behaviour and practices can be more malleable and open to suggestion. Finally, emerging fields do not have any preconceived institutional structures and processes. Although there may be power struggles in an attempt to establish a dominant logic, there will also be opportunities for institutional entrepreneurs to grasp the potential to influence how the field develops.

Tourism is one area of entrepreneurship where the work of the institutional entrepreneur can be exploited to benefit whole communities.

Questions for Discussion

1. What is institutional entrepreneurship and what are the main characteristics of institutional entrepreneurs?
2. What are the main barriers to institutional changes?
3. Why is the process of institutionalization very much relevant to the tourism context?
4. Identify and explain the common issues in the two case studies.

References

Aldrich, H.E., and Fiol, C. (1994). Fools rush in? The Institutional Context of Industry Creation, *Academy of Management Review*, 19(4), 645–670.

Zucker, L. (1977). The Role of Institutionalization in Cultural Persistence, *American Sociological Review*, 42(5), 726–743.

Chapter 7

Entrepreneurship and Innovation in Tourism: Public Sector Experiences of Innovation Activity in Tourism in Scandinavia and Scotland

Julie Franchetti and Stephen J. Page

Learning Outcomes

After reading this chapter, you should be able to:

- Understand the role of innovation in tourism;
- Identify how the public sector can shape and create an environment conducive to tourism innovation;
- Explain the importance of knowledge management and research in stimulating innovation at a business level;
- Describe the role and value of individual case studies from Scandinavia and Scotland in helping to provide examples of best practice in tourism innovation; and
- Identify the impact of specific factors in shaping innovative behaviour in tourism.

Introduction

Tourism has traditionally been viewed by governments and public sector agencies as a growth sector since the 1980s with potential to stimulate entrepreneurship, new firm formation, employment growth and regeneration of local economies. There has been little questioning of these fundamental relationships as towns, cities and districts face global competition to retain, develop and nurture national and local economies. The public sector has largely endorsed the role of tourism and economic development to maximize the use of the unique assets to differentiate their tourism offering, but there is now global competition amongst localities pursuing these strategic goals. In other words, global competition and serial reproduction of the same ideas and models of development mean that individual businesses and destinations now need to embrace innovation as a process to address the global competition, making an even greater use of research and market intelligence to understand customer needs and preferences.

Research is also used as a process to inform public sector decision-making to promote tourism as an investment decision to assist localities in building a service economy, often using studies commissioned by specialist consultants which provide the blueprint or strategic direction for change, along with potential business opportunities. Individual businesses typically develop these new commercial opportunities, frequently undertaking or commissioning consultants to prepare feasibility studies and subsequent business plans (Page, 2006) as a precursor to implementing the innovation process to develop new businesses or to grow existing business capacity and capabilities. To assist with the further research needs of businesses, including gathering market intelligence, relevant and usable research studies are often produced by public sector agencies such as economic development agencies (typically Tourist Boards) and are normally available in report or web-based formats to help inform innovation decision-making.

This chapter argues that research is not only an important part of the innovation process in tourism but suggests that entrepreneurship and new firm formation in tourist destinations alone will not enable them to compete globally without a constant innovation process, akin to the Total Quality Management (TQM) philosophy of the 1980s and 1990s (Oakland, 1990).

This chapter also argues that innovation now has to permeate tourism businesses because of the fast changing nature of tourism at a global level, so that innovation becomes a value-adding process akin to the way in which TQM was heralded as vital to retaining a loyal customer base. Businesses need to embrace the same philosophical stance if they are to retain and develop their customer base and product offering, since whilst TQM processes are paramount to delivering a quality visitor experience, there is now a growing recognition among public sector agencies, governments and academics that innovation is vital to maintaining a vibrant, exciting and dynamic tourism sector to develop the unique and distinctive assets of the destination.

We argue in this chapter that innovation (including case studies of best practice) as evident through the leading-edge practices of Scandinavian agencies and Scottish Enterprise, illustrate how entrepreneurship can be enriched, developed and operationalized by innovation approaches which are a total philosophy towards tourism business development.

The chapter commences with a brief review of the link between innovation, tourism and productivity, focusing on the critical role of knowledge to inform the innovation process to remove obstacles to product development and business improvement. The examples of Norway and Scotland are used to illustrate how the leading role of the public sector in each successful tourist destination has adopted innovation as the starting point for developing their business potential. This stance has been embraced to enhance their destination competitiveness given its global significance as reflected in the recent World Economic Forum report (World Economic Forum, 2007). However, prior to examining these issues it is pertinent to consider the link between tourism and innovation to understand why it is vital to the well-being of a successful tourism economy and destination.

Tourism and Innovation: The Conceptual Basis

There is a growing recognition by transnational agencies such as OECD (2006) that tourism is a highly fragmented industry sector, often reliant upon small and medium-sized enterprises (SMEs), with a high labour intensity (i.e. a high ratio of staff to clients). It is also characterized by low levels of productivity (Blake et al., 2006). For example, Blake et al. (2006) observed that productivity levels in the hotel and restaurant sector were 49% of the UK average. These low levels of productivity also translate into low levels of competitiveness, compounded by poor awareness of and involvement in the process of innovation, especially in the SME sector which is well documented in academic studies (e.g. Thomas and Augustyn, 2006). Interestingly, OECD (2006) argue that innovation should now be a matter of routine for many businesses, which can be incorporated into normal business practices as a series of incremental steps.

When a failure to innovate across the tourism sector occurs at a destination level, there is a high likelihood that a loss of destination competitiveness could lead to a downward spiral of decline in the destination lifecycle. This would then require, as is the case in many former UK seaside resorts, a massive capital reinvestment programme to reposition and regenerate the resort to stimulate further development of the lifecycle stage from decline and decay to growth. Therefore, pursuing a strategy based on innovation in a destination whilst it is still developing, to avoid stagnation, is a more cost-effective intervention and business-led rather than needing to regenerate an entire destination.

What is Innovation?

Innovation is a process whereby change can occur in the way businesses and organizations perform their activities and functions in more efficient, profitably and meaningful ways to remain competitive. The term originates from the Latin word 'innovation', which means 'to create something new' (Peters and Pikkemaat, 2005). Innovation is the essence of tourism as a service sector and vital to remain competitive as well as ensuring continuous improvement to the visitor experience. According to Solow (1970), the role of innovation in economic growth was firmly established using economic research to demonstrate that innovation rather than capital investment was a key catalyst for growth. Solow (1970) indicated that capital investment only accounted for 20% of the growth in economic productivity, illustrating the importance of innovation to economic development.

However, tourism is often characterized as one of the least productive sectors of the economy. Within tourism, Sundbo et al. (2007) observed that innovation normally occurred at the level of the firm, at the level of a network and at a systems level (i.e. within government, institutions and organizations which influence the management and operation of tourism). Hjalager (2002) expands upon the typical areas of innovation, basing her observations on the initial work of Schumpeter (1954) which outlined the main areas for industrial innovation that include product innovations, process innovations (e.g. new ways of delivering services), market innovations (i.e. new ways of communicating with the customer such as the internet) and logistical innovations (i.e. innovations in supply chain delivery of services such as vertical integration to deliver a seamless tourism experience).

Hjalager (2002) has reviewed many of the academic studies of tourism and innovation, highlighting that to repair the limited levels of innovative behaviour which characterize the tourism industry is not an insurmountable problem, a feature also observed by Hall and Williams (2008). Indeed, Sundbo et al. (2007) suggest that most innovation that occurs in tourism is not technological; it comprises a change in behaviour by businesses – a culture shift. Some of the principal factors that affect the culture of innovation in a country are the attitude, support structures and approach of the state.

International research suggests that to foster innovation to promote competitiveness and improved business performance requires leadership to champion the notion and to create a focal point to increase adaptation and implementation of innovation-fostering initiatives. Leadership is a key element in promoting innovation in tourism, in bringing innovations to market. This leadership role is important given the ability of entrepreneurs to tolerate uncertainty, frustration, express confidence in their ideas and communicate and network to interact with other players in an industry with multiple inter-relationships and other service providers who create the visitor experience. Pechlaner et al. (2005) point to where leadership needs to occur for innovation to flourish in a destination, also requiring cooperation among different actors and players as necessary to the extent that the innovation process can only be successfully implemented if the following are involved:

- *Leaders* – for example political authorities and members of regional development agencies, such as Scottish Enterprise, with an understanding of the regional context and destination;
- *Managers* in tourism businesses, including entrepreneurs who understand the market and likely take-up of an innovation.

The recognition of these different players illustrates why networking and encouragement of cooperation and collaboration by agencies to facilitate this activity is vital. Norway is an interesting example of a country which has sought to strengthen innovation in tourism. As the following case study shows, Norway has radically redesigned the relationship between its public sector tourism and innovation organizations to place innovation at the heart of its tourism support mechanism, recognizing the need to create these synergies so that innovation becomes the driving philosophy for public sector involvement in tourism to aid and develop the industry.

Case Study: Tourism and Innovation in Norway – 'Innovation Norway'

In January 2004, a new state-owned company called Innovation Norway was created from the amalgamation of four state organizations:

- The Norwegian Tourist Board;
- The Norwegian Trade Council;
- The Norwegian Industrial and Regional Development Fund (SND); and
- The Government Consultative Office for Inventors (SVO).

As a relatively peripheral tourist destination within a European context with low levels of innovation in tourism, Innovation Norway was created to promote innovative behaviour at a national and regional level. The dispersed nature of Norway's business sector and tourism industry means that most of its tourism business development is regionally based, with clustered networks of SMEs working alongside larger tourism interests such as Color Line As. Innovation Norway views innovation, district and regional development and internationalization of the country's tourism sector as inter-related. In other words, Innovation Norway views competing internationally as a prerequisite for succeeding in commercializing new products and ideas: the tourism sector needs to adopt an outward-looking international approach to tourism rather than a local and parochial approach. Innovation Norway views networking as crucial to safeguarding and developing over 9000 jobs a year in Norway's tourism sector.

One important stimulus for Innovation Norway to maintain its activities to promote innovation is its participation in the Global Entrepreneurship Monitor (GEM) where its position in the country rankings slipped between 2000 and 2005, but then improved after 2005 as the newly created organization's activities started to embed themselves in tourism and non-tourism business practices. However, GEM highlighted that the state was spending too little on innovation which was facing obstacles due to bureaucratic processes and obstacles to new firm formation.

One outcome of GEM's observations is the focusing of resources on the Arena programme in mountain areas to promote regional clusters of tourism business activity. To add value to the innovation process to harness the creative talents and knowledge base at a regional level, a conscious attempt to coordinate and facilitate cooperation via a Triple Helix model (see Figure 7.1) has been promoted. The Triple Helix model in simple terms suggests that where mutual benefits exist in the intersection of the three stakeholders (public sector, private sector and universities/research institutes) it may be possible to foster innovation. To lead the nurturing of mutual benefits, it is vital that one of the stakeholders (e.g. the public sector) leads and champions the process, initially through networking and then through the creation of a smaller community of like-minded individuals committed to promoting innovation. This particular focus in Norway on the Triple Helix has informed its thinking on collaboration and cooperation in many of the networks which Innovation Norway has supported and funded.

A recent study by Vikane (2006) examined the innovation process for destinations in Norway and Sweden and the results in Tables 7.1 and 7.2 show that information, collaboration, networking and the public sector's role were critical, and that in all of these the Triple Helix model plays a crucial part. When entrepreneurs were asked how they might improve innovative activity, a range of public sector-led activities was noted as being formative to the innovation process. In fact a study by the Nordic Innovation Centre cited cooperation with public sector agencies as the most important factor in shaping innovative behaviour in tourism. This involvement by the public sector was vital as a lead role in

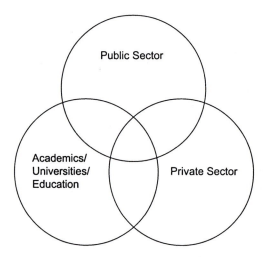

Figure 7.1: The Triple Helix Model

Table 7.1: Innovation in Åre, Hamesdal and Hovden: entrepreneur views.

Innovation	Business Examples
Clustering in office space	• Linkages between businesses • Local supply of services and food stuffs for hospitality sector
Meetings	• Sharing competencies and learning from others
Product focus	• Local/regional foods
Business mentor	• Worked with own ideas to see if there was a market for their idea or product
Local cooperation	• Advice and sharing of expertise from other destinations • Sharing experiences via informal and formal business association meetings
Public sector assistance	• Municipality business assistance and political commitment to innovation • Innovation Norway funding to develop new ideas • Innovation Mountain, tourism project and infrastructure investment

Source: Vikane (2006).

Table 7.2: How businesses may increase innovative activity – entrepreneur views.

- Networking, brainstorming, meeting with local businesses.
- Funding from Innovation Norway; benchmark experiences.
- Learn from other destinations; Innovation Mountain Project.
- 'Lighthouses to make the destination visible' – such as an event.
- Examine the long-term sustainability of innovative projects once pump-priming funding is removed.
- Need to watch trends (but when given a large book of results [from research] no one will read it).
- Learning journeys (from restaurant sector in Åre).
- Event development in the locality.
- Increase academic involvement (in the Triple Helix model) although no current use of academic research.

Source: Vikane (2006).

coordinating networks, in providing funding and support, promoting quality enhancement of tourism products and services, and, lastly, in terms of knowledge of the market.

This last point, as Hjalager's (2002) research reaffirms, means that the public sector has a pivotal role in the transfer process of research into usable knowledge for businesses. If the public sector research needs to be distilled down, codified and modulated before it can flow into tourism organizations to influence innovation. For this reason, attention now turns to Knowledge Management (KM) and Knowledge Transfer (KT) in tourism as these have a crucial role for the public sector in assisting businesses to become more innovative by sharing the knowledge, know-how and wider awareness of how trends and developments of the tourism sector require ongoing adaptation, development and innovative behaviour to remain ahead of the competition.

Knowledge Management to Promote Innovation in Tourism

Unlocking the human potential and knowledge which exists inside an organization is probably one of the greatest challenges for tourism at an operational level, since other challenges like service quality can be allocated to process-driven policies and manuals. In contrast, innovation cannot easily be treated as a formulaic process which is policy and manual driven when much of the impetus is about creative thinking and harnessing in-house knowledge and ideas to make a business activity, process or product better in terms of its qualitative or operational features, with a view to improving satisfaction with it and enhancing profitability. For example, Scottish Enterprise's highly successful Innovation Toolkit, which seeks to foster innovation as a process in a semi-structured manner in businesses, still relies on unlocking the human potential and creative knowledge within an organization. The following case study outlines how the Innovation Toolkit was developed to facilitate this process.

Case Study: Scottish Enterprise's Tourism Innovation Toolkit – A personal view

Julie Franchetti

The Innovation Toolkit was developed to help change the culture of the tourism sector, where businesses were encouraged to work together and to work together within organizations. This was based on a widely held view that Scottish tourism needed to improve its performance as new destinations and competitors were challenging the competitive position of Scottish tourism. In essence the Innovation Toolkit as a concept was designed to help businesses to understand:

- What does the market and consumer want?
- What are the key assets and attractors which can be harnessed for people to visit Scotland?

Linked to this was the desire to get groups of businesses to enhance the experience of tourism for visitors. One key element here was to help businesses to think and act more creatively in a sector which is driven by the visitor experience and word of mouth recommendation.

But how did the toolkit concept evolve as an innovative idea?

In 2000, I organized a 'learning journey' with 12 businesses to visit Disney Corporation in the USA. One of the learning outcomes on the last day of the learning journey was to get businesses to identify one thing they would do differently when they returned to Scotland. My own 'one thing' was to identify the need to create a nucleus and focal point for businesses to change their existing behaviour. The Toolkit idea emerged from the best practice evidence gleaned from the Disney learning journey alongside two pieces of internal research I conducted: an international benchmarking study of what tourism businesses were doing and a study to understand what innovation looked like as a process.

The Innovation Toolkit was informed by the transfer of knowledge from the learning journey and two internal research studies which identified that:

- It needed to embrace functional techniques to drive collaboration as a total philosophy to ultimately improve the experience for the visitor;
- It needed to be fun and practically based;
- It needed to recognize key success factors associated with driving innovation (discussed below) and to stimulate these through the toolkit process.

To date the success of the Toolkit, which is introduced and explained to businesses through participation in a workshop, is reflected in the 4000 businesses which have participated.

To support the innovation process, Scottish Enterprise funds the most promising outcomes through its Tourism Innovation Development Awards with funding and business support. Ultimately, the toolkit is one process which helps to turn ideas, supported by knowledge, into reality to make a positive change in the visitor experience.

In this context, Knowledge Management is a process to identify relevant knowledge, capture it, transfer and share it, and optimize its flow is crucial to the innovation process (Ahmed et al., 2002). One recent attempt by the European Union to create the KM process at a destination level has led to the notion of a learning destination (Schianetz et al., 2007), but this is still at a pilot stage and will inevitably prove more complex and bureaucratic than encouraging distinct clusters of businesses and stakeholders to collaborate to foster innovation within and between partners in a network. One of the principal challenges in KM, particularly in the use and dissemination of research knowledge, is in shifting the organizational culture to recognize how knowledge can enhance competitiveness, by adding value. Conceptually, this requires the differentiation between:

- *Tacit knowledge*, which is often not written down and is experience-based so is not communicated or codified, and;
- *Explicit knowledge*, which is found in documents, data and written forms.

In some studies of KM, explicit knowledge is only around 10% of total knowledge and, therefore, understanding how all forms of knowledge are transferred is critical if it is to be harnessed to promote innovation from existing knowledge. According to Nonaka (1991), the transfer of knowledge occurs in four distinct ways:

- Tacit to tacit transfer, via meetings and team discussions;
- Tacit to explicit, via external brainstorming;
- Explicit to explicit, by moving knowledge around a network from one organization to another one;
- Explicit to tacit, taking explicit knowledge and generating new ideas.

What Nonaka (1991) highlights is the key role of the diffusion of ideas, which helps to explain how an idea passes through certain channels to individuals and groups. In other words, networking remains a major activity in developing knowledge flows within and between organizations.

As most international research argues that the public sector has an important mobilizing and facilitating role in leading the innovation process, then the ability to transfer knowledge and the ability of the private sector to absorb it is a crucial starting point in the innovation process in tourism. Research in Australia reported by Cooper (2006) found that research knowledge transfer was only effective among SMEs where the information being transferred was relevant, easy to access and uncomplicated to use.

KT is also most effective and utilized where it is shared as part of a network, led by a public sector agency. As Morrison et al. (2004) suggest, tourism networks can enhance the learning and exchange function in tourism (including KT) as well as improving business activity as Tables 7.3 and 7.4 show. Yet establishing, nurturing and facilitating these networks in many countries requires an active role by a public sector agency because of the lack of collaboration where businesses view competition as the prevalent ideology among private sector tourism businesses. The public sector can assist in educating these stakeholders about the wider collaborative and cooperation benefits for their own

Table 7.3: The benefits of tourism networks.

Learning and Exchange	Improved Business Activity	Community Effects
Knowledge transfer	Cooperative activity	Developing a common
Communication	(e.g. joint marketing)	purpose for tourism
Developing a new culture	Increasing visitor	in destinations
and values	numbers through	Engagement with SMEs
Increasing the speed of agency	collaboration	Retaining tourist
implementation of	Pooling of SME	spending locally
initiatives	resources	
Assisting SMEs in their	Inter-trading within the	
development stage	network	
Improved understanding of	Repeat business	
tourism as a sector and its	Stronger lobby for	
complexities and foibles	public sector	
	investment	

Source: Developed from Morrison et al. (2004, p. 198).

enterprises. For this reason, attention now turns to the role of one agency in Scotland to illustrate its influential role in fostering tourism innovation.

Scottish Enterprise: Its Role in Economic Development

Scotland has a long history of entrepreneurship in industrial development dating back to the eighteenth century and much of the innovation in the post-war period was associated with heavy industrial sectors which dominated the national economy. With the structural changes in the Scottish economy in the 1970s and 1980s, state aid via regional development agencies such as the Highlands and Islands Development Board and the Scottish Development Agency sought to promote regional development. Whilst innovation was also an implicit objective of these earlier agencies, their successors – Highlands and Islands Enterprise (covering the Highlands and Islands of Scotland) and Scottish Enterprise – both sought to encourage regional economic development and industrial diversification as traditional sectors (e.g. agriculture and fishing in the Highlands) and heavy industry/manufacturing in the industry centres (e.g. Glasgow, Edinburgh, Dundee and Aberdeen) experienced rapid decline in the 1980s and 1990s as coal mines, steelmaking and shipbuilding entered a state of almost terminal decline.

Whilst these agencies assisted in promoting new industrial sectors, such as technology and services, another notable growth sector since the early 1990s has been tourism. Tourism is not a new sector in Scotland, with a rich history going back to the eighteenth century, but the potential of its towns and cities as business and leisure destinations able to lead regeneration objectives was a comparatively new concept for much of the public sector prior to the 1980s. Much of the growth in tourism has occurred through new firm formation. As tourism expanded as a new service sector in the early 1990s, promoted by

Table 7.4: Functions and benefits of tourism networks.

	Academic	Private	Public/private
Learning and exchange	Collaboration for the creation and dissemination of new knowledge	Peer learning and knowledge sharing	Peer and partner learning and transfer of knowledge
Business activity	Through more increased understanding and *perfect* knowledge, impacts at policy, agency, business and societal levels	Effective use of pooled resources and resource leverage contributes to enhanced innovation and market development	Support of umbrella organizations contributes to the stimulation of cooperative practices to enhance innovation and market development
Community	Provides for a sustainable sense of community and active engagement in tourism destination development	Facilitates engagement of micro and small enterprises in sustainable tourism destination development at community level	Foster a private/public sector community including SMEs with a common purpose in terms of tourism destination development

Source: Developed from Morrison et al. (2004, p. 198).

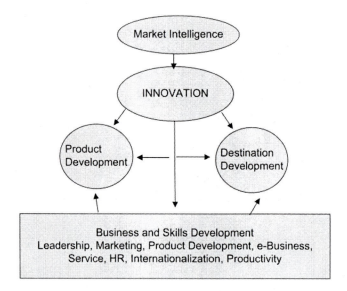

Figure 7.2: The innovation process at Scottish Enterprise for the Scottish tourism sector.

successful re-imaging strategies for cities such as Glasgow with its 1990 European City of Culture and 'It smiles better here' campaign, agencies such as Scottish Enterprise recognized the importance of investing in enterprising and forward-looking businesses.

Scottish Enterprise's philosophy in the 1990s viewed public sector intervention in the market place as a broader strategy to address 'market failure' where a perceived lack of private sector investment would not occur without their assistance. One area which emerged in numerous market and economic studies of Scotland commissioned by Scottish Enterprise in the 1990s was the perceived lack of innovation behaviour needed to be fostered to enable Scotland to develop as a world class tourist destination able to compete on a global stage. This public sector intervention was compounded by poor performance in Scotland's visitor markets in the late 1990s, culminating in the restructuring of the Scottish Tourist Board to Visit Scotland in the period 2000–2002 alongside the realization of the value of tourism with the Foot and Mouth outbreak in 2001 and the impact of 9/11.

Against this background of perceived stagnation in industry investment in Scotland's tourism product, Scottish Enterprise embarked on a long-term programme of investment in measures to promote innovation in tourism businesses, to complement the marketing and market development activities of VisitScotland. Scottish Enterprise is funded by the devolved government – the Scottish Government. Tourism is funded as one of the priority industries within Scottish Enterprise on a root and branch model, with the main team managed from its Glasgow main office and other team members located throughout the Scottish Enterprise offices based in different discrete regions. This structure is based on the following principles:

1. The tourism team based in Glasgow is responsible for strategic issues and leadership in the key areas of innovation, product development, destination development, and business and skills development.

2. At the local level (i.e. in the Enterprise Company region), the strategic issues are translated into operational issues.

This is illustrated more fully in Figure 7.2. More specifically, Scottish Enterprise's role in tourism is reflected in Table 7.5 which is derived from its Industry Demand Statement.

One key cultural change which Scottish Enterprise has engendered through a process of innovation is to shift the notion of industry leadership to a dedicated body to champion the idea – The Tourism Innovation Group (see Inset 1).

Table 7.5: Scottish Enterprise Industry Demand Statement, 2007

To guide the strategic development of tourism in Scotland and to align its activities with the tourism framework for change and the Scottish tourism industry stategy, the Scottish Enterprise (SE) Industry Statement outlines the major areas of SE's intervention to grow tourism spend by 50%. The pricipal areas of action to 2011 include:

- **Innovation** to establish a culture of innovation in the tourism industry with tourism businesses showing evidence of all of the following:

  - a process for gathering and utilizing market intelligence (including feedback from customers)
  - involvement in creating new products and services
  - participation in collaborative activity with at least two other businesses resulting in new products/services.

- **Product Development** so tourism businesses can enhance Scottish tourism assets structural around whisky, high quality Scottish food, Scottish forests and golf tourism.

- **Destination Development** where investment activity is focused on the six key tourism destinations (Glasgow, Edinburgh, St Andrews, Loch Lomond and Trossachs, Perthshire and Deeside/Cairngorms).

- **Skills** to ensure tourism business leaders and the workforce are enabled to deliver innovation, higher levels of productivity and improved service standards. An underlying concept is 'workforce development', particularly strengthening recruitment and retention initiatives in the six key destinations.

- **Internationalization** to support the objectives above with support from Scottish Development International to assist with inward investment for the six key destinations to improve the tourism real estate at the higher end of the market.

Source: Developed from Scottish Enterprise (2007) Industry Demand Statement, Scottish Enterprise: Glasgow.

Inset 1: The Tourism Innovation Group (TiG)

Formed in 2002, The Tourism Innovation Group (TiG) is a private-sector-led group which aims to stimulate tourism operators into taking action to add to the quality, scope and success of tourism businesses, thus improving Scotland's competitiveness in tourism markets – in other words, to 'innovate'. This means doing things differently, exploring new avenues, collaborating effectively and taking risks.

TiG comprises an active membership of over 50 businesses, representing a cross-section of tourism operators and entrepreneurs. Members of TiG are determined that Scotland should participate fully in the global growth of tourism – and are prepared to do something to help achieve this. The proposition is simple: 'what can we, TiG do – here, now and in a practical sense – to remove barriers that hold our industry back and accelerate change where the real opportunities lie'.

TiG aims to stimulate tourism business success. Businesses that develop new products and services or significantly improve business practices are almost twice as likely to increase turnover as those that don't.

TiG is funded by key stakeholders in the Scottish tourism sector: Scottish Enterprise, Highlands and Islands Enterprise, and Visit Scotland, each making valuable contributions through senior staff involvement as members, in addition to their financial support. TiG has provided a very effective and valuable mechanism for public sector agencies to network and engage with industry at a strategic level.

There are two permanent members of staff based in the Edinburgh office – Sue Crossman, Project Director, and Claire-Jayne Fordyce, Project Coordinator.

The Tourism Innovation Group's vision is to be the driver of long-term strategic change in Scottish tourism.

The group agrees that this vision will be achieved by a mission centring around:

- Identifying and focusing on key strategic issues where TiG can bring about change;
- Fostering innovation across the industry;
- Incubating specific projects to the point of implementation (with TiG's help) by delivery partners, often public sector agencies;
- Supporting public-sector-/industry-led innovation;
- Encouraging members to meet, listen to specialists, and discuss issues: functioning as an ideas 'think-tank';
- Integrating closely with the Pride & Passion initiative (see below).

TiG concentrates on innovative thinking and brainstorming ideas as well as influencing via effective channels. TiG members have formed four teams, reflecting interests and concerns about a number of priorities. TiG members were also involved with the conception of the Pride & Passion movement.

Pride & Passion is an industry-led movement to improve the quality and reliability of the visitor experience in Scotland. It focuses on how businesses and individuals can improve their own lot as well as that of the visitors by working together and looking at

Continued

Inset 1: The Tourism Innovation Group (TiG) – Cont'd

how they do what they do from the perspective of their customers. The idea is to improve our tourism industry from within so we move with the market's expectations rather than resting on any laurels we may have.

A network of people from within the trade exists to motivate, support and advise other businesses through existing groups and on a one-to-one basis.

Source: www.tourisminnovation.com

The Scottish Enterprise region, which covers 93% of the Scottish population through its regional offices, has a fourfold approach to involvement in tourism to promote a competitive edge and improvement to the visitor experience. The areas are:

- Business leadership;
- Destination development,
- Product development; and
- Innovation.

Scottish Enterprise is involved in business leadership to assist business owners and key staff to develop their skills and knowledge of tourism through master classes and learning journeys along with understanding best practice from the international tourism sector.

It has developed a working relationship with industry partners to develop a number of key destinations in Scotland as a hub and focal point for investment and activity, and alongside this it promotes product development by encouraging specific initiatives such as whisky tourism, food- and drink-related tourism development and the wildlife sectors. However, probably most significant in the context of improving future tourism products and experiences is the work on innovation which informs its other activities as total philosophy.

Scottish Enterprise and Innovation

According to Scottish Enterprise's own research commissioned on innovation, based on the work of de Bono (1999) it considers that:

> innovative organizations encourage and capitalize on new ideas. Innovative processes and/or services are market-led and have a positive impact upon internal processes and business services and/or products. Innovation entails both invention and design and continuous improvement of existing products, services and processes.

Or, put more simply, for individual businesses you need to:

1. *Do things right* – follow the correct procedures.
2. *Do the right things* – set priorities.
3. *Do away with things* – stop doing things that do not count.

4. *Do things better* – think of ways to improve continuously.
5. *Do things others are doing* – find the best practices.
6. *Do things that have not been done.*
7. *Do things that can't be done* (de Bono, 1999).

The innovation activities and economic impact of these activities are summarized in Inset 2.

Inset 2: Scottish Enterprise's Tourism Innovation Programme

The Tourism Innovation Programme has changed the thinking across the tourism sector as the following extract from the Scottish Enterprise (2006) innovation report findings shows.

1. To date over 3800 individuals from around 2600 companies have participated in the Tourism Innovation Approach, which includes events and business development programmes such as the annual Tourism Innovation Development day, Innovation Toolkit workshops, Innovation learning journeys and the highly successful Tourism Innovation Development Awards.
2. The net impacts delivered by the programme so far are considerable – nearly £15 million in turnover for the industry, generating over 190 new jobs in the sector with additional Gross Value Added (GVA) estimated to be £6.1 million –10 times the actual cost of the Innovation Programme to the public purse.
3. It is also estimated that the programme will continue to reap dividends over the next three years with net GVA expected to reach around £12 million, helping to create around 510 new jobs in the sector as many of the new experiences are just being launched to market.

Source: Scottish Enterprise (2006).

In fact, in-house research by Scottish Enterprise shows that the following have been identified as success factors for innovation in a tourism context:

• Leadership;
• Culture;
• People;
• Customers;
• Collaboration;
• Tools;
• Clarity;
• Information Technology.

What follows is a brief discussion of each factor and a number of small case studies of tourism businesses to illustrate how these success factors can contribute towards a tourism business's innovation activity.

Scottish Enterprise Success Factors for Innovation

Leadership.   Innovation starts with the leader. The leader has to inspire commitment and passion. The leader has to communicate a clear focus, develop structures, ensure all ideas are given equal airspace and follow through with them. The leader must create a culture which gives ownership to staff, where people feel empowered and free to try new things.

Case Study: Kids' Leisure Attraction, Mexico

The background

Kids' City is an innovative children's attraction which provides an entertaining and educational environment themed around the activities of a typical city. Their approach to business strategy and planning is evolutionary and heavily influenced by the fact that it is a small business. The company is characterized by a start-up mentality with clear leadership and a very open culture.

The solution

Kids' City follows the philosophy of 'leading by example' in managing the people and the culture. The company believes that informality in culture leads to innovation. The communication is open, and there are no titles on their business cards. Full-time staff are free to come and go as they please as long as results are achieved. One of the key planning tools that Kids' City utilizes is the *Junta Creativa* (creative meeting), which takes place every two weeks. The meeting typically lasts from a half day to one full day. The participants include management (the two partners – COD/CEO), architects/theming, graphic designers and operational/front-line staff. The meeting is used for discussing front-line feedback 'what works and what does not work', new initiatives and ideas, and overall strategy. The meetings are very creative where they 'put words into pictures' by prototyping and drawing or illustrating new things/concepts.

The impact

Kids' City is extremely successful. It receives the highest attendance and per capita expenditure of any indoor attraction in Mexico, and has generated profit results which supersede most indoor children's attractions worldwide.

Culture.   Innovative organizations develop a culture that actively encourages creativity and innovation. People will be more innovative working in an environment where they feel trusted and supported. In order to have an innovative culture in the workplace, you must create a safe environment where collaboration, trust and cooperation flourish; where people feel comfortable taking risks and bold initiatives; where it is acceptable to make mistakes.

Case Study: The Edinburgh Playhouse

The background

A large city theatre hosting major touring productions.

The issue

Before it could begin to develop new ideas, the Playhouse needed to improve internal communication and staff knowledge, as well as motivation and the business culture.

The solution

A 'bible' for the Playhouse was created to improve staff knowledge. This is kept up to date (on an almost daily basis) with new information on shows, ticketing and facilities. A special section allows staff to note down new ideas that will help improve the business.

The impact

Staff motivation has improved markedly and customer service has improved – as evidenced by the excellent customer feedback. A number of new ideas have been implemented and this is helping the Playhouse to increase productivity.

People.   The right people in an organization can make a real impact to the innovation process. Innovative companies tend to hire staff for their positive attitude and train them to achieve the necessary skills, thereby avoiding the impact of 'laggards' who resist change and innovation. Innovative companies listen to those who do the job and involve people with many different skill sets.

Customers.   The customer's perspective must be at the heart of the business. Innovation should ultimately lead to an improved visitor experience and high customer satisfaction. Tourism businesses need to understand their customers, utilize customer relationship management tools and work with customers to identify solutions and create new ideas. Companies need to consider how new and innovative ideas will impact on their visitors. Experiencing life as a customer at other tourism businesses will help inspire new ideas.

Case Study: The Freedom of the Glen Family Hotels

The background

A group of three independently owned hotels.

The issue

A high turnover of staff – particularly those from overseas using the hotels as a temporary workplace – meant there was little continuity and constant staff training was required.

Continued

The solution

To help seasonal staff see some of the country, while continuing to earn money, the group purchased a car for exclusive staff use. Rented out at a nominal £5 a day, staff had to respect the car, i.e. refrain from smoking in it and return it spotless.

The impact

Staff were immediately very positive as it allowed them to see more of Scotland at little cost. Because they felt more valued, they were happy to stay with the group for a longer period.

Collaboration.   Internal and external collaboration is key to stimulating innovation as discussed earlier. Examples internally include multidisciplinary project teams or forums that help with idea creation or exchange. External collaboration can include developing strategic alliances with competitors, customers, partners, other sectors and key industry players, through web-based technology and around specific product themes.

Case Study: Welcome to Edinburgh

The background

A collaborative industry group of 10 private and public sector bodies.

The issue

The group realized the need to improve the welcome visitors receive on arrival in Edinburgh and to communicate the events and activities on offer in the city.

The solution

An initial scheme saw flat screen TVs installed on the Lothian Buses Airlink service, each showing a 20-minute video timed to last the length of the journey from the airport to the city centre. The video is also being shown, on a trial basis, in each room in the Sheraton Grand Hotel and Spa, before further roll-out across the city.

The impact

Existing research has shown that a high quality welcome and information service can enhance the whole visitor experience, thus encouraging repeat visits.

Tools.   Building prototypes and describing ideas in more than words (e.g. drawing, acting, and pictures) can help stimulate creativity and ideas exchange. Getting away from the working environment encourages people to think differently, highlighted earlier in relation to Scottish Enterprise's Tourism Innovation Toolkit.

Clarity.   Creativity requires parameters. That is why it is important that tourism organizations clarify the purpose or aim of new ideas. These ideas will only add real value if you are clear about your customers, product, values and operating environment.

Case Study: Crieff Hydro

The background

A family-owned hotel and spa in Scotland.

The issue

A disused sand and gravel quarry next to the hotel had lain dormant for 20 years. Well screened with trees and natural vegetation, this large site – over 30 acres – had potential. But what for?

The solution

It was decided to use the greatly uneven terrain to its best advantage by creating an off-road driving centre. Using a JCB, a suitable course was landscaped including mounds and 'river' crossings.

The impact

Within three years, a turnover of £135,000 was achieved, with a projected pre-tax profit of £30,000. The company has taken on four full-time employees.

Information.   A constant appetite for new information can help stimulate new thought. For example:

- Observing and understanding customers;
- Keeping up to date with competitors, the industry and the latest trends;
- Searching the internet;
- Attending conferences and work shows;
- Networking.

Case Study: Disney and Universal in the USA

The background

These companies own and operate major visitor attractions/theme parks in the USA

The issue

In order to generate new ideas and identify opportunities, innovative companies have a voracious appetite for information and everything new – they need to research, read, travel, talk, listen and observe.

Continued

The solution

Universal Studios has a master contract with a market intelligence research firm to provide customized research reports. They provide concise reports on key topics and trends in the toy industry, fashion, retail, hotel and teenage market. This service is provided free to all employees – reports every two weeks – in order to keep current. Both Disney and Universal also track all the theme park rumour sites on the internet for possible new industry developments. Both companies emphasize the importance of market research and reading a broad range of magazines (entertainment industry and non-industry related) and articles enhancing the understanding of the market trends and what people are experiencing.

The impact

The enjoyment of a visit to a crowded theme park is lessened by the ever-present necessity of waiting in long lines in order to experience a very popular attraction. This situation grew more prevalent during the 1990s. Both guests and park operators are adversely affected. A guest will have less chance of enjoying additional attractions, while the operator will have less guest flow through food and merchandise locations. Disney's Fastpass took on the challenge of a totally comprehensive approach to this well-known theme park problem, and Disney is delivering outstanding results for its efforts. Fastpass encompasses an almost infinite variety of detailed solutions, which can be fine-tuned virtually immediately as situations change during the day.

Technology. Businesses need to harness technology to develop new products and services so that they can:

- Identify areas where technology can enhance the visitor experience;
- Investigate how other sectors have used the internet and other technologies, and think about how this could be adopted to a tourism environment;
- Collaborate with others to package new and innovative e-products and services.

However, as Scottish Enterprise shows, there may also be barriers to innovation that are reflected in a resistance to change which might take the form of clinging to standards, procedures, rules and regulations, and resisting new ideas. These barriers may include:

- Threat/fears – others may pose a threat to security or status; fear of competition or that ideas will be stolen; isolation.
- Lack of time or interest – constant interruptions and the necessity to be busy leave no time to create.
- Corporate structure or atmosphere – corporate attitudes, status, lack of cooperative efforts.
- Continuity – it is more convenient to continue on a familiar path than make a change.
- Rushing to judgement – failure to invest time, so new ideas are too quickly rejected.

Barriers can also exist at a personal level due to:

- Improper motivation – a failure to welcome challenges.
- Fear of risk-taking – a fear of making a mistake, letting others down, losing money and being viewed as unsuccessful.
- Lack of mental/expressive facilities – a failure to use all senses, imagination and being very left-brain dominant.
- The nature of the human brain – which functions best at processing information, not perceptions or the generation of new directions.

The actual culture of a company can also act as a barrier to innovation. The organization may be one where staff are not encouraged to be creative. It may be that the culture is one where people's ideas are stifled and there is no opportunity for people to interact, create or exchange ideas.

Implications of the Scottish Enterprise to Innovation in Tourism

It is increasingly being recognized that the role of Scottish Enterprise in global settings is almost unique in tourism with its proactive involvement in innovation, product development, destination development and business leadership ensuring that a destination's tourism experience continues to grow in sophistication and apace with international developments in consumer demand.

At one level, innovation has been viewed in public sector contexts outside of Scotland and Scandinavia as a short-term activity that needs intervention to stimulate collaboration and to build competencies to create a new generation of tourism products and experiences. This has often been a response amongst policy-makers as a quick fix to perceived problems of a sluggish or unresponsive tourism industry and such responses are not conducive to building an innovative culture amongst tourism stakeholders where it is simply short-term initiative led. The Scottish Enterprise approach is more aligned to a medium to long-term culture change so that businesses grow in confidence and are more open towards collaborating with each other.

The approach in Scandinavia and Scotland demonstrates that this needs to be a continuous process akin to TQM. Entrepreneurship, new firm formation and new product and service development in existing firms is a long-term process which seeks ultimately to change the culture and mindset of the tourism sector to be more responsive, customer-oriented and able to evolve to meet the new challenges and customers for the twenty-first century. The series of short case studies used by Scottish Enterprise to demonstrate the value of innovation in individual businesses is part of a much wider innovation programme that seeks to demonstrate the benefits using exemplars of best practice to show that they can offer for other like-minded businesses.

Innovation is also part of building a knowledge base and in disseminating good practice and expertise across the tourism sector, exemplified by the champion role which the Tourism Innovation Group (comprised of influential business leaders who demonstrate an interest, ability and willingness to drive innovation) seeks to promote in areas of Scottish tourism. Being industry-led and supported by Scottish Enterprise, the TIG adds credibility for other businesses so that innovation can be something that individuals can take ownership over rather than perceive as a top-down initiative which a public sector agency seek to promote. Again, innovation is viewed as a philosophy and 'can-do' approach to inspire, educate and stimulate further collaboration through showcase events such as the annual Tourism Innovation day.

The Scottish Enterprise approach to innovation also incorporate the conceptual elements of innovation research and practice, which are communicated in a simplified and direct manner to businesses to assist them in harnessing corporate knowledge and expertise so that they can unlock much of their latent potential to stimulate the innovation process.

The use of different facilitation tools and techniques assists in the leadership role which Scottish Enterprise performs in a national and local setting via its Scotland-wide events. It also has a range of more targeted events in conjunction with its network of economic development companies and networks of businesses with which it engages. The success to date has been impressive using both economic measures, as reflected in Inset 1, and also at a qualitative level through the gradual inroads into culture change across the Scottish tourism sector. Innovation activity at Scottish Enterprise is based on the principle of collaboration-led activity, which is a core feature of the Scottish Enterprise organization, and more specifically the workings of its tourism team. Such a collaborative approach recognizes, as Table 7.2 and 7.3 suggest, that collaborative groups have a particular role to play in bringing together the public and private sector. Having said that Scotland has not widely adopted the Triple Helix model, utilizing instead the university sector where specific areas of research and knowledge are required to benefit innovation and business development to mutual benefit.

Summary

Innovation in tourism still remains, from an academic perspective, poorly understood and few good studies of how to evaluate and measure the effectiveness of innovative behaviour exist. Hjalager (2005) observes from international research that in tourism, generally businesses tend to be imitators and adaptors rather than innovators. However, the experience in Scandinavia and Scotland shows that where the public sector intervenes, it may be able to change this culture and foster successful examples of innovation. Hjalager's (2005, p. 10) comment that 'research into innovation in tourism is still sparse and fragmented, in spite of the fact that innovation is considered a prerequisite of economic development' remains broadly valid aside from the recent review by Hall and Williams (2008). What is lacking, as this chapter has highlighted and addressed, is a blend of academic thinking alongside practical examples and demonstrable benefits from the changes which innovation brings.

Innovation as a process to precisely identify the triggers and tipping points which shift the corporate culture from one where the status quo is acceptable to one where change and new ideas are positively welcomed, examined and adopted is still poorly understood conceptually at an individual firm level. The future research agendas for innovation research in tourism will surely have to foster a greater understanding of the microprocesses of how to permeate the individual business. It will have to demonstrate, where the 'bottom-line' impact on the organization is able to justify the investment of time, energy and know-how into growing innovative staff, products and experiences to keep abreast of the changes in the tourism market.

The destination as a concept, and its constituent parts, remains a valid focal point for looking at how innovative the product and experiences are, and this approach is one which Scottish Enterprise are pursuing in their destination investment strategy for Scottish tourism. That said, innovation will still occur without state intervention where a pro-active and go-ahead entrepreneur decides to create a new product or experience. But with the growing clusters of products and experiences that make destinations attractive and appealing, collaborative and cooperative behaviour will be a valuable form of innovation in itself if competitors can be encouraged to work together to share and grow the business activity at a destination level. This is certainly the experience in Scandinavia and Scotland with networks that can work to the mutual benefit of their participants, as shown in Table 7.4; the private sector illustrates the areas for further development for many countries and individual destinations.

Questions for Discussion

1. Why is innovation important to a business sector such as tourism?
2. Why does the public sector need to intervene to promote innovation?
3. How would you set about stimulating the innovation process among private sector businesses?
4. What do the experiences of innovation in Scotland and Scandinavia illustrate in how the public sector leads the process of tourism innovation?

References

de Bono, E. (1999). *Six Thinking Hats*, Back Bay Books: Boston.

Oakland, J. (1991) *Total Quality Management*, 2nd ed. Oxford: Heinemann.

Schumpeter, J. (1954). *The Theory of Economic Development*, New York: Oxford University Press.

Part 3

Tourism Entrepreneurship Mediating the Global–Local Divide

Chapter 8

Entrepreneurial Crafts and the Tourism Industry

Ian Fillis

Learning Outcomes

After reading this chapter, you should be able to:

- Understand the cultural and economic importance of the craft industry;

- Identify and explain links between the craft sector and tourism;

- Understand how the craft sector provides a source of creativity and innovation in relation to the process of entrepreneurship;

- Identify and describe the profile of a typical craft firm and its owner/manager;

- Identify the main barriers to the growth of the craft industry; and

- Illustrate the Celtic connection and the link with tourism.

Defining Craft and the Craft Enterprise

This chapter evaluates how the craft firm engages with tourism and other economic sectors to ensure profitability through creative, entrepreneurial ways of overcoming a range of physical and perceptual barriers to growth. Any research into the craft sector should recognize from the outset that it makes a vital contribution to the wider economy, especially with regard to the impact of the smaller firm. This wider impact is facilitated through, for example, its relationship with the tourism industry and its role with the wider creative and cultural industries, as well as its contribution to rural economies through its entrepreneurial endeavour (Irvine and Anderson, 2004; Fuller-Love et al., 2006).

The craft sector is also a source of creativity and innovation, something which both other small- and medium-sized enterprises and larger businesses should recognize and learn from. Those working in the sector exhibit many entrepreneurial attributes, from idea generation, opportunity recognition and risk-taking in terms of product design and in relation to business decisions. In the UK there are approximately 3.75 million enterprises of which 99.1% employ fewer than 50 people. These enterprises accounted for 55.4% of employment and 51.4% of turnover (Small Business Service, 2003).

Most of the growth in overall business numbers has been in microenterprises which employ fewer than 10 people, and most of this growth has tended to involve one or two people businesses. Ignoring those craft firms that have embraced mass production techniques, and which therefore are no longer strictly craft based, the vast majority of craft businesses are microenterprises. A smaller number of firms have grown in terms of numbers of personnel and in markets served. The craft sector offers the same possibility for business formation, growth and development as in the broader SME sector. Craft enterprises also tend to face problems similar to those of other SMEs (Carson et al., 1995; Fillis, 2002a).

Benchmarking the crafts sector with other industries, the divisions of 'other mining and quarrying', 'manufacture of food products and beverages', 'manufacture of leather and leather products' consist of lower percentages of self-employed owner/manager businesses, with 39%, 33% and 41% respectively. Industry divisions with higher percentages include 'manufacture of tobacco products' (60%), and 'manufacture of chemicals and chemical products' (64%). Although there are no Department of Trade and Industry statistics which directly relate to the craft sector, it is possible to deduce that divisions such as 'publishing, printing and reproduction of recorded media' (64%), 'manufacture of wearing apparel' (63%) and 'manufacture of textiles' (67%) are craft and creative industries-related fields.

Examining the collective contribution of all firms employing less than 10 people, microenterprises account for over 82% of businesses in the private sector in the UK. Fielden et al. (2000, p. 296) note that small businesses 'have been the main source of new jobs in this country for many years, with enterprises consisting of fewer than 50 workers being responsible for 46% of all private sector employment in the UK. Reaching a detailed understanding of the craft microenterprise has direct implications for other firms of a similar size across sectors. Assuming slow but steady growth as the results indicate, the craft sector has now overtaken the forestry and logging division (£596 m), the manufacture of wood and wood products (SIC (standard industry classification) 020; £478 m), the manufacture of motorcycles and bicycles (SIC 354; £470 m) and the manufacture of sports goods (SIC 364; £574 m). So it is clear that the economic contribution of the craft sector is sizeable and yet still does not attract the attention of support agencies to the same degree as other similar sized sectors.

Historically, the craft firm can be traced to the medieval period (Heslop, 1997), the Italian Renaissance (Greenhalgh, 1997; Welch, 1997) – reaching a peak of popularity during the Arts and Crafts Movement (Naylor, 1971) – and onwards to the present day where the craft firm is situated within the general SME community small- and medium-sized enterprise (SME) community. The nature and meaning of craft has altered during this time, from its early vernacular status to the more recent aesthetic appreciation of the craft product (Aslin, 1981). A major problem relating to tracing the development of the crafts as a recognized industry is that when examining historical documents there is a lack of agreement over the definition of craft (Dormer, 1997). In the last 300 years, for example, there has been a change in the etymology of craft, from describing political acumen and shrewdness in the eighteenth century to the current understanding of its meaning, which has its origins in the Arts and Crafts Movement (Greenhalgh, 1997). It was not until the eighteenth century that a system of fine arts was formulated in Britain, in which the crafts could be placed aesthetically (Kristeller, 1951, p. 510):

> It is known that the very term 'aesthetics' was coined at that time ... it is generally agreed that such dominating concepts of modern aesthetics as taste and sentiment, genius, originality and creative imagination did not assume their definitive modern meaning before the eighteenth century ... scholars have noticed that the term 'Art' with a capital 'A' and in its modern sense, the related term 'Fine Arts' (beaux Arts) originated in all probability in the eighteenth century.

Greenhalgh (1997) notes that it was not until the latter part of the nineteenth century that the words 'craft' and craftsman' were in popular usage, derived mainly from discussion in the visual arts at that time. Metcalf (1997, p. 67) remarks that many of those currently working in the craft industry look back to writers such as Ruskin and his *Nature of Gothic* 1853) in order to promote the idea of craft as art and that:

> To assert that craft is art assumes that the two are comparable, and implies that the conceptual tools and vocabulary of the fine arts can be applied to any craft object, and vice versa. ... both craft and art are visual, and thus subject to the same formalist visual analysis. However, an examination limited to the formal aspects of craft overlooks the way craft objects are made and used, resulting in a highly distorted view.

Its present connotation encapsulates a number of ideas drawn from philosophy, aesthetics and technology. This contrasts to the way in which commentators viewed how art and craftwork were produced as early as the fourteenth century in Italy, an example being those involved in making frescoes being called mastercraftsmen. In other craft-related industries at that time, such as weaving, it was the capitalist entrepreneur who developed the business, not the craftsperson (Antal, 1948).

Metcalf (1997) makes a distinction between contemporary craft and art in a scientific sense, in that there are inherent biological and social differences. Dormer (1997, p. 7) indicates that current thinking in the crafts has resulted in two schools of thought about its definition:

> Either craft means 'studio crafts' covering everyone working with a craft medium. This includes producers of functional ware as well as abstractionalist sculptors working in textiles, clay or glass. Or craft means a process over which a person has detailed control, control that is the consequence of craft knowledge.

Danto (1964, 1981) applied this practice to the arts and crafts movements while Metcalf distinguishes between craft as skilful labour and craft as a class of objects. Concentrating on the latter category, he sees this as embracing the idea that the object must have a high degree of handmade input, either by using the hand itself, hand tools and even hand-held power tools. Furthermore, the craft object does not necessarily have to be wholly produced using traditional materials, only that they have been utilized as part of the production process. Metcalf (1997, p. 71) differs from Danto in making the following distinction between the artist and craftsperson in terms of the methods used in the manufacturing of the work:

> While an artist might freely choose any form for his or her artwork, the craftsman must make an object, must make it substantially by hand, and must utilise to some extent the traditional materials and usage of craft.

Developing this argument, those makers of objects who consider themselves to be artists rather than craftspeople, but who fall into Danto's categorization, cannot then be artists in the strictest sense. However, organizations such as the Crafts Councils appear not to make this distinction and continue to promote contemporary craft as art. Metcalf goes further and believes that there are inherent biological differences in the makers of craft and art:

> ... craft grows directly from the human cognitive potential for fine motor control, and that this potential is actualised as a cultural response to late industrial conditions. While the artworld places its highest values on verbal and logical cognitive abilities, the craftworld places its value elsewhere. (p. 72)

Furthermore, he believes that the current craft culture in Western society does not have any meaningful relationship with the past but that it is mainly a development of twentieth century phenomena. He interprets its occurrence scientifically:

> It is rooted, initially, in the biology of the brain. People use craft to exercise a gifted bodily intelligence, partly because Western society provides few other vehicles for self-determined and dignified handwork. Having made a choice about their life's work, people then seek out others who share the same experiences, ultimately inventing an adaptive culture based on the value of handwork. (p. 79)

Although many craft businesses promote their products as being handmade, there may be some elements of the production process which require mechanical assistance. The weaving and mass production process has its origins in the industrial revolution, where inventors such as Cartwright and Crompton developed equipment which enabled the process to be greatly enhanced in terms of increasing the number of units being produced and the number of people employed in the industry (Berg, 1994; Floud and McCloskey, 1994). Now, in the post-industrialization era, the craftsperson has to compete with both domestic and foreign competition where many products appear handcrafted even though they are often mass produced using advanced technological processes. This threat from advancing technology may mean that, although the craftsperson is endeavouring to sell the work as a one-off or in small batch runs, they will now have to differentiate the work even more from mass produced pieces.

Although some craft products are closely associated with or even deemed art, vernacular crafts derive from the culture of the society in which they have developed and tend to be linked to the more traditional view of the crafts based in rural communities (Dean, 1994). Both craft as art and craft in the vernacular or traditional form are marketed to domestic and international tourists. Recent literature suggests that the crafts industry be viewed as part of the greater cultural and creative industries, comprising designer trades, book publishing, the music industry, television and radio broadcasting, independent film and video, the art trade and cinema (Myerscough, 1996), and it has even been located within the field of visual culture (Walker and Chaplin, 1997).

There is no overall agreed definition of the composition of the cultural industries but Myerscough (1988) viewed them as commercial providers of goods and services which convey to the public cultural ideas and experiences. Coopers and Lybrand (1994) identified cultural industries as embracing heritage and tradition, contemporary entertainment and art, and innovation or experiment. Their report notes that cultural industries are a source of economic activity, employment and added value. Girard (1982) categorized the cultural sector into those industries involving an original small-scale creative activity which can then be reproduced *en masse* through some sort of industrial process (such as books, art reproductions and records), other areas incorporating considerable industrial input such as cinema and television, and photography. The Creative Industries Mapping Document (Department for Culture, Media and Sport, 1998, 2001) views the creative industries as including advertising, architecture, the art and antiques market, crafts, design, designer fashion, film and video, interactive leisure software, music, the performing arts, publishing, software and computer services, television and radio.

The Craftworks survey (Leeke, 1994) chose to define crafts in the widest possible sense, involving individuals through to firms making or manufacturing a functional or decorative product that has a handmade element at some stage in its production. Hillman-Chartrand (1988, p. 39) defines crafts as:

> embracing individual craftspersons, their cooperatives and collectives engaged in the production of and distribution networks for handmade articles, generally of a utilitarian nature embodying varying degrees of artistry.

Neapolitan (1985) makes the distinction between industrial crafts, which were of paramount importance during the era of the industrial revolution, and the handicrafts which involve production of utilitarian household goods sold to individual consumers. Coopers and Lybrand (1994) distinguish between the production of handcraft and craft-based industries involved in larger scale manufacturing practices. Craft production involves a single person completing the entire process, from conceptualization to fabrication. The craft product itself must exhibit aesthetic appeal, be of individual design and contain a large degree of manual skill in its production. In recent studies, the author has defined craft as having a high degree of handmade input, but not necessarily produced or designed using traditional materials. It should be produced as a one-off or as part of a small batch – the design of which may or may not be culturally embedded in the country of production – and sold for profit (Fillis, 2002a, 2002b, 2002c, 2003, 2004, 2007).

Cultural and Economic Impacts of the Craft Firm

Production of crafts can be found throughout the global economy (Dickie and Frank, 1996). In a study of American craft businesses, for example, Neapolitan (1985, p. 313) noted that 'sales of craft objects have become a multi-billion dollar business and large numbers of people use income from craft sales as a significant source of income'.

The impact of arts and crafts is becoming increasingly significant as far as the performance of national economies is concerned (Radich, 1987). Most studies have been concerned with the implications surrounding employment and/or associated expenditure. Economic contribution can be seen in international or even global terms (Royal Commission on the Economic Union and Development Prospect for Canada, 1985, pp. 115–116):

> There is another aspect to culture, namely good taste, good design and creative innovation, that should enable smaller industrial economies to compete effectively in the world economy. Higher quality implies an organic relationship between business and engineering, on the one hand, and design and craftsmanship, on the other.

Hillman-Chartrand (1988) believes that crafts have a significant role to play in what he refers to as the post-modern economy where the traditional economic weaknesses of the arts and crafts are becoming strengths. He views the craftsperson as a risk-taking entrepreneur, where risks are taken in terms of time and talent. The craft industry is compared similarly to high technology industries where both are characterized by small entrepreneurial businesses operating in an economic environment where technological change occurs quickly. Also, consumers now have almost complete access to fashions and styles of previous historical times, with the result that demand has risen for reproductions of many types of craft. Demand has also increased for non-mass produced goods generally since consumers tend to be influenced increasingly by design and aesthetic appearance (O'Brien and Feist, 1995).

A major difficulty in assessing the economic impact of the cultural industries is the lack of availability of relevant data. However, Davies and Lindley (2003) have carried out a study which found that 760,000 people were employed in the year 2000 in a cultural occupation. Many craft producers cannot be identified from Census data using the Standard Industrial Classifications system adopted in other industry surveys (Green, 1971). This lack of identification stems from the nature of the craft sector, which contains significant numbers of part-time workers and businesses that are often too small to register for tax purposes. Debate surrounding the definition of craft has also contributed to lack of clarity regarding the numbers working in the sector. There are a limited number of available reports concerning the economic contribution of the craft industry, while other relevant articles remain outside of the public domain or out of print and data collected in previous studies may have been destroyed because of data protection issues (Leeke, 1994).

The Craft Firm in the United Kingdom and the Republic of Ireland

Some methods of measuring the impact of the arts in general encompass a broad economic catchment area, such as assessing the impact of the arts on tourism and studies that make the distinction between amateurs and professionals (Brosio, 1994). The study discussed here involves an examination of craft which is viewed as both a business and as a way of life, and not a pastime. During the 1980s there was an overall growth in the domestic market for crafts and an associated increase in the number of craft fairs and specialist shops, and, more recently, a heightened interest in selling overseas (Knott, 1994). This survey identified almost 17,000 craftspeople in England, Scotland and Wales. The creative sector in general has evolved over the last 30 years (Adorno and Horkheimer, 1977; Healy, 2002). Creativity is not just applicable to the arts and the artistic product but should also be viewed in a wider sense, where it embraces entrepreneurship and innovation.

In the United Kingdom, recent figures suggest that 1.4 million people are employed in the industry and that the economic contribution is more than £90 billion per year (Smith, 2001). The typical range of craft products being sold has been identified by Fillis (2000) in an examination of the craft sector in Northern Ireland, the Republic of Ireland, England, Scotland and Wales. This examination also shows that both traditional and contemporary products are being created and that the handmade factor is an essential ingredient for both the general consumer and the tourist alike.

An illustrative example of the range of craft products

Lamps

Bowls

Tableware

Hand-thrown ceramics

Porcelain giftware and tableware

Table mats

Wood carved furniture

Wood-turned bowls

Wooden toys

Hand-painted timber mobiles

Hand-pyrographed and painted wood

Guitars, Bodhrans and other musical instruments

Embroidery kits

Stained glass windows, panels and lamps

Glass engraving

Decorative mirrors

Crystal figures

Wall hangings/tapestries

Bags

Shirts

Jewellery: silver, gold, paper, costume

Trinket boxes

Willow baskets

Handmade felt products

Games

Lap trays

Writing tops

Invitation boards

Screen-printed and embroidered garments

Wedding gowns

Horse-riding clothes

Decorative ironwork

Handmade papers

Handmade greetings cards

Leather goods

Bookends

Book bindings

Bookmarks

Fire screens

Batik and collage pictures

Candles

Candelabras

Plaster mouldings

Silk paintings

Papier mache items

Woven fabric

Textiles/Fabrics

Rugs

Knitwear

Fashion accessories: hats, jackets, scarves, skirts, cushions

Clocks

In a survey of the economic impact of the craft sector in Scotland, McAuley and Fillis (2002) found that the dominant craft disciplines were ceramics, textiles, wood and jewellery. Over three quarters of respondents were sole traders of microenterprises employing up to two people, and more females than males were involved in the sector. Market channels were dominated by commissions, selling from a workshop (17.3%), direct to retailers and through craft fairs. Turnover in the Scottish craft sector was estimated to be up to £151 m.

In a similar study of the socio-economic impact of the craft sector in England and Wales, McAuley and Fillis (2004) found that turnover here was around £826 m while in their latest study in Northern Ireland, McAuley and Fillis (2006) estimated turnover to be around £8 m but with indications that this value was set to rise due to increasing tourist visits and a general upturn in the economy following the cessation of political violence. Many of the findings from these surveys compare similarly to the patterns and characteristics found in the wider small and medium enterprise (SME) sector. Ceramics, textiles, wood and jewellery are the main forms of craft produced here. As with those making crafts in Scotland, England and Wales, the main ways of generating sales include commissions, selling directly to the public from a workshop or from craft fairs and markets.

A Profile of the Craft Firm and its Owner/Manager

Analysing both the qualitative and quantitative data collected in the various surveys discussed in this chapter has enabled the identification of the following orientations: there are those who have chosen to work in the craft industry because of the type of lifestyle involved and are unwilling to sacrifice this in order to expand the business (the *lifestyler*). Another type of craft owner/manager is the business-oriented entrepreneur who is willing to take risks and recognizes the importance of developing a customer base (the *entrepreneur*). Networking and relationship building are deemed very important for business success (Morison et al., 2004). This partly confirms the view held by Hillman-Chartrand (1988) that the craftsperson is really a risk-taking entrepreneur.

The third type can be described as an artist/designer who is unwilling to view the craft as a product but as a creative piece (the *idealist*). Their stance is uncompromising when producing the work; they do not tend to take note of customer demand but instead make art/crafts which they feel have artistic integrity. In other words, they embrace an 'Art for Art's sake' philosophy, rather than 'Art for Business sake'. They do take risks as far as the craft itself is concerned in order to break new ground, and they can be innovative and certainly creative with the craft product.

There is a fourth type who may enter the industry much later than the other groups; this type tends to have gained previous work experience in unrelated areas and has decided to make a career change (the *late developer*). Depending on their background, a number of key skills can be brought into the new venture, but the importance of lifestyle quality appears to be significant here too. This has relevance as far as expansion in terms of sales, markets and numbers being employed in the business are concerned. The following table illustrates some of the characteristics found in the four craft business types (Table 8.1).

Table 8.1: Craft business owner/manager characteristics.

THE LIFESTYLER	THE ENTREPRENEUR
• expansion of business not important	• risk-taker (in terms of carrying out business and with the craft product itself)
• unwilling to take many risks	
• importance of quality of life	• may or may not export; proactive
• may or may not export; generally reactive	• most likely to embrace business and marketing philosophy in the longer term
• unwilling to follow business and marketing philosophy and develop related skills	• realization of the importance of customer relationships/networking
THE IDEALIST	**THE LATE DEVELOPER**
• risk-taker (with the craft product)	• tends to come from non-creative background
• unwilling to accept business and marketing philosophy	• less motivated to expand business; less likely to export
• dominance of 'Art for Art's sake' beliefs	• unlikely to accept *new* ideas
• may or may not export	• believes in valuing own experience of business and life
• realization of importance of establishing and building relationships and generating reputation	• able to bring *outside skills* to the business
• views self as artist rather than craftsperson	• may find problems with accessing existing networks

Although the above analysis has identified these four groups of owner/manager characteristics it should be noted that they are not always mutually exclusive. Several characteristics can be found in more than one group although their interpretation varies: for instance, both the entrepreneur and the idealist are prepared to take risks. However, it is the nature of the risk that is inherently different. The former is prepared to indulge in risk-taking at the business and product level, while the latter is really only concerned with artistic risk. Each of these orientations will also have implications for the tourist market and the type of tourist; for example, it is expected that variations will be found in those visiting galleries with craft objects for sale and those shopping in larger retail stores in towns and cities. In the former scenario, many craft objects are positioned as art and have normally been assigned a higher price to those sold in other retail outlets. In addition, many tourists seek out the crafts for sale in rurally located workshops, building this visit into their overall holiday experience. Some may also purchase various craft objects via the craft business' own website or shared portal.

Ateljevic and Doorne (2000) evaluate the wider implications of lifestyle orientation as part of entrepreneurship in tourism. They note that non-economic factors such as lifestyle serve as major stimuli for tourism entrepreneurship as well as impacting on the growth of the small-business sector in general. Although economic interpretations of business behaviour are still valid, the ways in which we lead our lives today also mean that more qualitative, subjective factors also play a part in shaping the behaviour of the business and the motivations of its owner/managers. Rather than viewing lifestyle as an impediment to economic development (Morrison et al., 1999; Morrison and Teixeira, 2004), it should be seen as a positive influence within the wider context of flexible working and the notion of liquid lives (Chartered Institute of Personnel and Development, 2004).

Ateljevic and Doorne's research of New Zealand lifestyle entrepreneurs focuses on non-economic motivating factors, revealing that the conscious rejection of economic and business growth opportunities can be explained by the entrepreneur's socio-political ideology. This would also help to explain the diversity found in craft business owner/manager characteristics. Dewhurst and Horobin (1998) also acknowledge the need to recognize those entrepreneurs who do not view maximization of profits as an absolute priority and who therefore may only employ small numbers of personnel, influenced by a highly personalized form of managerial decision-making. Craft firm owner/managers exhibit a variety of creative competencies which determine how products are designed and how the business is shaped, including how the owner/manager leads the employees (Fillis, 2002c). This also has implications for the degree of engagement with customer groups, including the tourist market, where market orientation and creation issues and relationship building influence profitability (van Zyl and Mathur-Helm, 2007).

Creating the Market for Crafts

As can be seen from the profile of the craft firm and its owner/manager, there are differences in the ways in which the maker perceives and embraces marketing. For some, the marketing concept is wholeheartedly followed and the craftsperson produces what the customer wants. For others, however, this is not an option and there is no following of the market. Instead, demand for the particular craft is created by the efforts and competencies of the makers who often view themselves as artists. Hirschman (1983, p. 46) suggests that the marketing concept does not match the behaviour and philosophy of the artist as a producer of products because of the personal values and the social norms which impact on the artistic production process:

> … artists … do not bring forth products according to … the marketing concept [which] holds that products should be created in response to the … desires/

> interests of their consuming public ... creators of aesthetic ... products
> frequently exhibit exactly the opposite pattern. An artist ... may first create
> a product that flows from their own internal desires ... and then present this
> product to consumers who choose to either accept or reject it.

Artists create mainly to express their subjective conceptions of beauty, emotion or some
other aesthetic ideal (Becker, 1978; Holbrook, 1981). Aesthetic creativity is the central
influence in the process, and is expressed or experienced purely for its own sake rather than
responding to customer demand (Holbrook and Zirlin, 1983).

The Crafts as Part of a Creative Cluster

Positioning the crafts within the cultural and creative industries also means that they can be
located within a wider economic cluster which includes festivals, cultural tourism,
education, intellectual property management and new technology promotions (Fillis and
Rentschler, 2006). An extensive complement of industries exists which supports cultural
activities, tourism, the environment and sustainable innovation. These include specialized
publicity and marketing firms, universities, and numerous publications, pamphlets and
media promotional material aimed at consumer and trade audiences. There are special
committees at local government level devoted to developing the region's tourism, as well
as academics researching the subject for the betterment of their local community. The
cluster also enjoys linkages to other clusters, such as cultural tourism and hospitality.
Figure 8.1 illustrates how the crafts sector is located within a wider network of directly and
indirectly related bodies.

The significance of geographically defined clusters arises from their capture of
intellectual property needs but also from the nature of networked knowledge entrepreneurship (Flew, 2002). Clusters are integral to everyday life and commerce and are
a central component in the new economy. Landry (2000) draws attention to the hard
and soft infrastructure in creative clusters. Hard infrastructure comprises buildings,
institutions and other tangible entities in a region or city. Soft infrastructure comprises
the social networks and human interactions that underpin and encourage the flow of
ideas between individuals and institutions. These concepts of infrastructure are
a reminder of the importance of creativity in the development of new products and
services as well as dynamic regions and cities. As regions and cities are increasingly
sites of leisure, entertainment, hospitality and tourism sectors, such developments
require innovative public policy which seeks and identifies new opportunities for
creative development.

Clusters enjoy common marketing media and are both cooperative and competitive.
Their boundaries are defined by the linkages across industries and institutions that are
important to their growth and survival; they may extend beyond regional or state
boundaries or political frameworks. As Porter (1998) argues, clusters represent a new kind
of spatial organizational form. However, it is more than that: clusters are also a social
structure of creative marketing comprising (1) new systems for technological creativity
and marketing, (2) new and more effective modes of conceiving goods and services, (3)

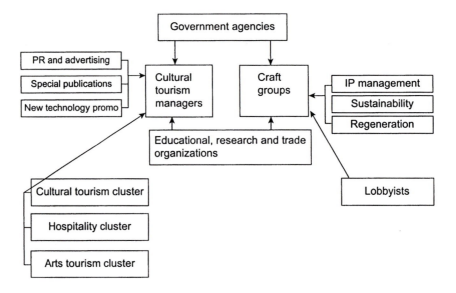

Figure 8.1: Anatomy of a Crafts Cluster.

a broad, social, cultural and geographic milieu conducive to creativity of all sorts. Clusters enable creative growth as they stimulate competition for ideas and innovative solutions for bringing them to market. They drive the pace of innovation and they stimulate the formation of other new enterprises as well as encouraging their institutional support services to thrive. A cluster allows each person in it to benefit as if it had greater scale or formality, but without it needing to sacrifice its flexibility.

The Celtic Connection and the Link with Tourism

Many Irish, Scottish and Welsh craft businesses deliberately incorporate an element of Celtic design into their work, relying on the symbolism and associated meaning to sell the product to culturally close markets through exporting processes as well as through retailing from their own premises or via shops and galleries to visiting tourists and local consumers. There may be a degree of exploitation here among the more entrepreneurially inclined Celtic makers who freely admit that shamrock imagery sells well in the USA and that they don't mind compromising their artistic ideals. Others refuse to capitalize on this and prefer, instead, to draw on design influences they have experienced while travelling or as freer flowing subconscious-level creative outputs. To describe some Celtic craftspeople as lazy and complacent would be wrong. Instead, they feel that by exploiting their historical and cultural connections in an entrepreneurial sense, there is no need to look further afield for business. The success of the Celtic craft product has even led to some makers from non-Celtic backgrounds copying their designs and passing off their work as Celtic or Celtic inspired.

In-depth interviews with respondents from Scotland and Ireland show that, despite apparently similar Celtic backgrounds, there are some differences in business practices. This is also evidenced by the differences between the two in terms of achieving business success and engagement with the tourist market. The Irish maker seems more able to exploit intuitive marketing competencies whilst the closeness to the English border may mean that Scottish business methods tend to sometimes veer towards the more formal mechanisms of formalized thinking. There can also be negative connotations associated with exploitation of Celticness. Some makers feel that having a Celtic ethos can impede development of the business while others openly exploit the connection. It seems to depend on whether or not the maker believes in the Celtic aesthetic and subsequently has the nerve and ability to make use of this connection in the market place. Compare these contrasting attitudes:

> I quite like those kind of games if you like, where you can hide your ethnic background. But I would be hiding it rather than exploiting it up front. I don't find that up front business very interesting. I think it leads to divide rather than harmony. (English maker intent on hiding their identity)

> I don't like to get bogged down in that avenue because that can be restricting. That holds down the talent, the potential for ideas coming from within the person. A lot of people would say that's a load of rubbish – do the Celtic thing and make millions ... I don't know if they do or not. (Northern Irish maker refusing to exploit Celtic connection)

> We use Celtic design in the work. It does sell a lot of things – a wee individual style of it. You can sort of look around and say 'That's one of Kevin's'. (Northern Irish maker exploiting the Celtic connection)

> Selling something to the Americans, if you put a shamrock on it or a Celtic pattern they think it's great. And it doesn't matter if it's from Ireland, England, Scotland or Wales, they love it. (Republic of Ireland maker discussing the Celtic factor)

So the Celtic dimension can be seen to assist in the marketing and selling of the product to tourists and other consumers. Even non-Celtic craftspeople, either by accident or through deliberate courses of action, utilize the mistaken belief by the customer that their work is Celtic in order to sell the product. Some Irish exporters have come to incorporate a degree of Celticness in the design of the product but in a more subtle way by:

> get(ing) the Irish idea across without the leprechauns, without all the tourism, without the Walt Disney.

The notion of the Celtic aesthetic grounded in pre-Christian and Christian iconography is embraced by some makers while others intentionally dismiss it and instead incorporate a more personal creative approach that includes influencing factors such as overseas travel and exposure to alternative design influences.

Conclusions: Using Creativity to Attract Interest from Potential Customers

One of the strengths of the crafts sector is the ability of those working within it to utilize their creativity both to overcome the limited resources at their disposal and to work out how to create and appeal to potential customers. The customer base ranges from long-term local, national and international loyal buyers to one-off purchases made by tourists as they travel through the locality. Another strength of the craft firm owner/manager is the ability to develop a firm-specific form of marketing which has a strong product focus. Being creative is not normally sufficient on its own in ensuring success. Leadership skills and visionary competencies are also essential (Frisch, 1998). Creativity in business is often viewed as feeding into a structured planning process, but Carson (1990) makes it clear that formal business methods must be adjusted to suit the needs of the SME manager. It is not disputed that creativity impinges on marketing and business strategy; it is the degree of formality and the extent of the process, however, which varies depending on the size of the firm and the characteristics of the key decision-makers (Wolff and Pett, 2000).

This chapter has detailed how important it is to develop profiles or typologies of owner/managers and not to treat them as a generic entity with similar thought processes and outputs. The craft sector is unique in that the products made tend to be one-off designs – a fact that very often appeals to the discerning consumer who views quality over price every time. Factors such as risk-taking behaviour, being able to control rather than be controlled, being independent, not being afraid to fail and having the perseverance to succeed all feed into some sort of creative output and are not only central to success in the craft sector but are also found across the smaller firm environment where owner/managers have set up businesses to serve an inner need to succeed on their own terms. Creativity has been identified as a competitive strength (Kao, 1989), a key competency (Carson et al., 1995) and an entrepreneurial attribute (Bridge et al., 1998).

The successful craft firm develops a key set of creativity-related competencies, linked to networking, relationship building, opportunity recognition and exploitation (Shaw, 1998; Hulbert and Brown, 1998). Those working in the craft sector can be viewed as a metaphor for successful marketing and entrepreneurial practice, where many firms operate within very limited budgets but are able to differentiate themselves from other firms through application of creativity of both thought and practice. This is in line with other firms in the creative industries. If creativity is viewed as rejection of established modes of practice in favour of alternative methods, then the lifestyler owner/manager has been creative in following a philosophy where quality of existence is much more important than business expansion and profit-making. The entrepreneurial owner/manager embraces creativity in the approach to business and in the design of the product. The idealist follows creative artistic practice in the selling of the craft object, relying on reputation rather than business and marketing skills. The late developer has been creative in terms of making the decision to switch vocations and in the ability to apply experience gained in other industry sectors.

Questions for Discussion

1. How would you define the craft industry?
2. Why and how does tourism provides an important distribution channel for the craft industry?
3. What are the main characteristics of craft entrepreneurs?
4. Identify and discuss, with an illustration, problems of the craft industry.

References

Carson, D. (1990). 'Some Exploratory Models for Assessing Small Firms' Marketing Performance – A Qualitative Approach, *European Journal of Marketing*, 24(12), 8–51.

Coopers and Lybrand ((1994)). *The Employment and Economic Significance of the Cultural Industries in Ireland*. Coopers and Lybrand.

Department for Culture Media and Sport (1998). *Creative Industries Mapping Document*. Department for Culture, Media and Sport.

Department for Culture Media and Sport (2001). *Creative Industries Mapping Document, update*. Department for Culture, Media and Sport.

Chapter 9

Tourism Entrepreneurship and Regional Development

Jovo Ateljevic

Learning Outcomes

After reading this chapter, you should be able to:

- Understand the way tourism contributes to regional development;

- Identify the key actors from both private and public sectors in the process of regional tourism development as well as the relationship between them while shaping an environment conducive to tourism innovation;

- Identify specific and generic issues and constraints affecting development of the small tourism sector;

- Understand the bottom-up theory that underpins the entrepreneurial behaviour of a multiplicity of stakeholders in rural localities; and

- Describe the role and value of the Wairarapa case study from New Zealand in helping to provide examples of good practice in tourism development.

Introduction

The process of tourism development is being seen as the path to enhance local economies (Thomas and Augustyn, 2007) and deliver more appropriate development to marginal and/ or peripheral social, cultural and physical environments (Doorne, 2008). In this context, the contribution of small and innovative tourism firms has been particularly significant. Small tourism firms (STFs) have been linked to creative product development and innovative entrepreneurship (Shaw and Williams, 1998; Ateljevic and Doorne, 2000; Getz and Carlsen, 2004; Thomas and Augustyn, 2007).

Despite their emerging significance and entrepreneurial behaviour, STFs-like small firms in general face numerous difficulties due to an increasing number of reasons related to: their managerial weaknesses (Stokes, 2000); limited access to expertise in core business disciplines as well as lifestyle motivations (Irvine and Anderson, 2004; Marcjanna, 2004; Ateljevic and Doorne, 2000); limited access to external finance (Jarvis, 2006); and a unfair institutional regulatory environment that inhibits business growth and new entry (Smallbone and Wyer, 2006; Storey, 1994).

These disadvantages present barriers to successful tourism development, particularly in isolated areas dominated by small family-owned businesses (Morrison, 2006). In such situations the role of government, working through specific agencies, has been to identify good practices, benchmark, provide financial support, and invest in the skills of the labour force (Wanhill, 2000). However, it remains unclear how the relationship between STFs/SMEs and the institutional sector works and how it might be improved upon (Fuller-Love et al., 2006).

While the tourism literature helps us to understand specific issues facing STFs in rural regions, regional economic development literature provides a broader understanding of regional development strategies. The latter suggests that regional development strategy has shifted from the conventional 'one-for-all' approach to more customized development strategies suitable for different types of regions (Scrimgeour et al., 2002; Moulaert and Sekia, 2003; Bull and Baudner, 2004).

An increasing number of countries have adapted 'bottom-up' strategies for their lagging regions. The approach is largely associated with the concept of sustainability in which local communities are increasingly proactive in facilitating the regional development. Few studies have examined the bottom-up approach more critically in the context of tourism (Agrusa et al., 2003). Amongst an increasing number of theories on local and regional development the bottom-up concept seems to be the most appropriate to explain reality in a country periphery. The discussion in this chapter draws on a study of Wairarapa, one of the first sheep farming regions in New Zealand. The area is dominated by rural settings with a few provincial towns, providing a unique opportunity to explore the entrepreneurial behaviour in the growing tourism sector. In many respects this example reflects broader issues elsewhere.

In order to cover the contextual conditions of STFs the research relies on a wide range of sources of primary information at different levels through participant observation, in-depth interviewing and a survey. Most of the variables related to the regional development including entrepreneurship and civil leadership cannot be precisely measured as the standard measurement could be inappropriate or misleading. Therefore, a close examination of the personal opinion of individuals from both private and public sectors was the dominant method in collecting and interpreting the empirical data. Although the qualitative paradigm was used in guiding research action, the quantitative method was carried out to analyse demographic and historical characteristics of entrepreneurs and their firms.

A total of 47 interviews were conducted during 1999, 2000, and 2001 with a range of tourism firms from the Wairarapa region (34), and public and private sector representatives from Wairarapa and Wellington (13). A number of repeated in-depth interviews were conducted with representatives from the following public and private sector organizations and agencies: the local RTO; National Tourism Organization (NTO); Central Stage Macro Region (CSMR); the Department of Conservation (DoC); Small Business Link (BIZinfo), Wellington; Central Government representatives; the local small business enterprise; New Zealand Tourism Industry Association (NZTIA); Motel Association of New Zealand; Homestay Association; several local promotion/interest groups and, finally, four representatives from the banking and accounting sectors.

The aim of this chapter is threefold. Firstly, it will examine the small tourism businesses' entrepreneurial behaviour and their ability to contribute to regional development in the context of a transitional economy. Secondly, to see to what extent the bottom-up theoretical model underlying a new regional development paradigm accommodates the selected case study. Thirdly, to identify specific and generic issues and constraints affecting STFs' development in order to inform decision-making in the policy and regulatory environment with a view to more effectively integrating the small-firms sector into wider regional and national economies.

Following this introduction, the chapter commences by providing the contextual significance of New Zealand and the theoretical underpinning. This is followed by an overview of structural changes that have brought about a rise in importance of small tourism firms, identifying the range of perspectives that inform contemporary understanding. The chapter then discusses the extent to which economic factors have remained central to the analyses and concurrently point to evolving studies of tourism entrepreneurship and STFs that have begun to play an important role in regional development.

Understanding of the New Zealand Context

By the mid-1980s, New Zealand had undertaken a massive programme of economic restructuring moving an agrarian economy dependent on concessionary British market access toward a more industrialized, free market economy that can compete globally (Le Heron, 1998; Kelsey, 1995). The process of restructuring and deregulation at the national level created significant changes at the local and regional levels that had major implications for regional tourism developments (Pearce, 1998). Some of the main measures that government has introduced since 1984 include: removal of all major subsidies by government including ones for agriculture, liberalization of imports and implementation of a freely floating exchange rate. Controls on interest rates, wages, and prices have been removed, and marginal rates of taxation reduced.

The changes in the early stage of the reform had created opportunities for overseas investors, including the financial sector which by the mid-1990s was entirely in foreign ownership (Statistic NZ, 2000). These changes spread quickly throughout all economic and social activities, and within all organizations, industries, and regions of the country, regardless of scale and operation (Kelsey, 1995). Economic and political restructuring opened up the economy to international investment and led to the economic diversification that has now shaped much of the existing pattern of tourism developments in the country (Pearce, 1998). New Zealand central government recognized tourism as a key sector for national and, particularly, regional economic development. Major tourism developments, mainly driven by foreign investments, were limited to the major cities and resorts. The sector was also seen to provide new opportunities for diversification for small entrepreneurs in the New Zealand periphery.

At the regional level, local government has played an important role through a mix of regulatory initiatives. On the other hand, having just emerged as autonomous entities, inadequate funding and revenue sources are now serious problems for local governments. Therefore, local governments are actively campaigning to attract new businesses and industries to their respective areas as a means of both increasing revenue sources and expanding their economic base. With limited finance and intense regional competition some regions have found it hard to be successful (Doorne, 1998). Local authorities have taken a proactive role trying to reverse population decline and regenerate regional growth by developing economic tourism plans, investing in tourism infrastructure and establishing Regional Tourism Organizations (RTOs).

Theoretical Context of the Bottom-up Approach to the Regional Development

Economic development in many industrial as well as developing countries has tradition-ally been driven by a top-down approach, where the central government uses power to create growth centres around a few large cities and priority is given to urban and industrial capital-intensive development. In the context of the contemporary approach of the regional development theory the top-down model has become less effective as most peripheries depend largely on the local conditions, including regional policy assistance, physical infrastructure, structure of the labour market, social qualifications and population density.

As opposed to the top-down or centre-down approach known as a classical development theory, the new regional development paradigm is based on an assumption of the bottom-up model (Hansen, 1990, 1992). It is argued that the new paradigm was born out of the weaknesses of the classical regional development theory that was not sufficient for the current global and ever-dynamic business environment (De Montricher, 1995; Stohr, 1990; Stohr et al., 2001). The general force of the top-down or centre-down theory, in which government makes decisions without inclusion of local people, is relatively small; large investments are mainly made in specific sectors of the economy or geographical areas, and the benefits will spread and help other areas.

It is also argued that a top-down regional development policy approach is associated with subsidization and protectionism and is therefore seen as less productive than a locally based industry-driven model (Jackson, 2005). The top-down model, according to tradi-tional theories, assumes that development starts in a few dynamic sectors and geographical areas and then spreads to other sectors and areas. The emphasis is normally on urban and industrial, capital-intensive development, the advance technology and maximum exercise of economies of scale (Stohr et al., 2001).

The lack of a uniform regional development pattern in recent decades is used to cast doubts on the success of the traditional models and is put forward as a reason to support the need for a bottom-up approach (Illeris, 1993; Bingham and Mier, 1993). Regional development patterns, as Illeris observes, exhibit a mosaic of dynamic and declining regions with no consistent core/periphery polarization. This has replaced the former uniform concentration of economic growth in the national core areas. This shift of para-digm was an attempt made by Illeris (1993) to explain regional disparities in economic performance. The concept is labelled as an inductive theory for regional development and has two main bearings: first, the structural composition of the economy in terms of declining and growing sectors that might influence regional total development; and second, the regional dependency on local conditions. The local conditions, Illeris stressed, 'do not only affect the performance of sectors inside the region, but may also contribute to attracting inward investments and building interregional networks' (cited in Terluin and Post, 2003, p. 11). Well-performing regions are those with comparative advantage created with one or more expanding sectors such as energy production, high tech industries, producer services, tourism and international organizations.

The concept of a bottom-up approach is part of several broader theoretical perspectives on local/regional development, including the neo-Schumpeterian theory associated with entrepreneurship and innovation (Morgan, 1997) and the endogenous development model that is principally associated with institutional dynamics of all groups in the local population and its empowerment (Friedman, 1992). Shifting responsibilities from the central to local government to encourage bottom-up development has been actively promoted across the globe. The central–local power shift was one of the major EU reforms of regional development policy in 1988 with the aim of reducing regional disparities within the EU (CEC, 2004). The implementation of such policy requires an effective local and regional governance system. Therefore, the endogenous development approach sees regional development as a product of increased local potential achieved by building institutional capacity (CEC, 2004; Bull and Baudner, 2004). The importance of local institutional structure and its adaptability was initially recognized by the French model of the milieu innovator (produced by GRAMI) more than two decades ago (see Aydalot, 1986).

While an effective government policy framework has long been regarded as the main prerequisite for regional development, in recent times a constructive regional institutional capacity on the 'bottom' (local government authorities and non-government institutions, business and other organizations) has become more efficient in sustaining or re-inventing local/regional economies. This shift has become apparent with the decline of the direct government intervention in the state economy; since the early 1980s it has stimulated the rise of governance – the exercise of authority by non-government institutions (Painter and Goodwin, 1995). Non-government institutions particularly play a critical role in creating a broader environment for regional tourism development and subsequently STFs.

Moulaert and Sekia (2003) advocate that the key implication of the bottom-up approach is the 'decentralization of decision-making to lower territorial levels'. Given the complex nature of tourism development, due to the number of stakeholders involved, this devolution of power is a complicated process. While governments may take actions that are expressed through specific tourism policies implemented by various government agencies at the national, regional, and local level, Pearce (2001) implies that there are frequently no clear-cut responsibilities and well-developed policies for tourism planning and development. Instead, the public sector gets involved in tourism in a variety of ways, at different levels, and through many agencies and institutions often lacking in coordination. Many disparate interest groups simultaneously vie for the power to influence government policy at various levels (Hall and Jenkins, 1995).

Importance of Small (Tourism) Firms: An Overview

An increasing number of scholars believe that a healthy small-firms sector, after the structural economic crisis, is essential for countries seeking to encourage economic development opportunities (Storey, 1994; Dicken, 1998; Carter and Jones-Evans, 2006; Scase, 2000). Indeed, the revival of small firms in the late 1970s became a feature of development across the whole of the industrial world, and as the OECD notes, 'small firms are particularly important in net job growth' (1985, p. 80). Drucker (1992) observed that the growth of SMEs during the 1980s is not seen as an independent process, but is attributed to various developments including: the decentralization strategies of large firms; a shift from labour-intensive to knowledge-intensive industries; and the shift of manufacturing production/assembly to developing countries for cheaper labour.

The changing nature of developed economies has, in turn, led towards service-based economies including marketing, distribution, media, communications, and leisure (Morgan and Pritchard, 2000) and the resurgence of small firms. New modes of production based on technological advancement, and new organizational and management strategies along with ever-increasing consumerism have created a range of additional products and services (Greene and Mole, 2006).

The implications of the production/consumption changes are not merely confined to the commercial environment. They have also affected the social context, which is coincidental with a 'cultural turn', and the realignment of social groups (gender, ethnicity, vocation, education level) – changes which in turn inform the context of entrepreneurship, consumer practice and regional development. An increasing number of individuals are attracted to enter the world of the small sector for employment opportunities, and in opposition to the increasingly competitive corporate environment in which many entrepreneurs 'would have found it almost impossible to work' (Carter and Jones-Evans, 2000, p. 4). Indeed, this global transition has become apparent in the travel, tourism, and leisure sectors. As the range of tourism products has expanded rapidly (Pearce et al., 1998), opportunities have been created worldwide for a wider array of specialized small-scale tourism firms. In the context of this shift, and a corresponding demand for differentiated, 'tailor-crafted' tourism products, the importance of small-scale firms has been widely recognized (Thomas, 2004; Page et al., 1999).

Wairarapa

Wairarapa is officially part of the greater Wellington area (see Figure 9.1), which encompasses most of its rural setting and is split into three separate districts: Masterton, Carterton and Martinborough (Southern Wairarapa) with a total population of 39,200. The majority of the population (24,000) lives in Masterton, which is the main urban area (Statistic NZ, 1997). Disturbance of the New Zealand equilibrium in the 1970s was highly visible in Wairarapa due to its agricultural background. The region was once the most important sheep-farming region in New Zealand and its economy was traditionally dominated by meat and wool. However, as at the national level, both products' earnings – which underpin the agricultural sector – have significantly decreased (Kelsey, 1995).

As a result of the demise of the regional agrarian sector many small regional servicing businesses supplying living essentials, farm inputs and services to farmers went out of business. Many of the redundant people moved out of rural communities seeking employment or business opportunities in larger towns. Decline of the regional population, mostly between 18 and 35 years old, was identified as one of the major problems the Wairarapa region has faced since the mid-1980s (Statistic NZ, 2000). After fruitless expectations of government help, farmers and communities across the Wairarapa region realized that the future prosperity of the region was very much dependent upon their own

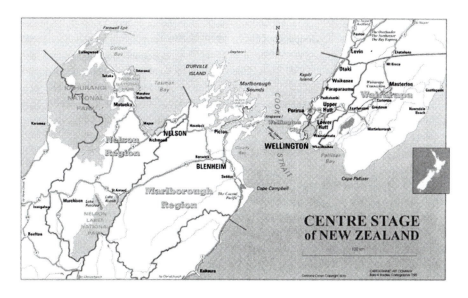

Figure 9.1: Wairarapa – part of the centre stage tourism macro-region,
New Zealand. (*Source*: Totally Wellington, 1999.)

ability and initiative. Emerging entrepreneurial spirit was stimulated by two opposite
forces: individual initiatives and government readjusted policies.

In Wairarapa, tourism has been seen as a means of regional rejuvenation in many rural
localities faced with the challenges of economic restructuring. Recent tourism development
has been associated with the emergence of wine growing as well as an increasing visitors'
demand for a country retreat in the regional pristine environment. The majority of businesses in the Wairarapa tourism industry are micro in size, and their orientation reflects the
region's farming background, particularly with respect to home-stay, farm-stay and nature-
based businesses. Intensive marketing of the region over the last six years has focused on its
proximity to the capital city, with the wine industry as a key product of the region.

Martinborough (Southern Wairarapa) is indeed a major draw for visitors to the Wairarapa
region. The area is becoming the fastest growing wine region in the country, increasing
from four vineyards first established in 1997–80 to 27 wineries by the end of 2000 (Tourism
Wairarapa, 2000). As a result, the area has become the heart of the regional tourism development (the managing director of economic development department, South Wairarapa
District Council, personal communication). According to the SWDC (South Wairarapa
District Council) (1998/9, p. 32), almost 100 new liquor licenses and 457 building consents
were issued and over 80 land use applications were considered in 1989–99.

Development of the institutional support for the increasing number of small businesses
in the region still lags behind entrepreneurial needs (the managing director of Wairarapa
RTO, personal communication). Currently there are two semi-public business development
organizations in the Wairarapa region. The MBE offers support for economic analysis,
facilitates joint venture partnerships, helps analyse investment opportunities, and builds
government relationships and immigration assistance. The South Wairarapa Enterprise

Board in Martinborough (SWEB), unlike the previous organization, has been specifically designed to encourage and provide assistance for local business initiatives. The support is mainly based on the information supply and upskilling programme for SMFs (SWEB's manager, personal communication). This form of the government support configuration in New Zealand was in fact shifted in 1996 from a purely grant-based system. The previous concept, it is argued, was not efficient and was based on a complicated formula often targeting those lacking any business ability and missing out the wider areas.

STFs and Regional Development

The majority of STFs were relatively new; over 50% were in operation for less than 4 years, which strongly reflects the regional economic (re)development introduced in the early 1990s followed by a growing institutional presence encouraged by public–private partnerships. Also, an increasingly proactive role of local communities, through various informal and formal actions, has been critical in supporting tourism development initiatives (the manager of the Wairarapa RTO, personal communication).

Most of the tourism businesses were characterized by being small in scale and scope, and by having operations and financial support revolving around family units. Financially, most ventures were based on personal assets such as family homes, farms, or savings, particularly in the start-up phase, whereas bank borrowing tended to be more important for financing subsequent product development. The average gross income was relatively low, in most cases below NZ$ 50,000.

The home-based accommodation sector accounted for over 60% of businesses with a turnover of under $30,000. Only 4.7% of businesses (e.g. motels, small hotels and restaurants) achieved a turnover of over NZ$ 500,000 per annum. However, the survey-based evidence shows that the vast majority of respondents (67.2%) increased business profitability between 1999 and 2001 suggesting a steady growth of tourism businesses turnover. Only 4.1% of the businesses suffered profit decline.

Many interviewees spoke of business opportunities, lack of employment and career prospects, the opportunity to change lifestyle (for a number of reasons), and meeting different people. Both the survey and in-depth interviews suggest that *changing economic conditions* (i.e. one income is not sufficient to support most families with children), *redundancy* and a *lack of job opportunities*, and the growing opportunities in *tourism* were the main reasons for many respondents to start their own business. The tourism business was often cited as an opportunity to generate additional income and diversify economic activities, mostly because the necessary assets for the proposed activity, such as land in a tourist location, farm or vineyard were already in place. 'Another egg in the basket' is an increasingly common practice by farmers across the Wairarapa region; at the time of the fieldwork, 16% of all tourism businesses were combined with farming or other activities. Winemakers also saw the tourism and hospitality component as increasingly valuable in their overall business activity.

Push and Pull factor-motivation concepts have been established to explain some of the main reasons for becoming involved in small tourism operation. The matrix presents individual factors in the context of different tourism activities (Table 9.1). While motivation is largely linked to the participants' characteristics, those characteristics that shape

Table 9.1: Push and pull factors.

Type of Business	Push Factors	Pull Factors
Home-based accommodation establishments: B&B, home-stays, farm-stays	Increasing monetary requirements; to be economically productive (desire to have own income – wife); lack of suitable jobs; self-fulfilment	Spare space (large house); low capital requirements to work at home; business opportunity to combine with family commitments; 'easy' made additional income; natural environment; to learn about other people
Commercial accommodation (e.g. motel, lodge)	Entrepreneurial challenge; corporate lifestyle; lack of career prospects; lack of particular education	Tourism seen as an opportunity to work with partner/spouse and employ family members; less structured lifestyle; natural environment, lack of experience or business knowledge
Restaurants/cafes, catering	Low pay for working long hours; to express more creativity; personal/family savings; language barriers to find suitable job	Opportunity to be well-off; to employ family members; to apply previous experience or cultural background (e.g. ethnic restaurants, arts and crafts shops)
Tourist attraction/ activities	Low level of job security and career prospects	Opportunity to make a living doing what one enjoys; often low level of capital required
Vineyards (tourism and hospitality part)	Increasing demand for the product	To add another egg to the basket (with a few additional costs overall profitability is increased); improves door selling and direct marketing; employment of family members

entrepreneurship in the small tourism sector are also inevitably created within a broader social-economic context. More detailed analysis shows that those factors reflected the past work experience and the skills and psychological disposition of the owner/manager toward entrepreneurial activity. In the broader picture, the social context of the family, educational and socio-economic backgrounds exert a strong influence over the prospective STF owner/manager. Another important issue concerning respondents was their geographical background. According to the survey, 16% of the respondents were originally from overseas, and over 40% from other parts of New Zealand.

Participants had followed a diverse range of career paths (e.g. farmers, builders, teachers, doctors) before entering the tourism industry. Farming activity was the most common occupation for operators in the Wairarapa region. Farming communities in the region have become increasingly entrepreneurial, combining both tourism and agriculture activities to remain economically sustainable.

One of the interesting features of the Wairarapa small tourism sector was the increasing participation by women (58.5%),[1] reflecting the region's strong farming tradition in which activity women are less involved, therefore have become proactive in creating their own employment by creating their own business in the tourism industry. According to the managing director of South Wairarapa Enterprise Board, Wairarapa women are crucial in the rapid growth of small businesses. Redundancy and a lack of job opportunities in Wairarapa also mostly affected women. Changing economic conditions mean that one income is not sufficient to support most families with children. The wife's part-time job (away from home) was seen as an extra source of income yet put more pressure on family life, particularly for families with small children. Therefore, a small tourism business (run from home) is seen as a solution to meet both extra income needs and family requirements. Tourism also provided a fitting context for women to meet their social and personal needs.

Regional Tourism Development: The Institutional Context

Obstacles and Supports for the Development of Small Tourism Firms

The study identified a number of perceived constraints to the growth of STFs and their success, as well as to regional socio-economic prosperity. The main concerns for owner/managers were competition, particularly from other small businesses (44.5%), labour costs (22%), lack of demand (36.7%), limited access to finance (16.6%), high operational costs associated with regulatory and financial obligations, followed by high interest rates, lack of skilled workers and larger businesses.

Government plays an active role in each of the issues above, either at the central or local level, in terms of policy development, legislation and regulatory compliance enforcement, or indirectly through setting social and economic market mechanisms and standards. Specific issues were identified, including changes to taxation, which incurred additional costs through external accountancy assistance, and the processes and cost of compliance, especially when conflicts with front-line staff were perceived to influence administrative efficiency. Increasing competition ('saturation') from growing numbers of new entrants was seen as the most influential factor affecting the performance of STFs. There were obvious tensions between part-time home-based accommodation providers and established businesses. The local authorities welcomed such a competitive environment as tourism development created new economic conditions and demand for premises in the second half of the 1990s.

Regulatory Requirements

There was almost a unanimous consensus amongst the interviewed owner/managers that the tourism sector could only be developed to its full potential with adequate public sector support and an appropriate infrastructure and a constructive regulatory and policy framework. Even

---

1. Such high participation by women might be misleading as many businesses were run by family.

so, many respondents stressed that an increasing number of regulatory compliances were not fully justified and were expensive. Some respondents regarded that much compliance as being inappropriate to the microenvironment and also regarded the administration process as similarly unfavourable to small business development.

Tourism operators argued that many policy advisors have a 'large business' concept because they have rarely or never worked for the small sector, or even in the private sector in general. The concept of the small sector is fundamentally different from the large sector. The operators believe that government compliances are not fairly imposed, creating hostility between commercial (which provide the main source of income) and non-commercial businesses (hobby, lifestyle enterprises). While 'commercial' businesses such as motels see an increasing number of home-based or casual lifestyle operations competing unfairly as they have few requirements to meet, the latter 'non commercial' group argues that they have far fewer resources to get to grips with government regulations.

Nature-based tourism enterprises that are required to gain resource consent from the Department of Conservation (DoC) to use natural resources raised similar issues related to scale. Many of these businesses differentiated their product according to demonstrated environmental values and argued that their small scale facilitated more sensitive environmental practices, yet also anticipated that these activities would translate into structural and administrative support.

External Support Structures: Enhancing Local Entrepreneurship

Despite the availability of a limited amount of government grants, only a few respondents received government financial support in the start-up phase. Those who tried to obtain it explained that the process was too complicated. The limited resources and expertise of some owner/managers highlighted differences in the expectations of administration and STFs. Other operators had lower expectations of support but raised further issues, as one of the owner/managers illustrates: 'I don't think one should expect much help from the government. You are in the industry to make money, but certainly local government needs to be more efficient in providing information'.

On the other hand, from the local government perspective, the level and availability of financial and other supports depends largely upon the industry's contribution to the local economy, although, as local authority representatives admitted, in other economic activities it is easier to calculate the spin-off. Obviously, other benefits (e.g. social) are not factored in as part of the equation. Local government representatives participating in the research had argued that a number of the owner/managers were still not aware of the changes (the economic reforms) or were not mentally adapted to the new situation and retain unrealistic expectations towards government support. As one of the participants commented:

> 'Most of these [local] people get into tourism for a hobby not as a serious business to depend on. However, once they start doing that they come to realise that, even on a small scale, it is complex and difficult to maintain and the return is far less than they expected. This could have huge negative impact on the region ... numerous entrepreneurs from overseas, particularly Europeans, tend to be faster in detecting opportunities in the tourism sector.'

Government support has, however, been more indirect in the form of creating better economic conditions by investing in various forms of both tangible and intangible infrastructure. One of the government initiatives in the early 2000s was a nationwide project aimed at lifting education and economic development in regional New Zealand, with the launch of high speed internet access. It is, according to the Economic Development Minister Jim Anderton,

> '... a critical infrastructure investment that will ensure students and families, businesspeople and workers will have the same opportunities, in education and in economic development, regardless of where they live and work. It will enable rural businesses to access quickly and efficiently all the resources and business information that's available on the internet. It means rural businesses will be able to tap into the same internet capability as businesses in the cities.'

The establishment of several eCentres across the region was a consequence of this initiative. These are public computer facilities (usually in schools), where people can get free access to equipment and tuition to gain computing skills.

On the regional/local level, government authorities offer an increasing range of services that include business training, events planning and promotion, tourism marketing, visitor information and booking services, inward investment opportunities and advice related to business retention in Wairarapa. These services are delivered by economic development (and tourism) agencies including Go Wairarapa (the regional tourism organization) and several local business enterprises from Masterton and Martinborough. The Wairarapa Regional Economic Development Strategy (2000–2007) clearly identified action steps that need to be taken to reverse regional economic decline. According to Kelvin Speirs, the Go Wairarapa General Manager, these actions are related to a holistic approach to regional development, specifically focusing on key sectors and the needs of individual members of the Wairarapa business community.

Management Training and Information. Personal interviews identified that STF owners are not always aware of the relevant policy changes in a newly elected government. However, those aware of the changes do not perceive much benefit to small firms; for example, shifting support from grants to training was not found very useful. These claims were best indicated by the low proportion of respondents using government-arranged training courses. Only the minority of STFs plan for training in any formal sense and learning approaches are not sequential and rational, but are developed and executed in an incremental trial-by-error manner.

The types of training were very diverse ranging from personal training management, ICT, small business management and marketing. The most common course completed, by owner/managers from all sectors was related to small business management and marketing – skills which appear to be essential in running a small business. Only one quarter (27.6%) of respondents were aware of the existence of free business advice services offered by various government agencies. Respondents indicated that marketing and promotion were their most pressing concerns, although these did not feature in the workshops provided. However, those using the services expressed problems with their pitch, content, and relevance to the STF environment.

Public–Private Sector Relationships: Tourism Organizations. As part of understanding the context within which SFTs operate, it is important to understand the organizations that support enterprises in the New Zealand tourism sector. The following section profiles the nature of STFs' relationships with public sector tourism organizations at national and regional levels.

Tourism New Zealand (TNZ). Tourism New Zealand is the National Tourism Organisation (NTO) responsible for promoting New Zealand overseas. One of the key messages emerging from the research was that operators would welcome a more proactive role by the agency in industry development activities at the local level. Over half of the respondents knew little or nothing about TNZ and its role, despite the fact that the establishment of the Tourism Marketing Network is supposed to develop more direct communication across the tourism industry.

The network operates through 12 units, based on particular products (e.g. wine, rural tourism farm-stay, adventure activities), with the goal being 'to find these little people and to get them working on international marketing, otherwise they are not able to do that as they lack resources and knowledge' (TNZ representative). From the STF perspective, a perceived absence of local involvement by the NTO contributed to feelings of alienation at the local level and a perception of the agency as 'distant' and encouraging unrealistic expectations. Small operators' demands centred on practical ('appropriate') help with, for example, information technology and website development.

Centre Stage Macro Region (CSMR). This CSMR marketing group (established in 1998 to integrate the central part of New Zealand into a single marketing entity) was unknown to the majority of operators. Only 7% of respondents, mainly those targeting international markets, were formally associated with the organization, which was commonly assumed to be part of the NTO. RTOs themselves raised a number of issues but most of all were concerned about the group marketing activities. In this context smaller members of CSMR did not receive adequate attention compared to larger ones. Indeed, tour operators and wholesalers, rather than local industry, are the key focus for the CSMR initiative through which it attempts to change the perception of the region and to reshape domestic air transport routes. Larger businesses are also more financially capable of supporting regional marketing and other activities.

Regional Tourism Organization (RTO). The local RTO (currently called Go Wairarapa) plays a vital role in tourism development in the region. A central role of the RTO is getting an increasing number of stakeholders to work together to ensure a common long-term goal, while at the same time avoiding conflict and the desire for short-term personal gain. In order to achieve this in the emerging tourism destination it required a great degree of entrepreneurial capacity.

Relationships with the RTO were perceived as the most significant institutional linkages across the STF sector. Equity and the distribution of resources were the main concerns of operators, particularly those in more remote locations with the most perceptions of unequal treatment between sectors or scales of operation. Relationships between STFs and the RTO were most commonly through Visitor Information Centres (VICs). More formal relationships with the RTO were generated through the payment of annual subscriptions, although few operators noted tangible benefits because booking fees and a presence in promotional material were additional costs. Compounded with perceptions of preferential treatment to high profile sectors (e.g. the wine industry) or larger operators, these were the core reasons behind the lack of STF support for collaborative marketing initiatives. Conversely, under-resourced RTO offices were often frustrated by demands from small operators who 'don't understand the structure of the industry and the dynamics of the market place' (an RTO representative). Further constraints to RTO initiatives are 'a groundswell of antipathy' towards tourism development, and jealousies between small communities over their respective tourism attention.

Local Networking: Barriers and Incentives for Tourism Development

Growing competition and a level of jealousy are clearly seen as barriers to more effective formal and informal interactions with the local institutions and organizations. Local authorities saw the proliferation of the local market groupings as potentially inconsistent with current RTO marketing initiatives. Marketing and promotion activities undertaken by local groups may undermine other marketing cooperations within the region. A competitive business attitude by individual operators was increasingly seen by the RTO as an obstacle to more constructive and comprehensive collaboration in the region. Given the composition of regional councils, these issues are sometimes transferred to the political realm and policies guiding the roles, resources and functions of the RTO.

However, competition or rivalry between small towns in Wairarapa has had a number of positive implications, such as raising awareness of local communities and increasing their participation in tourism development. Indeed, members of the Wairarapa communities are very active in a number of ways. For example, at the time of the research there were over a hundred volunteers participating in various tourism activities, such as organizing special events, tour guiding, etc. In fact, the region is made up of a number of local communities, each with its own local issues and aspirations. Regional organizations, such as the RTO, facilitate participation of local communities by developing strong linkages between each other.

Generally, as many 'outsiders' (originally from overseas and other parts of New Zealand) agreed, most of the communities across the region are very closed and conservative despite an increasing number of people with different cultural backgrounds. The following quote reflects their experiences:

> We have had both positive and negative experiences with the community. Some of them are very conservative and do not like changes. We had problems in getting resource consent. It was opposed by a few community members, despite our high level of environmental consciousness. We collect rainwater; we built our own water tanks and built our own septic system using the very latest technology.

Communities in the Wairarapa region were perceived as *open* for visitors and *closed* and conservative for new residents. On the other hand most of the *real local* respondents felt that investors from outside were mainly interested in a quick capital return. As one local respondent said:

> Cooperation in our community is not only important to improve business performance (to get more customers) but for the long run in community development and the direction that tourism takes. However, this is not the major concern of many of them especially those outside the local area.

Entrepreneurial Behaviour of Small Business Owner/Managers

Small business owners/managers demonstrated entrepreneurial abilities in different areas of business activities. In this context the STFs' managerial areas of planning, marketing, networking, ICT (information and telecommunication technology) and HR, which are crucial to the sector performance, are examined. A theme that runs through all of these areas and integrates them is informality of managerial style. Only 25% of the STFs surveyed had some kind of documented business plan. Decisions are normally made by one or two persons who tend to respond to sudden opportunities. As the small business owner makes a multitude of decisions almost on a daily basis, they are prevented from acting more strategically.

One of the areas where tourism operators demonstrated their entrepreneurial attitude was ICT. Small business owner/managers are taking advantage of ICT and have developed their own in-house 'research centre', incorporating marketing activities, extensive customer information, and analysis. The internet has been extensively used as a marketing tool, challenging many entrepreneurs to learn new skills including website design for their own business. In this regard, the owner/manager of an independent travel agency stated:

> Even though we have a presence on the internet through others, I'd like to have my own site. By doing so I will have control over it. That is the best way to learn things too and to be more confident and able to establish an effective communication with our customers.

It is fair to say that a lack of financial resources to delegating outside experts forces the entrepreneurs to adopt a learning-by-doing business strategy.

Small businesses put great effort in to marketing activities. Those surveyed used an extensive range of advertising tools. Lower-cost advertising approaches, such as publicities and direct marketing communication, were the preferred options and well suited to limited marketing budgets. Tourism operators competed successfully with modest advertising budgets by taking advantage of free promotions, as the owner of a luxury lodge explained:

> This industry has an advantage really, if you are good you can actually have a lot of free promotion ... when people come here we make sure they have a better time than they expected to have ... it's a lot cheaper to get someone back than to get new customers.

In order to overcome capacity problems during weekdays and off-peak periods, more 'entrepreneurial' operators tried to capture international markets either via the internet or by establishing business relations with NZ-based international wholesalers. These initiatives are often accompanied by in-house computerized databases indicating priority listings of their customers and their consumption behaviour. The following was stated by one of the respondents:

> Each year I keep a marketing/advertising folder and at the end of the year I analyse it. I select the most effective marketing tools and work out our budget. We also try new promotion tools every year.

Formal and informal networking has proven to be an effective way for STFs to compensate their intrinsic weaknesses and disadvantages. Apart from a number of formal arrangements with various tourism or business organizations, STFs tend to network through various informal occasions locally as well as nationally. In so doing they get more opportunity to discuss individual concerns, exchange valuable experiences, learn specific skills (e.g., workshops, conferences, training programmes) as well as lobby their interests to the government. For example, after long negotiation and a campaign coordinated by the Farm-/Home-stay Association, the Liquor Licensing Authority exempted these businesses from the obligation in 1999.

Informality in human resource management practice was the main issue for many according to both sources of empirical information. This approach, as the survey shows, was particularly dominant in the recruitment process. Word-of-mouth was by far the most important tool for recruiting staff (45.3%) as opposed to the Employment Service (11.5%).

In the Wairarapa region the lack of skilled or formally trained workers seems to have been compensated for by their good attitudes, as a restaurant owner/manager claimed:

> People from the region are not skilled, or experienced in the industry. The good side of that is when you have got somebody in you can train them the way you want and also that you get people who have not been exposed to the service industry. They bring a totally different feeling, and still get great satisfaction working in this environment ... you can rely on them always to get the job done in time. Satisfaction in working in the industry has been highlighted by a number of other participants, some of whom have extensive tourism and travel experience. They feel it is the biggest single aspect that New Zealand needs to concentrate on.

In order to overcome the seasonal nature of the tourism industry, Wairarapa STFs work collectively by establishing a database of potential employees prepared to work in the region.

In order to reduce the labour costs, adventure-oriented tourism businesses take advantage of many New Zealanders as well as international travellers who like outdoor activities. The owner of a diving operation explained that most of his employees are volunteers:

It is easy to get them any time. They want to get involved, to meet people. I provide the boat – they want to practise their diving skills. Not only do these volunteers reduce the labour cost but they are also an excellent distribution channel. I have some people to maintain the boats mechanically but I'm actually the only one employed for the diving.

Tourism Sustains the Local Economy

Small tourism firms are linked to a local/regional community via purchasing physical material (goods), business services and employment. The interviews clearly show that the price and the product/service quality (to some extent loyalty to social networking) dictate the nature and level of economic cooperation.

Up-market businesses are more mindful about the quality rather than the price of goods they purchase, therefore they developed a widespread network with local suppliers. For example, one manager of a successful business combining the accommodation and restaurant facilities described how they establish linkages with local suppliers:

> We have got more than a hundred local suppliers. They are mainly related to food and beverage. In fact we work with every single person in the area who has got top quality stuff; some supply us, for example, with tea, wine, chocolate, venison and so on. The main difficulty is delivery but our chef has developed a special system of drop off points in Wairarapa.

The attitude 'working for the community' was not always possible. In some of the remote areas lack of goods and service supply as well as the price level reduce the local interdependency as pointed out by one of the respondents from a remote village in Wairarapa: 'It is extremely difficult running a business in an isolated area. We normally get our supplies from the city as they are cheaper at the larger firms. We can't go to the local shops otherwise our profit dwindles considerably.' The Wairarapa's towns were bypassed by those capable enough to organize supplies from large centres such as Auckland and Wellington.

'Outsiders' Drive Regional Tourism Development

Entrepreneurs from overseas and outside the local areas, as the fieldwork suggests, contribute significantly to the quality of tourism products and services in Wairarapa. Often coming from Europe, bringing their savings, international market connections and a more professional business approach, these entrepreneurs tend to create innovative business models (at least in the New Zealand context). Most 'outsiders', particularly from overseas, also appeared to be more proactive. New product development, or incremental adjustment to existing products and services, and other innovative 'tweaking' create a competitive advantage over the 'local' orthodox business approach.

In contrast, local small business owner/managers tend to overvalue their 'knowledge' of the local environment and often overlook important changes such as market trends and dynamic visitor behaviour. Another significant association with this group is their willingness and ability to network with the specific external environment including local authorities and tourism-related organizations. Such an entrepreneurial dichotomy creates a healthy competitive environment in the regional tourism sector.

Private Sector Relationships – Financial Services

This section details the issues affecting STFs in their relationships with financial service providers in the private sector, notably banks and accountancy practices.

Banks

An important part of the STF business environment is the relationships developed with accountants and bank managers. Both the survey and personal interviews displayed relatively low levels of bank borrowing for business set-ups. Some 35% of the businesses introduced external capital during the study period, most commonly through banks in the form of commercial/personal loans or overdraft arrangements. All participants from the banking sector noted that the failure rate of small businesses in the first years of operation shaped lending policies, which commonly limited loans to 3–5 years. Interest rates were cited by owner/managers as barriers to development. Small businesses commonly pay higher interest rates than larger companies and borrowing was less negotiable.

Banks were increasingly prudent where loans were dependent on evidence (financial statements – cash flow, trading history) and consequently the tourism and hospitality industry, which was regarded as the least attractive sector for lending, accounted for only a small percentage of clients. Most STFs, particularly restaurants and cafes, were required to meet all lending criteria as well as higher levels of collateral. As one bank manager commented: 'We are not really keen in taking on cafes or restaurants. It involves a very high risk. We are looking at professionals such as lawyers, accountants, dentists – solo credential businesses/people; also manufacturing we regard as good.' Those owner/managers seeking financial facilities would have to fulfil strict borrowing criteria including a well-developed business plan, cash flow history and more often a full credit security.

Even if they were aware of the financial shortage, many entrepreneurs would still pursue further business. Indeed, undercapitalized STF owners often have a strong belief in the potential of their operation. They often have a *hunch* or are following their 'gut instinct' that success can be obtained only through risk. Overdrafts were the most popular form of borrowing as many STFs were heavily reliant upon short-term finance for their day-to-day operation. In an increasingly competitive financial sector, banks have become more proactive in relationships with their clients. They often recommended borrowing structures (e.g. family trust, mortgage, personal needs) and provided advice on how to bridge gaps in loan costs and how to manipulate money.

Accountants

Interviews with accountants suggest that there have been significant changes in recent years to their services. Most had moved away from pure accounting and compliance roles (e.g. tax returns) to providing assistance in marketing and business planning. Information technology

(IT) has had a considerable impact on the accountant–STF relationship. IT developments have enhanced the efficiency of communication and enables owner/managers to do much of the paperwork, significantly reducing fees for small firms. As one respondent noted: 'four or five years ago we had more paperwork, and we would charge on the basis of the amount of time and job.' Despite changes to the charging structure of advice, costs remained prohibitive for micro-STFs. Accountants also reiterated owners' concerns that, despite government claims, small businesses faced increased tax compliance costs.

Accountants were generally proactive in tracking small business concerns. As one respondent noted: 'before I would spend most of my time in the office, whereas now I spend half of my day outside the office, because I get a far better feel if I visit a particular business.' Sitting with small business owner/managers on a more regular basis certainly raises the question of the accountant's service charges that have traditionally been based on the amount of time spent with clients. Such commission structure, as it was argued by one of the accountants, often creates obstacles in the relationships with their clients, thus they prefer to have fixed annual fees. Besides finance, accountants have begun focusing on other aspects of small businesses, including business plan preparation, feasibility studies, valuations, marketing and management reporting, and monitoring business performance. There was agreement amongst the accountants interviewed that most STF owners spent excessive time 'running but not managing' the business, subsequently losing sense of direction.

Accountants have also become mediators between STFs and banks, contributing professional expertise which many managers lack. Finally, accountants have emerged as advisors in the day-to-day running of businesses as well as providing strategic decision-making for STFs. Few, however, claimed more than a superficial understanding of the tourism industry and its markets, and most had only limited experience in the tourism and hospitality sector.

Summary of the Findings

The overall political and economic changes particularly affected peripheral regions that were dominated by agricultural communities in New Zealand. Such geographic and economic isolation is a significant contextual dimension for STF studies that are also identified elsewhere, such as in Northern Ireland (Gillmor, 1998), Portugal (Lewis and Williams, 1998), Greece (Buhalis, 1999) and South Africa (Tassiopoulos and Nuntsu, 2005). Tourism development in these countries has for a long time suffered from uneven regional development as the government priority was given to selected and more accessible regions. New development policy initiatives have been designed to address these inequalities, with the tourism industry playing a leading role in regional development.

In the process of economic adjustment in New Zealand, the case of Wairarapa, which has only recently emerged in the gaze of international and domestic visitors, provides a fitting context to study regional tourism development. Regional tourism, dominated by small-scale business, might not generate that much direct employment and regional income, but it certainly reversed the negative trends related to the population decline, the demise of the main economic activities and social sluggishness.

Part of the regional income created directly from an increasing number of visitors (from 55,000 in 1996 to 320,000 in 1999) sustains many dwellings in Wairarapa. Tourism in the region is also seen as a source of entrepreneurial spirit demonstrated through innovative tourism products. Deregulation of the welfare state and the 'mean-lean' policy pushed many individuals in the region to perceive the increasing entrepreneurial opportunities in the steady growth of the tourism industry, underpinned by global trends and progressive market diversification. In Wairarapa, STF's resilience to economic change requires the ability to access a range of skills in management, production, strategic marketing, finance and law. In order to sustain their vulnerable businesses the owner/managers of STF are forced to learn fast. An important element of the Wairararapa STF's value lies in its flexible organizational structure, informal management style, and the regular and personalized interaction with the other stakeholders.

Generally speaking, small firms including those from the tourism sector have come to assume a strategic significance in the developmental aspirations of developed, transitional and developing economies, and their importance is reflected in various government initiatives: policy adjustment, grants schemes, training programmes, and research (OECD, 1999; Moulaert and Sekia, 2003). As the study shows, the capacity of governments to shape regional development outcomes was perceived as weak and indirect in Wairarapa.

While the central government considers the tourism industry as one of the main drivers of regional and national economic development, the support 'on the ground' remains, as perceived by many small business owner/managers, well below the political rhetoric. At the central government level the implementation of blanket policies for regulation and compliance often affects STFs adversely. These direct policy initiatives are part and parcel of a broader, more indirect, shift towards a more competitive financial environment. In times of financial uncertainty, financial institutions are reluctant to take risks and, increasingly, banks are wary of STFs.

Continuous tension between tourism entrepreneurs and the public sector appeared to have positive implications on the overall tourism development in Wairarapa. An increasing number of tourism operators put pressure on the local government to fully recognize tourism potential and constructively approach its development. However, as the study shows, government activities were more directed towards a constructive long-term sustainable tourism development reflected in different indirect forms of intervention: improvement of regional infrastructure, protection of the natural environment, establishment of institutional support for small business development, financial support for the RTO, support for special events (e.g. wine and food festival) and regional tourism publicity.

The transfer of power from the top to local government level, as a consequence of the comprehensive restructuring commenced in the mid-1980s, has major implications at the local level and for the small tourism sector where both public and private institutional infrastructure has become more complex and interconnected. A high degree of market liberalization has forced local authorities to become entrepreneurial, entering into various forms of partnerships with private sector, particularly large and profitable, businesses from different sectors.

A prudent set of the government regulations/compliances that most concern small business owner/managers seem to be justified by the quality of tourism product and a competitive advantage of the tourism destination as a whole. This was also agreed by a number of tourism entrepreneurs in the region. In addition, high expectation by small businesses for government to fulfil their needs often is not justifiable. Obviously those businesses owned and managed by committed and entrepreneurial individuals were less concerned with the government policy framework.

The study demonstrates that recent New Zealand immigrants appeared to be more mindful of the strategic business philosophy (see also Ateljevic, 2002). These entrepreneurs as opposed to the 'locals' have clearer business vision and expect less external help. Bringing new and innovative business ideas, fresh financial capital and their entrepreneurial spirit the 'outsiders' are regarded as important contributors to the regional tourism (economic) development.

Women in Wairarapa, as the study suggests, are certainly active participants in shaping the regional tourism industry. An increasing number of women across the region saw tourism as an opportunity to exhibit their creativity and commitment in order to improve their economic and social positions. This leads us to believe that women entrepreneurship in Wirarapa is more likely to emerge from the regional rural culture and long farming tradition.

Key Lessons from the New Zealand Experience – Theoretical Implications

It is clear from the example of Wairarapa that this reform in New Zealand represents a move from a traditional top-down approach to regional development towards a more pluralist model that involves numerous interactions between national regional actors and agencies. This partly reflects the regional development policies as a part of the broader process of the country's reform, where a shift has occurred in central governed policies from 'above' to 'below' in order to promote regional entrepreneurship and wide participation in regional development through a constructive public–private partnership. The present study shows how an increasing number of national, regional and local actors from both the public and private sector are interplaying in regional tourism development. In Wairarapa, for the three centres of local authorities, this shift has not been a straightforward process; a number of conflicting situations underpinned by local interests tended to undermine the overall regional well-being. Tourism seems to be a good agent to excavate these parochial attitudes on the one hand and galvanize key regional stakeholders on the other.

Although in the Wairarapa region both top-down and bottom-up approaches occur simultaneously, more credit for the regional rejuvenation goes to local forces including individual businesses, business associations and proactive local authorities. Indeed, central government has been more focused on a regulatory environment to meet free market requirements. Such interventions were perceived by many local entrepreneurs more as business barriers than constructive measures; small business owner/managers expecting an immediate result or investment return often do not see the big picture of the regional future prospect. In between the two, local authorities are obligated to serve the best interests of the local economy in an environment of volatile markets and shifting policy infrastructures. This situation has major implications on STFs and their owner/managers as broader development decisions are beyond their influence, thus, to a degree, undermining the key principles of the bottom-up approach.

The interests of STFs might be protected collectively through formal organization structures such as the local RTO. In order to solve local problems, Stohr et al. (2001)

suggests that '... government must be more decentralized and make increasing use of civil society and the private sector'. Wairarapa local authorities have learned this lesson; however, given limited financial resources, strategic alliances tend to be formed with a few large businesses in the region. In the context of tourism, this practice is increasingly exercised at the national level where national and macro-regional tourism organizations seek partnership with large businesses including airlines and international hotel chains while paying little attention to the country periphery.

In light of the above discussion the theoretical implications can be summarized in the following points: firstly, there is a strong link between entrepreneurship and the bottom-up approach. Secondly, tourism development provides an appropriate context that directly contributes to that link. Thirdly, the sector distinctiveness is reflected in its ability to stimulate broad cooperation and a collective entrepreneurship[2] in a given locality. Fourthly, the emerging shift in rural development policy from the top-down towards bottom-up approach is a long process that requires changes in the institutional structure, changes in competences between different administrative levels, and the adequate capacity of local actors to initiate and sustain the regional economic growth.

Policy Implications and Further Research

What makes insular regions such as Wairarapa more or less successful is an open-ended question. Further research is needed to identify common factors contributing to regional developments and subsequently to decide on possible theoretical as well as policy readjustments. What has become clear is that the rural Wiararapa has become part of a global–local nexus reflecting the process of globalization. The success of both the small tourism sector and the Wairarapa region at large depends on how well they respond to the changing circumstances. Wairarapa has emerged from a traditional rural area into a dynamic region not only because of its geography, which fits into the framework of 'new tourism', but also because of economic necessity that has pushed local communities to yield their entrepreneurial capabilities.

The structure of the local economy also played a part: the decline of one sector (farming), created room for another (tourism). This transition is very much in line with the Illeris' (1993) inductive theory of regional development. Yet, other elements underpinning this theory (e.g. recruitment of qualified staff, political conditions) do not seem to be part of the Wairarapa equation. Some commentators argue that a regional development bottom-up approach can leave things to chance. However, leaving things to chance is sometimes risky; therefore a top-down approach can be more certain in its outcomes. There may be a role for both approaches – one to let things happen and the other to make sure that certain things happen.

STFs are clearly an integral, dynamic and rapidly growing sector of the fragmented industry. Underlying all of the identified issues are the constraints of small scale and scope, the very qualities that contribute to the responsiveness and sectoral diversity of destinations as well as the spatial penetration of tourism for marginal economic areas. Transecting the tourism industry based on the common constraints of scale reveals a diversity of needs

---

2. The concept of the collective entrepreneurship is synonymous with entrepreneurial culture.

for policy prioritization, yet given their spatial and sectoral diversity STFs remain a considerable challenge for effective support delivery.

Policy coordination and integration are required across the breadth of government agencies either directly (e.g. regulation, compliance) or indirectly (e.g. interest rates, regional tourism marketing) involved in small firm development. Given that the small firm is by its very nature both multifaceted and relatively impotent politically, there is an imperative for research to demonstrate not only the issues affecting development within the sector but also the benefits that the sector contributes to the wider processes of regional economic development. Whilst there is evidence that small firms often carry a creative energy of product development and have the capacity to initiate development in marginal economic environments, more evidence is required which demonstrates the value of the sector to broader development initiatives. It is through this process that appropriate levels of policy attention and support can be directed to address the sort of issues identified here.

Questions for Discussion

1. Why is tourism an important agent for regional development?
2. To what extent does the Wairarapa case fit into the bottom-up theory?
3. What factors contribute to a continuous tension between tourism entrepreneurs and the public sector in Wairarapa?
4. What are the key lessons that the Wairarapa local authorities have learned from the case study?

References

De Montricher, N. (1995). L'Aménagement du Territoire. La Découverte, Paris.

SWDC (1999). *Annual Report 1998/1999*. Martinborough, Wairarapa: South Wairarapa City Council.

Chapter 10

Entrepreneurial Wildlife Exploitation in Sub-Saharan Africa: An Overview

Peter Rosa and Patricia Joubert

Learning Outcomes

After reading this chapter, you should be able to:

- Comprehend the history and state of conservation of wildlife areas in sub-Saharan Africa;

- Identify and understand entrepreneurial opportunities of the African wildlife;

- Understand the dual role of tourism in terms of the protection and commercialization of African wildlife resources;

- Identify the main obstacles to local communities benefiting more from wildlife resources;

- Understand the nature of the impact of the media industry on the African wildlife; and

- Understand the role of international organizations and institutions in protecting the African wilderness.

Introduction

> The [African] plains are alive with droves of strange and beautiful animals whose like is not known elsewhere ... it is an never ending pleasure to gaze at the great herds of buck as they move to and fro in their myriads; as they stand for their noontide rest in the quivering heat haze; as the long files come down to drink at the watering places; as they feed and fight and rest and make love. There are no words that can tell the hidden spirit of the wilderness, that can reveal its melancholy and its charm.
>
> (Theodore Roosevelt, 1910, p. ix)

> Not another bloody elephant. Lets head for the bar.
>
> (Ex-patriate Company Director, to the author on visiting Tsavo National Park)

The African wilderness and its wildlife have inspired contrasting reactions over the years. There are those who see the African wilderness as a kind of garden of Eden (Akama, 1999, p. 13), a living artistic landscape full of wonderful plants and animals. They view it as a precious heritage, to be carefully preserved for future generations. Our television companies offer us a diversity of African wildlife programmes featuring cute elephants, lions, cheetahs, leopards and meerkats. Africa's wildlife, we are constantly reminded, is a vulnerable heritage, constantly under threat from greedy entrepreneurs and politicians who wish to gain undeserved profits from what has taken nature thousands of years to evolve.

It is a landscape being degraded by a rapidly increasing population, who need more and more land to live on, and who create unsustainable demands on wilderness resources. Our newspapers regularly contain images of elephant carcasses without tusks or rhinoceroses without horns; of forest areas being deforested by fire; of monster trucks with large irreplaceable rainforest logs driving past bemused indigenous hunters, such as pygmies, who need the forest to survive; of dead gorillas on sale in West African markets for meat; of eroded dustbowls that were once pristine woodland; or of dams and irrigation schemes bringing in industrialization and pollution. Hardly a wildlife programme is made without some reference to the animal or wilderness area in question disappearing soon unless severe action is taken.

Many people, however, see the wilderness and its wildlife as a resource to be exploited. If there is a profit to be made out of wildlife, why not take it? In any case, if the opportunity is not taken now, someone else will take it in the future. African politicians face high expectations from their people, who are desperate for more economic development, the eradication of poverty, and the creation of jobs. For most politicians the land is primarily there to sustain livelihoods and contribute to GDP. Wilderness set aside for what many would regard as the aesthetic indulgence of westerners is a luxury that poor nations cannot afford. The wilderness needs to pay its way; otherwise it will be converted to other uses. Conversion of wilderness to farmland, for example, is especially attractive when it provides sustainable food production and cash crops. Wildlife is usually incompatible with this, and its destruction provides a short-term bonanza while the wilderness is being converted.

Once wildlife is eliminated farming becomes easier and more profitable. Where an area of wilderness contains some advantages for specialist intensive agriculture, agribusiness tends to have a clear priority. For example in Kenya, large areas of the Narok District bordering the famous Masai Mara Game reserve were found to be ideal for wheat production and in the 1960s the land, hitherto rich in wildlife, was cleared. Today in Uganda, large wild areas of Northern Uganda are being gazetted to grow sugar cane to convert to bio-fuels. Only in areas where wildlife has a chance to pay its way, and its preservation does not entail high opportunity costs, is its presence welcome. In this context mass wildlife tourism has provided a welcome source of foreign exchange, justifying the setting aside of national parks and game reserves.

The maximization of wilderness resources is thus an unsentimental aim of most African governments and this process often conflicts with conservation. Business leaders, entrepreneurs and multinationals from outside Africa often take a pragmatic view of wilderness exploitation, and provide the inspiration and capital for new exploitative projects. What of indigenous African people themselves, who actually live in or close to wilderness areas and wildlife? The Swahili word for wildlife is 'nyama' or meat. Traditionally wildlife has been a source of protein for large numbers of Africans and is naturally viewed as food.

It is also a nuisance, with a host of potential crop predators from monkeys to elephants ready to pillage a family's growing food supply and cash crops. It is also a source of danger, with people killed or maimed by wild beasts throughout Africa.[1] Where conservation laws are actually enforced, it is a source of resentment. This is particularly so when people have been trans-located from their original homes to free wildlife areas from people. Overall many African people would view conservation as a problem of development, and largely irrelevant to their lives.

Some Africans would go further than this, and view conservation as a direct threat to their jobs and livelihood. There is a surprising number of conservation 'martyrs' in Africa who have been killed because their conservation campaigns have conflicted with the economic interests of some local people. These include Dian Fossey whose conservation of gorillas provoked a local Rwandan poacher to murder her on Boxing Day, 1985; George Adamson, who was shot when fearlessly combating local Somali poachers in the Kora Game Reserve in August 1989; and Joan Root, a wildlife film maker, whose vigorous campaign to preserve the wildlife of Lake Naivasha in Kenya provoked a fatal raid on her house by assassins who shot her in her bed in January 2006. In the case of Joan Root it appears local people feared that her campaign would compromise the cut flower industry which had grown around the lake, and cost them their jobs.[2]

The modern conservation movement in Africa owes a great debt to individuals such as these, but there are also powerful and proactive institutional lobbies stressing on African

Figure 10.1: Former goat killer trapped and tamed: Nairobi. (*Source*: author.)

---

1. Between August 2002 and April 2004 a man-eating lion killed 35 people and injured at least nine in a 350 sq. km area along the Rufiji River. The most frequent method of attack was by the lion forcing its way through the mud wall or the thatched roof of a hut, and then seizing a person and leaving by the same way. This is one example of hundreds of deaths a year caused by wildlife including elephants, buffalos, lions, leopards, hippos and crocodiles. (www.ippmedia.com/ipp/guardian/2006/08/28/73305.html)
2. www.telegraph.co.uk/news/obituaries/1507979/Joan-Root.html

leaders the need to conserve wilderness and wildlife in Africa. In recent years the areas protected by African governments through gazetting national parks and game reserves has been increasing, largely as a result of pressure from external organizations such as the EU, IUCN, UNESCO, the WWF and western governments. The governments of nearly all sub-Saharan African countries have signed up to the IUCN and UNESCO principles.

Large areas of wilderness have been set aside as national parks of wildlife reserves. By 1980 over 90 national parks or wildlife areas had been created, covering over 250,000 square miles (Parker and Amin, 1983, p. 152), and this number has increased considerably since then. In Kenya alone, for example, there are now 55 national parks and wildlife reserves compared to 38 in 1980 (Williams, 1981), covering some, 8% of the land area (Okello and Kiringe, 2004, p. 55). Tanzania has 15 national parks compared with seven in 1980 but, when game reserves and other protected areas are included, the total is 28. This includes the Selous ecosystem which, at 81,000 sq. km, is Africa's largest game reserve complex (Blanc et al., 2007, p. 102) – twice the size of the Netherlands and a third of the size of the United Kingdom. Overall 27% of Tanzania's land area is gazetted either as a national park, game reserve or national forest, with people prohibited or severely restricted from settling or grazing animals in these areas (Brockington, 2005, p. 7).

Even in West Africa, not renown for its wildlife, there are over 90 national parks and protected areas. In Gabon alone, President Omar Bongo Ondimba created 12 new national parks in 2002 following favourable publicity on the unique wildlife of the area. The total area now covered by national parks and protected wilderness areas in Africa conservatively exceeds 1 million sq. km, and many of these parks are also surrounded by very large areas of a gazetted wilderness, with low population densities. The total area of protected wilderness is greater than the Roman Empire of Trajan.

The need to protect the wilderness has been strengthened by the system of World Heritage sites established under the 'convention concerning the Protection of the World Cultural and Natural Heritage adopted by the General Conference of UNESCO at its 17th session on 16 November 1972'.[3] The convention stresses two important principles: firstly, the fact that there are wilderness or cultural sites that are of worldwide interest and importance, not just to the inhabitants of the countries in which the sites are located; and, secondly, that it is the duty of people today to preserve these sites for future generations. A World Heritage site once designated can no longer be just regarded as a resource to be exploited commercially. Governments have a responsibility to conserve it and manage it properly. The list of World Heritage sites is growing, and since the 1980s includes a number of African national parks.[4] Each site receives focused conservation advice and even funding from UNESCO.

While increasingly honouring international commitments to preserve wilderness areas, African governments face pressures from their own people whose immediate interests are probably much better served by taming the wilderness, as Europeans and North Americans have done. In so doing they open up protected land for the commercialization of wildlife products, attain new land for agriculture and settlement, and increase their economic and

---

3. whc.unesco.org/en/comittee/
4. See whc.unesco.org/en/list

personal security by eliminating game which would otherwise prey on them, raid their crops or provide reservoirs of disease that could attack their livestock. This conflict of interest is increasing as Africans become more numerous and consumer orientated. There are in essence conflicting sets of entrepreneurial opportunities on how wildlife and wilderness areas should be exploited.

Theoretical Issues

The economic theory of 'consumptive wildlife utilization' treats wildlife as a kind of commodity that can be 'consumed' for various raw materials such as meat, oil, fur, hides, feathers and bones. Where there is no ownership of such resources, no protection or regulation, large profits can be made by wildlife entrepreneurs, especially when advances in technology reduce the problems and costs of harvesting and transport. Following a period of bonanza, stocks soon dwindle, often leading to the commercial extinction of species. While a species is abundant, high prices occur if it is difficult to harvest or process. If technology overcomes these difficulties, then it is possible to kill animals in large quantities. Being able to harvest more animal units, hence maintaining profitability, offsets the decrease in price per unit. Prices increase as the resource becomes scarce through overexploitation. This encourages even more intensive hunting, leading to commercial extinction or, in extreme cases, the disappearance of the whole species (Roth and Mertz, 1996; Macgregor et al., 2004). With their disappearance, attention turns to alternative species and new markets grow. The cycle is repeated. In time the whole wilderness will be irretrievably degraded.

Open commercial access contains no incentive for sustaining the wildlife resource (MacGregor et al., 2004). Faced with rapid depletion of stocks, conservation through legal protection has been the traditional answer. Conservation of resources reduces open access to wildlife exploitation and theoretically should lead to a reversal in the decline of

Figure 10.2: Cow killed by lions in Kenya: an expensive loss. (*Source*: author.)

wildlife stocks, and eventually to a sustained increase in numbers. Unfortunately conservation requires not only an effective system of laws, but that they should be accepted by interested stakeholders, and effectively implemented and enforced. Legal protection just does not work without all three conditions being satisfied.

Legal protection which is imposed on local people, for example, leads to resentment and little will to comply. If protection is ignored, and not enforced, it becomes little more than a form of open access to wildlife exploitation. Indeed it could be worse, as open exploitation in this form is illegal, and hence what is poached is not monitored. This can lead to even faster depletion of wildlife stocks than legal commercialization. Enforcement of the law tends to be expensive, and not easily justifiable when governments are faced with multiple demands for limited revenue resources. It has only worked either when most people are behind the laws (hence only a small number of criminal poachers have to be dealt with), or when the enforcement of the law is draconian (as was the case, for example, in some royal medieval hunting reserves in Europe, when poachers faced extreme penalties).[5]

The need to provide incentives to local people to preserve wildlife is being increasingly acknowledged. 'Consumptive' strategies (i.e. those based on the killing of wildlife for products) need to provide mechanisms where local people can benefit economically from the killing of their wildlife, either for local consumption or for profit, but in a way that is sustainable. One method for achieving this is to transfer ownership of the wildlife to individuals or cooperatives and let them develop systems for accessing markets and for sustainably harvesting their wildlife. This requires laws permitting individual ownership of wildlife at the macro level, and laws permitting the sale of wildlife products. A second method is to retain government ownership of wildlife, but to allow access by wildlife entrepreneurs to exploit a sustainable harvest of wildlife. This can be achieved by quotas, or permit systems, with special priority being given to local people (Macgregor et al., 2004).

There are also 'non-consumptive' strategies for conserving wildlife, where the wildlife is not killed, but exploited in other ways such as tourism or wildlife film-making. This requires transferring rights to exploit these markets, including concessions and leases for accommodation facilities and game viewing, and retail facilities for selling local produce and handicrafts. How far local people benefit from these activities is a crucial dimension to the conservation of the wilderness and its wildlife. It is also possible to combine both consumptive and non-consumptive strategies for economically exploiting the wildlife of an area. This usually requires some separation between areas used for tourism and those used for direct harvesting of wildlife.

The theories of wildlife conservation have mainly been associated with neoclassical economics, where economic laws of demand and supply account for the way economic resources are allocated, and the economy is assumed to be in equilibrium. There is little room for the entrepreneur in this type of theory. In practice, however, the real world is not in perfect equilibrium, nor does it operate with perfect information or competition. Hence entrepreneurship theory does have a place, potentially adding new dimensions and insights

---

5. www.smr.herefordshire.gov.uk/education/Medieval_Countryside.htm states that 'Medieval law stipulated that a poacher could have a hand chopped off, be blinded or have his testicles severed'.

to supplement those of neoclassical environmental economic theories. In the context of wildlife and wilderness resources, knowledge of these resources, and the commercial opportunities they represent, is unevenly distributed.

Kirzner (1973, 1984) predicts, for example, that successful entrepreneurs are those with superior alertness and knowledge who see opportunities where others do not. In a global economy, the markets for wildlife products and services are varied, and require specialist knowledge to not only see the opportunity, but to know how to exploit it. Faced with local wildlife, a local African will see quite different opportunities than, say, a European or Chinese entrepreneur. It is not just a question of rationally weighing up which opportunity will pay best based on supply and demand. It is a complex interaction of opportunities in which most potential entrepreneurs do not have the awareness or information to make optimum choices. There are in fact different value systems that vary across cultures (Barth, 1967), which only certain entrepreneurs can bridge. In the domain of wildlife exploitation, several distinct spheres of values can be identified. These include:

a) Traditional tribal values in which the relationship between animals and people is symbolic. Many tribal clans, for example, have associations with particular animals, and this in turn can influence the way particular species are treated.

b) Traditional subsistence values in which wild animals traditionally have no commercial value (as in most pre-Colonial societies there was no money). Rather they were seen as a source of food, and of materials for making key artefacts. In Kenya, for example, peoples such as the Kamba and Lliangulo, who relied on hunting for meat, killed giraffe for their tendons, which were made into bowstrings.[6]

c) Values hostile to the presence of wildlife, which is seen as a danger to humans and a source of predation on crops and livestock. This is deeply ingrained in European rural areas, for instance, where any damaging wildlife is treated as vermin.

d) Economic enterprising values where animals are viewed as commodities to be killed and sold. This is a capitalist phenomenon, where profit and free enterprise are dominant factors.

e) Farming values where wild animals are regarded as forms of livestock to be managed, farmed and harvested.

f) Pragmatic conservation values, where wild animals are viewed as a scarce and valuable resource which will disappear quickly unless properly managed. This system stresses the need for protection, and the desirability of developing sustainable commercial uses to preserve stocks and habitats. These conservationists dislike the killing of wildlife, but are prepared to condone it in the interests of preserving habitats and species.

g) Idealistic conservationist values, which see wildlife and wild places as precious and irreplaceable. Wildlife is not a resource but fellow creatures which have a right to live undisturbed from the exploitation and predation of people. Killing is wrong under any circumstances. When problems occur they should be left to nature to sort out. The duty of people is to provide strict protection so that wildlife and their habitats can continue to exist harmoniously and undisturbed.

---

6. Strings for powerful bows are very difficult to make from vegetable fibres.

It is evident from this list that theoretically there is a large difference between traditional values such as (a) and (b), enterprising values such as (d) and (e), and modern conservation values (f) and (g). In the context of African wildlife, local rural Africans have values predominantly located in spheres (a), (b), (c) and a bit of (d); but conservationist attitudes are almost lacking. It is westerners, however, that predominantly hold conservation values. There is thus considerable asymmetry in opportunity awareness, know-how and capital between western-driven forms of wildlife exploitation and those of indigenous Africans.

This chapter examines various ways in which both Africans and non-Africans have exploited wildlife in Africa from both a consumptive and non-consumptive basis. It demonstrates the existence of a dual economy in wildlife: one based on consumptive exploitation dominated by poaching and the sale of products from the dead animals, the other based on non-consumptive exploitation dominated by tourism and wildlife film-making. The abilities of local Africans to engage with these opportunities differ markedly.

Consumptive Exploitation of African Wildlife

Mass Exploitation and Protection in the Imperial and Colonial Eras

During the latter decades of the nineteenth century European explorers and travellers opened up large areas of wilderness in the Americas, Australia and Africa. These vast regions contained a wealth of wildlife, which provided food and material resources for local tribal peoples, who lacked the technology or incentives to make much of an impact on their local wildlife. This sustainable utilization of wildlife resources came to an abrupt end as explorers of European origin opened up the wilderness and were followed by adventurers, entrepreneurs and settlers. They were able to take advantage of advances in firearm technology and of access to industrial markets to commit wholesale extermination of wildlife in the newly annexed territories.

The most famous slaughter of wildlife took place on the American prairies. According to the American Bison Society[7] an estimated 25–30 million bison in the eighteenth century were reduced to less than 2000 by the late 1880s. Between 1871 and 1975 alone, 4 million were killed and over 1 million hides (worth $3 each) were shipped from Dodge City. By 1990 not only buffalo but also buffalo hunters and traders had disappeared. In another example, in the late nineteenth and early twentieth century millions of Koala bear in Australia were killed for their fur and almost became extinct (Australia Koala Foundation).[8]

In South Africa, the only part of sub-Saharan Africa in European control in the mid-nineteenth century, the trend was similar. At the same time as American Bison were being shot out in their millions, huge herds of elephant, buffalo, blesbok, bontebok, zebra and white wildebeest in South Africa were reduced to remnant populations. The demise of the southern white rhino is particularly instructive. It was abundant in South Africa and

---

7. www.americanbisonsocietyonline.org
8. www.savethekoala.com

modern Zimbabwe until the mid-nineteenth century, when it attracted the attention of commercial hunters (mostly white) for its hide and horns. The first IUCN Red Data Book on endangered species noted that 'one trader supplied firearms to more than 400 natives to hunt rhinos on his behalf' (Fisher et al., 1969, p. 118). By 1900 a handful of survivors remained in Natal.

The opening up of Central and East Africa in the late nineteenth century provided unique opportunities for commercial elephant hunters. There were countless herds of elephants in millions of square kilometres of savannah and forest that had never seen or heard a modern rifle and who, virtually undisturbed, contained large numbers of tuskers with very heavy ivory.

A Scotsman, William 'Karamoja' Bell, an intrepid but literary hunter entrepreneur, described extensive hunting expeditions to areas of Uganda and the Sudan in the early twentieth century – areas that had not yet been brought into colonial administration. He shot hundreds of elephant, all with prime ivory, and was able to buy a Scottish estate with his profits (Bell, 1923). He was an entrepreneur with a canny appreciation of risk. He tended to target little explored areas of Africa, with fearsome reputations, to hunt elephants in. Experience had taught him that such areas were less dangerous than their reputation, but full of elephants with very heavy ivory, who had never been shot at before. He was but one of a host of white hunters who found unrestricted elephant hunting lucrative at that time. Few indigenous Africans in this period had access to the capital, technology or knowledge of markets to participate in this mass exploitation of elephants.

The years of colonial administration saw a dual policy develop between the protection of wildlife, and its control when it conflicted with the interests of farmers and local Africans.

A series of international conventions from 1890 to the 1930s led to a series of conservation measures (Parker and Amin, 1983, pp. 123–4), involving the restriction of firearms for local Africans, the legislation of game laws protecting certain species and the shooting of females of valuable species, and the creation of game reserves. By the First World War these measures had effectively stopped the mass unregulated commercial exploitation of elephants and other herbivores by white hunter entrepreneurs.[9]

The measures created a network of game reserves which grew into modern famous national parks, such as the Dinder National Park in the Sudan (1935); the Garamba National Park in the Congo (1938); Tsavo National Park in Kenya (1948); the Mt Kenya National Park (1949); The Murchison Falls National Park in Uganda (1952); and the 'W' Park Niger in (1953). At the same time game was ruthlessly shot out where it conflicted with people. In a famous incident, the Kenya colonial government in the 1940s sanctioned the elimination of black rhino from the Makueni district, occupied by the Kamba tribe, to make more land available for resettlement. John Hunter, a Scottish white hunter, shot over 163 in three months and in a series of follow-up hunts killed over a thousand. He wrote 'is it worth killing off these strange and marvellous animals just to clear a few more acres for people that are on the increase?' (Hunter, 1952, p. 175). This is a very 'Western' view.

---

9. A hard core of hunter/poachers remained until the First World War, who plied their trade in the Belgian Congo. They were not prosecuted by the British who actually encouraged this trade as long as elephants were not killed on British territory (Parker and Amin, 1983, p. 107). The dangers of arrest or even being shot (Bell, 1923) kept white poaching to levels low enough not to damage the overall stock of elephants.

The protection of wildlife during the colonial period was motivated less by idealism and more by the need to protect the stock of game for the dominant aristocratic sport of the time: big game hunting. Many African countries were able to attract very rich celebrities, such as President Theodore Roosevelt, the Prince of Wales and the Duchess of York, to go on big game hunting safaris. This developed into a major industry in Kenya, where over 350 professional white hunters had access to some 80% of the country's wildlife areas through a system of hunting blocks (Parker and Amin, 1983).

Illegal Exploitation of African Wildlife by Hunter Entrepreneurs and Traders in the Post-colonial Era

The wildlife policies of the colonial period directly prevented mass exploitation of wildlife by white hunter entrepreneurs through regulation and indirectly deprived local African hunter entrepreneurs the means and incentives to kill valuable game *en masse* by controlling the possession of modern firearms and monopolizing markets for wildlife products. Thus, at independence, most sub-Saharan former colonial countries still had plentiful numbers of valuable wildlife species such as leopards, elephants and rhinoceros.[10] As new global markets developed for ivory and rhino horn in the Middle and Far East, so did the means to exploit these on a large scale. The escalation of the Cold War saw the sale of thousands of semi-automatic AFK rifles to Africa, and political instability in some countries removed even a pretence of protection. Instability not only allowed more elephants and rhino to be shot without risk of arrest but, more importantly, allowed rules governing the trade of wildlife products to be relaxed. Burundi, for example, which has no rhino, became a leading exporter of rhino horns in the 1980s, no questions asked.

The slaughter of the 40–100,000 black rhino and 4–8000 northern white rhino reputed to inhabit Africa in the 1960s began in earnest in the 1970s. So did the killing of Africa's then reputed population of up to 2 million elephants. By the early 1980s the slaughter had been so great that the total black rhino population had been reduced to less than 5000. By the end of the 1990s the last large poorly protected population in Zambia and Zimbabwe had been reduced to low numbers. Today there are less than 3000, mostly in South Africa and Namibia. The 1000 or so white rhino of Garamba National Park in the 1960s were reduced to nine by 2002 and are thought to have completely gone since the recent troubles in the Democratic Republic of the Congo erupted in the early 2000s.

Elephant numbers have declined sharply – to less than a third of the numbers in 1980 – currently estimated at around 750,000 for the whole continent (Blanc et al., 2007). In most African countries elephant ranges have been greatly reduced and in many west and central African countries their numbers are very low; many populations are on the edge of viability. The total ban on the Ivory trade in 1989 has seen numbers recover slightly in some countries, but prices are rising again in China. In a recent article Wasser reports that Chinese demand for ivory is driving the black market where the material sells for $750 per kilogram, up from $100 in 1989 and $200 in 2004. The high prices have attracted organized crime, which runs sophisticated trafficking networks (Wasser, 2007).

---

10. i.e. where there natural range occurred. Rhino did not occur in West Africa.

Additionally, the market for other species is also increasing rapidly. There is a growing underground demand for exotic pets (reptiles and birds). A market has developed in China for bones of large cats such as leopards and lions. There has been an explosion of demand for bush meat of all types, especially in West Africa. Despite being illegal, bush meat is openly on sale in most European cities where Africans are present in any numbers. The stock of ungulates has diminished considerably in West Africa, where the bulk of the trade has taken place. The Niokola Koba National Park, for example, in Senegal, has lost over 90% of its herbivores in the last 10 years (Table 10.1). In East Africa too there has been considerable attrition of herbivores. Table 10.2 shows that though elephants registered their greatest loss in the years before 1980, when Idi Amin was in power, herbivore numbers crashed between 1980 and 1995, when the country was recovering from insecurity and tyranny following the removal from power of Idi Amin.

The slaughter of wildlife in the last 30 years is *de facto* a continuation of the nineteenth century 'open access' trends, except that it is now black rather than white hunter entrepreneurs and traders who are doing most of the killing. Most of the wildlife has disappeared in countries where wildlife laws and conservation measures have been in place but not enforced. The killing has been technically illegal, but condoned by authorities. This has benefited a large network of entrepreneurs, while still permitting African governments to claim that they are complying with their international conservation commitments. Entrepreneurs include local hunters, who are recruited to actually kill the game, local traders who collect the products and sell them on to global traders, and middlemen who derive the main share of the profits. Politicians and other African leaders also gain a share by protecting the poachers and traders from legal prosecution.

Kenya provides an example of this set-up. It banned hunting in 1977, but this was followed by a wholesale slaughter of rhino and elephants. The ban on hunting was necessary to eliminate monitoring by big game safari hunters who until that time regularly took clients to most parts of Kenya where wildlife flourished. The illegality of poaching

Figure 10.3: Poached elephant carcass: Kibwezi, Kenya. (*Source*: author.)

was reinforced by the ban, whilst enforcement of the ban was, in practice, totally relaxed. There was in essence a substitution of entrepreneurs: of white hunters by black poachers and traders.

From a conservation perspective, the widespread slaughter of wildlife in sub-Saharan Africa was, and indeed is, a tragedy, but in terms of resource utilization and opportunity, the picture is more complex. African leaders regarded wildlife as a resource to be utilized. It was a large resource, which appeared to be benefiting few people, and certainly not local people. It was also an impediment to rural development, which stopped many local people expanding into new land, and made existing land more difficult to farm. It needed drastic culling. (Would a Western developed country regard it as desirable or politically sustainable to allow three quarters of its land area to be roamed by elephants, rhino and predators?)

The politicians effectively allocated concessions for entrepreneurs to harvest this surplus. Everyone who participated did well out of it, even poor local people who provided hunters on the ground. Non-hunters gained new land when wildlife had been cleared. Even those politicians who gained large profits often gave much of it back by investing the profits in development projects within their local constituencies or in new more conventional business enterprises which generated jobs. Like most commercial forms of entrepreneurship, the lead entrepreneurs gained the most benefit, but there was also a considerable trickle down effect.

Sustainable Legal Wildlife Exploitation: The Growing Role of the Private Sector

The precondition for sustainable wildlife exploitation is protection. National parks and game reserves do provide legal protection, but this, as just discussed, is only effectively enforced in a relatively small percentage of the land technically legally protected. The public sector through national ownership owns most of the wildlife resources in sub-Saharan Africa, but on the whole has proved to be an inefficient and even reluctant custodian of the thousands of square kilometres of wilderness resources under its charge. Revenues from park fees are low, except for a small number of frequently visited parks. Hence there is little money to pay for an efficient ranger service and there are few rangers to protect park animals. In many parts of Africa the skeleton staff are not paid much, or

Figure 10.4: Zebra poached for its skin: Kitengela Plains, Kenya. (*Source*: author.)

Table 10.1: Depletion of game stocks in Niokola Koba National Park, Senegal.

Species	Population 1990/91	Population 2006	% change 1990–2006
Hartebeest	5000	149	− 97%
Buffalo	8000	457	− 94%
Kob	24,000	92	− 99%
Waterbuck	3300	10	− 99%
Giant Eland	150 (max)	171	+ 14%
Roan antelope	6000	710	− 88%
Elephant	30 (max)	10 (max)	− 66%

Source: Howard et al. (2007).

sometimes not paid at all for long periods. These circumstances breed corruption and staff will be tempted to participate in poaching themselves, or to turn a blind eye. A road engineer in Uganda told me over a drink in 2005 that when in Kenya in the 1980s, he would bribe park officials to allow him to hunt game within the boundaries of a famous game reserve.

The private sector is arguably a more efficient way to utilize wildlife resources and exploit wildlife sustainably. Since the 1970s there has been a growing trend to establish private game reserves, usually sited at the borders of large state-owned national parks. This has been particularly developed in South Africa; for example there are over 30 private game reserves surrounding the Kruger National Park alone. They provide a lucrative buffer zone between the park and farmers, and much greater choice on how the wildlife and the wilderness can be exploited.

An example of the differences between public and private sector managed national parks can be found in Senegal. The largest state run national park, Niokola Koba, is listed as a world heritage site and was established to protect rare West African subspecies of eland, roan antelope and giraffe. Since the 1980s, large mammal populations have fallen by over 90%. Giraffes have disappeared and elephants were down to less than 10 (Howard et al., 2007). This conservation record is in direct contrast to Bandia National Park, a small private game reserve 30 kms from Dakar, the capital of Senegal. Bandia was gazetted as

Table 10.2: Depletion of game stocks in Murchison Falls National Park, Uganda.

Species	Population 1969	Population 1980	Population 1995
Elephant	14,500	1420	201
Buffalo	26,484	15,250	1087
Hartebeest	16,234	14,000	3068
Uganda Kob	?	30,700	6355
Waterbuck	?	5500	539

Source: Mann (1995).

a private reserve in the early 2000s and contains an impressive list of large mammal species, including giraffe, rhinoceros and Western Derby Eland. The animals are increasing and making a profit for the owners. Bandia, however, is unlikely to attract world heritage status, as the fauna is introduced, much of it from East and South Africa: there is nothing much that is locally distinctive about its fauna.

Related to private game reserves are game ranches, where core ranching of cattle is supplemented by income derived from game. The number of game ranches and private protected areas in Africa is difficult to estimate, but figures do exist for some countries. Table 10.3 shows that the number of such areas is highest by far in South Africa, where nearly 7% of the total land area is privately protected. The number of such areas, however, has been increasing elsewhere, especially in Namibia and Kenya. Unlike private game reserves, game ranches can combine a number of income streams from both domesticated and wildlife stocks. An example of a pioneering game ranch is the Galana Ranch, whose 1 million acres border Tsavo East National Park in Kenya. The Galana Ranch not only has large herds of cattle, but of game as well. It has been experimenting since the 1960s in the domestication of wildlife species such as oryx and eland, not just for meat but also for milk.

Sustainable Consumptive Strategies for Wildlife Exploitation

The slaughter of African wildlife has occurred with no incentive for its renewal. Yet the potential for sustainable harvesting of wildlife is considerable. It has long been recognized that the biomass of wild animals in the African savannah is much greater than can be attained by ranching cattle or goats alone. Different animals exploit different types of vegetation and are more resistant to unfavourable arid conditions. For example zebra eat much coarser grass than cattle, giraffe thrive on high branches that other browsers cannot reach. African wildlife has evolved to be tough and resilient in the face of heavy natural predation and frequent natural disasters such as disease and drought. The rinderpest outbreaks of the 1890s severely reduced herbivore populations throughout Africa. Large numbers of elephants and rhinos died in the 1963 drought in Kenya. Yet populations soon bounced back where allowed to do so.

When Bernhad Grzimek wrote 'Serengeti Shall not Die' in 1959, there were around 200,000 wildebeest in the Serengeti, suffering from a great deal of human as well as animal predation. Since strict protection measures were introduced, there are now over 2 million. Elephants were nearly extinct in the Kruger National Park in the early 1900s. There are so many now that they have to be culled or translocated. In the Nyika National Park in Malawi one of the most common antelope is the reedbuck, which now number several thousand. In the 1950s poaching reduced them to less than 50 individuals. In fact, freed from hunting pressures, most African animals can register spectacular rates of increase in their numbers. Higginbottom reports that 'without large predators and operating at economic carrying capacity, the wildlife population increases at about 23 percent per annum' (Higginbottom and King, 2006, p. 4). This opens up considerable opportunities for sustainable wildlife entrepreneurship.

The most basic way to exploit this capacity for regeneration is to cull the game when stocks are large. Culling of game in Africa has generated considerable passions over the years. In South Africa it became a common practice, from the 1960s to 1990s, for the national park authorities to cull excess game, including elephants, and to sell the meat, hide and horn to local markets. This is not only in the form of fresh bush meat, but also dried meat or biltong (estimated to be worth $33 million in South Africa in 2005).[11] Large herbivores are still being culled, but pressure from conservationists and animal welfare groups has halted the culling of elephants. The translocation of live animals and the holding of live animal auctions has deflected some of the pressure for dealing effectively with surplus stock, but the revenue potential for harvesting game directly from national parks has still to be fully realized in South Africa.

In the rest of sub-Saharan Africa, conservation lobbies are so strong that no national park allows the culling of game for meat or hides. Many conservationists are appalled by any form of killing of wildlife; others view any commercial exploitation as running counter to the principles of the national park movement as defined by IUCN and UNESCO. Others view the African wilderness as a natural balanced ecosystem that should not be interfered with. In the 1960s, for example, elephant and hippo numbers had increased to such high levels in the Tsavo National Park, Kenya and the Murchison Falls National Park, Uganda, that the vegetation of these parks was being seriously degraded, often at the detriment of other species. Proposals to cull elephant and hippo numbers met with stern resistance from idealistic conservationists. They argued that such population increases ran in cycles and that people should not interfere. In the end it was left to poachers to do the culling in the late 1970s.

To idealist conservationists the requirement to leave nature alone, free from human interference, is a paramount article of faith. This has led to local inhabitants being evicted from their former homelands to preserve the ecosystem in its primeval state

Table 10.3: Private protected areas in selected East and Southern African Countries in 1996.

Country	Number of private conservation ranches	Total sq. km	% of country land area
Kenya	50	12,211	2.10
Namibia	148	7642	0.93
South Africa	4035	80,932	6.85
Tanzania	1	465	0.05
Zambia	12	219	0.03
Zimbabwe	3	6500	1.67

Source: Watkins et al. (1996).

---

11. www.american.edu/ted/biltong.htm

Figure 10.5: Semi-domesticated Eland on a Kenyan Game Ranch. (*Source*: author.)

(Brockington, 2002). Arguments based on the pristine state of the African wilderness, however, are more idealistic than real. It is now realized that the virgin pristine wilderness is largely a myth in Africa. People have always lived, albeit at low densities, throughout most parts of Africa's apparently 'untouched' wilderness areas and have helped shape the landscape.

Lake Mburo National Park in Uganda, for instance, appears at first to be an untouched wilderness of rolling savannah bush and grassland, where herds of impala, zebra, buffalo and eland graze. The glades are interspersed by characteristic copses of tress surrounding a termite hill. These typically consist of a mixture of acacia, African olive and euphorbia trees. Research has shown that these copses are not natural, but have evolved from the grass burning practices of the local Ankole pastoralists (Snelson and Wilson, 1994). The vegetation would be radically different if people did not burn the grass.

The setting up of national parks can disrupt the workings of natural ecosystems. Without human predation and competition, well-protected national parks can contain far more animals than used to be the case before they were gazetted. For example in the Serengeti and Masai Mara, the migration of 2 million wildebeest is artificial in the sense that numbers have increased from under 250,000 in the 1950s to nearly 2 million today. Complete protection has involved not only stopping poaching of wildebeest, but also freeing them from competition for food from the livestock of local Masai pastoralists.

The infrastructure of parks itself has also caused changes. The most visited national parks and reserves in Africa have developed road systems, which eat away land and compartmentalize the bush. Additionally, wildlife suffers from being crowded by a constant stream of visitors, which may be detrimental to their feeding and social behaviour. Off-road driving damages sensitive flora and litter pollutes the ground. Catering for the needs of thousands of visitors requires a settlement of employees within the parks, which in turn creates a degree of urbanization that is incompatible with the ideal of a virgin wilderness. Overall, therefore, the wilderness is already managed and under the influence of people.

It could be legitimately argued, therefore, that national parks in Africa should contain a human presence and a defined role in the utilization of park resources. Parks such as the Serengeti, the Masai Mara, Amboseli, Lake Mburo and Kagera in their natural state require a degree of pastoralism and range management, as occurred before the parks were gazetted and people removed from within their boundaries. Parks such as Tsavo in Kenya, Garamba in the Congo and Waaza in the Cameroons (indeed most West African Savannah parks), where local people have always traditionally relied on wildlife for food, would now benefit from some wildlife harvesting to maintain their traditional balance of species.

Once the idea is accepted that local Africans have a legitimate role in managing wilderness areas, then the harvesting of wildlife products becomes less contentious. The South African Park model of culling game and distributing profits amongst the local people is the most basic. There are other more sophisticated models that directly appeal to the spirit of enterprise of local people. One model is based on the concept of co-managed areas, where local people are given permission to hunt and participate in the development of the local area using revenue from wildlife resources. An example of this model is Zimbabwe's Communal Areas Management Programme for Indigenous Resources (CAMPFIRE) where local people have a direct stake in the management of their own wildlife. Poaching has been significantly reduced since the scheme was instigated. Another example is the Nazinga Game Ranch, Burkina Faso, which was established in 1979 as a communal wildlife park. The people surrounding the park are permitted to hunt through a quota system, and fees from big game hunting are also ploughed back into the local community (Brodlie and Hanselmann, 2003).

These schemes involve debates about how to utilize wildlife resources in national parks and reserves owned by the government. South Africa has also demonstrated that wildlife can provide significant revenues in private ranches and reserves. The wildlife on private ranches in South Africa belongs to the rancher, and it can be managed like any other farm resource. The efficient and entrepreneurial rancher will thrive; the inefficient will lose their wildlife stocks. (It is expensive to replace game once it disappears, and hence the incentive to harvest it carefully is a strong one.) This kind of scenario depends on markets for wildlife products to be open and legitimate. In countries such as Kenya and Uganda, where hunting is banned or heavily restricted, legitimate markets are hard to come by and the entrepreneurialism of ranchers is suppressed. In Uganda, for example, I recently came across some local luxury restaurants selling impala and crocodile meat. It all came frozen from South Africa. It was legal to import game meat from reputable sources, but illegal to use local game.

High Value Consumptive Use of Wildlife: Big Game Hunting

The value of meat per kilo, or an individual skin from a common game species, is significant, but not high per unit. Only by shooting a volume of animals can significant revenue be generated. In contrast, big game hunting provides a high value return. It has a number of advantages over culling of animals for meat. Firstly, only a small number of selective animals are shot. These are usually male animals, conforming to high trophy standards (antelope with well-developed horns, lions with prime manes, elephant with long and heavy tusks). Very often an animal with large horns, tusks or manes is already old, past its prime. With knowledge of breeding dynamics of individual species, the effect of killing prime males can be monitored so that the impact on the overall breeding stock will be minimal. Secondly, high fees can be charged to shoot individual animals.[12] Thirdly, a great deal of money can be made by organizing luxury hunting safaris, which can last several weeks. Fourthly, big game hunting is most prized where it is difficult to locate and hunt the game (usually in the remoter less developed wildlife areas, which are usually outside national parks).

Big game hunting occurs throughout most African countries in low volumes, where game stocks and security allow it. However it is particularly well developed in Southern Africa and parts of Central and West Africa, such as Benin, Burkina Faso, the Cameroons and the Central African Republic. In Kenya it used to be a major revenue earner, with over 350 professional white hunters who had the right to book one of over 100 hunting blocks. There was a hunting map clearly outlining their boundaries. This industry collapsed in 1977 when the Government of Kenya banned all hunting. There is now no value to wildlife in the thousands of square miles of Kenya where population densities are low, but do not lie within gazetted game reserves and national parks.

Non-Consumptive Exploitation of Wilderness Areas

In some parts of Africa, wildlife tourism took off in a big way in the 1970s when cheap air travel became possible. Over one million tourists a year visit the Kenya wildlife parks, a figure that has been increasing until the 2007–8 troubles (Kenya Ministry of Tourism). Most visitors combine a seaside holiday on Kenya's white beaches, with a 'safari' to a game park. Tourism has become Kenya's major foreign exchange earner.

There are other wildlife tourist hotspots in other countries, such as the Serengeti in Tanzania, the South Luangwa National Park in Zambia, the Etosha National Park in Namibia, the Okovanga Delta in Bostwana, and the Victoria Falls complex of parks in Zimbabwe and Zambia. South Africa has experienced the largest increase in tourism in Africa since the early 2000s. Tourism is now its third largest earner of foreign exchange and adds 8% to the country's GDP each year (South Africa Info, 2004).[13] The wildlife parks and reserves, such as the Kruger National Park and Addo Elephant National Park, contribute a significant proportion to national earnings. Additionally, unlike other sub-Saharan African countries, South Africa's national parks and reserves also attract significant numbers of local tourists. Kruger National Park attracts nearly a million visitors a year (see note 13).

Luxury Tourism.   One area that has seen considerable expansion is the provision of luxury accommodation for visitors. Government lodges have been replaced with a new generation of luxury lodges leased to private companies or entrepreneurs. These include large enterprises which are not multinationals but local African companies.

---

12. Fees for a hunting safari in Burkina Faso, for example, range from Euro 6000 to Euro 8900 for 6 and 12 day hunting safaris run by Nazinga safaris. A bull elephant hunting safari in the Gwayi Valley, Zimbabwe, costs $US 21,000 (www.huntinafrica.com/packages/).

13. www.nps.gov/yell/planyourvisit/upload/176(4-08).pdf; www.southafrica.info/doing_business/economy/key_sectors/tourismforecast.htm

A leading example is the TPS (Tourism Promotions Services) Eastern Africa Ltd, which has a number of subsidiaries in Kenya, Uganda, Tanzania and Rwanda trading under the 'Serena' brand. The TPS Group has built or renovated 16 luxury hotels and lodges, nearly all located in premier game parks and reserves (for example the Lake Manyara Serena Safari Lodge, the Serengeti Serena Safari Lodge and the Samburu Serena Safari Lodge). In 2006 the TPS Group was floated on the Nairobi Stock Exchange. In 2007 its turnover was 3.67 billion Kenyan Shillings (some £30 million) and it made a profit of 617 million shillings (some £5 million). This is a very large local company by African standards. Most of the directors and shareholders are local East Africans.[14] In Uganda the Idi Amin years led to the neglect and ruin of former luxury lodges in the Queen Elizabeth and Murchison Falls Parks. In the 1980s and 1990s these were restored by the Madhvani Family and are now the basis of a growing tourist industry.

These premium lodges provide core luxury accommodation in frequently visited parks, and serve the mass tourist markets. These successes, however, have been achieved on a low utlization of the overall wilderness capacity. In Kenya, for example, most tourists only visit a small number of national parks and reserves (the Masai Mara, Tsavo National Park, Amboseli, Nairobi National Park, Mt Kenya National Park). Many parks and reserves attract just enough visitors to get by and some, such as the South Turkana National Reserve, Rahole National Reserve and Malika Mari National Park, hardly get any. Even within the most visited parks, there are many areas that are never visited by tourists. Large areas of Tsavo National Park, for example, are not accessible by road, and some areas are even out of bounds. Even the Masai Mara, the most visited of the Kenya parks, has sections that are not visited.

It has been left to smaller businesses, particularly family businesses, to provide more customized luxury wildlife experiences, concentrating on low volumes of tourists. The Masai Mara Game Reserve in Kenya, in addition to mass tourist lodges, contains concessions for exclusive luxury tented camps such as the family run 1920s Cottar's Camp, which has a 22,000-acre exclusive concession. Tena Tena camp in the South Luangwa National Park in Zambia is but one of several exclusive small tented camps within the park. This practice has accelerated in recent years as the number of national parks has increased. In Gabon the creation of Loango National Park in 2002 has resulted not only in the creation of the Loango Luxury Safari Lodge, but in a cluster of new camps.[15]

Opportunities for luxury accommodation and high value tourism have spread outside state game parks and reserves. In South Africa in particular there has been a growth of facilities to cater for high value safari experiences on private game reserves and ranches. The private game reserves surrounding the Kruger National Park contain some 45 luxury lodges catering for visitors.[16] The private game reserves are able to provide attractions and activities that go well beyond the limitations of heavily regulated game viewing in the state-owned national parks. These include night drives, horse riding, foot safaris, fishing

14. TPS Annual Report, 2007.
15. www.africas-eden.com/accommodations/loango_lodge.html
16. www.sa-venues.com/accommodation/np_game_lodges.htm

Figure 10.6: Elephant shot under big game hunting licence, 1970: Mt Elgon Kenya.

and even balloon flights. The few visitors have a minimal impact on the environment, while still generating significant revenue.

In Kenya, game ranches and private game reserves have also expanded the range of luxury tourist facilities and activities since the early 1990s. They have been mostly constructed by private entrepreneurs or family businesses, and offer customized activities and luxury accommodation. Considerable value is added by facilities for game viewing. Commercial returns per hectare for wildlife viewing have been estimated to be up to four times that for livestock alone (Boyd et al., 1999).

An example is the Loisaba Ranch, founded by Peter and Tom Sylvester and Giles Davies in 1997, which comprises 150 sq. km of savannah rangeland and is well stocked with big game and other wildlife (50 species of mammal have been recorded). Guides and employees are recruited from the local Samburu people. The luxury lodge has spectacular views and has 'a swimming pool, tennis court, bocce court and croquet lawn. The spa offers massage, beauty treatments and a romantic open-air bubble bath, all with a tranquil view of the unspoilt Karissia Hills' (Source: Loisaba Ranch Brochure). The owners are proud of their hand-designed and hand-built furniture, and of several highly original features including a private 'cliff top swimming pool – the ultimate hideaway' and a 'wildlife blind', nestling in a rocky outcrop and 'charismatically' furnished. The entrepreneurs are also thrilled with their helicopter, which offers customized flights

Figure 10.7: Lion shot under a big game licence, Narok, Kenya, before the 1977 hunting ban. (*Source*: author.)

throughout the spectacular northern Kenya hills and valleys. Incidentally, the helicopter 'is exceptionally well appointed with air-conditioning, a CD music system and handmade picnic and cocktail set for six people'.[17]

This enterprising attention to luxury and detail, and a constant search for new novelties and experience, is demonstrated by many of the newly established Kenyan game ranches. White African entrepreneurs, often the descendents of colonial settlers, have started most of these ranches. However there has been some development by local Africans, who have been helped by neighbouring ranchers to set up communal eco-ranches. An example is the Il Ngwesi Ranch, a communally owned Group Ranch, representing over 6000 people, with a formal governance structure. Established in 1997 it made $40,000 in 2000. Restocking of big game has taken place from neighbouring ranches and wildlife has been increasing, as poaching has ceased in the area.[18] Another communal initiative is the Trans Mara Conservancy, near the Masai Mara Game Reserve. A number of Masai Ranches have pooled resources and their game is now being managed by a private company to attract visitors, arrange game viewing and collect revenues. The ranch owners get a share of the proceeds.

In Uganda, high value tourism has been developed for viewing mountain gorillas in the Bwimbi and Mgahinga National Parks. Visitors pay a premium fee (US $500) to travel on foot to visit habituated gorilla groups. Numbers of visitors are severely restricted. Other high value, low volume tourist activities include a chimp habituation experience at Kibale National Park (US $150) and mountaineering on the Rwenzori Mountains (US $560). Although still in its early phases of development, high value tourism has acted as an incentive for the renovation and construction of new camps and lodges both outside and

---

17. www.loisaba.com
18. www.lewa.org/ilngwesi.php

Figure 10.8: Ngulia Lodge: Tsavo West National Park, Kenya. (*Source*: author.)

inside park boundaries. For example from virtually no facilities in the 1980s, Bwimbi Impenetrable Forest National Park now boasts over seven luxury hotels and camps.[19]

The development of high value 'ecotourism' is accelerating and is viewed by conservationists as the most acceptable way to exploit wildlife and wilderness resources.

The Wildlife Media Industry

The market for wildlife television programmes has grown exponentially since the 1960s, and today there are even whole television channels that show nothing else. Programme makers have found rich pickings in Africa, from the original Disney classics of the 1950s, such as the African Lion (1955), to modern animal soap operas such as Meerkat Manor (a mongoose soap opera first aired in 2005 and now in its fourth series)[20] and Big Cat Diary (a lion, cheetah and leopard soap set in the Masai Mara and running since 1996).

Some are linked to conservation projects, such as those providing income and publicity for the private Lewa Game Ranch in Kenya. One may wonder, however, who these programmes actually enrich? What do local Africans get out of them? Many African countries charge fees for commercial camera teams or programme makers, but these fees are miniscule compared to the profits to be made in distributing the films on world television networks. Paradoxically, local African wildlife photographers and film-makers are almost non-existent. Africans, who include amongst their number wildlife hunter entrepreneurs capable of risking prison to sell elephant tusks worth hundreds of dollars on the black market, are unable to produce wildlife programmes potentially worth hundreds of thousands of dollars. The filming of wildlife programmes

19. Mantana Lodge, The Gorilla Resort, Bwindi Lodge, Gorilla Forest Summit Lodge, Lake Kitandara Bwindi Camp, Buhioma Homestead Lodge, Gorilla Forest Camp. (*The Eye Magazine*, April/May 2008.)
20. animal.discovery.com/fansites/meerkat/meerkat.html

in African parks would add much greater income if fees were increased, and contracts signed to include a share of the profits at distribution. Their perceived value would also be enhanced when local Africans become motivated to make their own wildlife programmes.

South Africa also contains examples of some innovative companies, who use webcams sited around waterholes to bring wildlife experiences to a global audience. This business model has been pioneered by Africam.com, who made enough money by 2006 to allow it to be floated on the Johannesburg stock exchange. The large audience attracted by the webcams provides the basis for a diverse revenue stream based on subscription and advertising.[21] So far this potentially lucrative model has yet to take off in the rest of Africa.

The commercial media exploitation of African wildlife is already a major industry, and is likely to grow much more once local Africans learn to exploit their share of opportunities. Quite simply, few Africans are aware of these opportunities and even fewer about how to exploit them.

Restocking Wildlife

South Africa was the first sub-Saharan African country to lose most of its wildlife. By the early twentieth century, as related earlier, there was very little left, especially large mammals. This situation has been reversed through strict conservation policies, and the realization that wildlife does add value to economy and society. In terms of society, many South Africans have realized that wildlife is part of their heritage and that it has an important cultural role to play in modern South Africa. In terms of economics, the realization that wildlife can produce sustainable economic value through tourism and sustainable harvesting has created conditions where private game reserves and ranches thrive.

As the number of game ranches and reserves increases, there is a growing market for restocking wild animals in areas where game has been eliminated. In the case of prized species such as rhino and elephants, and rare species of antelope, the supply is well short of demand. Prices have escalated for live animals to restock new areas. In South Africa, wildlife auctions are regularly held to dispose of surplus stock and to service a growing market for restocking. For example, the KZN Wildlife Game Auction held at the Centenary Game Capture Centre in the Hluhluwe-iMfolozi Park on 22 June 2002 realized R11.4 million from the sale of 2018 head of game gathered from the 110 protected areas under the control of KZN Wildlife. White rhino, the most prized species, averaged R227,000 each. Hippos fetched R41,000 each and an adult male Nyala fetched R35,000. As a means of disposing of surplus game in highly protected areas this is much more lucrative than allowing poachers a free reign, or selling it as meat.

'This annual game auction is important to us in many ways. In the first place it provides a means of disposing of our surplus game – which in the days before the auctions began – up to 14 years ago – we used to cull and sell our surplus antelope as venison at about R2-00 per kilogramme. That same antelope now sells live for R650. It provides the game industry of

---

21. See for example, africam.com or wavelit.com/index.php?view=africam

South Africa with excellent breeding stock, and it provides KZN Wildlife with much needed funds,' said Khulani Mkhize, KZN Wildlife Chief Executive Officer. It is likely that as the free game disappears from large parts of Africa, its replacement will provide a lucrative industry for those better managed wildlife areas who retained their stocks. The example of Bandia in Senegal has shown that the market is growing outside South Africa as well.

It is interesting to note that most non-consumptive revenue generation of wildlife has occurred through the entrepreneurial efforts of Africans of European or Asian origins. This is particularly true in South Africa and Kenya, where descendants of European and Asian settlers have been able to see new opportunities arising from ecotourism and wilderness management. Indigenous Africans have succeeded through partnerships to share in some of the profits (particularly in mass tourist enterprises such as the Serena Hotel Group), and in some cases are beginning to establish small ecotourist operations on their own. However, in the main they have lacked the imagination, awareness and skills on how to exploit wildlife from a non-consumptive perspective. This is in direct contrast to consumptive wildlife entrepreneurship, where the skills required are highly compatible with African traditions.

Discussion and Conclusions

The period from the mid-1970s to the mid-1980s saw a move back to the mass commercialization of wildlife of the nineteenth century, with a dramatic reduction of valuable wildlife stocks, including the near elimination of the rhino. Despite the world ban on ivory sales by CITES in 1989, there is still mass poaching going on in many African countries, moving now to other species to serve fast growing markets in bush meat and the pet trades. Okello and Kiringe (2004, p. 61) report that illegal killing of animals for bush meat occurred in 96% of Kenya's protected areas. It is a remorseless tide that appears unstoppable; a situation where entrepreneurial vigour is combined with very profitable markets and low risk (poaching and the trading of wildlife products is illegal, but not enforced). It is a situation where everyone wins in the supply chain, from the local hunters who kill the animals, to the middlemen that sell on the products, to the politicians that shield or protect entrepreneurs from the law, and to the entrepreneurs outside Africa that process and retail the final products.

The benefits of this process to local economic development have not been researched, as the activity is illegal, unmonitored, and subject to hostile reactions from conservationists. Western conservationists view mass poaching as greedy criminal exploitation of irreplaceable resources, rather than a source of income and development for Africans. Global conservation organizations such as WWF, UNESCO, CITES and western governments have lobbied African governments to increase protection and to allocate more areas as national parks or game reserves. The number of these, as reported earlier, has increased dramatically in the last 20 years – the very period during which mass poaching has accelerated. (One could argue that there is nothing better than gazetting a national park to alert commercial poachers that this is an area which contains a large volume of lucrative wildlife).

However, although African governments have made commitments to conservation, often under considerable external pressures, the politicians themselves have not been brought up as idealized conservationists, but as citizens of countries where poverty is prevalent and economic development a priority. One former Uganda Minister of State told me that he was sick of wildlife and the arrogance of western conservationists. He contrasted the policies of Western countries towards their wildlife with what they expected Africans to do. No European government tolerates the presence of damaging or dangerous wildlife near crops, livestock or people. Wildlife is mostly tolerated only in remote areas far from people. Countries such as the UK who have long since eliminated dangerous wildlife are extremely resistant to its reintroduction. Whereas in the West food production is a priority for land usage, and little productive land is allowed to become wild, in Africa these same people expect huge areas of the country to give wildlife a priority on potentially productive land. Finally, no foreign expert tells US or European governments how to manage their wildlife, yet Africa is full of such experts.

African governments face a dilemma as there is a conflict between mass poaching, which as argued brings in visible and tangible benefits to large numbers of people, and valuable foreign exchange and mass tourism, which also brings large and varied benefits to local development. The benefit chain for tourism is quite different to that for mass poaching and involves a complex chain of interdependent entrepreneurial interactions, involving multinationals and large public companies, local suppliers to luxury lodges, and local people selling handicrafts and services. There is a large complex of intermediaries providing goods and services for a range of tourist related niche markets. The tourist industry requires safe and well-regulated game parks, free from mass poaching. The carcasses of poached animals are distressing to tourists, animals become frightened, shy and less visible when shot at, and dangerous game becomes much more prone to attack vehicles and people when constantly hunted.

How to balance the two sources of revenue is one of the issues African governments have had to face. The obvious solution has been to concentrate tourists in areas which are well protected, where poachers are excluded, and where wildlife is easy to see and plentiful. The rest of the wilderness, i.e. the majority, can then be informally allocated for illegal poaching. This is effectively what has happened in countries such as Kenya and Uganda where wildlife in areas that are not visited by tourists is disappearing fast, or has mostly disappeared.

South Africa is the only country to have experienced the near elimination of its wildlife following unrestricted commercial exploitation in the nineteenth century. The vigorous resilience of its wildlife has been such that wildlife stocks have recovered strongly under protection. Rather than just rely on the law for protection, modern wildlife management has been opened up to the private sector, and a host of practices have been evolved to make wildlife profitable on a sustainable basis.

Wildlife is thriving not so much because South Africans value its beauty (though many do) but also because it makes money. South Africa's private game reserves and ranches have demonstrated that multiple and often compatible income streams can be generated. These income streams include farming some species (such as ostrich and eland), creating luxury accommodation for ecotourists, and diversifying the enjoyment of the wilderness through walking, horse riding, mountain bike safaris, night drives and even balloon rides.

Sensitively culling surplus game can add additional income for meat and hides, and high value game management can be pursued by allowing big game hunting and selling of live animals to restock other areas. Many private reserves and ranches now host wildlife programme makers, and even internet webcams which form the central attraction of some thriving websites. On ranches all these activities bring in income additional to the more conventional raising of farm livestock and agriculture.

These sustainable practices are now well developed throughout Southern Africa (including Namibia and Botswana). The countries in the rest of Africa, however, have lagged behind. This is due to several reasons. Firstly, game stocks until recently have been plentiful and much more easy to exploit through poaching than management. Secondly, the market for dead animal products such as meat and hides has been illegal and driven underground in many countries. Big game hunting has flourished in some countries, where hunting has not been banned, but this has been localized and largely invisible. The development of game ranches and private game reserves requires capital, and has only taken off so far in Kenya. The private game ranches and reserves have been forced to restrict their revenue streams to ecotourism, as big game hunting and the harvesting of venison has been illegal. Pilots to allow game cropping on some ranches in the 1990s proved unprofitable, as there was no developed legal market for venison (Boyd et al., 1999).

The absence of legal markets for the most valuable wildlife products is the result of international conservation treaties. They have provided some short-term respite in some areas of Africa, and for some species, but they may well prevent entrepreneurs evolving sustainable strategies of wildlife exploitation. Until the 1970s, ivory auctions had occurred annually since early colonial times, yet elephants were common and continued to be so. The plentiful supply of ivory kept prices down, and the incentive to over-hunt was curbed. Indeed, where elephant numbers are large and stable, the yield of ivory from natural mortality alone is considerable. Parker and Amin (1983, p. 153) calculated that the then estimated 1.3 million elephants would have yielded between 58,000 to 117,000 tusks annually from natural deaths alone.

Since 1989 there have been no legal ivory markets, and countries where elephants are well managed cannot sell their ivory legally. The legal value of elephants is very low, but the illegal value is high. Illegal poaching is the only way left to supply demand, through the black market. Elephants continue to disappear anyway despite prohibition. Moreover, by not setting up conditions where local people own their own wildlife resources (obviously such ownership would have to be communal in the case of elephants), the incentive to manage such a valuable resource in a sustainable manner is also minimal. Killing an elephant in a natural wilderness owned by the state is poaching. Killing an elephant owned by a consortium of people is theft. There needs to be a radical change of policy for entrepreneurs to evolve effective sustainable systems of elephant and rhino harvesting if their commercial extinction is to be avoided. It is interesting to note that the numbers of species that have become extinct through human hunting activities are few, but persecution can result in a severe reduction in numbers and range (Woodroffe et al., 2008). What unmanaged hunting does is drive the species to levels that are so low that it is no longer worthwhile to hunt its members. It is the hunter entrepreneurs of a species who become extinct, not the species.

The establishment of regulated and legal markets for wildlife products is one of the most controversial conservation issues. Trade in the most valuable commodities (ivory, rhino horn, leopard skins, parrots and reptiles) is banned under global agreements. Lucrative markets for all these products exist, but the bans prevent entrepreneurs from legally accessing them. The local ban on hunting in some African countries further restricts the market for meat and hides. The net effect is to make wildlife uneconomic to retain on private land on a sustainable basis. However it makes it even more lucrative to poach. You do not even have to pay taxes on poacher derived revenues. Countries who manage their wildlife well and who reward legal enterprise, such as South Africa, are prevented from reaping their full profits by global bans. In the meantime, countries that do not manage their wildlife in a sustainable way still continue to kill off their stocks and sell them on the black market.

By establishing free unrestricted markets, the entrepreneurial potential of wildlife exploitation in Africa would find its own level, and in the long term lead to sustainable populations of wildlife throughout the continent. In the short term whole areas might become denuded of large mammals,[22] but there would still be areas that are better managed where stocks are maintained. In time, depleted areas would be restocked if markets justified it. As mentioned earlier, it does not take long for wildlife numbers to recover if protected. The restocking of wildlife in itself becomes a lucrative market, as demonstrated in South Africa. The main problem with restocking is the potential loss of biodiversity. Whole subspecies can become extinct, and restocking might require introductions from areas which have different forms of the animal. For example in Senegal there are no Nubian giraffes left, so the restocking of the Bandia Game reserve was with South African giraffe. Conservation projects would arguably be better spent ensuring that pockets of diversity typical of a country survive in highly protected areas, which could then be used to restock, rather than on blanket bans.

Another factor that affects the take up of new opportunities to exploit wildlife in Africa is information asymmetry. Africans, on the whole, lack the education and exposure to the global economy to enable them to access and develop new opportunities presented by wildlife. A large proportion of Africans live in urban or highly populated rural areas where wildlife is absent or very scarce. Most have never seen an elephant, rhino or antelope, never mind know its worth. Those who actually live in areas where game are present are focused on making a livelihood in terms of conventional agriculture or pastoralism. Of these only a few actually poach and of these, few have any awareness beyond local markets for meat. Most of the mass poaching is organized by middle-class entrepreneurs in cities, who already know how to trade both legally and illegally. They recruit, equip and train local hunters to poach for them.

Local Africans also are mostly unaware of the opportunities associated with game ranching, ecotourism or wildlife filming. Most of these ventures have been developed by Africans of European of Asian origin, especially the descendants of colonial settlers and migrants, who have the knowledge, capital and networks to develop these businesses. It will take some time before awareness of these opportunities spreads to the African

---

22. It takes a great deal of effort to totally remove large mammals from an area, and it only becomes desirable if the area is to be cleared for intensive agriculture. Hunting pressure in a favourable environment will always contain a nucleus of survivors to base a restocking programme on.

population at large. Even where awareness is present, most Africans lack the resources to exploit opportunities presented by ecotourism. Boyd et al. (1999) comment that the conditions for successful wildlife ranching in the Liakipia region of Kenya requires capital and an acreage of land well beyond the means of most local Africans.

African governments set the framework conditions which allow entrepreneurship to flourish. Since early colonial times, wildlife as a resource has been managed directly, with governments defining what is permissible to harvest and directly setting aside land for conservation without engaging local people. The mass exploitation of wildlife through poaching or through tourism has mostly benefited elite entrepreneurs and politicians. There has been a trickle down effect, but of a limited kind. To exploit wildlife more sustainably and equitably governments must learn to manage entrepreneurial opportunities as well as assets. They must free markets and develop the capabilities of local entrepreneurs to exploit these markets.

Theoretical Thoughts

This chapter illustrates that the consumption and exploitation of African wildlife has many facets, and there are many income streams to tempt enterprising entrepreneurs. Left to market forces alone, the commercialization of wildlife is compatible with the predictions of environmental economics, i.e. that wildlife stocks of any commercial value will soon drastically reduce under the onslaught of hunter entrepreneurs and traders who have no incentive to preserve the resource in the longer term. In time, as the resource gets scarce, it

Figure 10.9: South African White Rhino translocated to Meru National Park, Kenya.[23]

---

23. Kenya lies outside the white rhino traditional range. This translocation is thus inappropriate from a purist view of preserving zonal biodiversity.

will command even higher prices, which will increase the pressure to target remaining stocks even more. This will lead to commercial extinction of the resource.

This kind of theory, however, assumes open markets, freely available information, and perfect competition. The wildlife markets in Africa today, however, do not fulfil these criteria. Markets for the consumption of valuable wildlife are not open, but suppressed by the global conservation lobbies in the interests of the preservation of biodiversity and a sense of stewardship. There has been considerable pressure to divert entrepreneurs from consumptive to non-consumptive forms of exploitation, such as tourism and commercial wildlife film-making. The growth of the ecotourist movement is especially compatible with forms of wildlife exploitation that does not require the killing of wildlife, and is highly endorsed by idealized conservation lobbies.

In the absence of open free markets there has arisen a black market for valuable wildlife products. To exploit these opportunities the matching of supply and demand has been a complex process for African entrepreneurs to master, as it involves establishing networks of hunters, middlemen, international traders and politician protectors.

In terms of Barth's (1967) theories of spheres of value, entrepreneurs have been able to exploit synergies between traditional value systems that see wildlife as a resource to be killed for subsistence and local profit, and new forces of commercial entrepreneurialism in Africa where the need for self-advancement and economic development are highly valued. At the same time the western-led forces of conservation have encouraged the development of sustainable exploitation of African wildlife, particularly tourism and wildlife film-making. The entrepreneurs associated with these markets have tended to be westerners or African of recent western origin, who have the awareness of these opportunities and the capital and knowledge to exploit them. They have been 'alert' to new opportunities, especially those presented by ecotourism, and have acted as classic Kirznerian entrepreneurs. In terms of Barth's (1967) theory of spheres of value, they have been able to bridge entrepreneurially the values of enterprise and ideal conservationists – values that are alien to most local Africans.

South Africa is the only region in Africa where laws are compatible with the legal exploitation of wildlife from both a consumptive and non-consumptive basis. The growth of private game reserves and game ranches has seen the development of both high value consumptive exploitation of wildlife (game meat, big game hunting, wildlife for restocking) and high value non-consumptive activities (high value tourism, wildlife film-making). This model is based on synergies between pragmatic conservation values and entrepreneurial consumer values. It is a system that will benefit most if and when bans in the international markets for the most valuable wildlife products (rhino horns, ivory) are finally lifted.

Questions for Discussion

1. What do you consider to be a sustainable tourism development in the context of sub-Sahara destinations?
2. How are business opportunities in the African wilderness exploited by tourism entrepreneurs?
3. What are the key factors that have contributed to the large scale of commercialization of the African wildlife stock over the last three decades?

4. Who are the most influential actors (stakeholders) in shaping the tourism industry in the sub-Sahara region?

References

Boyd, C., Blench, R., Bourn, D., Drake, L., and Stevenson, P. (1999). *Reconciling interests among wildlife, livestock and people in Eastern Africa: a sustainable livelihoods approach.* Natural Resource Perspectives, 45, Overseas Development Institute, London.

Brodlie, R., and Hanselmann, R. (2003). Gh Development of Methodologies at the Nazinga Game Ranch for use in a Piloted Integrated Conservation Program in Burkino Faso. IUCN, Burkino Faso.

The Eye Magazine, (2008). April/May, Kampala.

Chapter 11

Bridging the Global–Local Divide: Lessons from Indigenous Entrepreneurship on Vatulele Island, Fiji

Stephen Doorne

Learning Outcomes

After reading this chapter, you should be able to:

- Better understand tourism development in the developing world including its importance in the Pacific region;

- Comprehend and dismiss some of the main misconceptions related to an alternative form of tourism development;

- Understand the process of tourism entrepreneurship in a number of South Pacific microstates;

- Identify and understand the role of the public sector in developing sustainable tourism in Fiji through policies to support indigenous SME development;

- Understand and explain some of the key barriers to sustainable and ecotourism development in the Fiji Island;

- Understand the cultural distance between consumers and producers in the context of a sustainable and commercially viable ecotourism development on Lomanikaya island, Fiji; and

- Link the empirical findings from the Lomanikaya case study to other similar contexts around the globe.

Introduction

In 2002, the village of Lomanikaya on Vatulele Island in Fiji established the Lomanikaya Ecotourism Project (LEP) with a view to providing supplementary income, employment, and development opportunities for local people. Adjacent to Fiji's mainstream tourism complex of the Coral Coast on the neighbouring island of Viti Levu, the project approached the Canada Fund, the small grants facility of the Canadian International Development Agency (CIDA) to fund a boat to facilitate day trips to the island. The product proposed included a village visit, cross-island walk taking in heritage sites, lunch and cultural performance. After some consideration and consultation with the University of the South Pacific (USP) the Canada Fund opted not to fund the proposal fearing that concerns over aspects of product quality would jeopardize the sustainability of the venture. It appeared that the project would follow a path of similarly labelled ecotourism ventures in villages throughout the country in offering marginally viable low quality cultural experiences with little or no environmental integrity.

Contrary to expectations the village persisted with the idea for the next three years and significantly reconfigured their proposal and business plan. In 2005 they succeeded in obtaining funding from the Canada Fund and later launched their product that, in the context of Fijian ecotourism, was of very high quality. This chapter describes the way in which such a turnaround was achieved amidst an industrial context long noted for its neo-colonialist foreign dominated dependency relations, and re-examines the theoretical implications for the traditional structuralist core-periphery paradigm.

Thanks to the work of Britton and Clarke (1987), Fiji has been at the forefront of discussions involving tourism, global political economy and local people. The neo-colonial tourism model, it is argued, assumes a spatial character reminiscent of a pre-existing pattern of the 'colonial space economy' (Bianchi, 2002), namely the plantation economies based on sugar and the foundation of the confection industry in the west. Weaver (1988) observes a similar process in the Caribbean where the tourism industry's resemblance to these economic systems goes beyond the spatial but mirrors an insidious hegemonic control of political and social structures, particularly at the level of corporate and state governance.

In the intervening decades since Britton's work, theorists have largely sidestepped classical neo-colonial arguments around discussions of contemporary tourism, resulting in a collective tendency to throw the theoretical baby out with the bathwater. An overt emphasis on mass tourism in the 'third world' was seen to sit uncomfortably with new tourisms. The occasionally zealous championing of benefits from ecotourism and community-based tourism, for example, preferred a less dismal theoretical context (see Murphy, 1985; Honey, 1999). Similarly the spatial concentration of the mass model set up a core-periphery dichotomy more readily apparent at macro scales. The focus of new tourisms in the local context has brought with it a multitude of theoretical perspectives and methodologies that run counter to overarching structuralist argument (see Poon, 1996; Scheyvens, 2002). The very unevenness of 'globalization' processes demands a reconsideration of contextual dilemmas as a connected series of changes rather than the somewhat misleading homogeneity implied by the singular term.

Structural inequalities between markets and destinations, at the core of the neo-colonial model, emerge with a renewed transparency in the periphery (Britton, 1991; Bianchi, 2002; Mowforth and Munt, 2003). What is perhaps most marked in the persistence of global change is the now relative spatial proximity of what was previously a remoteness implied by the term 'periphery'. Tourism in the 'here and now' sees these equal opposites as charged adjacents, at best dynamic and interactive, at worst exploitative and parasitic. Indeed Mowforth and Munt argue that such has been the neglect of academic interest in classical political economy that the systemic entrenchment of the overarching capitalist system is more apparent than ever in the management-driven era of tourism studies.

Central to the seemingly exponential growth in power and control is the localization and multiplicity of its processes. Not only has there been a centralization of power at the upper echelons through consolidation, amalgamation and conglomeration, the post-modernistic diffusion of product and the penetration of 'market places' create an insidious localization of power through which the separation of core and periphery is difficult to distinguish. In this context the neo-colonial 'cliché' is perhaps better understood as a *cultural* as much as a *structural* paradigm (Clifford, 1992; Featherstone, 1987; Featherstone, 1990; Kirschenblatt-Gimblett, 1988; Rojek, 1995; Appadurai, 1996).

A dismal irony surrounds the homogenization of destinations in which endless product diversification and differentiation is pursued by tourism/property investment and speculation creating the net effect of drawing an ever-widening sphere of influence. As the once periphery ceases to be defined through geographical remoteness more and more people are finding themselves face to face with the core of globalization (Silver, 1993; Ateljevic et al., 2003). Responses to change are, however, never far away and can be observed in an array of forms as varied and colourful as the places where they are situated. Whilst we can readily observe and quantify the steady seepage of tourism into the local context the comprehension of the net effect of the response is more difficult to evaluate (Bianchi, 2002). Similarly, structuralist arguments often fall foul of their own concerns by neglecting to localize perspectives of resistance, preferring a big picture genre of macro proportions (Crick, 1989; Franklin and Crang, 2001).

Post-structuralist interpretations have taught us the value of equal and opposite in bringing to life otherwise passive victims of globalization. Bianchi, however, cautions that 'further empirical investigation of the hierarchical relations of power which bind different networks of local, regional, national and transnational tourism actors and institutions together within specific development circumstances is, therefore, needed in order to enable a more concrete assessment of the changing structures of power within an increasingly transnational tourism industry' (2002, p. 297).

At the heart of structuralist concern is the extraordinary expansion of tourism as a global industry and the rapidity with which places, and particularly peripheral places, are drawn into the tourism process beginning with Turner and Ash's (1975) interpretation of the massification of tourism and continuing through diversification in subsequent decades (Mowforth and Munt, 1998, 2003). The tourism process is not only a spatial and economic phenomenon but is intrinsically bound within expressions of cultural and symbolic capital in developed societies. Mowforth and Munt identify this complex as being driven by 'the emergence of specialist agents and tour operators (and its adjunct, more individually centred and flexible holidays); the de-differentiation of tourism as it becomes associated with other activities, and the growth of interest in *Other* cultures, environments and their association with the emergence of new social movements (2003, p. 116). Further to the process is its unevenness through which inequalities of power, control and, most importantly, knowledge emerge.

The ability of hosts to 'read' the cultural context of the guest is critical for the creation of viable, quality experiences yet must be balanced with an awareness of the capacity for the mainstream complex to voraciously consume places and cultures (Morgan and Pritchard, 1998; Mowforth and Munt, 2003). Focusing on the Fijian context, Ateljevic and

Doorne (2005) observe the need for tourists to enact the role of their particular tourist group as central to the success and thus sustainability of experiential products wherein the act of consumption is an act of reproduction (Ateljevic and Doorne, 2004). It follows that a sophisticated understanding of niche marketing and constructs of social identity are critical to entrepreneurial behaviour and it is here that Foucault's (1980) power/knowledge becomes central to the equation (Morgan and Pritchard, 1998).

Throughout the last two decades the benefits of alternative tourisms have been widely extolled with particular emphasis on their accessibility for local communities (see Murphy, 1985; Fennel, 1999; Honey, 1999; UNEP, 2001 and, in the context of Fiji, Bricker, 2003). Alternative tourism is normally associated with relatively low barriers of entry particularly in economic terms. These forms of tourism do not rely heavily on infrastructural investment or other capital-intensive developments but instead make use of social and cultural capital for the development of products.

Ecotourism as a concept has, however, been embraced at the village/community level on a global scale to the extent that tourism industries are rapidly becoming saturated with products espousing alternative tourism values (Cater and Lowman, 1994; Rudkin and Hall, 1996; Lindberg and McKercher, 1997). This combined with the rapid segmentation and fragmentation of tourism markets effectively raises sustainable entry barriers to a very high level in terms of product development and understanding of consumer psychology (Ateljevic and Doorne, 2005). This chapter argues that whilst the economic barriers of entry may be relatively low, the cultural barriers, particularly for remote and isolated communities, may be growing higher. As travel and tourism become ever more globalized, encounters between discerning experienced tourism consumers and remote peripheral communities increase, raising a range of complex issues surrounding the commodification of experience, the definition of quality and the consumption of culture (Rojek, 1995; Lury, 1996; Sharpley, 1996).

This chapter draws on the case of the Lomanikaya Ecotourism Project on Vatulele Island to argue that responses to change do not necessarily conform to established patterns and that the existing social, economic and political structures of local people have the capacity to facilitate positive engagement with global tourism. In the process the discussion takes up the challenge of revisiting what has been a persistent theoretical paradigm for Fiji and asks questions as to its contemporary relevance and, more specifically, how the contemporary growth of the tourism phenomenon is reconfiguring peoples lives in the 'periphery'.

Literature Review – Cultural Challenges for Entrepreneurial Modelling

The inherently fluid and localized nature of entrepreneurship continues to confound 'conventional' model-based interpretations of the process. As Bygrave and Hofer comment 'there is little likelihood of an entrepreneurial model ever being developed that will meet our "ideal" specifications. In fact, we hope that we have shown that it is extremely difficult to develop even "useful" entrepreneurship models' (1991, p. 20). Characteristic of the definitional approach they argue that the difficulties of adequate modelling confound attempts at understanding and interpretation (see also Wortman, 1987; Keats and Bracker, 1988).

Given the difficulties of establishing a unifying concept a range of theoretical trajectories have been mined in the name of entrepreneurship, which even collectively reconfirm Bygrave and Hofer's argument. Hannan and Freeman (1977), for example, drew extensively on a biological metaphor in terms of their population–ecology paradigm in which the lifecycle processes of living things are replicated in the various stages and fortunes of enterprises. Martin (1984) explored the initiation of new ventures through the inner motivations of individuals in relation to their conditional context (see also Bull and Willard, 1993), and Krueger and Brazeal (1994) draw on Shapero's (1982) model and Ajzen's (1991) 'Theory of Planned Behaviour' to illustrate the significance of particular events in stimulating entrepreneurship and venture dynamics.

More recently, however, researchers have explored more interpretive perspective-centred approaches to understand change – a paradigm which achieves its objectives as much through a subjective process as through empirical truth. In this context the small business sector in tourism has long been the focus of attention due to a range of issues which constrain productivity, innovation and quality (Shaw and Williams, 1998; Getz and Carlsen, 2004). Not least of the constraints is that of aspiration and entrepreneurial drive in the sense of following a growth-orientated development model.

Ateljevic and Doorne (2004), for example, present a litany of problems endemic to the SME sector focusing on a series of case studies in New Zealand describing the net effect of serial replication of business problems as creating 'diseconomies of scale'. Similarly, Ioannedes and Petersen (2003) identify a persistent problem in tourism entrepreneurship – that of 'non-entrepreneurship' as characteristic of small enterprises adding little or no innovation to the industrial and product mix but simply replicating existing formulaic patterns of small tourism business. Within this environment, however, there are difficulties of generalizing. Ateljevic and Doorne (2000), for example, provide evidence of SMEs driving innovation in the sector through entrepreneurs who are motivated not specifically by non-economic goals but more by lifestyle and were thus able to approach product development in less conventional but more creative ways.

It should be noted however that these cases and arguments reflect conditions in developed economies where aside from issues of lifestyle, niche and style in the marketing mix there is little real cultural distance between producers and consumers. For SMEs in developing countries there are significant cultural barriers and constraints to business and entrepreneurship. Indeed the particular context 'indigenous' as distinct from 'ethnic' entrepreneurship in developing countries makes it possible to consider 'indigenous entrepreneurship' as a distinct realm of activity (Peredo et al., 2004; Dana and Anderson, 2007).

The interpersonal nature of cultural perspectives, all too apparent in tourism SMEs, adds a further dimension to the discussion, particularly when cultural distance is both the attraction and the source of many of the problems (Ateljevic et al., 2003). Richards and Hall's (2000) accumulation of case studies illustrates the diversity of contexts in which the localization of global tourism takes place. The cases similarly reinforce the argument that amongst the diversity are commonalities in terms of the issues and general dynamics tourism displays in the community setting.

The 'problem' of entrepreneurship in the Pacific has been a regular feature of small business studies for a number of decades (see Fairburn, 1988). The issues of inadequate skills, collective responsibilities, and relative economic and political impotence echo

Britton's structural arguments and have spawned a myriad of similarly top-down policy responses articulated through programme strategies implemented at the local level. The persistent reference to the problem nature of the situation highlights the relative impotence of the responses themselves, and in turn demands a re-conceptualisation of the ways and means by which change can positively reciprocate in the village environment.

Rao (2004) in the context of Fiji argues for the context of culture to be placed at the forefront of entrepreneurial research, in particular pointing to the extent to which entrepreneurship is more likely to emerge from cultures valuing individualism than those articulating collectivism. His comparative study of Fiji's two main ethnic groupings observes, 'in the context of Fiji it may be expected that an ethnic grouping which espouses individualism would exhibit a greater degree of an entrepreneurial disposition and achieve greater success in entrepreneurship' (2004, p. 144). In spite of this, Rao also urges caution against assumptions that generalize on the basis of ethnicity and culture,

> Whilst Fijian society is often viewed as being traditional and collective, there is a category of urbanised and educated Fijians who espouse modern thoughts and ideas. Some of these Fijians operate business ventures based on modern business principles. To characterise this class of Fijian entrepreneurs as being traditional and collectivist is inappropriate. They should be viewed differently. (2004, p. 145)

Whilst Rao's observations based on a traditional–modern continuum are familiar to cultural studies of entrepreneurship the world over, the obligations to extended families in the Fijian context cannot be overstated. It is rare to encounter an urbanized modern Fijian divorced from their responsibilities to the wider tokatoka (group of family units) and tikina (tribal district). Qalo (1997) illustrates the extent to which these relationships can impede entrepreneurial inertia and produce a creative drag by syphoning time, resources and often cash. It is also apparent, as this chapter illustrates, that the values and skills of significant individuals are often instrumental in shaping the entrepreneurial perspectives, aspirations and skills of people in places culturally and spatially remote from classical modernity.

A theoretical foundation for this discussion underlies Chang et al.'s (1996) discussion of a global–local nexus, expressed in their case in an urban heritage context, where an argument against the theorization of macro global political economy as a one-way-street is presented. Instead, they observe, local influences colour and shape the way in which places are articulated. The urban context of the study more readily lends itself to the term 'nexus' given that the cultural conditions of consumers and producers are more closely aligned than the cultural distance that characterizes Fijian villagers encountering visitors from suburban Australasia. In a different cultural context but still with an urban theme, Chang (1999) provides an up-beat prognosis of place commoditization – the cultural differences perhaps accounting for his description of a 'divide' across which values are negotiated.

A similarly optimistic discussion of the global–local dichotomy is presented in Baldacchino's (1999) study of small business in Fiji. Against a typically Britton-esque background, the responses of small businesses to return opportunities to their local environment again illustrate the dynamics of benefit accrual which only local knowledge can utilize. Despite theoretical recognition of the importance of local knowledge in facilitating entrepreneurship, policies and programmes implemented through international development agencies and local government programmes often adhere to a more conventional top-down approach.

Echtner's (1995) programme for encouraging entrepreneurship in developing countries illustrates a predominantly top-down-driven implementation strategy commonly favoured by international development agencies in conjunction with host country policy initiatives (see also Scheyvens, 2002). Indeed in the Fiji context the approaches to facilitating small business activity and entrepreneurial skills amongst the indigenous Fijian population reflect the overall approach advocated by this paradigm. This chapter illustrates at the local level how a similar set of initiatives implemented by the Fiji Ministry of Tourism met significant problems in generating socially and economically sustainable businesses and were ultimately discarded in favour of more meaningful relationships and learning experiences based on traditional learning systems and knowledge.

The following discussion examines the case of the Lomanikaya Ecotourism Project (LEP) on the island of Vatulele south of Fiji's main island of Viti Levu. The case study illustrates a cultural distance between consumers and producers of tourism experiences, particularly with respect to their expectations of the other. It is argued that this distance is widening to the extent that the development of community managed, sustainable and commercially viable ecotourism products in such places presents considerable challenges. The discussion identifies key issues emerging throughout the development of the project and discusses strategies for bridging this divide.

Background and Context

The Fiji Islands are made up of over 300 islands located in the South West Pacific Ocean. They are firmly branded in the global tourism industry as a 'tropical paradise' destination (Harrison, 2004). As Hall and Page observe, Fiji lives in the minds of prospective tourists as the 'quintessential tourism image of sun, sea, surf and sand' (1996, p. 1).

Since the 1960s, Fiji's tourism development has been largely dominated by transnational capital investment in the hotels and resorts sectors, for the most part targeting families, couples and honeymooners (Douglas and Douglas, 1996a). As such Fiji is regarded by many as a 'classic' example of tourism dependency, leakage and 'enclave tourism' (e.g. Britton and Clarke, 1987; Britton, 1991; Plange, 1996; Stanley, 1996; Harrison, 1997; Douglas and Douglas, 1996b). In recent years, however, with political unrest and changing tourism market structures, the emergence of alternative tourism markets is being encouraged as a mechanism for overcoming the inherent problems produced by the structure of the tourism industry in Fiji.

In recent years financial support mechanisms have become crucial components of the Government's tourism policy largely due to its perceived contribution to Fiji's 'triple bottom line' development goals integrating economy, employment and the conservation of culture and tradition (Fiji Taskforce, 2001). For the most part however the 'mainstream' tourism industry dominated by multinational investment and foreign ownership continues to shape the profile of tourism in Fiji (Harrison, 1997).

The military coup in 2000 effectively collapsed tourism in Fiji. More recently, prior to the coup of 2006, annual visitor arrivals were restored in excess of numbers preceding the previous unrest (Fiji Visitors Bureau, 2005). The largest two visitor markets are Australia and New Zealand closely followed by the United States and the United Kingdom. As noted earlier virtually all visitor markets to Fiji seek rest and relaxation experiences. Even rapidly growing backpacker markets, traditionally noted for seeking alternative and more adventurous experiences, mirror the experiential demands of other segments (Ateljevic and Doorne, 2005).

It is on the back of this plan that 'ecotourism' became a significant differentiating element in the national marketing strategy (Bricker, 2003; Fiji Visitors Bureau, 2003). Ecotourism in the context of Fiji lends itself more strongly to a cultural and social interpretation than that favoured in the West, which equates the concept more centrally with environmental integrity (see Honey, 1999). Indeed it is the scant regard paid to environmental issues that is a major concern to the tourism industry in terms of finding appropriate representations of environmental quality in and around Fijian villages, thus rendering village experiences marketed as 'ecotourism' highly suspect and barely viable. Although the Ministry of Tourism has adopted an Ecotourism Certification scheme, the Green Globe 21 programme, and bases its policy initiatives on WTO guidelines, the implementation of environmental management in accordance with these guidelines proves problematic at the local level.

For Australian and New Zealand visitors – the bulk of the tourist arrivals – Fiji similarly represents a traditional 'holiday' destination and is commonly regarded as something of a playground in the 'backyard' of these two countries. The tourism plant catering to these markets is typified by large-scale resort complexes providing all-inclusive holiday deals to family groups across a broad age spectrum. The largest of these resorts are located along the southern Coral Coast running between Nadi in the west and Suva in the east. Although many of these resorts are rather dated, such as the Shangri-La's Fijian built in the 1960s, demand for these kinds of experiences remains strong.

Challenges to these markets however include niche-oriented tourism products offering more interactive experiences with both the natural and cultural environments. These emerging markets elsewhere in Fiji and the region have led the mainstream resort complexes to seek differentiating products that will take guests out of the traditional enclave environment of the resort. To this end these resorts represent fertile ground for the marketing of experiential products by neighbouring villages and communities encouraged to enter the tourism economy through government subsidies and donor support. The following discussion focuses on the issues emerging from the planning process for the LEP and illustrates the divide between the expectations of tourists and villagers as to what constitutes a Fijian village experience.

Encountering the Global–Local Divide: Issues of Cultural Distance and Product Development

There are four villages on Vatulele Island located on the eastern coast. Most of these villages have some relationship with the exclusive and very expensive Vatulele Resort located on the picturesque western shore. Some villagers are employed in the resort in semi-skilled jobs such as security, laundry services or room servicing. The more high profile positions are filled from elsewhere and management is the exclusive domain of expatriates. The experiences of living with the resort led the elders of Lomanikaya village to initiate their own tourism venture to provide alternative economic opportunities for the village, particularly its young people. The product outlined in the original funding proposal to Canada Fund featured a number of issues discussed below.

Transportation to the island is central to the development of the product. The local boats which normally ply the waters between Vatulele and the Coral Coast take over three hours to complete the 25 km journey and have limited capacity. The boats are old, barely seaworthy, and are normally filled above capacity with villagers and their produce. The boat sought by the project would complete the 25 km journey in approximately 40 minutes and would seat up to 17 passengers in relative comfort and safety. This then became the number of visitors for whom the experiential product was designed. The boat would also double as a safe alternative travel option for villagers on days not allocated to the project.

Once arriving at Lomanikaya village on Vatulele Island the project proposed that visitors would be traditionally welcomed at a purpose-built shelter adjacent to the beach just to the north of the village. The welcome would normally include a 'kava ceremony' or *sevusevu* following which the group would be taken on a guided walk through the village congregating at the central 'bure', a large traditionally thatched meeting house in the centre of the village. On their tour of the village visitors would be able to observe the making of 'masi', a cloth made from the mulberry tree bark and beaten to form large sheets which are painted in traditional patterns, principally for ceremonial use. In recent years the village has become one of the major producers of masi for the tourist trade and has a standing order with the Government Handicrafts Centre in Suva.

Following the village tour visitors would embark on a cross-island walk with discussions on points of interest along the way. Vatulele Island is home to the locally renown red fresh water prawns which live in springs close to the village of Lomanikaya. The walk would take visitors through the village's subsistence plantations and through a forested area where traditional medicines are gathered. Further along the walk visitors would be taken to a cultural *taboo* site with fortifications from the tribal warfare period preceding the Christian era. Also nearby is an archaeological site with scattered remnants of ancient pottery and other evidence of early human habitation.

At the end of the cross-island walk visitors would arrive at the spectacular western beach owned by the Lomanikaya village. The proposal suggested that visitors would have lunch provided for them here and they could take the opportunity to swim and relax before returning to the village along a more direct route. In effect, the various elements, including the natural resource base on which the product was designed, were of very high quality and of significant interest if interpreted well. The project in its initial appraisal had the capacity to offer high quality experiences to potentially lucrative and well-established markets. Each visitor would expect to pay around $120 per head for the experience, on a par with top-end day trips operating elsewhere in Fiji – providing appropriate levels of service and plant quality could be achieved.

Despite the promising opportunities detailed by the proposal some significant challenges emerged for the development of a viable visitor experience. The first and perhaps the most intractable problem facing the villagers was that of rubbish littering the beaches, villages and all areas where there is a human presence. The beach at Korolevu on

It is this core-safety concern which features highly on the hierarchy of needs for both visitors and the resorts in which they stay. Any suggestion of food poisoning or other concerns emerging from the village would result in instant withdrawal of support and the collapse of business operations for the village. Again, the structure of relationships in this instance demands that producer standards conform to the needs and demands of visitors. Given that issues emerging from the product development phase would result in considerable changes to lifestyle practices to cater for the targeted visitor markets, the question emerges as to the extent to which the experiences created retain the integrity of a contemporary Fijian village environment. An unfortunate reality is that the daily lives of remote Fijian villages often display few characteristics marketable in an industry predominantly dedicated to producing iconic and contrived experiences.

Other issues emerged as 'soft spots' in the initial proposal including the need for guides to develop their language skills sufficiently to communicate adequately with guests, and the need for interpretation to be planned, structured and developed uniformly amongst guides in order to mesh with other elements of the product and sequences of activities. The beach environment on the western side of the island represents a significant resource in terms of its iconic appeal, especially given that the quality of beaches on the Coral Coast scarcely resemble the dominant imagery. The western coast of Vatulele, where there are no villages, has the environmental integrity and iconic characteristics which allow the Vatulele resort to charge up to US $1500 per night. The resort offers a first class service environment and accommodation, yet the significance of a high quality natural environment cannot be ignored.

The ultimate irony of the project is that although the venture articulates the vision of government in terms of developing locally based tourism enterprises, the 'alternative' model is expressed in terms of the production process and structures rather than the visitor markets. It remains that the most viable market open to the project is precisely the market which policy agencies are not actively seeking to further develop. Many of the issues identified above emerge directly from the need to cater to the demands of these markets.

Bridging the Divide: Institutional Strategies and Local Networks

What makes the Lomanikaya case study significant is the way in which a very high quality product (including several years of rubbish removal efforts) was ultimately created by local villagers largely independent of any centralized facilitation processes targeting indigenous Fijians wanting to enter the ecotourism sector. Indeed their success occurred *in spite of* the efforts of government ministries that have created a succession of generally poor quality 'ecotourism' projects nationwide. Not only are quality issues at the fore of concerns, but the situation is symptomatic of a more generalized core-periphery relationship and the serialization of neo-colonial dependencies.

As noted earlier the Tourism Ministry in Fiji has in the last decade been proactively fostering 'ecotourism' as a strategy for facilitating largely economic benefits for-indigenous Fijians who otherwise rank poorly amongst indicators of social, economic and political welfare. Seduced by a dearth of normative writing in the late 1980s and 1990s, the Ministry embraced a series of policies expressed as strategies through subsequent development plans to encourage the initiation of business ventures, mostly focusing on accommodation and activities, amongst villages throughout the country. The issues facing Lomanikaya village described above are typical of those attempting to engage with the wider mainstream industry which is largely foreign owned and controlled.

Aside from several high profile projects receiving international donor assistance, such as the Abaca and Bouma projects sponsored by what is now New Zealand International Aid and Development (NZAID), little in the way of consultative or knowledge support has filtered down to villages. The majority of support given has been delivered through the Ministry in the form of roaming workshops offering instruction to villagers, through the traditional village hierarchies, on basic elements of tourism business operation. As such the percolation of knowledge often bypassed those villagers most critical to the implementation of the product, namely women. Secondly, the nature of delivery mirrors the way in which the Fijian education system delivers its teaching, i.e. largely based on a top-down, rote system of learning. The delivery of the tourism workshops, whilst accepted as the norm in terms of up-skilling methodologies by government and villagers alike, bears little resemblance to the ways in which villagers learn traditional life skills in the village environment.

In the case of Lomanikaya, the way in which, for example, masi making was learned by young women involved a more interactive 'sit by nellie' approach where understanding was achieved by 'doing' but, most importantly, was conceived, structured, delivered, and evaluated by the people most important to the individual doing the learning. As such, issues of quality are regulated not by a willingness to reproduce what is taught but is inherently embedded within wider social structures and relationships of family, kinship, seniority and village life in general.

An irony is apparent here in the fact that the issues impeding the flow of information delivered through the modernist paradigm, and rendering it relatively impotent, is the very mechanism through which real learning opportunities can be realized. There are other examples throughout the village where the mode of learning differs significantly from the normal approach to teaching. These include subsistence activities such as fishing, food preparation, cooking, building construction, health care, animal husbandry, resource management, as well as what are regarded as traditional cultural practices such as the aforementioned masi making, herbal medicines, song and dance (meke), and the performance of ceremonial ritual.

In Lomanikaya village virtually all of the above skills feature in the development of the tourism product. What is of critical concern is the introduction of other cultures into the mix. The quality management 'standards' employed for village based skills are however of little practical application in the host–guest tourism relationship and quality management 'systems' are however directly relevant. What is of critical concern is the knowledge implemented by the system. Foucault's power–knowledge paradigm in this context is central to the generation of positive development benefits capable of mitigating potential dependency relations.

The final bridging of the cultural divide came from the utilization of existing extended family networks in the form of *tokatoka* and *tikina* spread throughout the country and, given the predominant role of tourism in the Fiji economy and employment statistics, a sector in which many extended family members have significant knowledge and expertise. Distinct from a situation in which representatives of the Ministry of Tourism or other government agency travel the country delivering tourism training workshops, sometimes to tribal groups who were historical enemies only a handful of generations previously, the difference in learning outcomes was vast.

The role of individuals facilitating the training visits to the island by distant family members was significant. These individuals were able to wield sufficient status to attract those with skills to the island within the overriding systems of reciprocity which dominate Fijian socio-economic relations. Extended family members working in seemingly non-influential positions in the mainstream industry, such as laundry workers, restaurant kitchen hands and groundkeepers, assumed roles of critical importance amongst villagers – not necessarily for their particular industrial skills but more for their familiarity with the culture of mainstream resorts and the tourists themselves. Their ability to read the needs of these tourists should not be confused with a familiarity with nuances of Australasian cultures, but more significantly with the needs and concerns of those cultural groups 'on holiday'. Here the opportunity for tourists to perform the act of being a tourist is central to the delivery of a successful and quality product – a fact fully appreciated by the management and training systems of resorts and the wider industry in general. As well as the more mundane roles, incorporated in this system of indigenous knowledge transfer were the more high profile tourism-specific activities such as tour guiding, food preparation, and cultural performance (*meke*).

Around these activities some further ironies were observed whereby, in the case of food preparation, a marked reversal of social status for a particular individual was a notable outcome of the tourism power–knowledge relationship. In the male dominated social structures of the Fijian village the status of homosexual men is accorded relatively little significance, individuals regarded more as women than men. For one young gay man in Lomanikaya the development of the tourism product dramatically shifted that position to the extent that he became a highly respected and valued leader within the tourism venture. His job as a flower arranger in the dining room of the Vatulele Resort on the other side of the island was in one context a typically menial role in the neo-colonial system yet that same role empowered him with important understanding of the significance of the aesthetic in the food environment, particularly the creation of ambience in the dining setting. As such this individual assumed an instrumental role in the establishment and maintenance of quality standards and management processes around the preparation of food and its presentation as well as playing an important role in the design and layout of the previously mentioned purpose-built *bure* adjacent to the village.

This *bure* is used as a 'meet and greet' point for visitors arriving off the boat and was fringed by several new flush toilets with running water. The *bure* doubled in use as a dining room for the visitor group on their return from the cross-island walk, by which time the structure had been transformed by the adornment of flowers, weaving and attention to detail commonly seen in dining areas of upmarket resorts. Such is the importance of this aesthetic element that the dining experience branded the product as distinctly 'top-end' when combined with high quality ingredients. Octopus, shellfish, fish, fruit are all grown organically and harvested locally in contrast to the largely imported and often processed ingredients characteristic of mainstream resorts. The individual was able to work effectively with extended family members brought to the village as trainers to establish quality systems across and through the product. Quality systems in this context work through a largely oral culture and revolve around embedding a sense of pride, work ethic and collective adherence to quality consistent with the ways in which standards are maintained in aspects of collective domestic life outside the tourism product.

This last point returns the discussion to the critical element of facilitating a positive entrepreneurial outcome, one that set this particular tourism venture apart from other attempts to establish ecotourism ventures elsewhere in Fiji. At the centre of the process is the difference in the way in which people are taught versus the way they learn. The Ministry of Tourism's approach to facilitating tourism entrepreneurship by implementing a series of workshops throughout the country, whilst consistent with the Fijian education delivery system in general, is at odds with the way in which individual and collective learning takes place in the village environment.

The launch of the LEP product created a welcome addition to the product portfolio of the Coral Coast industry. A positive start, however, by no means ensures a positive future and some difficult issues loom on the horizon that will continue the steep learning curve for all concerned. As well as obvious ongoing concerns about rubbish and quality, carrying capacity in particular will present significant pressures on local resources, especially the management of time.

The tourism product creates a multitude of additional roles for village women. It is notable, for example, that as the project progresses, male members of the operation are more inclined to advocate a growth model whereas women are generally more cautious and aware of the way in which other domestic responsibilities are displaced when in 'tourism mode'. At present the village hosts at the most two trips per week, although some are advocating that this be expanded to four or five trips. Also at issue are the collective responsibilities surrounding funerals in which all village members prepare gifts (weaving, *masi*, food) for reciprocal ceremonies. In such circumstances it is not uncommon for all villagers to vacate the village in order to visit other villages. Such practices will need to be carefully considered in a business environment where their product is potentially able to be booked and paid for from thousands of miles distant.

Conclusions: Global Lessons from Local Learning

The Lomanikaya case, whilst raising some important issues around mechanisms for entrepreneurial facilitation, should also be considered in a wider context. Not only are there implementation issues in terms of establishing effective and sustainable quality management standards and systems, but the top-down process reflects the wider neo-colonial structures of power–knowledge in which the tourism industry in Fiji has featured as a prime example for the last three decades (Britton, 1987; Mowforth and Munt, 2003).

The collapse of time and space reminds us that the process of globalization is an inherently spatial one. The context of tourism concentrates cultural collision to produce geographies of change; the inherently spatial becomes the implicitly spatial, necessarily demanding that the local co-exists with any consideration of the global. The significance of the role of culture in this entrepreneurial dynamic cannot be understated. Indeed the cultural context surrounding entrepreneurship in marginal environments is apparent in the former periphery the world over. Rather than attempting a unifying perspective consistent with more conventional non-tourism entrepreneurial modelling (Keats and Bracker, 1988; Bygrave and Hofer, 1991; Peredo et al., 2004), the Lomanikaya case suggests that some form of aggregate understanding is necessary to form collective strategies which subsequently emerge at the policy and programme level.

Similarly a specific focus on issues of tourism entrepreneurship in this context should be careful to avoid a fragmentation from tangential theorization as characteristic in the more generalized realm of entrepreneurial study (Bull and Willard, 1993). It is here that the structuralist backdrop provided by the likes of Britton (1987) and reinvigorated by Mowforth and Munt (2003) serves to focus attention on a series of discourses and dichotomies which are the unifying element of an otherwise disparate and multifaceted phenomenon (Featherstone, 1987; Morgan and Pritchard, 1998). Whilst each case naturally assumes its own particular point of focus from the theoretical to the operational, the march of globalized tourism is both the actual process and contextual reality. Human cultural encounters at the local level should not mask the structures and political economies that facilitate them.

Following the discussion at the start of this chapter, the currency of such theoretical perspectives is a function of their applicability. In response to Bianchi's (2002) call for understanding the dynamics of change at the local level, the Lomanikaya village case study illustrates that the neo-colonial model does not necessarily create a succession of orbiting dependency relations around a spatially central core. Rather the juxtaposition of these core-periphery relations at the local level has the capacity to facilitate empowering opportunities through the introduction of interpersonal relationships, not only between hosts and guests, but also by drawing elements of the wider industry into the local context through already existing familial relationships and social structures.

It follows that the challenge for entrepreneurship researchers, practitioners and policy-makers seeking to draw lessons from examples such as Lomanikaya is to explore mechanisms and methodologies for facilitating the networking of this and similar examples in such a way that local people can empower themselves against the encroachment of a formidable political economic phenomenon. As such, centrally driven approaches to developing entrepreneurship need to be balanced with methodologies working through local social systems and cultural structures rather than on top of, or indeed in spite of, them.

Questions for Discussion

1. What are the core arguments of the Britton's theorists on contemporary tourism development in the Developing World?
2. What are the main barriers to tourism entrepreneurship in the Fiji Islands?
3. What would be the most effective way to bridge the cultural divide between the local producers and global consumers?
4. What are the key lessons learned to help policy-makers and practitioners?

References

Ajzen, I. (1991). The Theory of Planned Behaviour. *Organisational Behaviour and Human Decision Processes*, 50, 179–211.

Appadurai, A. (1996). *Modernity at Large: Cultural Dimesions of Globalisation.* Minneapolis: University of Missesota Press.

Atelijevic, I. and Doorne, S. (2000). 'Staying Within the Fence': Lifestyle Entrepreneurship in New Zealand. *Journal of Sustainable Tourism*, 8(5),378–392.

Ateljevic, I., Doorne, S. and Bai Z. (2003). Representing Identities Through Tourism: Encounters of Ethnic Minorities in Dali, Yunnan Province. *International Journal of Tourism Research*, 5(1),1–11.

Ateljevic, I and Doorne, S. (2004a). Cultural Circuits of tourism: Commodities, Place and Reconsumption. In *Blackwell Companion to Tourism Geography.* (A. Lew, C.M. Hall, and A. Williams eds.), Oxford: Blackwell, pp. 291–302.

Ateljevic, J. and Doorne, S. (2004b). Diseconomies of Scale: A Study of Development Constraints in Small Tourism Firms in Central New Zealand. *Journal of Tourism and Hospitality Research*, 5(1), 5–24.

Ateljevic, I. and Doorne, S. (2005). Tourism Performance as Metaphor: Enacting Backpacker Travel in Fiji Islands. In *Tourism, Discourse and Communication*, (A. Pritchard, and A. Jaworski, eds.), pp. 173–198.

Baldacchino, G. (1999). Small Business in Small Islands: A Case Study from Fiji. *Journal of Small Business Management*, 37, 254–259.

Bianchi, R.V. (2002). Towards a New Political Economy of Tourism in the Third World. In *Tourism and Development: Concepts and Issues*, (R. Sharpley, and D. Telfer, eds.), Clevedon: Channel View Publications, pp. 265–299.

Bricker, K. (2003). Ecotourism Development in Fiji: Policy, Practice and Political Instability. In *Ecotourism Policy and Planning*, (R.K. Dowling, and D.A. Fennel, eds.), London: CABI Publishing, pp. 187–204.

Britton, S. and Clarke, W. (eds) (1987). *Ambiguous Alternative: Tourism in Small Developing Countries.* Suva: University of South Pacific.

Britton, S. (1991). Tourism, Capital and Place: Towards a Critical Geography of Tourism. *Environment and Planning D: Society and Space*, 9, 451–478.

Bull, I. and Willard, G.E. (1993). Towards a Theory of Entrepreneurship. *Journal of Business Venturing*, 8(3), 183–196.

Bygrave, W.D. and Hofer, C.W. (1991). Theorizing about entrepreneurship. *Entrepreneurship Theory and Practice*, 16(2), 13–22.

Cater, E. and Lowman, G. (eds) (1984). *Ecotourism: A Sustainable Option.* Chichester: John Wiley and Sons.

Chang, T.C. (1997). Heritage as a Tourism Commodity: Traversing the Tourist-Local Divide. *Singapore Journal of Tropical Geography*, 18(1), 46–68.

Chang, T.C., Milne, S., Fallon, D. and Pohlmann, C. (1996). Urban Heritage Tourism: The Global-Local Nexus. *Annals of Tourism Research*, 23(2), 284–305.

Clifford, J. (1992). Travelling Cultures. In *Cultural Studies*, (L. Grossberg, C. Nelson, and P.A. Treichler, eds.), London: Routledge, pp. 96–116.

Crick, M. (1989). Representations of International Tourism in the Social Sciences: Sun, Sex, Sights, Savings and Servility. *Annual Review of Anthropology*, 18, 307–344.

Dana, L.P. and Anderson, R. (2007). *International Handbook of Research on Indigenous Entrepreneurship*, London: Edward Elgar Publishing.

Douglas, Ngaire and Douglas, Norman (1996a). Social and Cultural Impack of Tourism in the Pacific. In *Tourism in the Pacific: Issues and Cases*, (C.M. Hall and S.J. Page, eds.), London: International Business Press, pp. 49–64.

Douglas, Norman and Douglas, Ngaire (1996b). Tourism in the Pacific: Historical Factors. In *Tourism in the Pacific: Issues and Cases,* (C.M. Hall and S.J. Page, eds.), London: International Business Press, pp. 19–35.

Echtner, C. (1995). Entrepreneurial Training in Developing Countries. *Annals of Tourism Research*, 22(1), 119–134.

Fairburn, Te'o, I.J. (ed) (1988). *Island Entrepreneurs: Problems and Performances in the Pacific*, The East-West Centre. Honolulu: University of Hawaii Press.

Feathersone, M. (1990). Perspectives on Consumer Culture. *Sociology*, 24(1), 5–22.

Featherstone, M. (1987). Lifestyle and Consumer Culture. *Theory, Culture and Society*, 4, 55–70.

Fennel, D.A. (1999). *Ecotoursim: An Introduction*, London: Routledge.

Fiji Visitors Bureau (2003). *Market Overview*. National Tourism Forum, 27–29 November, Suva.

Fiji Visitors Bureau (2005). *Fiji International Visitors Survey*, Suva: Fiji Visitors Bureau.

Fiji Taskforce (2001). *Enquiry into the Backpacker Segment of Fiji's Tourism Industry*, Bangkok: PATA.

Foucault, M. (1980). *Power/Knowledge*, Brighton: Harvester Press.

Franklin, A. and Crang, M. (2001). The Trouble with Tourism and Travel Theory? *Tourist Studies*, 1(1), 5–22.

Getz, D. and Carlsen, J. (2004). Family Business in Tourism: State of the Art. *Annals of Tourism Research*, 32(1), 237–258.

Hall, C.M. and Page, S.J. (1996). Introduction: The context of tourism development in the South Pacific. In *Tourism in the Pacific: Issues and Cases*, (C.M. Hall, and S.J. Page, eds.), London: International Thomson Business Press, pp. 1–15.

Hannan, M. and Freeman, J. (1977). The Population Ecology of Organisations. *The American Journal of Sociology*, 82(5), 929–964.

Harrison, D. (1997). Globalisation and Tourism: some themes from Fiji. In *Pacific Rim Tourism*, (M. Opperman, ed.), Wallingford: CAB International, pp. 83–166.

Harrison, D. (2004). Introduction: Tourism in Pacific Islands. *The Journal of Pacific Studies*, 26(1&2), 1–28.

Honey, M. (1999). *Ecotourism and Sustainable Development: Who Owns Paradise*, Washington DC: Island Press.

Ioannides, D. and Petersen, T. (2003). Tourism 'Non-Entrepreneurship' in Peripheral Destinations: A case study of small and medium enterprises on Bornholm, Denmark. *Tourism Geographies*, 5(4), 408–435.

Keats, B.W. and Bracker, J.S. (1988). Toward a Theory of Small Firm Performance: A Conceptual Model. *American Journal of Small Business*, 12(Summer), 41–58.

Kirschenblatt-Gimblett, B. (1998). *Destination Culture: Tourism, Museums, and Heritage*, Berkeley: University of California Press.

Krueger, N. and Brazeal, D. (1994). Entrepreneurial Potential and Potential Entrepreneurs. *Entrepreneurship Theory and Practice*, 18(3), 91–104.

Lindberg, K. and McKercher, B. (1997). Ecotourism: A Critical Overview. *Pacific Tourism Review*, 1(1), 65–79.

Lury, C. (1996). *Consumer Culture*, Cambridge: Polity Press.

Martin, M.J.C. (1984). *Managing Technological Innovation and Entrepreneurship*, Reston, VA: Reston Publishing.

Morgan, N. and Pritchard, A. (1998). *Tourism Promotion and Power: Creating Images, Creating Identities*, Chichester: John Wiley and Sons.

Mowforth, M. and Munt, I. (1998). *Tourism and Sustainability: New Tourism in the Third World*, London and New York: Routledge.

Mowforth, M. and Munt, I. (2003). *Tourism and Sustainability: New Tourism in the Third World*, 2nd Edn. London and New York: Routledge.

Murphy, P. (1985). *Tourism: A Community Approach*, New York: Routledge.

Peredo, A., Anderson, R., Galbraith, G., Honing, B. and Dana, L.P. (2004). Towards a Theory of Indigenous Entrepreneurship. *International Journal of Entrepreneurship in Small Business*, 1(1/2), 1–20.

Plange, N. (1996). Fiji. In *Tourism in the Pacific: Issues and Cases*, (C.M. Hall, and S.J. Page, eds.), London: International Thomson Business Plan, pp. 205–218.

Poon, A. (1996). *Tourism, Technology and Competitive Strategies*, London: Oxford University Press.

Qalo, R. (1997). *Small Business: A study of a Fijian family*, Suva: Mucunabitu Education Trust.

Rao, D. (2004). *Culture and Entrepreneurship in Fiji's Small Tourism Business Sector*. PhD. Thesis, Melbourne: Victoria University.

Richards, G. and Hall, D. (2000). *Tourism and Sustainable Community Development*, London: Routledge.

Rojek, C. (1995). *Decentring Leisure: Rethinking Leisure Theory*, London: Sage Publications.

Rudkin, B., and Hall, C.M. (1996). Unable to see the forest for the trees: ecotourism development in the Solomon Islands. In *Tourism, Indigenous, Peoples*, (R. Butler and T. Hinch, eds.), London: International Thompson Press, pp. 203–226.

Scheyvens, R. (2002). *Tourism for Development: Empowering Communities*. Pearson Education: Harlow.

Shapero, A. (1982). Some Social Dimensions of Entrepreneurship. In *The Encyclopedia of Entrepreneurship*, (C. Kent, D. Sexton, and K. Vesper, eds.), Englewood Cliffs, NJ: Prentice Hall.

Sharpley, R. (1996). Tourism and Consumer Culture in Postmodern Society. In *Tourism and Culture Towards the 21st Century Cultural Change*, (M. Robinson, N. Evans, and P. Callaghan, eds.), Sunderland: The Center for Travel and Tourism Conference Proceedings.

Shaw, G. and Williams, A. (1998). Entrepreneurship, small business culture and tourism development. In *The Economic Geography of the Tourism Industry*, (D. Ioannides, and K.D. Debbage, eds.), London: Routledge, pp. 235–255.

Silver, I. (1993). Marketing Authenticity in Third World Countries. *Annals of Tourism Research*, 20, 302–318.

Stanley, D. (1996). *South Pacific Handbook*, California: Moon Publications.

Turner, L., and Ash, J. (1975). *The Golden Hordes: International Tourism and the Pleasure Periphery*. London: Constable.

UNEP (2001). *Ecotourism and Sustainability*, Paris: United Nations. Environment Programme.

Weaver, B. (1988). *Ecotourism in the Less Developed World*, London: CAB International.

Wortman, M.S. (1987). Entrepreneurship: an integrating typology and evaluation of the empirical research in the field. *Journal of Management*, 13(2), 259–279.

Chapter 12

Building Institutional, Economic and Social Capacities: The Role of NGOs in the Context of Bosnia–Herzegovina & Serbia

Jovo Ateljevic and David Gallagher

Learning Outcomes

After reading this chapter, you should be able to:

- Explain how an NGO (non-governmental organization) engaged in entrepreneurship through social capacity building (SCB) helps local communities to convert their economic and social weaknesses into strengths;

- Understand essential concepts of social and other capacities building, regional tourism development, institutional/social entrepreneurship as well as of discourse analyses as a useful theoretical framework for understanding the social construction of organizational changes;

- Appreciate the specific political and historical context of the studied region and be able to compare it to other similar or different environments;

- Identify and explain the complexity of the regional development process burden by various political influences as well as personal interests by a multiplicity of actors.

Introduction

This chapter attempts to explain how an NGO (non-governmental organization) engages in activities of social and institutional entrepreneurship in developing capabilities at different levels: social, human, economic and institutional. In this study, tourism provides the empirical context in the cross-border regional tourism development of the eastern part of the Republika Srpska[1] (RS), BiH (Bosnia and Herzegovina) and western Serbia. The region, known as the

---

1. The state of BiH has a highly complex political system: it consists of a confederal government in which power is rotated between three ethnic communities (Bosniacs, Croats and Serbs). Within this, there are two political entities. One is the Bosniak–Croat Federation (FBIH), mainly made up of Bosnian Croats and Bosnian Muslims (the latter now termed 'Bosniacs'). The other is Republika Srpska (RS), a state in which Bosnian Serbs form the majority.

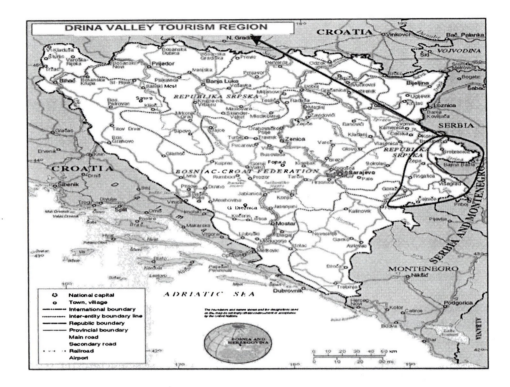

Figure 12.1: Drina Valley Tourism Region. (*Source*: Ateljevic et al., 2004.)

Drina Valley Tourism Region (DVTR), encompasses eight municipalities, four from each side of the Drina river which forms the border between the two countries (see Figure 12.1). The DVTR, situated in the Drina river valley, comprises fragile ecosystems and equally fragile open economies facing unique sustainable development problems and opportunities. The economy is strongly dependent upon agriculture and a few tourism activities with good prospects for innovative tourism development. A sizeable influx of concessionary finance, official grants and net private transfers from abroad sustain development programmes in some parts of the region, particularly in the two municipalities of Srebrenica and Bratunac (RS-BiH). One of the main problems facing all the municipalities is negative population growth and an increasing number of younger people permanently leaving the region.

The area provides a specific political and historical context due to its dynamic history associated with perpetuated ethnic and religious struggles amongst the communities[2] along the Drina river since the Ottoman invasion in the fifteenth century. The dissolution of the former Yugoslavia followed by the civil war in the early 1990s revived the historical tensions that were controlled in the former Yugoslavia. Bridges over the Drina river have never lasted

---

2. The local communities are divided by religious beliefs – Christian Orthodox (the Serbs living on both sides of the River) and Islam (the Muslim living on the left river bank i.e., the BiH territory).

long. In such context, the local communities from the region are 'closed' characterised by parochial thinking and lack of constructive initiatives for collaboration. As a result, despite abundance of natural resources, local econimies are in a poor state. Thus, any new initiative or disturbance of the traditional thinking is an increasingly challenging task.

In this light, any major changes would require a large amount of both entrepreneurial and social skills. Creating new practice and institutional infrastructure is essentially an example of institutional and social entrepreneurship as it relates to the alteration of existing practices (see Fligstein, 1997) in order to add economic and social values to the local communities through tourism development. The process of sustainable regional tourism development in this complex socio-political context is not well understood; therefore, a number of questions need to be asked. Who instigates the process? How is the process negotiated and maintained? Who gets involved in the process and how are decisions made? In this research, apart from addressing these questions, we are essentially interested in the role played by the international NGO Social Solutions and its ability to facilitate the process of this cross-border sustainable tourism development.

Our empirical investigation is limited to the international NGO sector that is regarded as the main force in institutional capacity building (ICB) (Thomson and Pepperdine, 2003). ICB refers to the provision of technical or material assistance to strengthen one or more elements of organizational effectiveness including governance, management capacity, human resources, financial resources, service delivery, external relations and sustainability. The concept of ICB is also associated with building civil society or democratization. Building organizational and institutional capacity is an essential development intervention towards the strengthening of civil society. Indeed, it is the heart of development practice. International and indigenous NGOs and many governments in developing countries recognize the importance of capacity building for development (James, 1994). Collectively and separately, the elements of capacity are often thought of as assets, or 'capital', which, in the context of capacity building refers to human capital: the knowledge and skills of people (as individuals) (Thomson and Pepperdine, 2003). Thus, capacity building relates to a range of activities by which individuals, groups and orga- nizations improve their capacity to achieve sustainable development, which is often associated with the empowerment and mobilization of local communities.

The Research Approach

Tourism as the empirical context used for this study has particular significance and it presents methodological opportunities, since its development generally involves an array of stakeholders. Tourism provides an avenue for overall economic development and is strongly embedded into a broader social fabric; as such the sector has the potential to bring more equitable, sustainable, and net benefits to local people. In the context of former Yugoslavia, tourism also has a political significance in bringing people from different ethnic/religious groups together. In other words, tourism is considered a passport for regional development and an agency for social reconciliation.

Therefore, in our study the strategy adopted by the NGO was a community approach to regional tourism development through discourse as an analytical framework to accom- modate the complexity of the two countries' (Serbia and BiH) 'distance' context. By the notion of distance or distal,[3] we mean a multiplicity of social structures in terms of classes, culture, religions, ethnic composition and institutions (Fairclough, 1992). By using discourse analysis we are able to explore and explain the process of social movement and its (re)construction. In our study discourse ascertains the role, position and actions (discursive) of different actors involved in the process of building social capacity infrastructure in the given context.

Moreover, the intrinsic reason for the existence of most of the NGOs is related to their role in changing civil society. Therefore, discourse analysis is not only able to explain how social reality is constructed but 'how it is maintained and held in place over time' (Phillips and Hardy, 2002, p. 6). In other words, we focus on the ability (or inability) of individual actors, involved in the process of institutional capacity building through discourse, as a resource to bring about sustainable changes. Discourse analysis is also an interrelated set of texts and practices of production, dissemination and consumption that bring an object into being (Fairclough, 1992; Phillips and Hardy, 2002).

Empirical data was obtained during the 3-year-long fieldwork in the DVTR. The fieldwork began with conducting initial interviews with a number of key individuals including three managing directors of Social Solutions, local NGOs and the tourism development project. The managers provided a useful background of the project and gave us an opportunity to obtain all the data we needed. Unstructured interviews were also conducted with eight mayors of the municipalities (four from each side of the Drina river) at different stages during the fieldwork. During this time the authors (one of whom was employed by Social Solutions) attended a number of formal and informal meetings, workshops, seminars and social events organized in different settings: municipal buildings, community centres, local business centres, pubs, hotels and other social settings including special tourism events such as white water rafting, regattas on the (Drina) river and fishing. In most of these meetings and events the NGO was an active participant. The collected data helped us to uncover the various layers of the reality in the eight munici-palities that emerged from the negotiations and struggles between the various actors (see also Verbole, 2000).

The Geopolitical Context

In order to understand the process of economic and social changes in the former Yugoslav states including BiH and Serbia, it is necessary to understand the Balkan context in which external influence is one of the main characteristics in the process of political and economic transformation known as the transition process. The transition process is a concept coined in the early 1990s after the dissolution of the Soviet Union and its republics, and defines the replacement of the centrally planned socialist economic system by the market economy (Blanchard, 1997). The economic and political model of the former Yugoslavia was significantly different from the mainstream model of communism

---

3. As opposed to distal proximate, 'context' refers to the immediate features of the interaction (e.g. a consultation, an interrogation, a family meal-time) in which particular events occur and the capacities in which people speak [Phillips and Hardy (2002, p. 19)].

exercised in the former Soviet Bloc. Essentially, Yugoslavia was a non-aligned, socialist state with less strict government state intervention. The command economy was looser, allowing different forms of private ownership, although on a smaller scale and mainly in the service sector (tourism, hospitality and craft industries).

Thus the process of transition from a socialist economy to a market economy could not be viewed as entirely novel for the Balkan successor states which emerged after the Yugoslav civil war, and, arguably, they should have had a much easier transition than the remainder of the former Soviet bloc (Ateljevic et al., 2004). However, the process of transition has frequently been seriously hampered by stubborn remnants of the former ideology and a new set of institutions created in the aftermath of the civil war.

Economic and political transformation in the context of former Yugoslavia, which has often been solicited by various international actors, has created a specific political and socio-economic environment in some of the newly formed countries of the former Yugoslavia, including BiH. Due to its complex ethnic/cultural structure as well as geopolitical significance, BiH has attracted a considerable international presence in the region. In spite of the extensive external help, which has continued well after the peace agreement signed in 1995,[4] the country is still somewhere halfway between transition and economic and political consolidation. The effectiveness of the intervention of foreign actors is strong not only in the light of its financial significance, but also of its concepts and strategies. In both countries, BiH and Serbia, a lack of an adequate institutional infrastructure has been regarded as the main obstacle in the transition process. Particularly in BiH, an increasingly slow process of political consolidation amongst the constituencies has undermined economic and social development. Thus, building institutional and social capacities in such a complex environment is not a straightforward process; it requires significant resources and diplomacy to negotiate many interests between an increasing number of stakeholders (Strauss and Corbin, 1990).

Research Site: Social Solutions – An International NGO

Non-governmental organizations, collectively described as the independent sector, vary greatly in scope, size, resources and impact. NGOs can be community based, or multinationally-organized-grass-roots or policy oriented. They have proven to be effective in mobilizing the support of the international community for many creditable causes in the public interest. Their missions involve a range of different activities: research-based, service-oriented, geographically focused, educationally-driven, faith-based, ideologically focused or engaged in public advocacy. Regardless of such a wide focus their

---

4. The General Framework Agreement for Peace in Bosnia and Herzegovina, also known as the Dayton Agreement, Dayton Accords, Paris Protocol or Dayton-Paris Agreement, is the peace agreement reached in Dayton, Ohio in November 1995, and formally signed in Paris on December 14, 1995. These accords put an end to the three-and-a-half-year-long civil war in BiH – one of the armed conflicts in the former Yugoslavia. According to the Agreement, BiH became a confederation consisting of two Entities: the Federation of Bosnia and Herzegovina (FBH) and the Republika Srpska (RS).

fundamental principles are more likely to be consistent with the objectives for which they receive funds.

Donations are the main source of an NGO's funding and can come from governments, the UN, private trusts, individual donors, religious institutions and other NGOs. NGOs are non-party/politically affiliated organization and have no explicate political missions; however, given the nature of their activities and funding, dependency and political significance of NGOs should not be underestimated (Bossuyt and Develtere, 1995). They often have strong influence on policy decisions and shaping political perspectives on various social and economic issues. It is believed that NGOs are capable of leveraging their influence through strategic alliances with other NGOs and government authorities. One of the major avenues through which NGOs exercise their political role is the media. It is becoming increasingly common for NGOs to establish broad and deep relationships with local communities; indeed establishing such relationships, with a strong sense of mutual trust and respect, is one of the key priorities for any NGO.

The effectiveness of NGOs is largely dependent on their leaders having the right skills in public policy negotiations, building social alliances, strategic planning, and other competencies that enhance their capacity to bring about changes. In order to do so, NGOs need to be at the forefront of many innovations that have provided ideas and models replicated or adapted in other settings and situations. Generally, non-profit organizations are seen as a growing source of solutions to issues facing today's society such as poverty, pollution, etc. (Amankwah and Anim-Sackey, 2003). This is very much associated with the concept of social entrepreneurship which is often (but not exclusively) related to not-for-profit organizations with strong social missions as well as the individuals that manage and work in such organizations (Dees et al., 2002).

Social Solutions is an international NGO that operates in a number of counties and is one of the world's largest such organizations. Social Solutions International was one of the first NGOs to operate during the wars in the former Yugoslavia. The organization is working to increase economic opportunities by supporting the establishment and growth of small and medium-sized businesses. Another major focus of their work is promoting peace and democracy in the region. Social Solutions works with forward-thinking local organizations and student associations to help them influence decision-makers to become a positive force for change.

One of the organization's missions is strengthening local organizations and capacity building by strengthening networks between organizations from different communities and through development projects that benefit members of all ethnic groups. One of the current Social Solutions projects in BiH is strengthening democracy in Eastern BiH by supporting local organizations. They provide local organizations with training and resources in order to help them increase their influence over decision-makers and promote democratic values. Part of this project is tourism development in the region.

One of the reasons for selecting an international NGO as a research site was its increasingly important role in building social capacities in the Balkans in the last 10–15 years. In so doing, the organization has established an extensive network with various government and non-government institutions and individuals in the country. It has particularly developed strong links with local NGOs that are commissioned by the organization for specific tasks. The organization also attracts some of the best local employees who seek international experience and good learning environments combined with a significant monetary reward (the salary package is approximately five times the average salary in BiH).

Tourism Development: 'Social Solutions' in Action

The project conducted by Social Solutions is based on the community and multi-stakeholder approach, which required the need for intense negotiation with various stakeholders at local, regional and national levels. The process involves various formal and informal activities including a number of workshops, with the intention to bring representatives from the eight municipalities together with an ultimate objective to establish institutional mechanisms to achieve long-term sustainable tourism development (Figure 12.2).

The tourism development project, of which building institutional capacity is the essential pillar, began with the formation of an Action Development Plan that included a number of strategic steps carried out by a Tourism Action Group (TAG) consisting of 16 people (two representatives from each municipality) whose activities were coordinated by a Liaison Officer (LO) appointed by Social Solutions. The LO ensured full participation and transparency of activities within the TAG while the TAG members extended these concepts to their municipalities through engagement of the key stakeholders. Actions undertaken by the TAG and other interest groups representations were translated into

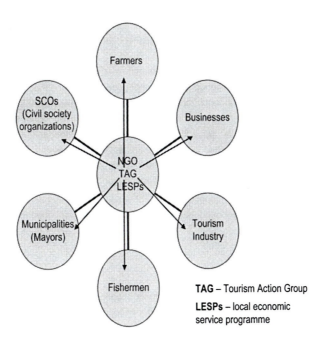

Figure 12.2: Social Solution's strategic framework.

consumer-friendly and accessible texts. The participants would receive the contextualized material and had the opportunity to contribute their opinions.

For an NGO like Social Solutions, whose focus leans mainly towards marginalized peoples' rights, the implementation of an economic development programme that emphasizes entrepreneurship and job creation was always going to be a challenge. But the key to this challenge was not only economic regeneration of an extremely poor region, across international borders with subsequent creation of community jobs within the tourism supply chain, but the issue of building sustainable institutions. This implies cooperation and partnerships (both between ethnic groups and across borders in the context of the aftermath of a bitter war in the 1990s), the development of a common tourist product based around a common natural resource – the Drina River Valley – and the equal involvement of the local state (municipalities), the private sector (SMEs) and the communities targeted (community groups, associations and NGOs) through multi-stakeholder entities.

This project was designed to assist the economic regeneration of the Drina Valley by fostering and promoting a quality and sustainable visitor industry in the region. In practice, this meant that the state – at national, regional and local (municipal) levels – would invest in the infrastructure needed (roads, signing, nature trails, river clean-up, solid waste disposal, municipal tourist associations). The private sector would help develop SMEs within the tourism supply chain (accommodation, restaurants, internet cafes, hiking trails, rafting enterprises, river boating). Community associations would look to coordinate efforts of fishing, hunting (photo safaris), hiking and rafting associations and employment opportunities for community members (ideally the most marginalized, for example single mothers, women in general, and young people). Associations would look at common licensing, monitoring, etc., whilst environmental groups would look at possibilities for river clean-up (working in cooperation with dam operators), solid waste disposal and vital environmental education.

Given the multidimensional nature of the tourism industry the project emphasized the need to view tourism from a number of different perspectives. For the producers of tourism goods and services, the project offered enhanced promotion, increased yield, better access to services and information, and greater responsiveness from the eight municipalities. For the municipalities and those that plan tourism related activities and infrastructure, there was the prospect of a coordinated approach between different stakeholder groups to develop a crucial component of the economy through a strategy focused on economic yield and environmental, social and economic sustainability. For the community there was the opportunity to play an increased role in the planning of future tourism development, in order to be more aware of the issues associated with the industry and to benefit from extra revenue and job creation.

The Process

Whilst the Social Solutions approach is bottom-up and participatory, it was clear that given recent history it was necessary to first get the main political actors on board, in both countries, BiH and Serbia. In order to begin this educational and advocacy process, a multi-stakeholder workshop was held to develop a SWOT analysis of the situation (Table 12.1). Given the nature of the tourism sector and its wider geographical and political significance this analysis was not limited to the DVTR but placed in the broader context of Serbia and BiH. The analysis confirmed that the two countries are blessed with a treasure of natural diversity, historical and cultural heritage and traditions that reflect the new trends of market travel. As a result, tourism in both countries has a strong potential for development and, if adequately planned, could play a significant role within the two

Table 12.1: SWOT analysis for DVTR.

Strengths	Weaknesses
Diversity of *natural resources* in a small area; Unpolluted land – *clean and green image*; Favourable *climatic* conditions; Wealth of *culturo-historical heritage*, values and traditions; Strategic geographical position – *proximity to markets*; Residents are keen hosts of their visitors, friends and family – *traditional hospitability* – and a determination to develop tourism; *Awareness* of the value of tourism and its potential by local government, and their determination to support tourism development; Serbia's long experience in tourism.	*Poor infrastructure*, especially transportation (roads), public utilities and visitor facilities; *Poor institutional capacity* and linkages between key stakeholders; *Lack of ecological conscience* by local residents – prevailing *take it for granted attitude*; *Litter and waste management* is an outstanding problem; Outdated and *limited knowledge, skills* (marketing in particular) and motivation of young people to stay in local areas; Lack of distinct brand or identity.
Opportunities	**Threats**
Establishment of *DVTR*; Build the *Tourism Action Group* as a business and information networking tool; Involvement of the *local community* in tourism development; *Tourism synergy* with other commercial activities (e.g. *farming*) in the region and stimulation of local *entrepreneurship* and *SMF* development; Commercialization and *conservation of cultural* and *historical* heritage; *Protection of ecosystem*.	*Legal instability* – inconsistent and unfavourable legal/policy framework for tourism development; *Inadequate privatization* of tourism-related business facilities; *Slow infrastructure improvement/ development* in BiH and SCG; Infrastructure and *environmental degradation*; *Cross-border regulation* and service; *Lack of external funding*; *Decline of population* among young and educated.

Source: CARE, (2005).

economies, becoming increasingly important over the next 10 years. Moreover, tourism occupies the central stage of both countries' economic strategy.

BiH and Serbia have major tourist assets to offer for people who seek contact with nature, away from crowds, whether they are lovers of quiet walks or enjoy skiing, rafting, hunting or patient bird-watching. Those in search of more cultural tourism will be able to relive centuries of history by visiting many heritage sites, dating back to Roman times. Within the context of tourism, the Drina Valley tourist project, as a cross-border tourism entity of BiH and Serbia, represents a blend of the best features of the two countries. The SWOT analysis was an important phase of the development process in raising awareness about the tourism opportunities amongst stakeholders. More importantly, the outcomes of the SWOT analysis were used as an effective and convincing tool during the process of negotiation.

Apart from many opportunities, the exercise addressed a number of regional weaknesses and external impediments that were subsequently translated into actions to be undertaken within an agreed and realistic timeframe of 3 years.

These actions were to:

- Identify the key stakeholders from the eight municipalities;
- Build for tourism development institutional capacity starting with the Tourism Action Group;
- Tourism planning and strategy;
- Lobby for infrastructure improvement at all government levels;
- Identify the most effective mechanism for education and training;
- Identify those with most tourism and marketing knowledge and experience in the eight localities; and to
- Provide recommendations to government (local, regional, national) for developing a simulative regulatory and policy framework for sustainable tourism development and to provide incentives to outside investors.

State Structures

These findings were presented to the Ministry of Tourism in Serbia and in Bosnia–Herzegovina (BiH – the Serb Republic entity in whose territory the project lies), emphasizing not only the potential for economic regeneration and the encouragement of entrepreneurship but also the aspect of political and social reconciliation. The discussion emphasized the necessity for multi-stakeholder partnerships (state, private sector, civil society) and the need for political and financial input from the state. Both ministries reacted positively with promises of high involvement.

Municipalities.   With this endorsement, the next set of workshops gathered the eight municipalities (Ljubovija, Bajina Basta, Priboj and Uzice in Serbia and Bratunac, Srebrenica, Visegrad and Rudo in BiH) together – this included the mayors, economic departments and municipal tourist associations. Each had been approached individually already. In order to understand the level of stakeholders' representatives' commitments towards partnership, reconciliation as well as commitment of their time and resources, a SWOT analysis was made. The results of the workshop led to a Memorandum of Understanding on support, commitment of key personnel and cooperation, which was signed by all eight mayors in the presence of high media coverage. Initially, the media based in the Federation of BiH (Bosniak[5] and Croat entity) were sceptical, especially given that Srebrenica was an integral part of the arrangement and the role of the international community had been less than positive over the past 10 years. Social Solutions dedicated a lot of time to the media subsequently and, although there are still sceptics, managed to drive the point across that economic regeneration and reconciliation were keys to the future of this depressed region and that the local state, local businesses in the tourism supply chain and community groups were in favour of moving forward.

Meanwhile, the eight mayors each designated a representative to sit on a committee that would become the overall strategic board (with Social Solutions as managers) of the initiative from the municipal side, meeting monthly and agreeing (by majority vote) on all strategic directions. This became known as the Tourist Action Group or TAG. In order to unlock the economic potential of tourism development in the Drina Valley, the major challenge was to stimulate and harmonize tourism development and marketing strategies to meet the changing needs of the consumer while at the same time creating a sustainable industry – one which maximizes economic benefits while reducing socio-environmental costs.

It was also vital to achieve some form of balance between the potentially conflicting uses of common pool resources in a cross-border context encompassing the eight municipalities. For the municipalities and the state tourism ministries, this worked very well. Strategies were developed along common lines in each municipality, financial input for infrastructure was forthcoming and overall parameters for the common Drina Valley product development were made and put out to tender. It is interesting to note that, during a stakeholder analysis workshop carried out with all stakeholders, the state actors were at the top of the scale in terms of potential investment since FDI and even local private investment was seen as only potentially forthcoming once the product and marketing of the Drina Valley Tourist Region was up and running (envisaged for 2009/10).

Entrepreneurs. Following the high profile signing of the MOU, Social Solutions began a series of both explanatory and more specific workshops with local business people, NGOs and community groups. During this first six months there were few people in the area that were not aware of the Drina Valley Tourist Project and its potential.

Local or indigenous entrepreneurs are key agents for economic change and regional development in BiH and Serbia. In this context, tourism plays an important role in a number of ways. As a result of the growth in international tourism, small (tourism) enterprises have gained political importance in both developed and less developed countries, as governments have assumed the strategic direction of regional development goals using small firm programmes to target specific geographical or demographic groups.

---

5. The new term for the Muslim population in BiH.

Therefore, in the context of the Drina Valley, tourism and small tourism enterprises were to be used as development tools for the empowerment of the economically and socially depressed communities, and were particularly focused on the empowerment of socially marginalized groups (e.g. women, youths, returnee families).

Social Solutions held a series of workshops, public meetings and training sessions with local entrepreneurs, from both existing businesses and potential SMEs. As a result, some 200 business people were clear about their potential to receive grants from the programme. Workshops were based on 5 years of experience, in the Balkans, of working with SMEs. Thus, detailed business and financial planning, proposal preparation and presentation and strategic thinking were highlighted. An important result of these deliberations was that a group of local businesses (agrobusiness, restaurants, and hotels) decided to set up a Business Association. They were assisted by Social Solution workshops in all main areas of business establishment including small grants for essential office equipment.

This was established for eastern BiH (such things already existed on the Serbian side). Over 75 businesses registered and paid membership dues, hired support staff, elected a chair at a general meeting and, after one year of operation became self-supporting. This is the first of its kind in eastern BiH and serves as a model for other areas. With some help from Social Solutions, the association has become a key player in advocacy and lobbying for better business services from the municipalities, in debates on strategies for SME development and in stakeholder decision-making on SME start-up grants. There has been an increasing interest in Bed and Breakfast accommodation in these discussions and in the key idea of using these to display local produce (jams, fruit wines, crafts). This is an area to be explored fully in the next stage (2010).

Community Groups.   During the first six months of the initiative there was much interest and involvement of local NGOs (women's groups, youth organizations, and environmental organizations), local sports associations (fishers, hunters, hikers, climbers, rafters) and community associations that represent villages on the municipal assemblies. Results included a community voice in all deliberations and, more specifically, a unified licensing, fees and calendar for fishing throughout the region through the Drina River Valley Fishers Association. This includes a grant to supply boats for policing the river. Hunters Associations are traditionally more organized with national laws already in place to regulate the sport. Social Solutions introduced the idea of photo-safaris and hiking/viewing. Rafting SMEs already exist and are well established. The assistance they needed was related mainly to marketing and river clean-up.

Organizational Forms

The Tourist Action Group (TAG) and the Business Association, along with the Fishers and Hunters Associations, have to date been the strongest participants in the ongoing development of this initiative. However, a mid-term review by Social Solutions pointed to the reality that TAG had become the key player in terms of strategy development, grant-making and infrastructure funding (see above Stakeholder Analysis). In this sense, the Business Association and the NGOs have become recipients of grants rather than full stakeholders. In 2008, this was be rectified with an expanded TAG to incorporate them.

Grants to Entrepreneurs, Municipalities and NGOs/Community Associations. The TAG decided to combine the concept of grant funding for strategic interventions associated with furthering the goals of a regional tourist product with a fair share of funding for each of the eight areas (municipalities) in order to avoid conflict later on. Also, a decision was made to spread project funds equally between municipalities, SMEs and community initiatives. Thus, at the first round and only for projects within the strategic criteria, there would be three projects per area for a total of 24 projects funded.

Within the context of the Balkans, the jury is still out on the issue of grant funding vs. soft or commercial loans. The fact is that this project has a grant fund (available, in a competitive process, to all stakeholders to enhance knowledge and to increase tourism assets) worth approximately € 1 million over 3 years. Some feel that grants distort the market and promote opportunism from those applicants with the better skills in writing proposals, good contacts with municipalities and the like. On the other side, commercial loans from banks and microcredit organizations are seen as expensive (12–18%) and often impossible (lack of collateral).

We did our best to give all potential applicants equal training in business and financial planning – some 10 workshops per municipality – and chose a project approval committee from as wide a range of stakeholders as possible. Our experience, in the end, is that whilst grants make for quicker and more visible results (donors tend to favour this), it does distort the market and leads to much social and political disturbance. Given the delicate context of this region, especially on the BiH side (returnees vs. residents, Bosniak vs. Serb to name only two), we were inundated with complaints when project approvals were posted publicly, and spent much valuable staff time holding commissions and enquiries (none of which resulted in any changes, incidentally). In future, soft loans or administrative subsidies to the lending institutions might be a fairer and less contentious approach rather than direct grants.

The nature of the proposals received and assessed by an independent business consultant was interesting. Entrepreneurs generally had solid business and financial plans and were, as encouraged in workshops, able to post their own funding (usually as much as 50%) in initiatives that basically called for imported equipment, e.g. stainless steel tanks for wine-making, furniture and equipment for Bed and Breakfasts, machines for jam-making, irrigation and frost prevention sprays for fruit and vegetable production, vehicles.

Social Solutions also encouraged a number of Public Private Partnerships (one per municipality in the first phase) whereby the municipality would supply land (often beachfront), roads and bulk services to entrepreneurs who would provide buildings, equipment and management staff for tourist initiatives. Municipalities generally asked for equipment (computers) and office furnishings as well as specific staff training for tourism related activities (economic and spatial planning departments, tourist associations, publications). NGOs and community associations were generally modest in their applications and concentrated on basic equipment, e.g. boats as mentioned above, and publications and supplies for campaigning.

The Main Obstacles

Quantitatively, there have been very many workshops around the principles embodied in the project, about business and financial planning, about strategic planning, about product development and about the huge potential in this initiative.

Qualitatively, however, there have been successes and failures and it is perhaps best to describe these in relation to the weaknesses and threats in the SWOT analysis in order to examine the difficulties presented, even though the quality of the training, workshops and knowledge transfer is high.

Poor Infrastructure and Slow Infrastructure Improvement. This is especially a problem on the BiH side due in part to the war, but there have been improvements. As an example, the Serb Republic government (one of the two entities from the Dayton Peace Accords of 1996, the other being the Federation of BiH) has improved the river road from Bratunac to Skelani/Baijna Basta and tourist associations have been set up in all eight municipalities, but progress is slow in other areas of concern (e.g. internet access, signing, nature trails, waste disposal).

Poor Institutional Capacity and Linkages Between Key Stakeholders. The project has greatly assisted municipalities in planning and human resource upgrading and, as a result, the Tourist Action Group (TAG) has developed a strategic plan for the region and the tourist 'product' has been defined. At the moment a marketing plan is being developed which entails a series of tours throughout the region as a whole with key features within each municipality highlighted, e.g. the Bridge on the Drina in Visegrad (over 300 years old), rafting, hunting, fishing, etc. The TAG, as a new institute, now has a secretariat and has funding from the state tourism offices of BiH and Serbia and, following the completion of the marketing plan, will focus some of its efforts on investment into the region.

Lack of Ecological Conscience, Environmental Degradation, Litter and Waste Management. Whilst many workshops and connections with environmental groups have been made, this remains one of the weaknesses of the programme. Municipalities find it hard to find funds for solid waste disposal and little progress has been made. It's the same with river clean-up campaigns and this is mainly due to the periodic sluicing of the dams and the low consciousness of communities. This is seen as a major design fault in the programme, in that insufficient funds were made available and reliance on local and international environmental groups has proved to be erroneous.

Outdated and Limited Knowledge and Skills (Marketing in Particular). This is gradually being addressed by bringing in marketing expertise from outside. The issue for the future is how to get the TAG and other players to interact with professional tour operators from target countries in the Balkans and in Europe.

Lack of Motivation of Young People to Stay in Local Areas and General Population Decline. Whilst some jobs have been created via the 30-odd SMEs already in operation, the overall population continues to decline, especially in BiH. This is a general phenomenon as young people move to the cities to seek employment and, ultimately, to emigrate. The consequences of the Dayton Peace Accord (especially the formation of high cost entities and cantons) and the continuing ethnic tensions make EU entry a distant prospect. Consequently, the economy generally is not performing well as inflation rises.

Lack of Distinct Brand or Identity. The development of the product and the marketing plan is making this a reality.

Legal Instability – Inconsistent and Unfavourable Legal/ Policy Framework for Tourism Development, Cross-Border Regulations and Services. This has improved in that regional Drina valley tours will have much improved cross-border regulations as agreed by both countries. Another positive example is that a common policy framework now exists on fishing licences, seasons, etc. via the integrated Drina Valley Fishing Association.

Inadequate Privatization of Tourism Related Business Facilities. This is still a problem, but gradually joint public/private ownership is being consolidated as well as some instances of privatization, especially when a facility receives a grant from the project.

Lack of External Funding. As donor funding declines in BiH and Serbia (although most of what is left is designated for economic development), foreign direct investment still tends towards energy, forestry and telecommunications. Once the marketing is launched it is hoped to attract investors, local and foreign, but this is still a way off.

Key Implications and Conclusions

With hindsight, this stakeholder analysis tended to move the focus more towards the state as the prime mover and the underdeveloped private and community sectors became more the recipients of resources rather than prime movers in the decision-making process. The result was the separation of activities between the sectors. However, much work was done with the private sector, e.g. setting up a Business Association for eastern BiH, and with civil society groups, especially those related to fishing, hunting, and bed and breakfast accommodations. However, what is beyond doubt is that an organization is needed as a catalyst for this process to succeed, in this case Social Solutions. It is important that this is an organization that is not only objective – an outsider if you like, that has no political affiliation – but that is an NGO which keeps the social aspects to the fore whilst, at the same time, encouraging local initiatives, especially those of local entrepreneurs.

Power relations are a key facet of any development initiative anywhere and this underdeveloped area attempting a cross-border cooperative initiative is no exception. The war in eastern BiH saw many atrocities committed and the inadequacy of the international community was clearly exposed – this has left deep wounds and suspicions. Add to this the fact that Srebrenica Municipality is essentially run by the SDA (Muslim party) and the rest by a variety of Serbian nationalist parties. However, Srebrenica Municipality officials are masters at donor relations and they quickly endorsed the project.

The point here is that municipalities in Republika Srbska (BiH) and in Serbia itself are directly linked to line ministries in Banja Luka (administrative centre of RS) and Belgrade, but also to the political parties in Sarajevo, Banja Luka and Belgrade so their propensity to seek the power in a project arrangement like this is strong. They will cooperate between themselves and see to it that project resources are shared equally between them but, perhaps because of the continued mentality of socialism, they are reluctant for community associations and NGOs to take much power in the arrangement. The problem with this is that most elected local officials and bureaucrats have an expectation of some personal gain wherever there are outside resources at play. This usually translates into friends and relatives receiving entrepreneurial grants. Social Solutions was very aware of this and built the necessary selection criteria, capacity building and equality into workshops, meetings, conferences and grants.

In eastern BiH there has been a large transfer of foreign funding since the end of the war in 1995, so you have this strange mentality, mentioned above, of entitlement amongst all groupings – state, business and civil society.

Local NGOs are sons and daughters of international NGOs (INGOs) and are thus extremely competitive and tend to follow INGO trends – youth, women's rights, anti-trafficking, violence against women, etc., which, though laudable in themselves as issues to be faced, tend to link them nationally and internationally into UN statistics rather than focus on local issues of employment, education and health care. Thus, in this tourism project, the local NGOs seemed interested only in possible grants on their salaries and were therefore not a force within the overall power relations. This was left to the community groups and community-based organizations (CBOs) who were not only much more representative of people in the area but forceful and creative in workshops and meetings. Those community organizations that were organized around specific activities, i.e. fishing, hunting, rafting, and hiking, were especially active and pertinent to the tourism focus. Entrepreneurs and local business people in general, whilst fulfilling their mandate to get profitable businesses going, make money and indeed invest their own money, were also very active in enhancing the 'contact sport' of influencing municipal officials in order to acquire the grants.

There can be no doubt, from experiences to date, that a neutral, creative, participatory oriented organization like Social Solutions is essential, given the political context and the potential for power imbalances. However, it must be said that the prevailing entitlement attitudes, the power of the local state and the virtual non-existence of relevant local NGOs presented a high potential for failure. But consistent efforts towards maximum participation and transparency have borne some fruit and the process continues quite successfully even though setting up the TAG (municipalities – see above) to the exclusion of other stakeholders was a mistake and will be rectified in the future.

The DVTR model is specific in a number of ways, however it helps to enhance our general understanding of the process of local/regional development – beyond the context of BiH and Serbia or the Balkans – by emphasizing two key issues. These are related to the participatory approach of multiple stakeholders from the state, the private sector and civil society and giving them equal weight in discussion and planning (this latter being a good lesson learned by Social Solutions). The other relates to donors and it is important that they be persuaded towards loans rather than quick-fix grants. Both of these have a better chance of enhancing the sustainability of the initiative.

Questions for Discussion

1. What are the key strengths of a discourse analysis for understanding the social construction of organizational changes?
2. Why have international NGOs often limited autonomy in delivering their services?
3. What was the main miscalculation that Social Solutions made during the process of the tourism development in DVTR?

References

Amankwah, R. K. and Anim-Sackey, C. (2003). Strategies for Sustainable Development of the Small-scale Gold and Diamond Mining Industry of Ghana. *Resources Policy*, 29, 131–138.

Ateljevic, J., O'Rourke, T. and Todorovic, Z. (2004). Entrepreneurship and SMEs in Bosnia and Herzegovina: building institutional capacity. *The International Journal of Entrepreneurship and Innovation*, 5(4), 241–254.

Blanchard, O. (1997). *The Economist of Post-Communist Transition*. Oxford: Clarendon Press.

Bossuyt, J. and Develtere, P. (1995). Between autonomy and identity: The financing dilemma of NGOs. Full text of an article from *The Courier* ACP-EU No. 152, July–August: pp. 76–78. www.hiva.be/docs/artikel, accessed on 29/05/2006.

CARE (2005, October). *Regional Economic Develoment: a Cross-Border Partnership between Bosnia and Herzegovina (BiH) and Serbia and Montenegro (SCR)*. Sarajev: CARE International for the Balkans.

Gregory, Dees, J. et al. (Eds) (2002). *Strategic Tools for Social Entrepreneurs: Enhancing the Performance of Your Enterprising Non-Profit*. New York: Wiley.

Fairclough, N. (1992). *Discourse and Social Change*. Cambridge: Polity Press.

Fligstien, N. (1997). Social Skill and Institutional Theory. *American Behavioral Scientist*, 40, 397–405.

James, R. (1994). *Strengthening the Capacity of Southern NGO Partners: A survey of current Northern NGO approaches. International NGO Training and Research Centre*. INTRAC Occasional paper, *Vol. 1*, no. 5. Oxford: INTRAC.

Phillips, N., and Hardy, C. (2002). *Discourse Analysis: Investigating Processes of Social Construction, Thousands*. Oaks, CA: Sage.

Strauss, A., and Corbin, J. (1990). *Basics of Qualitative Research: Grounded Theory Procedures and Techniques*. London: Sage Publication.

Verbole, A. (2000). Actors, Discourses and Interfaces of rural Tourism Development at the Local Community Level in Slovenia: Social and Political Dimensions of the Rural Tourism Development Process. *Journal of Sustainable Tourism*, 8(6), 479–490.

Part 4

Sectoral Strategies and Policy Issues for Tourism Entrepreneurship

Chapter 13

The Public Policy Context of Tourism Entrepreneurship

C. Michael Hall

Learning Outcomes

After reading this chapter, you will be able to:

- Comprehend and analyse the role of government in the tourism sector;

- Identify the main reasons for public sector involvement in the tourism industry and its contribution to tourism development;

- Identify and explain an institutional structure at a range of geographical scales ranging from the local to regional, national and international level and how these might be directly or indirectly related to the tourism industry;

- Understand the complexity of the tourism policy system;

- Understand and illustrate the embeddedness of tourism entrepreneurs and firms within institutional structures in which the activities of government and the state are dominant.

Introduction

At first glance a chapter entitled 'the public policy context of tourism entrepreneurship' may seem to be something of a misnomer, linking as it does the notion of government bureaucracy at one level – often regarded as slow and unwieldy – with the dynamism of the individual entrepreneur. Typical of negative perceptions of government in relation to entrepreneurship and innovation is the oft-quoted statement of Ronald Reagan, at his first inaugural address as President of the USA in 1981 (Reagan, 1981), that 'government is not the solution to our problem; government is the problem'. To which may be contrasted the comments of Ateljevic and Doorne (2000a, p. 280) who concluded, in a tourism context, that 'Key descriptors of the entrepreneur have come to include: risk-taking, innovation, creativity, alertness and insight'. However, nothing could be further from the truth than a supposed dichotomy of individuals as entrepreneurial and government as anti-entrepreneurial.

Governments throughout the world are seeking to maximize economic growth by providing a framework for economic development of which entrepreneurship is regarded almost universally as an integral component. In some cases government actors are also significant economic and social entrepreneurs (Boyett, 1996). Indeed, entrepreneurship is typically regarded as integral to national and regional competitiveness, including at the level of the destination. For example, Blake et al. (2006, p. 1104) comment that 'Entrepreneurial ability is an important source of competitiveness, as entrepreneurs who start up new businesses introduce innovative practices and new technology that challenge incumbents' performance'. Furthermore, Hall and Williams (2008) also argue that 'Although entrepreneurialism is usually understood as being a characteristic of individuals, it can also be understood ... that it also represents a form of collective behaviour, whether of the entrepreneurial state or the entrepreneurial company'. In fact in tourism the state has long been a major entrepreneurial actor in many jurisdictions (Hall, 2008a).

In most European countries with a significant welfare state tradition, along with some countries with a colonial heritage such as Canada, New Zealand and Singapore, government has usually had an entrepreneurial role in tourism. Although entrepreneurship is often primarily seen as a private sector activity from more of an American entrepreneurial model, governments have historically acted to develop businesses opportunities where the private sector has not been willing to undertake investment risks. This has often been particularly important in tourism where returns may be relatively low as compared to other sectors. This means that national and local governments have often acted to own and operate businesses such as airlines, travel companies and accommodation along with what is widely regarded as more traditional government tourism ventures such as national parks, art galleries and museums as well as some transport and visitor infrastructure (Mattson et al., 2005).

For example, in the Nordic countries government ownership in transport infrastructure, such as railways and airlines, has long been significant for tourism although several of these ventures have now been corporatized or privatized (Hall et al., 2009). Nevertheless, the 'entrepreneurial state' is still extremely strong at the regional level in terms of municipal support for tourism related ventures (Ateljevic and Doorne, 2000b; Pike, 2004). For example, in Europe municipal entrepreneurial developments, usually undertaken through wholly or partly-owned companies, have also often been supported through European Union funding as part of a broader process of entrepreneurial development in more peripheral regions and responses to issues of 'market failure' (Müller and Jansson, 2007; Neubauer et al., 2007; Hall et al., 2009), especially in relation to

- Improving economic competitiveness at regional and national scales;
- Amending property rights;
- Enabling state decision-makers to take account of externalities, particularly in the environmental and social policy spheres;
- Providing widely available public benefits;
- Reducing risk and uncertainty;
- Supporting projects with high capital costs and involving new technologies;
- Educating and providing information.

Although there is a significant tradition of policy analysis and research related to the ways that government may be able to stimulate entrepreneurship and business start-up in general (Mokry, 1988; Dutz et al., 2000; Audretsch, 2004; Spencer and Gómez, 2004), it is a topic which has been insufficiently considered in tourism where the entrepreneur and the firm are often treated in relative isolation from the structural context in which they are embedded (Hall and Williams, 2008). Moreover, little research has been done to place tourism entrepreneurship into a comparative context and explain why government measures with respect to encouraging tourism entrepreneurship in one jurisdiction may be more effective than in other jurisdictions (Morrison and Teixeira, 2004a), even though the role of the environment is widely recognized as important to tourism business success (Dahles, 1998; Page et al., 1999; Lerner and Haber, 2000; Florida, 2002; Koh, 2002, 2006; Irvine and Anderson, 2004; Morrison and Teixeira, 2004b; Morrison, 2006; Zapalska and Brozik, 2007).

Figure 13.1 presents a diagram of a tourism entrepreneurial and innovation system to help illustrate the embeddedness of entrepreneurs and firms within institutional structures in which the activities of government and the state are central both in terms of direct intervention, for example financial support of business start-up activities, and indirect influence, for example broader regulatory structures and funding for infrastructure and education. In the context of tourism and innovation Hall and Williams (2008) argued that as well as understanding individual entrepreneurial behaviour we also need to understand that tourism entrepreneurship is being shaped at various scales by structural conditions, in which the role of government and the state is particularly important (see also Hébert and Link [2006] for a more generic discussion of the interrelationships between innovation and entrepreneurship).

Within the innovation literature these are also termed 'innovation systems' and within the entrepreneurship literature such structural conditions are also closely related to concepts such as entrepreneurial development systems (Lichtenstein and Lyons, 2001, 2006) or entrepreneurial climate (Goetz and Freshwater, 2001). However, given their recognized importance with respect to innovation and firm survivability there is a surprising dearth of literature on the extent to which such entrepreneurial systems and the entrepreneurial climate affect tourism (Deller et al., 2001; Wilson et al., 2001; Acs and Armington, 2004; Lordkipanidze et al., 2005; Wilkinson, 2006).

One of the key points of such a structural and institutional approach is that location matters, and that entrepreneurship needs to be understood as embedded in a place and in the set of socio-cultural, economic and political structures that operate there. As Hall and Williams (2008) observe, 'Essentially, some environments – for reasons related to how markets are constructed and their institutions – are more favourable than others to innovation'. The particular reasons are necessarily complex and centre on capital markets, the specific roles of state intervention, the existence of inter-agency relationships and trust, and the existence of a cosmopolitan social environment which is not only tolerant of but encourages and rewards difference and dissent. The state, and its associated set of policy, regulatory and financial interventions, is therefore an essential ingredient of tourism entrepreneurship.

This chapter is divided into two main parts. The first section discusses the policy context for tourism entrepreneurship with respect to understanding policy mechanisms while the second discusses some of the policy categorization and implementation relationships that exist. The chapter concludes by emphasizing the need to move beyond tourism policy if trying to understand the policy environment for tourism entrepreneurship.

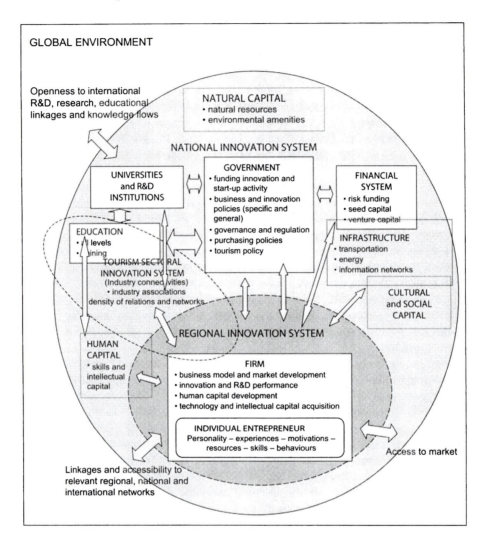

Figure 13.1: The embeddedness of tourism entrepreneurship in entrepreneurial and innovation systems (Hall, 2008b).

Tourism Policy

A key starting point for understanding the policy dimensions of tourism entrepreneurship is the nature of the state that determines 'public policy'. Unfortunately, this is not a simple matter as the state is now increasingly seen as a multilayered institution (Rhodes, 1997). A state is the political association of governing institutions that has effective sovereignty over a given spatial area and set of people. The term is often used by the layperson to refer to government. However, in a more formal sense government is only one component of the broader set of state institutions that also includes administrative departments, the courts and judiciary, enforcement agencies, other levels of government, government business enterprises, regulatory and assistance authorities, and a range of semi- and quasi-state organizations (Hall, 2008a). The state performs a number of functions as:

- Developer and producer;
- Protector and upholder;
- Regulator;
- Arbitrator and distributor; and
- Organizer.

The functions of the state will affect tourism entrepreneurship to different degrees (Wood and Valler, 2004). The state and its institutions shape the economic climate for industry, help provide the infrastructure and educational requirements for tourism, establish the regulatory environment in which business operates and take an active role in promotion and marketing. However, the extent to which individual functions are related to particular tourism entrepreneurship policies, decisions and developments will depend on the specific objectives of institutions, interest groups and significant individuals relative to the policy process as well as the nature of the specific jurisdiction within which policy is being developed

Furthermore, the state, in terms of the sense of a nation state, is only one level of governance, and therefore only one level at which policy is articulated. In addition to the nation state, other levels of governance can be recognized at the international and supranational level – for example multistate institutions such as the various UN agencies as well as the World Trade Organization and the World Bank, both of which have enormous impacts on business opportunities in many jurisdictions (Coles and Hall, 2008) – as well as the sub-state level or what is often referred to as the local state. In many jurisdictions there will be multiple sub-state levels of governance; for example in federal systems there is a state/provincial level, which may have powers that in other jurisdictions would be undertaken by the national government, as well as a local government level. The important point is that each level of governance produces public policies that can directly and indirectly influence entrepreneurship capacities in different economic sectors (Evans and Jovanovic, 1989; Malecki, 1994; Kuratko et al., 1999; Thomas, 2000; Goetz and Freshwater, 2001; Wood and Valler, 2004).

The government, elected or unelected, is clearly one of the central institutions of the state. Consisting of the ministers of the state and the head of state, government maintains political authority within the state. From a western democratic perspective government legitimacy can only be provided through an electoral process. Therefore, parliamentary institutions provide the main forum for the articulation of alternative policies and act as a decision-maker in conjunction with cabinet, individual ministers and the head of state. However, while a lay perception may exist that policies go through parliament, this is certainly not the case in most jurisdictions. Policies may be discussed but it is usually legislation and regulation that is the focus of parliamentary activity, and such legislative dimensions are only a rather narrow aspect of what constitutes policy. Furthermore, it also needs to be recognized that in the majority of jurisdictions around the world, tourism is not a significant electoral issue in comparison with broader policy fields such as employment, crime, security, the environment or the cost of energy (Padgett and Hall, 2001), which itself may be a general reflection of the tourism industry's lack of persuasion in influencing public policy (Crouch and Ritchie, 1999).

Public policy is the focal point of government activity. Public policy 'is whatever governments choose to do or not to do' (Dye, 1992, p. 2). Public policy-making, including tourism policy-making, is first and foremost a political activity. Public policy stems from governments and/or public authorities—'A policy is deemed a public policy not by virtue of its impact on the public, but by virtue of its source' (Pal, 1992, p. 3). The economic, social and cultural characteristics of society as well as the formal structures of government and other features of the political system influence public policy. Pressure/interest groups (e.g. tourism industry associations, conservation groups, community groups), significant individuals (e.g. local government councillors, business leaders), members of the bureaucracy (e.g. employees within tourism organizations or economic development agencies) and others (e.g. academics and consultants) all influence and perceive public policies in significant and often markedly different ways. Policy is therefore a consequence of the political environment, values and ideologies, the distribution of power, institutional frameworks and of decision-making processes (Hogwood and Gunn, 1984; Hall and Jenkins, 1995; Kerr, 2003).

Tourism public policy is whatever governments choose to do or not to do with respect to tourism (Hall and Jenkins, 1995). However, such a deceptively simple statement hides an extremely complex policy situation. As any student of tourism recognizes, tourism is a complex field to define because of its service characteristics, its variability in space and time, and the extent to which it can be difficult to distinguish it from other forms of human mobility (Hall and Page, 2006). The difficulty of definition is not just an academic issue, as failure to clearly define a policy field can severely limit the capacities of governments and public agencies to effectively undertake action.

In fact Hall (2006, 2008a) stresses the importance of distinguishing between tourism policies, i.e. policies generated by government tourism agencies, authorities and departments that have been developed specifically for the purpose of managing, regulating or promoting tourism and policies that affect tourism, i.e. public policies that either through their scope or because of their specific intent affect or influence tourism. In the case of the latter, policies with respect to industrial policy, labour law, international trade, education and training, and regional development, for example, may be far more significant for the operation of tourism firms and entrepreneurial behaviour than 'tourism policies' per se (Coles and Hall, 2008; Hall, 2008a).

Nevertheless, the policy situation is also complicated by the different institutional structures of tourism related public organizations. Table 13.1 outlines the four basic designs of public tourism organizations in relation to the main functions of such tourism bodies, which may be characterized as policy, marketing and development (Hall, 2008a). There is therefore no one universal model of what the policy related functions of a tourism agency should be; instead there are four main variants, which may also differ in their emphasis given the scale of governance, and which clearly will have different perceived functions with respect to their role in encouraging tourism entrepreneurship.

Table 13.1: Approaches to the institutional design of public tourism organizations.

Institutional Design	Nature	National Level Example	Other Scales of Governance
1. Unified	Tourism policy, marketing and development combined into a single agency	China National Tourism Administration	Sometimes occurs at a regional scale in Europe
2. Policy/Marketing split	Different government agencies are responsible for developing tourism policy (including undertaking research) and national tourism marketing and promotion.	Minister for Tourism (Department of Resources, Energy and Tourism)/ Tourism Australia; Minister of Industry (Industry Canada)/Tourism Canada; Ministry of Tourism/Tourism New Zealand	Sometimes occurs at the provincial/state scale in federal systems such as Australia and Canada
3. Policy only	A government body with a degree of autonomy is responsible for policy and research but there is no single government agency responsible for national tourism promotion.	Office of Travel and Tourism Industries, USA	Extremely common at the supranational scale where policy is also sometimes tied to regulatory regimes, such as the WTO's General Agreement on Trade in Services
4. Integrated	Tourism functions are integrated within a larger government agency that has other areas of responsibility. Although there may be a tourism-specific section it is not an autonomous body.	Innovation Norway; Innovation Wales; Ministry of Trade and Industry (Finland)	Extremely common at the regional/local/municipal scale

Source: Hall (2008b).

In the case of Nordic tourism businesses Hall et al. (2009) argue that outside of regional promotion and marketing, the bulk of public policy that affects tourism is not usually categorized under tourism policy at all and instead point to the importance of national and EU policies as the most important institutional influences on tourism entrepreneurship and business development, as they represent a limit on the direct public support that individual firms, whether tourism related or otherwise, can receive. In Nordic regions that are considered weak from an EU or EEA perspective, or have a very low population density, a maximum of 30–35% net investment support is allowed for small and medium-sized businesses. For regions that are considered weak from a national perspective, a maximum of 20–25% net investment support is allowed (the aid ceilings are 5–10% points lower for companies with more than 250 employees).

Outside the support areas, up to 10% investment aid is allowed for SMEs independent of location. The population in Nordic support areas that received investment aid in 2000–06 was substantial: Denmark (17.6%); Finland (41%); Iceland (38.1%); Norway (25.3%); and Sweden (15.9%) (Hanell et al., 2002, pp. 31–32); much of this investment aid was directed into tourism related businesses. Furthermore, indirect support via short-term EU and national projects to encourage networks and clusters may also be important for tourism entrepreneurship (Hjalager, 2005; Mattson et al., 2005; Hjalager et al., 2008). Yet recognition of the significance of institutional policy factors for entrepreneurship highlights the importance of taking a far more macro-view of policy than just what is produced by public tourism bodies and, for that matter, students of tourism.

Therefore, in order to understand the public policy dimensions of tourism entrepreneurship it is important that we utilize a larger perspective of public policy and tourism entrepreneurship that goes beyond the role of tourism agencies, and it is to this that the chapter will now turn.

Public Policies Affecting Tourism Entrepreneurship

Given that it is clear that there is a range of public policies that influence tourism entrepreneurship, how might they be best understood? One of the most influential approaches to classifying public policy has been that of Lowi (1972). Lowi focused on the outputs of policy and argued that different policy types could be identified that reflect different policy processes. Lowi identified these distinct policy types as being distributive, constituent, regulative, and redistributive in character. These categories were based upon Lowi's contention that the principal concept underlying public policy-making is coercion:

> Institutions are means of moralizing coercion. Administration is a means of routinizing coercion. Government is a means of legitimizing it. Power is simply the relative share a person or group appears to have in shaping and directing the instruments of coercion. (Lowi, 1970, p. 314)

From this perspective all policies are interpreted as deliberate coercion as they are attempts to define the purpose, means, subjects and objections of coercive activity. The nature of each policy category and its relationship to tourism entrepreneurship is outlined below and in Table 13.2.

Table 13.2: Characteristics of different policy types.

Policy type	Characteristics of the policy	Characteristics of the policy arena	Tourism entrepreneurship policy examples	Policy and regulatory instruments
Distributive	Groups receive desired outputs without directly competing with other groups. Collective public provision although taxpayers have small role. Each interest group received a benefit specific to itself; little confrontation occurs and little emerges in the way of 'policy'	Consensual, mutual non-interference. Conflict invisible.	Research grants; general tax reduction for business	Business incentives; deregulation
Redistributive	Relation between costs and benefits obvious. A conscious decision to satisfy aspirations of some groups at the expense of others	Conflict; polarization between winners and losers; ideologically driven. Pluralist politics.	Labour market policy; economic assistance programmes	Imposed by state

(continued)

Table 13.2 — *cont'd*

Policy type	Characteristics of the policy	Characteristics of the policy arena	Tourism entrepreneurship policy examples	Policy and regulatory instruments
Regulative	Legal and institutional norms for behaviour. Principle issues often involve an attempt to alter the distribution of benefits and costs in society, and frequently centre upon issues related to levels and rates of taxation, public spending and subsidies	Changing coalitions according to the distribution of costs and benefits. Often class rather than sectoral based.	Consumer protection; occupational health and safety; environmental protection	Varied: imposed by the state; persuasion; self-regulation (allowed by the state)
Constituent	Public–private partnerships; institutional norms	Specific policy networks, especially sub-governments	Setting up of a tourism specific agency; new procedures; allowing self-regulation; sectoral funding	Imposed by the state

Source: Lowi (1972); Heinelt (2005); Hall (2008a, b).

Distributive policies involve the distribution of benefits to particular groups in society. Parker (1999, p. 320) argues that distributive policy is 'fundamentally promotional in nature and governments rely heavily upon it to stimulate the tourism and ecotourism industries'. To an extent that is true although it should be noted that from a distributive policy perspective the use of such measures as investment tax credits, accelerated depreciation, leasing of property, subsidization and market support tend to be available to all business interest groups, rather than just tourism, and are a generic policy approach towards business and entrepreneurship as a result of a broader 'business friendly' government policy perspective (Holtz-Eakin, 2000; Acs et al., 2001; Audretsch, 2004).

Redistributive policies are specific policies to move the distribution of wealth or other resources from one group in society to another. This may be undertaken on the basis of income levels, wealth, class, ethnicity or region. For example, in the 1980s ecotourism was conceived as a means of improving the level of economic well-being of otherwise marginal communities in peripheral areas (Hall and Page, 2006). More recently, the notion of pro-poor tourism has become increasingly significant as it reflects a policy idea that tourism can be used as a targeted means of redistribution of wealth through encouraging consumers to undertake certain tourism activities in specific locations that require poverty reduction strategies, and in which small and microentrepreneurs can be encouraged (Ashley, 2006).

Regulatory policy refers to the placement of restrictions and limits on the actions of some individual persons or organizations and not others. Self-regulatory policy is a subset of regulatory policy in that it refers to controls on the behaviour of identified groups or individuals but is undertaken by the regulated group or non-government organization. Self-regulation may be utilized as a government policy as a form of public–private partnership so as to reduce its own costs or to satisfy the demands and needs of particular producer groups to reduce their compliance costs. However, it is only as effective as the extent to which compliance with regulatory standards is actually sought (Hall, 2008a).

Constituent policy refers to the development of specific policies to meet the interests of specific groups. Such policies are often developed through public–private partnerships but may also be developed with respect to the issue networks surrounding particular policy concerns, such as the environment or security. Examples of constituent policies include the development of new public agencies with specific constituent developed mandates and/or specific sectoral specific financial packages. As noted above, the tourism industry rarely has the political power to enable significant constituent policies in most developed countries, simply because of their diverse economic base as well as the perceived higher value of other industries. However, in small island and less developed countries which have a narrow economic base, and in which tourism may play a significant part, there are far more opportunities for constituent policies in relation to tourism entrepreneurship.

The above classification can be an extremely useful way of identifying the effects of different policies, although it does not necessarily recognize the split between tourism and non-tourism agencies and the accompanying direct and indirect affects on tourism entrepreneurship (Table 13.3) which can be a useful tool to compare policy measures between jurisdictions.

A good example of the split between tourism and non-tourism government bodies with respect to developing tourism entrepreneurship, as well as the connection to different types

Table 13.3: Simple framework for categorizing public policies that affect tourism entrepreneurship.

Organizational base	Direct	Indirect
Tourism		
Non-tourism		

of policy outputs, is that of post-apartheid South Africa where tourism is often regarded as integral to the empowerment of previously disadvantaged groups (Binns and Nel, 2002; Kirsten and Rogerson, 2002; Rogerson, 2002a, 2002b, 2004a, 2005, 2006; Rogerson and Visser, 2004; Ashley, 2006). For example, the African National Congress (ANC) regard tourism as an important mechanism to generate employment, with their 2004 report on *Delivery to Women* stating:

> The Tourism Policy is also enabling, so that by 2010, more than 174,000 new jobs can be created directly in the travel and tourism industry, and 516,000 jobs can be created, directly and indirectly, across the broader South African economy. These will involve high levels of training, pay higher than average wages and be particularly accessible to women, unskilled people and new entrants to the job market. Most of the new jobs will be in areas where structural unemployment is most high. (African National Congress, 2004)

The South African experience with respect to the development of public policy initiatives is regarded as particularly significant because of its transformation dimension with respect to Black Economic Empowerment (BEE) as well as the introduction of dedicated tourism specific support programmes for SM(M)Es that may provide 'good practice' for support of tourism entrepreneurship in other parts of Africa and the developing world (Rogerson, 2007). For example, like South Africa, Namibia has developed a tourism industry BEE charter, while BEE legislation and strategies have also been developed for Botswana, Malawi, Namibia, Tanzania and Zimbabwe.

Tourism has developed as one of the major foreign exchange earners for South Africa and is regarded as an important employment generator because of the perceived relatively low skill base that is required. South Africa also expects to attract 10 million foreign tourists by 2010 when the country hosts the FIFA World Cup (Parliament of the Republic of South Africa, 2007). However, no member of the tripartite governing alliance between the African National Congress (ANC), the South African Communist Party (SACP) and the Congress of South African Trade Unions (COSATU) has a separate tourism policy, although tourism can be identified as an element in parliamentary submissions, speeches and other organizational documents including the 1996 white paper on the development and promotion of tourism (Government of South Africa, 1996).

The ANC in particular appears to link government tourism policy documentation and organization, particularly with respect to bringing tourism and the environment together under a single ministry as synonymous with party policy. In contrast other political parties, such as the Democratic Alliance (DA) and the Inkatha Freedom Party (IFP) have separate tourism policy documents. Nevertheless, the entrepreneurial potential of tourism was clearly recognized in the 1996 white paper:

> ... tourism, perhaps more than any other sector, has the potential to achieve the objectives of the Reconstruction and Development Programme (RDP) of the new government. Tourism creates opportunities for the small entrepreneur; promotes awareness and understanding among different cultures; breeds a unique informal sector; helps to save the environment; creates economic linkages with agriculture, light manufacturing and curios (art, craft, souvenirs); creates linkages with the services sector (health and beauty, entertainment, banking and insurance); and provides dignified employment opportunities. Tourism can also play a strategic role in dynamizing other sectors of the economy ... (Government of South Africa, 1996, p. 2.1)

The South African government supports industry by means of the following national institutions: Department of Environmental Affairs and Tourism (DEAT) – the main policy organization; the Tourism, Hospitality and Sport Sector Education and Training Authority (THETA); South African Tourism (SAT) – the national tourism marketing organization; and the Tourism Grading Council of South Africa.

An example of tourism policy aimed at encouraging and supporting entrepreneurship was the Department of Environmental Affairs and Tourism's (2001) Tourism Transformation Strategy launched in November 2001. The strategy had a specific focus on empowerment initiatives, with three key objectives:

- To sustain black-owned enterprises in tourism;
- To create a demand for the establishment of new business (especially via SME development and poverty relief programmes); and
- To develop linkages between the government as travel consumer and black-owned companies.

The effort to create government–industry linkages incorporated a three-year action plan which included:

- The development of a database of black businesses in each tourism segment for local, provincial, national departments and parastatals. This database is to be updated on a quarterly basis;
- The joint publication with the Department of Trade and Industry of *The Support Programmes for Tourism Businesses Handbook* which aims at increasing demand for government support;
- A public–private sector forum to address empowerment, the gaps between public and private initiatives, and share information and ideas.

However, in a review of the programmes it was noted that participants were 'in general not aware of the DEAT's (2001) Tourism Transformation Strategy. Furthermore, some expressed concern that government should not impose rigid or restrictive empowerment targets' (Mason, 2003, p. 28). Although the Tourism Business Council of South Africa (TBCSA) (2003) regarded such concerns as perhaps misplaced, it did suggest that there was a clear need for better communication of policy to target audiences.

In relation to marketing, SAT also has a number of initiatives that are regarded as supporting empowerment objectives which include:

- A national tourism awareness campaign;
- The Emerging Tourism Entrepreneur of the Year Award (ETEYA) – an annual award aimed at SMME development;
- An annual tourism trade show;
- Strategies for tourism growth and e-business.

However, 'marketing support was highlighted ... as a sine qua non for industry development, particularly for small businesses' (TBCSA, 2003, p. 28). Financial and other support for small and emerging tourism enterprises comes from four main sources: The Tourism Enterprise Programme (TEP) (see Rogerson [2007] for an indepth analysis of the two phases of this programme) and the International Tourism Marketing Aid Scheme (ITMAS) supported by DEAT; and two initiatives supported by the Department of Trade and Industry: Khula Enterprise Finance and the Small Medium Enterprise Development Programme (SMEDP). (Details of these programmes are provided in Table 13.4.)

Reviews of the transformation and empowerment initiatives in the tourism sector have been generally positive (TBCSA, 2002, 2003, 2004), with Rogerson (2004b, 2007) focusing on the TEP in particular, which he described as 'the jewel in the crown' with regards to the upgrading and development of tourism SMMEs (Rogerson, 2004b, p. 253). Rogerson (2007) regards the TEP as an innovative institution in relation to being a dedicated programme for the support of tourism SMMEs, especially as it represents an important break from the existing style of SMME support on offer in South Africa since 1995 in which the focus of support was upon generic packages of assistance rather than tailored support for the needs of enterprises in different economic sectors.

The South African example illustrates the importance of identifying public policy influences on tourism entrepreneurship from more than just public tourism organizations. However, South Africa has been fortunate to have been subject to considerable tourism policy analysis in recent years. This stands in stark contrast to the virtual absence of such studies in many other countries and jurisdictions.

Conclusions

This chapter has sought to provide an overview of some of the public policy issues associated with tourism entrepreneurship. It has highlighted the importance of developing a broad understanding of public policy with respect to its effects on entrepreneurship, and the role of multiple organizations and institutions in influencing the climate of entrepreneurship as well as the development of tourism related entrepreneurial systems. However,

Table 13.4: South African tourism entrepreneurship support programmes.

Organizational basis	Government Department	Direct	Indirect
Tourism	Environmental Affairs and Tourism; funded by the Business Trust; operates as an independent Section 21 (not for profit) company that works with Government, parastatals, and the private sector, in developing and managing partnerships including public–private partnerships	Tourism Enterprise Programme: Goal is to create jobs in and through the tourism economy by helping SMEs to grow and create linkages. It works with SMEs directly involved in the tourism industry and also with those who provide non-tourism products or services, such as office supplies or outsourced cleaning, to larger tourism companies.	

(continued)

Table 13.4 — *cont'd*

Organizational basis	Government Department	Direct	Indirect
		The aim of TEP is to support, guide and assist small and medium enterprises in the tourism sector. Through TEP focusing on increasing the business activities of small businesses in tourism, by providing greater market access opportunities, the challenge of facing a very serious economic downturn is addressed. This must equate to increased occupancy, increased production of craft and increased trips by wheel operators, all of which lead to job creation, sustainability and transformation – the ultimate objectives of the new TEP.	

Environmental
Affairs and
Tourism

International Tourism Marketing Aid
Scheme: Assists SMEs by sponsoring
part of the cost of attending international exhibitions, as well as
producing and distributing international marketing material. An SME
can qualify for assistance if it
complies with any three of the
following criteria:

– The business is owned by historically
  disadvantaged individuals;
– The business is owned by disabled
  individuals;
– The business has been in operation
  for between one and four years;
– The business has a turnover of less
  than R1m per annum;
– The business has operational assets
  worth less than R1m.
Applicants must also be registered
members of an official tourism trade
organization and have formal SA
Tourism approval to attend an international marketing exhibition.

• Tourism Transformation Strategy

– including public–private sector forum
  to address empowerment, the gaps
  between public and private initiatives,
  and share information and ideas.
– development of a database of black
  businesses in each tourism segment
  for local, provincial, national
  departments and parastatals. This
  database is to be updated on a quarterly basis.

• Conservation strategies and their relationship to ecotourism and pro-poor
  tourism initiatives

(continued)

Table 13.4 — *cont'd*

Organizational basis	Government Department	Direct	Indirect
	Tourism, Hospitality and Sport Sector Education and Training Authority		Overall improvements in level of tourism skills and knowledge via education and training programmes
	Tourism Grading Council of South Africa		Quality evaluations of businesses
	South Africa Tourism	The Emerging Tourism Entrepreneur of the Year Award (ETEYA): An annual award aimed at SME development.	– A national tourism awareness campaign – An annual tourism trade show – Strategies for tourism growth and e-business

| Non-tourism | Trade and Industry | • Khula Enterprise Finance: Does not directly fund small enterprises, but facilitates access to private sector finance by helping small enterprises develop business plans, and providing (if necessary) credit guarantees for up to 80% of a R1m loan and ongoing free mentorship services after a loan has been concluded | General departmental activities in relation to trade and economic development |
| | | • Small Medium Enterprise Development Programme: Offers cash grants to tourism related businesses to invest in buildings, furniture, equipment or tourism vehicles. The two-year grants are offered tax free to businesses that have been in operation for less than six months, or plan to increase their current capacity by more than 25% | |

Sources: Mason (2003); Rogerson (2007); Tourism Enterprise Partnership (2008).

it has also noted that the application of such concepts to tourism entrepreneurship has been extremely limited because of the lack of research on firm embeddedness.

Public policy is something that inherently exists 'beyond the firm' yet is of great importance to the entrepreneurial process and firm success. This is something which has been recognized with respect to issues of tourism innovation but has not been investigated to any great extent directly with entrepreneurship. Perhaps more seriously for the study of public policy and tourism entrepreneurship, the majority of research that has been conducted is usually not comparative and often fails to recognize that policy 'solutions' in one jurisdiction may not apply to another. In fact issues of entrepreneurial and policy cultures, as well as the differential role of institutions, is a 'blind spot' in tourism entrepreneurship research. Nevertheless, work in some jurisdictions, such as the examples provided from South Africa and the Nordic countries, does highlight the potential value of research on policy settings and therefore the potential for policy learning. In particular, research on the policy dimensions of tourism entrepreneurship suggests that the relative range of outcomes for policy is related to the spread of benefits within a jurisdiction as well as the desire for immediacy of policy impact. These observations are summarized in Figure 13.2.

As this chapter has emphasized, if the policy dimensions of tourism entrepreneurship are to be best understood it is vital that researchers look beyond what is usually regarded as tourism policy conducted by tourism organizations. Instead researchers must seek to understand the broader scope of policy initiatives that affect tourism entrepreneurship and their interplay at different levels of governance. While individual entrepreneurs and their firms will no doubt remain the primary research focus, their behaviours cannot be fully understood without a better understanding of the entrepreneurial systems in which they are embedded.

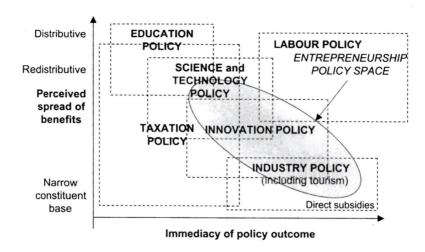

Figure 13.2: Relative positioning of state policies towards entrepreneurship.

Questions for Discussion

1. What are the key reasons for government involvement in tourism planning and development?
2. Identify and discuss the main public policy issues associated with tourism entrepreneurship.
3. What would be the most constructive government policies for an innovative tourism model?
4. What do you understand by the embeddedness of tourism entrepreneurship in entrepreneurial and innovation systems?

References

Florida, R. (2002). Bohemia and economic geography. *Journal of Economic Geography*, 2, 55–71.

Rogerson, C.M. (2004b). Financing tourism SMMEs in South Africa: a supply-side analysis. In *Tourism and Development Issues in Contemporary South Africa*, (C.M. Rogerson and G. Visser, eds.), Pretoria: Africa, Institute of South Africa, pp. 222–267.

Chapter 14

A Multi-stakeholder Approach to Tourism Development

Marko Koscak and Tony O'Rourke

Learning Outcomes

After reading this chapter, you should be able to:

- Understand the key principles of the multi-stakeholder approach to tourism development;

- View this specific approach within an environment in which public funding is an integral part of a mixed private sector and community-led programme;

- Understand that a bottom-up model of development tourism in rural settings requires entrepreneurship and entrepreneurial skills by all those involved in the development;

- Appreciate the Slovenian model of rural tourism development as a good, if not best, practice that could be applied in comparable situations elsewhere.

Introduction

One of the beneficial methodologies for growing and developing a level of tourism which is sustainable and enhances the totality of local and regional environments is a multi-stakeholder approach to tourism development. In this chapter, we explore the methods by which sustainable rural development[1] takes an integrated approach in terms of start-up, implementation and development, and how it is supported by and benefits from the notion of a core of multiple stakeholders.

It is clear that entrepreneurship and entrepreneurial skills, harnessed in a bottom-up model of development, will have a huge impact on rural and agritourist microeconomies at a local community level. The effect in driving wealth creation and expanding employment is measurable in a very tangible and transparent way. Furthermore, multi-stakeholder tourism projects benefit the ownership transformation process by forcing public[2],

---

1. We take this to include cultural, heritage, vinicultural and gastronomic as well as ecological tourism.
2. By 'public' we mean municipal/local government, state agencies and international organizations operating in a local or regional framework.

private[3] and social[4] ownership agents and enterprises to work together for common benefit. Because of the bottom-up approach the measurable value at an enterprise or agency level is also more tangible and obvious. We can also see that by engaging local public agencies, the dimension of environmental planning and protection can be assured. In this way the sustainable nature of tourism and its impact on the local environment can be assessed and given due priority.

At the same time, in such integrated projects individual entrepreneurs begin to comprehend and understand the value of cooperation as well as of competition. A key feature is often the need for small-scale tourism entrepreneurs to develop a promotional mechanism to market their product or service at a wider national and international level. Individually the costs of such an activity are too great for microenterprises, but they are possible for groups of enterprises. This evidences how an integrated model enables participants to benefit from the totality and complexity of resources and skills held by all stakeholders.

Thus in this chapter we will explore aspects of tourism multi-stakeholding from the perspective of a very specific model of tourism connected through sustainable rural development. Primarily this relates to a model, based on international precedents, which was developed in Slovenia – a country which joined the European Union in 2004. At the same time we will also observe situations where similar or related models have been implemented in less advanced Central and Eastern European economies.

Clearly the model we are referring to, as demonstrated in the case study in this chapter, has a very precise local/regional orientation. The heritage trail of Dolenjska and Bela krajina case study has a rural base and is profoundly affected by the necessity to attract tourism inputs without damaging the sensitivities of the rural environment. It also has a strong multi-stakeholder approach which in many ways illustrates the impact in EU-funded programmes of the concept of 'subsidiarity'[5] – aiming at seamless connectivity between EU supranational policy and funding, member state objectives in macroeconomic harmonization, and stabilities and local microeconomic needs.

The Content

First we will examine the European and international perspective. The most successful models of multi-stakeholder action have been those which combine elements of international and national intervention as well as the distinctive inputs of regions and local communities, whether public, private or mutual. We will then review the progress of sustainable rural development by looking at research and practical projects over the past few

---

3. By 'private' we mean privately owned companies, including quoted or unquoted companies, as well as partnerships or self-employed individuals.
4. By 'social' we mean entities established for mutual benefit, including cooperatives, societies and not-for-profit agencies.
5. The principle of subsidiarity is defined in Article 5 of the Treaty establishing the European Union and was intended to ensure that decisions are taken as closely as possible to the citizen and that constant checks are made as to whether action at supranational level is justified in the light of the possibilities available at national, regional or local level. The Edinburgh European Council of December 1992 issued a declaration on the principle of subsidiarity, which lays down the rules for its application. (*Source*: European Commission, 2007)

decades, including the immediate antecedents to the Dolenjska and Bela krajina heritage trail case study. After considering the case study we will consider the extent to which similar models have been successfully implemented, before assessing the critical success factors and, finally, concluding with the pivotal role of the multi-stakeholder approach.

The European and International Policy Dimension

Tourism has been strongly interwoven into various policies which have emerged from international agencies, such as various UN programmes, as well as from the institutional structures of the European Union (Council, Commission and Parliament). It is seen to have impacts on employment, the environment, rural development, urban regeneration and sustainability. Importantly, the concept of bringing together various stakeholders has been an important and powerful element in the concept of sustainable rural tourism development. The role of international organizations always appears to have been underpinned by the actions of the UN Environment Programme with ICLEI (the international association of local governments and national and regional local government organizations that have made a commitment to sustainable development) resulting in programmes related to training and capacity building at a local level.

During 2002–03, with support from the European Commission, UN/ICLEI (2003) engaged in a local action-planning project 'Agenda21' which sought to deal with problems of unemployment as well as maintaining environmental sustainability. This was a particularly important element in the heritage trail project, where there has always been the risk of over-activity resulting in environmental damage. Working with seven EU partners from six member states, the project included in its focus the issues of employment and sustainability as well as employment generation for tourist destinations. A key element in the 'Agenda21' process has been the importance of the multi-stakeholder public–social–private participation model.

More recently, the European Parliament has made a clear and unambiguous policy on European tourism development which not only underlines the values of sustainability and the rural environment,[6] but strongly identifies the important role of the multi-stakeholder approach. The parliament's policy resolution spelled out, *inter alia*, the guiding principles for a European sustainable tourism policy in an attempt to develop a consistent cross-policy approach to tourism at EU level. In such a policy the environmental and social dimension of tourism require to be strongly emphasized in the interest of sustainability. Furthermore, the parliament took the step of stressing the need to protect, preserve and restore the European cultural heritage whilst calling for more stringent management of heritage sites.

Within the overall concept of socially, economically and environmentally sustainable tourism, it is evident that European legislators are now greatly concerned to ensure that tourism is sustainable in economic, social, territorial, environmental, and cultural terms. This takes cognisance of the fact that sustainably developed tourism is required to offer local economies (especially in disadvantaged regions) a long-term source of revenue, help

---

6. European Parliament resolution of 29 November 2007 (2006/2129[INI] on a renewed EU Tourism Policy: Towards a stronger partnership for European Tourism)

in promoting stable employment structures whilst at the same time safeguarding and enhancing the cultural, historical, landscape and environmental heritage.

In welcoming the Commission's ongoing initiative in creating an agenda for sustainable and competitive European tourism as a basis for tourism policy, the parliament has also requested the Commission to provide member states with guidance to improve political coordination in the development of tourism at national, regional and local levels, and enhance the sustainability of tourist activities. This is likely to involve candidate and pre-accession states in the West Balkan Stability Pact[7] where short-term economic gain often triumphs over the threat of long-term environmental degradation caused by uncontrolled tourism exploitation.

Important future elements, in light of the focus of this chapter being on the Heritage Trail model, are the EU wide initiatives now in progress that seek to enhance the common cultural heritage, through the creation of a European Heritage label. Cultural heritage, as we will see in the case study, also includes the protection of traditional culture, and in particular endangered folk arts, crafts, trades and knowledge. A further key element, related to the variety of stakeholders in sustainable tourism development, is the role of SMEs and particularly of micro and smaller-sized enterprises. EU institutions share a common view that SMEs/MSEs should have greater involvement in tourism related entrepreneurship and that possibilities for simplifying procedures to obtain financial support should be found, especially in the new member states.[8]

Background: Analysis of Research and Evidence From Projects

The Situation in Slovenia.   The initial work in Slovenia dates from the period when Slovenia became the first republic to secede from the Yugoslav socialist federation. This removed the country from the dynamics of the overall Yugoslav tourism product while leaving Slovenia without a clear tourism identity. In the initial period the inflow of tourists slowed considerably. In retrospect this had advantages; primarily that a country with three main tourism products or 'icons' – the northern lakes and mountains, the karstic caves and the Adriatic littoral of some 45 km of coast – was able to look at alternative forms of tourism which would appeal both to traditional group related activities as well as to individual tourism. It is an important factor that since independence in 1991, Slovenia has never accounted for more than 0.3% of total tourist visits in Europe. At the same time, tourist activity contributes around 9% to GDP and employs over 50,000 people. Earnings from tourism are calculated as EUR 1.2 billion in income flows and as providing around 10% of total exports of goods and services within the balance of payments.

The relatively rapid stabilization of the economy, and Slovenia's appearance as an island of political and economic stability on the edge of the Balkan madhouse from 1991–95, also assisted in driving a highly marketing-oriented tourism development policy from the beginning. As a result, significant studies were carried out in the Ministry of

---

7. Albania, Bosnia and Herzegovina, Croatia, Macedonia, Montenegro and Serbia.
8. Bulgaria, Czech Republic, Cyprus, Estonia, Hungary, Latvia, Lithuania, Malta, Poland, Romania, Slovakia and Slovenia.

Economy, especially those led by Sirše et al. (2004). The overall strategy, which began to unfold with the support of the various EU pre-accession and candidate country programmes, had two main strands – the local and regional, and the national. The model was evidently driven by:

- Willingness to bring a number of stakeholders into the development and implementation process – domestic and international, private and public;
- The decision at a relatively early stage to launch the 'Integral Development of Rural Areas and the Renovation of Villages' project, known by the acronym CRPOV. This project was backed by the Ministry of Agriculture, Forestry and Food, which played a very important role and at one time was involved in more than 250 projects throughout the country.

One project from this period, by M. Koščak (1998), dealt with the issues arising from the delineation of Slovenia's new southern border with Croatia, especially in the rural areas along the Slovene–Croatian border. These issues were seen as connected to the problems of border areas and marginal regions, and thus were both specific and new for this region of Dolenjska and Bela krajina. The transformation of the Slovene rural areas, as well as of the rural areas in the region investigated, was seen as having been affected by the creation of urban centres and towns, with the concentration of the population residing in them for economic, social, and cultural purposes. Against this has been the rise of less populated areas with poor demographic structure, loss of agricultural activity, and deficient social and technical infrastructures.

The author had researched the structure of the farm holdings in the regions of Posavska and in Dolenjska and Bela krajina, which occupy a significant stretch of the Slovenian state frontier in the south east of the country. Drawn from the 1991 data, this research indicated that in the region of Dolenjska and Bela krajina, dominated by the large industrial and services centre of Novo mesto and by two comparatively large health-tourism centres, there were 14,647 farms. These holdings had an average size of 6.2 hectares of which approximately 40% was under cultivation. However, the data indicated that 50% of these farms were inhabited by occupants who did not derive any income from farming activity. Only 11% of farms had inhabitants whose sole form of income was farming – in those cases the size of the cultivated land was some 15% larger. A similar pattern occurred in the Posavska region, where 10,845 farms had an average size of 4.6 hectares, but where 49% of the holdings were occupied by those who derived no income from farming. In Posavska 12% were dependent on farming for their complete income, with cultivated land also some 15% larger.

The socio-economic shift from rural communities to urban centres mentioned above, which had its origins in the industrialization of the Sava-Krka valley from the nineteenth century, was given added impetus by the modernization programmes implemented by the Communist leadership in the post-1945 period. However, it also resulted in a pattern in which a significant number of those employed in non-agricultural jobs continued to live in rural areas and for at least a third of these people to supplement their salaries with agricultural activity. Further pressure on the rural environment came after 1991 as traditional manufacturing industries downsized to remain internationally competitive, and as EU membership brought pressures on what was essentially a peasant farming structure. Ecotourism and tourism sensitive to the cultural heritage and environment therefore presented an attractive answer to rural decline, as the following examples and the main case study indicate.

The Trebnje Case Study.   The case study by Koščak mentioned above, which he began in 1998, brought attention to the fact that the quality of the environment was rapidly becoming an integral part of modern people's perceptions. Thus, the countryside offered a variety of the almost forgotten traces of the past, handicrafts and centuries-old customs. It is also home to three wine regions that produce not so much quantity (1 million litres annually) as a superior quality of renowned European and autochthonous wine varieties.

Gosar (1990), in a paper for the Slovenian Urban Planning Institute, made the assertion that:

> Rural development policy must be multidisciplinary in concept, and multisectoral. It must be based on an integrated approach, encompassing within the same legal and policy framework: agricultural adjustment and development, economic diversification – notably small and medium-scale industries and rural services, the management of natural resources, the enhancement of environmental functions, and the promotion of culture, tourism and recreation.

Thus the definition of a strategy at government level which sought to place equal emphasis on agricultural production goals and the protection of rural areas and villages, their further harmonious development, the preservation of regions of cultural significance, the protection of farmlands and the sustained presence of the population in rural areas was intended to take place within a multi-stakeholder framework.

It was also intended to take account of the view, at the risk of offering a generalization, that there is a definable contemporary trend towards individuals giving an increasing priority to ecological and environmental quality in deciding where to spend a holiday or choose a travel destination. This current trend in tourism arguably indicates that 'mass' tourism is declining, while individual experiences are becoming more popular, and consequently this segment of the tourist market is on the rise. This trend certainly favoured Slovenia, which had little potential for mass tourism but at the same time matched government desires for the expansion of tourism, the development of the rural economy and the preservation of the rural heritage. In an article for the Slovenian Tourist Board, Koščak (1993–95) wrote that:

> As for the future strategy of Slovenian tourism, it is perfectly clear that the exposure of the cultural landscape of the region and its heritage are of primary importance.

The use of the Trebnje municipality as one of the pilot case studies in how the new policy could be developed and implemented with formidably wide range of players was ideal. The town of Trebnje is located 50 km southeast of the capital city of Ljubljana along the Ljubljana-Zagreb motorway. Geographically it stands at the centre of the historic

Dolenjska region consisting of two different parts. The northern and northeastern parts are of an alpine structure with impermeable soil and an abundant network of watercourses, while the south and southwest have karst features with permeable soil and therefore underground streams. The municipality is predominantly rural with about half of the area is covered with forests, while the remainder is under arable cultivation.

The authorities of the Trebnje municipality entered the Ministry of Agriculture, Forestry and Food's CRPOV programme at the end of 1991. The project initially covered two communities. The success of the initial work, which pre-dated the wider development of the regional programme 'heritage trail' (see case study below) was to a great extent the result of the fact that the predominantly rural character of the Trebnje municipality pointed logically to the development of tourism in villages, and of rural tourism in general. In the past, tourism had not played a particularly important role in the Trebnje municipality, although an interest in tourism has gradually been on the increase. However the impetus of the development projects driven by the programme had an exponential effect on the development of interest within the community, which was increasingly directed towards promoting tourism in accordance with the natural and contemporary human environments and the historic heritage.

Cultural Tourism Impacts. The work by Bachleitner and Zins (1999) predicated the view that cultural tourism develops at a considerable speed and diversifies continuously in a multifaceted way. It boosts support for the rapid expansion in European city tourism and is, in addition, important in increasing interest in tourism in rural areas. A focus of rural development, as we have seen from the work conducted in Slovenia, is to maintain or improve the quality of life of the local people. Bachleitner and Zins (1999) analysed the impacts of a particular kind of cultural tourism (exhibition tourism) as perceived by local residents in several small rural communities in the Austrian province of Steiermark. The study examined the psychometric characteristics of the tourism impact and attitude scale (TIAS) developed by Lankford and Howard (2004).

It is interesting that the geographic area for their work was centred on a number of Styrian rural localities which have some historical and cultural heritage parallels with Slovenia. Bachleitner and Zins put forward the view that the development of cultural tourism – an activity with a strong degree of multiple stakeholders and an undeniably larger public, social and voluntary sector component – was dependent on:

- Cultural supply (which to a degree was related to the attractiveness of the cultural object);
- Social and organizational structure in the local environment;
- The perceived prestige of the cultural object.

Furthermore, they saw that there were three differing levels of interest, especially in the case of cultural exhibitions (which would also broadly include heritage and historical interpretative centres). These were:

- Enterprise related: boosting tourism visits and overnight levels; expanding jobs; creating new tourism segments;

- Economic related: improving business prospects in a local economy and growing the business birth rate primarily in the service sector;
- Local community related: conflicting levels of interest and involvement based on improving job prospects and economic growth against which the environmental effect of additional visitors, strains on the existing cultural and social heritage, and the potential for dilution of quality of life need to be considered.

The latter point was the real focus of the study, and looked specifically at how cultural exhibition tourism impacted in rural conservative areas. It is clear that in such areas critical factors such as loss of cultural identity (e.g. local dialect, local customs and festivals) and of cultural authenticity (e.g. insertion of rural hotel and catering establishments) have to be carefully controlled by those responsible for policy and implementation.

The study analysed the attitudes of a sample of around 12% of the 8400 inhabitants in six local communities in the federal province of Steiermark towards a 1994 exhibition with the theme 'Pilgrimage: Paths to Strength'. This was held in a local monastery during the summer of 1994 and highlighted the mysteries of the pilgrimage; pilgrimage tourism is popular in Austria, Hungary, Croatia and Slovenia and there are a large number of sites in the region covered by the heritage trails of Dolenjska and Bela krajina (see case study). The region under study had a poor tourism penetration rate – four overnight stays per resident compared to 17 for Austria as a whole. Agricultural activity was however three times higher than the federal average and twice as high at the provincial average. Some 170,000 visits were made to the exhibition – of which only 6% stayed overnight. Bachleitner and Zins (1999) questioned the sample at the time of the exhibition (August 1994) and again in June 1995. The conclusions made by the authors can be summarized as:

- There was a significant shift from those actively favouring the tourism developments (26%) in 1994 to those favouring the developments in 1995 (19%), which would indicate that over time individual residents began to develop concerns about cultural and social impacts;
- Residents opposing the tourism development remained the consistently largest number of respondents at around one-third.

This would imply that whilst inhabitants may be more compliant regarding such projects during the implementation stage, over time the environmental effect might become more obvious to them. It would further imply that local residents form one of the most important stakeholders in the multi-stakeholder process of sustainable tourism development.

Cairngorms National Park. The Cairngorms were made a National Park in September 2003, both to protect the wildlife and countryside in them and for the benefit of those people who live in the area as well as visit it as tourists. It is the UK's largest national park, but comes under the control of the Scottish Government. The Cairngorms National Park (CNP) has the largest area of arctic mountain landscape in the British Isles and is home to 16,000 people as well as 25% of the UK's threatened birds, animals, and plants. It includes moorlands, forests, rivers, lakes and valleys. Since finalizing its Sustainable Tourism Strategy, the Cairngorms National Park became the first UK National Park to be awarded the European Charter for Sustainable Tourism in Protected Areas in July 2006.

The policy of the National Park Authority has included some important actions which focus on multi-agency and multi-level cooperation. These include:

- *Environmental management and conservation* – this has involved maintaining a high quality environment in the Cairngorms, encouraging sound environmental management practices and support for conservation by all those involved in tourism. This requires collaboration not only of the CNP management, but also residents and tourists. For example, all those now entering the CNP by car are invited to make a £1 carbon tax donation which is allocated to environmental use;
- Multi-stakeholder collaboration at a structural level – to ensure effective involvement by all stakeholders in the planning, development and management of tourism in the Cairngorms, and to maintain good communication;
- Marketing – which includes raising awareness of the Cairngorms as a year-round, rural tourism destination by branding and by working with public and private sector actors in the CNP area;
- Visitor information and interpretation systems – this includes signage to convey a sense of place (branding at Tourism Information Centres (TICs)), a sense of arrival (markers at road and rail entry points to the CNP) as well as targeted training courses for those working in the tourism front-line;
- Strengthening viability – this enables a direct relationship with the local (CNP), regional (Highlands of Scotland) and national (Scottish Government) actors to ensure a flexible workforce, adequate training, enterprise development in the micro–small enterprise sector and the coordination of different transport modes in one of Europe's peripheral regions. It also engages private, voluntary and social sector providers with the various public agencies;
- Community development – the importance of involving the local community, who live in the CNP area, is seen as highly pivotal. The Cairngorms Local Plan, setting out detailed planning policies to guide development, was finalized after extensive consultation. Research has also been conducted on residents' viewpoints and, whilst it is apparent that a large majority of those who live permanently in the CNP area are supportive of tourism, significant concerns were expressed regarding traffic congestion and the escalation of house prices by those seeking weekend homes.

Case Study: Dolenjska and Bela Krajina Heritage Trail

Introduction

It is a paradox that the 1960s, which saw the emergence of modern sustainable tourism, through the global movement for resource conservation and the limiting of development, also gave rise to a destructive counter-phenomenon! That counter-problem was the explosive rise in air-based international tourism, given added impetus as the result of the deregulation of airline routes in the European economic space. This revolution in low-cost and accessible air transport, which grew exponentially in the 1990s with the emergence of low-cost budget carriers, has become damaging to the environment and culture of many tourist destination regions. It has taken 40 years to respond effectively to this demanding global process, and to start to achieve sustainable rural regional tourism products and realities.

The rural case study presented here is one from a region in Slovenia along the border with Croatia, where we track a 10-year process – from the preliminary idea to the operational reality of sustainable international tourism in a strategically located destination region.

Origins and Catalysts

The 30-year period from 1960–90 saw distinct phases of evolution in tourism, planning, conservation-focused thinking and actions in the Western world. This led to the concepts and processes of sustainable tourism planning. For example in the UK, by the end of the 1980s, a National Task Force on 'Tourism and the Environment' had been established in order to provide sustainable tourism guidelines for three problem categories:

a) the countryside;
b) heritage sites;
c) historic cities and towns.

In the case of the Slovene example explained in this case study, an additional factor is the multiple dynamic of international, national, regional and local agencies involved in the project. These were drawn from public, private and social sources, but the key actors and catalysts who can be identified in this story were the Slovenian Ministry of Agriculture, the Bavarian State Ministry for Agriculture, the Faculty of Architecture in Ljubljana, the European Commission's Tourism Directorate, a Regional Chamber of Commerce, a commercial tourism operator and, at later date, an international market research consultant.

Integrated Rural Community Development Project

The CRPOV Programme (Integrated Rural Development and Village Renovation), which commenced in 1990, was associated both with the UN Food and Agriculture Organization (FAO) and with the Bavarian Ministry for Agriculture. Bavaria helped in the initial phase, transferring experience and know-how. CRPOV was based on a bottom-up approach, involving an initial 14 local project areas, starting in 1991. Two of the project villages were located in the Slovene municipality of Trebnje, with around 500 local residents involved in the project. During this period some 250 local projects were developed in Slovenia, primarily aimed at development possibilities for rural economic diversification.

The community development role of CRPOV involved many local village meetings, linked to the economic need for diversification of the rural economy. CRPOV worked together with an expert team on strategy and action. Critically, this case study relates to a rural region which sits strategically between Ljubljana and Zagreb, on the international motorway from Belgrade to Ljubljana. This has a high location potential for selling locally sourced food and wine products, as well as craft and tourism products. Tourism is based on the appeal of a gentle landscape of hills and river valleys – for walking, horse riding, cycling, angling, rafting, or the simple enjoyment of its unspoilt character!

The CRPOV, as an Integrated Rural Community Development programme, led the way towards rural product development and, as a by-product, community-based sustainable tourism. Such tourism requires partnership and cooperation between the public, private and the NGO voluntary sectors. Cooperation of this sort was not common in the period 1992–95 in Slovene tourism. It was clear, however, that sustainability – in Slovenia or anywhere else – requires community involvement together with the firm commitment of local actors and producers of products and services. The appeal of such action is to add tourism products to the other rural products which they complement.[9]

CRPOV resulted in the creation of a themed tourism product, linked to the state railways operator, in the development of a one-day tour programme. This theme was the main idea of a development strategy, one outcome of which was the 18 km long Baraga walking trail. Initially, this product was offered to school pupils. The response was limited, as there was no commercial partner to market and sell the product on the domestic market. However, there were improvements in infrastructure and housing, plus local training schemes to create business opportunities. In 1996, the project was given an award in Munich, as part of the ARGE 'Landentwicklung und Dorfeneurung' development competition. This was also a confidence-building phase for rural people locally, which later enabled them to become part of a broader, regional project, with its tourism elements. The wine trail was a parallel project to CRPOV, at the national level. The idea behind it was to promote wine products as well as the culture, customs, and traditions of wine-making areas of Slovenia. The effort resulted in 25 wine trails being created all round the country.

International Team Heritage Trail Consultancy

This early stage of the CRPOV programme, as well as the parallel development in terms of wine trails, prompted the Regional Chamber of Commerce of Dolenjska and Bela krajina to accept an invitation by a consortium (which had in 1996 secured European Union funding to launch two pilot projects in Slovenia and Bulgaria) to create heritage trails. The consortium included Ecotourism Ltd (a British consultancy firm), PRISMA (a Greek consultancy firm) and ECOVAST (The European Council for the Village and Small Town). All of these were supported by regional and national institutions in the field of natural and cultural heritage.

The UK/Slovene heritage trail team conducted a 'Tourist Resource Inventorization and Selection', based upon natural, built and living cultural heritage resources in the selected

---

9. NB. Community-based rural development is thus an ideal starting point for sustainability, whether in agriculture, and/or in tourism. This creates an 'environment' in which new opportunities for economic diversification, new job creation, added value to agricultural products, local guiding, and new farm services can occur. In this process, institutions like an Agricultural Extension Service and others play a very important role in terms of capacity building and human resource development.

region. Some 150 sites were identified and proposed by the different partners involved in the participation process for the heritage trail. From this large number, 28 sites were selected to be networked in a trail system for the area. The idea was to develop a tourist product which was capable of offering opportunities for stays of up to seven days in the region. Two key access forms were used for the clustering of attractions: one a 'flower structure' and the other a 'garland structure' (see Figures 14.1 and 14.2). Existing tourist assets and potentials were the basis of these groupings.

A major result of this work was the creation of a Regional Partnership of 27 organizations from the public, private and NGO sectors, which signed an agreement to cooperate in the heritage trail's implementation phases of marketing and product development. This partnership – working under the umbrella of the Regional Chamber of Commerce – is now 10 years old, and remains a vibrant and robust operating entity. The partnership supports coordinates and brings together the provider partners. Work in general consists of marketing activities, product development, and training activities, where different combinations of partners, institutions, and individuals are involved.

For marketing purposes, a local commercial partner – Kompas Novo mesto – was invited into the partnership in 2001, in order to articulate a stronger and more effective assault on foreign markets. Kompas was engaged to act as the marketing agency, on behalf of the heritage trail partnership. Although the official launch of the product was in 1997 at the World Travel Market in London, followed in 1998 by a presentation at the ITB/Tourist Fair in Berlin, there was no significant response. Foreign markets at that time had limited awareness about any Slovene tourist products, other than what can be described as the constantly featured traditional Slovene Tourist icons such as Lake Bled, Kranjska Gora ski resort, Postojna cave, and Portoroz seaside resort.

The effective commercial launch of the heritage trail at an international level, with a foreign tourist industry adviser and a much greater professionally coordinated national approach, was delayed until 2002. At the World Travel Market in London the launch had the active support of the Slovenian Tourism Board, together with other relevant institutions.

Stages of Commercial Product Adaptation and Implementation

Despite the launch of the heritage trail in the domestic market, followed by the international launch at the World Travel Market in 2002, the level of response by foreign tour operators and travel agents was weak. It became clear that external help was required to target appropriate foreign tourism-trade partners as well as to identify and select niche markets. An external consultant, Professor A.S. Travis of East–West Tourism Consultancy Ltd, was employed in this role.

From the market research conducted by Professor Travis on Slovenia's key foreign markets, the special interest markets with a focus on either cultural tourism or nature-tourism (ecotourism) were selected. Independent operators and some major commercial ones were to be approached by phone, fax, or online. Two hundred firms were identified in seven European countries; of these, 60 firms were contacted by at least two contact modes, but only six showed some degree of interest.

It became apparent that although there was much interest in Slovenia as a high-growth destination country, it was seen by the international industry as one with only three major

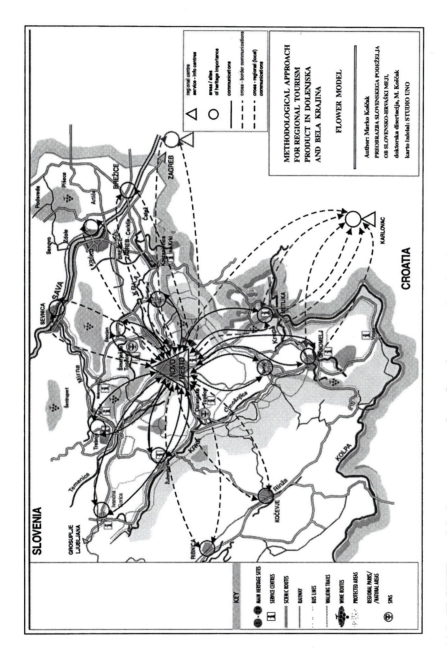

Figure 14.1: FLOWER model, shows concentration of tourism around regional centre and day visits from here to other "tourism destinations" in the region and immediate vicinity. Sustainability and long-term development were not satisfactory in the situation some 10 years ago.

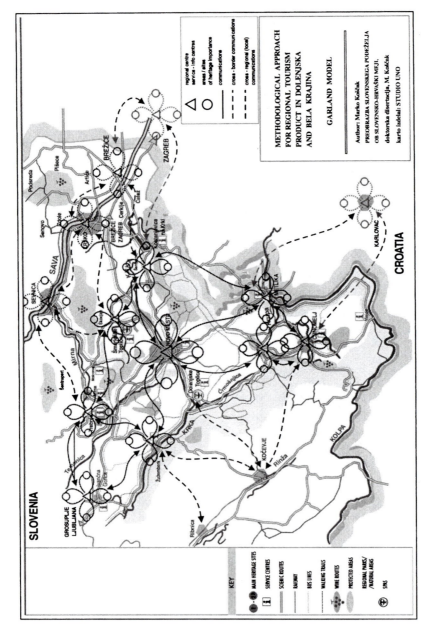

Figure 14.2: GARLAND model, represents aim to develop arrange of attractions around the region, which together with quality of accommodation and services provides a successful network for sustainable and long-term tourism as well as opportunities for cross-regional and cross border co-operation.

attractions – the 'tourism icons' already mentioned, i.e. lakes and mountains, caves and sea. For a significant period of time Slovene overseas marketing has tended to focus only on these well-known destinations!

By 2003, low-cost airlines made Slovenia easily accessible to high-spend markets. Air travel cannot be a basis for sustainability, but may have to be used as the initial opening-up phase for a new destination or product. Ultimately, connected rail travel access must be the longer-term primary aim. However, at this initial stage of opening the heritage trail market, the transport access methodology was via the low-cost airline destination airports of Ljubljana (easyJet), Klagenfurt (Ryanair) and Graz (Ryanair), with access ground transport routing via Ljubljana. In-depth contact with key operators by phone showed that there were two viable special interest packages, which could appeal commercially:

a) A 'heritage trail add-on' tourism package to offers at Bled (lakes and mountains) or Ljubljana (city and culture);
b) An integrated new 'highlights of Slovenia' holiday which started with 25% of the time allocation spent at two existing icons (Bled and Ljubljana), then the remaining 75% spent on the heritage trail.

Testing of this product with a group of six UK travel professionals was extremely successful. A second tour with tour operators from Germany and the UK in 2004 was less successful. In 2005 a specialist walking tour firm assembled its bespoke and individualized heritage trail offer and, at the time of writing, independent tour operator firms were preparing to launch two individualized, alternative packages online.

Learning Points

1. It is evident from the case study that the Heritage Recycling for Tourism phase was preceded by the work on integrated rural community development. This stimulated a community-based approach to development, in which context tourism was a part of the economic mix. This created a real hope of sustainability via the local communities' support for a new mixed economy, thus indicating that sustainable development can underpin successful tourism, if the correct strategy is chosen.
2. The evidence from the project has also revealed that heritage resource-based tourism development, if it is to be sustainable, must: a) show respect for the carrying capacity of resource zones – be they robust or fragile; and b) have rural community involvement and commitment to tourism, as the rural community has a stake in tourism, and thus acquires net economic gains from it.
3. Much tourism development arises because people in the destination create potential tourism products because they wish to acquire economic gain from them. Rural tourism products have to be adjusted to fit niche market demands that are highly competitive sectors internationally. Thus market awareness and understanding must be built in early in the development process, or the process becomes much longer and harder.

4. New tourist destinations are very difficult to launch internationally, even if they have high accessibility, unless they can be linked and tied in to existing tourism icons or magnets. This new Slovene offer had to be adjusted to do just that.

5. The 'gateway' identification is critical in new product formulation – whether this be a selected airport, seaport, railway station, or whatever. If the gateway is the airport of an attractive heritage city (such as Ljubljana), then both add-on package possibilities as well as links to a popular 'short city break' destination add great value.

6. Continuity of personnel in a development process is of real importance. The role of the Project Manager in initiation and continuity is critical, and the continuing interaction with external partners – who are supportive and share a belief in the integrity of the development over the long term – is also valuable.

7. This model ultimately is one of community-based multiple stakeholders, with equal support from small rural operatives and major agencies. The support from several levels – local, regional, national, and international – has enabled the 13-year development cycle of the Dolenjska and Bela krajina heritage trail project to be achieved.

Implementation of the Heritage Trail Model in Less Advanced Situations

Fundamental Issues

Whilst the Heritage Trail (HT) model of sustainable environmental and balanced economic development remains a strongly applicable model to be followed by regional development agencies in transition economies, a major issue has to be faced in the implementation process. The HT model has the implicit and inbuilt concept of the multi-stakeholder structure: both in the development stage and in the implementation stage the ability of all the actors to work together – irrespective of nature and background – is a fundamental demand. This demand is not always easily met in those transition economies where at a local level the psychosocial structures of the socialist economy as a power mechanism remain. The HT model has an almost prescriptive requirement for each interest group involved to surrender some element of power and control for the overall benefit of the development of the project as a whole. Almost paradoxically, such a mechanism appears to be difficult both for those who are steeped in the structures of the former economic system as well as the new entrepreneurs who seem to have the idea that a free market confers absolute freedom without socio-economic restraints.

The Vojvodina Case Study

There are a number of situations where the concept of the HT as a model has failed at an early stage. However, both authors of this chapter had an experience of a very early-stage breakdown of the multi-stakeholder approach in a potential transfer of the HT concept to a regional project in the Serbian autonomous province of Vojvodina.

The project was envisaged as covering a national park region in the Danube valley, close to the eastern frontier of Croatia, which had suffered from severe lack of funding as the result of the conflicts in the former Yugoslavia between 1991 and 1999. The potential actors were the municipality which covered the local region, the provincial tourism authorities, a local development agency with public/private status, a number of socially-owned entities (hotel and catering companies) and also a wide range of private entrepreneurs (e.g. vineyard owners, travel agencies, leisure activity organizations, etc). Primarily, all of these organizations had been driven together by the dynamic leadership of the municipality to enhance the status of the national park whilst ensuring that all future tourism development was sustainable, environmentally sensitive and took care of the apparently fragile nature of the communities in the park area. The latter had suffered not only from the economic collapse of Serbia during the period of the Balkan wars, but also from their proximity to what was initially a war front and latterly a frontier of marked hostility.

The first stage in the process was therefore calling all participants to a meeting, in which the Heritage Trail model was presented, together with examples of rural, sustainable tourism projects (e.g. wine trails) and an overview of a process of development and potential implementation. The authors and other experts also took part in a tour of the target tourism area, meeting local actors and discussing the development of a project.

Unfortunately, although the project would have been exceptionally favourable in dynamizing the local economy whilst also protecting a fragile and already damaged environment, it was undermined by antagonism between the development agency, the municipality and a number of the private sector enterprises which had strong political contacts. The development agency took control of the project, without external support or expert inputs, primarily for the purpose of improving their project list and gaining additional international funding. Furthermore, the leading role of the municipality was undermined when the more internationally focused leadership was replaced by a xenophobic political party which resented international cooperation and any concept of cross-border links with neighbouring countries.

This exemplifies the fact that projects are only as good as those involved in managing them and their ability to create a team dynamic. Here the project is overlaid with mutual suspicion and distrust, and the whole multi-stakeholder approach collapses.

A Success Story

Nonetheless there have been a number of successful transfers of the conceptual model where the multi-stakeholder approach has worked despite significant problems at a political and structural level. A good example has been an internationally funded project in Bosnia and Herzegovina, the 'Bosnian Kingdom Trail'[10] project, whose aim is to use the medieval Bosnia theme in improving competitiveness of BiH in cultural tourism, attracting foreign tourists and further developing local tourism.

The project is a continuation of the 'heritage trails' project which the Foundation successfully implemented between 2004 and 2007 within a framework of a living heritage

---

10. http://www.mozaik.ba/eng/heritage.html#trail

programme, developed in partnership with four local communities contributing to the development of tourism in terms of field research, design, restoration, marketing, and tourist product. There has also been a focus on local and regional networking in terms of developing a single cultural product as well as promoting a tourist 'historical route' at local and international level.

It is expected to be operational within a 3-year time span and includes the central Bosnian towns of Travnik, Vranduk, Kraljeva Sutjeska, Visoko, Prusac, Tešanj, Fojnica, Vareš, Jajce and Maglaj. The main focus is to unite these medieval Bosnian citadels into a single tourist product in order to present the rich cultural and historical heritage of the country more efficiently. It has been mainly funded by the European Commission through the Mozaik Foundation but has also been seeking support from the private sector.

The Entrepreneurial Community

Community involvement for ecotourism projects, within which the concept of sustainable rural tourism is included, is seen as a critically important area. Studies and programmes conducted by the World Wildlife Fund (Denman, 2004) and associated international agencies (GTZ, 1999), which have sought to manage the preservation of endangered species of animals and their environments together with economic development for sensitive rural communities, have found that ecotourism provides a valuable balance between what are often competing demands.

Community involvement in the planning and implementation process has often boosted community economic development and therefore precluded the need to adopt more exploitative types of development such as quarrying, mineral extraction or mass-scale tourism. The WWF PAN Parks initiative was established for the purpose of protecting wildlife in vulnerable European environments through tourism limited by sustainable carrying capacity. This has ensured that the quality of the natural and cultural heritage of an area is not damaged whilst also creating opportunities for entrepreneurship through community-driven tourism actions. This may involve micro and small businesses which are creating products and services derived from local or regional traditions or ethnography, and which create a unique selling point without creating cultural devaluation.

At the same time there is evidence, as Denman (2004) and others commented, that some ecotourism and rural development products fail because of the failure of the entrepreneurial vision. Projects fail to dynamize enough interest and generate visits, poor marketing decisions are made, or inadequate marketing channel utilized. In some cases, whilst the actual project location may be attractive, the surrounding region is sufficiently unattractive or poorly structured, and thus blocks access in marketing and logistical terms.

The role of specialist or niche market tour operators can often be critical, as seen in the heritage trail case study in this chapter, and can be an important component of the multi-stakeholder mix. This also applies to the quality of the accommodation and catering product: whilst ecotourists and heritage-cultural tourists may not seek five star hotel products or standards, they will normally demand clean, comfortable and appropriate facilities. The level of those facilities and the pricing may depend on whether, for example, the overall visitor profile is directed towards backpackers rather than the 'grey tourism' market (i.e. the over 55s). But quality is an important consideration and one which has been seen as essential to the community–entrepreneurship balance.

Analysis: Critical Success Factors

There are good reasons why the Slovene Heritage Trail model is being successfully adopted in several neighbouring countries as an initiative for rural regeneration through sustainable tourism, namely:

Factor 1 – Economic regeneration. A heritage trail is created as a tool for rural economic regeneration. The heritage trail extends tourism from existing centres into new and undervisited areas, by increasing the number of visitors, extending their stay, and diversifying the attractions and services offered to them, i.e. expansion, extension and diversification.

Factor 2 – Contributing to regional tourism development. The heritage trail is a tourism product which makes the natural and cultural heritage of a region the focal point of the offering. The development of such a product is, therefore, an integral component of the development of the whole region as a tourism destination. However, a heritage trail is only one product, and many regions have other tourism products on offer which may not be included in the trail. In creating heritage trails in Slovenia, there was frequently a temptation to include all tourism attractions and services in the region. But to give in to such a temptation would have been to lose the focus of a well-defined tourism product.

Factor 3 – Complementing other tourism products. Although a heritage trail focuses on only some of the attractions of a region, it can be complementary to other tourism products on offer. For example, it can contribute to economies of scale in regional promotion: in Slovenia, the heritage trail and spa tourism were promoted jointly, and costs of this shared. A heritage trail can also contribute to a wider choice of products for target markets. Taking the example of Slovenia again, spa tourists may be interested in the heritage trail product, and heritage trail tourists may enjoy the spa facilities.

Factor 4 – Transferability. The heritage trails concept is transferable to other regions and countries where there is sufficient natural and cultural heritage to attract tourists and where there is a local desire both to benefit from tourism and to safeguard that heritage. This is particularly the case in parts of central and eastern Europe where established settlement patterns and rural economies have developed similarly to those in Slovenia.

Factor 5 – Sustainable tourism. A heritage trail focuses on the natural and cultural assets of a rural region. This runs the risk of exposing some of the most vulnerable sites in a region to excessive numbers of tourists. The preparation of a heritage trail, therefore, must include a 'tourism carrying capacity' study at each proposed tourism site. If a sudden increase in tourists risked damaging the physical or natural attributes of a site, or if it were to exceed the tolerance of the local people, it should not be included in the heritage trail until preventive measures can be implemented.

Conclusion: Role of the Multi-stakeholder Approach

We have seen that one of the beneficial methodologies for growing and developing certain tourism sectors by interventionist systems is the multi-stakeholder model. In this chapter, we have explored the specific case of sustainable rural development through a case study of a multi-stakeholder approach in action and through reference to other cases and to research in this area.

It has been noted that multi-stakeholder tourism projects have:

- The capacity to benefit the ownership transformation process by forcing public, private and social ownership agents and enterprises to work together. This is of particular benefit in that public agencies will bring in concerns and structures in relation to spatial planning whilst the private sector will bring in important questions about quality, marketing and financial sustainability;
- We determined that the business enterprise issues are important as community-based organizations do need to have external inputs of these skills, as long as they have a clear local focus. We saw that some concepts fail because of the failure of the entrepreneurial vision, i.e. poor marketing, low levels of inter-agency coordination, and a lack of forward planning and futurism about markets;
- An integrating role in which individual tourism entrepreneurs begin to comprehend and understand the value of cooperation as well as of competition. In the case of common promotional activity and branding, the multi-stakeholder model of integration benefits from the totality and complexity of resources and skills.
- The ability to provide the important harmonization of what should be complementary but which may become conflicting aims, i.e. entrepreneurial dynamism, the demands of the macro-economy, and the aspirations of inhabitants. In this way growth can benefit communities without the erosion of the cultural heritage.

Essentially, we are of the view that:

- The heritage trail case study shows that the model was very firmly focused on community-based multiple-stakeholders, with equal support from small rural operatives and major agencies. In the Dolenjska and Bela krajina project the multiple levels – local, regional, national, and international – and the variety of actors have been instrumental in enabling the 14-year development cycle to be achieved;
- Importantly, the case study, as with other similar projects, makes a key point about tourism development in countries proceeding through the transitionary process. The model we have explained has quite undeniably the prescriptive requirement for each interest group involved to surrender an element of power and control for the overall benefit of the development project as a whole. Where there has been failure it may often

be ascribed to an unwillingness of private entrepreneurs to embrace what they often see as the socialistic concepts of planning and cooperation. Equally, local bureaucracy often remains under the semi-political control of former party cadres who desire an almost feudal model of control and leadership.

Questions for Discussion

1. Does the concept of the multi-stakeholder approach imply the need for a variety of organizational hierarchies (e.g. international, national, regional, local, community-level) as well as a range of actors (e.g. public, private, social and voluntary)?
2. Is it possible at the start of the development process to ensure that a successful tourism development project, with a multiplicity of stakeholders, can be underpinned by an environmental sustainability policy?
3. What are the key success factors that small and microenterprises in rural regions need to employ to develop effective tourism programmes?
4. Is there evidence that the development of multi-stakeholder projects in European transition economies has been assisted by the structures of European Union financial intervention?

Reference

European Parliament (2007). Resolution of 29 November 2007 (Commission recommendation 2006/2129-INI) on a renewed EU Tourism Policy: *Towards a stronger partnership for European Tourism.*

Chapter 15

Information Communication Technologies (ICTs), Entrepreneurship and SMTEs

Dimitrios Buhalis and Hilary Murphy

Learning Outcomes

After reading this chapter, you should be able to:

- Understand the role of SMTEs in the tourism sector;

- Gain an understanding of the key advantages of SMTEs as well as their disadvantages as firms;

- Appreciate the role of ICT in the tourism industry and SMTEs;

- Understand the ICT applications for SMTEs; and

- Understand diffusion of innovations and the different stages of ICT engagement in SMTEs and the tourism sector at whole.

The Strategic Role of SMEs in the EU

Small and Medium-sized Enterprises (SMEs) dominate most markets worldwide. They are increasingly being recognized as the engine of growth and as the backbone of the European economy. The significance of SMEs becomes more obvious as they are recognized as providers of a diversity of products and services for a wide range of cultural and national backgrounds. Across the EU there are around 23 million SMEs; that is 99% of all enterprises providing two-thirds of all private sector jobs, accounting for about 75 million jobs. In some key industries, such as textiles, construction and furniture-making, they account for as much as 80% of all jobs (European Commission, 2003). SMEs are particularly important in developing and less industrialized countries. For example microbusinesses (those with fewer than 10 employees) dominate employment in countries such as Italy (47%) and Poland (41%). More importantly, due to their flexibility, SMEs are capable of operating successfully even during periods of economic turbulence and recessions. The overriding challenge for the European Union and its member states is to create conditions in which entrepreneurs are encouraged to follow their ideas through, where the attractions and potential gains outweigh more clearly the costs and inevitable risks of starting an enterprise.

The definition of an SME varies significantly depending on geographic location. The EU has defined an SME as having less than 250 employees, less than €50 million in turnover and as being independent of larger enterprises (Buhalis and Deimezi, 2004). Downie (2002) states that a similar definition is adopted in the USA, whereas in Australia an enterprise with less than 50 employees is considered an SME. These definitions are somewhat simplistic in the sense that only quantitative parameters are used. Though size measurements are certainly relevant as they may indicate levels of resources available and the complexity/simplicity of organizational structure, there are other qualitative criteria that need to be considered. MacGregor and Vrazilic (2004) provide a more detailed definition of SMEs. They argue that both quantitative and qualitative parameters should be used when defining SMEs.

Small and Medium-sized Tourism and Hospitality Enterprises

SMTEs play a dominant role in the tourism industry worldwide (Getz et al., 2004; Morrison et al., 1999; Morrison and Thomas, 1999; Morrison, 1998). To define these particular SMEs, a wide range of qualitative criteria can be used such as: the organizational structure; participation in hotel consortia or chains; turnover; responsibility distribution in decision-making; financial strength; operational procedures; recruitment and training practices; decision-making process; entrepreneurial involvement and control; integration level; family domination in running the property; internationalization of operation; the marketing functions and managerial experience (Buhalis, 1993, p. 367; Poon, 1990, p. 110). When hotels are classified, the number of beds criterion can be applied. Most authors seem to agree that accommodation establishments with less than 50 rooms are small (Go and Welch, 1991, p. 14; Moutinho, 1990, p. 104). Moutinho (1990) also characterizes as small all hotels and travel agencies employing less than 10 people.

However we define these particular SMEs, they dominate the tourism economic landscape around the world and share certain characteristics that are both quantitative in terms of employment and turnover, and qualitative in terms of management structures, flexibility in production and ability to operate in regional clusters.

However, these SMTEs globally lack the expertise and resources to follow those developments (Levy and Powell, 2000; Buhalis and Main, 1998). They often find it increasingly difficult to transform their operational and strategic management to face the new realities and the challenges they introduce. These SMEs are typically family run and most researchers agree that financial restrictions in terms of available capital are characteristic of this sector (Main, 2002; Buhalis and Main, 1998; Chapman et al., 2000; Collins et al., 2003). SMTEs, in most cases, operate informal organizational structures with a greater involvement by proprietors' family. Often traditional household roles are adapted in the everyday running of the business. As a result, a business is usually run according to family principles, rather than proper business practices, while people in the SME rarely have formal education or training. This often causes both managerial and emotional problems.

Smaller hotels are not simply smaller versions of larger hospitality organizations but have distinct managerial/owner cultures of their own. SMEs, therefore, have special needs and requirements which affect their competitiveness and their ability to grow. Morrison and Thomas (1999) explain that assertions made by those who see small hospitality firms as merely miniaturized versions of larger organizations are ill-conceived. However the minority of SMTEs which can be classed as entrepreneurial represent dynamic engines that have the potential to drive the hospitality and tourism industries.

Despite their structural weaknesses emerging from their management, marketing and training deficiencies, SMTEs are particularly important for the prosperity of a destination, not only by enabling tourists to experience the destination character, but also by facilitating the rapid infusion of tourist spending into the local economy. In addition, they contribute significantly to the range, variety, authenticity and quality of the tourism experience. Often SMTEs formulate value-added networks or clusters of product and service delivery, which enhance tourist satisfaction and stimulate the multiplier effects of the tourism activity at the destination (Braun, 2002; Buhalis, 1998). Since a wide number of SMEs are involved in order to deliver a tourism product and service, the destination is literally an amalgam of SMEs which address the consumer's needs. Most importantly, SMEs are regarded as flexible and capable of providing personalized services for the new era of tourism.

Public sector support for networking schemes is also of great significance, as it assists SMEs to achieve synergies, economies of scope and system gains. In this context, the public sector in several regions has recently financed destination management systems in order to strengthen SMEs' visibility and competitiveness in the tourism distribution channel. Other programmes include training and incentive policies aiming to reduce SMEs' strategic disadvantages and to ameliorate their tourism product. Hence, as a result of the recognition that SMEs are the backbone of the tourism industry, a variety of supporting agents, funds and programmes become available to support not only the enterprises at the micro-level, but also their regions at the macro-level.

Information Communication Technologies, the Internet and SMEs

Tiessen et al. (2001) assert that globalization, the internet and e-commerce pose new challenges and provide new competitive opportunities, especially for small and medium-sized enterprises (SMEs) seeking to broaden their involvement into new international markets. Yet SMEs need to use e-commerce to respond to market changes and industry norms. Integrating technology into the business process and operating in an e-business environment can offer SMEs many advantages in daily operational procedures such as in sales, marketing, distribution and procurement, tactical and strategic management (O'Connor and Frew, 2000; Main, 2002).

The fragmentation of the market has made the internet ideal for promoting SMEs online and has rapidly become an important channel of distribution. This has a profound effect on the structure of the industry as well as the communications, promotions, operations and strategy of SMEs. The internet is increasingly becoming one of the most successful channels for SMEs to communicate directly with consumers. This direct contact should improve customer relationship management, giving direct access to customers without the cost of utilizing a third party, and thus avoid commission payments. In reality this occurs only for those entrepreneurial owner/managers who are able to acquire the skills (or access those who do have them) in terms of website design, database management and the ability to exploit the internet and keep current of the continuous evolution of this challenging media.

The rapid development of the internet in the late 1990s has had a strong impact on the tourism and hospitality industry SMEs (Buhalis, 2003; O'Connor, 1999). However, only a small number of innovative SMEs have fully realized the utility of the internet as their main communication and distribution channel. This enabled them to eliminate the barriers of global reach which they faced hitherto due to their under-representation in Global Distribution Systems (GDSs) (Werthner and Klein, 1999). Despite all of the benefits and opportunities that can be achieved, the internet and new technologies have failed to make a major impact on the majority of SMTEs. Many SMTEs can be characterized as laggards, and have yet to fully realize the actual benefits of applying ICT to their business (Buhalis, 2003; Morrison et al., 1999; Mutch, 1998). However, those SMTEs that are taking full advantage of the electronic market place are benefiting from the many opportunities that it provides for 'early adopters' or 'innovators'.

In particular, the level of Information Communication Technologies (ICT) adoption is also closely linked to the skills and ICT attitude of owners and managers (Buhalis and Main, 1998; Martin and Matlay, 2001). Main (1995) further argues that this adoption is heavily influenced by the profile of the owner/manager in terms of gender, age and education. This lack of skill is further aggravated by the negligence of training of often low skilled employees. Further research has also identified a general reluctance towards ICT (Main, 1995; Collins et al., 2003) and what Paraskevas and Buhalis (2002) call 'techno-phobia'. Buhalis and Main (1998) further argue that SMEs often perceive ICT adoption as requiring a heavy dependency on ICT experts. They further state that lack of ICT adoption is often linked to how marketing is performed by SMEs in general and the fact that they often focus on short-term marketing planning and activities. Furthermore, Collins et al. (2003) note that SMEs' low bargaining power with suppliers impacts significantly on their level of ICT adoption in the wider e-commerce environment, with little indication of supply chain management through optimizing technology solutions.

However, the internet may enable innovative small organizations to build their 'virtual' size and expand their reach. Low-cost access to network infrastructures, the ability to communicate directly with consumers and the availability of new distribution channels are a few of the key internet benefits for SMEs (Poon and Swatman, 1997; Levy and Powell, 2000). Never before have SMTEs had the opportunity to address and communicate global audiences so cost-effectively. e-Commerce can support them to trade globally, through enhancing direct distribution to consumers as well as through a global network of intermediaries (Brown and Lockett, 2004; Kalakota and Whinston, 1996; Lauden and Traver, 2002).

The hospitality European studies show that SMEs, in general, have to innovate both from a technological and an organizational perspective to take advantage of the emerging opportunities. They also need to build partnerships with other organizations through clusters of integrated activity in order to address strategic opportunities and challenges successfully (Dutta and Evrard, 1999; Poon, 1998). As far as the hospitality sector is concerned, it is increasingly evident that SMTEs have little choice. They can either enter into ICT-empowered strategic alliances with their stakeholders (and expand the opportunities to communicate directly with their clientele) or risk being sidelined as few SMEs have the capacity or expertise to fully exploit technology on a global scale.

There is abundant evidence that many medium-sized hotels have moved away from the clerical use of IT (record keeping and word processing) and have begun to use it in decision-making (yield management and data management). However, poor planning and a lack of core competences in internet management persist in many tourism and hospitality businesses (Carson and Sharma, 2001) and there is still an abundance of SMEs that hope to move towards retirement without adopting technology.

The rapid growth of the internet and web-based applications as mainstream communication and transaction media have enabled, and perhaps forced, dramatic changes in the way of doing business. As the digital economy develops, hotels increasingly need greater technology, regardless of their size, as customers continue to migrate to this new media in increasing numbers and for a wider range of uses (Connolly et al., 1998). In many cases, SMTEs are forced to adopt new technology; for example they are required by tax authorities to fill in forms electronically, to link inventory to the destination management system (DMS), or manage their availability and rates online for third-party distributors. This is clearly a push factor that is emerging in the market place and it is often forced by larger organizations that had to re-engineer their processes in order to reduce their transaction and operational costs.

More recent factors that impact on ICT adoption include: the demand for dynamic packaging, where customers can put together their own travel/tour package in one website visit; the governmental push towards a digital economy (e-commerce and m-commerce) and the associated incentives; the technically savvy, 'wired' consumer and consequent demand-side pull; the web 2.0 proliferation which reinforces the need for organizations to follow and manage online content for them; and the increasing technology role of the DMSs (Buhalis, 1993).

ICT Applications and Technologies for SMEs

The lack of suitable, affordable and easy to operate ICT systems for SMEs will continue to be problematic for the tourism SME sector. This is mainly due to the heterogeneous nature of these businesses, which makes them unattractive to vendors and developers of technology solutions. They are hard to reach, expensive to service and reluctant to spend on technology solutions. They frequently have inadequate infrastructure, networks, or up-to-date processing power to run current technology-based solutions. Quite often there is no qualified staff to operate the technology, and most SMTE staff and entrepreneurs are far too busy with their operational tasks that they cannot take sufficient time to familiarize themselves with technology.

This complicates the development of solutions, even with vendors and software developers who may be willing, or subsidized, to provide technology support and investment in this sector. This, along with the diverse language requirements required for the software in various EU states, means that vendors, who may initially get enthusiastic about the volume of available businesses in this sector, quickly discover the barriers to working towards technology-based solutions with SMEs. Consequently, there does not seem to be a 'business case' for all interested parties to pursue and often they change their business interests.

As the internet becomes ubiquitous and robust, global connection using internet protocol (IP) becomes more possible and preferable. Converged IP solutions are likely to become more widespread throughout the tourism and hospitality sector, with the convergence of data, voice and video onto a single network. This is particularly important as Voice Over Internet Protocol (VoiP) is increasingly utilized for voice communications.

Hospitality Application Service Providers (ASPs) offer remotely hosted hospitality software applications for hotels over an intranet or the internet, charging them a negotiated monthly fee for their use. ASPs and Software-as-a-Service (SaaS) offer cheaper high-end applications with specialized IT support and expertise, though a recent study showed that there is perceived weaknesses in the ASP model (Paraskevas and Buhalis, 2002). Increasingly the major technology providers to the industry, for example the property management system for the hotel sector, such as Fidelio, are promoting Software-as-a-Service (SaaS) or on-demand application hosting versions of their software. These are particularly targeted towards the SMEs sector, providing a low-risk–lower-cost solution. Even the major players, the GDS systems such as Amadeus, have launched affordable platforms tailored to the SME business sector.

Software-as-a-Service (SaaS) is one of the fastest growing segments of the ICT industry because it provides a more cost-effective alternative for enterprises to achieve their business objectives than traditional packaged applications. Kincora (2006) suggests that some consider the new breed of Software-as-a-Service (SaaS) providers the best bet for on-demand application hosting. Their predecessors, Application Service Providers (ASPs), offered application services in a hosted data centre style: a costly approach that led to service-level and financial failures. Back in the 1980s and 1990s, ASPs got the application outsourcing business rolling by hosting third-party, client-server applications. Essentially, ASPs transferred a customer's application sets into mini-data centres housed in a massive, extravagant data centre. Since one ASP was running so many customer-specific applications, the ASPs couldn't provide much expertise in each application. Customers still had to have in-house expertise to make sure the applications were operating correctly. The high cost of building and maintaining data centres and running customer-specific applications crippled many ASP ventures.

In contrast the typical SaaS provider offers applications specifically designed to be hosted and delivered over the internet to many customers. As a result, the providers can create and offer value-added features, which would be expensive in the ASP model. With SaaS, SMTEs don't have to buy the software and then pay for the provider to host it. With SaaS, the customers' ICT people have access to a number of different features or capabilities within the software set and can tweak them via a web interface to fit the needs of their company. The interface makes it easy for administrators to customize for simple changes. The SaaS model is a good fit for companies with many geographically dispersed and/or mobile software users or users who collaborate with each other or outsiders (Kincora, 2006).

Cost and Benefits of ICTs for SMTEs

Despite the great investments in information and communication technologies (ICT), research has not persuasively established corresponding productivity increases and many studies have also found no significant relationships between productivity and ICT (Sigala, 2003). However, the study also reveals that productivity gains do not accrue from ICT investments per se, but rather from the full exploitation of ICT networking and building the information capabilities in the organization. Although it is becoming evident that using technology and the internet is becoming inelastic for SMTEs, the questions 'are SMTEs too small to benefit from technology?' and 'does it make financial sense for SMTEs to use ICTs?' must be considered (Buick, 2003). Some SMEs have so few rooms or products that they cannot afford the investment in equipment and expertise. They also have such as small capacity that they cannot allocate rooms and guarantee the release of inventory to web-based retailers. Peacock and Evans (1999) propose a similar viewpoint in that technology has still much to prove in terms of reducing costs and increasing productivity.

It is also mooted that the internet and web-enabled technologies may prove to be merely 'intermediate technologies' and that mobile technology will be the future platform, with diffusion of mobile technology surpassing that of internet-based technology. A number of applications are already deployed on mobiles. For example, the destination management system TISCOVER is using an SMS application for informing small hotels of reservations as and when they are confirmed (Buhalis et al., 2006). However, this speed of evolution of technology is relentless and likely to continue into the next decade, according to Moore's Law. Waiting, therefore, is not a viable option for these SME businesses as it only further exacerbates their ICT confidence and capacity, and alienates them from their markets. As we move towards a more mobile market place, SMEs need now to be in a position to reach their wired, mobile customers and operate in the digital economy.

Table 15.1 illustrates a comprehensive framework of all cost and benefit elements for developing an internet presence for SMTEs (Buhalis, 1999). All items have been suggested as important during discussions with entrepreneurs and tourism marketing experts. The majority of the costs and benefits are management and marketing based, rather than ICTs based. Hence it can be concluded that competent and innovative entrepreneurs will find the internet more beneficial than their counterparts who lack marketing or management skills, abilities and knowledge. It is evident therefore that the costs can be reduced by intensive management, marketing and ICTs training for SMTEs, which will enable them to develop a more comprehensive marketing strategy and to utilize ICTs as a strategic tool for their long-term development.

However, from a business culture and entrepreneurial viewpoint, adoption of technology could be in complete conflict with the 'lifestyle' choice that Morrison et al. (1999) and Peters and Buhalis (2004) identify as a key characteristic of the SME owner/manager. Collins et al. (2003), demonstrated that SMTEs are not utilizing information technology in their businesses to its full potential. They primarily see the internet as a mechanism for promoting their hotel rather than for training, inter-, intra-organizational and e-commerce purposes. SMTEs therefore need to educate themselves on technology and other critical

Table 15.1: Cost and benefit analysis for developing internet presence for SMTEs.

Costs
- Purchasing hardware, software and communication package;
- Training of users;
- Design and construction of internet presence;
- Hosting the site on a reliable server;
- Ongoing maintenance and regular updating;
- Marketing the internet service and registration of domain;
- Development of procedures for dealing with internet presence;
- Commissions for purchases online by intermediaries;
- Advertising fees for representation in search engines and other sites;
- Interconnectivity with travel intermediaries such as Expedia, booking.com

Benefits
- Direct bookings, often intermediaries and commission free;
- Global distribution of multimedia information and promotional material;
- Low cost of providing and distributing timely updates of information;
- Global presence on the internet, 24 hours a day, 365 days a year;
- Durability of promotion (in comparison to limited life of printed advertising in press);
- Reduction of promotional cost and reduction of brochure waste;
- Great degree of attention by visitors to website;
- Reduction of time required for transactions and ability to offer last minute promotions;
- Low marginal cost of providing information to additional users;
- Support of marketing intelligence and product design functions;
- Development of targeted mailing lists through people who actively request information;
- Great interactivity with prospective customers;
- Niche marketing to prospective consumers who ask to receive information;
- Interactivity with local partners and provision of added value products at destinations;
- Ability to generate a community feel for current users and prospective customers.

Based on Buhalis (1999).

subjects, perhaps through online e-learning applications, in order to be able to take full advantage of the ICT potential (Cheng and Piccoli, 2002; Piccoli et al., 2001).

Diffusion of Innovations and Stages of ICT Engagement in SMEs

The utilization of technology in SMEs follows the diffusion of innovation theories as well as a number of critical pull and push factors (Buhalis and Main, 1998). Rogers' (1995) 'diffusion of innovation' theory identified the characteristics of innovation which determine the rate of diffusion in the market place. These include both hard/rational and soft/personal factors, such as complexity, trialability, compatibility and relative advantage. Although Rogers' theories can be applied to many SMEs, their particular needs and requirements, as well as their perceptions, need to be understood better. Lebvre et al. (1991) identified four categories of factors that influence the adoption of new technologies by SMEs and their attitude towards adoption, including:

- Characteristics of the firm;
- Competitiveness and management strategies of the firm;
- Influences of international and external parties on the adoption decision process; and
- Characteristics of new technologies adopted.

However, the limited adoption of ICT innovation in SMEs generates considerable concern at local, national and EU levels about their ability and readiness to use the ICTs and the internet as a business tool. A number of barriers can be identified, including lack of resources, lack of skilled employees, lack of easy to use technology adapted to SMEs, and also lack of awareness of the potential benefits (Main, 2002; Anckar and Walden, 2001). The European Commission, as well as national governments, has therefore been undertaking a number of initiatives to reduce the digital divide and to support SMEs to enhance their technology capabilities (European Portal for SMEs, 2007).

Nachira (2002) has demonstrated that the adoption of internet-based technologies can be represented as a continuous process with sequential steps of evolutions (Figure 15.1). In the early stages, email and information-only web presence allow SMEs to communicate and present their products online. Comprehensive e-commerce and e-business applications enable not only interaction with external entities but also integration with internal systems,

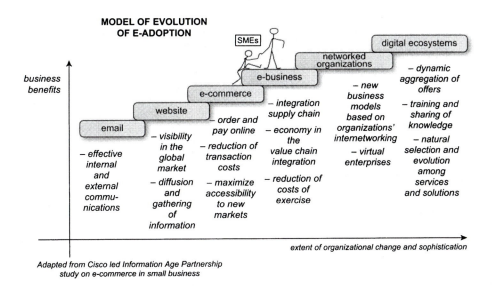

Figure 15.1: Model of evolution of e-adoption. (*Source*: Nachira, 2002.)

processes and data. A certain degree of business process re-engineering is required to achieve those objectives, although organizations do not need to change fundamentally. At the networking stage new business models are required to support organizations to concentrate on their core business and to develop internet working and partnerships with complementary organizations. Finally, the digital ecosystem supports dynamic networking and collaboration through the development of a community that shares business, knowledge and infrastructures towards maximizing their collective benefit. This changes dramatically the way that businesses are constructed and operate, and makes organizations much more fluid with structures being shaped dynamically by alliances, partnerships and collaboration (Nachira, 2002).

It is evident therefore that SMEs in different locations and industries will have variable factors affecting their ICT adoption, since the competitive forces and industry structures differ. Perhaps the most significant factor that affects the ICT acceptance is the attitude and ability of entrepreneurs to appreciate the opportunities and potential that ICTs can introduce to their business (Buhalis and Main, 1998). This also determines their benefits and perceptions towards the internet and technologies.

SMEs and e-Marketing

Most authors in the wider context of SMEs comment on the strategic marketing competencies and incompetencies of SMEs in that their marketing planning, essential to strategy and long-term viability, is 'both under utilized and misunderstood' (Hill, 2000, p. 217). Hill (2000) comments that SMEs lack 'routine marketing decision-making policies' and reaffirms their reliance on 'intuition' as a key determinant in marketing success. This, however, only works for a small number of SME operators who are equipped with the marketing expertise to exploit new products, services and markets. Sadowski et al. (2002) further note the fact that SMEs are not 'active sellers' and critiques their 'reactive selling' approaches.

Prior to the internet, in the offline world, this may have been sufficient. However, the internet environment has increased transparency dramatically in the market place and has also created a vibrant environment where time is one of the key determinants of competitive advantage (Buhalis, 2003). It also demands the creation of value systems that need to bring all contributors to the tourist experience together. Though 'co-opetition' exists within destinations, for example referring customers to other hotels when fully booked or recommending complementary products and services, their dependence on personal contact networks still dominates, reducing their ability to develop comprehensive value systems. Although it is becoming increasingly evident that 'network competency' should be considered critical to SME marketing success, most of these SMEs fail to take advantage of the value these networks can offer. This is particularly detrimental in the current 'customer-empowered' environment where the internet has built an expectation of instant recognition and response.

Additionally, along with the growth of the digital economy (e-commerce and m-commerce), the technically savvy, 'wired' consumer and consequent demand-side pull, even traditional marketing activities are less relevant. Reliance on traditional partners who are disappearing creates obvious threats to the SME, which must acquire new e-marketing skills and competences.

SMEs have less bargaining power when it comes to online distribution partners and may have to accommodate what these stakeholders dictate (e.g. what partners to work with, what target markets it attracts, how is distribution executed). Therefore they often have to rely heavily on the marketing plans of powerful members of their distribution channels and suppliers (Shiels et al., 2003). This results in them failing to make best use of these relationships and this failure contributes significantly to internet visibility, where linkages and traffic generation increase search engine rankings. Unfortunately, intermediaries are often seen as a threat to pricing integrity and distribution costs by hotels, despite serving a purpose in terms of gaining visibility and market reach (O'Connor and Frew, 2004). Similarly, DMSs are often viewed by SMEs as being inefficient and too competitive in their undifferentiated selection and listing of properties (Murphy and Keilgast, 2008).

Innovative SMEs gradually realize that once advanced technologies have been introduced, they need to use them dynamically in order to support their operational and strategic marketing. As online bookings and e-marketing increase in importance and customers use Search Engines (SEs) to filter their information seeking, SMTEs need to increase their visibility on SEs. Potential customers rarely look past the first page and less than 5% look past the first three pages of the search results, therefore investment in a website is wasted if not optimized for both organic and paid search. If the SME hotel operator does not have the necessary skills and e-marketing experience then they should consider strategic alignment(s) with distribution channel(s) that provide visibility in target markets, e.g. the DMS (public or private). Collaboration through other partners and becoming part of electronic clusters of value creation is another way to ensure that SMTEs are visible and also associated with local conferences, attractions, events and other developments.

Increasingly, entrepreneurial businesses are considering how to reach the 'unmanaged customers'. With the growth of social media, smart marketers are utilizing this media space to reach individual customers. Web 2.0 reflects the rapidly growing popularity of online communities, such as Facebook, MySpace and many other local and global sites. Hitwise, a UK-based research agency, states that in June 2007, the 20 top social networks accounted for 4% of UK internet visits – up 79% year on year. Hitwise (2007) further mentioned the growing importance of social networks in a commercial context, either as upstream traffic generators or as promotional platforms. Whether Web 2.0 is an appropriate term or not, the quintessence is that the web is becoming more and more user generated, which has significant implications for information-sharing and market communication. People are listening more and more to other amateur writers rather than to traditional mass media and marketing.

Entrepreneurial SME operators are tuned in to the changing market conditions and take advantage of new medias (e.g. they create and read blog sites, use their Facebook page to connect continually online, and use linkage to make their website more visible). They exploit the relatively inexpensive (in some cases subsidized) destination marketing website, and use it is as an additional distribution and booking channel. Developing their profile on Tripadvisor, MySpace, Facebook, YouTube, etc., they can relate to these audiences and put their related message forward, although there remains some debate as to how to best operate in social networks and social media space, i.e. will they need to develop their brand on those channels, should they join in the discussion as well as monitor reviews and comments, etc.? It will become difficult to ignore this phenomenon completely and the more progressive of the tourism and hospitality businesses are already incorporating 'user generated' content in both their own sites and also on the social networking sites. An example of that is Hotel Segas in Loutraki – see case study below – that incorporates destination content and engages in all possible communication channels to reach the widest audience possible. This hotel generates more that 25% of its revenue through its website.

Case Study: Hotel Segas in Loutraki, Greece

Following the termination of an 18-year exclusive contract with a major Scandinavian Tour Operator, Hotel Segas found itself in a very difficult situation. Having only 24 rooms and a fairly undifferentiated product, apart from the superb personal attention, the hotel had no resources and only little strength to approach prospective customers. Having over-relied on a single tour operator for so many years, they had abandoned all other markets and could not easily attract new customers at such a short notice. Given the limitation of the destination, the lack of funds for marketing activities, and the insufficiency of marketing expertise internally, the hotel trusted a willing, close relative to develop and maintain a web page promoting the hotel. There was no budget for the development of the site and as a result the hotel could not initially register its domain name, and could only be registered as a free server (netfirms.com).

The web design and text developed were significantly different from normal web pages. A much more personal and informal approach was adopted, giving a life story and introducing members of the host family. Also, emphasis was put on the destination and the practicalities. The web page went live in September 2000 and gradually was registered with most search engines by March 2001. The lack of funds delayed the registration as multiple submission through free submit engines was made. In 2005 the hotel registered its domain name although it continued to host its pages on the free servers. A yahoo email account was set for communications. The hotel decided to answer all emails and booking requests personally, engaging with prospective travellers and assisting with all their travel planning rather than the reservation with the hotel. In the period January to July 2001 the web pages had generated about 1000 viewings from areas as remote as Japan, Nicaragua and Canada. By 2007 the web generated about 50,000 unique visits to its website and about 200,000 page impressions whilst the web generated bookings reached 25% of the total turnover of the hotel. Although there was a displacement effect where people booked online through email rather than calling the hotel, most of the revenue generated was incremental. The cost of developing and maintaining the web page was only the volunteering time of the helpful relative, demonstrating clearly that the internet can enable even tiny, but innovative, organizations to maximize their potential.

Additional innovations were added to maximize customer service. For example, in 2007 the hotel offered free WiFi internet access to all guests, boosting customer satisfaction especially for business travellers. The website also continued to develop in parallel to the hotel renovation. Recent innovations include the provision of Google maps on the website as well as the addition of content to Google Earth. Finally, the hotel encouraged guests to post reviews on Tripadvisor and to share their experience – whether positive or negative – with the world. This has made them consistently one of the top of the hotels in the area. They also started to experiment with Facebook through the creation of a Fun Club and a business online. The hotel will continue to innovate in the future, using as many channels as possible to reach more potential customers worldwide and addressing the needs of its clientele.

For more information see: Greece http://www.hotelsegas.com

The Future ICT Landscape and SMEs

ICTs evolve constantly, providing new tools for tourism marketing and management. They support the interactivity between tourism enterprises and consumers and, as a result, they re-engineer the entire process of developing, managing and marketing tourism products and destinations. Buhalis and O'Connor (2005) predicted that increasingly ICTs will provide the 'info-structure' for the entire industry and will overtake all mechanistic aspects of tourism transactions. Innovative tourism enterprises will have the ability to divert resources and expertise to servicing consumers and provide higher value-added transactions. Social networking and Web 2.0 demonstrate that the web is becoming more and more user generated, which has significant implications for information-sharing and communication. Consumers rely more on their peer group for objective views and opinions about products and services, making the market more transparent and difficult to compete in.

New technologies will need to be engaged to ensure that consumers are touched at the channels that they use. Google and search have now moved into the mobile space, and new PDAs and smart mobile phones are loaded with internet and search tools. The expansion of both WiMax and fixed cost GPRS, as well as low-cost and increasingly free Wi-Fi within locations around the world, allows individuals to be connected all the time. The next generation of customers are net-savvy and even net-dependent – expecting to be connected with their preferred content and devices anywhere, anytime … and the future entrepreneurial SMTE operator has to ensure that they are present and visible in the online environment as well as able to make this connection seamlessly. Like all other organizations around the world, SMTEs will require agile strategies at both strategic and tactical management levels to ensure that the ICT-raised opportunities and challenges are turned to the advantage of tourism organizations by enhancing their innovation and competitiveness.

Questions for Discussion

1. Why are SMTEs important for tourism development and growth?
2. What are the main advantages/disadvantages of SMTEs?

3. Explain how ICTs, particularly the internet, create competive advantages and add value to SMTEs?
4. What are the key rudiments that tourism businesses must adapt in order to develop innovative and competitive e-business models?

References

Cheng, C. and Piccoli, G. (2002). Web-Based Training in the Hospitality Industry: A Conceptual Definition, Taxonomy and Preliminary Investigation, *International Journal of Hospitality Information Technology*, 2(2), 19–33.

Downie, G. (2002). Internet marketing and SMEs, *Management Services*, 14(7), 8–20.

Dutta, S. and Evrard, P. (1999). Information Technology and Organisation within European Small Enterprises, *European Management Journal*, 17(3), 239–251.

Hill, J. (2001). A multidimensional study of the key determinants of effective SME marketing activity: Part 1, *International Journal of Entrepreneurial Behaviour and Research*, 7(5), 171–204.

Lebre, R. (1998). Small and medium-sized enterprises and IT diffusion policies in Europe, *Small Business Economics*, 11(1), 1–9.

MacGregor, R. and Vrazalic, L. (2004). *Electronic commerce adoption in small to medium enterprises (SMEs): a comparative study of SMEs in Wollongong (Australia) and Karlstad (Sweden)*. University of Wollongong, Wollongong, May.

Morrison, A., Taylor, S., Morrison, A., and Morrison, A. (1999). Marketing Small Hotels on the World Wide Web, *Information Technology and Tourism*, 2(2), 97–11.

Murphy, H. and Keilgast, C. (2008). Do small and medium sized hotels exploit search engine marketing? *International Journal of Contemporary Hospitality Marketing*, 20(1), 90–97.

Piccoli, G., Ahmad, R. and Ives, B. (2001). Web Based Virtual Learning Environments: A research framework and a preliminary assessment of effectiveness in basic IT skills and training, *MIS Quarterly*, 25(4), 401–427.

Poon, A. (1990). Flexible specialization at small size: The Case of Caribbean Tourism, *World Development*, 18(1), 109–123.

Prescott, L. (2007). Buzznet and iMeem: Fast growing socialnetworks. http://weblogs.hitwise.com/leeannprescott/2007/03/buzznet_and_imeem_fast_growing.html

Chapter 16

Access to Finance: Delivery Structures and the Problems Faced by Micro and Small Tourism Entrepreneurs

Tony O'Rourke

Learning Outcomes

After reading this chapter, you should be able to:

- Understand the specific issues for European micro, small and medium-sized enterprises with regard to their ability to access finance;

- Have an overview of the issues surrounding delivery structures for debt and equity finance and how these relate to entrepreneurial imperatives;

- Be aware of the specific situation for the financing of tourism in the European transition economies and the funding gaps that remain a significant barrier to the more effective development of small-scale tourism activity.

Introduction

This chapter is concerned with issues connected to the delivery of financing structures which match the demands and requirements of tourism entrepreneurs. More specifically, this chapter tends to focus on the micro and small-scale tourism sector whilst at the same time providing examples from similar issues facing tourism SMEs in a selection of European transition economies.

We will first seek to define what we mean by micro, small and medium-sized enterprises. Thereafter we will address the problematic area of financing SMEs and then look at such issues concerning SME finance relating to peripheral regions and the value of the social economy. This will be followed by a brief survey relating to the delivery mechanism for SME financing and then we conclude by looking at the extent to which tourism is financed in a selection of European transition economy capital markets.

Definitions

It is important from the outset to define what is meant by the term 'micro and small enterprise', a definition which falls within the wider description of 'small and medium-sized enterprises', i.e. SMEs (European Commission, 2003). This wider SME definition has a particularly wide ranging scope in terms of business activities and formats, covering enterprises which are, for example:

- A *micro* enterprise with one owner/manager (e.g. a tourism guide business) or with an owner/manager and less than 10 employees (e.g. small travel agency, guesthouse or arts/crafts shop);
- A *small* enterprise with up to 50 employees (e.g. hotel, tour operator, transport services company, contract caterer, ethno-cultural centre);
- A *medium-sized* enterprise with more than 50 but less than 250 employees (small hotel chain, road or air transport operator, a chain of tourism agencies, providers of support or ancillary services, a chain of restaurants, etc.).

Data from the European Commission (European Parliament, 2007) indicate that whilst over 99% of all EU enterprises are SMEs, 90% of those SMEs are microenterprises with an average of five employees. These enterprises account for around 50% of employment in the EU, which ensures that their importance to the overall Union economy is very high. For the last two decades European policy-makers and legislators have been aware that this sizeable sector of Europe's economy faces very specific problems due to their size and accessibility to resources. Not only is there the challenge of locating finance for start-ups or the development of existing business, there is also the significant problem of coping with the same level of local and national regulatory structures as apply to enterprises with over 250 employees. As part of the Lisbon Strategy, the European Parliament agreed on 1 February 2007 to recommend to the Commission and the Council that micro and small enterprises would be able to register as European Private Companies, with wide ranging exemptions from much of the bureaucracy and regulatory hurdles affecting larger enterprises.

We tend to be well aware of the problems of access to finance that impact on SMEs as an entity, despite the wide array of flexible financial instruments which are perceived to be available to entrepreneurs. However, in tourism (especially in transition economies) the accessibility of finance tends to be heavily focused on larger enterprises (big hotels, big resorts, big tourism agencies) and very often the smaller entrepreneur fails to have the same level of access. Furthermore, there is increasing evidence that smaller enterprises, particuarly those located in peripheral regions, have a poor understanding of the methodology of entrepreneurial finance as well as limited access to finance in the start-up as well as the developmental stage.

In many transition economies, those enterprises with more than 50 employees are more than likely to have been state-owned or, as in the case of the ex-Yugoslav republics, socially-owned.[1] Microenterprises in such economies either escaped state control or were among those which were privatized in the initial stages of the privatization process.

---

1. Social-ownership was a methodology of economic activity developed by Josip Broz Tito, President of the Socialist Federative Republic of Yugoslavia, as a 'third way' between Marxist-Leninism and capitalism. The primary author of the system was Tito's chief ideologist, Edvard Kardelj, who developed the doctrine of theory of associated labour in which the right to decision-making and a share in profits of companies was based on the investment of labour (Prunk, 1997).

The Financing Needs of SMEs

Apart from the number of employees, each of the examples given above will also have approaches to financing. A medium-sized enterprise may be (or have the potential to be) quoted on a local capital market or have access to standard debt instruments (loans, secured loan facilities, leasing, etc.). Such enterprises, due to their size, may also tend to have greater visibility to foreign investors. In comparison, the microenterprise will traditionally favour debt financing, as this does not incur any dilution of ownership and the prospect of external management control. Although there has been a growth of informal equity activity (e.g. the 'business angel movement') where SME owners cannot or choose not to access debt capital, owners will often turn to internal financing from surplus profits or to meeting the demand for additional capital from family and friends. This is particularly the case in respect of micro and small enterprises (MSEs), especially family concerns.

Another problem is that despite the fact that debt appears the most obvious and accessible financing vehicle, it is not always the most appropriate. For example, with tourism MSEs debt financing may lack flexibility; debt finance requires a constant stream of repayment and is thus inconsistent with the income patterns of small-scale tourism. It may be suggested that this is particularly the case with regard to accommodation and catering services, although there would be an exception in the case of personal service type tourism businesses (e.g. guides) where set-up costs are minimal. In general, equity investment would seem a more appropriate option, in that no repayment is involved until such time as the investor seeks to exit the investment. However, as we shall consider further in this chapter (see 'Financial Access Delivery Structures' section below) the problem is a lack of recognition of the investment potential as well as the frequently negative attitude of entrepreneurs themselves towards equity investors, especially with the concept of sharing control of the enterprise.

A related issue is the sense of double jeopardy: financial institutions and investors frequently fail to understand the complexities facing small business owners in general and small-scale tourism entrepreneurs in particular, not only in terms of access to finance but also in relation to the regulatory and legal burden which effectively discriminates against MSEs in comparison to medium-sized and large-scale enterprises (Barbieri and Lo Moro, 1996; Institut für Mittelstandsforschung, 1995). At the same time, evidence has been identified showing that enterpreneurs themselves have tended to have a very poor comprehension of the risk and portfolio constraints limiting investors (formal and informal) and effectively self-limit their investment-attracting potential (O'Rourke, 2000).

Peripherality

A specific issue in the 27-country European Union (EU) has been that of higher availability of finance for small-scale tourism activity in countries and regions closer to the main economic and business centres. Businesses in peripheral regions, where physical infrastructure and access to contemporary ideas and technologies are less developed, tend to be less favourably treated in terms of access to finance. Peripherality affects not only regions on the geographic edges of the EU (e.g. the North-West of Ireland and Eastern

Hungary) but also peripherality within relatively prosperous member states (e.g. the Danish Freisland, Italian Friulia and Austrian Burgenland). The revised EU Inter-reg IV Programme[2] has included, as one of its major objectives, mechanisms for improving access to finance in the North-East Atlantic Maritime Region (i.e. the North-West of Scotland, West of Ireland, Britanny, North-West Spain and Portugal). Importantly, EU institutions have recognized that there is now a limited development of informal (e.g. business angels) and formal (e.g. venture capital) risk capital providers in such peripheral regions.

The need to provide such a level of public sector co-funding (i.e. EU plus national/regional/local authorities) tends to illustrate a further problem identified by the European Commission. Where public funding through EU structures has taken place in peripheral regions (e.g. the former Objective 1 regions), private sector inputs have been almost invisible. EU funds have generally provided the largest proportion for projects which are concerned with improving transport links, enhancing the environment or developing the cultural heritage. Private sector investment, for example where projects have a clear profit advantage for local tourism entrepreneurs, is generally low; in the 12 new member states there is also evidence that tourism entrepreneurs are unwilling to work with and to react with EU and national funding agencies (European Parliament, 2008).

Thus a vicious circle exists in such regions where a lack of risk capital – informal or formal – tends to minimize the entry of MSE start-ups, thus reducing the number of mature and developing SMEs, which in turn deflates the opportunities for risk capital vehicles and structures. Added to this is the physical and psychological distance from major capital markets, which are a necessary component as one of the choices for a structured and orderly exit route for investors (see 'Financial Access Delivery Structures' section below).

Inevitably, and especially in the case of tourism, we appear to be faced with the fact that the major form of investment will need to flow from public sources, unless small entrepreneurs themselves can be energized to develop methods of cooperation to make a collective investment approach.

The Concept of the Social Economy

This leads to a further dimension of issues relating to entrepreneurship and access to finance: the unwillingness of many entrepreneurs to operate though mutual or cooperative structures for their common benefit. It is a fact that a significant proportion of Europe's economy is not organized solely to make profits for investors; there are around 10 million jobs in the social economy across Europe, but membership of social economy enterprises is much wider, with estimates ranging as high as 150 million. In many European countries (especially Austria, Denmark, France, Germany, Italy, Sweden and The Netherlands) there has been a long tradition of organizations based on *raiffeissen* – cooperative or mutual principles. Furthermore, it is frequently the case that a number of these mutual institutions are in reality common-interest collectives of entrepreneurs gathered to conduct some activity that is more efficient or less costly, for example marketing or purchasing.

---

2. European Council Regulation Number 1080/2006 established the programme which is financed through the European Regional Development Fund.

However, the Anglo-Saxon principle of a more individualistic approach to entrepreneurship seems to have become the norm in many countries in Central and Eastern Europe. Even in the former Yugoslavia, where socialism was far more decentralized and where the system allowed the development of MSEs as well as of profit-taking in medium- to large-scale enterprises, there is a strong degree of individualist reaction to cooperation between competing entrepreneurs. Frequently, entrepreneurs see any form of structure or planning as a threat of socialism. This is particularly evident in tourism where small entrepreneurs have frequently failed to understand the value of cooperating for mutual benefit, especially in such areas as marketing and international promotion – highly costly actions which tend to benefit from economies of scale. By failing to promote themselves adequately, they restrict the likely market in which they can be effective. In addition, in some transition economies evidence has occurred of a strong reluctance by small-scale tourism entrepreneurs to cooperate with former state- or socially-owned tourism companies in terms of promoting their local resorts or similar types of tourism product (e.g. spa-health tourism, sports tourism).

Financial Access Delivery Structures

The object of this section is to consider some of the issues relating to the structure of financing for smaller enterprises (O'Rourke, 2001, 2002); it is not intended as a review of financing methodologies.

The Obstacles

The previously referred to work by the European Commission and European Parliament indicates that micro and small businesses face three serious obstacles:

- The constraints of regulation, and the application of legal and fiscal regimes which tend to have a lesser impact on medium-sized and large-scale companies;
- The effects of strategic weakness which is often characterized by a lack of long-term planning and management development skills;
- A lack of adequate capitalization from the outset – the critical issue of access to structured finance.

All of these problems in access to finance are interconnected and, again, experience in transition economies indicates that problems in financing compound problems in management. Resourcing dysfunctionality then magnifies the effects of the regulatory, legal and fiscal environment. However, without doubt, the most frequent cause of failure is the lack of access to structured finance. Prior to 1995, there was a discernable divide between the method of financing for large companies and that utilized for small business. Large businesses had access to the financial markets in terms of raising capital through equity or bond issues, or by tapping the international syndicated debt markets. Small business was reliant on classic bank financing (overdrafts or fixed period loans) or self-financing. From the 1990s, the rapid expansion of the venture capital industry has tended to blur the distinction between financing large-scale and medium-sized enterprises.

In addition to venture capital financing, there has also been the development of the second markets, e.g. AIM, EASDAQ, Nouveau Marché and Neuer Markt. In parallel to these actions, the European Commission has taken a proactive stand in providing financing support facilities. However, blurring the distinction between medium-sized and large-scale companies has tended to obscure the problem of the 'equity gap' for relatively small-scale entrepreneurs seeking financing for start-ups or development projects in the EUR 50.000 to EUR 500.000 range. This tends to be too large an amount for straightforward bank credits, but too small for formal equity financing. The costs of seeking formal equity financing (through venture capital or on a regulated market) would tend to be disproportionate to the amount of capital raised.

Access to Finance

In general terms the problem areas in financing MSEs can be seen as:

- *Higher rates of interest for bank credits due to a perception of greater risk.* This particularly applies to European transition economies; what can be described as the innovation risk premium was highly evident in Slovenia in the period from 1993–96. Banks charged excessive rates of interest to entrepreneurs, whilst loans for new car purchases were considerably lower. The phenomenon has now surfaced in Bosnia and Herzegovina, Macedonia and Serbia;
- *Lack of understanding and communication between banks and SMEs.* This problem has moderated in the 'old' EU countries (the EU15) through closer links between banks and SMEs and more intensive training and education of banking staff. In transition economies, banks were previously lacking in understanding about entrepreneurship and had a low level of ability to evaluate entrepreneurial projects. That situation continues in less advanced transition economies, but has been minimized by the significant expansion of Western European owned banks into Central and Eastern Europe;
- *Poor structure of financing.* Simply and bluntly, providing money is not enough, irrespective of whether it derives from international, public or private sources. Adequate capitalization will not assist in an enterprise where management ability is inadequate.

Structures of Enterprise Financing

- Classic stock exchanges – blue chip, low risk companies with international prospects. In European markets 80% of capitalization is devoted to low-risk stocks compared to 60% in the USA. However, inevitably these markets are dominated by institutional investors and for larger-scale companies. Tourism tends not to feature highly, as it is regarded by analysts as cyclical and prone to shifts in consumer sentiment;

- Second markets – conceived in the 1990s for fast growth medium-sized companies, initially in technology and other growth sectors, but essentially became waiting rooms for the senior markets and failed to match the aspirations of smaller enterprises for access to equity finance. Some tourism companies listed on them;
- Debt financing – provision of loan related financial instruments through banks, credit funds and other similar private or public financial institutions. Also includes commercial paper and commercial bonds;
- Venture capital funds and companies (includes public sector equity funds) – entities investing equity (as well as debt instruments in larger deals) in small and medium-sized companies where the investor regards the risk–return ratio to be advantageous;
- Semi-formal venture capital – groups of investors (e.g. archangel groups or investment circles) formed in non-regulated collective vehicles to invest equity venture capital in enterprises which would not attract standard VC interest;
- Business Angel Networks – public or mutual structures which introduce investors seeking risk opportunities to entrepreneurs seeking funding;
- Informal equity investment – simple individual investors (including Business Angels) taking a stake in a business in return for a share of profitability.

Bank Debt versus Equity?

There is really no significant contest between financing entrepreneurship through bank debt, e.g. traditional term credits or overdraft facilities, and through equity participation. Equity financing is not a threat to traditional bank financing of enterprises and this is illustrated by the role of the European Savings Banks in providing and facilitating equity finance. In the majority of the European Single Market states (EU27 plus EFTA4) savings banks are the primary providers of banking services to SMEs and particularly to MSEs. But after almost two centuries in the provision of traditional credit instruments, they have enthusiastically embraced equity participation as a positive advantage. In Spain, the savings banks have created specialist venture capital companies to take equity financing stakes in a large number of enterprises; in Germany, the Sparkassen and Cooperative banks have been responsible for 40% of all market floatations of SMEs on the Neuer Markt as well as providing EUR3 billion in equity funding to German SMEs.

BANs

An important answer to this problem regarding access to finance which has been identified has been the development of the Business Angel concept and its expansion through Business Angel Networks (BANs). It is therefore valuable to consider this method given its importance to MSEs, especially those in the tourism sector. Over the next decade, we should be aware that on the whole enterprises will have a shorter life cycle and faster start-up stages than has been the case in the past. Enabling structures will be required not simply to provide risk capital, but to deliver it efficiently and effectively to the point of need.

The Business Angel movement has been highly successful in providing financing, with funding normally occurring in the EUR 40.000 to EUR 500.000 range. The main advantage of business angel capital is that it provides financing with a lower financial burden in the early stages – because there are no capital or interest payments as in debt finance. The role of the networks, which effectively match investors with entrepreneurs, is as a source of unbiased advice, providing introductions to those with capital with the underlying premise that the costs of finding that finance are generally low. In addition, there is good evidence that where a business angel invests in a small business that business will then find it far easier to access more traditional methods of financing (e.g. credits from a bank or equipment financing).

A key feature of angel financing is its inherent flexibility, i.e. the fact that it can be packaged to meet the needs of the investor and investee, rather than to fit the structure of a financial institution. The core financing methodology is equity financing where, in return for their capital, the investor angel takes a percentage of the shares in the enterprise. However, due to the 'informal' nature of angel financing, it is also possible to attach secured loan, deferred loan, loans convertible to equity or mezzanine-type finance (for example) to the core equity package.

Tourism and Financial Markets

One of the features of access to finance already identified, for tourism MSEs, is regarding access to equity risk capital. We have already noted that in some regions peripherality brings dysfunctionality in relation to the development of informal and formal risk capital finance, to the point where venture capital is not readily available and therefore there is no demand for venture capitalists. Equity markets present the ultimate stage in the risk capital process as they represent a mechanism by which both investors and entrepreneurs can exit from the enterprise – partially or fully if they so wish. In general only large-scale tourism enterprises tend to present on major global and European capital markets. However, due both to the process of privatization (e.g. listing of state or other publicly-owned companies on local markets) and the smaller scale of those markets, there was a view in the mid-1990s that stock exchanges in transition economies would be attractive to smaller-scale tourism enterprises. This is generally seen to include hotels, other forms of tourism accommodation, tour operators, tourist agencies, tourism transport and visitor attractions.

However, the reality has in general been significantly different, as can be seen by looking briefly at the tourism component on capital markets in five countries of the former Yugoslavia (UN World Travel Organization, 2008).

Croatia (population 4.4 million)

Croatia is one of the most developed tourism markets in Central and Eastern Europe; in 2005 foreign tourist visitors stood at 8.5 million, represented 16.5% of GDP and showed a 470% rise over 1995. In 2007, of the 359 companies listed on the Zagreb Stock Exchange (Zagrebačka Burza, 2008) 60 were in the tourism sector; yet despite the important role of tourism in the economy, these companies only generated 2% of the turnover of the Croatian capital market – a market dominated by energy, telecoms and banking stocks. The majority of tourism companies are listed on the second tier market, and their listing is primarily due to their conversion from social-ownership status to public limited companies. As a result around half of the tourism companies listed would be regarded as SMEs.

However, despite the relative ease of listing on both the Zagreb market and the OTC market in Varaždin, there has been little evidence that tourism MSEs have considered tapping the equity market for even modest capitalizations in the region of EUR 50.000.

Slovenia (population 2.0 million)

Whilst Slovenia's international tourism offer was previously focused on mountains and a small Adriatic littoral, in 2005 foreign tourist visitors stood at 1.6 million, represented 4.1% of GDP and showed a 112% rise over 1995. Ljubljana Stock Exchange (Ljubljanska Borza, 2008) is the most advanced capital market in the region, quite recently having merged with the Vienna Stock Exchange to create a significant force in Central Europe. Yet out of the 98 listed equities in 2007, there were only 10 from the tourism sector accounting for 2.9% of turnover in 2007, although this included leading tourism industry players like Terme Čatež. Although very close to enterprises in geographical terms given the size of the country and having sought to attract smaller enterprises to list on the secondary trading tiers, there has been little appetite from Slovenian entrepreneurs in general, and tourism in particular, to seek investment capital.

Serbia (population 10.0 million)

Generally, apart from the hotel sector in Belgrade (and other large cities) and the two main resorts of Kopaonik and Zlatibor, much of the domestically-owned tourism industry is poorly developed and lagging behind neighbouring countries. The loss of the relatively well-developed coastal region with the final separation from Montenegro in 2006 has combined with the slow growth of international and domestic tourism. In 2005 foreign tourist visitors stood at 0.2 million, represented 1.0% of GDP and showed a 125% rise over 1995. Although a large number of small companies have listed on the Belgrade Stock Exchange's secondary tier markets (Beogradska Berza, 2008), this has been primarily as it is one of the chosen formats for transition from social or state ownership towards private ownership or hopeful sale to a foreign investor. In 2007 an average of 99 tourism companies were listed out of the average of 1010 listings on all equity markets, yet only accounted for 2.1% of turnover. It is probable that almost half of these companies could be described as MSEs and therefore have no great attraction to investors – domestic or foreign.

Macedonia (population 2.0 million)

Tourism in Macedonia, inevitably focused on the resort of Lake Ohrid and a number of historical and religious sites, was badly damaged by the conflict in 2000–01 between the Macedonian government and an ethnic-Albanian terrorist group. Tourism activity only began to pick up in 2006–07. In 2005 foreign tourist visitors stood at 0.2 million, a 34% rise over 1995. Currently, four companies at the higher end of the SME spectrum are quoted out of the 354 equity listings on the Macedonian Stock Exchange, but these companies only accounted for 1.6% of turnover in 2007 (MSE Inc., 2008). The majority of tourism enterprises are in the MSE category and it is likely that those which do not have some degree of foreign investment (e.g. hotels in the Ohrid resort), or are in receipt of credits through the banking system, are being financed through remittance flows from Macedonian workers in EU countries (Narodna Banka Republika Makedonija, 2007).

Montenegro (population 0.6 million)

The exception to the rule is Montenegro, which is the smallest of the former Yugoslav republics but heavily dependent on tourism for foreign currency earnings and to support employment. In 2005 foreign tourist visitors stood at 0.5 million, a 291% rise over 1995. Apart from a handful of medium to large-scale enterprises (energy, telecoms, agro-industry), the economy is dominated by SMEs in tourism. Within this sector there is a sharp distinction between the larger hotel groups and tourism companies, and the MSEs engaged in micro-scale tourism (guides, small tourist agencies, providers of apartments and rooms, etc.) and in small hotels and tourism transport. As a result, 12 hotel and tourism companies were listed in 2007 on Montenegro's NEX Stock Exchange (NEX Crna Gora, 2008) out of the 77 equities listed; these enterprises accounted for 7.2% of the turnover on the NEX market.

Conclusions

• Despite significant levels of funding, as well as direct intervention at a European level, smaller-scale enterprises which we have defined as MSEs continue to face problems in accessing finance;
• Peripherality continues to remain a problem, whilst the structural support through EU funds, which is beneficial in some respects, appears to actively discourage private sector investment and dampen the business birth rate;
• There appears to be a good degree of scope for MSEs to cooperate in mutually beneficial activities – including access to finance. Social economy structures (cooperatives and mutuals) would have a powerful role in such a development;
• In general, insufficient use is being made of equity finance by MSEs. It is unclear whether this is due to the fear of losing control of the enterprise or lack of investors;
• In the five countries covered in the brief survey of tourism and capital markets, the apparent lack of tourism enterprises on those markets has resulted in generally low turnover. This situation may improve if the overall liquidity of those markets improves.

Questions for Discussion

1. What options are open to small-scale tourism entrepreneurs in funding business start-ups from the expansion of existing enterprises?
2. It may be argued that in EU peripheral maritime regions EU and public co-financing are crowding out potential investors in tourism. What is a possible solution?
3. Define instances where tourism entrepreneurs may gain advantage by cooperating with competitors to undertake joint activities.
4. What observations can be made in comparing the tourism industries of Croatia, Serbia and Slovenia with the activity of tourism stocks on their capital markets?

References

European Commission (2003). Annex 1, Article 2 of European Commission Recommendation 2003/361/EC, cited in the European Commission's Official Journal OJ 2003, p36, Bruxelles.

European Parliament (2007). European Parliament Policy Documentation under PE 2006/ 2013(INI).

UN World Travel Organization (2008). *World Travel Barometer*, vol. 6, January 2008.

Chapter 17

Tourism Distribution: From Structure to Strategy

Douglas G. Pearce

Learning Outcomes

After reading this chapter, you should be able to:

- Understand the complexity and importance of the tourism distribution value chain;

- Identify the most recent theoretical contribution and empirical research on tourism distribution systems;

- Understand the impact of technological change (the internet and associated technologies) on tourism distribution; and

- Understand innovation in New Zealand tourism through improved distribution channels.

Introduction

Tourism is a very competitive business. Worldwide demand has increased continuously and dramatically over the last five decades but so too has the supply-side as an ever-growing number of individuals, enterprises and governments have identified opportunities in tourism and actively entered this sector. As a result, tourism markets are crowded, competition is often intense and tourism suppliers need to take a more concerted and strategic approach to the distribution of their products and services if they wish to be successful.

Distribution is the part of the marketing mix that 'makes the product available' to consumers (Wahab et al., 1976, p. 96) and that serves as 'the link between the producers of tourism services and their customers' (Gartner and Bachri, 1994, p. 164). It is increasingly being recognized as a critical source of competitive advantage in the marketing mix. Rosenbloom et al. (2004, p. 4) assert in general terms that 'the reason for this is straightforward – it has become too difficult to hold onto a competitive edge via product, pricing and promotional strategies ...' Dev and Olsen (2000) identified the management of distribution costs as one of the major concerns facing hospitality firms in the present decade due to the spiralling cost of distribution, pressure from financial markets and opportunities afforded by the internet to make significant cost reductions. Likewise, Green (2005, p. 7) contends that 'Distribution strategy has quickly become the function in hotel marketing that can have the greatest impact on profitability'. Distribution can account for a quarter or more of a business's operating costs and returns can vary significantly from one channel to the next with each channel having its own set of costs and benefits (Choi and Kimes, 2002; Pearce and Taniguchi, 2008).

In addition, technological advances and changing consumer preferences have expanded the range of channels that tourism suppliers might use to distribute their products; multichannel distribution is now common. Each channel or path to the market may appeal to different segments, suit some products more than others and have a simple or complex structure. Deciding which distribution channels to use and in what combination is not only critical and but also challenging. Getting it right is not a question of 'just doing it'; developing an effective distribution strategy is a process which requires careful consideration and ongoing management.

It is in this context that this chapter provides an overview of the emerging body of research on tourism distribution that has appeared over the last decade or so. Links with the more established wider distribution literature are often not well developed and, as with other emerging fields, much of the work on tourism distribution remains rather fragmented and lacks a common sense of direction and purpose (Pearce, in press). The overview is structured around five approaches, starting with the most common and ending with perhaps the most important: structural, behavioural, functional, evaluative and strategic. In keeping with the theme of this book, emphasis is given to the supplier's perspective though mention is made of other channel members, namely the intermediaries and consumers. The overview is based on an extensive review of the literature and informed by the experience of leading a major 5-year project that took a systematic and integrated approach to the study of distribution channels in New Zealand (Pearce, 2003, 2007a).

A Structural Approach

The essence of distribution is captured in Stern and El-Ansary's (1992, p. 1–2) statement that marketing channels are:

> sets of interdependent organizations involved in the process of making a product or service available for use or consumption … not only do marketing channels satisfy demand by supplying goods and services at the right place, quantity, quality and price, but they also stimulate demand …

They then suggest that these channels might be considered as 'an orchestrated network that creates value for the user or consumer through the generation of form, possession, time and place utilities'.

To date, however, comparatively little of the work on tourism distribution explicitly recognizes the wider networks of interdependent firms that make up larger distribution systems in the sense that the basic components of a network are nodes and connections, actors and social ties (Rocks et al., 2005). Rather, the work on tourism distribution has generally taken a more structural approach in which researchers have concentrated on a tier-by-tier discussion of direct and indirect distribution channels and the ways in which these are linked (Pearce, 2007a). According to Morrison (1989, p. 274) 'direct distribution occurs when the organization assumes total responsibility for promoting, reserving and providing services to customers.' Conversely, indirect distribution exists when part or all of the responsibility for these functions is given to a third party, usually a travel trade intermediary.

Various attributes have been employed to describe or depict the structure of tourism distribution channels:

1. Channel depth or the number of intermediaries (e.g. retail travel agents, tour operators/ wholesalers and incoming agents) that occur between providers and end-users (the tourists) is the most widely used attribute and is commonly found as the basis for structural diagrams of tourism distribution (Wahab et al., 1976; Gee et al., 1989; March, 1997; Buhalis and Laws, 2001; Wynne et al., 2001).
2. The intermediaries' characteristics: size, geographical coverage, accreditation and, in the case of retail travel agencies, orientation to leisure or business travel (Buhalis, 2001).
3. The degree of integration that occurs between channel members and the extent of concentration (the share of business held by key members at each level) that exists (Chaintron, 1995; Casarin, 2001).
4. The amount of channel specialization that occurs by market (e.g. special interest, budget/upscale), by destination (e.g. short- and long-haul) or by functions (especially the mix of retail and wholesale activities) (Pearce et al., 2007).

International Studies

In addition to more general overviews (Wahab et al., 1976; Gee et al., 1989; Buhalis, 2001), a structural approach has generally been undertaken either of channels linking particular international markets and destinations or of particular sectors. The market-based studies reveal important differences exist in their distribution structures as a result of such factors as market and industry maturity, forms of tourism and cultural and economic characteristics. Casarin (2001, p. 140) provides a very useful overview of distribution in the major national markets of Europe, noting: 'At the beginning of 2000, tourism production in North and South Europe exhibits marked differences in industrialization which have grown out of disparate maturity levels for supply and demand. The distribution structures reflect this contrast'.

In particular, differences are found in the levels of concentration and in the type and degree of vertical integration. Japan, the most mature of the Asian markets, also exhibits a high level of concentration and vertical integration (Forsyth and Smith, 1992; Taniguchi, 2006). Both China and Korea are characterized by the blurring of wholesale and retail functions but they differ in their levels of concentration – the former is dominated by a few major outbound operators, a consequence of strict licensing procedures (Guo and Turner, 2001), whereas the outbound industry in Korea is still very fragmented (King and Choi, 1999).

Pearce et al.'s (2007) comparative study of the distribution channels for New Zealand tourism in that country's three major English-speaking channels – Australia, Great Britain and the USA – revealed variations around a common traditional structure. While a proportion of visitors from these markets make their travel arrangements independently, the common intermediated structure is characterized by wholesalers sourcing products from providers, either directly or through an inbound operator (IBO), bundling them together in varying degrees and distributing them to consumers through retail travel agents (Figure 17.1). One or more of these sets of intermediaries may be displaced to give rise to channels of differing depth, for example when wholesalers and other channel members source their products directly from providers rather than through an inbound tour operator, or when retail travel agencies are bypassed as other intermediaries deal directly with the customer (e.g. direct sellers in Great Britain or online distributors in the USA). The broader distribution structures in Britain serving primarily packaged travel to short-haul destinations in the Mediterranean described by Chaintron (1995) and Casarin (2001) appear to be much more concentrated and integrated than those involving the distribution of longer-haul travel to New Zealand.

The patterns for the more established markets contrast with those of the emerging market of India where the current structure of distribution channels for Indian travel to New Zealand is characterized by: fragmentation; multiple, multi-layered Indian intermediaries exhibiting little specialization; a heavy dependence on the bundling functions of a handful of New Zealand-based IBOs; and a comparative lack of direct sales (Sharda and Pearce, 2006). Similar contrasts occur in terms of Korean travel to Australia (King and Choi, 1999).

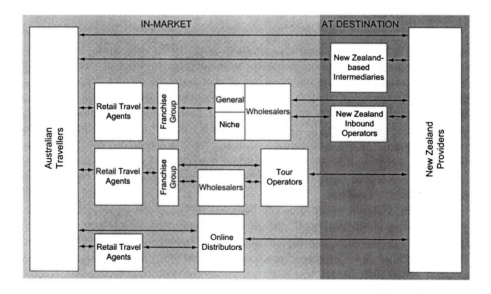

Figure 17.1: Major distribution channels for Australian travel to New Zealand. (*Source*: Pearce et al., 2007.)

Figure 17.2 provides a synthesis of three sets of interrelated characteristics that might be taken into account in analysing international tourism distribution systems: market characteristics, destination characteristics, and channel structure characteristics (Pearce et al., 2007). These are moderated by intervening distance. Further work is now needed along these lines in different contexts in order to develop a more comprehensive understanding of international tourism distribution. Firstly, parallel in-market studies might be undertaken for other destinations to determine whether the similarities and differences found for New Zealand are repeated elsewhere. Secondly, the focus might be reversed and the distribution channels for several destinations within a given market might be examined in order to differentiate further the impact of destination and market characteristics.

Where differences exist within and between markets, suppliers need to be aware of and make decisions regarding the most appropriate channels through which to distribute their particular products. A key decision is on the point of entry into each market, whether to distribute in the market or attempt to reach visitors once at the destination. If the former, when is it appropriate to deal directly with offshore wholesalers and other intermediaries and when is it more effective to work through an inbound operator? In view of the variation that occurs from one international market to another, multiple channels may be necessary. Understanding the other parts of the distribution structure is also important so that rates

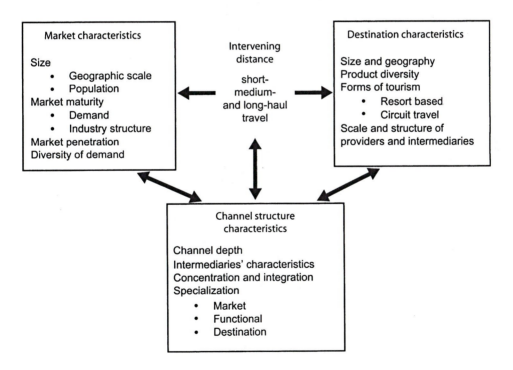

Figure 17.2: An analytical framework for international tourism distribution systems. (*Source*: Pearce et al., 2007.)

and commissions can be determined by taking account of the roles of all the channel members and the costs associated with the functions they perform.

Sectoral Studies

Other research has focused on distribution in particular sectors, especially transport and accommodation. Within these sectors attention has been directed primarily at air transport and hotels, industries characterized by larger players and ones which have often led the way in the adoption of new distribution technologies.

The role of distribution, the impact of external changes and the development of alternative distribution systems have been graphically demonstrated by the developments that have occurred over the last decade in the airline industry, particularly with the advent of low-cost carriers whose distribution has depended heavily on direct online reservations and sales (Morell, 1998; Ali-Knight and Wild, 1999; Buhalis, 2004). Distribution relating to other forms of transport has attracted much less attention even though surface transport may play a significant role for both domestic and international tourism, especially where a large amount of touring is involved. In contrast to air travel, which is predominantly sold in the market, many surface transport transactions are made once international travellers reach their country of destination, necessitating local or regional coverage.

Pearce and Sahli (2007) found considerable variation in the structure of distribution channels used by various forms of surface transport in New Zealand: coaches, rental cars, campervans, rail and inter-island ferries. This diversity is a function of their characteristics, the demand mix and the nature of tourism in the country. The far-reaching changes witnessed in the airline industry have few parallels to date with these forms of surface transport. Direct sales are important for some forms (budget rental cars, the ferry line and domestic coach charters) but for other others, notably those dealing in group tours (tour coaches and certain rail trips), the conventional three-tier system of travel intermediaries remains dominant. Local intermediaries play a key role in distributing some forms of surface travel (scheduled and backpacker bus services, rail and ferries) to independent international and domestic travellers.

In the accommodation sector, most of the studies have focused on hotels, particularly on the impact of technological change on distribution structures and costs (O'Connor, 1999; Bote Gómez and Alvarez Cuervo, 2001). The increasing array of electronic distribution systems has given rise to a high level of multichannel distribution with the importance of particular channels varying from property to property, market to market and segment to segment.

Figure 17.3 depicts the diversity of channels used by independent leisure travellers in chain hotels in Wellington, New Zealand (Pearce et al., 2004). Most of the domestic leisure demand is handled by direct sales. These are complemented by a wide variety of intermediaries, especially in the case of the smaller number of independent leisure travellers from abroad, with up to six layers of intermediaries being identified from the perspective of the individual property. Much corporate travel is now handled by travel management companies (Garnham, 2005) and professional conference organizers play a role in the distribution of rooms and facilities to conference attendees (Smith and Garnham, 2006). Distribution to the inbound group tour market usually involves the

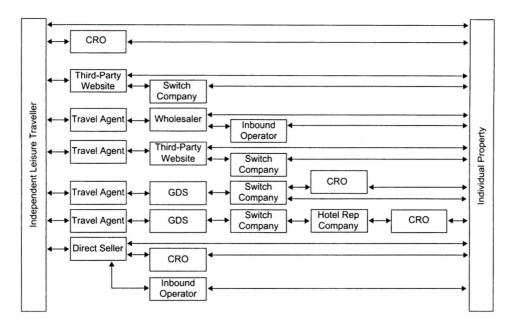

Figure 17.3: Distribution channels for chain hotels in Wellington by independent leisure travellers. (*Source*: Pearce et al., 2004.)

traditional travel industry intermediaries (inbound operator–wholesaler–retail travel agent), often with the participation of the chain's national sales office – the largest chains being able to offer properties throughout the country and negotiate on this basis.

The general tendency amongst the other accommodation providers in Wellington (motor inns, motels, and bed and breakfasts) is to use simpler systems and to carry out their own distribution activities aimed primarily at independent leisure visitors and, to a lesser extent, business travellers and conference goers. In these cases, distribution essentially concerns the dissemination of information (e.g. advertising in accommodation handbooks or online, racking brochures at the visitor information centre), heavy reliance on word of mouth, and reservations made directly with the property concerned (Pearce et al., 2004). This is a function of more limited marketing resources and the segments being served.

In contrast to transport and accommodation, the distribution of attractions has until recently been largely neglected (Origet du Cluzeau, 1995; Richards et al., 2001). This neglect may reflect the relative lack of work on this sector in the broader literature as well as a perception that attractions have comparatively simple distribution systems (Middleton and Clarke, 2001; Alcázar Martínez, 2002). Nevertheless, as a core part of the tourism product and a sector which offers many opportunities for small and middle-sized suppliers, enhanced understanding of the distribution of attractions is needed.

Results from various aspects of the New Zealand project (Pearce and Tan, 2004, 2006; Pearce et al., 2004; Schott, 2007; Smith, 2007) highlight the diversity that is to be found in the distribution channels for attractions, while at the same time showing that these are often shorter and simpler than for the larger transport and accommodation businesses.

There is, however, a tendency for group visitors (essentially international) to be reached through multi-layered channels that extend through to the market, while those attractions that draw a greater share of independent visitors have a higher share of direct sales, usually on site (Figure 17.4). Bookings and sales through local intermediaries (e.g. visitor information centres or accommodation providers) are also common. Some effort is also made to reach independent travellers en route to the destination, again usually involving visitor information centres and regional intermediaries.

The use of 'at destination' strategies for independent travellers is in large part a response to the travel behaviour of this segment: most attractions are decided on and purchased once at the destination or possibly en route to it (Pearce and Schott, 2005). Adventure tourists in particular are perceived to be reluctant to commit to a structured itinerary, to have a tendency to make spur of the moment decisions and believe products and prices can be assessed most effectively once at the destination (Schott, 2007). The breadth of product appeal, capacity issues and the non-commissionable nature of some products are other factors that come into play (Pearce and Tan, 2004).

Similar patterns are evident elsewhere. Pearce (2005) found the distribution channels for cultural tourism in Catalonia, Spain, were generally short, characterized by a high level of direct sales to tourists and a concentration on 'at destination' activity. Even where group travel is concerned there is a relative lack of layering and complexity; this largely involves the 'culture as complement' excursionist market from the coast rather than specialist group tours from further afield. Factors accounting for this simplicity include the nature of the demand for cultural tourism, the attributes of the providers and the broader structure of

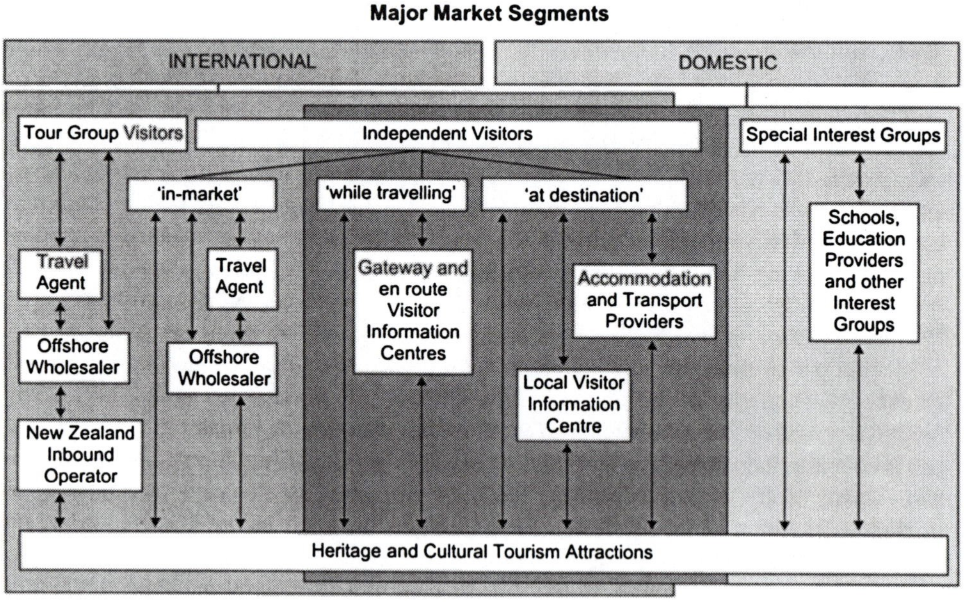

Major Market Segments

Figure 17.4: Distribution channels for heritage and cultural attractions in Rotorua and Wellington. (*Source*: Pearce and Tan, 2004.)

tourism within Catalonia. In contrast, Yamamoto and Gill's (2002) analysis of Japanese ski tourism in British Columbia reveals a strongly industrialized, integrated, multi-tiered distribution structure characteristic of Japanese group tourism to other destinations.

These differences point to the role of both cultural attributes and the ways in which distribution channels are influenced by the segments being targeted, with a particular distinction between package groups and independent travellers.

A Behavioural Approach

Structural studies have been complemented by research which has focused on the behaviour of one or more sets of channel members. The rationale for this approach is articulated clearly by Bitner and Booms (1982, p. 40) who observed: 'While structural factors give clues to how the system operates, motivational and behavioural factors provide more complex explanations for why intermediaries do what they do, what influences their decisions and how they interact with customers and suppliers'. The significance of studying channel relationships is also highlighted by Rosenbloom et al. (2004, p. 4) who note: 'the broader dynamics of how firms relate to each other in the interorganizational context of the marketing channel has taken on real practical significance. Channel members have to be moulded into a coordinated team to provide added value to final customers'. These relationships take on a particular significance in tourism where many tourism products involve the bundling together and sale of a variety of different components from a range of suppliers using the services of one or more intermediaries (Crotts et al., 1998).

This means going beyond and beneath the structural linkages depicted in Figures 17.1, 17.3 and 17.4 to examine the factors that influence the behaviour of the different channel members and the relationships between them. Two key features of this approach are the type of channel members considered and the constructs examined. While all channel members are important, from the supplier's point of view the most critical are relationships with those intermediaries with whom they have the most immediate contact (usually inbound operators, wholesalers and perhaps travel agents) and the distribution behaviour of the end-user (the tourist).

Particular emphasis has been given to relationships between tour operators and hotels, especially amongst researchers working in Europe, the Mediterranean and the Caribbean (Kimes and Lord, 1994; Buhalis, 2000; Karamustafa, 2000; Medina-Muñoz et al., 2003). Others have considered the links between hotels and other intermediaries, for example travel agencies and meeting planners (Dubė and Renaghan, 2000; Medina-Muñoz and García-Falcón, 2000). Crotts et al. (1998) examined the antecedents of small New Zealand activity businesses to wholesale buyers. March (2000) took a more comprehensive approach in surveying Australian inbound tour operators' attitudes to supplier attributes for hotels, coach companies and restaurants. This research is almost invariably limited to analysing the perspective of one set of channel members, for example hoteliers or wholesalers rather than both.

Two basic models of buyer–seller relationships have been identified: the adversarial and the cooperative (Wilson, 1995; Crotts and Turner, 1999; Kalafatis, 2000). As Wilson (1995, p. 336) notes: 'In an adversarial model, buyers pit suppliers against each other to achieve lower costs. In a cooperative model, both parties achieve lower costs by working together to lower both buyer's and seller's operating costs'. The constructs researchers have employed to explore these relationships vary depending upon which of these two models is adopted.

Much of the work on wholesalers and hotels takes an adversarial perspective examining constructs such as conflict, control and power (Kimes and Lord, 1994; Buhalis, 2000; Karamustafa, 2000; Medina-Muñoz et al., 2003). Others taking a cooperative perspective have investigated satisfaction, success and trust (Crotts et al., 1998; Dubé and Renaghan, 2000; Medina-Muñoz and García-Falcón, 2000). Crotts et al. (1998, p. 132) concluded: '... social bonding, cooperation and trust – though highly intercorrelated – appear to be critical factors in the development and management of business relationships among ... small New Zealand businesses'. Business-to-business relationships evolve, however, with studies showing many variables are active at different times (Wilson, 1995), such as in the initiation and maintenance stages of a relationship (Kalafatis, 2000; Medina-Muñoz and García-Falcón, 2000).

The New Zealand project adopted a more open approach to examining the supplier selection process and identified three major sets of factors that are taken into account by offshore intermediaries when selecting New Zealand suppliers: those related to products (market fit, market demand and product quality); people (the attributes of the suppliers – their keenness and perceived ability to work with the intermediaries); and competitive prices (Pearce, 2007b).

Product dissatisfaction expressed through complaints and negative feedback from clients is the prime reason intermediaries change suppliers. Suppliers are also changed because of people-related factors, especially those associated with bad service delivery and poor administration. Pricing changes are the third major reason. In other words, in both the initial selection decision and subsequent decisions to change, intermediaries take account of what is being supplied, who is supplying it and at what price.

Suppliers must be aware of these factors and respond to them. To deal successfully with some forms of international tourism, particularly package tours, their businesses must be 'export ready', that is, they must have staff and operational systems in place to deal with offshore distributors and be prepared to adopt pricing structures that reflect the functions carried out by multi-layered intermediaries (Figure 17.1). Suppliers must also pay constant attention to maintaining the quality of the product and service they offer, together with the competitiveness of their pricing structures.

Account must also be taken of the distribution behaviour of the tourists themselves, particularly of independent tourists who are dealing directly with the suppliers. In an early study, Buckley (1987, p. 7) advocated a transaction chain analysis, arguing: 'An analysis of transactions ... proceeds from the main actor – the tourist – and examines all the actor's transactions'. There appears to have been no empirical or theoretical development of Buckley's approach and relatively little attention has been given to considering how tourists perceive and use different distribution channels (Öörni, 2003; Wolfe et al., 2004). While a body of related research does exist, this is often not set squarely in the context of distribution. Nor does it usually deal jointly with the different functions of distribution but instead focuses separately on information search, purchasing or, less commonly, booking.

In terms of information search, a large discrete body of work has developed as 'an enduring interest in consumer behaviour' (Schmidt and Spreng, 1996, p. 246). Snepenger and Snepenger (1993), Fodness and Murray (1997), Gursoy and McCleary (2003) and Cai et al. (2004) all provide good reviews and syntheses of the information search process. These studies demonstrate the complexity of the information search process, illustrate a range of approaches (psychological/motivational and cost/benefit being the most prominent) and emphasize a concern with determinants, information sources, decision-making and segmentation. Less attention has been directed at the purchase phase of tourism behaviour (Duke and Persia, 1993; Woodside and King, 2001) although increasing interest is being shown in the use of the internet for travel transactions, for booking rather than just looking (Susskind et al., 2003; Fam et al., 2003).

Many of the information search studies consider a range of information sources, but much of this work, especially that involving transactions, tends to focus on a single channel, emphasizes packaged rather than independent travel and commonly deals with destination selection rather than with sectoral decisions (for example information about or purchase of accommodation, transport and activities). Where sectoral behaviour has been explored, differences have been reported between products and user groups. Important sectoral differences were found by Wolfe et al. (2004) in the buying behaviour of online travel purchasers and users of travel agents: both groups made more use respectively of online or agency purchases of airline tickets but tended to book accommodation and rental cars directly from suppliers.

Pearce and Schott (2005) adopted a more comprehensive approach by examining the information search, booking and payment behaviour of domestic and international tourists making travel, accommodation and attractions arrangements in two New Zealand destinations and analysing the factors that influence the channels selected for each of these functions. This analysis revealed both intersectoral similarities and differences; for example in the type of information used and the extent of booking, especially between transport (high) and attractions (very low). Ease and simplicity were the single most important factors influencing how visitors book their transport and accommodation. Differences were also found between domestic and international visitors in terms of the sources of information used and the extent of direct and indirect booking. Some variation also occurred between the two destinations, Rotorua and Wellington. Smith (2007) took a similar approach to information search and the booking and purchasing of tickets for events in Wellington. These studies underscore the need for suppliers to carefully consider visitor behaviour as well as their relationships with intermediaries when making decisions about distribution.

A Functional Approach

Within the wider distribution literature considerable importance has been attached to taking a functional approach to distribution. In one of the seminal works, Lewis (1968, p. 2) argued: 'The purpose of a ... "channel of distribution" ... is to bridge the gap between the producer of a product and the user of it.' The functions or activities he identifies to achieve this bridging include the transfer of title (buying and selling), the physical movement of goods, the search for markets or sources of supply, and the payment of goods. More recent writers have stressed the critical role of functions in channel design. Anderson et al. (1997, p. 68), for example, observe that 'Channel functions are the basic building blocks of the design process. While functions cannot be eliminated, they can be combined creatively to reduce cost and to improve responsiveness and be dispersed among several players'. Likewise, Frazier (1999, p. 235) asserts that 'Channel functions reflect the job tasks ... that must be performed within the distribution channel. They represent the basic building blocks of any distribution channel.'

Such an emphasis is, however, less apparent in the work on tourism distribution where there is often little attempt to go beyond the description of the general or empirically derived structural diagrams and examine the functions being performed. In most cases the discussion is limited to an outline of the functions of tourism distribution followed by an account of the way in which various intermediaries perform these. According to Buhalis (2001, p. 8):

> The primary distribution functions for tourism are *information*, combination and travel arrangement services. Most distribution channels therefore provide information for prospective tourists; bundle tourism products together; and also establish mechanisms that enable consumers to make, confirm and pay for *reservations*.

Middleton and Clarke (2001) see the main functions of distribution as extending the number of points of sale or access away from the location at which services are performed or delivered, and facilitating the purchase of products in advance of their production. Wynne et al. (2001) contextualize the likely impact of the internet on tourism distribution in South Africa. They draw on the wider distribution theories and stressing the economies to be obtained by increasing the efficiencies which intermediaries may bring to the distribution process by creating time, place and possession utilities. These may be summarized as:

- Adjusting the discrepancy of assortments;
- Making transactions routine so as to minimize the cost of distribution;
- Facilitating the search process of both buyers and sellers.

Wynne et al. then go on to consider the functions performed by such intermediaries as travel agents and inbound and outbound operators. Kotler et al. (1996), Ujma (2001) and Alcázar Martínez (2002) draw on the work of Stern and El-Ansary (1992) in applying an economic transactions perspective to tourism distribution, though this is not incorporated fully or explicitly in the structural diagrams they use.

Synthesis of the various strands of the empirical research undertaken in the New Zealand project and their reinterpretation in the light of the fundamental principles of distribution resulted in the elaboration of a needs–function model of tourism distribution (Pearce, 2008). This model emphasizes the needs of tourists and the functions required to meet those needs. International leisure tourists are segmented by their distribution behaviour into three segments: independent, customized and package. Their needs are expressed in terms of time, place, form and possession utilities. The functions required to meet them are information provision, assortment, bundling, and booking and purchase. The model also has a strong geographical component with significant implications for channel design. Some needs are expressed in the market ahead of travel, others at the destination, and a third group en route between the two. This reflects the underlying characteristics of tourism distribution: facilitating the movement of tourists from their home region to destinations where the consumption of goods and services essentially occurs *in situ* rather than the physical distribution of products, which is the focus of much of the wider literature.

Further work is needed in this area if tourism suppliers are to understand fully the implications of these diverse and interrelated functions of distribution and use these building blocks effectively in the design of their distribution strategies. Focusing on functions rather than structures opens up a potentially wider range of choice.

Consideration of functions also provides a useful perspective on the impact of technological change on tourism distribution. Effectively, use of online distribution channels has meant much of the effort in looking for information and carrying out transactions has been transferred from intermediaries and suppliers to the consumer. The ease of information search is related to several factors including the technology available and the degree of sorting which occurs. Increasingly sophisticated search engines facilitate the search and sorting of information on individual suppliers' websites (Hewitt, 2006), while third-party websites provide varying levels of assortment, depending on whether they serve a particular sector (e.g. transport and accommodation) or destination.

Advances in online distribution also offer growing scope for dynamic packaging whereby travellers are to bundle their own products together and purchase these in a single transaction rather than just make discrete selections (Green, 2005). Opportunities for booking and purchase also vary depending on the level of sophistication of the online channel. Some, such as those provided by major carriers, hotel chains and e-intermediaries might offer instant confirmation and transaction. As noted earlier, extensive adoption of online booking and purchase has been particularly evident in the airline industry, especially with short-haul point-to-point travel, where timing, availability and price are the key factors, and where the businesses concerned have had the means to introduce progressively sophisticated systems. Major accommodation chains have followed the airline industry's extensive adoption of online booking and purchase. In contrast, many attractions still use online channels mainly for promotion and information provision, in part because advance booking and purchase are often less necessary, in part because other channels correspond better to visitors' needs (Pearce and Schott, 2005; Tan and Pearce, 2004).

An Evaluative Approach

Given the importance of distribution to the success of their businesses and the range of distribution channels available, tourism suppliers need to carefully evaluate the performance of particular channels and the distribution mix as a whole. While this need has been recognized in the tourism distribution literature, there is very little guidance on how such an assessment should be carried out and a virtual absence of published empirical work in this field (Kotler et al., 1996; Middleton and Clarke, 2001; Green, 2005).

Table 17.1: An example of net revenue per channel for a small attraction.

Channel	Channel Share		Net revenue per visitor	Average rate	Average cost	Total distribution related costs					
	Visitors	Revenue				Advertising	Other promotional	Set-Up	Comms.	Staff	Total
	%	%	$ c	$ c	$ c	%	%	%	%	%	%
Direct	40	45	41.13	50	8.84	35.5	7.5	2.9	18.2	36	100
Travel trade intermediaries	20	18	17.67	40.99	23.33	13.5			10.9	75.6	100
Visitor information Centres	34	32	34.52	43.37	8.85	35.6	19.5		13.5	31.4	100
Other intermediaries	6	5	28.62	35.82	7.2	43.7	0		17.6	38.6	100
All channels	100	100	33.57	45.08	11.51	27.3	7.5	0.9	14.1	50.3	100

Source: Pearce and Taniguchi (2008).

Two key factors appear to account for the neglect of channel performance in the tourism sector. Firstly, as Choi and Kimes (2002, p. 26) note with regard to the American hotel industry:

> ... distribution channel management has been considered as a marketing tool, and distribution costs have generally been seen as inflexible. Little attention has been paid to the revenue management implications of using various distribution channels although the implications for hotel profitability could be substantial.

Secondly, measuring cost structures across multiple distribution channels presents many methodological challenges. Middleton and Clarke (2001, p. 302), for example, outline a range of fixed and variable distribution costs before noting: 'In practice, although database technology is making it much easier to trace the costs and revenue of individual channels, the exact margins are often too difficult to measure. But producers have to monitor and endeavour to balance the costs of distribution ....'. O'Connor and Frew (2003) and Green (2005) make similar points.

To address this issue Pearce and Taniguchi (2008) developed a systematic methodology for measuring net revenues across multiple distribution channels based on a comprehensive spreadsheet which assembled and interrelated revenue and costs on a channel by channel basis. While the collection of the necessary data was demanding, analysis of the results of a range of attractions and accommodation businesses in New Zealand revealed substantial variations in net revenue across different channels (Table 17. 1). In four of the eight cases examined direct channels are the best performing, with a variety of intermediaries generating the highest net returns in the other four. Travel trade intermediaries feature most frequently in the worst performing channels. Differences are also found in the structure of channel costs with staff costs being particularly important.

Further research on net revenue variation in multichannel distribution systems is needed to develop the broader managerial implications of this line of enquiry. At the same time it must be recognized that net revenue generation is only one measure of performance and, while migrating business to the better performing channels on this metric will be a key aspect of an effective distribution strategy, consideration will also need to be given to other factors such as consumer preferences, market coverage, volume, seasonality, development of new segments, control and dependence. Each of these elements merits detailed research in its own right as well as investigation of the relationships between them. What is needed in most cases to facilitate this line of research is a better integration of booking systems with financial records and greater emphasis on channels as a unit of analysis and a focus for management. Some online systems such as those associated with search engine marketing provide very sophisticated metrics or analytics which might be taken into account.

A Strategic Approach

Despite the acknowledged importance of tourism distribution outlined in the introduction, and the complexity of the topic discussed in subsequent sections, surprisingly little published research has dealt explicitly with issues of channel design in tourism and developing a more strategic approach to the distribution of travel products. This is in marked contrast to manufacturing and some service sectors where the importance of channel design has been explicitly recognized for some time and is now a distinctive field of study (Fava Neves et al., 2001).

One reason for the relative lack of attention to channel design in tourism may be that it is a sector composed predominantly of small and medium enterprises (SMEs) and as Simons and Bouwman (2004, p. 246) observe: 'Generally speaking, SMEs put very little time and resources into analysis and design'. The distribution practices reflected in structural diagrams such as Figure 17.4 indicate that SMEs have some underlying strategy to what they do (Pearce and Tan, 2004, 2006) but often this does not appear to be the outcome of formally developed strategic practices; many would seem to be ad hoc and based on prior experience. Certainly larger tourism enterprises, such as airlines and major hotel chains, will have formal distribution strategies but these are not generally publicly available. More attention has been given to the strategic issues and implications, particularly the impact of new technologies, facing these businesses rather than to the way in which their strategies have been developed (Ali-Knight and Wild, 1999; O'Connor, 1999; Piga and Filippi, 2002; Buhalis, 2004; Alamdari and Mason, 2006).

In the wider distribution literature, Anderson et al. (1997) define a channel strategy as 'a series of trade-offs and compromises that align the company's resources with what it should do to satisfy its target customers and stay ahead of its competitors'. Channel design commonly involves working through these trade-offs and issues in a sequence of steps (Fava Neves et al., 2001). In one of the few tourism applications, Kotler et al. (1996) are less graphic in depicting the sequence of steps but discuss the process in terms of four stages: analyzing consumer needs, setting the channel objectives and constraints, identifying major channel alternatives and evaluating them. Green (2005), focusing on online distribution in the hotel sector, does not propose a sequence of steps, outlining instead a set of elements for a distribution strategy: metrics, risk assessment, branding, channel analysis and web strategy.

As the last phase in the New Zealand project a seven-step process to developing an effective tourism distribution strategy was developed (Pearce, 2007c). Adoption of a more systematic and strategic approach to distribution was seen to be the best means of increasing the effectiveness of the distribution practices of New Zealand suppliers. This in turn required developing a robust and practical approach to channel design for the distribution of tourism products, which could be readily applied by tourism suppliers who had generally not been in the practice of taking a strategic approach to this side of their business.

A key consideration here was breaking what can be quite a complex process down into manageable steps. Seven basic steps are involved:

1. Identify the distribution needs and preferences of each customer segment targeted.
2. Identify the supplier's distribution needs.
3. Identify the functions to be performed to meet the distribution needs of the customers and the supplier.
4. Evaluate the alternative ways by which these functions might be performed.

5. Decide on the distribution mix.
6. Implement the distribution strategy.
7. Monitor and evaluate the distribution strategy.

Taking a structured step-wise approach to designing a distribution strategy makes the task of developing it more straightforward and also readily enables the strategy to be revisited to take account of changes in the market or the operating environment; for example, as new market opportunities or threats appear, new products are developed or technologies improve.

Elaboration of the strategy process involved consideration of issues identified in the wider distribution literature, and consolidation and integration of the results from other parts of the project. Step 1, for example, was informed by the research on visitor behaviour (Pearce and Schott, 2005), Step 3 was heavily influenced by the needs–function model (Pearce, 2008), and Steps 5 and 7 incorporated elements of the methodology for evaluating channel performance (Pearce and Taniguchi, 2008).

Conclusions

As this chapter has illustrated, a significant body of work on tourism distribution has emerged in the past decade. Many of the studies that have been completed have been carried out using either a structural or behavioural approach. Research undertaken from a functional, evaluative or strategic approach is much less common. Moreover, there have been few explicit linkages made between these different approaches. The structural studies in particular have provided a very useful starting point for understanding the basic dimensions of distribution channels, but only rarely has much deeper significance been attached to the structures described by interpreting them in behavioural, functional, evaluative or strategic terms.

The focus in many of these studies is on distribution channels rather than on the process of distribution, on how providers make their products available, how they bridge the gap between supply and demand, and how this might be done more effectively and more efficiently. What is needed now is a more purposeful direction in tourism distribution research, one whereby the various approaches are linked more explicitly to each other and directed more expressly at addressing strategic issues. Such research will in turn assist tourism suppliers to take a more strategic approach to distribution and be more competitive in what they do.

Questions for Discussion

1. Why is distribution of tourism products more complex than, for example, those from the manufacturing sector?
2. Why have the structural studies appeared to be important in understanding the basic dimensions of distribution channels?
3. How do the internet and associated technologies add value to the tourism distribution system?

4. What makes the New Zealand tourist destination distinctive in the context of the distribution system?

Acknowledgement

This research was undertaken as part of the Public Good Science Fund project: Innovation in New Zealand Tourism through Improved Distribution Channels, funded by the Foundation for Research, Science and Technology.

References

Alcázar Martínez, B. del. (2002). *Los Canales de Distribución en el Sector Turístico*. Madrid: ESIC Editorial.

Alamdari, F. and Mason K. (2006). The future of airline distribution. *Journal of Transport Management*, 12(3), 122–134.

Ali-Knight, J. and Wild S. (1999). British Airways' inbound leisure market to Manchester, England: is direct marketing the answer? *Journal of Vacation Marketing*, 6(1), 9–20.

Anderson, E., Day, G.S. and Rangan, V.K. (1997). 'Strategic channel design.' *Sloan Management Review*, 38(4), 59–69.

Bitner, M.J. and Booms B.H. (1982). Trends in Travel and Tourism Marketing: the Changing Structure of Distribution Channels. *Journals of Travel Research*, 20(4): 39–44.

Bote Gómez, V. and Álvarez Cuervo, R. (2001). *Promoción y Comercialización del Turismo Cultural de la Ciudad de Sevilla: Diagnóstico y Orientaciones Estratégicas*. Documentos de Trabajo Serie A, no. 20018. Madrid, Spain: Universidad de Alcalá, Escuela Universitaria de Turismo.

Buckley, P.J. (1987). Tourism: An Economic Transactions Analysis. *Tourism Management*, 8(3), 190–194.

Buhalis, D. (2000). Relationships in the distribution channels of tourism: conflicts between hoteliers and tour operators in the Mediterranean region. *International Journal of Hospitality & Tourism Administration*, 1(1), 113–139.

Buhalis, D. (2001). Tourism distribution channels: practices and processes. In *Tourism Distribution Channels: Practices, Issues and Transformations*, (D. Buhalis and E. Laws, eds), London: Continuum, pp. 7–32.

Buhalis, D. and Laws, E. (2001). *Tourism Distribution Channels: Practices, Issues and Transformations*. London: Continum.

Buhalis, D. (2004). eAirlines: strategic and tactical use of ICTs in the airline industry. *Information and Management*, 41(7), 805–825.

Cai, L.A., Feng, R. and Breiter, D. (2004). Tourist Purchase Decision Involvement and Information Preferences. *Journal of Vacation Marketing*, 20(2), 138–148.

Casarin, F. (2001). Tourism distribution channels in Europe: a comparative study. In *Tourism Distribution Channels: practices, issues and transformations*, (D. Buhalis and E. Laws, eds), London: Continuum, pp. 137–150.

Chaintron, B. (1995). Industrie touristique: le choc des modèles anglais et français. *Cahier Espaces*, 44, 31–36.

Choi, S. and Kimes S.E. (2002). Electronic distribution channels' effect on hotel revenue management. *Cornell Hotel and Restaurant Administration Quarterly*, 43(3), 23–31.

Crotts, J.C., Aziz, A. and Raschid, A. (1998). Antecedents of suppliers' commitment to wholesale buyers in the international travel trade. *Tourism Management*, 19(2), 127–134.

Crotts, J.C. and Turner G.B. (1999). Determinants of trust in buyer-seller relationships in the international travel trade. *International Journal of Contemporary Hospitality*, 11(2/3).

Dev, C.S. and Olsen M.D. (2000). Marketing challenges for the next decade. *Cornell Hotel and Restaurant Administration Quarterly*, 44(1), 41–47.

Dubè, L., & Renaghan, L.M. (2000). Marketing your hotel to and through intermediaries, *Cornell Hotel and Restaurant Administration Quarterly*, 41(1), 41–47.

Duke, C.R. and Persia M.A. (1993). Effects of Distribution Channel Level on Tour Purchasing Attributes and Information Sources. *Journal of Travel and Tourism Marketing*, 2(2/3), 37–55.

Fam, K.S., Foscht, T. and Collins, R.D. (2003). Trust and the Online Relationship – an Exploratory Study from New Zealand. *Tourism Management*, 25(2), 195–207.

Fava Neves, M., Zuurbier, P. and Cortez Campomar, M. (2001). A model for the distribution channels planning process. *Journal of Business & Industrial Marketing*, 16(7), 518–539.

Fodness, D. and Murray B. (1997). Tourist Information Search. *Annals of Tourism Research*, 24(3), 503–523.

Forsyth, P. and Smith N. (1992). Corporate organization and distribution channels in Japan: the tourism industry case. In *International Adjustment and the Japanese Firm*, (P. Sheard, ed), St Leonards: Allen and Ashwin, pp. 177–199.

Frazier, G.L. (1999). Organizing and managing channels of distribution. *Journal of the Academy of Marketing Science*, 27(2), 226–240.

Garnham, R. (2005). Corporate travel agents: Channels of distribution–an evaluation. In *Sharing Tourism Knowledge. Proceedings of the CAUTHE Conference, Alice Springs. CD-Rom*, (P. Tremblay and A. Boyle, eds), Darwin: Charles Darwin University.

Gartner, W.C. and Bachri, T. (1994). Tour operators' role in the tourism distribution system: an Indonesian case study. *Journal of International Consumer Marketing*, 6(3/4), 161–179.

Gee, G.Y., Makens, J.C. and Choy, D.J.L. (1989). *The Travel Industry*. New York: Van Nostrand Reinhold.

Green, C.E. (2005). *De-Mystifying Distribution: building a distribution strategy one channel at a time*. HSMAI Foundation.

Guo, W. and Turner L.W. (2001). Entry strategies into China for foreign travel companies. *Journal of Vacation Marketing*, 6(1), 49–63.

Gursoy, D. and McCleary K.W. (2003). An Integrative Model of Tourists' Information Search Behavior. *Annals of Tourism Research*, 31(2), 353–373.

Hewitt, C. (2006). 'Online Accommodation Bookings–The Future Innovation Through Disruption'. Paper presented at the Tourism Futures Forum, Melbourne.

Kalafatis, S.P. (2000). Buyer-seller relationships along channels of distribution. *Industrial Marketing Management*, 31(3), 215–228.

Karamustafa, K. (2000). Marketing-channel relationships: Turkey's resort purveyors' interactions with international tour operators. *Cornell Hotel and Restaurant Association Quarterly*, 41(4), 21–31.

Kimes, S.E. and Lord D.C. (1994). Wholesalers and Caribbean resort hotels. *Cornell Hotel and Restaurant Association Quarterly*, 35(5), 70.

King, B. and Choi, H.J. (1999). Travel industry structure in fast growing but immature outbound markets: the case of Korea to Australia travel. *International Journal of Tourism Research*, 1(2), 111–125.

Kotler, P., Bowen., J. and Makens, J. (1996). *Marketing and Hospitality for Tourism*. Upper Saddle River: Prentice Hall.

Lewis, E.H. (1968). *Marketing Channels: Structure and Strategy*. New York: McGraw-Hill.

March, R. (1997). An exploratory study of buyer-supplier relationships in international tourism: the case of Japanese wholesalers and Australian suppliers. *Journal of Travel and Tourism Marketing*, 6(1), 55–68.

March, R. (2000). Buyer decision-making behaviour in international tourism channels. *International Journal of Hospitality and Tourism Administration*, 1(1), 11–25.

Medina-Muñoz, D. and García-Falcón J.M. (2000). Successful relationships between hotels and agencies. *Annals of Tourism Research*, 27(3), 737–762.

Medina-Muñoz, J., Medina-Muñoz, D. and García-Falcón, J.M. (2003). Understanding European tour operators' control on accommodation companies: an empirical evidence. *Tourism Management*, 24, 135–147.

Middleton, V. and Clarke, J. (2001). *Marketing in Travel and Tourism*, 3rd edn. Oxford: Butterworth-Heinemann.

Morrel, P.S. (1998). Airline sales and distribution channels: the impact of new technology. *Tourism Economics*, 4(1), 5–19.

Morrison, A.M. (1989). *Hospitality and Tourism Marketing*. Delmar Albany, NY.

O'Connor, P. (1999). *Electronic Information Distribution in Tourism and Hospitality*. Wallingford: CABI Publishing.

O'Connor, P. and Frew A.J. (2003). An evaluation methodology for hotel electronic channels of distribution. *International Journal of Hospitality Management*, 23(2), 179–199.

Origet du Cluzeau, C. (1995). Distribution de Produits Touristiques Culturels: Le Sceptre d' autocar. *Cahiers Espaces*, 44, 98–102.

Öörni, A. (2003). Consumer search in electronic markets: an experimental analysis of travel services. *European Journal of Information Systems*, 12(1), 30–40.

Pearce, D.G. (2003). Tourism distribution channels: a systematic integrated approach. In *6th International Forum on the Sciences, Techniques and Art Applied to Marketing*, (E Ortega, L. González and E. Pérez del Campo, eds), Madrid: Universidad Complutense de Madrid, pp. 345–363.

Pearce, D.G. (2005). Distribution channels for cultural tourism in Catalonia, Spain. *Current Issues in Tourism*, 8(5), 424–445.

Pearce, D.G. (2007a). 'Tourism distribution networks: research issues and destination management implications'. Paper presented at the Advances in Tourism Marketing Conference: Destination and Event Marketing: Managing networks, Valencia, 10–12 September 2007.

Pearce, D.G. (2007b). Supplier selection in the New Zealand inbound tourism industry. *Journal of Travel and Tourism Marketing*, 23(1), 57–69.

Pearce, D.G. (2007c). *Paths to the Market: developing an effective tourism distribution strategy.* Wellington: Victoria Management School, Victoria University of Wellington.

Pearce, D.G. (2008). A needs-function model of tourism distribution. *Annals of Tourism Research*, 35(1), 148–168.

Pearce, D.G. (in press). Researching tourism distribution. In *Handbook of Tourism Research*, (W.C. Gartner and C.H.C. Hsu, eds), The Haworth Hospitality Press.

Pearce, D.G. and Sahli M. (2007). Surface transport distribution channels in New Zealand: a comparative analysis. *Journal of Travel and Tourism Marketing*, 22(2), 57–73.

Pearce, D.G. and Schott C. (2005). Tourism distribution channels: the visitors' perspective. *Journal of Travel Research*, 44(1), 50–63.

Pearce, D.G. and Tan R. (2004). Distribution channels for heritage and cultural tourism in New Zealand. *Asia Pacific Journal of Tourism Research*, 9(3), 225–237.

Pearce, D.G. and Tan R. (2006). The distribution mix for tourism attractions in Rotorua, New Zealand. *Journal of Travel Research*, 2(44), 250–258.

Pearce, D.G., Tan, R. and Schott, C. (2004). Tourism distribution channels in Wellington, New Zealand. *International Journal of Tourism Research*, 6(6), 397–410.

Pearce, D.G., Tan, R. and Schott, C. (2007). Distribution channels in international markets: a comparative analysis of the distribution of New Zealand tourism in Australia, Great Britain and the USA. *Current Issues in Tourism*, 10(1), 33–60.

Pearce, D.G. and Taniguchi, M. (2008). Channel performance in multi-channel tourism distribution systems. *Journal of Travel Research*, 46(3), 256–267.

Piga, C.A. and Fillippi, N. (2002). Booking and flying with low-cost airlines. *The International Journal of Tourism Research*. May-June, 4(3), 237–249.

Richards, G., Goedhart, S. and Herrijgers, C. (2001). The cultural attraction distribution system. In *Cultural Attractions and European Tourism*, (G. Richards, ed), CAB International London, pp. 71–89.

Rocks, S., Gilmore, A. and Carson, D. (2005). Developing strategic marketing through the use of marketing networks. *Journal of Strategic Marketing*, 13(2), 81–92.

Rosenbloom, B., Larsen, T. and Smith, B. (2004). The effectiveness of upstream influence attempts in high and low context export marketing channels. *Journal of Marketing Channels*, 11(4), 3–19.

Schott, C. (2007). Selling adventure tourism: A distribution channels perspective. *International Journal of Tourism Research*, 9(4), 257–274.

Schmidt, J.B. and Spreng R.A. (1996). A proposed model of external consumer information search. *Journal of the Academy of Marketing Science*, 24(3), 246–256.

Sharda, S. and Pearce, D.G. (2006). Tourism distribution in emerging markets: the case of Indian travel to New Zealand. *Asia Pacific Journal of Tourism Research*, 11(4), 339–353.

Simons, L.P.A. and Bouwman H. (2004). Designing a channel mix. *International Journal of Internet Marketing and Advertising*, 1(3), 229–250.

Smith, K.A. (2007). Distribution channels for events: supply and demand-side perspectives. *Journal of Vacation Marketing*, 13(4), 321–338.

Smith, K.A. and Garnham, R. (2006). Distribution channels for convention tourism: association conventions in Wellington, New Zealand. *Journal of Convention and Event Tourism*, 8(1), 1–30.

Snepenger, D. and Snepenger, M. (1993). Information search by pleasure travellers. In *Encyclopedia of Hospitality and Tourism*, (M.A. Kahn, M.D. Olsen and T. Var, eds), Van Nostrand Reinhold, New York, pp. 830–835.

Stern, L.W. and El-Ansary, A.I. (1992). *Marketing Channels,* 4th edn. Englewood Cliffs: Prentice-Hall.

Susskind, A.M., Bonn, M.A. and Dev, C.S. (2003). To look or book: an examination of consumers' apprehensiveness toward Internet use. *Journal of Travel Research*, 41(Feb), 256–264.

Tan, R. and Pearce, D.G. (2004). Providers' and intermediaries' use of the Internet in tourismdistribution. In *Proceedings of the New Zealand Tourism and Hospitality Conference 2004*, (Smith, K.A. and Schott, C. eds.), Wellington, 8–10 December 2004, pp. 424–432.

Taniguchi, M. (2006). The structure and function of the tourism distribution channels between Japan and New Zealand. *Proceedings of the 2006 New Zealand Tourism and Hospitality Research Conference*.

Ujma, D. (2001). Distribution channels for tourism: Theory and issues. In *Tourism Distribution Channels: Practices, Issues and Transformations*, (D. Buhalis and W. Laws, eds), Continuum, London, pp. 33–52.

Wahab, S., Crampon, L.J. and Rothfield, L.M. (1976). *Tourism Marketing*. London: Tourism International Press.

Wilson, D.T. (1995). An integrated model of buyer-seller relationships. *Journal of the Academy of Marketing Science*, 23(4), 335–345.

Wolfe, K., Hsu, C.H.C. and Kang, S.K. (2004). Buyer characteristics among users of various travel intermediaries. *Journal of Travel & Tourism Marketing*, 17(2/3), 51–62.

Woodside, A.G. and King, R.I. (2001). An updated model of travel and tourism purchase-consumption systems. *Journal of Travel and Tourism Marketing*, 10(1), 3–27.

Wynne, C.P., Berthon, L., Pitt Ewing, M. and Napoli, J. (2001). The impact of the Internet on the distribution value chain: the case of the South African Tourism Industry. *International Marketing Review*, 18(4), 420–431.

Yamamoto, D. and Gill A. (2002). Issues of globalisation and reflexivity in the Japanese tourism production system: the case of Whistler, British Columbia. *The Professional Geographer*, 54(1), 83–93.

Chapter 18

Understanding and Influencing the Entrepreneurial Intentions of Tourism Students

Andreas Walmsley and Rhodri Thomas

Learning Outcomes

After reading this chapter, you should be able to:

- Understand higher education policy in the UK with an emphasis on entrepreneurial behaviour amongst university students and the role of innovation in tourism;

- Understand the role of internships (placements) as a mechanism to inculcate positive dispositions towards entrepreneurship;

- Appreciate the impact of internships on tourism students undertaking internship programmes in SMEs;

- Understand the theoretical context of the entrepreneurial event based on Ajzen's theory of planned behaviour and Shapero's theories; and

- Understand the interconnections between internship programmes and entrepreneurial intentions and how these will be of value to policy-makers.

Introduction

In a recent review of British research on small business and entrepreneurship, Blackburn and Smallbone (2007) argued persuasively that the area of enquiry has now become part of mainstream academic activity. To support their case, they draw on selective metrics such as the number of active researchers, the quality and quantity of research output, and the fact that government research funding mechanisms now recognize the distinctive nature of the field. This probably reflects the position in many other countries. Their explanation for this growth of academic interest included the observation that it has found resonance with public policy-makers over the past 25 years or more. Such public policy interest has also applied to tourism over the years (e.g. Thomas, 1995) and there has been some growth of academic interest in entrepreneurship related to tourism (e.g. Getz, Carlsen and Morrison, 2004). However, there has been insufficient attention paid to a range of policy themes, such as those implied by the title of this chapter, that merit further investigation.

Although small firms dominate the tourism industry, graduates have generally neglected them as a source of employment. Moreover, in spite of the growing research in this field, graduate (self-) employment in small tourism businesses has also tended to be neglected by researchers. Indeed, our understanding of tourism graduate career decision-making more generally is weak. Only sparingly is reference made to career decision-making theory, in studies of careers in tourism (Marhuenda et al., 2004; Ladkin, 2002; Ayres, 2006).

This chapter begins to address this gap in knowledge by investigating the entrepreneurial intentions of tourism students who had undertaken a year's work placement in a tourism SME. Although the discussion takes place largely within a British context, the insights offered into entrepreneurial intentions are likely to be of wider relevance. Notwithstanding ongoing debates on the meaning of 'entrepreneurship' (e.g. Brazeal and Herbert, 1999; Atherton, 2004), for the purposes of this chapter 'entrepreneurship' is defined loosely, and quite traditionally (see Gartner, 1988; Shook et al., 2003), as primarily encompassing business start-up.

The chapter begins by underlining the policy relevance of research into graduate entrepreneurship and discusses briefly attempts to stimulate entrepreneurial aspirations in higher education (HE) in the UK. It then proceeds to review literature on the process of entrepreneurship focusing on the concept of entrepreneurial intent, paying particular attention to Shapero's model of the Entrepreneurial Event and Ajzen's Theory of Planned Behaviour as applied to entrepreneurship. These frameworks are then used to make sense of data collected on tourism students' placement experiences in SMEs and their relation to graduate entrepreneurship. On the basis of this discussion the chapter concludes by making a number of practitioner and research recommendations.

Entrepreneurial Intent and Pathways to Entrepreneurship

The British government recently declared that it wanted Britain to become the 'best place to start and grow a business' (Small Business Service, 2002) and that 'creating an enterprise culture is vital. It is business and entrepreneurs that create wealth and the young people of today are the entrepreneurs of tomorrow' (Rae and Woodier, 2006, p. 11). Such statements, and those made by others, make a case for the potential economic contribution of graduate entrepreneurship (ISBA, 2004). Not surprisingly, agencies such as the National Council for Graduate Entrepreneurship (NCGE) (www.ncge.com) and Centres of Excellence for Teaching and Learning Entrepreneurship (e.g. www.leedsmet.ac.uk/enterprise) have been established to advance the graduate entrepreneurship agenda.

Notwithstanding an apparent latent desire among the student and recent graduate population for business start-up (Greene and Saridakis, 2007), there exists a multitude of initiatives designed to raise awareness of entrepreneurship among students of higher education (McKeown et al., 2006; Carter and Collinson, 1999). Their effectiveness in raising levels of graduate business start-up, however, remains unclear. One major review of graduate pathways into entrepreneurship conducted by the Institute for Small Business Affairs Consortium concluded that education could influence students' perceptions of the desirability and feasibility of entrepreneurship (ISBA, 2004). However, some (Moreland, 2004; Robertson et al., 2003; Rae and Woodier, 2006) regard current HE provision as deficient with regard to entrepreneurship, particularly the *experience* of entrepreneurship (Moreland [2004], for example, highlights the need for students to understand what it means to be an entrepreneur). Robertson et al. (2003) suggest reading case studies and inviting entrepreneurs to lectures is a useful way of enhancing self-efficacy beliefs, particularly where students lack work experience.

Morrison (2000) highlights the role of culture in determining entrepreneurial behaviour. Dyer Jr (1994) emphasizes the effect of economic scenarios, specifically the post-internet boom, on attitudes towards business start-up among college students. Krueger (1993a) assesses the impact of exposure to family business on attitudes to entrepreneurship. These are just some examples of studies that have in common an interest in situations and events external to the individual that have led to entrepreneurial behaviour. By contrast, much early writing about entrepreneurship focused on the individual and personality traits (Robinson et al., 1991). The nature rather than nurture debate was initially highlighted as explaining why some people rather than others were entrepreneurial. Indeed, we can trace the person–environment (context) interaction back to Lewin (1951) who argued persuasively that behaviour is a function of the person and their interaction with the environment, leading others to argues some 40 years later that 'The interactionist position is that, above all else, entrepreneurship involves an individual operating in the environment' (Robinson et al., 1991, p. 15).

Much of the discussion surrounding factors that foster entrepreneurship has revolved around the notion of intent. Support for the focus on intentions is often provided with reference to Bird's (1988) conceptual work on this matter. The premise is quite simply that business start-up is an intended act and that therefore intent and factors that lead to it should be investigated. Shapero (1975, 1982) proposed an intentionality-based model of the entrepreneurial event (also known as Shapero's model of the Entrepreneurial Event, henceforth SEE). SEE, together with Ajzen's Theory of Planned Behaviour (TPB), also an intentions model, has provided frameworks upon which to investigate exposure to factors prone to increase the likelihood of business start-up. These frameworks are clearly relevant to this study and its discussion of the impact of the placement experience on career intentions.

SEE in its original form suggests intent is the result of perceived desirability and perceived feasibility of the entrepreneurial event, as well as a propensity to act on opportunities. Desirability is defined as the degree to which one finds the prospect of starting a business to be attractive. It reflects, so Krueger (1993b) argues, one's affect toward entrepreneurship. Perceived feasibility is the degree to which the individual feels capable of starting a business. Propensity to act is less straightforward than the other two factors in Shapero's model. It is the disposition to act upon one's decisions, in particular when faced with an opportunity. It might, as Krueger (1993b) points out, have a moderating relationship to other factors in the model. Clearly, propensity to act and intentions are related. This is where the already mentioned 'problem' with intentions models arises, in particular with regards to entrepreneurial intent. Not only do degrees of intent exist – 'buddingness' according to Krueger (1993b) – but the process of venture creation and intent to start a business can be simultaneous (Nabi et al., 2007).

Krueger with colleagues (1993a, 1994, 2000) has based a number of studies of entrepreneurship on SEE. In his earliest paper on this matter (Krueger, 1993b) he argues, and subsequently provides supporting empirical evidence, that exposure to entrepreneurship is one potential influence resulting in situational intentions and attitudes towards entrepreneurship. Exposure to entrepreneurship indirectly influences perceived feasibility.

In a further paper, Krueger and Brazeal (1994) discuss SEE but also Ajzen's Theory of Planned Behaviour. TPB assumes attitudes are the best predictors of intent, which as we have seen is the best predictor of behaviour. There is much similarity between TPB and SEE. The three factors TPB uses to predict entrepreneurial intent are attitude towards the act, social norms and perceived behavioural control. Attitude towards the act can be set next to perceived desirability and perceived behavioural control approximates perceived feasibility (Autio et al., 2001). The greatest discrepancy between the two models then lies in a focus on social norms in TPB although this is subsumed in Krueger and Brazeal's (1994) model of entrepreneurial potential (Figure 18.1), which is an extension to SEE.

Krueger et al. (2000) also conducted a comparison of SEE and TPB with regards to entrepreneurial intent. The comparison indicated statistical support for both models although all components of SEE were statistically significant at the $p < 0.05$ level, whereas for TPB the component 'social norms' was not. Krueger et al. (2000) propose that this could be related to the role of social norms in varying societies and cultures. For example, it is suggested that social norms may only be important in ethnic groups who have strong traditions of entrepreneurship.

Apart from Krueger's research into SEE and TPB, Autio et al. (2001) also investigated TPB in relation to entrepreneurial intent. Their findings add to the literature that supports the robustness of TPB in predicting entrepreneurial intent. All the more astonishing, so Autio

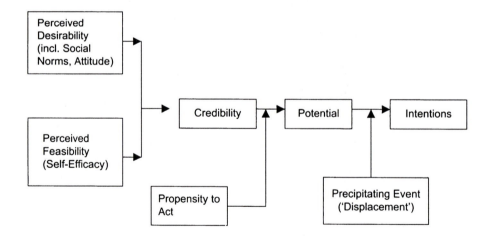

Figure 18.1: Model of entrepreneurial potential. (*Source*: Krueger and Brazeal, 1994.)

et al. (2001) suggest, was the robustness of the model across cultures (albeit all 'western'). Perceived behavioural control was found to be the strongest influence on intent. Their study also incorporated the situational variable 'small firm employment experience', the extent of which was measured by years of employment. One may question this measure as it is unclear why length of employment experience in an SME should be positively or negatively correlated to attitudes towards entrepreneurship. Other factors such as sector, SME growth orientation or level of autonomy, for example, may be more important than length of service. In any case, this matter requires further investigation.

The above discussion has provided a backdrop upon which making sense of the empirical data on SME placement experiences with regard to entrepreneurial intent is facilitated. In particular, perceived behavioural control, akin to perceived feasibility, or, more commonly, perceived self-efficacy, that is the perceived personal ability to execute a target behaviour (see also Bandura, 1986), appears to be a major influence of entrepreneurial intent, as also robustly argued in a paper by Boyd and Vozikis (1994).

The Experience of Tourism Students in SMEs

What follows draws on in-depth interviews with 20 tourism students in the UK who were in the process of completing, or had very recently completed, a year's placement in a tourism SME. While there has been much discussion as to the purpose of placements, a theme that is frequently highlighted relates to the development of career intentions. West and Jameson (1990) are very specific in their discussion of placements in hospitality suggesting that the placement should assist students to identify career paths within hospitality businesses and related organizations. Notwithstanding the recurring study of placements in tourism (McMahon and Quinn, 1995; Busby et al., 1997; Waryszak, 1999; Leslie, 1991; Leslie and Richardson, 1999; Busby, 2005; Collins, 2002), a focus on placements specifically in tourism SMEs has to date managed to elude attention. Thus, we know very little about how such experiences in fact affect career intentions.

Only a handful of studies exist that have investigated SME placements. One of these was conducted by Westhead (1998) and relates to the Shell Technology Enterprise Programme (STEP). Here he found that the placement resulted in a slight increase in the propensity to start a business. Westhead and Matlay (2005) then revisit longitudinal data related to STEP and concluded that there is little evidence that a SME placement increases the likelihood of SME employment. Other studies of placement experiences in SMEs have largely focused on the employer perspective (see a range of studies discussed by Otter, 2005, p. 488 and Bowen et al.'s [2004] discussion of the University of Glamorgan's Network75 initiative). Jones et al.'s (2001) study points out that 44% of respondents in their study claimed they were more likely to seek SME employment as a result of the placement experience. Given the conflicting views and the paucity of research in this area it is at this stage difficult to draw any firm conclusions as to the SME placement's impact on career intentions generally, and business start-up intentions more specifically.

A possible reason for the lack of research into SME placement experiences is the difficulty in pinpointing individuals who have actually undertaken such a placement. All of the above studies related to schemes aiming to introduce students or graduates to SME employment experiences rather than drawing on larger populations of placement students and then identifying those who were undertaking the placement in SMEs. Finding participants for the research reported here was in fact more difficult than anticipated, partly because it was difficult to identify students who had undertaken a placement in an SME. This may be because many HE institutions have traditionally targeted large firms in the tourism sector because larger organizations are more proactive in establishing links with HEIs for the purpose of work placements.

Two interviews were conducted with each individual: the first focusing primarily on the placement experience itself, the second on participants' career development and career intentions. The interviews were loosely structured which provided scope for participants to offer their own narrative while allowing a reasonable degree of cross-case comparisons to be made. Data were transcribed and analysed using the software NVIVO. This consisted of identifying themes and sub-themes in the data whilst also attempting not to lose insight into the individual case itself. This relates to Lieblich et al.'s (1998) identification of a holistic and categorical reading of interview data. Thus, to support the holistic interpretation of the data, familiarity with the individual's case was important and therefore interviews were listened to twice rather than solely once for purpose of transcription. This aided a 're-living' of the initial interview and a recollection of tone fall and expression when then working with the transcribed data. This is very much in the interpretive understanding ('*verstehen*') tradition of sociology and contrasts somewhat with Peterman and Kennedy's (2003) views on how to further research into entrepreneurship; they are unconvinced of the merits of more qualitative methodological approaches. The data gathered from the 20 cases provide rich insights into individual cases. Some of the key themes are discussed below.

Perceived Feasibility/Perceived Behavioural Control

One of the overriding themes from the interviews was that the SME placement and placements more generally (Busby et al., 1997; Brennan and Little, 2006) were found to increase confidence quite substantially. Although this appears to be a frequent finding in studies on placements, the placement may not automatically lead to increases in confidence. Both Krueger (1993b) and Peterman and Kennedy (2003) found associations between positiveness of experience and self-efficacy beliefs. It is conceivable that where placement students are anxious and unsure about their competence or abilities and then receive positive feedback, their confidence or self-efficacy beliefs with regards to a particular skill are augmented. Alternatively, the situation may arise where a student believes they are fairly competent at something only to then realize through critical feedback that they are not quite as competent as initially presumed. This may then dent confidence or self-efficacy beliefs with regards to a particular skill.

The data also suggest a connection between confidence and career development, particularly intentions, as one participant's comment illustrates:

> I think it's (the placement) made me more confident that I can achieve,
> like before I wasn't sure what I could do, now it's, well I know I can do

almost better than I thought I would. It's given me more confidence and go and look for the job I want, it's just really been a big sort of learning experience for me.

It appears that as confidence levels rise, the range of potential career options broadens. This is supported by Gottfredson's (1981, 2002) career development theory which encompasses circumscription and compromise. That is, individuals first circumscribe a set of career options based on personal preferences and then narrow their career options further (compromise) given, amongst other things, personal ability. Here, however, increased confidence may increase the zone of acceptable alternatives. Therefore, if feasibility towards business start-up increases as a result of SME placements so that entrepreneurship now falls within the expanded zone of acceptable alternatives, this would be, according to proponents of increased levels of graduate entrepreneurship at least, a positive outcome of the SME placement.

The role of practical as opposed to academic work in granting some students confidence is outlined in the following quotation and supports the practical application of knowledge as mentioned by Krueger (1993b) who maintains that teaching a relevant skill is not enough. It will be recalled that this was also a view favoured by Robertson et al. (2003) and Moreland (2004) who claimed that students lacked experience of what being an entrepreneur entailed. To illustrate, one participant commented:

It's also given me confidence cause … academically I've never been a hard worker, I get bored very easily of academic work… But as I say, for the first … when I worked really hard, I was quite happy with myself that I was working so hard, I got commented by everybody who worked there, I was told that I'd kind of set standards …

It appears then that the placement may provide confidence in particular to students who, from their perspective, are under-performing at university. Clearly, the reverse may also be true. One respondent had a number of years' experience working in the sector when he realized that to progress he would need to obtain a degree. He did particularly well at university and is strident in asserting that this built up his belief in his abilities, something that had been gradually eroded while working in industry.

Reasonably high levels of confidence may be beneficial in increasing the perceived feasibility of business start-up, more specifically though it is useful to investigate whether self-efficacy beliefs towards the act of business start-up were influenced by the placement. Self-efficacy is described by Bandura (1986) as the perceived personal ability to execute a target behaviour. The question then arises as to whether the SME placement led to increased self-efficacy towards business start-up. Applying Yin's (1994) notion of generalization to theory, this study generalizes from in-depth understanding of individual cases to the wider population of tourism students.

As well as augmenting levels of confidence, the SME placement also impacted on the perceived feasibility of starting a business by increasing self-efficacy beliefs towards venture creation. At this point, further quotations from participants are helpful to illustrate some of the analysis:

'... this has given me the opportunity to observe how things are done, how a good bar, a good popular bar, the steps that they make, you know, they make the profits for years and years, is run, what could be the wrong things to do, what would be the right things to do, so I definitely feel more confident, and ... the whole placement has been absolutely great because if I didn't do this then I wouldn't have felt confident, so confident basically, yes.'

'I've never been able to actually run a place before ... so it was all really about running a small business ... '

'As to what makes the place run: yes, I think I could pretty much do it. I know all the suppliers, I know the level, the electrics, where the electrics lie, I know where the problems with the service stations are. I think, you know, I've got a well-rounded knowledge now of how this place runs.'

'...'cause the hotel I work at is such a small operation ... you can see how they've (the owners) set it up, and while I've been there they've actually bought another company and renovated it and I've like seen that process, so ... if I hadn't seen that I might have thought "oh, this might be quite difficult to ... open your own business...".'

While it was established that undertaking a placement has the potential to increase general levels of confidence, confidence as mentioned above relates to running a small business, i.e. a specific behaviour, hence it is justified to speak of self-efficacy beliefs towards running a small business. This is as expected: a student enters an SME and, because of its size, gains an overview of the entire organization rather than, as may occur in larger enterprises, solely one department or facet of it. The individual shadows the owner/manager, observes how the business is run and perhaps also engages him or herself in running the enterprise. This in turn leads to increased self-efficacy vis-à-vis running a similar business. Both from a motivational as well as practical perspective the SME placement has the potential to enhance a successful business start-up.

From participants' responses it became evident that those who worked for the smallest firms were more likely to gain an overview of how the business as a whole functioned. This is in itself not surprising as the relationship between size and understanding of the organization as a coherent unit has already been established. In other words, as organizations grow, formality and clearly delineated functions are required, which includes the managerial function (Bacon and Hoque, 2005; Drucker, 1993). This also renders it more difficult for any one individual to grasp the organization in its entirety although this is clearly one of the functions of (senior) management.

Furthermore, some of the placement firms were relatively new businesses seeking to grow. Here in particular it was possible for participants to witness attempts at growing a small tourism firm. Interestingly, none of the participants appear to have been dissuaded from starting a business. This may, of course, be down to a selection bias in those businesses that are the focus of our attention. Notably, one may expect owner/managers of tourism SMEs that offer placements to be more open-minded in a business sense than those that do not. This may have led to an over-representation of growth SMEs in the sample. However, since the aim is not to generalize to all tourism SMEs but to explain how undertaking a placement in a tourism SME may impact upon entrepreneurial intentions, this is not of immediate concern.

The unit of analysis is the individual rather than the organization. Here then it seems that the *processes* of inculcating entrepreneurial intent in the student remain the same regardless of the growth aspiration of the placement owner/manager. This does not preclude the possibility that the student who is exposed to a dynamic organization may be more inspired towards entrepreneurship than those who undertake placements in organizations that are simply surviving. There are always exceptions of course. One student in our sample was sufficiently animated by seeing how his placement firm was generating income despite its poor management that this encouraged him to start his own business.

Perceived Desirability

Having discussed the notion of perceived feasibility according to SEE, or perceived behavioural control as per Ajzen's TPB, we now turn to the second factor that leads to entrepreneurial intent – the notion of perceived desirability and/or attitude towards the act. Participants commented less on the desirability of starting a business than they did on the feasibility of doing so. Although there was no hostility towards business start-up, those participants who did mention the fact that they would like to set up a business usually did so with reservations (for example only after initially working for a large firm, concern about financial constraints, etc.). There were exceptions; on the evidence of these interviews the placement appears to have affected desirability mainly through the concept of feasibility. That is, because business start-up was now seen as feasible it also became more desirable. Generally, however, little was said about desirability itself (for example, for greater autonomy, lifestyle considerations, escaping the rat race, choosing place of work, etc.).

The interaction between perceived desirability and perceived feasibility should be noted, as this is not clearly demonstrated in Krueger and Brazeal's (1994) model (see Figure 17.1). In fact, Krueger (1993b) tacitly concedes that the intentions models of the sort expounded in Figure 17.1 may obfuscate the true nature of the entrepreneurial process. He claims that 'since starting a business constitutes a complex, distal behaviour, intentions (end) and the plan (means) will likely co-evolve' (1993b, p. 6). Thus, the move from perceptions to intent is not so much linear as mutually shaping. This receives further attention below.

Propensity to Act

On the basis of foregoing discussion, propensity to act is a critical factor in making sense of graduate entrepreneurial intent. Whilst attitudes towards business start-up were on the whole positive, this is no guarantee that a business will be established. Though SEE and TPB help explain the provenance of entrepreneurial intent, intent in itself is not the act.

Indeed, we would argue that the prominence of entrepreneurial intent in studies of entrepreneurship is too readily accepted as a predictor for entrepreneurial behaviour.

The career intentions of the sample, although apparently very clear at first glance, were also often tentative when examined closely. Pathways to graduate entrepreneurship are less planned and more evolutionary. This was recently highlighted in a study that analysed how 15 graduate entrepreneurs had started their businesses (Nabi et al., 2006). Likewise, the early career development of the participants in this study also showed a great deal of oscillation between various ambitions, goals and interests. For most, their career development had been anything but planned. Overall then, although the SME placement played an important, and for some a critical, role in bolstering perceived feasibility of business start-up (which also had a knock-on effect on perceived desirability of starting a business by way of raising awareness of business start-up as a career option), propensity to act was weak. As we have seen, perceived feasibility is not lacking, desirability is present, and yet converting this latent desire into an entrepreneurial act is not straightforward. Our study seems to suggest that the focus of policy-makers as well as researchers should now be on the propensity to act.

Conclusions

Research into tourism graduates' career decisions in relation to entrepreneurship has been almost completely ignored by academics. This is surprising given its policy resonance. Drawing on Ajzen's Theory of Planned Behaviour and Shapero's model of the Entrepreneurial Event, this chapter has sought to make sense of tourism students' placement experiences in SMEs in relation to graduate entrepreneurial intent. SME placements enhance graduates' general levels of confidence as well as the more specific self-efficacy beliefs vis-à-vis business start-up. Perceived desirability is largely shaped by increases in perceived feasibility. The real task for policy-makers trying to increase levels of graduate entrepreneurship resides in turning latent desire for entrepreneurship into the act itself. In terms of Shapero's model of the Entrepreneurial Event, focus would be required on the propensity to act.

The chapter has provided a theoretical as well as an empirical foundation for those who might argue for increasing the number of tourism SME placements, in particular from a business start-up perspective. In this sense we concur with Brizek and Poorani (2006) who advocate increased emphasis on small business management and entrepreneurship courses in tourism and hospitality. While this study has provided an initial insight into how placements in SMEs influence entrepreneurial intent, further studies are required. In particular, longitudinal research should help overcome the weakness of studies that stop at entrepreneurial intent.

Questions for Discussion

1. Why does the tourism industry, particularly small tourism firms, attract a relatively small percentage of university graduates?

2. Why are Shapero's model of Entrepreneurial Event and Ajzen's Theory of Planned Behaviour relevant to the context of entrepreneurship and student internships in smaller enterprises?
3. What are the key lessons that this chapter provides for the policy-makers?

References

Atherton, A. (2004). Unbundling enterprise and entrepreneurship. From perceptions and preconceptions to concept and practice. *Entrepreneurship and Innovation*, 5(2), 121–127.

Brazeal, D. and Herbert, T. (1999). The genesis of entrepreneurship. *Entrepreneurship Theory and Practice*, 23(3), 29–45.

Busby, G. (2005). Work Experience and Industrial Links. In *An International Handbook of Tourism Education*, (D. Airey and J. Tribe, eds.), pp. 93–107. Oxford: Elsevier.

Collins, A.B. (2002). Gateway to the real world, industrial training: dilemmas and problems. *Tourism Management*, 23(1), 93–96.

Dyer Jr., W.G. (1994). Toward a theory of entrepreneurial careers. *Entrepreneurship Theory and Practice*, 7–21.

Getz, D., Carlsen, J., and Morrison, A. (2004). *The Family Business in Tourism and Hospitality*. CABI Publishing, Wallingford.

Gottfredson, L.S. (2002). Gottfredson's Theory of Circumscription, Compromise, and Self-Creation. In *Career Choice and Development*, (D. Brown, ed.), 4 edn., pp. 85–148. San Francisco: Jossey-Bass.

ISBA (2004). *Making the Journey from Student to Entrepreneur: A Review of the Existing Research into Graduate Entrepreneurship*, Birmingham: The National Council of Graduate Entrepreneurship.

Jones, A.J., Woods, A., Coles, A.-M., and Rein, M. (2001). Graduates as strategic change agents in small firms: a case study of graduate placements and lifelong learning. *Strategic Change*, 10(1), 59–69.

Krueger, N.F.J. (1993a) The impact of prior entrepreneurial exposure on perceptions of new venture feasibility and desirability. *Entrepreneurship Theory and Practice*, 18(1), 5–21.

Krueger, N.F.J. and Brazeal, D. (1994). Entrepreneurial Potential and Potential Entrepreneurs. *Entrepreneurship Theory and Practice*, 18(3), 91–104.

Krueger, N.F.J., Reilly, M.D. and Carsrud, A.L. (2000). Competing Models of Entrepreneurial Intentions. *Journal of Business Venturing*, 15(5/6), 411–432.

Otter, S. (2005). Graduate placement evaluation study, pp. 1–52; Otter Consulting Limited.

Shapero, A. (1982). Social dimensions of entrepreneurship. In *The Encyclopedia of Entrepreneurship* (C. Kent et al., eds.), pp. 72–90. Englewood Cliffs, NJ: Prentice Hall.

Thomas, R. (1995). Public Policy and Small Hospitality Firms. *International Journal of Contemporary Hospitality Management*, 7(2/3), 69–73.

Chapter 19

Tourism in Wartime Britain 1914–18: Adaptation, Innovation and the Role of Thomas Cook & Son

Stephen J. Page and Alastair Durie

Learning Objectives

After reading this chapter you should be able to:

- Understand the role of crisis in the business environment and how one large entrepreneurial and international company, Thomas Cook & Sons Ltd, responded to a major crisis – the First World War;

- Outline the challenges posed by operating in a wartime setting, where travel is not able to operate in a free market setting and with government intervention a dominant feature to meet national wartime efficiency objectives;

- Explain the types of evidence and research methods used by business historians and historians of tourism to reconstruct the way in which entrepreneurial businesses adapted and operated in wartime conditions;

- Appreciate the problems of having partial and incomplete evidence in reconstructing tourism patterns and activities;

- Illustrate how to use specific sources of historical data, such as newspapers, to challenge conventional interpretations of how tourism was impacted by war.

Introduction

The outbreak of war in August 1914 at the peak of the tourism season created a crisis for the tourism sector. It came at the end of the Edwardian period (Read, 1982) after a sustained period of affluence during which the British travelling elite developed a taste for travel to Europe and indeed beyond Europe. Tourism had become a major industry, with longer distance flows of considerable size: Americans travelling to Europe, Britons to the Mediterranean and the Middle East as well as world tours. The working classes were increasingly participating in domestic tourism in Britain, with the seaside a favourite destination (Walton, 1983).

Many tourism histories either end in 1914 or dismiss the wartime period as one in which tourism was at a standstill or relegated to a minor activity for the fortunate few. This is not dissimilar to the way the Second World War is treated by historians, as Sladen (2005, p. 215) makes a similar observation that 'academic and popular [published histories] say little or nothing about civilian holidays; the implication is that for most people they did not exist', which is analogous to the arguments in relation to the First World War. It might have been thought, therefore, that travel firms would have been at high risk with their staple activity so threatened and disrupted by war, and Thomas Cook & Son (hereafter Cook) as the largest firm in the British tourist industry, the most vulnerable of all. But it did survive. Indeed, despite heavy losses, it was able to come through the crisis and be in a position to quickly rebuild its operations and move into profit when peace came.

The response and behaviour of such a well-known and entrepreneurial organization offers many lessons for modern day companies in the management of crises. In particular it illustrates how one organization, noted for its entrepreneurial corporate culture (Brendon, 1991), was able to innovate, adapt and accommodate rapidly changing situations over which the organization had no control. This study provides a useful contribution to the study of entrepreneurship and tourism by drawing lessons and evidence from historical sources and illustrating how a contemporary focus on this area of research may be enriched and expanded by the application of the principles of business history and the historical analysis of tourism.

While the wartime years of 1914–18 have been widely studied by historians with an interest in war *per se* and its impact on domestic society and the economy (e.g. Broadberry and Howlett, 2005), little attention has been given to tourism. This can, in part, be attributed to the focus on the war economy and the war effort. It has been assumed that the war years led to a cessation of tourism. While there is no doubt that the war certainly had a major impact on tourism, what we shall be arguing here, using contemporary primary and secondary evidence, is that tourism did not end but rather changed its direction and nature. The *where*, *how* and *who* of tourism altered, but not the *fact*. Some once highly significant destinations in enemy countries were out of bounds for the duration of the war, in Europe and the Middle East. There were major problems of getting to destinations during wartime by either sea or land transport. Many men were away on military service, and American tourists, once they had got home in 1914 were not to be seen again in Europe until 1919; an annual loss of 150,000 visitors, if pre-war estimates are to be believed. Yet even in this difficult situation there were opportunities; there might be no foreign or American visitors in Britain, but the fact that British tourists could no longer holiday abroad, or not in any number at least, gave some domestic resorts an opportunity.

In the absence of a rich historiography of the period in relation to tourism, this chapter sets out to reconstruct from contemporary sources the effects of war on tourism and leisure behaviour in Britain. This is followed by a review of the types of challenges and opportunities tourism operators faced during the First World War and of the shift towards domestic tourism. There is a difficulty which dogs this discussion. Unlike other industries there are no neat statistical series to show how many tourists travelled where and when, which might confirm the thesis that during the war as British tourism to Europe ended, so domestic tourism grew.

Table 19.1: Late Victorian travel from the UK to Europe.

Year	Total passenger movements
1891	418,003
1892	405,998
1893	395,362
1894	477,318
1895	493,946
1896	479,913
1897	569,150
1898	590,226
1899	609,570
1900	669,292

Source: Lickorish and Kershaw (1953, p. 37) based on Board of Trade statistics.

Table 19.1, for example, shows the volume of *travel* from Britain to Europe in the 1890s, but some proportion of that would have been business and commercial travel. Were these annual figures broken down on a monthly basis, it would be a reasonable inference that the higher figures during the spring and summer do reflect the movement of tourists. Board of Trade figures record that in wartime August 1915, 47,055 passengers left the UK for all destinations compared to 111,843 in August 1914, and only 55,005 passengers arrived in the UK in August 1915 compared with 144,900 in August 1914. Much of the fall in the volume of travel is likely to have been in the number of tourists, because of the war. But there can be no precision.

Given the absence of tourism statistics to assist with the measurement and analysis of tourist flows and the value and volume of tourism in Britain between 1914–18, other data sources, of a more qualitative than quantitative nature, have to be utilized to gauge the nature of tourist travel in the years 1914–18. An analysis of the leading newspaper of the period – *The Times* – provides a commentary from a national perspective, in contrast to the local and regional focus of other studies (e.g. Walton, 1996; Durie and McPherson, 1999). Against this background, the role of Cook as the leading tour organizer responding to these conditions is examined using information from the company's rich, but again incomplete, historical archive, which limits how fully we can reconstruct how Cook responded to war. Nevertheless, this analysis serves as a detailed case study for the study of entrepreneurship and the response of innovative companies, as well being a significant contribution to documenting, analysing and explaining the way in which tourism adapted and developed during the period 1914–18 to create constraints and opportunities for the tourism industry.

Thomas Cook: Its Role as a Travel Company and its Operational Performance in Wartime Conditions

According to Brendon (1991, p. 245), 'the House of Cook dominated the Edwardian travel scene'. It was growing and profitable. Between 1909 and 1913 (inclusive), it made an average annual profit of over £119,000, more than double what it had been achieving a decade earlier. There were other travel firms with which it was in competition, of which Henry Lunn's was one, but Cook was far and away the leading tourism business in Britain, with substantial interests in Europe and elsewhere. In 1911 it had over 170 branches and agencies worldwide, only 40 of which were in Britain. Europe accounted for another 40, North America over 50. There were eight in Egypt and others in South Africa, Australia and the Far East, with even one in Japan.

While the firm was interested in any form of attraction which might draw crowds from a distance – Victoria's Diamond Jubilee, the English Cup final, the 1908 Olympics – and would assist the independent or business traveller to almost any destination at any time of the year, its main reputation lay in the conducted tour for the visitor, within Britain or Ireland, to Europe or the Middle East. These tours were tightly costed and carefully choreographed as to transport and accommodation. Cook had special arrangements for its tourists (with the Cook 'coupon') at hotels everywhere on the tourist trail: 234 hotels in Switzerland and 41 in Algeria, for example. It provided through its banking and foreign exchange department travellers' cheques, which were universally accepted, and its shipping department took care of the masses of luggage with which many tourists travelled.

The firm was well aware of the value of advertising and of promotion. Its magazine, *The Excursionist*, which later became Cook's monthly *Travellers Gazette,* was very widely read, which illustrates the level of destination marketing and promotion needed to attract the growing travelling elite. It published guidebooks for mainstream destinations, such as Florence, and for some more distant ones, including Burma. Its posters were attractive although their use in destination marketing remains largely unresearched. While the company's focus was perceived to have been tours within Britain and Europe, the importance of Egypt, where the company invested heavily in a fleet of Nile steamers, should not be underplayed nor its profitability within Cook's tourist operations underestimated. One American view in 1897 was that from the perspective of tourism 'Cook's simply owns Egypt'. Of the company's 2692 staff in 1891, one-third was located in Egypt.

Advertisements placed in *The Times* on 3 April 1911 and 24 July 1911 as part of the newspaper's regular tourism advertising (including railway timetables) highlight the nature of the company's investment in tourism, thus:

> In this special Easter edition of Cook's *Travellers Gazette*, particulars will be found of facilities for travelling to a large number of places in the British Isles and on the continent to which tickets at special holiday fares are issued. Among the features of Messrs. Cook's arrangements are combined travel and hotel tickets and conducted parties to Paris, Brussels and other parts of the Continent, including the Riviera. Messrs. Cook announce that their Ludgate Circus office and the more important of their branch offices in London will remain open until 9 o'clock from April 10 to April 20 for the transaction of tourist and excursion business (3 April 1911).

> Messrs. Thos. Cook and Son, who inform us that it is just 70 years ago that the first excursion train was run by Mr. Thomas Cook, the founder of the

firm, have just published a special Bank Holiday issue of *The Traveller's Gazette*, which is practically devoted to excursions. Cheap tickets can be purchased for most resorts in England and for short trips to the Continent, whether for travel only or combined with hotel accommodation. Messrs. Cook announce that their Ludgate Circus office and the more important of their branch offices in London will remain open until 9 o'clock each evening from July 31 to Saturday August 3 for the transaction of tourist and excursion business (24 July 1911).

This was a British family firm, owned in 1914 by the grandsons of the founder, but efficiently – with the odd hiccup – and successfully run. It was paternalistic in its management: John Cook (the founder's son) insisted that younger staff (those under 25) had to seek his permission first before they married. But they seem to have been paid well, with bonuses and commission part of the equation. There was a strong and experienced Accountant's Department, which kept a close check on what returns were being made from which activities and in what markets. Cook was able to monitor changes in the markets and had already had experience, thanks to the Sudan campaign and the Boer War, of what war might do either to disrupt the company's business or to offer new opportunities. Its Nile steamers were leased to the Army for Wolsey's expedition to relieve General Gordon: it was not Cook's fault that they reached Khartoum too late.

Of all the industries that war is likely to affect, tourism is surely the most vulnerable. No firm within the tourism industry in 1914 was more at risk than Cook with so much of their business within the European sphere of war operations, and also in the Middle East halted by the entry of Turkey into the First World War in November 1914. If the tourism industry as a whole was caught unprepared, with many thousands of British and American tourists stranded in Europe (although these were eventually evacuated), the outbreak of war also caught the company unprepared to a large degree. Brendon (1991, p. 255) has argued that Cook initially sought to operate 'business as usual', advertising tours to Europe, North America, Egypt, South Africa, Australia and the Far East, with 60 escorted tours abroad in October 1914. Yet by 1915, evidence of a slow down in tourism was evident, with no interest even in battlefield tours, a type of tourism to become very important in the 1920s.

There was no short-term crisis, i.e. over in a few months, with normal trading resumed quickly thereafter. One objective of this study is to show how the firm coped with a severe crisis that proved to be prolonged over four years, with the firm's main peacetime business being severely disrupted. Indeed, every aspect of the firm's operations was affected. In wartime, military and naval demands had first call on transport and the movement of people for non-military reasons by land or water was greatly restricted. The firm lost many of its pre-war clientele and destinations, staff and business alike. This state of affairs was reflected in the company's financial performance (Tables 19.2 and 19.3): the profitability of pre-war was changed into year after year of loss.

Some pre-war destinations were out of bounds, namely those in Germany and Austria, or in the war zone of France and Belgium, and even neutral countries were hard to reach. Tourism to, and in, Switzerland, once a profitable market for travel firms, collapsed completely. American tourists, a significant part of Cook's clientele, vanished from the

European scene for the duration of the war. Some of the company's assets overseas, as in Palestine, were seized by the Turks, whilst in Egypt they were taken over by the British Army or lay underused as with the Vesuvius railway in Italy. Tourism was used to good years and to bad – to some disruption – but the degree of difficulty experienced during the First World War was without precedence, either in intensity or in duration. It was a hard time, and one which savagely hit the firm's profits and left a legacy in the form of substantial provision for those staff wounded and unable to return to work: an allowance of £40,000 for 'war losses' was to feature each year in the post-war accounts.

Yet Cook, despite several years of heavy losses, as Table 19.3 shows, did survive. A central question of this study is how this occurred, given the vulnerability of a business devoted to leisure and pleasure in a world of total war, a war which was not over by Christmas but which dragged on year after year. In attempting to find an answer to why there was not a collapse, our analysis is handicapped by the absence of key records which might shed light on the firm's planning and operations, such as the Directors' Minute Books. There is no statistical data which would indicate the volume of the firm's tourist business, nor financial information to show earnings from particular activities. *The Travellers' Gazette* that the firm published throughout the war years, and of which Brendon (1991) makes imaginative use, is valuable in showing what products the company was still marketing, but it offers little insight into how Cook's management controlled the firm's response.

We shall be examining how far, given the nearly total closure of European and Middle Eastern operations, Cook was able to continue their staple business of providing services for the tourist traveller, albeit with an enhanced focus on New World tourism and British domestic tourism. It will be argued that while the war put a stop to tourism within Europe, from North America to Europe and in the Middle East, there were still areas of opportunity outside Europe. Additionally, judicious redeployment of the firm's expertise in the logistics of travel allowed it to participate directly and indirectly in the business of war in, for example, handling enemy mail through Holland. There may also have been an element of luck in the short term; the effort in retrieving stranded tourists in Europe in the early autumn of 1914 used staff resources which otherwise would have lain underemployed. In any case staff numbers and the wages bill were being trimmed by the enthusiasm of younger employees to enlist, with over 500 by the early months of 1915 joining as volunteers at the peak of enlistment prior to the introduction of conscription in 1916. Costs were cut to match falling revenue, and the company's trading loss did fall in the latter stages of the war.

Table 19.2: Financial performance of Thomas Cook 1909–23 (5-year average). [£'000]

Period	Trading surplus [Loss]	Profit [Loss] after depreciation, etc.	Aggregate profit [Loss]
1909–13	+136	+119	+ 596
1914–18	−18 [loss]	− 55	− 274
1919–23	+266	+214	+1068

Source: Figures compiled by the Chief Accountant in the 1970s, using company records which have since disappeared.

Table 19.3: Financial performance of Thomas Cook 1913–19 (£').

	Trading Profit [Loss]	Final Profit/Loss
1913	+164,396	+132,714
1914	+42,259	+ 14,821
1915	− 40,195	− 94,485
1916	−28,160	− 70,247
1917	−46,454	− 74,713
1918	−18,062	− 21,037
1919	+194,498	+139,268

Tourism and the First World War: A General Perspective

The First World War and its aftermath, whilst widely studied for its military, social and economic effects, remains almost a virgin territory for tourism researchers with only a limited number of incursions by historians (e.g. Durie, 2006; Walton, 1996; Durie and McPherson, 1999). Moreover many of these studies have been place-specific rather than examining generic tourism trends and issues. There seems to have been a general assumption, only recently challenged, that as far as Britain and Europe were concerned there was no tourism. A brief overview may therefore be helpful to challenge the conventional interpretations that argue that war led to a cessation of all tourist travel in this period.

The outbreak of war in early August 1914, at the peak of the tourism season, was a crisis for the tourism sector in Britain and the Continent. Durie (2006, p. 106) noted that 'the immediate impact of the start of hostilities was a general departure from all holiday resorts [in Britain]. Everywhere bookings were cancelled'. The situation was just as bad on the Continent where there was a rush of tourists trying to get back home – Britons to avoid internment, and Americans to escape the war zone. American Express found itself left with over 15,000 pieces of heavy luggage and hundreds of motor cars abandoned at their European offices. The British press was full of stories of flight and escape, and readers found pictures of 'refugees and tourists seeking safety in Britain' (*The Motor World*, 3 September, 1914).

What is important to note is that tourism in Britain, after the initial panic, was to recover; tourism within Europe (with very limited exceptions) was not. There were optimistic noises made by *The Times* on 12 December 1914 in an article entitled 'Visiting France', which noted that the French Riviera was feasibly accessible and the war had led to a drop in hotel prices there. Cook had recently re-opened their offices on the French Riviera (at Mentone and Nice). But as the war progressed, the British visitor to the Continent became increasingly uncommon though a few still ventured to Paris. The domestic situation was not much better. Easter 1915 in Britain saw Easter and Whitsun excursion trains suspended and *The Times* 27 March 1915 was reporting on 'a blank and depressing prospect'. There are, of course, no neat statistical series to confirm how domestic tourism in Britain fared, but a number of proxy sources can be examined to confirm this picture.

The Times *Newspaper as a Source of Wartime Travel Conditions in Britain 1914–18*

The value of newspapers – national, regional or local – has been widely recognized by historical researchers as a vital source of information about issues and events. While they may inevitably be a source of bias over what was covered, the use of a leading newspaper tracks general tourism in some degree of detail. *The Times* newspaper, typically a 16-page broadsheet during wartime Britain, which was produced 6 days a week, carried reports on everyday matters as well as political and military affairs, on music, sport and travel as well as battlefield news. Their advertising for hotels, resorts, excursions and sailings, as well as specific articles described the state of the holiday industry, the level of travel to resorts and the impact of specific events on the sector.

On 10 December 1914, after four months of conflict and when it had become evident that the war would not be over by Christmas, *The Times* carried a lengthy article entitled 'Christmas at Home: War Hindrances to Foreign Travel' in which it discussed what might be on offer. It had traditionally focused on travel in the run up to Christmas when it usually published the programmes of railway companies and tourist agencies for the coming year. The article commenced with a tongue in cheek quip by noting a 'conspicuous lack of advertisements this year urging visits to spend Christmas in Berlin, Vienna, in Constantinople and Belgium'. It did suggest, however, that Christmas in Paris, Boulogne and the French Riviera was practicable, if adventurous, despite the French and Belgian railway system being geared up to military requirements. Whilst Egypt was not available for winter sun holidays, much of the Mediterranean region remained open: Spain was at peace and Portugal and the North African coast were open. Winter sport destinations in neutral Switzerland, Norway and Sweden were also available.

There were, therefore, options for the traveller, though they were warned that they should expect delays with increased scrutiny of passports and formalities highlights the disruption caused by war. It might cost more and take longer, but in France an increase in rail travel prices because of the war was partially compensated for by 'war tariffs' which limited hotel prices. But the same article, while arguing that travel abroad for pleasure was feasible, questioned whether it was 'right' at such a time of national emergency but:

> ... for those who can still feel the holiday spirit, the home railways are making the usual arrangements for excursions and holiday tours and the usual attractions ... numberless hotels and similar places to tempt the Christmas visitor.

This article was accompanied by a page of advertising for resort hotels and the principal Christmas train services in Britain including options for day trips as shown in Table 19.4. This summary of the main advertisements illustrates a confirmation of the ongoing promotion and encouragement of wartime travel. Indeed tourism was possible beyond Britain. Throughout the war, *The Times* listing of Foreign Sailings, Home Arrivals and Home Sailings continued to show a wide range of passenger vessels sailing outside of the main war zones even after the torpedoing of a Cunard liner, The Lusitania, off the Irish Coast in 1915.

Table 19.4: Christmas Railway Company Advertising (December 1914) from London Termini.

Company	Type of service over Christmas
Great Western Railway	Paddington to Ireland, Wiltshire, Somerset, Devon, Cornwall, Wales and Gloucestershire services. Day trips/half-day trips to: Cardiff, Swansea, Birmingham, Leamington, Warwick, Cheltenham Races (the steeplechase on 26 December).
Midland Railway	Fenchurch Street to Leigh, West Cliffe, Southend on Sea, Thorpe Bay. Cheap Weekend Tickets to Shoeburyness (61 – First Class; 3/10 – Third Class) Cheap Day Returns to Leigh, West Cliffe and Southend on Sea (2/6 – Third Class).
Southeast and Chatham Railway	Charing Cross to Kent Christmas Day – Sunday Service.
Great Eastern Railway	Liverpool Street to Harwich/Colchester Christmas Day and Boxing Day Cheap Day Return 4/3 – Third Class
Brighton and South Coast Railway	Cheap Period Return to South coast resorts.
London and North Western Railway	Euston to the Midlands, Lake District – Christmas Day special trains.
Furness Railway	Rock climbing in Lakeland holidays.
London and South West Railway	Waterloo to Bournemouth/West Country trains.

Shipping Services during the War

Table 19.5 provides a summary of one such entry for 6 March 1915 to illustrate the geographical extent of the passenger shipping even during wartime. (An in-depth analysis of passenger arrival lists might help to illustrate the scale of tourist travel during wartime but it is outside the remit of this study.) What is notable from Table 19.5 are the interruptions noted by some shipping lines passing through shipping lanes with enemy patrols but it is clear that there was no general suspension of passenger travel, although 'fear' of submarine actions was a real deterrent to potential travellers. Even so, the history of P&O

Table 19.5: Advertisements in The Times newspaper of Shipping Lines from the UK, 6 March 1915.

Company and Principal Services and Destinations Peninsula and Oriental Steam Navigation Company – Mail and Passenger Services – Egypt, India, Straits, China, Japan, Australasia Services departing March 11–March 27 to: Colombo/Calcutta; Bombay and Karachi; Australia and Indo China; Colombo and Calcutta; Straits, China, Japan; Bombay and Karachi (with intermediate stops at Gibraltar/Malta).

'All sailings are liable to cancellation or deviation without notice due to the war'.

'Every Third Week from London via the Cape to Australian ports, conveying one class of passenger only at Third Class rates'.

British India Co. Services to Egypt, Ceylon, India, Persian Gulf, East Africa, Burma, Straits, Mauritius, China, Japan and Australia.

Departures 6 March to 3 April to Karachi and Bombay; Colombo, Madras, Calcutta; Queensland; Karachi and Bombay; Colombo, Madras, Calcutta.

British India Steam Navigation Co. – passenger service to South of France, Egypt, Ceylon and India.

Ellerman's City and Hall Lines from Liverpool to Egypt and India. Owing to the war, the regular passage is suspended. The following special steamers have been arranged subject to government requisition 14 March to 2 April: Colombo and Calcutta; Karachi and Bombay; Calcutta direct; Bombay and Karachi; Colombo and Calcutta; Bombay and Karachi.

Harrison Line from Liverpool: Calcutta Direct.

Anchor Line East Passenger Line: Liverpool to Bombay.

Bibby Line. Twin Screw Mail Steamers fortnightly for Marseilles, Egypt, Ceylon, Burma and Southern India.

Aberdeen Line: Australia via the Cape First Class Fares from £45; Third Class from £18.

The Blue Funnel Line: Australia and South Africa only First Class carried.

SS&A Cos Royal Mail steamers calling at Tenerife, Cape Town and Hobart (New Zealand and Australia).

N.Z.S.Co (New Zealand Shipping Company) to New Zealand, Tasmania, Cape Town and Tenerife.

Nippon Yasen Kaisha: Japan direct in 45 days. From London and Marseilles to Colombo, Singapore, Hong Kong and Shanghai.

Union-Castle Line: South and East Africa (The Cape, Transvaal, Rhodesia and weekly for South Africa). Alternatives including deviation without notice.

E&B (Ellerman and Bucknall Steamship Company Ltd): London to South Africa, 'owing to the war all arrangements are subject to cancelment or alteration with or without notice'.

Elder Demster and Co Ltd: West Africa Express Service.

Harrison Rennie Line: Cape Town, Natal, East Africa.

Cunard Line: Liverpool to New York (ships: March 6 Orduna; March 13 Lusitania; 29 March Cameronia; 27 March Transylvannia).

The Pacific Steam Navigation Co: West coast of South America (Chile, Peru, Ecuador).

Yeoward Line: Lisbon, Madeira and Canary Island

---

for the period (Howarth and Howarth, 1986) shows that the company had continued passenger services on its steamship services to many Far Eastern destinations and maintained its passenger traffic. However the unrestricted U-boat campaign made sailing even to neutral countries risky (this reached a climax in 1917).

According to Howarth and Howarth (1986), despite the war P&O and many shipping lines continued to publish regular sailings to Imperial destinations and further afield. For example, *The Times* newspaper front pages for the period 1914–18 regularly feature such advertisements. P&O is a good example of the period having just amalgamated on the eve of war with British India (BI), which dominated the passenger, freight and mail services to the Far East. The merger created a company with 131 steamers, of which 60 were requisitioned during 1914–18 for war service but only two ships in total were lost in war service in the early days of war. As Howarth and Howarth observed, P&O's mail service was not restricted at all until June 1917 and in 1916 the Chairman of P&O addressed the Board stating that

> week after week with unfamiliar regularity, without exception, all through these 16 months of war, the P&O mail steamers have started on their voyages from this country to far ends of the earth with their usual complement of passengers, just as in times of peace'. (Howarth and Howarth, 1986, p. 120)

This underlines the continuity of business travel to the Empire, despite the initial onset of war. At an operational level, war-risk insurance proved a major financial burden for all shipping companies and P&O continued to acquire overseas shipping companies and new routes to spread the risk of its business. The year 1917 saw 44 ships lost to enemy action and an additional 14 in 1918. The company continued to expand its routes, purchasing the Orient Line towards the end of 1918 and the Khedivial Mail Line in 1919 along with the General Steam Navigation Company in 1920 and the Strick Line in 1923 to give the company around 500 ships as passenger traffic boomed in the early 1920s.

Domestic Tourism in the UK during the War

In terms of domestic tourism in Britain the war had several effects, which gained momentum as the war went on. The war created a new demand from soldiers, with many London and coastal hotels developing services for soldiers on leave looking for rest and recreation (R&R) trade. London was the focal point of the administration of troop movements by the War Department and benefitted from troops en route and on leave, from a wide range of nationalities as advertisements in *The Times* of the period show. Many hotels, hydros and hospitals were taken over for the treatment of wounded soldiers, particularly those at the spa resorts with medical facilities such as baths. For example, 134 wartime hospitals for military use were converted from civilian use. As the scale of injuries and psychological problems associated with trench warfare and shellshock emerged, more were converted. Sadly, this also generated leisure and tourist travel by friends and family who visited injured loved ones in many major cities and ports that were points of disembarkation for hospital ships and trains, as vividly described in Vera Brittain's *Testament of Youth* (Brittain 1978).

An article in *The Times* (25 March 1915) reported heavy volumes of cross-channel traffic to France for Easter of families visiting military wounded at the British Expeditions Force Hospitals. On the following day *The Times* also noted reported travel by families to visit enlisted men in military camps for Easter, and cheap tickets for travel by sea were available to such camps. On 24 December 1914 *The Times* mentioned day-excursions of wounded Indian troops who had itineraries planned in batches of 20 at a time to visit London and see the sights by charabanc. Visiting troops also feature: One response by the tourism industry, as an article on 6 March 1915 in *The Times* confirms, was a number of spa resorts advertising their wares, such as Buxton which was described as 'provincial and middle class' where 'soldiers can undergo ... special treatments ... recovering from wounds or illness contracted in conflict'. This advertising continued throughout the war in *The Times*: 23 identical 'Resorts, Spas and Hotels' features were published in 1914–16 alone.

While accommodation was more restricted, not all hotels were requisitioned and spas still found room for the non-military person who needed a tonic. An 1915 advertisement proclaimed 'The British Spa, where the Hot Springs bring health and strength to aching limbs, and good music and charming surroundings give rest and recuperation to the mind. Leave again fit and well'. A 'Resorts, Spas and Hotels' section in *The Times* on 25 March 1916 saw most leading spa resorts advertising and as Table 19.6 shows, these destinations were also being advertised in 1917 in Cook's *Travellers Gazette*.

A consequence of the war (and the virtual closure of the Continent) was that British tourists who would previously have gone abroad were now more likely to holiday at home. Heavy snow allowed Buxton a boom in winter sports, drawing in part from those who would presumably have gone in peacetime to Switzerland. In a similar vein,

Table 19.6: Thomas Cook & Sons of Great Britain: resorts promoted for health tourism.

Bath
Buxton
Cheltenham
Droitwich
Harrogate
Ilkley
Leamington
Llandrinod Wells
Malvern
Matlock
Strathpeffer
Tunbridge Wells
Woodhall Spa

Source: The Travellers Gazette, June 1917.

Brighton was advertised by the London Brighton and South Coast Railway: 'The South Coast Watering Places offer an Excellent Substitute for the Continental Resorts'. A further effect of the war was that tourism was geographically more concentrated in Britain. Following the German Navy's raids on Whitby and Scarborough in November and December 1914 these East Coast resorts saw their leisure trade slump due to fear of further attack. Other favourite pre-war destinations were handicapped by the transport situation, and the shortage of steamers (many of the steamers were requisitioned for war use in transporting troops across the English Channel) crippled travel to the Isle of Man and the Clyde coastal resorts alike – to the benefit of mainland destinations in the west.

The tourist industry in those areas of Britain that were still accessible was, therefore, in a strong position, and those hotels which were not requisitioned were in a good position to benefit. Theirs was not an easy life, particularly as the war continued, because of staff shortages and the cost of food, but demand had to come to them. Nor were there any new hotels to leech business away. Work on the great railway hotel at Gleneagles was suspended and did not resume until 1919. Interviews with leading hotels in 1915 indicated that business was good even if the American visitor had disappeared. It was noted regretfully in *The Times* (30 March 1915), under the heading of 'The American Summer Invasion: Prospects in London' that President Roosevelt had warned US citizens not to summer in London. But there was an opportunity for British domestic tourism to capitalize on demand from those who would in peacetime have gone abroad. Cook, as we shall see, had their eye on this.

Although tourism to the Isle of Man and Ireland was handicapped by the difficulties of transport, as was travel to the Highlands, seaside resorts in the south and west of mainland Britain (away from the east coast which the Germans had shelled) fared quite well. For example, in a letter to *The Times* 13 July 1916 titled 'East Coast Resorts: Holiday visitors wanted', the writer noted 'the hotel keepers on the brink of despair' as visitors deserted the resorts after shelling. This led the government, via a special fund to compensate Scarborough with a £10,700 grant for the loss of rates. The situation was worsened by the migration of workers out of the town to more lucrative munitions work elsewhere, replacing employment in tourism. *The Times* reported that up to £30,000 in total was distributed in compensation to a wide range of east coast resorts including: £16,000 plus £5000 to Margate; £14,750 to Great Yarmouth; £7500 to Bridlington; £7000 to Lowestoft; £5000 to Cromer; £4560 to Clacton; £4000 to Ramsgate; £3100 to Skegness; £3100 to Cleethorpes; £2400 to Sheringham; £2000 to Broadstairs; £16,000 to Filey; £1500 to Herne Bay and £1000 to Felixstowe. The Borough Councils saw this assistance as inadequate.

One consequence of wartime shelling of East Coast resorts was the geographical concentration of demand on West Coast, South Coast and West of England resorts. Add to this the redirection of European travel to domestic destinations, and it is then evident that tourism did not cease. In fact, evidence from *The Times* newspaper between 1915 and 1918 confirms this spatial impact, despite government attempts to restrict travel. For example, an article entitled 'Holidays at Home: Heavy traffic to South Coast resorts' (2 April 1915) noted the addition of relief trains to cope with Easter demand and the impact on 'Brighton, Folkestone, Eastbourne, Bournemouth and Torquay [which] attracted the bulk of holidaymakers', with hotels and accommodation establishments having 'full houses'.

Similarly, the Isle of Wight, Matlock and Buxton 'attracted thousands', while 'Blackpool and other resorts' were busier with a 'greater use of bicycles and special omnibuses' to reach the destinations. This was reiterated in an article 'Holiday Prospects: Busy season expected at chief resorts' (31 July 1915). A similar article for Easter 1916 'Seaside Resorts Crowded' (22 April 1916) commented on Brighton being a 'town full to eclipse all records' and on 25 April 1916 an article noted crowding in London at Easter ('Holiday Sightseeing: Crowds in London'), especially at key visitor attractions. At the main resorts, the short commentary 'Report from Seaside Resorts' observed the spatial reconfiguration of tourism demand: West Coast and South Coast resorts fared well but East Coast resorts remained quiet or devoid of their traditional visitor markets as the following summary (by resort) suggests:

- Blackpool: 'In spite of the curtailment of railway facilities and withdrawal of cheap bookings, Blackpool never had a busier Easter tide ... All the hotels and boarding houses were overflowing'.
- Bournemouth: 'The withdrawal of cheap travelling facilities on the railways militated against a Bank Holiday crowd ... visitors promenaded in large numbers on the Marine drive'.
- Brighton: 'No Bank Holiday trippers ... but was full of tourists since Thursday'.
- Clacton-on-Sea: 'The number of visitors was far in excess of last year [1915], the railway returns being double of the corresponding day in 1915'.
- Cromer: 'Few general holidaymakers'.
- Lake District: 'Large crowds and ... cragsmen (climbers)'.
- Ramsgate: 'Fewer visitors than 1915' but large numbers swelled by Canadian troops.
- Torquay: 'A drop ... [in visitors]' as the races were cancelled.
- Great Yarmouth: 'Fewer than 1915 and an absence of excursionists ... [with] ... two sports meetings for soldiers and sailors' which created a good spectator audience.

Source: *The Times*, 25 April 1916.

From the 1830s, London's pleasure steamers had provided daily services from London down the River Thames to Southend and the Kent resorts. But many of these vessels were requisitioned during the war for the carriage of troops to Europe. This accommodated the call to arms and voluntary recruitment of over 1.5 million soldiers from the UK from August 1914 to 1915, prior to the onset of conscription. The impact of such requisitioning was the curtailment of river-borne leisure and tourism trips, and of rail services which also had a key role in moving the rapidly formed regiments to the embarkation ports. For example, *The Railway and Travel Monthly* in March 1915 reported that in the 'last six months, LNWR provided 7000 special military trains, and 70,000 staff signed up for war. The military traffic takes precedence over the civil traffic'.

Whilst hotels had lost key staff, such as French and German waiters or staff, other hotels had been taken over for hospitals or convalescent homes, with the Adelphi in Liverpool being used for both purposes by 1917. The situation was to change thereafter, but not in a straightforward fashion. Clearly many young men were away on military service and, depending on what theatre of war they were in, their eye was on leave rather than holidays. The unfit, unconscripted, the elderly and the young were still able to holiday if they had the time and the income, but there was some pressure on them to restrict their travel in the national interest. 'It is not a time when time or money can be spent on idle holidays or extended pleasure seeking', thundered *The Times* in December 1914. Motor touring for pleasure, for example, was frowned on and luxury duties after 1915 (the McKenna Duties) sought to restrict such conspicuous consumption. But sporting tourism for the elite continued; the record bag in a day for grouse in Britain was set on a Lancashire moor at Littledale on 12 August 1915.

There was a group who presented a growing dilemma: the army of munitions workers whose output was essential to the war effort. The government found itself every summer caught between the desperate need for output, and the recognition that the efficiency of these workers would suffer without some holiday time – an issue explored in a Parliamentary Inquiry in 1917. In fact, the Prime Minister Lloyd George's speech, reported in *The Times* (27 May 1916) in 'The Deplorable Effect of Easter', criticized the impacts of Easter holidays on munitions output, which dropped by 50%, and sought to cancel the Whitsun Holiday to help the war effort. At the same time, in the summer of 1917, the government appealed to the population to forego the summer holidays of 7 and 14 days.

By January 1917, changes induced by the war led *The Railway and Travel Monthly* to carry an article, entitled 'Our Railways and the War. The Cooperation of Travellers', in which the government sought to reduce pleasure travel due to major logistical problems with the war effort and munitions, rationing and the knock-on effect of limited food supplies due to shipping losses associated with German U-boats. As the following extract from *The Railway and Travel Monthly*[1] shows, pleasure travel expanded in wartime alongside military traffic rather than contracting as military travel grew, despite government restrictions and price increases on travel. As the article explained:

> Pleasure travel has also increased as a result of the war. So many hundreds of thousands of people who are earning wages largely in excess of those obtaining in normal times spend a proportion of their income in pleasure trips, that the trains are crowded with unnecessary passengers. From January 1st new restrictions [apply] – an increase in fares (50% for long-distance) with exceptional consideration in cases of travelling on business of national importance.

This expansion of pleasure travel ran alongside restrictions in the number and use of restaurant cars and sleeping cars, except for official and strictly business purposes. There was also the suspension of all rail services for sporting events and the removal of outstanding cheap facilities. For the military, weekend leave for UK-based troops was also reduced to remove unnecessary travel alongside that of voluntary workers. The impacts of these major changes were reflected in the financial performance of the

---

1. *The Railway and Travel Monthly* has been published since 1900 on a monthly basis and was a popular magazine featuring rail-related issues and is located at the National Archives in the ZPER53 series, many of which are in a fragile state.

Midland Railway which saw fares rise 50% in 1916–17 and receipts were £250,000 more in 1917 than 1916. In other words, Midland saw its revenue stay virtually static in the period 1916–17, declaring a turnover of £14,430,000 in 1917 (although this was still £500,000 greater than the company's record earnings in 1913).

These changes, which sought to limit leisure travel, did not prevent the arrival of hordes of girls, the munitionettes, with money to spend, as many resorts commented during this period. This is reflected in the rise in the female workforce, where the proportion rose by 50% from 3.3 million women employed in 1914 (equivalent to 23.7% of the civilian workforce) to 4.9 million by July 1918 (37% of the workforce) at a time when the total civilian workforce dropped 15% (1914–18) due to war service. Broadberry and Howlett (2005) indicate that government statistics for employment show women to have been disproportionately employed in munitions production where they made up almost 47% of those employed. However, female employment dropped after 1918, returning to almost pre-1911 levels, comprising 2.4% of civilian employment in the 1921 census.

This illustrates the arrival during the war of a new leisure and tourism constituency – women with a new found employment status and disposable income. The munitions workers proved to be a powerful driver of tourism demand, with *The Times* carrying a one page advertising sheet on 18 May 1917 entitled 'Resorts for War Workers', with a diverse range of English resorts and establishments promoting their wares. These promotions probably led to a further growth in resort tourism, even in the austere conditions of 1917: *The Times* reported on 4 August 1917 that 'August Holiday: Holiday resorts crowded', commenting on the shift from East Coast to South and South West Coast resorts.

One indication of the new found wealth of the munitions worker was the government's provision of bonuses of 7.5–12% (depending on the type of work/grade and method of payment) in January 1918, reported on 24 January 1918 by *The Times* ('Munitions Workers Bonus'). This created disposable income but also industrial discontent in other trades, such as tramway workers, with London and several resorts seeing strikes in August 1918. *The Times* reported that, during the Bank Holiday of August 1918, stoppages occurred in Bath, Brighton, Hove, Bristol, Folkestone, Hastings and Weston-Super-Mare (aside from London) at 'seaside resorts crowded with holidaymakers'.

Tourism in Britain, therefore, though limited by the war, may have actually grown if the contemporary accounts of the railway companies and reports are indicative of the wider trends in tourism and leisure. But was that the kind of business in which Cook were interested and from which they could profit? While the founder Thomas Cook had started his business by providing temperance trips for the working class, in the later nineteenth century the firm had increasingly moved away from the mass market. The firm dealt with the tourist to Baden Baden, and traditional holidays, but not the day-tripper to Blackpool. It might cater for the group picnic or the respectable outing, but not the rowdy day excursion. That was not the area in which its expertise could be turned to profit. So the growth of working class tourism during the war, much of it short stay, was not Cook territory.

Middle class demand for tourism continued, as Durie (2006, p. 109) noted with reference to Scotland's hydro hotels. Hydro hotels continued to advertise in *The Times*, as did inland and seaside resort hotels. But this was not business that could benefit a tour organizer. It was mostly low key, shorter distance tourism, with a destination of a single hotel, which needed no agent's assistance. People got what information they needed either from direct contact with the hotels or through the advertising of the railway companies. This is very much borne out by the analysis of railway company advertising of holiday destinations and travel in *The Railway and Travel Monthly* for the period 1914–18. Throughout the war, the railway companies continued to pursue an active programme of destination marketing and advertising to encourage leisure and tourist travel.

A summary of the main advertising pursued in *The Railway and Travel Monthly* in 1915 is also shown in Appendix 19.1. These advertisements demonstrate, as studies of railway posters show (Williamson, 1998; Cole and Durack, 1992; Bennet, 2002), that destination promotion by the railway companies even before the heyday of the 1930s age of poster campaigns was sophisticated and aligned with destination attributes to build holiday traffic among all social classes.

But there were difficulties. The South East and Chatham Railway (SE & Chatham) imposed restrictions on travel to France in March 1915 whilst most mainline stations in London saw the temporary expansion of waiting room facilities for troops to separate civilian from military traffic and to avoid congestion. The Great North Railway withdrew its Sunday services in May 1915 to the north and south of London to allow increased troop movements, while staff shortages were addressed by employing female clerks, porters and ticket examiners on the London, North Western Railway (LNWR) and Caledonian Railway in 1915. Despite these changes to services, 1915 saw the continued promotion of tourist and leisure travel by train as well as many colour poster advertising campaigns to promote traditional summer season holidays and off-peak travel to resorts. The selection listed in Table 19.7, annually reviewed by *The Railway and Travel Monthly*, illustrated the diversity of coastal, inland, urban and remote scenery underpinned by the health giving properties of holidays where fresh air and a change from an urban industrial lifestyle could be enjoyed.

Whilst further changes to rail services, such as GER removing Sunday services in May 1916 and planning station closures due to staff shortages, there was no evidence to suggest tourist and leisure travel was being curtailed. Whilst statistical collection of passenger statistics ceased between 1914–18, *The Railway and Travel Monthly* did note that in 1915 NER carried 67 million passengers, 2 million troops and 250,000 tons of freight. However, the South East and Chatham Railway hotel operations were more widely affected by wartime conditions, posting a profit of £15,000 in 1914 but only £1,732 in 1915, which may account for the advertising by railway hotels as shown in Table 19.8. Even so, the same railway company that reported only £1,732 profit on income of £115,834 in 1915 saw a revival in its fortunes in 1916 with income of £153,076 and a profit of £29,841 despite government controls. Thus, wartime travel and tourism did prove variable and, as with any difficult operating environment, advertising and marketing was seen as necessary to maintained its customers' interest in travel.

The East Coast was not actively promoted but many other traditional holiday destinations accessible to major conurbations (e.g. the West Country, eastern England and North Wales) were regularly advertised. What Table 19.7 reviews is the almost constant promotion of rail-borne holiday travel for 1914–18, even despite the government attempts to restrict travel. The continued use of the famous railway poster, which achieved a contemporary art form in the 1930s (Bennet, 2002; Cole and Durack, 1992; Watts,

Table 19.7: Railway posters from 1915 and their main destination slogans.

Bournemouth by L&SW	'Bournemouth by the Southern Sea'
East Coast Route by GNR	'Quickest Route between London and Edinburgh'
North Staffordshire Railway	'Rudyard Lake – 200 acres of water'
Cambrian Railways	'Beautiful Holidays on the Shores of Cardigan Bay'
London Metropolitan Railway	'The Met – the Best Way' (for travel into London)
GWR	'Another Comparison: Home Riviera : Continental Riviera – where's the difference? See your own country first'
London, Brighton and South Coast Railway	'Come South – the South Coast Watering Places'
Furness Railway	'The English Lakeland'
London and South West Railway	'Exeter and Countryside'
Great Eastern Railways	'Country Holidays in East Anglia'
Festiniog Railway	'12 miles up mountainside through enchanting scenery'
London Electric Railway	'Southend and its pier poster'

Source: *The Railway and Travel Monthly*, July 1915 ZPER 53/13, National Archives, Kew.

2004) but was well developed by 1914, and the continuing use of railway guide books and destination guides linked with rail travel does not illustrate a drop in the promotion of tourist travel. Indeed, the London Underground throughout this period continued to promote off-peak and suburban travel to the urban fringe and London's accessible countryside despite wartime conditions. During 1914–18, the London Transport poster collection (www.ltmcollection.org) shows that some 152 posters promoting leisure travel were produced, epitomized by the promotion of travel to individual resorts in Essex, Suffolk, Kent and the South Coast as well as day trips to the countryside (Plate 19.3). But how do these findings and the evidence of tourism and leisure travel and advertising fit with the established literature on how firms react to crises in tourism?

How Firms React to Crises

During crises the tourism sector is not necessarily as passive and reactive as many researchers would imply. The analysis of crises in tourism and the impact upon the sector has a well-established generic literature (e.g. Lynch, 2004; Henderson, 2007; Glaesser, 2003; Beirman, 2003) along with a multitude of research papers which depict the impact of specific events on visitor volumes. Most of these studies are secondary source-dependent or based on interviews with industry organizations to understand how leaders of the sector reacted and responded to crises. In any crises, the underlying principles of how businesses

Table 19.8: Advertising of railway hotels 1916–18 in *The Railway and Travel Monthly.*

October 1916 – LNWR List of Hotels

Railway Station	Railway Hotel Name
London Euston	Euston Hotel
Birmingham New Street	Queens Hotel
Liverpool Lime Street	North Western Hotel
Bletchley	Station Hotel
Crewe	Crewe Arms
Greenore	Greenore Hote
Preston	Park Hotel
Dublin	North Western Hotel

'Hotel porters meet trains and boats to convey luggage free to/from hotels'

July 1917 – Furness Railway – Furness Abbey Hotel, Barrow in Furness.

January 1918 – Midland Railway Hotels

Railway Station	Railway Hotel Name
London	Midland Grand
Manchester	The Midland
Liverpool	The Midland Adelphi*
Morecambe	The Midland
Belfast Midland	Station Hotel
Leeds	The Queens
Bradford	The Midland
Derby	The Midland
Portrush	Northern Counties Hotel

January 1918 – Lancashire and Yorkshire Railway – Exchange Hotel, Liverpool to March 1918 and June 1918.

* Whilst the Midland Railway spent £547,000 on purchasing the Adelphi Hotel, and a further £6000 in 1915 on refurbishing it, by May 1917 declining visitor numbers led it to lease half of it to the government for use as a military hospital/recuperation centre.

and organizations (e.g. National Tourism Organizations) react and respond to the onset of the situation are based on business continuity.

Within the emerging field of business continuity and emergency planning,[3] the key principles are to retain or recover the business activity to allow a degree of normality to exist or, at the extreme, to implement strategies to survive. One area of activity in tourism is increased

3. In 2006, a new academic journal was launched around this theme – *The Journal of Business Continuity and Emergency Planning*, reflecting its key role in the public and private sector.

Figure 19.1: Easter 1915 (*Source*: London Transport Museum).

advertising and marketing activity to promote a destination and to convey a 'business as usual' image or 'open for business' during a crisis, as illustrated by railway companies. Much of the literature from the public and private sector (see Page and Yeoman [2006] for a recent review with a tourism example) is about making plans in advance (i.e. being proactive towards known and unknown threats, given the growing turbulence in tourism operations with the rise of global terrorism, natural disasters and other events. The application of management science to this area (i.e. business continuity planning) has also become enshrined in legislation in some countries (e.g. the UK) so that public sector agencies prepare plans for most eventualities.

In this context, scenario planning also has a key role to play in understanding how tourism organizations prepare for extreme events such as war. A hundred years ago, however, many of the scientific disciplines which now contribute to the study of crises (e.g. management science) and their application of planning principles to business settings were still in their infancy if not non-existent. Therefore, in any retrospective analysis of events such as the First World War, we need to recognize that many of the concepts and techniques of analysis we can apply to that period were not in existence. Nevertheless, what is important in the context of this book is that entrepreneurship in tourism was and the need to respond to crises not just a modern day phenomenon. Cook is a case in point since the company clearly embraced many of the modern day principles of survival, through ad hoc measures that involved adaptation and innovation, but this raises numerous questions on how these principles were developed and executed in an age that pre-dates information technology and global media.

Thomas Cook & Sons – Tourism and Entrepreneurship: Questions and Answers

In evaluating the response of the firm to the events of the war period, it is important to avoid the wisdom of hindsight as to how far Cook could and should have planned ahead. That war would come, and come so rapidly in August 1914, was by no means inevitable. Nor was it anticipated by popular or informed opinion that this war would last years rather than a few months. It is always promised that wars will 'be over by Christmas'. In other words, short-term policies in 1914 and the absence of a longer-term strategy may not have been defective management. Brendon (1991, p. 255) praises the firm for responding promptly to the first emergency, which involved the retrieval of thousands of stranded tourists and their luggage from around Europe in the early autumn of 1914, but equally criticises it for being 'slow to appreciate the implications of Armageddon'. Is this not hindsight? While the firm's past might have given it some experience on which to draw in planning for the effects of war, such as the Boer War and Sudan campaign, this was a very different kind of war in its intensity and in its geographical coverage. Previous military campaigns did not completely disrupt main destinations and travel routes, since Africa could easily be substituted by other destinations in the event of war.

While most attention has been focused on what happened to the demand for tourism and the closure of destinations, it is important also to review the firm's operations as the war progressed. After its impressive activity in 1914 to retrieve tourists stranded in Europe, which may have been profitable as well as good publicity, how far did it continue with tourism, accommodating its marketing to changing destinations and clientele? Was diversification Cook's aim? How far, and how successfully, did the firm try to find new markets for a changed clientele or, in the case of the Americans, a clientele who could no longer visit Europe?

Although international tourism withered, there was some business travel to Europe: the organization of travel for a number of business fairs arranged by the government including the Lyons Fair in 1916, 1917 and 1918 generated much needed income with around 57 million francs of business in 1916 and 18 million francs in 1917 – a surprising level of interest, given the location so near the Front. The 40 or so North American and Canadian offices of Thomas Cook did good business with tours to Alaska and the Pacific, and in February 1917 the claim was made there that 'the closing of once popular regions by war may be forgotten. It is a negligible factor in the situation' (Brendon, 1991, p. 257). Japan was much promoted; although on the Allied side, it was a long way from the conflict. In 1917, a 60-day tour from San Francisco was on offer at $750 (Williamson, 1998, p. 88).

In short, the loss of European (and Egyptian) business may have been at least partially compensated for by increased business elsewhere. The business data is not available to confirm this nor indeed to show which destinations – home, European, Egypt and Palestinian, or further afield – were the most important in terms of business pre-war. Were the losses from 1914 onwards the result purely of the downturn in the European (and Middle Eastern) markets alone? We do not know how much of the firm's business was 'domestic' as opposed to European or worldwide travel, either pre-war or between 1914–18. But there does seem to have been, if the publicity material is indicative, a shift to domestic promotion in June 1915 as noted in the *Travellers Gazette* (p. 7):

> It looks like Scotland will be the favourite holiday ground this summer. We have received an abnormal number of enquiries for our 'Tours in Scotland' programme 1915 edition and have already secured a large amount of hotel accommodation running right up to the end of September. The combined travel and hotel tickets to the principal golfing centre and hydros in Scotland are also in greater request this year.

The justification was 'the extreme tension experienced by all classes of the community owing to the war makes the summer holiday more necessary than ever ... A health policy against nervous breakdown'. Cook was still continuing in 1915 to promote overseas travel by steamer to India, China, Japan and Australia, and in September 1915 the London–Marseille Boat Train was re-established to provide improved access to the South of France. While, as discussed earlier, the unrestricted U boat campaign made sea travel problematic, Cook prepared its 'sunnynooks' domestic tourism programme in January 1916 in the *Travellers Gazette*, which emphasized the charms of Britain to the erstwhile traveller abroad.

> in times of peace they had spent their holidays abroad – the charms of their native land having been altogether neglected...war's lesson has taught them that Ventnor and Bournemouth, Sidmouth and Torquay, Falmouth, Penzance and other sunnynooks where palm trees and sub-tropical plants flourish in luxuriance, possess merits which they had never dreamed of.

Yet how successful this was is doubtful with the worsening of travel restrictions within wartime Britain. The company could plan, but it could not control the world in which it had to operate. In April 1916 the *Travellers Gazette* reported that:

> owing to the Great War, it is the second consecutive Easter without Cook's Excursions being available for the holidaymaker.

In July 1916 the Chancellor of the Exchequer made a decision to postpone the August Bank Holiday, for which Cook had planned a programme of tours such as 'Three Hundred miles by Motor Coach in Wales.' Yet again the company was a victim of events over which it had no control. Working class and weekend outings had not been their pre-war staple but they did continue to promote domestic travel in the *Travellers Gazette*. It was not easy given the pressure on the railways, which the government controlled although they were still in the hands of the private companies.

In December 1916, tourist tickets by rail were also suspended. The deepening demands of war were reflected in the increased austerity in 1917, with the *Travellers Gazette* reporting that the:

> Government have appealed to the public to forego pleasure travel to relieve railways to cope with conveyance of troops and material. As a deterrent, the Board of Trade have required fares to be increased and restrictions to be placed on personal baggage.

In February 1917 this led to a 50% increase in fares, resulting in Cook suspending booklets of information with the government hoping that it would curtail travel for all but the most pressing business and health reason. With the pressure – by persuasion rather than prohibition – by government to reduce leisure travel in 1918, Cook suspended active promotion of material to encourage travel for pleasure in January 1918. With increased rationing (i.e. food restrictions) the firm warned of pre-booking as a necessity for holidays, and in May 1918 publicized its arrangements for summer holidays in *The Travellers Gazette*. To relieve the pressure on the rail system, Cook advised mid-week holiday travel to avoid Saturday delays. Even so, *The Times* newspaper reported the resurgence of interest in holiday travel in summer 1918 with its article on 5 August 1918 'Holiday Traffic' observing that:

> The tide of holiday traffic which had been steadily rising during the week came to a flood on Saturday ... the crowds at the mainline station recalled those of pre-war times when competition in cheap excursions was not restrained by military needs ... the crush was greatest at London Bridge, Victoria and Waterloo ... At Victoria, the chief bookings appeared to be Brighton, Eastbourne and Hastings ... At London Bridge the queue of waiting passengers, which began to form at 4 am, extended from the booking office across into the station yard ... Waterloo was equally crowded ... Liverpool Street had its long queues which began at 6am.

Police were in attendance at all stations to monitor the crowds in case of disturbances. In a similar vein, the resurgence in leisure, stimulated by wartime earnings, led *The Times* a day later to carry a feature 'On Hampstead Heath: Sedate and Well Dressed Crowds' (6 August 1918) where:

> The crowds who went yesterday to Hampstead Heath, to the Zoo or the parks
> in a steady never-ending stream that widened during the afternoon were quite
> unlike any crowds before or since the war. Everyone was well dressed ...

The same article recorded visitor numbers at the National History Museum (7547 visitors) and the Victoria and Albert Museum (5343 visitors), which are significant for that era. Durie (2006) points to a growing affluence among many munitions workers and other war-related work, which boosted holiday and day trip travel in Scotland to west coast resorts, and was replicated in England and Wales, as noted earlier. But, to what extent was this kind of working class tourism that developed during the war in Britain a type of tourism from which Cook could benefit?

Cook: Questions and Answers

The changing landscape of wartime travel and conditions meant that, like many of the railway companies, Cook had to adapt and develop new markets and forms of business to survive. But the war did not provide demand, as it did for the railways: Cook and the other tourist firms had to find their own way forward. This study has raised a number of unanswered questions associated with wartime Britain which concern:

1. To what extent was the firm able to redeploy staff resources and expertise?

This remains largely unanswered because the vital documents relating to the period – the company Minute Books of the Board of Directors' Meetings or their working papers – do not survive. We can only speculate, therefore, whether the considerable expertise accumulated by Cook in logistics and the movement of people and goods was pressed into service by the military at a formal or informal level.

2. To what extent could the firm diversify away from its core business of the tour party?

Here we are on firmer ground. The company did move into related activities and this was useful, leading it to handle mail with the enemy and British citizens interned in Germany (and POWs) via its Amsterdam office in neutral Holland. Its shipping department and forwarding department did well, becoming, as Brendon (1991, p. 257) asserts, one of the most efficient freight services in the world. How much revenue these activities generated is not known, but at least it was a welcome addition to the firm's balance sheet. Against that has to be set the loss of some assets overseas, particularly those in countries with which Britain was at war, but these were not substantial; the seizure by the Turks of the camping equipment in Palestine for the tours there was scarcely a major item. The firm owned few offices or hotels other than the Hermitage near Naples and none in Germany or Austria–Hungary. The Nile steamers which had stopped running in 1914 were taken over by the British military, with the government paying compensation. The Vesuvius railway, which Cook owned, was a casualty of the war and the downturn in tourism in Italy; the working account showed losses of between £3–5000 every year after 1914, all the more galling as there had just been heavy investment.

On the staff front, a substantial element in Cook's costs must have been its wage bill, but the reduction in staff may have actually helped the firm reduce its costs in line with its reduced tourist activities. Out of 1000 staff who joined up, over half (580) were volunteers who joined up pre-1916 and the introduction of conscription. And indeed *The Travellers Gazette* does make several references to staff shortages during the war which made it problematic to handle client correspondence. It is worth asking what effect this loss of men to the military had on the company. We know from historical accounts of the railway companies that many of them began employing women after 1914 to fill the vacuum left by military volunteers but we do not have similar data for Cook. Among those who volunteered, we do not know if any of these were key personnel. Or did it actually work in favour of the firm by cutting the wage bill? The firm did have to implement redundancies and wage cuts in 1917; but there might have been more.

One hundred and fifty-three staff died, many of whom were in their twenties or even younger; for example, Robert Galliford, aged 18, died of wounds in Egypt in August 1915; Albert Albrey, aged 26, was killed in Flanders in July 1917. Amongst those listed on the Thomas Cook Memorial window, 'members of the staff of Thomas Cook & Co who lost their lives in the Great War 1914–1919' are a number who do not make any appearance in the British lists of casualties. They were Cook employees perhaps serving with the French army (Arnaud, F.C. or Gilquin, G.A.J), the Italian (Fabbrini, G.L.) or the German (Hirschorn, E.W. and Hochhaus, F.G.).

It was a British firm but with a cosmopolitan workforce reflected in its transnational operations and global offices. Tourism researchers have tended to suggest that tourism became a globalised business activity only in the 1990s but Cook pre-dates all of these examples as the first truly globalized tourism company. It was developed in an era when the UK and British Imperial interests meant that the company had a much greater control of travel and tourism, than many of the current day firms in this sector do.

Thomas Cook and Post-War Recovery

In any form of crisis management, how a company plans for the recovery stage during the crisis is very revealing of the calibre and mindset of its management. In terms of recovery, the performance of Thomas Cook & Sons is striking, even though the demand situation post-1919 was so very favourable. The losses of the war years were quickly transformed into record profits, as shown earlier in Table 19.2. A brief synopsis of the company's immediate post-war activities serves as a useful postscript to this study since it demonstrates the organization's ability to rebuild its business, both with the reopening of destinations which had been shut by the war and the development of new forms of tourism.

At the cessation of war in November, *The Travellers Gazette*, December 1918 acknowledged that demobilization would need to occur before international travel could resume. It was not until March 1919 that the government removed travel restrictions (i.e. the removal of permits required for travel to Holland, Norway, Sweden, Denmark, Spain, Portugal, South America and other destinations outside Europe), so normality did not return immediately. However, by April 1919 Easter travel had resumed and was promoted again and, in May 1919, the Board of Trade pledged to resume train services for holidaymakers in the summer. There were problems: the railways had been worked hard during the war and there was a danger of demand swamping their resources. *The Travellers Gazette* reported the communication from the wartime Railway Executive Committee:

> If, following the usual practice, the bulk of holidays is taken in July and August, there will be difficulty in coping with the traffic. If however, those who are able to do so will take their holidays in May and June, this will do much to obviate any overcrowding or discomfort.

It would especially help if holiday journeys were taken mid-week. By June 1919, Cook recommended reservations for accommodation and travel due to the rapid growth in demand. The company, in common with other travel companies, introduced a major innovation in July 1919 – 'Tours to the Battlefields of Belgium' – in two forms: either luxury travel or popular tours by motor car from Paris. These proved popular and built on the desire for many families to visit the battlefield sites, i.e. places where loved ones were lost, along with the morbid interest of others in what has now been termed 'dark tourism' (Lennon and Foley, 2000) and 'battlefield tourism' (Ryan, 2007).

By the summer of 1919, full recovery of the UK tourism industry was being reported in the press and *The Travellers Gazette* of September 1919 noted a record season, with the government taxing the railway companies with unprecedented demand during July to September 1919. This is even more remarkable given that in 1918–19 three waves of a deadly influenza virus had devastated the population. It is a hidden aspect of post-1918 history even though it led to major disruption to normal life and society in the UK and worldwide (Johnson, 2006), although it remains largely neglected in terms of tourism research. This pandemic saw the tourism and travel revival suddenly cease only months after the end of the First World War and was another severe short-run crisis which tourism and transport companies had to deal with.

It is not unrealistic to attribute much of the pent up demand for travel in 1919 to the recovery from both the war and the influenza epidemic, with reports of some destinations (e.g. Blackpool, see Walton, 1996) being completely full up by the summer of 1919. *The Times* on 6 August 1919 reported on 'Crowding at Resorts', where the two reasons given for the revival in 'the pleasure rush, [were], first, the general release from the anxiety after five years [of war] and hailing our freedom by doing as little work as possible'. This sentiment was reiterated in a poster produced by The Underground Electric Railways Company Ltd (the modern day London Underground) entitled 'Bank Holiday':

> Then: August 3rd 1914 – Five years ago the shadow of impending war cast a gloom over the holiday and exercised a restraint upon pleasure-making

> Now: August 4th 1919 – This year with the arrival of peace the holiday free from anxiety of war will permit full measure of pleasure again

> Train, omnibus and tram are at your service during the holidays.

The scale of peacetime demand for travel and tourism – 'the post-war holiday boom' – meant that Cook had to print a new edition of its Summer Holiday Programme in 1919. It was a bonanza time. 'After having been pent up for years, the public would have been taken with a passion for getting away somewhere even if travelling had been three times as bad and five times as expensive' said the *Daily Telegraph* newspaper. Regular London–Paris air services were inaugurated, providing a new luxury travel product for Cook's to promote. The firm also offered joy rides in converted Handley Page bombers.

One relief for the apparent congestion on the railways was the development of motor coach and charabanc tours with Cook promoting 6-day tours to Devon, Cornwall, the Thames Valley and Bournemouth in 1919 – another new innovation in transport and tourism. An article in *The Times* (3 August 1923) reported that 'motor coach travel' was now well established and Cook were providing 4-day to 14-day tours by coach, often using first class accommodation which suggests a comfortably well-off clientele. Other forms were also involved: Robert Bow of Wallace Arnold expanded his businesses after the First World War, organizing his first charabanc trip from Yorkshire to London, and by 1922 was providing 5-day tours from Yorkshire to Edinburgh and London, and others to the Highlands for 16 guineas (Davies and Barber, 2007).

This was a cut-throat business, however, with many demobbed soldiers purchasing redundant military vehicles to convert and operate businesses in the pursuit of the travel boom. October 1919 also saw Cook begin to re-promote winter sports in the High Alps in the *Travellers Gazette*, for example, at Chamonix. As well as winter sports, The Riviera Programme was recommended along with conducted Tours of the South of Spain, Tangier, Algeria, Egypt, India and other regions. By 1920, the company also saw a major expansion of Battlefield Tours, including France and Belgium, costing from £6 to 82 guineas in August 1920, and Italy in September 1920, with six pages of tours in *The Travellers Gazette* in October 1920. These compare with the company's Round the World and other tours in 1914, which started at £125 upwards. Opportunities post-1919 were as many as they had been restricted between 1914 and 1918.

Conclusion

The financial performance of Thomas Cook & Co during the war looks poor relative to pre- and post-war returns. But given the situation, could anything better have been achieved? Did any other firms in the British industry, e.g. Lunn, do any better? The important point is that the company's reserves and profitable pre-war operations would have enabled it to have raised loans to meet any downturn in profitability during the wartime conditions. There is evidence that the company did what it could to diversify into war-related services and to keep its core activities in tourism going, showing flexibility in marketing and in promotion. Cook was at the mercy of events over which it had no control. In some respects, its survival was no mean achievement, and the speed of its post-war recovery was remarkable. At such time it displayed its characteristic ability to innovate, see market opportunities and to provide what the travelling public wanted, e.g. battlefield tours. It took advantage of new means of transportation, e.g. charabanc trips and air travel.

The company demonstrated a strong degree of resilience, a feature which management researchers with an interest in crisis management acknowledge is fundamental to survival.

It retained core activities as far as it could, and weathered the storm of the crisis. It then went back to its pre-war activities. The modern day evaluation of entrepreneurship in tourism often tends to overlook the major challenges which companies faced in the past, with the assertion that the present is much more difficult than anything that has gone before, particularly in relation to global terrorism threats.

Yet as this chapter shows, the First World War – aptly named the Great War – was unlike any war ever seen before and with global consequences for society and the economy. Interestingly, some international tourism managed to survive in relation to business travel at a time when the UK's imperial interests required a large civil service and business travel to keep it functioning. But the pursuit of leisure travel on a global scale was severely curtailed. At the same time, much of the demand for leisure travel was played out in the domestic arena, where the pursuit of travel did not cease. Indeed, we argue that in some cases new forms of demand were created in the domestic market (e.g. the R&R function for troops in major cities and resorts) along with a growth in leisure travel by the munitions workers (particularly female labour). These groups were earning income that previously was not available to them and so the increased disposable income made leisure travel and entertainment more accessible. But whether Cook with their orientation to middle class touring reaped much benefit by this is questionable.

Whilst the government tried to limit domestic travel, the evidence from contemporary sources is that this did not achieve its desired aim. There was mooted in 1918 the introduction of a 'luxury duty tax' to impose additional restraint on the perceived unnecessary conspicuous consumption and expenditure on leisure, tourism and other 'luxury goods' (in addition to McKenna Duties), although the committee of inquiry decided not to introduce the measure. Tourism did not cease in wartime Britain and whilst Cook was faced with a loss of specific overseas and European markets and destinations, it sought to look at other options – some within tourism, others in related or derivative activities – to remain in business as the most established travel brand of the Edwardian period.

Ultimately, the survival and subsequent revival of the company was indicative of a very resilient organization in the most testing of conditions. The founding family was to reap the benefit in 1923 when the firm became a limited company: the brothers Frank and Ernest took £1.6 million each, dividing the share capital of £1 m between them. They and their firm had come through the years of wartime crisis.

Questions for Discussion

1. What are the principal features that characterize Thomas Cook as an entrepreneurial company?
2. How did the outbreak of war in 1914 affect tourism business for Thomas Cook? How did it adapt to continue in business?
3. How did domestic tourism develop and adapt during wartime in Britain?
4. How do contemporary accounts of tourism in the period 1914–20 in newspapers help us to reconstruct the evaluation and development of wartime and post-war recovery in tourism?

Appendix 19.1: Railway advertising to promote tourist visitation by rail 1915–18 in *The Railway Travel Monthly*.

Date	Railway company	Destination promoted	Key attributes of the advertisement/main slogans used
April 1915	GWR	South West England	'The Holiday Line – A Wonderful Playground' Sub-text of advertisement: 'Not in the whole of the British Empire – possibly not in all the world are more perfect holidaylands to be found than in Devon and Cornwall, the wonderful playground of Great Britain' Commentary: The emphasis is on fast express services connecting the tourist generating regions in the main cities and luxury services were combined with the leisurely and diverse resorts and places to visit in the South West.
	L & SWR	Devon	'Glorious Devon – The Fairyland of the West' Sub-text of advertisement: 'In the path of the sun for health and pleasure' Commentary: The mystical qualities of the South West, including the link with King Arthur, Tintagel and Fairy Tales is combined with the perceived health-giving qualities of South West air (away from the industrial cities) and the pursuit of pleasure.
	Midland Railway	Stratford upon Avon	Holiday Destination – simple place-specific advertisement.

Date	Railway	Destination	Advertisement / Commentary
May 1915	L & SWR	Cornwall	'By the Cornish Sea – for delightful bracing holidays' Commentary: Emphasizing escape and remoteness combined with health-giving properties.
	L & SWR	South Coast	Place-specific advertisement promoting travel to the South Coast.
	Furness Railway	Lake District	Place-specific advertisement promoting travel to the scenic qualities of the Lake District.
	Cambrian Railway	Cardigan Bay	Promoting travel to Wales and Cardigan Bay.
July 1915	SE & Chatham	Kent	'Visit the Garden of England for sea, sands, sunshine and scenery – a choice of resorts to suit all requirements' Commentary: This advertisement is a standard railway promotion which persisted into the 1950s, with the emphasis on the Kent resorts, the Downs and weather for the East Kent Coast.
	L&SW	Bournemouth	'Bournemouth by the Southern Sea' Commentary: The coastal resort at Bournemouth remained a major destination throughout the nineteenth and twentieth century as a resort attracting a higher social class of visitor.

(continued)

Appendix 19.1: Railway advertising to promote tourist visitation by rail 1915–18 in *The Railway Travel Monthly. — cont'd*

Date	Railway company	Destination promoted	Key attributes of the advertisement/main slogans used
	GER	East Anglia	'Country Holidays in East Anglia' 'Seaside Holidays in East Anglia' Commentary: GER carried two campaigns in the summer months of 1915 emphasizing both rural and more traditional east coast seaside destinations as getaway locations.
	Isle of Wight Central Railway	Isle of Wight	General promotion of services and destination.
	Midland Great Western Railway of Ireland	Ireland	General promotion of tourist visitation to Connemara, Achill, Galway, Sligo and West of Ireland with joint rail and motor coach holidays including staying in railway hotels. Sub-text: 'For health and pleasure by mountain, moor, lough and ocean' Commentary: Promotion of UK, but especially domestic Irish tourist travel by rail and road from the main cities such as Dublin.
	Cambrian Railway	Wales	'Cambrian Riviera – the value of a holiday on the Cambrian Riviera including Cardigan Bay coast – a most desirable resort for a happy and healthy holiday' Commentary: the health theme alongside the need to improve the population's morale is emphasized by the Welsh promotion.

North British Railway	Scotland	'Health beckons you to Scotland' Commentary:
L & SW	Cornwall	'By Cornish Sea and Moor' Commentary:
Glasgow & South West Railway	Scotland	'The popular route to the land o' Burns and the Clyde watering places (including golf and Turnberry)' Commentary: The regional promotion of the Glasgow-based railway company was emphasizing the heritage theme associated with Burns Country alongside the coastal destinations previously served by many of the Clyde steamers, some of which were requisitioned for war service and rail services replaced pleasure cruises.
East Cornwall Line	Cornwall	'Beauty spots of the West' Commentary: This branch line serving many of the North and East Cornwall resorts and tourist destinations is unusual given the reliance upon tourist use at the destination or as a connecting service to mainline services such as GWR.
Belfast and County Down Railway	Belfast and Districts	'Belfast Tourist District – to tourists, golfers, antiquarians and health seekers' Commentary:

(continued)

Appendix 19.1: Railway advertising to promote tourist visitation by rail 1915–18 in *The Railway Travel Monthly.* — *cont'd*

Date	Railway company	Destination promoted	Key attributes of the advertisement/main slogans used
August 1915	S.M.J.	Stratford upon Avon	'The Shakespeare Route' – spend your holiday in Stratford upon Avon Commentary: Similarly, a boat yard (A J Witty) was offering boats for hire according to its advertisement in the 1916 Kelly's Directory of Nottingham.
	Great Central Railway (GCR)	All holiday destinations served by the railway from the Midlands	The company produced and periodically updated its 'Health and Holiday Resorts Guidebook' which was a detailed listing of the delights of key holiday resorts accessible by GCR services.
	L & SW	Ilfracombe	'Ilfracombe – the Holiday Magnet of Lovely Devon' Commentary: The railway company was advertising the unique features and appeal of one destination as a centre for touring and to stay in.
	L & NW	Ireland	General advertisement promoting rail/ferry trail to Dublin, Cork and Belfast from the Midlands.
September 1915	Furness Railway	Lake District	'The English Lake District – Always Beautiful in sunlight or moonlight' Commentary: The advertisement was seeking to bring a sense of romance and cheer at a time of national loss of soldiers in the Western Front.

Date	Company	Destination/Type	Commentary
	GER	Norfolk	'For a rest and change – go to the Norfolk Broads' Commentary: The promotion of the Norfolk Broads as a leisure destination by the main railway company serving London and East Anglia was also complemented by more regionalized advertising in directories such as The Kelly's Directory of Nottingham 1916 in which the Norfolk Broads Yachting Company promoted 'spend your holidays on the Norfolk Broads' onboard a yacht or wherry.
	Great Central Railway	Hotel Advertisement	Promoting railway hotels and their restaurant facilities in London, Sheffield, Grimsby and New Holland.
October 1915	L & SWR	South West England	'Autumn Holidays' – promotion of the South West as an off-peak, autumn destination.
November 1915	L & SWR	Illustrated talks (Lantern Talks with slides)	Promotion by the Publicity Manager of travel to the Channel Islands, Paris, Devon, Dorset, North Cornwall and Normandy by rail/ferry.
December 1915	GWR	Cornwall	'The Cornish Riviera' Commentary: This is a popular advertisement from the period which reappears during 1915–18 and remains the basis of the promotion activities of the GWR through to rail nationalization. Changing imagery in the rail posters emphasizes the similarities with the South of France.

(continued)

Appendix 19.1: Railway advertising to promote tourist visitation by rail 1915–18 in *The Railway Travel Monthly*. — *cont'd*

Date	Railway company	Destination promoted	Key attributes of the advertisement/main slogans used
	L & SW	South West England	'Hints for Holidays' with a listing of destinations to visit in the region.
	London Underground	London	'Off the beaten track' 'Thames Street' 'The Quayside of Old London' By Underground Commentary: With the intensification of air raids in London, the Underground were promoting places to visit 'off the Beaten Track'.
	Wirral Railway	The Wirral, Merseyside	'Health and Pleasure and Holiday Resorts of the Wirral Peninsula' (West Kirby, Hoy Lake, New Brighton and Wallasey) Commentary: Promoting leisure travel to the wartime population in Liverpool and NW England.
	M.S.W.J.	Cotswolds	General promotion of antiquities and places to visit in the Cotswolds.
January to April 1916[4]			
January 1916	London Electric Railway	London	'Look! Shop! And Travel' Commentary: Promoting suburban travel into London to encourage leisure shopping despite the exigencies of supply imposed by wartime conditions.

June 1916	London Electric Railway	London	'Arcadia poster' which depicted London countryside as a place to visit with the slogan 'Alight here for air, sun, winds, flowers and birds – London 15¼ miles'. Commentary: The London Electric Railway was, in common with the GER poster of August 1916 below, seeking to encourage leisure and recreational travel in the countryside surrounding London, which it served.
August 1916	GER	London	'Walking Exercise Keeps you Fit – there are many charming walks through picturesque forest and country scenery in districts near London served by GER. Convenient train services, low fares'. Commentary: In common with the London Electric Railway, promoting leisure travel alongside activities with no commercial cost (aside from the rail fare) sought to encourage off-peak and weekend travel (where it remained available) for the wartime population, especially those working in factories and munitions production, as assisting with maintaining their health.
	Cambrian Railway	Cardigan	'Spend your Holidays at one of Cardigan Bays resorts'

(continued)

Appendix 19.1: Railway advertising to promote tourist visitation by rail 1915–18 in *The Railway Travel Monthly*. — *cont'd*

Date	Railway company	Destination promoted	Key attributes of the advertisement/main slogans used
July 1916	Cambrian Railway	Wales	'A Holiday Reflection – change of air and rest, Cardigan Bay Resorts – Haven of Convalescence' Commentary: For the first time, one railway company begins to market the role of wartime R&R (rest and recuperation) especially for wounded soldiers needing to convalesce. Given that around 70% of wounded soldiers returned to duty during the Great War, many wartime hotels saw a rise in post-injury convalescence or the requisitioning of premises as wartime hospitals.
	Mayport and Carlisle Railway	Lake District	'English Lake District'
	Underground (throughout 1916/17)	London	Promoting travel to/from London
July 1916	Glasgow & SW	Glasgow to England	'The most picturesque route between Glasgow and England'
	Plymouth, Devonport and South West Junction Railway	East Cornwall	'Visit East Cornwall' Commentary: A branch line promoting local travel from mainline connections.
	Grand Central Railway	Holiday Guide	Updated 'Health and Holiday Resorts Guide'

Date	Railway	Location	Advertisement
December 1916[5]	L&BR	South Coast	'The South Coast Watering Holes' advertisement
	Furness Railway	Lake District	Re-running of September 1915 advertisement
January and April 1917	Glasgow & SW	Ayrshire	'Land o' Burns' advertising
May 1917	Maryport and Carlisle Railway	Lake District	'English Lake District' (as per December 1916)

Key to Railway Companies

GWR	Great Western Railway
L & SWR	London and South West Railway
Furness Railway	Railway serving the Furness and Lake District area
LNWR	London and North Western Railway
GNR	Great Northern Railway
GER	Great Eastern Railway
Cambrian Railway	Wales-based railway services
L&NW	London and North Western Railway
SMJ	Stratford upon Avon and Midland Junction Railway

[4] Due to the binding of these four issues at the National Archives, the advertisement pages have been removed from 2PER53/14 with one exception.

[5] From December 1916, the tourist advertisements diminish as industrial sites for rent/sale on railway land dominate the advertising space.

Acknowledgements

The generous funding provided by the Carnegie Fund for Scottish Universities and the Department of Marketing, University of Stirling, is gratefully acknowledged. Assistance and advice from Mr Paul Smith, Thomas Cook Archivist was also crucial to the completion of this study together with material available at The British Library, London, The National Library of Scotland, the National Rail Museum, York, The Public Record Office, Kew and The Thomas Cook Archive, Peterborough.

References

Beirman, D. (2003). *Restoring Destinations in Crises: A Strategic Marketing Approach.* Wallingford: CABI Publishing.

Bennet, A. (2002). *Great Western Lines and Landscapes.* Cheltenham: Runpast Publishing.

Brendon, P. (1991). *Thomas Cook: 150 Years of Popular Tourism.* London: Secker and Warburg.

Broadberry, S. and Howlet, P. (2005). The UK during World War 1: Business as usual. In *The Economics of World War 1*, (S. Broadberry, and M. Harrison eds.), pp. 206-234. Cambridge University Press.

Cole, B. and Durack, R. (1992). *Railway Posters 1923–1947.* York: National Railway Museum.

Davies, R. and Barber, S. (2007). *Wallace Arnold.* Hersham: Ian Allan Publishing.

Durie, A. (2006). *Water is Best: The Hydros and Health Tourism in Scotland 1840–1940.* Edinburgh: John Donald.

Durie, A. and McPherson, G. (1999). *Tourism and the First World War: A Scottish Perspective.* The Local Historian, November.

Glaesser, D. (2003). *Crises Management in the Tourism Industry.* Oxford: Butterworth-Heinemann.

Henderson, J. (2007). *Tourism Crises: Causes, Consequences and Management.* Oxford: Butterworth-Heinemann.

Howarth, D. and Howarth, S. (1986). *The Story of P&O. The Peninsular and Oriental Steam Navigation Company.* London: Weidenfeld and Nicolson.

Johnson, N. (2006). *Britain and the 19918-19 Influenza Pandemic: A Dark Epilogue.* London: Routledge.

Lennon, J. and Foley, M. (2000). *Dark Tourism.* London: Continuum.

Lickorish, L. and Kershaw, A. (1953). *The Travel Trade.* London: Practical Press.

Lynch, M. (2004). *Weathering the Storm: A Crisis Management Guide for Tourism Businesses.* Leicester: Matador.

Page, S. J. and Yeoman, I. (2006). How VisitScotland prepared for a flu Pandemic. *Journal of Business Continuity and Emergency Planning,* 1(2), 167–182.

Read, D. (ed.). (1982). *Edwardian England.* London: Croom Helm.

Ryan, C. (ed.). (2007). *Battlefield Tourism.* Oxford: Butterworth-Heinemann.

Sladen, C. (2005). Wartime holidays and the 'myth of the Blitz'. *Cultural and Social History,* 2, 215–245.

Walton, J. (1983). *The English Seaside Resort: A Social History 1750–1914.* Leicester: Leicester University Press.

Walton, J. (1996). Leisure towns in wartime: The impact of the First World War in Blackpool and San Sebastian. *Journal of Contemporary History,* 31, 603–618.

Watts, D. (2004). Evaluating British railway poster advertising: The London and Norht Eastern Railway between the wars. *Journal of Transport History,* 25(2), 23–56.

Williamson, A. (1998). *The Golden Age of Travel: The Romantic Years of Tourism in Images from the Thomas Cook Archive.* Peterborough: Thomas Cook Publishing.

FURTHER READING

Chapter 2

Aldrich, H.E., and Baker, T. (1997). Blinded by the Cites? Has There Been Progress in Entrepreneurship Research? In *Entrepreneurship 2000*, (D.L. Sexton, and R.W. Smilor, eds.). Chicago: Upstart Publishing.

Archer, B.H. (1977). *Tourism Multipliers: the State of the Art. Bangor Occasional Papers in Economics, No. 11*. Cardiff: University of Wales Press.

Archer, B.H. (1982). The value of multipliers and their policy implications. *Tourism Management*, 3(4), 236–241.

Ateljevic, J. (2002). *Small Tourism Firms: Owners, Environment and Management Practices in the Centre Stage of New Zealand. Unpublished PhD Thesis*. Wellington, New Zealand: Victoria University of Wellington.

Begley, T. (1995). Using founder status, age of firm, and company growth rate as the basis for distinguishing entrepreneurs from managers of smaller businesses. *Journal of Business Venturing*, 10, 249–263.

Britton, S. (1991). Tourism, capital and place: Towards the critical geography of tourism. Environment and planning D. *Society and Space*, 9, 452–478.

Burkart, J. (1981). Tourism — A service industry? *Tourism Management*, 2, 2.

Busenitz, L.W., West, G.P., Shepherd, D., Nelson, T., and Zacharakis, E. (2003). Entrepreneurship research in emergence: past trends and future directions. *Journal of Management*, 29(3), 285–308.

Bussell, R., and Faulkner, B. (1999). Movers and Shakers: chaos makers in tourism development. *Tourism Management*, 20, 411–423.

Bussell, R., and Faulkner, B. (2004). Entrepreneurship, chaos and the tourism area lifecycle. *Annals of Tourism Research*, 8(1), 1–23.

Chambers, R. (1997). Paradigm shifts and the practices of participatory research and development. In *Power and Participation Development – Theory and Practice*, (N. Nelson, and S. Wright, eds.), pp. 30–42. UK: Intermediate Technology Publication.

Champion, R. (2005). Reviews by Rafe Champion. www.amazon.com, Accessed 23 March 2005.

Chandler, G.N., and Lyon, D.W. (2001). Issues of Research Design and Construct Measurement in Entrepreneurship Research: The Past Decade. *Entrepreneurship Theory and Practice*, 26(4), 101–113.

Cornelissen, S. (2005). *The Global Tourism System: Governance, development and Lessens from South Africa*. England: Ashgate.

Cressy, R. (2006). Determinants of Small Firm Survival and Growth. In *The Oxford Handbooks of Entrepreneurship*, (M. Casson, B. Yeung, A. Basu, and N. Wadeson, eds.). Oxford: University Press.

Cullen, T., and Dick, T.J. (1989). Tomorrow's Entrepreneur and Today's Hospitality Curriculum. *The Cornell Hotel Restaurant Administration Quarterly*, 13(8), 54–57.

Curtis, D. (1997). Power to the people: Rethinking community development. In *Power and Participation Development – Theory and Practice*, (N. Nelson, and S. Wright, eds.), pp. 115–124. UK: Intermediate Technology Publication.

Dahles, E., and Bras., A. (1999). Entrepreneurs in Romance: Tourism in Indonesia. *Annals of Tourism Research*, 26(2), 267–293.

Davidsson, P. (2003). The Domain of Entrepreneurship Research: Some Suggestion. In *Advances in Entrepreneurship, Firm Emergence and Growth*, (J. Katz and D. Shepherd, eds.), vol. 6. Greenwich, CT: JAI Press.

Davidsson, P. (2004). *Researching Entrepreneurship*. Boston: Springer Science & Business Media.

DiMaggio, P.J. (1988). Interest and agency in institutional theory. In *Institutional patterns and organizations: Culture and environment*, (L.G. Zucker, ed.), pp. 3–22. Cambridge, MA: Ballinger.

Edquist, C. (2001) The System of Innovation Approach and Innovation Policy: An Account of the State of the Art, DRUID paper, www.druid.dk.

Evans, D., and Jovanovic, B. (1989). Estimates of a Model of Entrepreneurial Choice under Liquidity Constraints. *Journal of Political Economy*, 97(4), 808–827.

Firth, T. (2002). *Business strategies & tourism: An investigation to identify factors which influence marginal firms to move into or remain on the fringes of tourism industries.* Ph.D. thesis. Southern Cross University.

Fligstein, N. (1997). Social skill and institutional theory. *American Behavioral Scientist*, 40, 397–405.

Freedmann, J. (1992). *Empowerment – The Polices of Alternative Development*. Cambridge: Blackwell.

Friedland, Roger, Robert, R., and Alford. (1991). In *'Bringing society back in: Symbols, practices, and institutional contradictions' in The new institutionalism in organizational analysis*, (W.W. Powell, and P.J. DiMaggio, eds.), pp. 232–263. Chicago, IL: University of Chicago Press.

Gardner, K., and Lewis, D. (1996). *Anthropology, Development and the Post-Modern Challenge*. London: Pluto Press.

Gartner, W.B. (1985). A conceptual framework for describing the. phenomenon of new venture creation. *Academy of Management Review*, 10, 698–706.

Gartner, W.B. (1988). Who is the entrepreneur? Is the wrong question. *American Journal of Small Business*, 12, 11–32.

Gartner, W.B. (1990). *'What Are We Talking About When We Talk About Entrepreneurship?' Journal of Business Venturing*, 5(1), 15–28.

Getz, D., and Carlsen, J. (2000). Characteristics and Goals of Family and Owner-operated Business in the Rural Tourism and Hospitality Sector. *Tourism Management*, 2, 547–560.

Hall, M.C., Jenkins, J., and Kearsley, G. (eds.) (1997). *Planning and Policy – in Australia and New Zealand, Cases, Issues and Practices*. Sydney: Irwin Publication.

Harrison, F. (1999). *The Managerial Decision-Making Process,* 5th edn. New York: Houghton Mifflin Company.

Harrison, R.T., and Leitch, C.M. (1996). Discipline Mergence in Entrepreneurship: Accumulative Fragmentatlism or Paradigmatic Science? *Entrepreneurship, Innovation, and Change*, 5(2), 65–83.

Hasse, J. (2001). *Stakeholder Perceptions of Tourism Development in Marahau / New Zealand: A Role for Participatory Approaches and GIS*. Unpublished PhD Thesis. Wellington New Zealand: Victoria University of Wellington.

Hirst, P. (1997). The global economy – myths and realities. *International Affairs*, 73(3), 409–425.

Hitrec, T. (2006). Vjerski Turizam, in Carak, S. and Mikacic, V. (Urednici), Hrvatski Turizam: plavo, bijelo, zeleno. Institut za Turizam Zagreb.

International Institute for Tourism (2005). *Program for Development of Mountain Tourism in Montenegro*. Ljubljana, Slovenia: International Institute for Tourism.

Ionides, D., and Debbage, K. (1997). Post-Fordism and flexibility: The travel industry polyglot. *Tourism Management*, 18, 229–241.

Ireland, R.D., Reutzel, C.R., and Webb, J.W. (2005). From Editor: Entrepreneurship Research in *AMJ*: What Has Been Published, and What Might the Future Hold? *Academy of Management Journal*, 48(4), 558–564.

ISIC (1990). *International standard industrial classification of economic activities, Statistical Papers, Series M, No. 4, Rev. 3, Annex II*. New York: ISIC.

Jogaratnam, G., Tse, D., and Olsen, M.D. (1999). An empirical analysis of entrepreneurship and performance in the restaurant industry. *Journal of Hospitality and Tourism Research*, 23(4), 339–353.

Jogaratnam, G. (2002). Entrepreneurial orientation and environmental hostility: an assessment of small, independent restaurant business. *Journal of Hospitality and Tourism Research*, 26(3), 258–277.

Keith, G., and Malcolm, P. (1997). Entrepreneurship in the small hotel sector. *International Journal of Contemporary Hospitality Management*, 9(1), 21–25.

King, N. (1992). Modelling the innovation process: An empirical comparison of approaches. *Journal of Occupational and Organizational Psychology*, 65, 89–100.

Kirby, D. (2003). *Entrepreneurship*. UK: The McGraw-Hill.

Kirzner, I. (1973). *Competition and Entrepreneurship*. Chicago: University of Chicago Press.

Kirzner, I. (1979). *Perception, Opportunity, and Profit,*. Chicago: University of Chicago Press.

Knight, K.H. (1921). *Risk, Uncertainty, and Profit*. New York: Houghton-Mifflin.

Komppula, R. (2001). New-product development in tourism companies – case studies on nature-based activity operators. Paper presented at *The 10th Nordic Tourism Research Symposium*, October 18–20, Vasa, Finland.

Koppl, R. (2007). Entrepreneurial Behavior as a Human Universal. In *Entrepreneurship: the Engine of Growth*, (M. Manniti, ed.), pp. 5–6. Westport, CT: Praeger Publishers.

Koppl, R., and Minniti, M. (2003). Market Processes and Entrepreneurial Studies. In *Handbook of Entrepreneurial Research*, (Z.J. Acs, and D.B. Auretsch, eds.), p. 81. Boston: Kluwer.

Landstrom, H. (2005). *Pioneers in Entrepreneurship and Small Business Research*. New York: Springer Science + Business Media Inc.

Larkin, L. (2008). Religious Travel Cover Story – Destinations of the World, April http://christiantourism.blogspot.com/2008/04/religious-travel-cover-story.html, accessed on 24/04/08.

Lee, T., and Crompton, J. (1992). Measuring Novelty Seeking in Tourism. *Annals of Tourism Research*, 19, 732–751.

Leiper, N. (2008). Why 'the tourism industry' is misleading as a generic expression: The case for the plural variation, 'tourism industries'. *Tourism Management*, 29, 237–251.

Low, M.B., and MacMillan, I.C. (1988). Entrepreneurship: Past Research and Future Challenges. *Journal of Management*, 35, 139–161.

Lynch, P. (1998). Female microentrepreneurs in the host family sector: key motivations and social-economic variables. *International Journal of Hospitality Management*, 17, 319–342.

March, R. (2003). Tourism Industry as a Service Industry: An Australian Perspective, Inbound Tourism Studies Centre. www.inboundtourism.com.au/article_three, accessed on 23rd of February 2008.

McClelland, D. (1961). *The Achieving Society*. Princeton, NJ: Van Nostrand.

McKercher, B., Law, R., and Lam, T. (2006). Rating Tourism and Hospitality Journals. *Tourism Management*, 2, 1235–1252.

Minniti, M. (2007). *Entrepreneurship: The Engine of Growth*. Westport: Praeger Publisher.

Montanari, A., and Williams, A.M. (1995). *European Tourism: Regions, Spaces and Restructuring*. New York: John Wiley & Sons.

Morgan, N., and Pritchard, A. (2000). *Advertising in Tourism and Leisure*. Oxford: Butterworth Heinemann.

Morrison, A., and Thomas, R. (1999). The Future of Small Firms in the Hospitality Industry. *International Journal of Contemporary Hospitality Management*, 11(4), 148–154.

Morrison, A., Rimmington, M., and Williams, C. (1999). *Entrepreneurship in the Hospitality, Tourism and Leisure Industries*. Oxford: Butterworth-Heinemann.

Mowforth, M., and Munt, I. (1998). *Tourism and Suitability – New Tourism in the Third World*. London: Routledge.

Mugler, J. (1997). Research into entrepreneurship and small business in Austria. In *Entrepreneurship and Small Business Research in Europe, An ECSB Survey*, (H. Landstrom, H. Frank, and J.M. Veciana, eds.), pp. 14–25. Aldershot: Avebury.

Murphy, P., Pritchard, M.P., and Smith, B. (1999). The destination product and its impact on traveller perceptions,. *Tourism Management*, 21, 43–52.

Özer, B. (1996). An investment analysis model for small hospitality operations. *International Journal of Contemporary Hospitality Management*, 8(5), 20–24.

Page, S., and Connell, J. (2006). *Tourism: A Modern System*, 2nd edn. London: Thomson.

Pearce, D.G. (1987). *Tourism Today*. Harlow: Longman.

Pearce, D.G. (1996). Tourism: growth, change and internationalisation. In *Changing Places: New Zealand in the Nineties*, (R. Le Heron, and E. Pawson, eds.), pp. 188–196. Auckland: Longman Paul.

Pearce, D.G. (2001). Tourism, trams and local government policy-making in Christchurch, New Zealand. *Currant Issues in Tourism*, 4(2-4), 331–354.

Perry, C., MacArthur, R., Meredith, G., and Cunnigton, B. (1986). Need for achievement and locus of control of Australian small business owner-manager and super-entrepreneurs. *International Small Business Journal*, 4(4), 56–64.

Poon, A. (1993). *Tourism, Technology and Competitive Strategies*. Wallingford, UK: CAB International.

Roberts, P.W.D. (1987). Financial Aspects. *Tourism Management*, 8(2), 147–150.

Rritton, S.G. (1982). The political economy of tourism in the Third World. *Annals of Tourism Research*, 9(3), 331–358.

Smith, K.G. et al. (1989). Selecting Methodologies for Entrepreneurial Research: Trade-offs and Guidelines, *Entrepreneurship Theory and Practice*, 14(1), 39–49

Sarasvathy, S.D. (2004). Making It Happen: Beyond Theories of the Firm to Theories of Firm Design. *Entrepreneurship: Theory & Practice*, 28(6), 519–531.

Schumpeter, J. (1934). *History of Economic Analysis*. New York: Oxford University Press.

Schuurman, F.J. (ed.) (1996). *Beyond the Impasse – New Directions in Development Theory*, London: Zed Books.

Shane, S. (2002). *The Foundations of Entrepreneurship*. Massachusetts: Northampton: Edward Elgar Publishing, Inc.

Shane, S., and Venkataraman, S. (2000). The promise of entrepreneurship as a Field of research. *Academy of Management Review*, 25(I), 217–226.

Sharma, A. (2006). Economic Impact and Institutional Dynamics of Small Hotels in Tanzania. *Journal of Hospitality & Tourism Research*, 30(1), 76–92.

Sharpley, R. (2002). Rural tourism and the challenge of tourism diversification: the case of Cyprus. *Tourism Management*, 23, 233–244.

Shaw, G., and Williams, A. (1998). Entrepreneurship, small business culture and tourism development. In *The Economic Geography of the Tourism Industry*, (D. Ioannides, and K.D. Debbage, eds.), pp. 235–255. London: Routledge.

Smith, K.G., Gannon, M.J., and Sapienza, H.J. (1989). Selecting methodologies for entrepreneurial research: tradeoffs and guidelines. *Entrepreneurship Theory and Practice*, 14(1), 39–49.

Spear, R. (2000). *The Nature of Social Entrepreneurship*. Dublin: The paper presented at ISTR conference, July 2000.

Stewart, W.H., and Roth, P.L. (2001). Risk propensity differences between entrepreneurs and managers: a meta-analysis review. *Journal of Applied Psychology*, 86(1), 145–153.

Stiglitz, J. (2002). *Globalisation and its Discontents*. Great Britain: Allan Lane the Penguin Press.

Thomas, R. (1998). *The Management of Small Tourism and Hospitality Firms*. London: Cassell.

Torrance, E.P., and Horng, R.G. (1980). Creativity and style of learning and thinking characteristics of adaptors and innovators. *Creative Child and Adult Quarterly*, 5, 80–85.

Tremblay, P. (1998). The economic organisation of tourism. *Annals of Tourism Research*, 25(4), 837–859.

Venkataraman, S. (1997). The distinctive domain of entrepreneurship research: An editor's perspective. In *Advances in Entrepreneurship, Firm Emergence, and Growth*, (J. Katz & R. Brockhaus, eds.), vol. 3, pp. 119–138. Greenwich, CT: JAI Press.

Vesper, K. (1980). *New Venture Strategies*. Englewood Cliffs: Prentice Hall.

Wanhill, S. (2000). Small and Medium Tourism Enterprises. *Annals of Tourism Research*, 27(1), 132–147.

Giddens, A. (1984). *The Constitution of Society.* Cambridge: Polity Presss.

Goss, D. (2005). 'Entrepreneurship and 'the social': Towards a deference-emotion theory'. *Human Relations*, 58(5), 617–636.

Granovetter, M. (1973). The strength of weak ties. *American Journal of Sociology*, 78, 1360–1380.

Hampson, S.E. (1988). *The Construction of Personality,* 2nd edn. London: Routledge.

Hansemark, O.C. (2003). 'Need for achievement, locus of control and the prediction of business start-ups: A longitudinal study'. *Journal of Economic Psychology*, 24(3), 301–319.

Harré, R. (1979). *Social Being.* Oxford: Blackwell.

Harré, R., and Gillett, G. (1994). *The Discursive Mind.* London: Sage.

Hashemi, S., and Hashemi, B. (2002). *Anyone Can Do It.* Chichester: Capstone.

Haugh, H. (2007). 'Community-led social venture creation', *Entrepreneurship Theory & practice*, 31(2), 16, 1–182.

Hofstede, G. (1980). *Culture's Consequences: International Differences in Work-Related Values.* Newbury Park, CA: Sage.

Hornaday, J.A. and Aboud, J. (1971). Characteristics of successful entrepreneurs. *Personnel Psychology*, 24, 141–153.

Homewood, III Irwin, McClelland, D.C. (1987). 'Characteristics of successful entrepreneurs'. *Journal of Creative Behavior*, 21 (3), 219–233.

Jack, S.L., and Anderson, A.R. (2002). The effects of embeddedness on the entrepreneurial process. *Journal of Business Venturing*, 17, 467–487.

Johannisson, B. (1987). Anarchists and organizers: entrepreneurs in a network perspective. *International Studies of management & Organisation*, 17, 49–63.

Johnson, B.R. (1990). 'Towards a multidimensional model of entrepreneurship: the case of achievement motivation and the entrepreneur.' *Entrepreneurship Theory & Practice*, 14 (1), 39–54

Kets de Vries, M.F.R. (1977). The entrepreneurial personality: a person at the crossroads. *Journal of Management Studies*, 14 (1), 34–57.

Kirzner, I.M. (1973). *Competition and Entrepreneurship.* Chicago: Chicago University Press.

Krueger, N., and Carsrud, A. (1993). 'Entrepreneurial intentions: applying the theory of planned behaviour'. *Entrepreneurship & Regional Development*, 5(4), 315–330.

Lee, S.M., and Peterson, S.J. (2000). 'Culture, Entrepreneurial orientation, and Global Competitiveness'. *Journal of World Business*, 35(4), 401–419.

Levenson, H. (1973). 'Multidimensional locus of control in psychiatric patients'. *Journal of Consulting and Clinical Psychology*, 41(3), 397–404.

Lewin, K. (1951). In *Field theory in social science: selected theoretical papers*, (D. Cartwright, ed), New York: Harper Row.

Littunen, H. (2000). Entrepreneurship and the characteristics of the entrepreneurial personality, *International Journal of Entrepreneurial Behaviour and Research*, 6, 295–306.

Locke, E.E. and Baum, J.R. (2007). Entrepreneurial Motivation, In *The Psychology of Entrepreneurship*, (J.R. Baum, M. Frese, R.A. Baron, eds), chapter 5, pp. 93–112. Mahwah, N.J.: Lawrence Erlbaum Associates.

Lumpkin, G.T., and Dess, G.G. (1996). 'Clarifying the entrepreneurial orientation construct and linking it to performance'. *Academy of Management Review*, 21(1), 135–172.

Magnusson, D. (1981). *Toward a Psychology of Situations – An Interactional Perspective.* Hillsdale, NJ: Lawrence Erlbaum Associates.

McClelland, D.C. (1961). *The Achieving Society.* Princeton, NJ: Van Nostrand.

McClelland, D.C. (1987). 'Characteristics of successful entrepreneurs'. *Journal of Creative Behavior*, 21(3), 219–233.

McGrath, R.G., and McMillan, I.C. (1992). 'More like each other than anyone else? A Cross-cultural Study of Entrepreneurial Perceptions'. *Journal of Business Venturing*, 7, 419–429.

Minniti, M., Bygrave, W.D., and Autio, E. (2005). *Global Entrepreneurship Monitor.* Babson College, Babson Park, MA and London Business School, London, UK.

Mischel, W. (1968). *Personality and Assessment.* New York: Wiley.

Mischel, W. (1973). 'Towards a cognitive social learning reconceptualisation of personality', *Psychological Review*, 80(4), 252–283.

Mischel, W. (1981). *Introduction to Personality,* 3rd edn. New York: Rinehart & Winston.

Mischel, W., and Shoda, Y. (1995). A Cognitive-affective System of Personality: reconceptualizing situations, dispositions, dynamics and invariance in personality structure,. *Psychological Review*, 102, 246–268.

Mischel, W. and Shoda, Y. (1998). 'Reconciling processing dynamics and personality dispositions', *Annual Review of Psychology*, 49, 229–258.

Mitchell, R.K., Smith, J.B., Seawright, K.E.A., and Morse, E.A. (2000). 'Cross-cultural cognitions and the venture creation decision,'. *Academy of Management Journal*, 43(5), 974–993.

Mitchell, R.K., Smith, J.B., Morse, E.A., Seawright, K.E.A., Peredo, A.M., and McKenzie, B. (2002). Are entrepreneurial cognitions universal? Assessing entrepreneurial cognitions across cultures. *Entrepreneurship Theory & Practice*, 26(4), 9–32.

Mueller, S.L., and Thomas, A.S. (2000). 'Culture and entrepreneurial potential: A nine country study of locus of control and innovativeness'. *Journal of Business Venturing*, 16(1), 51–75.

Ogbor, J.O. (2000). 'Mythicizing and Reification in Entrepreneurial Discourse: Ideology-Critique of Entrepreneurial Studies'. *Journal of Management Studies*, 37, 605–635.

Park, J.S. (2005). *'Opportunity recognition and product innovation in entrepreneurial hi-tech start-ups: a new perspective and supporting case study.'* Technovation, 25(7), 739–752.

Pervin, L.A. (ed). (1990). *Handbook of Personality: Theory and Research.* New York: Guilford.

Rauch, A., and Freese, M. (2000). 'Psychological approaches to entrepreneurial success: a general model and overview of findings'. In *International Review of Industrial and Organisational Psychology*, (C.L. Cooper, and I.T. Robertson, eds.), vol. 15, pp. 101–141. New York: John Wiley.

Rauch, A., and Freese, M. (2007). Born to be an Entrepreneur? Revisiting the Personality Approach to Entrepreneurship. In *The Psychology of Entrepreneurs Mahwah*, (R.J. Baum, M. Frese, and R. Baron, eds.), pp. 41–65. NJ &London: Lawrence Erlbaum Associates.

Robinson, P.B., Stimpson, J.C., Huefner, J.C., and Hunt, H.K. (1991). 'An Attitude Approach to the Prediction of Entrepreneurship'. *Entrepreneurship Theory and Practice*, 15(3), 41–52.

Rotter, J.B. (1966). 'Generalised expectancies for internal versus external control of reinforcement'. *Psychological Monographs*, 80(1, Whole No. 609).

Sarason, Y., Dean, T., and Dillard, J.F. (2006). 'Entrepreneurship as the nexus of individual and opportunity: a structuration view'. *Journal of Business Venturing*, 21, 3, 286–305.

Saravathy, D.K., Simon, H.A. and Lave, L. (1998). 'Perceiving and managing business risks: differences between entrepreneurs and bankers'. *Journal of Economic Behavior & Organization*, 33(2), 207–225.

Schumpeter, J.A. (1911/1934). *The Theory of Economic Development*. Cambridge, Mass: Harvard University Press.

Shane, S. (2000). Prior knowledge and the discovery of entrepreneurial opportunities. *Organization Science*, 11(4), 448–469.

Shane, S (2003). A General Theory of Entrepreneurship. Cheltenham: Edward Elgar

Stewart, W.H., Watson, W.E., Carland, J.C., Carland, J.W. (1998). "A proclivity for entrepreneurship: A comparison of entrepreneurs, small business owners, and corporate managers." *Journal of Business Venturing*, 14(2), 189–214.

Thiessen, J.H. (1997). 'Individualism, Collectivism, and Entrepreneurship: A framework for International Comparative Research'. *Journal of Business Venturing*, 12, 367–384.

Thornton, P. (1999). The sociology of entrepreneurship. *Annual Review of Sociology*, 25, 19–46.

Timmons, J.A., Smollen, L.E. and Dingee, A.L.M. (1985). *New Venture Creation*, 2nd edn. Homewood, III, Irwin.

Wortman, M. S. (1986). 'A unified framework, research typologies, and research prospectuses for the interface between entrepreneurship and small business', *The Art and Science of Entrepreneurship*, Cambridge, Mass.: Ballinger, 273–331.

Chapter 4

Amin, A. (2002). 'Spatialities of Globalisation'. *Environment and Planning A*, 34, 385–399.

Amin, A. (2004). 'Regions Unbound: Towards a New Politics of Place'. *Geografiska Annaler B*, 86, 33–44.

Archibugi, D., Howells, J., and Michie, J. (1999). 'Innovation Systems in a Global Economy'. *Technology Analysis and Strategic Management*, 11, 527–539.

Asheim, B.T., and Isaksen, A. (2002). 'Regional Innovation Systems: The Integration of Local 'sticky' and Global 'ubiquitous' Knowledge'. *The Journal of Technology Transfer*, 27, 77–86.

Balzat, M., and Hanush, H. (2004). 'Recent Trends in the Research on National Innovation Systems'. *Journal of Evolutionary Economics*, 14, 197–210.

Boschma, R. (2005). 'Proximity and Innovation. A Critical Assessment'. *Regional Studies*, 39, 61–74.

Braczyk, H.-J., Cooke, P., and Heidenrich, M. (1998). *Regional Innovation Systems*. London: UCL Press.

Camagni, R., and Capello, R. (1999). 'Innovation and Performance of SMEs in Italy: the Relevance of Spatial Aspects'. In *Innovation, Networks and Localities*, (M.M. Fisher, L. Suarez-Villa, and M. Steiner, eds.), pp. 181–214. Berlin: Springer.

Carlsson, B., Jacobsson, S., Holmén, M., and Rickne, A. (2002). 'Innovation Systems: Analytical and Methodological Issues'. *Research Policy*, 31, 233–245.

Cooke, P., Gomez, O.M., and Etxebarria, G. (1997). 'Regional Innovation Systems: Institutional and Organizational Dimensions'. *Research Policy*, 26, 475–491.

Drucker, P. (2006). *Innovation and entrepreneurship*, 2nd edn. New York: Harper Collins.

Edquist, C. (2001) The System of Innovation Approach and Innovation Policy: An Account of the State of the Art, DRUID paper, www.druid.dk.

Edquist, C. (2005). 'Systems of Innovation: Perspectives and Challenges'. In *The Oxford Handbook of Innovation*, (J. Fagerberg, D. Mowery, and R.R. Nelson, eds.), pp. 181–208. Norfolk: Oxford University Press.

Edquist, C., Hommen, L., and McKelvey, M. (2001). *Innovation and Employment. Process versus Product Innovation*. Cheltenham: Edward Elgar.

Etzkowitz, H., and Leydesdorff, L. (2000). 'The Dynamics of Innovation: from National Systems and 'Mode2' to Triple Helix of University-Industry-Government Relations'. *Research Policy*, 29, 109–123.

Fagerberg, J. (2005). 'Innovation: A guide to the literature'. In *The Oxford Handbook of Innovation*, (J. Fagerberg, D. Mowery, and R.R. Nelson, eds.), pp. 1–27. Norfolk: Oxford University Press.

Feldman, M.P., and Florida, R. (1994). 'The Geographic Sources of Innovation: Technological Infrastructure and Product Innovation in the United States'. *Annals of the Association of American Geographers*, 84, 210–229.

Fisher, M.M., and Frölich, J. (2001). *Knowledge, Complexity and Innovation Systems*. Berlin: Springer.

Flagestad, A., Hope, C.A., Svensson, B., and Nordin, S. (2005). 'The Tourist Destination; a Local Innovation System? The Creation of a Model', In *Innovation in Tourism – Creating Customer Value*, (P. Keller and T. Bieger, eds), Brainerd: AIEST.

Freeman, C. (1987). *Technology Policy and Economic Performance*. London: Pinter.

Freeman, C. (1995). 'The National Innovation Systems in Historical Perspective'. *Cambridge Journal of Economics*, 19, 5–24.

Fuchs, G., and Shapiro, P. (2005). *Rethinking Regional Innovation and Change*. Berlin: Springer.

Geels, F.W. (2004). 'From Sectoral Systems of Innovation to Social-Technical Systems'. *Regional Policy*, 33, 897–920.

Håkansson, H. (1986). *Industrial Technological Development: a Network Approach*. London: Croom Helm.

Henten, A., Falch, M., and Jensen, S. (2006) *Multi-National Innovation Systems, Paper,* Lyngby: DTU.

Hjalager, A.-M. (2000). 'Tourism Destinations and the Concept of Industrial Districts'. *Tourism & Hospitality Research*, 2, 199–213.

Hjalager, A.-M. (2006). 'The Marriage between Welfare Services and Tourism – a Driving Force for Innovation'. *Journal of Quality Assurance in Hospitality and Tourism*, 6, 7–30.

Hjalager, A.-M. (2007). 'Four Stages in Tourism Globalisation'. *Annals of Tourism Research*, 34, 437–457.

Hjalager, A.-M., Huijbens, E.H., Björk, P., Nordin, S., and Flagestad, A. (2008). *Innovation systems in Nordic tourism*. Oslo: Nordic Innovation Centre. http://www.nordicinnovation.net/prosjekt.cfm?Id=1-4415-282

Johnson, A. (2001). 'Functions in Innovation Systems Approaches', DRUID paper. www.druid.dk

Johnson, B., and Lundvall, B-Å. (2000). *'Promoting Innovation System as a Response to the Globalising Learning Economy', Draft paper.* Aalborg University.

Lundvall, B-Å. (ed.) (1992). *National Systems of Innovation.* London: Pinter.

Lundvall, B-Å. (2005) 'National Innovation Systems - Analytical Concept and Development Tool', Paper Presented at the DRUID Conference in Copenhagen.

Lundvall, B-Å. (2005). *'Innovation System Research and Policy: Where It Came from and where It Should Go'.* Paper. Aalborg University.

Lundvall, B-Å. (2007a). 'National Innovation Systems – Analytical Concept and Development Tool', *Industry and Innovation*, 14(1), 95–119.

Lundvall, B-Å. (2007b). 'Innovation Systems: Theory and Policy', In *Companion to Neo-Schumpeterian Economics*, (H. Hanusch, ed), Cheltenham: Edward Elgar.

Malerba, F. (2004). 'Sectoral Systems of Innovation: Basic Concepts'. In *Sectoral Systems of Innovation. Concepts, Issues and Analyses of Six Major Sectors in Europe*, (F. Malerba, ed.), pp. 9–41. Cambridge: Cambridge University Press.

Markusen, A. (1999). 'Sticky Places in Slippery Space'. In *The New Industrial Geography*, (T.J. Barnes, and M.S. Gertler, eds.), pp. 98–147. London: Routledge.

Maskell, P., and Malmberg, A. (1999). 'Localised Learning and Industrial Competitiveness'. *Cambridge Journal of Economics*, 23, 167–185.

Massey, D. (2004). 'Geographies of Responsibility'. *Geografiska Annaler B*, 86, 5–18.

Morgan, K. (2004). 'The Exaggerated Death of Geography: Learning, Proximity and Territorial Innovation Systems'. *Journal of Economic Geography*, 4, 3–21.

Moulaert, F., and Sekia, F. (2003). 'Territorial Innovation Models: a Critical Survey'. *Regional Studies*, 37, 289–302.

Nalebuff, B.J., and Brandenburger, A.M. (1997). *Co-opetition.* London: Harper Collins Business.

Nelson, R. (1993). *National Systems of Innovation. A Comparative Study.* Oxford: Oxford University Press.

Nooteboom, B. (2000). *Learning and Innovation in Organizations and Economies.* Oxford: Oxford University Press.

Nordin, S. (2003). 'Tourism Clustering and Innovation—Paths to Economic Growth and Development', Östersund: European Tourism Research Institute.

OECD. (1999). *Boosting Innovation. The Cluster Approach.* Paris: OECD.

OECD (2005). *Innovation Policy and Performance. A Cross-Country Comparison,* Paris: OECD.

Oinas, P., and Malecki, E.J. (2002). 'The Evolution of Technologies in Time and Space: From National and Regional to Spatial Innovation Systems'. *International Regional Science Review*, 25, 102–131.

Porter, M. (1990). *The Competitive Advantage of Nations.* London: Macmillan.

Schienstock, G., and Hämäläinen, T. (2001). *Transformation of the Finnish Innovation System.* Helsinki: SITRA. A Network Approach.

Schumpeter, J. (1934). *The Theory of Economic Development: An Inquiry into profits, Capital, Credit, Interest, and the Business Cycle.* Cambridge: MA: Harvard University Press.

Schumpeter, J. (1942). *Capitalism, Socialism and Democracy.* London: George Allen & Unwin.

Sundbo, J., and Gallouj, F. (2000). 'Innovation as a Loosely Coupled System in Services, International'. *Journal of Service Technology and Management*, 1, 15–36.

Trott, P. (1998). *Innovation Management & New Product Development.* Harlow: Prentice Hall.

Chapter 5

Allen, I.E., Elam, A., Langowitz, N. and Dean, M. (2008). *Global Entrepreneurship Monitor 2007*: Report on Women and Entrepreneurship. GEM.

Allen, S., and Truman, C. (1993). *Women in Business: Perspectives on Women Entrepreneurs.* London and New York: Routledge.

Anna, A.L., Chandler, G.N., Jansen, E., and Mero, N.P. (1999). Women business owners in traditional and non-traditional industries. *Journal of Business Venturing*, 15, 279–303.

Apostolopoulos, Y., Sönmez, S., and Timothy, D.J. (2001). *Women as Producers and Consumers of Tourism in Developing Regions.* Westport, CT: Praeger Publishers.

Apostolopoulos, Y., and Sönmez, S. (2001). Working producers, leisured consumers: women's experiences in developing regions. In *Women as Producers and Consumers of Tourism in Developing Regions*, (Y. Apostolopoulos, S. Sönmez, and D.J. Timothy, eds.), pp. 3–17. Westport, CT: Praeger Publishers.

Ateljevic, I., and Doorne, S. (2000). 'Staying within the fence': lifestyle entrepreneurship in tourism. *Journal of Sustainable Tourism*, 8(5), 378–392.

Bates, T. (2002). Restricted access to markets characterizes women-owned businesses. *Journal of Business Venturing*, 17, 313–324.

Becker-Blease, J.R., and Sohl, J.E. (2007). Do women-owned businesses have equal access to angel capital? *Journal of Business Venturing*, 22, 503–521.

Beeton, S. (2006). *Community Development Through Tourism.* Collingwood, VIC: CSIRO Publishing.

Berger, K. (2005). *A recipe for paradise? Gendered tourism in Rarotonga.* Msc. Thesis Master of Arts in Development Studies. Auckland: The University of Auckland.

Blanchard, L., Zhao, B., and Yinger, J. (2008). Do lenders discriminate against minority and woman entrepreneurs? *Journal of Urban Economics*, 63, 467–497.

Botha, M., Niemand, G., and van Vuuren, J. (2006). Enhancing female entrepreneurship by enabling access to skills. *Entrepreneurship Mgt*, 2, 479–493.

Bouquet, M. (1982). Production and reproduction of family farms in South-West England. *Sociologica Ruralis*, 22, 227–244.

Bras, K., and Dahles, H. (1998). Women entrepreneurs and beach tourism in Sanur, Bali: Gender, employment opportunities, and government policy. *Pacific Tourism Review*, 1, 243–256.

Brega, L. (1998). Women farmers: a resource for agriculture. *Mondo Macchina*, 7(1), 40–43.

Brindley, C. (2005). Barriers to women achieving their entrepreneurial potential: women and risk. *International Journal of Entrepreneurial Behaviour and Research*, 11(2), 144–161.

Bruni, A., Gherardi, S., and Poggio, B. (2004). Entrepreneurial-mentality, gender and the study of women entrepreneurs. *Journal of Organizational Change Management*, 17(3), 256–268.

Brush, C.G., Carter, N.M., Gatewood, E.J., Greene, P.G., and Hart, M.M. (2006). *Growth-oriented Women Entrepreneurs and Their Businesses: A Global Research Perspective.* Northampton, MA: Edward Elgar Publishing.

Butler, J.E. (2003). *New Perspectives on Women Entrepreneurs.* Greenwich, Conn: Information Age Publishing.

Buttner, E.H., and Rosen, B. (1988). Bank loan officers' perceptions of the characteristics of men, women, and successful entrepreneurs. *Journal of Business Venturing*, 3, 249–258.

Catley, S., and Hamilton, R.T. (1998). Small business development and gender of owner. *Journal of Management*, 17(1), 75–82.

Chhabra, D., Healy, R., and Sills, E. (2003). Staged authenticity and heritage tourism. *Annals of Tourism Research*, 30(3), 702–719.

Chiappe, M.B., and Flora, C.B. (1998). Gendered elements of the alternative agriculture paradigm. *Rural Sociology*, 63(3), 372–393.

Cohen, C.B. (2001). Island is a woman: women as producers and products in British Virgin Islands tourism. In *Women as Producers and Consumers of Tourism in Developing Regions*, (Y. Apostolopoulos, S. Sönmez, and D.J. Timothy, eds.), pp. 47–72. Westport, CT: Praeger Publishers.

Coughlin, J.H., and Thomas, A.R. (2002). *The Rise of Women Entrepreneurs: People, Processes, and Global Trends.* Westport, Connecticut, London: Quorum Books.

Das, M. (1999). Women entrepreneurs from Southern India: an exploratory study. *The Journal of Entrepreneurship*, 8(2), 147–163.

Della-Giusta, M., and Phillips, C. (2006). Women entrepreneurs in the Gambia: challenges and opportunities. *Journal of International Development*, 18, 1051–1064.

DeMartino, R., and Barbato, R. (2003). Differences between women and men MBA entrepreneurs: exploring family flexibility and wealth creation as career motivators. *Journal of Business Venturing*, 18, 815–832.

Doherty, L., and Manfredi, S. (2001). Women's employment in Italian and UK hotels. *International Journal of Hospitality Management*, 20(1), 61–76.

Elmas, S. (2007). Gender and tourism development: a case study of the Cappadoccia region of Turkey. In *Tourism and Gender: embodiment, sensuality and experience*, (A. Pritchard, N. Morgan, I. Ateljevic, and C. Harris, eds.), pp. 302–314. USA, UK: CABI.

Ericksen, G.K. (1999). *Women Entrepreneurs Only: 12 Women Entrepreneurs Tell the Stories of Their Success.* New York, Cambridge: John Wiley and Sons.

Fielden, S.L., and Davidson, M. (2005). *International Handbook of Women and Small Business Entrepreneurship.* Northampton, MA: Edward Elgar Publishing.

Fuller-Love, N., Lim, L., and Akehurst, G. (2006). Guest editorial: female and ethnic minority entrepreneurship. *Entrepreneurship Mgt*, 2, 429–439.

Garcia-Ramon, M.D., Canoves, G., and Valdovinos, N. (1995). Farm tourism, gender and the environment in Spain. *Annals of Tourism Research*, 22(2), 267–282.

Gartner, W.B. (1990). What are we talking about when we talk about entrepreneurship? *Journal of Business Venturing*, 5, 15–28.

Gentry, M.K. (2007). Belizean women and tourism work: opportunity or impediment? *Annals of Tourism Research*, 34(2), 477–496.

Getz, D., Carlsen, J., and Morrison, A. (2004). *The Family Business in Tourism and Hospitality*. USA, UK: CABI.

Gibson, H.J. (2001). Gender in Tourism: Theoretical Perspectives. In *Women as Producers and Consumers of Tourism in Developing Regions*, (Y. Apostolopoulos, S. Sönmez, and D.J. Timothy, eds.), pp. 19–43. Westport, CT: Praeger Publishers.

Gray, K.R., and Finley-Hervey, J. (2005). Women and entrepreneurship in Morocco: debunking stereotypes and discerning strategies. *International Entrepreneurship and Management Journal*, 1, 203–217.

Guijt, I., and Shah, M.K. (1998). *The Myth of Community: Gender Issues in Participatory Development*. London: Intermediate Technology Publications.

Hall, D.R. (2001). From the 'Iron Curtain' to the 'Dollar Curtain': women and tourism in Eastern Europe. In *Women as Producers and Consumers of Tourism inDeveloping Regions*, (Y. Apostolopoulos, S. Sönmez, and D.J. Timothy, eds.), pp. 191–207. Westport, CT: Praeger Publishers.

Harris, C., McIntosh, A., and Lewis, K. (2007). The commercial home enterprise: labour with love. *Tourism Zagreb*, 55(4), 391–402.

Heffernan, M. (2008). *Women on Top: How Women Entrepreneurs are Rewriting the Rules of Business Success*. New York: Penguin.

Heidrick, T., and Johnson, S. (2002). *Financing SMEs in Canada: barriers faced by women, youth, aboriginal and minority entrepreneurs in accessing capital – phase 2: gap analysis and recommendations for further research. Research Paper prepared for the Small Business Policy Branch as part of the Small and Medium-Sized Enterprise (SME) Financing Data Initiative*. Ottawa: Publishing and Depository Services, Public Works and Government Services Canada.

Heilman, M.E., and Chen, J.J. (2003). Entrepreneurship as a solution: the allure of self-employment for women and minorities. *Human Resource Management Review*, 13, 347–364.

Hisrich, R.D., and Öztürk, S.A. (1999). Women entrepreneurs in a developing economy. *The Journal of Management Development*, 18(2), 114–124.

Hughes, K.D. (2005). *Female Enterprise in the New Economy*. Toronto: University of Toronto Press.

ILO (International Labour Organization) (2008). *Women's Entrepreneurship Development and Gender Equality*. Available at http://www.ilo.org/dyn/empent/empent.Portal?p_prog= Sandp_subprog=WE (Accessed: 15 July 2008).

Iverson, K., and Sparrowe, R. (1999). Cracks in the glass ceiling? An empirical study of gender differences in income in the hospitality industry in the UK. *Journal of Hospitality and Tourism Research*, 23(1), 4.

Jennings, G., and Stehlik, D. (1999). *The innovators are women: the development of farm tourism in Central Queensland, Australia. Conference Proceedings of the 1999 annual ISTTE conference. One world, One community, One mission*. Canada: Vancouver. pp. 84–85.

Joppe, M. (1996). Sustainable community tourism development revisited. *Tourism Management*, 17(7), 475–479.

Kahn, M.R. (1995). Women entrepreneurs in the Bangladeshi restaurant business. *Development in Practice*, 5(3), 240–244.

Kempadoo, K. (2001). Freelancers, temporary wives and beach-boys: researching sex work in the Caribbean. *Feminist Review*, 67(1), 39–62.

Kinnaird, V., and Hall, D. (1994). *Tourism: A Gender Analysis*. Chichester: John Wiley and Sons.

Kyro, P., Aaltio, I., and Sundin, E. (2008). *Women Entrepreneurship and Social Capital: A Dialogue and Construction*. Copenhagen: Copenhagen Business School Press.

Lackey, A.S. (1990). Defining development. *Journal of Rural Development and Administration*, 22(4), 63–75.

Langreiter, N. (2004). Only a question of the right attitude: female innkeepers and hoteliers on handling of time and space. *Tourismus Journal*, 8(1), 111–131.

Lee-Gosselin, H., and Grisé, J. (1990). Are women owner-managers challenging our definitions of entrepreneurship? An in-depth survey. *Journal of Business Ethics*, 9, 423–433.

León, M.C. (2006). Women and empowerment: community participation in tourism in Ecuador. *Msc. Thesis Department of Environmental Sciences, Social-spatial Analysis*. Wageningen: Wageningen University.

Lerner, M., Brush, C., and Hisrich, R. (1997). Israeli women entrepreneurs: an examination of factors affecting performance. *Journal of Business Venturing*, 12, 315–339.

Li, J. (2003). Playing upon fantasy: women, ethnic tourism and the politics of identity construction in contemporary Xishuang Banna, China. *Tourism Recreation Research*, 28(2), 51–65.

Lituchy, T.R., and Reavley, M.A. (2004). Women entrepreneurs: a comparison of international small business owners in Poland and the Czech Republic. *Journal of International Entrepreneurship*, 2, 61–87.

Long, V., and Wall, G. (1995). Small-scale tourism development in Bali. In *Island Tourism: Management, Principles and Practice*, (M. Conlin, and T. Baum, eds.), pp. 237–257. Sussex: John Wiley and Sons.

Lynch, P. (1998). Female microentrepreneurs in the host family sector: key motivations and socio-economic variables. *Hospitality Management*, 17, 319–342.

MacCannell, D., and Lippard, L.R. (1999). *The Tourist: A New Theory of the Leisure Class. Berkeley and Los Angeles*. California: University of California Press.

Markham, S.E. (1997). *Women: the invisible pioneers in recreation and leisure research bibliography*. Available at http://ace.acadiau.ca/fps/srmk/markham/biblio.htm (Accessed: 15 July 2008).

Mattis, M.C. (2004). Women entrepreneurs: out from under the glass ceiling. *Women in Management Review*, 19(3), 154–163.

McClelland, E., Swail, J., Bell, J., and Ibbotson, P. (2005). Following the pathway of female entrepreneurs: a six-country investigation. *International Journal of Entrepreneurial Behaviour and Research*, 11(2), 84–107.

McGehee, N.G., Kim, K., and Jennings, G.R. (2007). Gender and motivation for agri-tourism entrepreneurship. *Tourism Management*, 28, 280–289.

Mills, B. (2004). Hucksters and homemakers: gender responses to opportunities in the tourism market in Carriacou, Grenada. In *Tourism in the Caribbean: Trends, Development, Prospects*, (D.T. Duval, ed.), pp. 257–270. London: Routledge.

Mitchell, R., and Reid, D. (2001). Community integration: island tourism in Peru. *Annals of Tourism Research*, 28(1), 113–139.

Momsen, J.H. (2004). *Gender and Development*. London: Routledge.

Moore, D.P., and Buttner, E.H. (1997). *Women Entrepreneurs: Moving Beyond the Glass Ceiling*. Thousands Oaks, CA: Sage Publications.

Mowforth, M., and Munt, I. (2003). *Tourism and Sustainability: Development and the New Tourism in the Third World*. London: Routledge.

Murphy, P.E. (1985). *Tourism: A Community Approach*. New York and London: Routledge.

Ng, C., and Pine, R. (2003). Women and men in hotel management in Hong Kong: perceptions of gender and career development issues. *International Journal of Hospitality Management*, 22(1), 85–102.

Oppedisano, J. (2004). Giving back: women's entrepreneurial philanthropy. *Women in Management Review*, 19(3), 174–177.

Overbeek, G. (2003). The income and property of women in the agriculture and tourism sectors. *International Journal of Agricultural Resources, Governance and Ecology*, 2(2), 125–139.

Pretty, J., and Hine, R. (1999). *Participatory Appraisal for Community Assessment: Principles and Methods*. UK: University of Essex.

Pritchard, A., Morgan, N., Ateljevic, I., and Harris, C. (2007). *Tourism and Gender: embodiment, sensuality and experience*. USA, UK: CABI.

Radovic Markovic, M. (2008). *The Perspective of Women's Entrepreneurship in the Age of Globalization*. Charlotte, NC: Information Age Publishing.

Richards, G., and Hall, D.R. (2000). *Tourism and Sustainable Community Development*. London and New York: Routledge.

Roehl, W., and Swerdlow, S. (2001). Sex differences in hotel employee training in the western United States. *Pacific Tourism Review*, 5(3, 4), 143.

Roomi, M.A., and Parrot, G. (2008). Barriers to development and progression of women entrepreneurs in Pakistan. *The Journal of Entrepreneurship*, 17(1), 59–72.

Runyan, R.C., Huddleston, P., and Swinney, J. (2006). Entrepreneurial orientation and social capital as small firm strategies: A study of gender differences from a resource-based view. *Entrepreneurship Mgt*, 2, 455–477.

Samir El-Sharif Ibrahim, N., Pritchard, A., and Jones, E. (2007). (Un)veiling women's employment in the Egyptian travel business. In *Tourism and Gender: embodiment, sensuality and experience*, (A. Pritchard, N. Morgan, I. Ateljevic, and C. Harris, eds.), pp. 290–301. USA, UK: CABI.

Scheyvens, R. (1999). Ecotourism and the empowerment of local communities. *Tourism Management*, 20, 245–249.

Scheyvens, R. (2000). Promoting women's empowerment through involvement in ecotourism: experiences from the Third World. *Journal of Sustainable Tourism*, 8(3), 232–249.

Smith, C.A. (2005). *Market Women: Black Women Entrepreneurs – Past, Present, and Future*. Westport, CT: Praeger Publishers.

Smith-Hunter, A.E. (2006). *Women Entrepreneurs Across Racial Lines: Issues of Human Capital, Financial Capital and Network Structures*. Cheltenham: Edward Elgar Publishing.

Spear, R. (2000) The nature of social entrepreneurship. The paper presented at ISTR conference, Dublin, July 2000.

Still, L.V., and Walker, E.A. (2006). The self-employed woman owner and her business: an Australian profile. *Women in Management Review*, 21(4), 294–310.

Timothy, D.J. (2001). Gender relations in tourism: revisiting patriarchy and underdevelopment. In *Women as Producers and Consumers of Tourism in Developing Regions*, (Y. Apostolopoulos, S. Sönmez, and D.J. Timothy, eds.), pp. 235–248. Westport, CT: Praeger Publishers.

Tosun, C. (2000). Limits to community participation in the tourism development process in developing countries. *Tourism Management*, 21, 613–633.

Tosun, C. (2001). Challenges of sustainable tourism development in the developing world: the case of Turkey. *Tourism Management*, 22, 289–303.

Tosun, C. (2005). Stages in the emergence of a participatory tourism development approach in the Developing World. *Geoforum*, 36, 333–352.

Tucker, H. (2007). Undoing shame: tourism and women's work in Turkey. *Journal of Tourism and Cultural Change*, 5(2), 87–105.

United Nations (1999) *Gender and Tourism: Women's Employment and Participation in Tourism*. Summary of UNED-UK's Project Report. Available at http://www.earthsummit2002.org/toolkits/women/current/gendertourismrep.html (Accessed 15 July 2008).

Venkataraman, S. (1997). The distinctive domain of entrepreneurship research: an editor's perspective. In *Advances in entrepreneurship, firm emergence, and growth*, (J. Katz, and R. Brockhaus, eds.), vol. 3, pp. 119–138. Greenwich, CT: JAI Press.

Walker, S., Valaoras, G., Gurung, D., and Godde, P. (2001). Women and mountain tourism: redefining the boundaries of policy and practice. In *Women as Producers and Consumers of Tourism in Developing Regions*, (Y. Apostolopoulos, S. Sönmez, and D.J. Timothy, eds.), pp. 211–234. Westport, CT: Praeger Publishers.

Walker, E.A., Wang, C., and Redmond, J. (2008). Women and work–life balance: is home-based business ownership the solution? *Equal Opportunities International*, 27(3), 258–275.

Walker, E.A., and Webster, B.J. (2007). Gender, age and self-employment: some things change, some stay the same. *Women in Management Review*, 22(2), 122–135.

Watson, J., and Newby, R. (2005). Biological sex, stereotypical sex-roles, and SME owner characteristics. *International Journal of Entrepreneurial Behaviour and Research*, 11(2), 129–143.

Watson, J., and Robinson, S. (2003). Adjusting for risk in comparing the performances of male- and female -controlled SMEs. *Journal of Business Venturing*, 18, 773–788.

Wells, S.J. (1998). *Women Entrepreneurs: Developing Leadership for Success*. US: Library of Congress Cataloging-in-Publication Data.

Wilkinson, P.F., and Pratiwi, W. (1995). Gender and tourism in an Indonesian village. *Annals of Tourism Research*, 22(2), 283–299.

Williams, S. (2004). *Tourism: Critical Concepts in the Social Sciences*. London: Routledge.

Winn, J. (2005). Women entrepreneurs: can we remove the barriers? *International Entrepreneurship and Management Journal*, 1, 381–397.

Chapter 6

Aldrich, H.E., and Fiol, C. (1994). Fools rush in? The Institutional Context of Industry Creation. *Academy of Management Review*, 19(4), 645–670.

Ardichvili, A., Cardozo, R., and Ray, S. (2003). A Theory of Entrepreneurial Opportunity Identification and Development,. *Journal of Business Venturing*, 18, 105–123.

Baldelt, C. (1997). *Entrepreneurship Theories of the Nonprofit Sector.* Voluntas, 8/2.

Barley, S., and Tolbert, P. (1997). Institutionalization and Structuration: Studying the Links between Action and Institution. *Organization Studies*, 18/1, 93–117.

Baumol, W. (1993). Formal Entrepreneurship Theory in Economics: Existence and Bound. *Journal of Business Venturing*, 8, 197–210.

Beckert, J. (1999). Agency, Entrepreneurs, and Institutional Change: The Role of Strategic Choice and Institutionalized Practices in Organizations,. *Organization Studies*, 20, 777–799.

Berger, P., and Luckman, T. (1967). *The Social Construction of Reality.* London: Penguin.

Bourdieu, P., and Wacquant, L. (1992). *An Invitation to Reflexive Sociology.* Chicago: University of Chicago Press.

Bridge, S., O'Neil, K., and Cromie, S. (2003). *Understanding Enterprise, Entrepreneurship and Small Business.* Basingstoke: Palgrave Macmillan.

Casson, M. (1982). *The Entrepreneur.* Totowa, NJ: Barnes and Noble.

Casson, M. (1995). *Entrepreneurship and Business Culture.* Aldershot: Edward Elgar.

DiMaggio, P. (1988). Interest and Agency in Institutional Theory. In *Institutional patterns and organizations: Culture and environment*, (L.G. Zucker, ed.), pp. 3–22. Cambridge, MA: Ballinger.

DiMaggio, P. (1991). Constructing an Organizational Field as a Professional Project: U.S. Art Museums 1920-1940. In *The New Institutionalism in Organizational Analysis*, (W.W. Powell, and P.J. DiMaggio, eds.), pp. 267–292. Chicago: University of Chicago Press.

DiMaggio, P.J., and Powell, W.W. (1983). The Iron Cage revisited: Institutional Isomorphism and Collective Rationality in Organizational Fields,. *American Sociological Review*, 48, 147–160.

DiMaggio, P.J., and Powell, W.W. (1991). Introduction. In *The New Institutionalism in Organizational Analysis*, (W.W. Powell, and P.J. DiMaggio, eds.), pp. 1–38. Chicago: University of Chicago Press.

Fligstein, N. (1997). Social Skill and Institutional Theory. *American Behavioral Scientist*, 40, 397–405.

Fligstein, N. (2001). Institutional Entrepreneurs and Cultural Frames: The Case of the European Union's Single Market Program,. *European Societies*, 3/3, 261–287.

Friedland, R, Alford, R (1991) Bringing Society Back in: Symbols, Practices, and Institutional Contradictions. In *The New Institutionalism in Organizational Analysis*, (W.W. Powell and P.J. DiMaggio eds.), pp. 232–263, Chicago, IL, University of Chicago Press.

Greenwood, R., and Hinings, C.R. (1996). Understanding Radical Organizational Change: Bringing together the Old and New Institutionalism. *Academy of Management Review*, 21/4, 1022–1054.

Greenwood, R., Suddaby, R., and Hinings, C. (2002). Theorising Change: The Role of Professional Associations in Institutional Change. *Academy of Management Journal*, 45, 58–80.

Hinnings, C., and Greenwood, R. (1988). *The Dynamics of Strategic Change*. Oxford, England: Basil Blackwell.

Jepperson, R. (1991). Institutions, Institutional Effects, and Institutionalization. In *The New Institutionalism in Organizational Analysis*, (W. Powell, and P. DiMaggio, eds.). Chicago: IL University of Chicago Press.

Khilstrom, R., and Laffont, J. (1979). A General Equilibrium Entrepreneurial Theory of Firm Formation Based on Risk Aversion,. *Journal of Political Economy*, 87, 719–748.

Lawrence, T., and Philips, N. (2004). From Moby Dick to Free Willy: Macro-Cultural Discourse and Institutional Entrepreneurship in Emerging Fields. *Organization*, 11/5, 689–711.

Maguire, S., Hardy, C., and Lawrence, T. (2004). Institutional Entrepreneurship in Emerging Fields: HIV/AIDS Treatment Advocacy in Canada. *Academy of Management Journal*, 47/5, 657–679.

Meyer, J., and Rowan, B. (1977). Institutionalized Organizations: Formal Structure as Myth and Ceremony. *American Journal of Sociology*, 83, 340–363.

Morrison, A. (2006). A Contextualisation of Entrepreneurship. *International Journal of Entrepreneurial Behaviour*, 12/4, 192–209.

Oliver, C. (1992). The Antecedents of Deinstitutionalization. *Organization Studies*, 13, 563–588.

Peredo, A., and Chrisman, J. (2006). Toward a Theory of Community-Based Enterprise. *Academy of Management Review*, 31/2, 309–328.

Philips, N, (2003). Discourse or Institution? Institutional Theory and the Challenge of Critical Discourse Analysis. In *Debating Organization – Point – Counterpoint in Organization Studies*, (R. Westwood and S. Clegg, eds.), pp. 220–131. Oxford: Blackwell.

Reay, T., and Hinings, C. (2005). The Recomposition of an Organizational Field: Health Care in Canada. *Organizational Studies*, 16/3, 351–384.

Rao, H., Morrill, C., and Zald, M. (2000). Power plays: How social Movements and Collective Action Create New Organizational Forms. In *Research in organizational behavior*, (R.I. Sutton, and B.M. Staw, eds.), pp. 239–282. Greenwich, CT: JAI Press.

Seo, M., and Creed, W. (2002). Institutional Contradictions, Praxis and Institutional Change: A Dialectical Perspective. *Academy of Management Review*, 3, 222–247.

Scott, W.R. (1995). *Institutions and Organizations*. Thousand Oaks, CA: Sage.

Scott, W. Richard, Ruef, M., Mendel, P., and Caronna, C. (2000). *Institutional Change and Healthcare Organizations*. Chicago, IL: University of Chicago.

Shumpeter, J. (1934). *Capitalism, Socialism and Democracy*. New York: Harper and Row.

Timmons, J. (1994). *New Venture Creation*. Boston, MA: Irwin.

Venkataraman, S. (1997). The Distinctive Domain of Entrepreneurship Research: An Editors Perspective. In *Advances in Entrepreneurship, Firm Emergence and Growth*, (J. Katz, and R. Brockhaus, eds.), vol. 3, pp. 119–138. Greenwich, CT: JAI Press.

Wijen, F., and Ansari, S. (2007). Overcoming Inaction Through Collective Institutional Entrepreneurship: Insights from Regime Theory. *Organization Studies*, 28/7, 1079–1100.

Young, D. (1987). Executive Leadership in Nonprofit Organisations. In *The Nonprofit Sector: A Research Handbook*, (W. Powell, ed.). New Haven: Yale University Press.

Zucker, L. (1977). The Role of Institutionalization in Cultural Persistence. *American Sociological Review*, 42(5), 726–743.

Chapter 7

Ahmed, P., Lim, K., and Loh, A. (2002). *Learning Through Knowledge Management*. Oxford: Butterworth Heinemann.

Blake, A., Sinclair, M., and Soria, J. (2006). Tourism Productivity: Evidence from the UK. *Annals of Tourism Research*, 33(4), 1099–1120.

Cooper, C. (2006). Knowledge Management and Tourism. *Annals of Tourism Research*, 33(1), 47–64.

de Bono, E. (1999). *Six Thinking Hats*. Boston: Back Bay Books.

Hall, C.M., and Williams, A. (2008). *Innovation in Tourism*. London: Routledge.

Hjalager, A. (2002). Repairing innovation defectiveness in tourism. *Tourism Management*, 23(5), 465–474.

Hjalager, A. (2005). The marriage between welfare services and tourism – a driving force for innovation. In *Innovation in Hospitality and Tourism*, (M. Peters, and B. Pikkmaat, eds.), pp. 7–30. Binghampton, NJ: The Haworth Hospitality Press.

Morrison, A., Lynch, P.A., and Johns, N. (2004). International Tourism Networks. *International Journal of Contemporary Hospitality Management*, 16(3), 197–202.

Nonaka, I. (1991). The Knowledge Creating Economy. *Harvard Business Review*, 69(6), 96–104.

Oakland, J. (1991) *Total Quality Management*, 2nd edn. Oxford: Heinemann.

OECD. (2006). *Innovation and Growth in Tourism*. Paris: OECD.

Page, S.J. (2006). *Tourism Management: Managing for Change,* 2nd edn. Oxford: Butterworth Heinemann.

Pechlaner, H., Fischer, E., and Hammann, E. (2005). 'Leadership and innovation processes – development of products and services based on core competencies'. In *Innovation in Hospitality and Tourism*, (M. Peters, and B. Pikkmaat, eds.), pp. 31–58. Binghampton, NJ: The Haworth Hospitality Press.

Peters, M., and Pikkmaat, B. (2005). Innovation in tourism. In *Innovation in Hospitality and Tourism*, (M. Peters, and B. Pikkmaat, eds.), pp. 1–6. Binghampton, NJ: The Haworth Hospitality Press.

Schianetz, K., Kavanagh, L., and Luckington, D. (2007). The learning tourism destination: the potential of a learning organization approach for improving the sustainability of tourism destinations. *Tourism Management*, 28(6), 1485–1496.

Schumpeter, J. (1954). *The Theory of Economic Development*. New York: Oxford University Press.

Scottish Enterprise (2007) Tourism and Innovation. www.scottishenterprise website, accessed 12 September 2007.

Solow, R. (1970). *Growth Theory: An Exposition*. New York: Oxford University Press.

Sundbo, J., Orfilas-Sintes, F., and Sørensen, F. (2007). The innovative behaviour of tourism firms – comparative studies of Denmark and Spain. *Research Policy*, 36(1), 88–106.

Thomas, R., and Augustyn, M. (eds) (2006). *Tourism in the New Europe*. Elsevier: Oxford.

Vikane, H. (2006). *What Influences the Entrepreneurial Activity in a Tourist Destination*. Stirling: University of Stirling.

World Economic Forum. (2007). *Travel and Tourism Competitiveness Report*. Geneva: World Economic Forum.

Chapter 8

Adorno, T., and Horkheimer, M. (1977). "The Culture Industry: Enlightenment as Mass Deception". In *Mass Communication and Society*, (J. Curran, M. Gurevitch, and J. Wollacott, eds.). London: Edward Arnold J.

Antal, F. (1948). *Florentine Painting and its Social Background – 14th and Early 15th Centuries*. London: Routledge and Kegan Paul Ltd.

Aslin, E. (1981). *The Aesthetic Movement – Prelude to Art Nouveau*. London: Ferndale Editions.

Ateljevic, I., and Doorne, S. (2000). "Staying Within the Fence': Lifestyle Entrepreneurship in Tourism". *Journal of Sustainable Tourism*, 8(5), 378–392.

Becker, H.S. (1978). "Arts and Crafts". *American Journal of Sociology*, 83(January), 862–889.

Berg, M. (1994). *The Age of Manufacturers 1700-1820, Industry, Innovation and Work in Britain*, 2nd edn. London: Routledge.

Bridge, S., O'Neill, K., and Cromie, S. (1998). *Understanding Enterprise, Entrepreneurship and Small Business*. Basingstoke: Macmillan Press.

Brosio, G. (1994). "The Arts Industry – Problems of Measurement". In *Cultural Economics and Cultural Policies*, (A. Peacock, and I. Rizzo, eds.). The Netherlands: Kluwer Academic Publishers.

Carson, D. (1990). 'Some Exploratory Models for Assessing Small Firms' Marketing Performance – A Qualitative Approach. *European Journal of Marketing*, 24(12), 8–51.

Carson, D., Cromie, S., McGowan, P., and Hill, J. (1995). *Marketing and Entrepreneurship in SMEs. An Innovative Approach*. UK: Prentice Hall.

Chartered Institute of Personnel and Development (2004). The Opportunity of a Lifetime, Reshaping Retirement, CIPD, London.

Coopers and Lybrand (1994). *The Employment and Economic Significance of the Cultural Industries in Ireland*. Dublin: Coopers and Lybrand.

Danto, A. (1964). "The Artworld". *Journal of Philosophy*, 61, 580.

Danto, A. (1981). *The Transfiguration of the Commonplace*. Cambridge, MA: Harvard University Press.

Davies, R., and Lindley, R. (2003). *Artists in Figures, Arts Council England*.

Dean, D. (1994). "A Slipware Dish by Samuel Malkin: An Analysis of Vernacular Design". *Journal of Design History*, 7(23), 153.

Department for Culture, Media and Sport (1998). *Creative Industries Mapping Document*. Department for Culture, Media and Sport.

Department for Culture, Media and Sport (2001). *Creative Industries Mapping Document, update*. Department for Culture, Media and Sport.

Dewhurst, P., and Horobin, H. (1998). Small business owners. In *The Management of Small Tourism and Hospitality Firms*, (R. Thomas, ed.), pp. 19–38. London: Cassell,.

Dickie, V.A., and Frank, G. (1996). "Artisan Occupations in the Global Economy: A Conceptual Framework". *Journal of Occupational Science*, 3(2), 45–55.

Dormer1997, P. (1997). "The Salon de Refuse?". In *The Culture of Craft – Status and Future*, (P. Dormer, ed.), pp. 19–38. Manchester: Manchester University Press.

Fielden, S.L., Davidson, M.J., and Makin, P.J. (2000). 'Barriers Encountered During Micro and Small Business Start-Up in North-West England'. *Journal of Small Business and Enterprise Development*, 7(4), 295–304.

Fillis, I. (2000). *An Examination of the Internationalisation Process of the Smaller Craft Firm in the United Kingdom and the Republic of Ireland, unpublished doctoral thesis*. University of Stirling.

Fillis, I. (2002a). Barriers to internationalisation: an investigation of the craft microenterprise. *European Journal of Marketing*, 36(7/8), 912–927.

Fillis, I. (2002b). "The internationalisation process of the craft firm microenterprise". *Journal of Developmental Entrepreneurship*, 7(1), 25–43.

Fillis, I. (2002c). "An Andalusian dog or a rising star: creativity and the marketing/entrepreneurship interface". *Journal of Marketing Management* 18(3/4), 379–395.

Fillis, I. (2003). "Image, reputation and identity issues in the arts and crafts organisation". *Corporate Reputation Review: An International Journal*, 6(3), 239–251.

Fillis, I. (2004). "The internationalising smaller craft firm: insights from the marketing and entrepreneurship interface". *International Small Business Journal*, 22(1), 57–82.

Fillis, I. (2007). *"Celtic Craft and the Creative Consciousness as Contributions to Marketing Creativity", Journal of Strategic Marketing*..

Fillis, I., and Rentschler, R. (2006). *Creative Marketing: an Extended Metaphor for Marketing in a New Age*. Palgrave Macmillan.

Flew, T. (2002). *"Beyond ad hocery: Defining creative industries" Cultural Sites, Cultural Theory, Cultural Policy The Second International Conference on Cultural Policy Research*. Wellington, New Zealand: TePapa. January 23–26.

Floud, R., and McCloskey, D. (eds.) (1994). *The Economic History of Britain Since 1700*, 2nd edn. Vol. 1, pp. 1700–1860. Cambridge: Cambridge University Press,

Frisch, B. (1998). 'A Pragmatic Approach to Vision'. *Journal of Business Strategy*, 19(4), 12–15.

Fuller-Love, N., Midmore, P., Thomas, D., and Henley, A. (2006). Entrepreneurship and Rural Economic Development: a Scenario Analysis Approach. *International Journal of Entrepreneurial Behaviour and Research*, 12(5), 289–305.

Girard, A. (1982). *"Cultural industries: a handicap or a new opportunity for cultural development?", Cultural Industries – a challenge for the future*. Paris: UNESCO.

Green, R.W. (1971). "Statistical Classifications – Structure and Development: The Government's Viewpoint". *IMRA Journal*, 7(4).

Greenhalgh, P. (1997). "The History of Craft". In *The Culture of Craft*, (P. Dormer, ed.). Manchester: Manchester University Press.

Healy, K. (2002). "What's New for Culture in the New Economy?". *Journal of Arts Management Law and Society*, 32(2), 86–103.

Heslop, T.A. (1997). "How Strange the Change from Major to Minor: Hierarchies and Medieval Art". In *The Culture of Craft*, (P. Dormer, ed.). Manchester: Manchester University Press.

Hillman-Chartrand, H. (1988). "The Crafts In The Post-Modern Economy,". *Journal of Cultural Economics*, 12(2), 39–66.

Hirschman, E.C. (1983). Aesthetics, ideologies and the limits of the marketing concept. *Journal of Marketing*, 47(Summer), 45–55.

Holbrook, M.B. (1981). "Introduction: the esthetic imperative in consumer research". In *Symbolic Consumer Behavior*, (E.C. Hirschman, and M.B. Holbrook, eds.). Association for Consumer Research. MI, Anne Arbor.

Holbrook, M.B., and Zirlin, R.B. (1983). "Artistic creation, artworks and aesthetic appreciation: some philosophical contributions to nonprofit marketing". In *Nonprofit Marketing*, (R. Belk, ed.), vol. 1. Greenwich, CT: JAI Press.

Hulbert, B. and Brown, R. (1998) 'Business Opportunity Explored in the Context of Entrepreneurial Marketing', In (B. Hulbert, J. Day, and E. Shaw eds). *Proceedings of the Academy of Marketing UIC/MEIG-AMA Symposia on the Marketing and Entrepreneurship Interface 1996-1998*, pp. 529-534. Northampton: Nene University College.

Irvine, W., and Anderson, A.R. (2004). Small Tourist Firms in Rural Areas: Agility, Vulnerability and Survival in the Face of Crisis. *International Journal of Entrepreneurial Behaviour and Research*, 10(4), 229–246.

Kao, J.J. (1989). *Entrepreneurship, Creativity and Organization*. New Jersey: Prentice-Hall.

Knott, C.A. (1994). Crafts in the 1990s. A Socio-economic Study of Craftspeople in England. *Scotland and Wales*. London: Crafts Council.

Kristellar, P.O. (1951). "The Modern System of the Arts". *Journal of the History of Ideas*, 510.

Landry, C. (2000). *The Creative City: A Toolkit for Urban Innovators*. London: Earthscan Publications Ltd.

Leeke, D. (1994). Audit of the Craft Sector in Northern Ireland, completed for Craftworks NI (Ltd).

McAuley, A., and Fillis, I. (2002). *Crafts Businesses in Scotland: A Study, a report for The Scottish Arts Council, Scottish Enterprise and Scottish Enterprise Glasgow.*

McAuley, A., and Fillis, I. (2004). *Making it in the Twenty-First Century: A Socio-Economic Study of Craftspeople in England and Wales 2003/2004, a report for Crafts Council and Arts Councils of England and Wales.*

McAuley, A., and Fillis, I. (2006). *A Future in the Making: A Socio-Economic Study of Makers in Northern Ireland 2006, a report for Craft Northern Ireland.*

Metcalf, B. (1997). Craft and Art, Culture and Biology'. In *The Culture of Craft -Status and Future*, (P. Dormer, ed.). Manchester: Manchester University Press.

Morrison, A., and Teixeira, R. (2004). "Small Business Performance: A Tourism Sector Focus". *Journal of Small Business and Enterprise Development*, 11(2), 166–173.

Morrison, A., Lynch, J., and Johns, N. (2004). "International Tourism Networks". *International Journal of Contemporary Hospitality Management*, 16(3), 197–202.

Morrison, A., Rimmington, M., and Williams, C. (1999). *Entrepreneurship in the Hospitality, Tourism and Leisure Industries*. Oxford: Butterworth & Heinemann.

Myerscough, J. (1988). *The Economic Importance of the Arts in Britain*. London: Policy Studies Institute.

Myerscough, J. (1996). *The Arts and the Northern Ireland Economy.* Belfast: Northern Ireland Economic Council.

Naylor, G. (1971). *The Arts and Crafts Movement, Studio Vista, Great Britain.*

Neapolitan, J. (1985). "Craft Media Workers: Success In Sales Generated Income,". *Sociological – Focus*, 18(4), 313–324.

O'Brien, J., and Feist, A. (1995). *Employment in the Arts and Cultural Industries: an Analysis of the 1991 Census, Policy Research and Planning Department, Arts Council of England.*

Porter, M. (1998). "Clusters and the new economics of competition". *Harvard Business Review*, 76(6), 77–90.

Radich, A.J. (1987). Economic Impact of the Arts – a sourcebook, National Conference of State Legislatures, USA.

Royal Commission on the Economic Union and Development Prospect for Canada (1985). Report: vol. 11, pp. 115–116. Ottawa, Canada: Minister of Supply and Services.

Shaw, E. (1998) 'Networks as a Strategic Entrepreneurial Marketing Tool – A Review of the Evidence', In *Proceedings of the Academy of Marketing UIC/MEIG-AMA Symposia on the Marketing and Entrepreneurship Interface 1996-1998*, (B. Hulbert, J. Day and E. Shaw eds), pp. 707–722. Northampton: Nene University College.

Small Business Survey (2003). Small and Medium-sized Enterprise: Statistics for the Regions 2001, Small Business Service Press Release, 3 April 2003.

Smith, C. (2001). *Culture and Creativity, Great Britain, DCMS.*

van Zyl, H.J.C., and Mathur-Helm, B. (2007). "Exploring a conceptual model, based on the combined effects of entrepreneurial leadership, market orientation and relationship marketing orientation on South Africa's small tourism business performance". *South African Journal of Business Management*, 38(2), 17–24.

Walker, J.A., and Chaplin, S. (1997). *Visual Culture: An Introduction.* Manchester: Manchester University Press.

Welch, E. (1997). *Art and Society in Italy 1350–1500.* Oxford: Oxford University Press.

Wolff, J.A., and Pett, T.L. (2000). "Internationalisation of Small Firms: An Examination of Export Competitive Patterns, Firm Size, and Export Performance". *Journal of Small Business Management*, 38(2), 34–47.

Chapter 9

Agrusa, J., Coats, W., and Donlon, J. (2003). Working from a Bottom-Up Approach: Cultural and Heritage Tourism. *International Journal of Tourism Sciences*, 3(1), 121–128.

Ansoff, I.H. (1990). General management in turbulent environnements. *The Practicing Manager*, II(1), 6–27.

Ateljevic, I., and Doorne, S. (2000). 'Staying Within the Fence': Lifestyle Entrepreneurship in New Zealand. *Journal of Sustainable Tourism*, 8(5), 378–392.

Ateljevic, J. (2002). Small Tourism Firms: Owners, Environment and Management Practices in the Centre Stage of New Zealand. Unpublished PhD Thesis, Victoria University of Wellington: Wellington New Zealand.

Aydalot, P. (1986). *Milieux Innovateurs en Europe.* Paris: GREMI.

Bingham, R.D., and Mier, R. (1993). *Theories of Local Economic Development, Perspectives from Across the Disciplines.* Newbury Park, CA: Sage.

Buhalis, D., and "Tourism in the Greek Islands: The issues of peripherally, competitiveness and development". (1999). International Journal of Tourism Research, Special issue. *Tourism in the European periphery*, 1(5), 341–359.

Bull, M., and Baudner, J. (2004). Europeanization and Italian policy for the Mezzogiorno. *Journal of European Public Policy*, 11(6), 1058–1076.

Carter, S., and Jones-Evans, D. (2000). Introduction. In *Enterprise and Small Business: Principles, Practice, and Policy*, (S. Carter, and D. Jones-Evans, eds.), pp. 3–6. Harlow: Pearson Education.

Carter, S., and Jones-Evans, D. (2006). Introduction. In *Enterprise and Small Business: Principles, Practice, and Policy*, (S. Carter, and D. Jones-Evans, eds.), pp. 1–4. Harlow: Pearson Education.

CEC, Commission of the European Communities. (2004). *Third Report on Economic and Social Cohesion. A New Partnership for Cohesion: Convergence, Competitiveness, Co-operation.* Luxembourg: Office for Official Publications of the European Communities.

De Montricher, N. (1995), L'Aménagement du Territoire. La Découverte, Paris.

Denzin, N.K. (1989). *The Research Act: A Theoretical Introduction to Sociological Methods*, 3rd edn. New Jersey: Prentice Hall.

Dicken, P. (1998). *Global Shift, Transforming the World Economy.* London: Paul Chapman Publishing.

Doorne, S.M. (1998). *The Last Resort: A Case Study of Tourism Policy, Power & Participation on the Wellington Waterfront*, Unpublished PhD Thesis. Wellington: Victoria University of Wellington.

Doorne, S.M. (2008). Bridging the Global–Local Divide: Lessons from Indigenous Entrepreneurship on Vatulele Island, Fiji. In *Progress in Tourism and Entrepreneurship: Global Perspectives*, (J. Ateljevic, and S. Page, eds.). Oxford: Butterworth Heinemann. (Forthcoming).

Drucker, P. (1992). *Managing for the Future.* Oxford: Butterworth-Heinemann.

Friedmann, J. (1992). *Empowerment: The Politics of Alternative Development.* Oxford: Blackwell.

Fuller-Love, N., Midmore, P., Thomas, D., and Henley, A. (2006). "Entrepreneurship and rural economic development: a scenario analysis approach". *International Journal of Entrepreneurship Behaviour & Research*, 12(5), 289–305.

Getz, D., and Carlsen, J. (2004). Family Business in Tourism: State of the Art. *Annals of Tourism Research*, 32(1), 237–258.

Gillmor, D.A. (1998). Republic of Ireland: an expanding tourism sector. In *Tourism and Economic Development: European Experiences*, (A. Williams, and G. Shaw, eds.), 3rd edn., pp. 221–240 Chichester: John Wiley & Sons Ltd.

Greene, F., and Mole, K. (2006). Defining and measuring the small business. In *Enterprise and Small Business: Principles, Practice, and Policy*, (S. Carter, and D. Jones-Evans, eds.), pp. 7–29. Harlow: Pearson Education.

Hall, C.M., and Jenkins, J.M. (1995). *Tourism and Public Policy.* London: Routledge.

Hansen, N. (1990). "Innovative Regional Milieux, Small Firms and Regional Development: Evidence from Mediterranean France". *Annals of Regional Science*, 6, 55–64.

Hansen, N. (1992). Competition, trust and reciprocity in the development of innovative regional milieux. *Pap. Reg. Sci*, 71, 95–105.

Harris, S., and Sutton, R. (1986). "Functions and parting ceremonies in dying organisations. *Academy of Management Journal*, 29, 5–30.

Hawkins, R., and Prencipe, A. (2002). *Business to Business e-commerce in the UK: A Synthesis of sector reports*. London: Department of Trade and Industry.

Henderson, R. (2005). Education, training and rural living: Young people in Ryedale. *Education + Training*, 47(3), 183–201.

Illeris, S. (1993). An Inductive Theory of Regional Development. *Papers in Regional Science*, 72, 2.

Irvine, W., and Anderson, A.R. (2004). "Small tourism firms in rural areas: agility, vulnerability in the face of crisis". *International Journal of Entrepreneurship Behaviour & Research*, 10(4), 229–246.

Jackson, J. (2006). Developing regional tourism in China: The potential for activating business clusters in a socialist market economy. *Tourism Management*, 27(4), 695–706.

Jarvis, R. (2006). Finance and the small business. In *Enterprise and Small Business: Principles, Practice, and Policy*, (S. Carter, and D. Jones-Evans, eds.), pp. 338–356. Harlow: Pearson Education.

Kelsey, J. (1995). *The New Zealand Experiment: A World Model for Structural Adjustment?* Auckland: Auckland University Press.

Kidder, T. (1982). *Soul of New Machine*. New York: Avon.

Le Heron, R. (1998). Business, finances and travel services. In *Changing Places: New Zealand in the Nineties*, (R. Le Heron, and E. Pawson, eds.), pp. 181–188. Auckland, NZ: Longman Paul.

Lewis, J., and Williams, A. (1998). Portugal: market segmentation and economic development. In *Tourism and Economic Development: European Experiences*, (A. Williams, and G. Shaw, eds.), 3rd edn, pp. 125–149. Chichester: John Wiley & Sons Ltd.

Marcjanna, A.M. (2004). Coping with Resource Scarcity: The Experience of UK Tourism SMEs. In *Small Firms in Tourism: International Perspective*, (T. Rhodri, ed.), pp. 257–275. Elsevier.

MBE (1999), Wairarapa: the Promise and the Potential. Masterton, NZ: Masterton Business Enterprise Inc.

Morgan, K. (1997). The learning region: institutions, innovation and regional renewal. *Reg. Studies*, 31, 491–503.

Morgan, N., and Pritchard, A. (2000). *Advertising in Tourism and Leisure*. Oxford: Butterworth Heinemann.

Morrison, A. (2006). A contextualisation of entrepreneurship. *International Journal of Entrepreneurship Behaviour & Research*, 12(4), 192–209.

Moulaert, F., and Sekia, F. (2003). Territorial Innovation Models: A Critical Survey. *Regional Studies*, 37(3), 289–302.

OECD. (1985). *Employment in small and large firms: Where have the jobs come from? Employment Outlook*. Paris: September.

OECD. (1999). *Stimulating private enterprise in transition economies*. Paris: OECD. Policy Brief, April.

Page, S. J., Forer, P., Lawton, G. R. (1999), "Small business development and tourism: Terra incognita?" *Tourism Management*, 20, 435–459.

Painter, J., and Goodwin, M. (2000). Local governance after Fordism: a regulations perspective. In *The new politics of British local governance*, (G. Stoker, ed.), pp. 33–53. Basingstoke: Macmillan.

Pearce, D.G. (1998). Tourism: growth, change and internationalisation. In *Changing Places: New Zealand in the Nineties*, (R. Le Heron, and E. Pawson, eds.), pp. 188–196. Auckland, NZ: Longman Paul.

Pearce, D.G. (2001). "Tourism, trams and local government policy-making in Christchurch, New Zealand". *Current Issues in Tourism*, 4(2–4), 331–354.

Pearce, P.L., Morrison, A.M., and Rutledge, J.L. (1998). *Tourism: Bridges across continents*. Sydney: McGraw-Hill.

Pezzini, M. (2000). Rural Policy Lessons From OECD Countries, Economic Review, Third Quarter.

Robbins, S.P., Bergman, R., Stagg, I., and Coulter, M. (2000). *Management*. Sydney: Prentice Hall Australia Pty Ltd.

Scase, R. (2000). The enterprise culture: the socio-economic context of small firms. In *Enterprise and Small Business: Principles, Practice and Policy*, (S. Carter, and D. Jones-Evans, eds.), pp. 32–47. Harlow, England: Pearson Education.

Scrimgeour, F., Chen, Hui-Chin and Hughes, W. (2002). Regional Economic Development: What Does The Literature Say? Department of Economics Waikato University, New Zealand. http://nzae.org.nz/files/%2321-SCRIMGEOUR.PDF. Retrieved on 23/05/07.

Shaw, G., and Williams, A. (1998). Entrepreneurship, small business culture and tourism development. In *The Economic Geography of the Tourism Industry*, (D. Ioannides, and K.D. Debbage, eds.), pp. 235–255. London: Routledge.

Smallbone, D., and Wyer, P. (2006). "Growth and development in the small business". In *Enterprise and Small Business: Principles, Practice, and Policy*, (S. Carter, and D. Jones-Evans, eds.), pp. 100–128. Harlow: Pearson Education.

Statistics New Zealand (1997), Regional Economic Profile: Statistics New Zealand.

Statistics New Zealand. (2000). *Key Statistics August 2000*. Wellington: Statistics New Zealand.

Stohr, W. (1990). *Global challenge and local response*. London: Mansell.

Stohr, W., Edralin, J., and Mani, D. (eds) (2001). *New Regional Development Paradigms: Decentralisation, Governance and the New Planning*, Vol. 3. London: Greenwood Press.

Stokes, D. (2000). Marketing and the small firms. In *Enterprise and Small Businesses: Principles, Practice and Policy*, (S. Crater, and D. Jones-Evans, eds.), pp. 354–366. Harlow: Pearson Education.

Storey, D.J. (1994). *Understanding the Small Business Sector*. London: Rutledge.

SWDC (1999). *Annual Report 1998/1999*. Martinborough, Wairarapa: South Wairarapa City Council.

Tassiopoulos, D.N. (2005). Cultural tourism in South Africa: a case study of cultural villages from a developing country perspective. In *International Cultural Tourism*, (D. Leslie, and M. Sigala, eds.). UK: Butterworth Heinemann / Elsevier.

Terluin, I.J., and Post, J.H. (2003). "Reinventing regions in the global economy". *paper presented at the International Conference of the Regional Studies Association* 12–15, Pisa, April.

Thomas, H., and Thomas, R. (1998). "The Implication for Tourism of Shifts in British Local Governance". *Progress in Tourism and Hospitality Research*, 4, 295–306.

Thomas, R. (ed.) (2004). *Small Firms in Tourism: International Perspective*. London: Elsevier.

Thomas, R., and Augustyn, M. (eds.) (2007). *Tourism in the New Europe: Perspectives on SME Politics and Practices*. Oxford: Elsevier.

Tourism Wairarapa. (2000). Tourism Industry Structure. Masterton. *Tourism Wairarapa*.

Wanhill, S. (1997). "Peripheral area tourism: a European perspective". *Progress in Tourism and Hospitality Research*, 3, 47–70.

Wanhill, S. (2000). "Small and medium tourism enterprises". *Annals of Tourism Research*, 27(1), 132–147.

Chapter 10

Akama, J. (1999). The evolution of tourism in Kenya. *Journal of Sustainable Tourism*, 7(1), 6–25.

Barth, F. (1967). Economic spheres in Darfur. In *Themes in Economic Anthropology*, (R. Firth, ed.), pp. 148–174. , London: Tavistock.

Bell, W.D.M. (1923) *The Wanderings of an Elephant Hunter,* Suffolk:Neville Spearman (1960 Edition).

Blanc, J, Barnes, R., Craig, G., Dublin H., Thouless, C., Douglas-Hamilton, I. and Hart, J. (2007) *African Elephant Status Report,* Occasional Paper of the IUCN Species Survival Commission, 13.

Boyd, C., Blench, R., Bourn, D., Drake, L., and Stevenson, P. (1999). *Reconciling interests among wildlife, livestock and people in Eastern Africa: a sustainable livelihoods approach.* Natural Resource Perspectives, 45, Overseas Development Institute, London.

Brockington, D. (2002). *Fortress Conservation, the Preservation of the Mkomazi Game Reserve.* London: James Currey and Sons. Tanzania.

Brodlie, R. and Hanselmann, R. (2003) Gh Development of Methodologies at the Nazinga Game Ranch for use in a Piloted Integrated Conservation Program in Burkino Faso. IUCN, Burkino Faso.

The Eye Magazine, (2008) April/May, Kampala.

Fisher, J., Simon, N., and Vincent, J. (1969). *The Red Book: Wildlife in Danger.* London: Colins.

Grzimek, B. (1961). *Serengeti Shall not Die.* New York: Dutton.

Higginbottom, K. and King, N. (2006), *The Live Trade in Free-Ranging Wildlife within South Africa and implications for Australia*, Government of Australia: Report for the Rural Industries Research and Development Corporation. No. 06/046 (Dec.).

Howard, P., Wangari, E., and Rakotoarisoa, N. (2007). *Mission Report UNESCO/IUCN joint monitoring mission to Niokola-Koba National Park.* Senegal: UNESCO.

Hunter, J.A. (1952). *Hunter.* London: Hamish Hamilton.

Johnstone, R. (2000). Talking ecotourism. *Swara*, 22(4), 5–9.

Kirzner, I.M. (1973). *Competition and Entrepreneurship.* Chicago: University of Chicago Press.

Kirzner, I.M. (1984). *The entrepreneurial process,* In *The Environment for Entrepreneurship.* (C.A. Kent, ed), pp. 33–43. New York: Lexington Books.

Lindberg, K., James, B., and Goodman, P. (2003). 'Tourism's contribution to conservation in Zululand'. In *Nature tourism, conservation and development in Kwa-Zulu Natal, South Africa,* (B. Aylward, and E. Lutz, eds.), pp. 203–244. Washington DC: World Bank.

MacGregor, J., Karousakis, K., and Groom, B. (Sept. 2004). *Using Economic Incentives to Conserve CITES-listed Species: a Scoping Study on ITQs for Sturgeon in the Caspian Sea. Environmental Economics Programme, Discussion Paper 04-02.* London: International Institute for Environment and Development (IIED).

Mann, S. (1995) A Guide to Murchison Falls National Park and the Surrounding Game Reserves. Uganda Wildlife Authority.

Okello, M., and Kiringe, J. (2004). Threats to biodiversity and their implications in protected and adjacent dispersal areas of Kenya. *Journal of Sustainable Tourism,* 12(1), 55–69.

Parker, I., and Amin, M. (1983). *Ivory Crisis.* London: Chatto and Windass Ltd.

Roosevelt, T. (1910). *African Game Trails.* London: John Murray.

Roth, H.H. and Merz, G. (1996) *Wildlife Resources: A Global Account of Economic Use* Springer-Verlag Berlin and Heidelberg GmbH & Co. KG

Snelson, D. and Wilson, A. (1994), *Lake Mburo National Park Guidebook.* African Wildlife Foundation.

Wasser, S., Mailand, C., Booth, R., Mutayoba, B., Kisamo, E., Clark, B., and Stevens, M. (2007). Using DNA to track the origin of the largest ivory seizure since the 1989 trade ban. *Proceedings National Academy of Sciences,* 104, 4228–4233.

Williams, J.G. (1987). *A Field Guide to the National Parks of East Africa.* London: Collins.

Woodroffe, R., Thirgood, S. and Rabinowitz, A. (2008) *People and Wildlife, Conflict or Co-existence?* Cambridge University Press.

Chapter 11

Ajzen, I. (1991). The Theory of Planned Behaviour. *Organisational Behaviour and Human Decision Processes,* 50, 179–211.

Appadurai, A. (1996). *Modernity at Large: Cultural Dimesions of Globalisation.* Minneapolis: University of Missesota Press.

Ateljevic, I., and Doorne, S. (2000). 'Staying Within the Fence': Lifestyle Entrepreneurship in New Zealand. *Journal of Sustainable Tourism,* 8(5), 378–392.

Ateljevic, I., and Doorne, S. (2003). Unpacking the Local: A Cultural Analysis of Tourism Entrepreneurship. *Tourism Geographies,* 5(2), 123–150.

Ateljevic, I., Doorne, S., and Bai, Z. (2003). Representing Identities Through Tourism: Encounters of Ethnic Minorities in Dali, Yunnan Province. *International Journal of Tourism Research,* 5(1), 1–11.

Ateljevic, I and Doorne, S. (2004a). Cultural Circuits of tourism: Commodities, Place and Reconsumption. In *Blackwell Companion to Tourism Geography*. (A. Lew, C.M. Hall, and A. Williams, eds.), pp. 291–302. Oxford: Blackwell.

Ateljevic, J. and Doorne, S. (2004b). Diseconomies of Scale: A Study of Development Constraints in Small tourism firms in Central New Zealand. *Journal of Tourism and Hospitality Research*, 5(1), 5–24.

Ateljevic, I., and Doorne, S. (2005). Tourism Performance as Metaphor: Enacting Backpacker Travel in Fiji Islands. In *Tourism, Discourse and Communication*, (A. Pritchard, and A. Jaworski, eds.), pp. 173–198.

Baldacchino, G. (1999). Small Business in Small Islands: A Case Study from Fiji. *Journal of Small Business Management*, 37, 254–259.

Bianchi, R.V. (2002). Towards a New Political Economy of Tourism in the Third World. In *Tourism and Development: Concepts and Issues*, (R. Sharpley, and D. Telfer, eds.), pp. 265–299. Clevedon: Channel View Publications.

Bricker, K. (2003). Ecotourism Development in Fiji: Policy, Practice and Political Instability. In *Ecotourism Policy and Planning*, (R.K. Dowling, and D.A. Fennel, eds.), pp. 187–204. London: CABI Publishing.

Britton, S. (1991). Tourism, capital and place: Towards a critical geography of tourism. *Environment and Planning D: Society and Space*, 9, 451–478.

Britton, S. and Clarke, W. (eds.) (1987). *Ambiguous Alternative: Tourism in Small Developing Countries*. Suva: University of South Pacific.

Bull, I., and Willard, G.E. (1993). Towards a Theory of Entrepreneurship. *Journal of Business Venturing*, 8(3), 183–196.

Bygrave, W.D., and Hofer, C.W. (1991). Theorizing about entrepreneurship. *Entrepreneurship Theory and Practice*, 16(2), 13–22.

Cater, E. and Lowman, G. (eds.) (1984). *Ecotourism: A Sustainable Option*. Chichester: John Wiley and Sons.

Chang, T.C. (1997). Heritage as a Tourism Commodity: Traversing the Tourist-Local Divide. *Singapore Journal of Tropical Geography*, 18(1), 46–68.

Chang, T.C., Milne, S., Fallon, D., and Pohlmann, C. (1996). Urban Heritage Tourism: The Global–Local Nexus. *Annals of Tourism Research*, 23(2), 284–305.

Clifford, J. (1992). Travelling Cultures. In *Cultural Studies*, (L. Grossberg, C. Nelson, and P.A. Treichler, eds.), London: Routledge pp. 96–116.

Crick, M. (1989). Representations of International Tourism in the Social Sciences: Sun, Sex, Sights, Savings and Servility. *Annual Review of Anthropology*, 18, 307–344.

Dana, L.P., and Anderson, R. (2007). *International Handbook of Research on Indigenous Entrepreneurship*. London: Edward Elgar Publishing.

Douglas, Ngaire and Douglas, Norman (1996a). Social and Cultural Impack of Tourism in the Pacific. In *Tourism in the Pacific: Issues and Cases*, (C. M. Hall and S. J. Page, eds.), pp. 49–64, London: International Business Press.

Douglas, Norman and Douglas, Ngaire (1996b). Tourism in the Pacific: Historical Factors. In *Tourism in the Pacific: Issues and Cases*, (C. M. Hall and S. J. Page, eds.), pp. 19–35. London: International Business Press.

Echtner, C. (1995). Entrepreneurial Training in Developing Countries. *Annals of Tourism Research*, 22(1), 119–134.

Fairburn, Te'o I.J. (ed.) (1988). *Island Entrpreneurs: Problems and Performances in the Pacific.* The East–West Centre. Honolulu: University of Hawaii Press.

Feathersone, M. (1990). Perspectives on Consumer Culture. *Sociology*, 24(1), 5–22.

Featherstone, M. (1987). Lifestyle and Consumer Culture. *Theory, Culture and Society*, 4, 55–70.

Fennel, D.A. (1999). *Ecotoursim: An Introduction.* London: Routledge.

Fiji Visitors Bureau (2003). *Market Overview.* National Tourism Forum, 27–29 November, Suva.

Fiji Visitors Bureau (2005). *Fiji International Visitors Survey,* Suva: Fiji Visitors Bureau.

Foucault, M. (1980). *Power/Knowledge.* Brighton: Harvester Press.

Franklin, A., and Crang, M. (2001). The Trouble with Tourism and Travel Theory. *Tourist Studies*, 1(1), 5–22.

Getz, D., and Carlsen, J. (2004). Family Business in Tourism: State of the Art. *Annals of Tourism Research*, 32(1), 237–258.

Hall, C.M., and Page, S.J. (1996). Introduction: The context of tourism development in the South Pacific. In *Tourism in the Pacific: Issues and Cases*, (C.M. Hall, and S.J. Page, eds.), pp. 1–15. London: International Thomson Business Press.

Hannan, M., and Freeman, J. (1977). The Population Ecology of Organisations. *The American Journal of Sociology*, 82(5), 929–964.

Harrison, D. (1997). Globalisation and Tourism: some themes from Fiji. In *Pacific Rim Tourism*, (M. Opperman, ed.), pp. 83–166. Wallingford: CAB International.

Harrison, D. (2004). Introduction: Tourism in Pacific Islands. *The Journal of Pacific Studies*, 26(1&2), 1–28.

Honey, M. (1999). *Ecotourism and Sustainable Development: Who Owns Paradise.* Washington DC: Island Press.

Ioannides, D., and Petersen, T. (2003). Tourism 'Non-Entrepreneurship' in Peripheral Destinations: A case study of small and medium enterprises on Bornholm, Denmark. *Tourism Geographies*, 5(4), 408–435.

Keats, B.W., and Bracker, J.S. (1988). Toward a Theory of Small Firm Performance: A Conceptual Model. *American Journal of Small Business*, 12(Summer), 41–58.

Kirschenblatt-Gimblett, B. (1998). *Destination Culture: Tourism, Museums, and Heritage.* Berkeley: University of California Press.

Krueger, N., and Brazeal, D. (1994). Entrepreneurial Potential and Potential Entrepreneurs. *Entrepreneurship Theory and Practice*, 18(3), 91–104.

Lindberg, K., and McKercher, B. (1997). Ecotourism: A Critical Overview. *Pacific Tourism Review*, 1(1), 65–79.

Lury, C. (1996). *Consumer Culture.* Cambridge: Polity Press.

Martin, M.J.C. (1984). *Managing Technological Innovation and Entrepreneurship.* Reston, VA: Reston Publishing.

Morgan, N., and Pritchard, A. (1998). *Tourism Promotion and Power: Creating Images, Creating Identities.* Chichester: John Wiley and Sons.

Mowforth, M., and Munt, I. (1998). *Tourism and Sustainability: New Tourism in the Third World*. London and New York: Routledge.

Mowforth, M., and Munt, I. (2003). *Tourism and Sustainability: New Tourism in the Third World*, 2nd edn. London and New York: Routledge.

Murphy, P. (1985). *Tourism: A Community Approach*. New York: Routledge.

Peredo, A., Anderson, R., Galbraith, G., Honig, B., and Dana, L.P. (2004). Towards a Theory of Indigenous Entrepreneurship. *International Journal of Entrepreneurship in Small Business*, 1(1/2), 1–20.

Plange, N. (1996). Fiji. In *Tourism in the Pacific: Issues and Cases*, (C.M. Hall, and S.J. Page, eds.), pp. 205–218. London: International Thomson Business Plan.

Poon, A. (1996). *Tourism, Technology and Competitive Strategies*. London: Oxford University Press.

Qalo, R. (1997). *Small Business: A study of a Fijian family*. Suva: Mucunabitu Education Trust.

Rao, D. (2004). *Culture and Entrepreneurship in Fiji's Small Tourism Business Sector.* PhD. Thesis. Melbourne: Victoria University.

Richards, G., and Hall, D. (2000). *Tourism and Sustainable Community Development*. London: Routledge.

Rojek, C. (1995). *Decentring Leisure: Rethinking Leisure Theory*. London: Sage Publications.

Rudkin, B., and Hall, C.M. (1996). Unable to see the forest for the trees: ecotourism development in the Solomon Islands. In *Tourism and Indigenous Peoples*, (R. Butler, and T. Hinch, eds.), pp. 203–226. London: International Thompson Press.

Scheyvens, R. (2002). *Tourism for Development: Empowering Communities*. Harlow: Pearson Education.

Shapero, A. (1982). Some Social Dimensions of Entrepreneurship. In *The Encyclopedia of Entrepreneurship*, (C. Kent, D. Sexton, and K. Vesper, eds.). Englewood Cliffs, NJ: Prentice Hall.

Sharpley, R., (1996). Tourism and Consumer Culture in Postmodern Society. In *Tourism and Culture Towards the 21st Century Cultural Change. Conference Proceedings*, (M. Robinson, N. Evans, and P. Callaghan eds.). Sunderland: The Center for Travel and Tourism.

Shaw, G., and Williams, A. (1998). Entrepreneurship, small business culture and tourism development. In *The Economic Geography of the Tourism Industry*, (D. Ioannides, and K.D. Debbage, eds.), pp. 235–255. London: Routledge.

Silver, I. (1993). Marketing Authenticity in Third World Countries. *Annals of Tourism Research*, 20, 302–318.

Stanley, D. (1996). *South Pacific Handbook*. California: Moon Publications.

Teye, V. (1988). Commentary: Tourism Plans and Planning Challenges in Ghana. *Tourism Geographies*, 1(3), 283–292.

Turner, L., and Ash, J. (1975). *The Golden Hordes: International Tourism and the Pleasure Periphery*. London: Constable.

UNEP (2001). *Ecotourism and Sustainability*. Paris: United Nations. Environment Programme.

Weaver, B. (1988). *Ecotourism in the Less Developed World*. London: CAB International.

White, C.M. (2007). More Authentic than Thou: Authenticity and Othering in Fiji Tourism Discourse. *Tourist Studies*, 2007(7), 25–49.

Wortman, M.S. (1987). Entrepreneurship: an integrating typology and evaluation of the empirical research in the field. *Journal of Management*, 13(2), 259–279.

Chapter 12

Aldrich, H., and Fiol, C. (1994). Fools rush in? The institutional context of industry creation. *Academy of Management Review*, 19, 645–670.

Amankwah, R.K., and Anim-Sackey, C. (2003). Strategies for Sustainable Development of the Small-scale Gold and Diamond Mining Industry of Ghana. *Resources Policy*, 29, 131–138.

Ateljevic, J., O'Rourke, T., and Todorovic, Z. (2004). Entrepreneurship and SMEs in Bosnia and Herzegovina: building institutional capacity. *The International Journal of Entrepreneurship and Innovation*, 5(4), 241–254.

Barley, S., and Tolbert, P. (1997). *Institutionalization and Structuration: Studying the Links between Action and Institution, Organization Studies*, 18(1), 93–117.

Blanchard, O. (1997). *The Economist of Post-Communist Transition*. Oxford: Clarendon Press.

Bossuyt, J. and Develtere, P. (1995). Between autonomy and identity: The financing dilemma of NGOs. Full text of an article from *The Courier* ACP-EU No. 152, July-August: pp. 76–78. www.hiva.be/docs/artikel, accessed on 29/05/2006.

CARE (2005, October). *Regional Economic Develoment: a Cross-Border Partnership between Bosnia and Herzegovina (BiH) and Serbia and Montenegro (SCR)*. Sarajev: CARE International for the Balkans.

Dees, J. Gregory, Emerson, J., and Economy, P. (2002). *Strategic Tools for Social Entrepreneurs: Enhancing the Performance of Your Enterprising Nonprofit*. New York: John Wiley & Sons, Inc.

DiMaggio, P.J. (1988). Interest and Agency in Institutional Theory. In *Institutional patterns and organizations: Culture and environment*, (L.G. Zucker, ed.), pp. 3–22. Cambridge, MA: Ballinger.

DiMaggio, P.J., and Powell, W.W. (1983). The iron cage revisited: Institutional isomorphism and collective rationality in organizational fields,. *American Sociological Review*, 48, 147–160.

Doh, P. Jonathan and Guay, R. Terrence (2006), Terrence, "Corporate Social Responsibility, Public Policy, and NGO Activism in Europe and the United States: An Institutional-Stakeholder Perspective". *Journal of Management Studies*, 43(1), 47–73.

Drucker, P. (1994). *Innovation and entrepreneurship: practice and principles*. Oxford: Butterworth/Heinemann.

Fairclough, N. (1992). *Discourse and Social Change*. Cambridge: Polity Press.

Fligstein, N. (1997). Social Skill and Institutional Theory. *American Behavioural Scientist*, 40, 397–405.

Garud, R., Jain, S., and Kumaraswamy, A. (2002). Institutional Entrepreneurship in the Sponsorship of Common Technological Standards: The Case of Sun Microsystems and Java. *Academy of Management Review*, 45(1).

Greenwood, R., Suddaby, R., Hinings, C.R. (2002). Theorising Change: The Role of Professional Associations in Institutional Change, *Academy of Management Journal*, 45, 58–80.

James, R. (1994). *Strengthening the capacity of Southern NGO partners: A survey of current Northern NGO Approaches. International NGO Training and Research Centre.* INTRAC Occasional paper, Vol. 1, no. 5. Oxford: INTRAC.

Lawrence, T. (1999). Institutional Strategy. *Journal of Management*, 25, 161–187.

Lawrence, T., Hardy, C., and Phillips, N. (2004). *Institutional Effects of Collaboration: The Emergence of Proto-Institutions, Academy of Management Journal*, 45(1), 281–290.

Lawrence, T., and Phillips, N. (2004). From Moby Dick to Free Willy: Macro-Cultural Discourse and Institutional Entrepreneurship in Emerging Fields. *Organization*, 11(5), 689–711.

Leblebici, H., Salancik, G., Copay, A., and King, T. (1991). Institutional change and the transformation of inter-organizational fields: An organizational history of the U.S. radio broadcasting industry. *Administrative Science Quarterly*, 36, 333–363.

Maguire, S. (2002). Discourse and adoption of innovations: A study of HIV/AIDS treatments,. *Health Care Management Review*, 27(3), 74–88.

Maguire, S, Hardy, C, Lawrence, T (2004) Institutional Entrepreneurship in Emerging Fields: HIV/AIDS Treatment Advocacy in Canada. *Academy of Management Journal*, 47(5), 657–679.

Meyer, J, Rowan, B (1977) Institutionalized organizations: formal structure as myth and ceremony, *American Journal of Sociology*, 83, 340-63.

Papic, Z. (2003). *'From dependency towards politics of sustainable development', Conference Proceedings, Business Activities in Bosnia and Herzegovina in Association with Development and Cohesion in SE Europe: Strategic and Politics in a Fragmented Region, Sarajevo, 10–11 November.* Melbourne: Victoria University.

Philips, N., and Hardy, C. (2002). *Discourse Analysis: Investigating Processes of Social Construction, Thousands.* Oaks, CA: Sage.

Phillips, N., Lawrence, T., and Hardy, C. (2004). Discourse and institutions. *Academy of Management Review*, 29, 635–652.

Rao, H., Morrill, C., and Zald, M. (2000). Power plays: How social Movements and Collective Action Create New Organizational Forms. In *Research in Organizational Behaviour*, (R. Sutton, and B. Staw, eds.), pp. 239–282. Greenwich, CT: JAI Press.

Scott, W.R. (1994). *Institutional analysis: Variance and process theory approaches. In Institutional Change and Healthcare Organizations* (W.R. Scott, M. Ruef, P.J. Mendel and C.A. Caronna, eds.). Chicago, IL: University of Chicago.

Strauss, A., and Corbin, J. (1990). *Basics of Qualitative Research: Grounded Theory Procedures and Techniques.* London: Sage Publication.

Thomson, D.M. and Pepperdine, S. (2003). Assessing community capacity for riparian restoration, National Riparian Lands Research and Development Program, Land & Water Australia, Canberra, ACT.

Verbole, A. (2000). Actors, Discourses and Interfaces of rural Tourism Development at the Local Community Level in Slovenia: Social and Political Dimensions of the Rural Tourism Development Process. *Journal of Sustainable Tourism*, 8(6), 479–490.

Zucker, L.G. (1977). The role of institutionalization in cultural persistence. *American Sociological Review*, 42, 726–743.

Chapter 13

Acs, Z., and Armington, C. (2004). The impact of geographic differences in human capital on service firm formation rates. *Journal of Urban Economics*, 56, 244–278.

Acs, Z.J., Morck, R.K., and Yeung, B. (2001). Entrepreneurship, globalization, and public policy. *Journal of International Management*, 7(3), 235–251.

African National Congress (2004) *Report on Delivery to Women, ANC Sub-Committee on Gender Issues*, http://www.anc.org.za/ancdocs/reports/2004/delivery_to_women/environ. html [accessed 1 April 2008]

Ashley, C. (2006). *Facilitating Pro-Poor Tourism with the Private Sector: Lessons Learned from Pro-Poor Tourism Pilots in South Africa. Pro-Poor Tourism Report No.2. Pro-Poor Tourism Partnership*. London: Overseas Development Institute.

Ateljevic, I. and Doorne, S. (2000a). Staying within the fence: Lifestyle entrepreneurship in tourism. *Journal of Sustainable Tourism* (8)5: 378–392.

Ateljevic, I. and Doorne, S. (2000b) Local government and tourism development: Issues and constraints of public sector entrepreneurship. *New Zealand Geographer* 56(2), 25–31

Audretsch, D.B. (2004). Sustaining innovation and growth: Public policy support for entre-preneurs. *Industry and Innovation*, 11(3), 167–191.

Binns, T., and Nel, E. (2002). Tourism as a local development strategy in South Africa. *The Geographical Journal*, 168(3), 235–247.

Blake, A., Sinclair, M.T., and Soria, J.A.C. (2006). Tourism productivity: evidence from the UK. *Annals of Tourism Research*, 33(4), 1099–1120.

Boyett, I. (1996). The public sector entrepreneur – a definition. *International Journal of Public Sector Management*, 9(2), 36–51.

Coles, T., and Hall, C.M. (2008). *Tourism and International Business*. London: Routledge.

Crouch, G.I., and Ritchie, J.R.B. (1999). Tourism, competitiveness, and societal prosperity. *Journal of Business Research*, 44(3), 137–152.

Dahles, H. (1998). Tourism, government policy and petty entrepreneurs. *South East Asia Research*, 6, 73–98.

Deller, S.C., Tsai, T.-H., Marcouiller, D.W., and English, D.B.K. (2001). The role of amenities and quality of life in rural economic growth. *American Journal of Agricultural Economics*, 83(2), 352–365.

Department of Environmental Affairs and Tourism. (2001). *A Transformation Strategy for the South African Tourism Industry*. Pretoria: DEAT.

Dutz, M.A., Ordover, J.A., and Willig, R.D. (2000). Entrepreneurship, access policy and economic development: Lessons from industrial organization. *European Economic Review*, 44(4–6), 739–747.

Dye, T. (1992). *Understanding Public Policy*, 7th edn. Englewood Cliffs: Prentice Hall.

Evans, D.S., and Jovanovic, B. (1989). An estimated model of entrepreneurial choice under liquidity constraints. *Journal of Political Economy*, 97(4), 808–827.

Florida, R. (2002). Bohemia and economic geography. *Journal of Economic Geography*, 2, 55–71.

Goetz, S., and Freshwater, D. (2001). State-level determinants of entrepreneurship and a preliminary measure of entrepreneurial climate. *Economic Development Quarterly*, 15(1), 58–70.

Government of South Africa (Department of Environmental Affairs and Tourism). (1996). *The Development and Promotion of Tourism in South Africa*. Pretoria: Department of Environmental Affairs and Tourism.

Hall, C.M. (2006). Policy, planning and governance in ecotourism. In *Ecotourism in Scandinavia*, (S. Gössling, and J. Hultman, eds.), pp. 193–206. Wallingford: CAB International.

Hall, C.M. (2008a). *Tourism Planning*, 2nd edn. Harlow: Pearson.

Hall, C.M. (2008b). Innovation Value Creation Points in the Tourism Firm, Presentation to 4th Creative Lapland Seminar, Rovaneimi, 17 April.

Hall, C.M., and Jenkins, J. (1995). *Tourism and Public Policy*. London: Routledge.

Hall, C.M., and Page, S. (2006). *Geography of Tourism and Recreation*, 3rd edn. London: Routledge.

Hall, C.M., and Williams, A. (2008). *Tourism and Innovation*. London: Routledge.

Hall, C.M., Müller, D., and Saarinen, J. (2009). *Nordic Tourism: Issues and Cases*. Clevedon: Channel View Publications.

Hanell, T., Aalbu, H., and Neubauer, J. (2002). *Regional Development in the Nordic Countries*. Nordregio Report 2005: 5. Stockholm: Nordregio.

Hébert, R.F., and Link, A.N. (2006). The entrepreneur as innovator. *Journal of Technology Transfer*, 31(5), 589–597.

Heinelt, H. (2005). *Do Policies Determine Politics? School for Policy Studies Working Paper Series Paper No. 11*. Bristol: School for Policy Studies, University of Bristol.

Hjalager, A. (2005). Innovation in tourism from a welfare state perspective. *Scandinavian Journal of Hospitality and Tourism*, 5(1), 46–62.

Hjalager, A.-M., Huijbens, E.H., Björk, P., Nordin, S., Flagestad, A., and Knútsson, Ö (2008). *Innovation Systems in Nordic Tourism*. Oslo: Nordic Innovation Centre.

Hogwood, B., and Gunn, L. (1984). *Policy Analysis for the Real World*. New York: Oxford University Press.

Holtz-Eakin, D. (2000). Public policy toward entrepreneurship. *Small Business Economics*, 15(4), 283–291.

Irvine, W., and Anderson, A.R. (2004). Small tourist firms in rural areas: agility, vulnerability and survival in the face of crisis. *International Journal of Entrepreneurial Behaviour & Research*, 10(4), 229–246.

Kerr, W.E. (2003). *Tourism Public Policy and the Strategic Management of Failure*. Oxford: Pergamon.

Kirsten, M., and Rogerson, C.M. (2002). Tourism, business linkages and small enterprise development in South Africa. *Development Southern Africa*, 19(1), 29–59.

Koh, K. (2002). Explaining a community touristscape: An entrepreneurism model. *International Journal of Hospitality and Tourism Administration*, 3(2), 21–48.

Koh, K. (2006). Tourism entrepreneurship: People, place, and process. *Tourism Analysis*, 11(2), 115–131.

Kuratko, D., Hornsby, J., and Naffziger, D. (1999). The adverse impact of public policy on microenterprises: An exploratory study of owners' perceptions. *Journal of Developmental Entrepreneurship*, 4, 81–93.

Lerner, M., and Haber, S. (2000). Performance factors of small tourism ventures: The interface of tourism, entrepreneurship, and the environment. *Journal of Business Venturing*, 16, 77–100.

Lichtenstein, G.A., and Lyons, T.S. (2001). The entrepreneurial development system: Transforming business talent and community economies. *Economic Development Quarterly*, 15(1), 3–20.

Lichtenstein, G.A., and Lyons, T.S. (2006). Managing the community's pipeline of entrepreneurs and enterprises: A new way of thinking about business assets. *Economic Development Quarterly*, 20(4), 377–386.

Lordkipanidze, M., Brezet, H., and Backman, M. (2005). The entrepreneurism factor in sustainable tourism development. *Journal for Cleaner Production*, 13(8), 787–798.

Lowi, T.A. (1970). Decision making vs policy making: toward an antidote for technocracy. *Public Administration Review*, 30, 314–325.

Lowi, T.A. (1972). Four systems of policy, politics and choice. *Public Administration Review*, 32(4), 298–310.

Malecki, E. (1994). Entrepreneurship in regional and local development. *International Regional Science Review*, 16, 119–153.

Mason, G. (2003). South African Tourism Industry Empowerment and Transformation Annual Review 2002. Randburg: www.workinfo.com

Mattsson, J., Sundbo, J., and Fussing-Jensen, C. (2005). Innovation systems in tourism: The role of the attractor and scene-takers. *Industry and Innovation*, 12(3), 357–381.

Mokry, B.W. (1988). *Entrepreneurship and Public Policy: Can government stimulate start ups?* New York: Quorum Books.

Morrison, A. (2006). A contextualization of entrepreneurship. *International Journal of Entrepreneurial Behaviour & Research*, 12(4), 192–209.

Morrison, A. and Teixeira, R. (2004a). Small firm performance in the context of agent and structure: A cross-cultural comparison in the tourism accommodation sector. In *Small Firms in Tourism: International Perspectives*, (R. Thomas Ed.). Oxford: Elsevier.

Morrison, A. and Teixeira, R. (2004b). Small business performance: a tourism sector focus. *Journal of Small Business and Enterprise Development* 11(2): 166–173.

Müller, D.K., and Jansson, B. (2007). *Tourism in Peripheries: Perspectives from the Far North and South*. Wallingford: CAB International.

Neubauer, J., Dubois, A., Hanell, T., Lähteenmäki-Smith, K., Pettersson, K., Roto, J., and Steineke, J.M. (2007). *Regional Development in the Nordic Countries 2007, Nordregio Report*. Stockholm: Nordregio. 2007:1.

Padgett, M., and Hall, C.M. (2001). Tourism at the polls. In *Tourism in New Zealand: An Introduction*, (C.M. Hall, and G. Kearsley, eds.), pp. 99–104. Melbourne: Oxford University Press.

Page, S., Forer, P., and Lawton, G. (1999). Business development and tourism: terra incognita? *Tourism Management*, 20, 435–459.

Pal, L.A. (1992). *Public Policy Analysis: An Introduction.* Scarborough: Nelson Canada.

Parker, S. (1999). Ecotourism, environmental policy and development. In *Handbook of Global Environmental Policy and Administration*, (D.L. Soden, and B.S. Steel, eds.), pp. 314–345. New York: Marcel Dekker.

Parliament of the Republic of South Africa (2007) The Strategic Imperatives for South Africa as Set Out in the 2007 State of the Nation Address: An Oversight Tool for Members and Committees of Parliament. Pretoria: Parliamentary Research Unit, Parliament of the Republic of South Africa [available from http://www.parliament.gov.za/live/content. php?Item_ID=224]

Pike, S. (2004). *Destination Marketing Organizations.* Oxford: Elsevier.

Reagan, R. (1981). Inaugural address, West Front of the U.S. Capitol, January 20. http://www. reaganfoundation.org/reagan/speeches/first.asp [accessed April 1, 2007].

Rhodes, R.A.W. (1997). *Understanding Governance: Policy Networks, Governance, Reflexivity and Accountability.* Buckingham: Open University Press.

Rogerson, C.M. (2002a). Tourism – a new economic driver for South Africa. In *Geography and Economy in South Africa and its Neighbours*, (A. Lemon and C.M. Rogerson, eds.), pp. 95–110. Aldershot: Ashgate.

Rogerson, C.M. (2002b). Driving developmental tourism in South Africa. *Africa Insight* 32(4), 33–42.

Rogerson, C.M. (2004a). Tourism, small firm development and empowerment in postapartheid South Africa. In *Small Firms in Tourism: International Perspectives*, (Thomas, R. ed.), pp. 13–33. Oxford: Elsevier.

Rogerson, C.M. (2004b). Financing tourism SMMEs in South Africa: a supply-side analysis. In *Tourism and Development Issues in Contemporary South Africa*, (C.M. Rogerson and G. Visser eds), pp. 222–267. Pretoria: Africa, Institute of South Africa.

Rogerson, C.M. (2005). Unpacking tourism SMMEs in South Africa: structure, support needs and policy response. *Development Southern Africa*, 22(5), 623–642.

Rogerson, C.M. (2006). Pro-poor local economic development in South Africa: The role of pro-poor tourism. *Local Environment*, 11(1), 37–60.

Rogerson, C.M. (2007). Supporting small firm development in tourism: South Africa's Tourism Enterprise Programme. *The International Journal of Entrepreneurship and Innovation*, 8(1), 6–14.

Rogerson, C.M., and Visser, G. (2004). *Tourism and Development Issues in Contemporary South Africa.* Pretoria: Africa Institute of South Africa.

Spencer, J.W., and Gómez, C. (2004). The relationship among national institutional structures, economic factors, and domestic entrepreneurial activity: A multicountry study. *Journal of Business Research*, 57(10), 1098–1107.

Thomas, R. (2000). Small firms in the tourism industry: some conceptual issues. *International Journal of Tourism Research*, 2(5), 345–353.

Tourism Business Council of South Africa (TBCSA). (2002). *South African Tourism Industry Empowerment and Transformation Annual Review 2002.* Johannesburg: TBCSA.

Tourism Business Council of South Africa (TBCSA). (2003). *South African Tourism Industry Empowerment and Transformation Annual Review 2003.* Johannesburg: TBCSA.

Tourism Business Council of South Africa (TBCSA). (2004). *South African Tourism Industry Empowerment and Transformation Annual Review 2004.* Johannesburg: TBCSA.

Tourism Enterprise Partnership (2008) About TEP, http://www.tep.co.za/about.php [accessed 1 April 2008]

Wilkinson, T.J. (2006). Entrepreneurial climate and U.S. state foreign trade offices as predictors of export success. *Journal of Small Business Management*, 44(1), 99–113.

Wilson, S., Fesenmaier, D.R., Fesenmaier, J., and van Es, J.C. (2001). Factors for success in rural tourism development. *Journal of Travel Research*, 40(2), 132–138.

Wood, A., and Valler, D. (2004). *Governing Local and Regional Economies:Institutions, politics and economic development*. Burlington, VT: Ashgate Publishing.

Zapalska, A.M., and Brozik, D. (2007). Managing family businesses in the tourism and hospitality industry: the transitional economy of Poland. *Proceedings of Rijeka Faculty of Economics Journal of Economics and Business*, 25(1), 141–165.

Chapter 14

Bachleitner, R., and Zins, A.H. (1999). Cultural Tourism in Rural Communities: The Residents' Perspective. *Journal of Business Research*, 44(19), 199–209.

Cairngorm National Park Authority (2006), Tourism and the Cairngorms National Park (Update report for the Board of the Authority in corporate plan discussions)

Denman, R., (2004) Report for WWF: *Guidelines for community-based ecotourism development*, Gland, Switzerland

European Parliament (2007). Resolution of 29 November 2007 (Commission recommendation 2006/2129-INI) on a renewed EU Tourism Policy: *Towards a stronger partnership for European Tourism.*

Gosar, L. (1990). *Celoviti razvoj ruralnih območij*. Ljubljana: Urbanistični Institut.

GTZ (1999). Sustainable Tourism as a Development Option: Practical Guide for Local Planners, Developers and Decision Makers. GTZ/Deutsche Gesellschaft für Technische Zusammenarbeit GmbH, Eschborn/Germany. Place = Eschborn as noted before

Koščak, M. (1998). Integral development of rural areas, tourism and village renovation, Trebnje, Slovenia. *Tourism Management*, 19(1), 81–86.

Koščak, M. (1993–1995). *Lipov List, Series of Articles on Rural Tourism*. Ljubljana: Turistična zveza Slovenije.

Lankford, S.V., and Howard, D.R. (1994). Developing a Tourism Impact Attitude Scale. *Annals of Tourism Research*, 21(1), 121–139.

Sirše, J., Černič, I., Kalin, J., and Vidjen, T. (2004). *Report Satelitski računi za turizem v Sloveniji*. Ljubljana: Ministry of the Economy of the Republic of Slovenia.

UNEP/ICLEI (2003), Tourism and Local Agenda 21 – Role of Local Authorities in Sustainable Tourism. UNEP/ICLEI, Vienna

Chapter 15

Anckar, B., and Walden, P. (2001). Introducing Web Technology in a small peripheral hospitality organization. *International Journal of Contemporary Hospitality Management*, 13(5), 241–250.

Braun, P. (2002). Networking Tourism SMEs: E-Commerce and E-Marketing Issues in Regional Australia. *Information Technology and Tourism*, 5, 13–23.

Brown, D.H., and Lockett, N. (2004). Potential of Critical e-Applications for Engaging in e-Business: a Provider Perspective. *European Journal of Information Systems*, 13, 12–34.

Buhalis, D. (1993). Regional integrated computer information reservation management systems as a strategic tool for the small and medium tourism enterprises. *Tourism Management*, 14(5), 366–378.

Buhalis, D. (1998). Strategic Use of Information Technologies in the Tourism Industry. *Tourism Management*, 19(3), 409–423.

Buhalis, D. (1999). Information technology for small and medium-sized tourism enterprises: Adaptation and benefits. *Information and Technology and Tourism*, 2(2), 79–95.

Buhalis, D. (2003). *eTourism: Information Technology for Strategic Tourism Management*. Prentice Hall.

Buhalis, D., and Main, H. (1998). Information Technology in small and medium hospitality enterprises: strategic analysis and critical factors. *International Journal of Contemporary Hospitality Management*, 10(5), 198–202.

Buhalis, D., and Deimezi, R. (2004). eTourism developments in Greece. *International Journal of Tourism and Hospitality Research*, 5(2), 103–130.

Buhalis, D., and O'Connor, P. (2005). Information Communication Technology – Revolutionizing Tourism. *Tourism Recreation Research*, 30(3), 7–16.

Buhalis, D., Kärcher, K., and Brown, M. (2006). TISCOVER: Development and Growth. In *Managing Tourism and Hospitality Services*, (B. Prideaux, G. Moscardo, and E. Laws, eds.), pp. 62–72. London: CAB, ISBN 1845930126.

Buick, I. (2003). Information technology in small Scottish hotels: Is it working? *International Journal of Contemporary Hospitality Management*, 15(4), 243–247.

Carson, P., and Sharma, P. (2001). Trends in the use of Internet Technologies. *World Hospitality and Tourism Trends*, 2(3), 116–128.

Chapman, P., Szczygiel, M., and Thompson, D. (2000). *Building internet capabilities in SMEs,Logistic Information Management*, 13(6), 353–360.

Cheng, C., and Piccoli, G. (2002). Web-Based Training in the Hospitality Industry: A Conceptual Definition, Taxonomy and Preliminary Investigation. *International Journal of Hospitality Information Technology*, 2(2), 19–33.

Collins, C., Buhalis, D., and Peters, M. (2003). Enhancing SMTEs Business performance through eLearning Platforms. *Journal of Education and Training*, 45(8/9), 483–494.

Connolly, D., Olsen, M., and Moore, R. (1998). *The Internet as a Distribution Channel, Cornell Hotel and Restaurant Quarterly* 42–54.

Downie, G. (2002). Internet marketing and SMEs. *Management Services*, 14(7), 8–20.

Dutta, S., and Evrard, P. (1999). Information Technology and Organization within European Small Enterprises. *European Management Journal*, 17(3), 239–251.

European Commission, (2003), SME definition, available at http://europa.eu.int/comm/enterprise/enterprise_policy/sme_definition/index_en.htm

European Portal for SMEs, (2007). http://ec.europa.eu/enterprise/sme/index_en.htm

Getz, D., Morrison, A., and Carlsen, J. (2004). *The Family Business in Tourism and Hospitality.* Oxford: CAB International.

Go, F., and Welch, P., (1991), Competitive strategies for the international hotel industry, The Economist Intelligence Unit, Special report No.1180, London.

Hill, J. (2001). A multidimensional study of the key determinants of effective SME marketing activity: Part 1. *International Journal of Entrepreneurial Behaviour and Research*, 7(5), 171–204.

Kalakota, R., and Whinston, A.B. (1996). *Frontiers of electronic commerce.* Addison Wesley Longman Publishing.

Kincora, M. (2006), IT/BUSINESS STRATEGIES: ASP vs. SaaS: What's the difference? http://searchcio.techtarget.com/tip/0, 289483,sid182_gci1216679,00.html [accessed 6 January 2008]

Lauden, K.C., and Traver, C.G. (2002). *E-Commerce, Business, Technology, Society.* Addison Wesley.

Lebre, R. (1998). Small and medium-sized enterprises and IT diffusion policies in Europe. *Small Business Economics*, 11(1), 1–9.

Levy, M., and Powell, P. (2000). Information Systems strategy for SMEs: an organizational perspective. *Journal of Strategic Information Systems*, 9(1), 63–84.

MacGregor, R., and Vrazalic, L. (2004). *Electronic commerce adoption in small to medium enterprises (SMEs): a comparative study of SMEs in Wollongong (Australia) and Karlstad (Sweden).* Wollongong: University of Wollongong. May.

Main, H. (1995). Information technology and the independent hotel failing to make the connection? *International Journal of Contemporary Hospitality Management*, 7(6), 30–32.

Main, H. (2002). The expansion of technology in small and medium hospitality enterprises with a focus on net technology. *Information Technology and Tourism*, 4, 167–174.

Martin, L., and Matlay, H. (2001). 'Blanket' approaches to promoting ICT in small firms: some lessons from the DTI ladder adoption model in the UK. *Internet Research*, 11(5), 399–410.

Morrison, A. (1998). Small firm statistics: a hotel sector focus. *Service Industries Journal*, 18(1), 132–142.

Morrison, A., Rimington, M., and Williams, C. (1999). *Entrepreneurship in the Hospitality, Tourism and Leisure Industries.* Oxford: Heinemann.

Morrison, A., Taylor, S., Morrison, A., and Morrison, A. (1999). Marketing Small Hotels on the World Wide Web. *Information Technology and Tourism*, 2(2), 97–111.

Morrison, A., and Thomas, R. (1999). The Future of Small Firms in the Hospitality Industry. *International Journal of Contemporary Hospitality Management*, 11(4), 148–154.

Moutinho, L. (1990). Strategies for destination development – the role of small businesses. In *Marketing tourism places*, (B. Goodall, and G. Ashworth, eds.), pp. 104–122. London: Routledge.

Murphy, H., and Keilgast, C. (2008). Do small and medium sized hotels exploit search engine marketing? *International Journal of Contemporary Hospitality Marketing*, 20(1), 90–97.

Mutch, A. (1998). Using Information Technology. In *The Management of Small Tourism and Hospitality Firms*, (R. Thomas, ed.), pp. 92–206. London: Cassell.

Nachira, F. (2002). *Towards a network of digital business ecosystems fostering the local development, Discussion Paper, DG IST.* Brussels: European Commission.

O'Connor, P. (1999). *Electronic Information Distribution in Tourism and Hospitality.* London: CAB International.

O'Connor, P., and Frew, A. (2000). Evaluating electronic channels of distribution in the hotel sector: a Delphi study. *Information Technology and Tourism*, 3(3/4), 177–193.

O'Connor, P., and Frew, A. (2004). An evaluation methodology for hotel electronic channels of distribution. *International Journal of Hospitality Management*, 23(2), 179–199.

Paraskevas, A., and Buhalis, D. (2002). Information Communication Technologies decision-making: The ASP Outsourcing Model from the Small Hotel Owner/Manager Perspective. *The Cornell Hotel Restaurant Administration Quarterly*, 43(2), 27–39.

Peacock and Evans. (1999). A comparative study of ICT and tourism and hospitality SMEs in Europe. In *Information and Communication Technologies in Tourism 1999*, (D. Buhalis, and W. Schertler, eds.), pp. 247–258. Wein-New York: Springer.

Peters, M., and Buhalis, D. (2004). Small family hotel businesses: The need for education and training. *Journal of Education and Training*, 46(8/9), 406–416.

Piccoli, G., Ahmad, R., and Ives, B. (2001). Web Based Virtual Learning Environments: A research framework and a preliminary assessment of effectiveness in basic IT skills and training. *MIS Quarterly*, 25(4), 401–427.

Poon, A. (1990). Flexible specialization at small size: The Case of Caribbean Tourism. *World Development*, 18(1), 109–123.

Poon, S., and Swatman, P.M.C. (1997). Small business use of the internet: findings from Australian case studies. *International Marketing Review*, 14(5), 385–402.

Prescott, L. (2007). Buzznet and iMeem: Fast growing socialnetworks. http://weblogs.hitwise.com/leeannprescott/2007/03/buzznet_and_imeem_fast_growing.html

Rogers, E.M. (1995). *Diffusion of Innovations*. New York: The Free Press.

Sadowski, B.M., Maitland, C., and Van Douyer, J. (2002). Strategic use of the internet by small and medium sized companies: an exploratory study. *Information Economics and Policy*, 14(1), 75–93.

Shiels, H., McIvor, R., and O'Reilly, D. (2003). Understanding the implications of ICT adoption: insights from SMEs. *Logistics Information Management*, 16(5), 312–316.

Sigala, M. (2003). The information and communication technologies productivity impact on the UK hotel sector. *International Journal of Operations and Production Management*, 23(10), 1224–1245.

Tiessen, J., Wright, R., and Turner, I. (2001). A model of e-commerce used by internationalizing SMEs,. *Journal of International Management*, 7(3), 211–233.

Werthner, H., and Klein, S. (1999). *Information Technology and Tourism – A Challenging Relationship*. New York: Springer.

Chapter 16

Barbieri, G. and Lo Moro, V. (1996). *Utenti e Pubblica Amministrazione*, il Mulino (Rome).

Beogradska Berza (2008). *Promet na Beogradskoj berzi u 2007* (Belgrade).

European Commission (2003). Annex 1, Article 2 of European Commission Recommendation 2003/361/EC, cited in the European Commission's Official Journal OJ 2003, p. 36, Bruxelles.

European Parliament (2007). European Parliament Policy Documentation under PE 2006/ 2013(INI).

European Parliament (2008). European Parliament Policy Department B: Structural and Cohesion Policies. *The Impact of Tourism on Coastal Areas: Regional Development Aspects*, PE 397.260, PE 397.260,CSIL Milano(Strasbourg).

Institut für Mittelstandsforschung (1995). Bürokratie – ein Kostenfaktor: eine Belastungsuntersuchung bei mittelständischen Unternehmen (Bonn).

Ljubljanska Borza (2008). Mesečna statistična poročila v letu 2007 (Ljubljana).

MSE Inc. (2008). Report on Trading 2007 Year (Skopje).

Narodna Banka Republika Makedonija (2007). *Economic Review October 2007* (Skopje).

NEX Crna Gora (2008). Statistika trgovanja 2007 (Podgorica).

O'Rourke, A. (2000). Issues in equity financing structures for small business in the European Union, AEFC *Research papers* 1996–2000. Issue 8 (Bruxelles)

O'Rourke, A. (2001). *Financing of SMEs in transition economies: incentives and boundaries* – Paper for 3rd CEBWA Workshop, Financing Women's Businesses, 6 October 2001 (CTS Research, Belgrade).

O'Rourke, A. (2002). *Small Business financing in the new environment – flexible financial engineering* – Paper for Fakultet organizacionih nauka, Beograd, International Symposium SYM-ORG, Zlatibor, Serbia 2–5 June 2002 (CTS Research, Belgrade).

Prunk, J. (1997). Idejnopolitični nazor Edvarda Kardelja v okviru evropskega socializma, in. In *Ferenčev zbornik*, (Z. Čepič, and Guštin, eds.), pp. 105–116. Ljubljana: Inštitut za novejšo zgodovino.

UN World Travel Organization (2008). *World Travel Barometer*, vol. 6, January 2008.

Zagrebačka Burza (2008). Godišnje izvješće 2007 (Zagreb).

Chapter 17

Alcázar Martínez, B. del. (2002). *Los Canales de Distribución en el Sector Turístico*. Madrid: ESIC Editorial.

Alamdari, F., and Mason, K. (2006). The future of airline distribution. *Journal of Transport Management*, 12(3), 122–134.

Ali-Knight, J., and Wild, S. (1999). British Airways' inbound leisure market to Manchester, England: is direct marketing the answer? *Journal of Vacation Marketing*, 6(1), 9–20.

Anderson, E., Day, G.S., and Rangan, V.K. (1997). 'Strategic channel design'. *Sloan Management Review*, 38(4), 59–69.

Bitner, M.J., and Booms, B.H. (1982). Trends in Travel and Tourism Marketing: the Changing Structure of Distribution Channels. *Journal of Travel Research*, 20(4), 39–44.

Bote Gómez, V., and Álvarez Cuervo, R. (2001). *Promoción y Comercialización del Turismo Cultural de la Ciudad de Sevilla: Diagnósticoy Orientaciones Estratégicas*. Documentos de Trabajo Serie A, no.20018. Madrid, Spain: Universidad de Alcalá, Escuela Universitaria de Turismo.

Buckley, P.J. (1987). Tourism: An Economic Transactions Analysis. *Tourism Management*, 8(3), 190–194.

Buhalis, D. (2000). Relationships in the distribution channels of tourism: conflicts between hoteliers and tour operators in the Mediterranean region. *International Journal of Hospitality and Tourism Administration*, 1(1), 113–139.

Buhalis, D. (2001). Tourism distribution channels: practices and processes. In *Tourism Distribution Channels: Practices, Issues and Transformations*, (D. Buhalis, and E. Laws, eds.), pp. 7–32. London: Continuum.

Buhalis, D. and Laws, E. (2001). *Tourism Distribution Channels: Practices, Issues and Transformations.* London: Continum.

Buhalis, D. (2004). eAirlines: strategic and tactical use of ICTs in the airline industry. *Information and Management*, 41(7), 805–825.

Cai, L.A., Feng, R., and Breiter, D. (2004). Tourist Purchase Decision Involvement and Information Preferences. *Journal of Vacation Marketing*, 20(2), 138–148.

Casarin, F. (2001). Tourism distribution channels in Europe: a comparative study. In *Tourism distribution channels: practices, issues and transformations*, (D. Buhalis, and E. Laws, eds.), pp. 137–150. London: Continuum.

Chaintron, B. (1995). Industrie touristique: le choc des modèles anglais et français. *Cahier Espaces*, 44, 31–36.

Choi, S., and Kimes, S.E. (2002). Electronic distribution channels' effect on hotel revenue management. *Cornell Hotel and Restaurant Administration Quarterly*, 43(3), 23–31, June.

Crotts, J.C., Aziz, A., and Raschid, A. (1998). Antecedents of suppliers' commitment to wholesale buyers in the international travel trade. *Tourism Management*, 19(2), 127–134.

Crotts, J.C., and Turner, G.B. (1999). Determinants of trust in buyer–seller relationships in the international travel trade. *International Journal of Contemporary Hospitality*, 11(2/3).

Dev, C.S., and Olsen, M.D. (2000). Marketing challenges for the next decade. *Cornell Hotel and Restaurant Administration Quarterly*, 44(1), 41–47.

Dubé, L., and Renaghan, L.M. (2000). Marketing your hotel to and through intermediaries. *Cornell Hotel and Restaurant Administration Quarterly*, 41(1), 73–84.

Duke, C.R., and Persia, M.A. (1993). Effects of Distribution Channel Level on Tour Purchasing Attributes and Information Sources. *Journal of Travel and Tourism Marketing*, 2(2/3), 37–55.

Fam, K.S., Foscht, T., and Collins, R.D. (2003). Trust and the Online Relationship – an Exploratory Study from New Zealand. *Tourism Management*, 25(2), 195–207.

Fava Neves, M., Zuurbier, P., and Cortez Campomar, M. (2001). A model for the distribution channels planning process. *Journal of Business and Industrial Marketing*, 16(7), 518–539.

Fodness, D., and Murray, B. (1997). Tourist Information Search. *Annals of Tourism Research*, 24(3), 503–523.

Forsyth, P., and Smith, N. (1992). Corporate organization and distribution channels in Japan: the tourism industry case. In *International Adjustment and the Japanese Firm*, (P. Sheard, ed.), pp. 177–199. St Leonards: Allen and Ashwin.

Frazier, G.L. (1999). Organizing and managing channels of distribution. *Journal of the Academy of Marketing Science*, 27(2), 226–240.

Garnham, R. (2005). Corporate travel agents: Channels of distribution – an evaluation. In *Sharing Tourism Knowledge. Proceedings of the CAUTHE Conference, Alice Springs. CD-ROM*, (P. Tremblay, and A. Boyle, eds.). Darwin: Charles Darwin University.

Gartner, W.C., and Bachri, T. (1994). Tour operators' role in the tourism distribution system: an Indonesian case study. *Journal of International Consumer Marketing*, 6(3/4), 161–179.

Gee, G.Y., Makens, J.C., and Choy, D.J.L. (1989). *The Travel Industry*. New York: Van Nostrand Reinhold.

Green, C.E. (2005). *De-Mystifying Distribution: building a distribution strategy one channel at a time*. HSMAI Foundation.

Guo, W., and Turner, L.W. (2001). Entry strategies into China for foreign travel companies. *Journal of Vacation Marketing*, 6(1), 49–63.

Gursoy, D., and McCleary, K.W. (2003). An Integrative Model of Tourists' Information Search Behavior. *Annals of Tourism Research*, 31(2), 353–373.

Hewitt, C. (2006) 'Online Accommodation Bookings – The Future Innovation through Disruption'. Paper presented at the Tourism Futures Forum, Melbourne.

Kalafatis, S.P. (2000). Buyer–seller relationships along channels of distribution. *Industrial Marketing Management*, 31(3), 215–228.

Karamustafa, K. (2000). Marketing-channel relationships: Turkey's resort purveyors' interactions with international tour operators. *Cornell Hotel and Restaurant Association Quarterly*, 41(4), 21–31.

Kimes, S.E., and Lord, D.C. (1994). Wholesalers and Caribbean resort hotels. *Cornell Hotel and Restaurant Association Quarterly*, 35(5), 70.

King, B., and Choi, H.J. (1999). Travel industry structure in fast growing but immature outbound markets: the case of Korea to Australia travel. *International Journal of Tourism Research*, 1(2), 111–125.

Kotler, P., Bowen, J., and Makens, J. (1996). *Marketing and hospitality for tourism*. Upper Saddle River: Prentice Hall.

Lewis, E.H. (1968). *Marketing Channels: Structure and Strategy*. New York: McGraw-Hill.

March, R. (1997). An exploratory study of buyer–supplier relationships in international tourism: the case of Japanese wholesalers and Australian suppliers. *Journal of Travel and Tourism Marketing*, 6(1), 55–68.

March, R. (2000). Buyer decision-making behaviour in international tourism channels. *International Journal of Hospitality and Tourism Administration*, 1(1), 11–25.

Medina-Muñoz, D., and García-Falcón, J.M. (2000). Successful relationships between hotels and agencies. *Annals of Tourism Research*, 27(3), 737–762.

Medina-Muñoz, J., Medina-Muñoz, D., and García-Falcón, J.M. (2003). Understanding European tour operators' control on accommodation companies: an empirical evidence. *Tourism Management*, 24(2), 135–147.

Middleton, V., and Clarke, J. (2001). *Marketing in Travel and Tourism*, 3rd edn. Oxford: Butterworth-Heinneman.

Morell, P.S. (1998). Airline sales and distribution channels: the impact of new technology. *Tourism Economics*, 4(1), 5–19.

Morrison, A.M. (1989). *Hospitality and Tourism Marketing*. Albany, NY: Delmar.

O'Connor, P. (1999). *Electronic Information Distribution in Tourism and Hospitality.* Wallingford: CABI Publishing.

O'Connor, P., and Frew, A.J. (2003). An evaluation methodology for hotel electronic channels of distribution. *International Journal of Hospitality Management*, 23(2), 179–199.

Origet du Cluzeau, C. (1995). Distribution de Produits Touristiques Culturels: Le Sceptre d'autocar. *Cahiers Espaces*, 44, 98–102.

Öörni, A. (2003). Consumer search in electronic markets: an experimental analysis of travel services. *European Journal of Information Systems*, 12(1), 30–40.

Pearce, D.G. (2003). Tourism distribution channels: a systematic integrated approach. In *6th International Forum on the Sciences, Techniques and Art Applied to Marketing*, (E. Ortega., L. González, and E. Pérez del Campo, eds.), pp. 345–363. Madrid: Universidad Complutense de Madrid.

Pearce, D.G. (2005). Distribution channels for cultural tourism in Catalonia, Spain. *Current Issues in Tourism*, 8(5), 424–445.

Pearce, D.G. (2007a). 'Tourism distribution networks: research issues and destination management implications', paper presented at the Advances in Tourism Marketing Conference: Destination and Event Marketing: Managing Networks, 10–12, September 2007, Valencia.

Pearce, D.G. (2007b). Supplier selection in the New Zealand inbound tourism industry. *Journal of Travel and Tourism Marketing*, 23(1), 57–69.

Pearce, D.G. (2007c). *Paths to the Market: developing an effective tourism distribution strategy. Victoria Management School.* Wellington: Victoria University of Wellington.

Pearce, D.G. (2008). A needs–function model of tourism distribution. *Annals of Tourism Research*, 35(1), 148–168.

Pearce, D.G. (in press). Researching tourism distribution. In *Handbook of Tourism Research*, (W.C. Gartner and C.H.C. Hsu eds.). The Haworth Hospitality Press.

Pearce, D.G., and Sahli, M. (2007). Surface transport distribution channels in New Zealand: a comparative analysis. *Journal of Travel and Tourism Marketing*, 22(2), 57–73.

Pearce, D.G., and Schott, C. (2005). Tourism distribution channels: the visitors' perspective. *Journal of Travel Research*, 44(1), 50–63.

Pearce, D.G., and Tan, R. (2004). Distribution channels for heritage and cultural tourism in New Zealand. *Asia Pacific Journal of Tourism Research*, 9(3), 225–237.

Pearce, D.G., and Tan, R. (2006). The distribution mix for tourism attractions in Rotorua, New Zealand. *Journal of Travel Research*, 2(44), 250–258.

Pearce, D.G., Tan, R., and Schott, C. (2004). Tourism distribution channels in Wellington, New Zealand. *International Journal of Tourism Research*, 6(6), 397–410.

Pearce, D.G., Tan, R., and Schott, C. (2007). Distribution channels in international markets: a comparative analysis of the distribution of New Zealand tourism in Australia, Great Britain and the USA. *Current Issues in Tourism*, 10(1), 33–60.

Pearce, D.G., and Taniguchi, M. (2008). Channel performance in multi-channel tourism distribution systems. *Journal of Travel Research*, 46(3), 256–267.

Piga, C.A., and Filippi, N. (2002). Booking and flying with low-cost airlines. *The International Journal of Tourism Research*, 4(3), 237–249, May–June.

Richards, G., Goedhart, S., and Herrijgers, C. (2001). The Cultural Attraction Distribution System. In *Cultural Attractions and European Tourism*, (G. Richards, ed.), pp. 71–89. London: CAB International.

Rocks, S., Gilmore, A., and Carson, D. (2005). Developing strategic marketing through the use of marketing networks. *Journal of Strategic Marketing*, 13(2), 81–92.

Rosenbloom, B., Larsen, T., and Smith, B. (2004). The effectiveness of upstream influence attempts in high and low context export marketing channels. *Journal of Marketing Channels*, 11(4), 3–19.

Schott, C. (2007). Selling adventure tourism: A distribution channels perspective. *International Journal of Tourism Research*, 9(4), 257–274.

Schmidt, J.B., and Spreng, R.A. (1996). A Proposed Model of External Consumer Information Search. *Journal of the Academy of Marketing Science*, 24(3), 246–256.

Sharda, S., and Pearce, D.G. (2006). Tourism distribution in emerging markets: the case of Indian travel to New Zealand. *Asia Pacific Journal of Tourism Research*, 11(4), 339–353.

Simons, L.P.A., and Bouwman, H. (2004). Designing a channel mix. *International Journal of Internet Marketing and Advertising*, 1(3), 229–250.

Smith, K.A. (2007). Distribution channels for events: supply and demand-side perspectives. *Journal of Vacation Marketing*, 13(4), 321–338.

Smith, K.A., and Garnham, R. (2006). Distribution channels for convention tourism: association conventions in Wellington, New Zealand. *Journal of Convention and Event Tourism*, 8(1), 1–30.

Snepenger, D., and Snepenger, M. (1993). Information search by pleasure travellers. In *Encyclopedia of Hospitality and Tourism*, (M.A. Kahn, M.D. Olsen, and T. Var, eds.), pp. 830–835, New York: Van Nostrand Reinhold.

Stern, L.W., and El-Ansary, A.I. (1992). *Marketing Channels,* 4th edn. Englewood Cliffs: Prentice-Hall.

Susskind, A.M., Bonn, M.A., and Dev, C.S. (2003). To look or book: an examination of consumers' apprehensiveness toward Internet use. *Journal of Travel Research*, 41(Feb), 256–264.

Tan, R. and Pearce, D.G. (2004). Providers' and intermediaries' use of the Internet in tourism distribution. In *Proceedings of the New Zealand Tourism and Hospitality Conference 2004*, (Smith, K.A. and Schott, C. eds.), Wellington, 8–10 December 2004, pp. 424–432.

Taniguchi, M. (2006). 'The structure and function of the tourism distribution channels between Japan and New Zealand'. *Proceedings of the 2006 New Zealand Tourism and Hospitality Research Conference.*

Ujama, D. (2001). Distribution channels for tourism: Theory and issues. In *Tourism Distribution Channels: Practices, Issues and Transformations*, (D. Buhalis, and W. Laws, eds.), pp. 33–52, London: Continuum.

Wahab, S., Crampon, L.J., and Rothfield, L.M. (1976). *Tourism Marketing.* London: Tourism International Press.

Wilson, D.T. (1995). An integrated model of buyer–seller relationships. *Journal of the Academy of Marketing Science*, 23(4), 335–345.

Wolfe, K., Hsu, C.H.C., and Kang, S.K. (2004). Buyer characteristics among users of various travel intermediaries. *Journal of Travel and Tourism Marketing*, 17(2/3), 51–62.

Woodside, A.G., and King, R.I. (2001). An updated model of travel and tourism purchase–consumption systems. *Journal of Travel and Tourism Marketing*, 10(1), 3–27.

Wynne, C.P., Berthon, L., Pitt Ewing, M., and Napoli, J. (2001). The impact of the Internet on the distribution value chain: the case of the South African Tourism Industry. *International Marketing Review*, 18(4), 420–431.

Yamamoto, D., and Gill, A. (2002). Issues of globalization and reflexivity in the Japanese tourism production system: the case of Whistler, British Columbia. *The Professional Geographer*, 54(1), 83–93.

Chapter 18

Atherton, A. (2004). Unbundling enterprise and entrepreneurship. From perceptions and preconceptions to concept and practice. *Entrepreneurship and Innovation*, 5(2), 121–127.

Autio, E., Keeley, R.H., Klofsten, M., Parker, G.G.C., and Hay, M. (2001). Entrepreneurial Intent among Students in Scandinavia and in the USA. *Enterprise and Innovation Management Studies*, 2(2), 45–160.

Ayres, H. (2006). Education and Opportunity as Influences on Career Development: Findings from a Preliminary Study into Eastern Australian Tourism. *Journal of Hospitality, Leisure, Sport and Tourism Education*, 5(1), 18–27.

Bacon, N., and Hoque, K. (2005). HRM in the SME sector: valuable employees and coercive networks. *International Journal of Human Resource Management*, 16(11), 1976–1999.

Bandura, A. (1986). *Social Foundations of Thought and Action. A Social Cognitive Theory.* New Jersey: Englewood Cliffs.

Bird, B. (1988). *Implementing Entrepreneurial Ideas: The Case for Intention. Academy of Management Review*, 13(3), 442–453.

Blackburn, R.A., and Smallbone, D. (2007). *From the margin to the mainstream: The Development of Research on Small Business and Entrepreneurship in the UK.* London: Kingston University: Small Business Research Centre.

Bowen, E., Lloyd, S., and Thomas, S. (2004). Changing cultural attitudes towards graduates in SMEs to stimulate regional innovation. *Industry and Higher Education*, 18(6), 385–390.

Boyd, N., and Vozikis, G. (1994). The influence of self-efficacy on the development of entrepreneurial intentions and actions. *Entrepreneurship Theory and Practice*, 94(18), 63–77.

Brazeal, D., and Herbert, T. (1999). The genesis of entrepreneurship. *Entrepreneurship Theory and Practice*, 23(3), 29–45.

Brennan, J., and Little, B. (2006). *Towards a strategy for workplace learning. Report to HEFCE by CHERI and KPMG.* London: Centre for Higher Education Research and Information.

Brizek, M., and Poorani, A. (2006). Making the Case for Entrepreneurship: A Survey of Small Business Mangement Courses within Hospitality and Tourism Programmes. *Journal of Hospitality, Leisure, Sport and Tourism Education*, 5(2), 36–47.

Busby, G. (2005). Work Experience and Industrial Links. In *An International Handbook of Tourism Education*, (D. Airey, and J. Tribe, eds.), pp. 93–107. Oxford: Elsevier.

Busby, G., Brunt, P., and Baber, S. (1997). Tourism sandwich placements: an appraisal. *Tourism Management*, 28(2), 105–110.

Carter, S., and Collinson, E. (1999). Entrepreneurship education: Alumni perceptions of the role of higher education institutions. *Journal of Small Business and Enterprise Development*, 6(3), 229–239.

Collins, A.B. (2002). Gateway to the real world, industrial training: dilemmas and problems. *Tourism Management*, 23(1), 93–96.

Drucker, P. (1993). *Post-capitalist Society*. London: Butterworth-Heinemann.

Dyer Jr., W.G. (1994). Toward a theory of entrepreneurial careers. *Entrepreneurship Theory and Practice* 7–21.

Gartner, W. (1988). 'Who is an entrepreneur?' Is the wrong question. *American Journal of Small Business*, 12(4), 11–32.

Getz, D., Carlsen, J., and Morrison, A. (2004). *The Family Business in Tourism and Hospitality*. Wallingford: CABI Publishing.

Gottfredson, L.S. (1981). Circumscription and Compromise: A Developmental Theory of Occupational Aspirations. *Journal of Counseling Psychology Monograph*, 28(6), 545–578.

Gottfredson, L.S. (2002). Gottfredson's Theory of Circumscription, Compromise, and Self-Creation. In *Career Choice and Development*, (D. Brown, ed.), 4 edn., pp. 85–148. San Francisco: Jossey-Bass.

Greene, F., and Saridakis, G. (2007). *Understanding the Factors Influencing Graduate Entrepreneurship*. Birmingham: National Council for Graduate Entrepreneurship.

ISBA (2004). *Making the Journey from Student to Entrepreneur: A Review of the Existing Research into Graduate Entrepreneurship*, Birmingham: The National Council of Graduate Entrepreneurship.

Jones, A.J., Woods, A., Coles, A.-M., and Rein, M. (2001). Graduates as strategic change agents in small firms: a case study of graduate placements and lifelong learning. *Strategic Change*, 10(1), 59–61.

Krueger, N.F.J. (1993a) The impact of prior entrepreneurial exposure on perceptions of new venture feasibility and desirability. *Entrepreneurship Theory and Practice*, 18(1), 5–21.

Krueger, N.F.J. (1993b) Some developmental consequences of early exposure to entrepreneurship. Academy of Management Proceedings. Atlanta.

Krueger, N.F.J., and Brazeal, D. (1994). Entrepreneurial Potential and Potential Entrepreneurs. *Entrepreneurship Theory and Practice*, 18(3), 91–104.

Krueger, N.F.J., Reilly, M.D., and Carsrud, A.L. (2000). Competing Models of Entrepreneurial Intentions. *Journal of Business Venturing*, 15(5/6), 411–432.

Ladkin, A. (2002). Career analysis: a case study of hotel general managers in Australia. *Tourism Management*, 23(4), 379–388.

Leslie, D. (1991) The Hospitality Industry, Industrial Placement and Personnel Management. *The Service Industries Journal,* 11(1), 63–74.

Leslie, D., and Richardson, A. (1999). Work placement in UK undergraduate programmes. Student expectations and experiences. *Industry and Higher Education*, 13(2), 142–150.

Lewin, K. (1951). *Field Theory in Social Science*. New York: Harper and Row.

Lieblich, A., Tuval-Mashiach, R., and Zilber, T. (1998). *Narrative research. Reading, Analysis, and Interpretation*. London: SAGE Publications.

Marhuenda, F., Martinez, I., and Navas, A. (2004). Conflicting vocational identities and careers in the sector of tourism. *Career Development International*, 9(3), 222–244.

McKeown, J., Millman, C., Sursani, S., Smith, K., and Martin, L. (2006). Graduate entrepreneurship education in the United Kingdom. *Education and Training*, 48(8/9), 597–613.

McMahon, U., and Quinn, U. (1995). Maximizing the hospitality management student work placement experience: a case study. *International Journal of Contemporary Hospitality Management*, 37(4), 13–17.

Moreland, N. (2004). *Entrepreneurship and higher education*. York: ESECT and HEA. an employability perspective.

Morrison, A. (2000). Entrepreneurship. What triggers it? *International Journal of Entrepreneurial Behaviour and Research*, 6(2), 59–71.

Morrison, A., Rimmington, M., and Williams, C. (1998). Entrepreneurship in the Hospitality. *Tourism and Leisure Industries*. Oxford: Butterworth-Heinemann.

Nabi, G., Holden, R., and Walmsley, A. (2006). *Career-Making: Graduating into Self-Employment. National Council for Graduate Entrepreneurship Research Report 009/2006*. Leeds: Leeds Metropolitan University.

Nabi, G., Holden, R. and Walmsley, A. (2007). From Student to Entrepreneur: Towards a Model of Graduate Career-making in Business Start-up. Paper presented at the 8th International Conference on HRD Research and Practice Across Europe, Oxford, 27–29 June, 2007.

Otter, S. (2005). Graduate placement evaluation study, pp. 1–52. Otter Consulting Limited.

Peterman, N.E., and Kennedy, J. (2003). Enterprise Education: Influencing Students' Perceptions of Entrepreneurship. Entrepreneurship. *Theory and Practice*, 28(2), 129–144.

Rae, D., and Woodier, N. (2006). *Graduate Career Choices and Entrepreneurship*. Birmingham: National Council for Graduate Entrepreneurship.

Robertson, M., Collins, A., Medeira, N., and Slater, J. (2003). Barriers to start-up and their effect on aspirant entrepreneurs. *Education and Training*, 45(6), 308–316.

Robinson, P.B., Stimpson, D.V., Huefner, J.C., and Hunt, K.H. (1991). An Attitude Approach to the Prediction of Entrepreneurship. Entrepreneurship. *Theory and Practice*, 15(4), 13–31.

Shapero, A. (1975). The displaced, uncomfortable entrepreneur. *Psychology Today*, 9, 83–88.

Shapero, A. (1982). Social dimensions of entrepreneurship. In *The Encyclopedia of Entrepreneurship* (C. Kent et al., eds.), pp. 72–90. Englewood Cliffs, NJ: Prentice Hall.

Shook, C., Priem, R., and McGee, J. (2003). *Venture Creation and the Enterprising Individual: A Review and Synthesis. Journal of Management*, 29(3), 379–399.

Small Business Service. (2002). *Small Business and Government – The Way Forward*. London: Small Business Service.

Thomas, R. (1995). Public Policy and Small Hospitality Firms. *International Journal of Contemporary Hospitality Management*, 7(2/3), 69–73.

Thomas, R. (2003). *Small Firms in Tourism: International Perspectives*. Oxford: Elsevier.

Waryszak, R. (1999). Students' expectations from their co-operative education placements in the hospitality industry: an international perspective. *Education and Training*, 41(1), 33–40.

West, A.J., and Jameson, S. (1990). Supervised Work Experience in Graduate Employment. *International Journal of Contemporary Hospitality Management*, 2(2), 29–32.

Westhead, P. (1998). The Shell Technology Enterprise Programme: Benefits reported by students and 'host' employers. *Journal of Small Business and Enterprise Development*, 5(1), 60–78.

Westhead, P., and Matlay, H. (2005). *Graduate employment in SMEs: a longitudinal perspective*. *Journal of Small Business and Enterprise Development*, 12(3), 353–365.

Yin, R.K. (1994). *Case Study Research. Design and Methods*. London: SAGE Publications.

Chapter 19

Beirman, D. (2003). *Restoring Destinations in Crisis: A Strategic Marketing Approach*. Wallingford: CABI Publishing.

Bennet, A. (2002). *Great Western Lines and Landscapes*. Cheltenham: Runpast Publishing.

Brendon, P. (1991). *Thomas Cook: 150 Years of Popular Tourism*. London: Secker and Warburg.

Broadberry, S., and Howlett, P. (2005). The UK during World War 1: Business as usual. In *The Economics of World War 1*, (S. Broadberry, and M. Harrison, eds.), pp. 206–234. Cambridge: Cambridge University Press.

Cole, B., and Durack, R. (1992). *Railway Posters 1923–1947*. York: National Railway Museum.

Davies, R., and Barber, S. (2007). *Wallace Arnold*. Hersham: Ian Allan Publishing.

Durie, A. (2006). *Water is Best: The Hydros and Health Tourism in Scotland 1840–1940*. Edinburgh: John Donald.

Durie, A., and McPherson, G. (1999). *Tourism and the First World War: A Scottish Perspective*. The Local Historian. November.

Glaesser, D. (2003). *Crisis Management in the Tourism Industry*. Oxford: Butterworth-Heinemann.

Henderson, J. (2007). *Tourism Crises: Causes, Consequences and Management*. Oxford: Butterworth-Heinemann.

Howarth, D., and Howarth, S. (1986). *The Story of P&O The Peninsular and Oriental Steam Navigation Company*. London: Weidenfeld and Nicolson.

Johnson, N. (2006). *Britain and the 1918–19 Influenza Pandemic: A Dark Epilogue*. London: Routledge.

Lennon, J., and Foley, M. (2000). *Dark Tourism*. London: Continuum.

Lickorish, L., and Kershaw, A. (1953). *The Travel Trade*. London: Practical Press.

Lynch, M. (2004). *Weathering the Storm: A Crisis Management Guide for Tourism Businesses*. Leicester: Matador.

Page, S.J., and Yeoman, I. (2006). How VisitScotland prepared for a flu pandemic. *Journal of Business Continuity and Emergency Planning*, 1(2), 167–182.

Read, D. (ed.). (1982). *Edwardian England*. London: Croom Helm.

Ryan, C. (ed.). (2007). *Battlefield Tourism*. Oxford: Butterworth-Heinemann.

Sladen, C. (2005). Wartime holidays and the 'myth of the Blitz'. *Cultural and Social History*, 2, 215–245.

Walton, J. (1983). *The English Seaside Resort: A Social History 1750–1914*. Leicester: Leicester University Press.

Walton, J. (1996). Leisure towns in wartime: The impact of the First World War in Blackpool and San Sebastian. *Journal of Contemporary History*, 31, 603–618.

Watts, D. (2004). Evaluating British railway poster advertising: The London and North Eastern Railway between the wars. *Journal of Transport History*, 25(2), 23–56.

Williamson, A. (1998). *The Golden Age of Travel: The Romantic Years of Tourism in Images from the Thomas Cook Archive*. Peterborough: Thomas Cook Publishing.

INDEX